Acclaim for Robert Kanigel's

EYES ON THE STREET

"Kanigel has written the definitive Jacobs biography . . . in prose that is as lively as her own." —*The Washington Post*

"[Kanigel delivers] fast-paced and nuanced storytelling in a crisp prose style that engages the reader. . . . This most complete biography of Jane Jacobs to date is a treat to read." —*New York Journal of Books*

"*Eyes on the Street* is the Jane Jacobs biography I've been waiting for." —Richard Florida, *CityLab*

"Kanigel has found the right tone for his subject, light but serious." —Adam Gopnik, *The New Yorker*

"Kanigel tells this story well. [And he] does a fine job of describing the shock [Jacobs's] book caused." —*The Wall Street Journal*

"Zestfully illuminating and entertaining. . . . Kanigel's delight in his subject . . . shimmers on every page." —*Booklist* (starred review)

"[A] first-rate story of one of the great independent thinkers of the twentieth century. . . . Kanigel handles [Jacobs's] story with respect, humor, and scrupulous scholarship." —*Shelf Awareness*

"Kanigel turns Jacobs's life into a fascinating narrative with an endearing, obstinate, brilliant protagonist." —*Publishers Weekly* (starred review)

"An outstanding chronicle of a provocative, influential, iconoclastic theorist of the American cityscape. . . . A well-rounded, illuminating narrative." —*Kirkus Reviews* (starred review)

Robert Kanigel

EYES ON THE STREET

Robert Kanigel is the author of seven previous books. He has been the recipient of numerous awards, including a Guggenheim fellowship and the Grady-Stack Award for science writing. His book *The Man Who Knew Infinity*, a finalist for the National Book Critics Circle Award and the Los Angeles Times Book Prize, has been made into a movie. His other books include *The One Best Way* and *On an Irish Island*. For twelve years he was a professor of science writing at M.I.T. He and his wife now live in Baltimore, Maryland.

www.robertkanigel.com

EYES ON
THE
STREET

EYES ON THE STREET

THE LIFE OF JANE JACOBS

Robert Kanigel

VINTAGE BOOKS
A Division of Penguin Random House LLC
New York

The Library of Congress has cataloged the Knopf edition as follows:
Names: Kanigel, Robert, author.
Title: Eyes on the street : the life of Jane Jacobs / Robert Kanigel.
Description: First edition. / New York : Alfred A. Knopf, 2016. |
Includes bibliographical references and index.
Subjects: LCSH: Jacobs, Jane, 1916–2006. | City planners—United States—Biography. |
City planners—Canada—Biography. | City planning—United States—
History—20th century. | City planning—Canada—History—20th century. |
Urban renewal—United States—History—20th century. | Urban renewal—
Canada—History—20th century. | Sociology, Urban—Philosophy.
Classification: LCC HT167.K325 2016 | DDC 711/.4092 [B]—dc23
LC record available at https://lccn.loc.gov/2015050758

Vintage Books Trade Paperback ISBN: 978-0-345-80333-7
eBook ISBN: 978-0-307-96191-4

Author photograph © Michael Lionstar
Maps by Robert Bull
Book design by Maggie Hinders

www.vintagebooks.com

146122990

For Sarah, Jessie, Duncan,
and all the Calvert Street gang

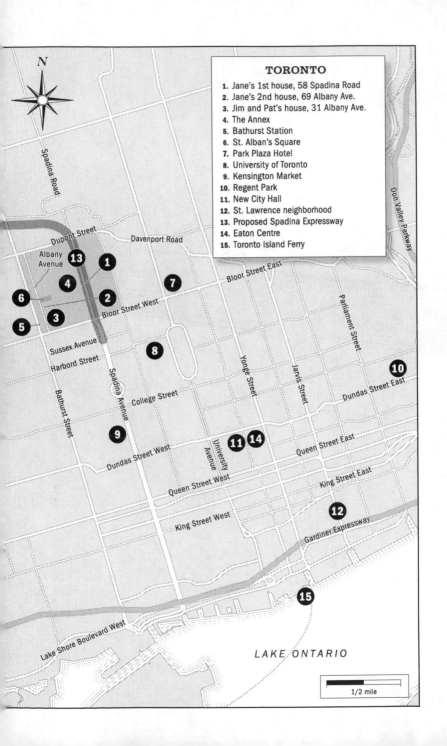

TORONTO

1. Jane's 1st house, 58 Spadina Road
2. Jane's 2nd house, 69 Albany Ave.
3. Jim and Pat's house, 31 Albany Ave.
4. The Annex
5. Bathurst Station
6. St. Alban's Square
7. Park Plaza Hotel
8. University of Toronto
9. Kensington Market
10. Regent Park
11. New City Hall
12. St. Lawrence neighborhood
13. Proposed Spadina Expressway
14. Eaton Centre
15. Toronto Island Ferry

N

Spadina Road

Dupont Street

Davenport Road

Albany Avenue

Bloor Street East

Bloor Street West

Sussex Avenue

Harbord Street

Spadina Avenue

College Street

Bathurst Street

Dundas Street West

University Avenue

Yonge Street

Jarvis Street

Parliament Street

Don Valley Parkway

Dundas Street East

Queen Street East

Queen Street West

King Street East

King Street West

Gardiner Expressway

Lake Shore Boulevard West

LAKE ONTARIO

1/2 mile

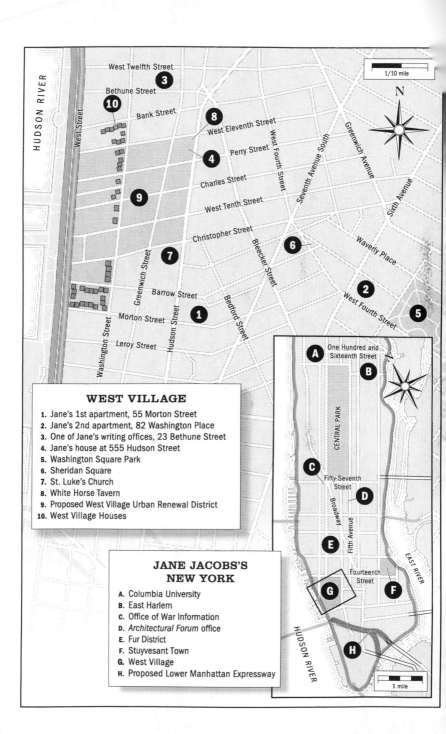

HUDSON RIVER

West Twelfth Street

3

Bethune Street

10

Bank Street

8

West Eleventh Street

4

Perry Street

West Fourth Street

Charles Street

West Tenth Street

Seventh Avenue South

Greenwich Avenue

Sixth Avenue

9

Christopher Street

Bleecker Street

6

Waverly Place

West Street

7

2

Barrow Street

Greenwich Street

Hudson Street

Bedford Street

West Fourth Street

5

Morton Street

1

Washington Street

Leroy Street

1/10 mile

N

WEST VILLAGE

1. Jane's 1st apartment, 55 Morton Street
2. Jane's 2nd apartment, 82 Washington Place
3. One of Jane's writing offices, 23 Bethune Street
4. Jane's house at 555 Hudson Street
5. Washington Square Park
6. Sheridan Square
7. St. Luke's Church
8. White Horse Tavern
9. Proposed West Village Urban Renewal District
10. West Village Houses

JANE JACOBS'S NEW YORK

A. Columbia University
B. East Harlem
C. Office of War Information
D. *Architectural Forum* office
E. Fur District
F. Stuyvesant Town
G. West Village
H. Proposed Lower Manhattan Expressway

One Hundred and Sixteenth Street

A

B

CENTRAL PARK

C

Fifty-Seventh Street

D

Broadway

Fifth Avenue

E

G

Fourteenth Street

F

EAST RIVER

HUDSON RIVER

H

1 mile

CONTENTS

EYES ON
THE
STREET

INTRODUCTION

THINK ABOUT what you'd want to say about Jane Jacobs and it's hard not to wonder what she'd say right back.

You might not want to get in a debate with Jane; she was sure to beat you. In verbal combat she was overwhelming. When she was in her thirties, before she'd written *The Death and Life of Great American Cities*, she wrote a provocative article for a major magazine whose publisher questioned her reporting. When the two of them met, Jane defended her account with, by one account, "a screed of facts and firsthand observations." Later, she asked a sympathetic colleague why he'd not stuck up for her more. "No need," said he. "The poor man"—the publisher—"thought he'd hit a buzz saw."

You could say Jane Jacobs didn't suffer fools gladly, which is true. But you don't want to say it, because it's such a damnable cliché, and you don't want to utter a cliché in front of Jane. You want to be at your best. If there's a flabbiness to your argument, a want of pointed example, a blurriness of vision, you probably wouldn't want it to show. Because if it did—around the kitchen table at her home in Greenwich Village, or later in Toronto, or at a public meeting, or among a bunch of academics—she'd just gobble you up. "There are ways to disagree with Jane Jacobs, but not as many as you might think," Roger Sale wrote of her in *The Hudson Review* in 1970, "because on her own terms she is almost invariably right and the real questions arise when you start to consider what she has left out."

Jane—which is what everyone called her, including her three children—wrote seven books, saved neighborhoods, stopped expressways, was arrested twice, basked in the glow of legions of admirers, and had a million discussions and debates around the kitchen table, which she always won. At least in her later years—though there's reason to think it went all the way back to grade school—she invariably dominated the conversation. She listened, she responded, she challenged. She thought about what she wanted to say and said it. Not honey coated, not smoothed over. It just came out. Call her brutal, call her honest. Someone once said of her, "What a dear, sweet grandmother she isn't."

Jane was perfectly normal, healthy and happy in all the important ways. She had friends who loved her. She was good to them, kind, and loving. She could be playful, even silly; at least once, she screwed up her face into ridiculous shapes and submitted herself to the camera. When you greeted her she'd throw her arms around you in a tight clasp. She took time out from the writing that was about the most important thing in the world to her to help her children, her friends, her neighbors. But always, she *said what she thought;* she didn't know how not to. Once, the editor of a magazine she worked for spoke to her when she said what she thought to *The New York Times.* "I believe you really should not have sounded off . . ."

Now, it's fair to ask: Was she always like this? Or was it a personality trait that blossomed over time? Perhaps only after she became famous with her first book? Or, having moved to Toronto, after she became a revered symbol of that city? Were these the affectations of Personality that a prominent person sometimes makes part of him or herself over the years? Or was she always this way?

Jane Jacobs wrote seven books, but is remembered most for one of them, *The Death and Life of Great American Cities,* published in 1961, continuously in print ever since, and heralded as the book that, more than any other single influence, has reshaped how people see cities and what they expect of them. When they talked about it later, readers sometimes made it sound as if *Death and Life* was near to a religious experience for them. That before reading it, they were as they were; then, after they read it, they were different. That henceforth they *saw* differently. That their Chicago or New York or Boston had been reshaped before their eyes, with a new balance as to what was important and what was not. For many today, certainly, Jane Jacobs verges on a cult figure, with *Death and Life* a kind of gospel, like Chairman Mao's Little Red Book in its time, or the Bible, or the U.S. Constitution—a repository of revealed Truth. I was among those early drawn to Jacobs through *Death and Life,* which I read in the early 1970s. Its unapologetic assertion of all a city could be at its best, its affirmation of urban sensibilities like those I'd absorbed growing up in New York, and later seen in Paris and San Francisco, was a revelation.

But these many years later, the subject of the book you are now reading is not cities, urban planning, or urban design. It's not a book that sets out to gather upbeat stories of rejuvenation and revitalization from the urban front lines. It does not take the reader by the hand and guide her through resurgent Station North in Baltimore or gentrified Williamsburg in Brooklyn; through old warehouses and office buildings made into homes, or downtowns set a-bustling again. Or exult in the reassuring drops in crime in New York and other cities. Or enjoy the vision of city-busting urban highways torn down in Boston and San Francisco. Each of these, seen through the right lens, can be laid at Jane Jacobs's door. And you'll find such happy stories in this book. But they are not its subject.

Rather, this is a biography of the remarkable woman who helped make such accounts possible. This book looks back, to a time when the rare upbeat report of city life was buried beneath stacks of press releases from new suburban developments, new interstate highways linked by cloverleafs, new rounds of corporate exodus to suburban office parks. To a time when old city neighborhoods were being erased, high-rise housing projects erected in their place; when slums were slums and everyone knew exactly what they were, or thought they did; when anyone who wanted to live in the city would have been seen as just a little weird. To a time into which Jane Jacobs strode, looked around her, and helped the rest of us see through new eyes.

During the last half of her life and since her death at the age of eighty-nine in 2006, she has inspired a devotion whose intensity one is tempted to greet with a lifted eyebrow. She's been called "the most influential urban thinker of all time," ahead of Frederick Law Olmsted, Lewis Mumford, Robert Moses, and Thomas Jefferson. She's been called "genius of common sense," "godmother of urban America," an "urban Thoreau," and "the Rachel Carson of the economic world." One of her books, *Systems of Survival*, was deemed "as bitchily observant as a Woody Allen film." In turn, one Woody Allen film was described as "channeling Jane Jacobs and her complaints . . . about the alienating scale of modern architecture and postwar urbanism." *The Death and Life of Great American Cities* was likened "to the paper Luther nailed to the Schlosskirche Wittenberg four centuries earlier." A man who described himself as a Jacobs groupie traveled to her residences in New York and Toronto, saying that for him, a "city geek," "this was like a trip to Graceland and Tupelo, Mississippi." In an essay, "The Society of Saint Jane," Mariana Mogilevich wrote how, after Jane's death, "not surprisingly, no time at all was wasted in beginning the canonization process." When the Occupiers occupied Wall Street, the economist Sandy Ikeda asked, "What would Jane Jacobs do?" And when Stewart Brand, originator of the *Whole Earth Catalog*, the counterculture bible of the 1960s, was asked who he'd like to be other than himself, he picked Jane Jacobs, a "one-lady Venice, fifteenth century. As good as it gets."

Individually, these attestations might be intriguing, but collectively they give us pause: you can admire Jane Jacobs, as I do, yet grow weary or suspicious of such a heaping-up of adulation; our understanding of any real human being doesn't profit from such hyperbole. For the moment we needn't decide whether Jane Jacobs really does qualify as "Mrs. Insight," or whether she ranks as the most influential urban thinker of all time, or attains only a lower, merely human standard. Indeed, as we'll see, plenty of revisionist thinking questions one or another facet of Jacobs's legacy. But we can find in such lionization at least one firm fact: that among thousands of architects, urban activists, city planners, economists, city dwellers generally, and champions of independent thought, Jane Jacobs is seen in just such larger-than-life terms; that something in what she said, or how she said it, inspired not cool, respectful admiration but ardency and awe; that many emerged from her books, or from hearing her in public, as fans or acolytes.

What makes this phenomenon all the more confounding is that Jane Jacobs didn't enjoy those superficial blessings that often arouse reverence. She was not male. She was not rich. She did not reach public recognition of any magnitude until she was pushing fifty. She was not beautiful. She was not even memorably *unbeautiful;* for long stretches of her public life, she was a pudding-faced old lady in ill-fitting jumper and sneakers. Her voice, which in its timbre could verge on squeaky, conveyed no hypnotic majesty. She didn't wholly avoid television interviews or other publicity on behalf of her books or the social issues she championed, but she didn't normally reach out for it, either. After the success of her first book, she would say, she had to decide whether to be a celebrity or to write books, and opted for the latter. How, then, we are left to wonder, did so many come under her spell?

They came under her spell, I think, almost solely through her words. Her words expressed ideas. And those ideas had a quality and resonance that were new and fresh and thrilling. They were memorably put, in distinctive aphorisms, in brick-like agglomerations of evidence and fact, that added up to a sense of irrefutable *rightness*. For many readers, too, what she said seemed to stand up for them. Maybe you thought you didn't want to march off to the suburbs like everyone else, that it was satisfying, or fun, or fascinating, to live amid a million strangers in an anonymous city, and here was a lady who thought so, too, who understood, and who helped you *see* your city, and maybe yourself, in a new and liberating way.

But there was more: her words conveyed a stance, a sensibility that to many were marvelously attractive and compelling. Her language was lucid, but you don't get a hold on people by being merely lucid. It was disruptive, too—combative, even bitchy. And defiantly independent, yet suggesting that it was all just common sense in the end, and that maybe anyone could be like her.

There's a scene in the classic Academy Award–winning 1940 film *The Philadelphia Story*, where a tabloid press reporter, played by Jimmy Stewart, and Tracy Lord, upper-class to her toenails, played by Katharine Hepburn, are both thoroughly smashed, with maybe the makings of romance burbling up between them.

"You're quite a girl, aren't you?" says Stewart.

"You think?"

"Yeah, I know."

"Thank you, professor, I don't think I'm exceptional."

"You are."

"There are any number like me. You ought to get around more."

Of course, every frame of film, every word uttered by Tracy Lord, every look and gesture, every syllable of her Main Line accent, adds to he conclusion that if anyone is exceptional it's her, and that to deny it is either willful faux modesty or evidence she's out of touch with herself or with the effect she has upon others.

Almost sixty years later, something like this scene was enacted with Jane Jacobs. It was 1997 and a Canadian interviewer was asking her why there were so few iconoclasts like her. Oh, but there were: "You must move in different circles than I do," says Jane. "Most of the people I know think for themselves, they really do."

"But you're a brilliant woman and you attract those sorts of people."

"No, I'm not that brilliant," Jane replies. "I'm really slow. I run across them [iconoclasts] all the time. I'm a very ordinary person."

And it's just as false coming from Jane Jacobs as from Tracy Lord.

Of course, Jane has the good grace to add, "But I'm articulate."

Jane Jacobs's words did not reach her admirers solely through her writings. Many of her acolytes knew her not through *Death and Life*, or her lesser-known books, but through her work as an urban activist. To them, especially during the 1960s and early 1970s, *that* was her day job. One time, city authorities wanted to run a road right through the park where Jane's kids played. Another time, they wanted to write off her whole Greenwich Village neighborhood as a slum, bringing it under Urban Renewal's dark, unlovely sway. Then they were going to all but lop off the whole bottom of Manhattan Island with a big expressway and, it looked like, destroy her whole way of life.

What else could she do but try to stop it? So she stood up and spoke at public meetings. She wrote forceful, sometimes angry letters. She had friends spy on city authorities. She helped organize protests; once, she managed to get herself arrested, and had four felony indictments thrown at her. Neighbors would come by for strategy sessions around her kitchen table, deciding on what facts and figures to gather, or how to maneuver some city official to come around. Jane wasn't the one to go around collecting signatures. Most often, she was the master strategist, often the public face of protest, getting up at public meetings to harangue the planners, or the developers, or city officials, or whoever else was the enemy this time. Most of the time, she won, as she did in fighting the New York planning czar Robert Moses to a standstill, defeating his Lower Manhattan Expressway; "Jane took an axe to Moses and killed him," her longtime editor, Jason Epstein, would say. And when her neighbors weren't a little put off by the sheer impudence of her urban battle strategies, the fierce single-mindedness with which she waged her wars, they loved her. That was how they remembered her—as protector and defender of the neighborhood. When she became famous and the magazines and newspapers needed something to call her they depicted her as "the Barbara Fritchie of the Slums," or as a "Madame Defarge leading an aroused populace to the barricades."

So prominent were some of these battles—they loom in collective memory in part thanks to books and articles that almost reflexively pair her with Robert Moses, her David to his Goliath—that they make it sound like this is what she *was*, that here, in this work on behalf of her community, was the real Jane Jacobs: organizer, activist, radical, a woman of the people who'd risen up out of the gritty city streets to fight city hall. She *was* all that, and though she never quite said so, she must have derived satisfaction from it. More often, though, she went on the record to say some something like this: "I resented that I had to stop and devote myself to fighting what was basically an absurdity that had been foisted on me and my neighbors." To listen to Jane, it all made for an interruption from her *real* work.

Indeed, each time she was through battling one civic opponent or another, it was not as if she sought out the next dragon to slay; rather, like Cincinnatus, the statesman who relinquished the scepter of leadership after defeating each challenge to Rome, Jane returned to the work she'd been forced to give up during the crisis of the moment. Now, once again, she'd mark off hours away from her family, instruct her husband and children to let no one in to see her. And there, amid her books and notes and typewriter, she'd resume the close reading, the hard thinking, the endless laboring over words and ideas, that made her one of the premier intellectual figures of the twentieth century.

After *Death and Life*, Jane wrote many other books, which got respectful hearings, significant readerships, critical hosannas, and had their own fans. She wrote particularly of economics, specifically about what makes for economically healthy cities and regions; these, a little idiosyncratic, have brought no consensus within the larger economics community as to whether, as some say, they represent real genius, or are quirkily irrelevant. Other books headed off in wholly uncharted directions. She edited a book about her great-aunt and her adventures in Alaska. She wrote a children's book. She wrote more philosophical works, structured as Platonic dialogues.

You could say these books were all on different "subjects," based on different bodies of fact, their author flitting from one to the other. But you could also look at them as bearing on a single overarching subject: Jane told the story of how one day when she was a child, sitting with her father on the front porch of her house in Scranton, their conversation wandered to the oak tree in their yard. "What is its purpose?" asked her father. It was a rhetorical question, of course. He was going somewhere with it, its answer embodying something like a philosophy. The tree's *purpose?* What purpose did it need, really? It was *alive*. "I made of the answer," Jane would recall, "that the purpose of life is to live." She said as much to her father. "Yes," he said, "that tree has a great push to live—any healthy, living thing does."

It's natural to view *The Death and Life of Great American Cities* as a book about cities, but it might better be seen as a book about death and life. The same really goes for the entirety of her work, as a chorus and conversation about life in glowing contrast to decay and death. Referring to *Death and Life,* she'd say she was never particularly interested in pushing one particular ideal city. Rather, "I just wanted to know how to keep the life" in it going, "which in my mind is the purpose of life." The epigraph to the book includes a quotation from Oliver Wendell Holmes Jr.: "Life is an end in itself, and the only question as to whether it is worth living is whether you have enough of it." An article she wrote during World War II about jobs opening up for women fairly hums with the happy clatter of machines and industrial vibrancy. Jane watched her father restore sick people to health. She was brought up on accounts of her uncle Billy's lusty energy, of her great-aunt's charge into the Alaskan bush. She was distraught at the decline of Scranton, and at how a hamlet in backwoods North Carolina she visited as a teenager had declined over the years. What impressed her most about the life of great cities was not just their diversity, but their energy. It was as if, all through her own life, she sought the conditions men and women needed to make good and vital lives.

When she was wrapped up in the Girl Scouts as a young teenager, Jane belonged "to what my friends and I thought was the finest Girl Scout troop in Scranton, Pennsylvania." But it got too popular, too big, and the powers-that-be decided to establish a second troop, meeting in the same church, only at a different time. Jane stayed with the original troop, but soon experienced it as "boring and lackadaisical." So one evening, she and a friend dropped in on the other troop. "What a contrast!" she'd remember thinking; it was all enthusiasm, older girls helping the younger ones, the whole "jumping with life." *Life*—measure of all things. *Life*—roots reaching for water, leaves reaching for the sun, cities exploding with vitality, businesses booming, economies flourishing, ideas aborning. Read enough of Jane Jacobs and you see these same themes and images running like a river all through her work. No need to understand why cities decline, she counseled, only why they prosper: "The most elementary point is the most startling. There are no causes of stagnation. There are no causes of poverty. There are only causes of growth."

But living things never stayed as they were. Jane's was a vision that resisted any hint of stasis, even of beauty remaining beautiful. "Think for a minute," she wrote, "what life would be like if all we had to do was to maintain things as they already are, living passively off the creativity of the past. In such a utopia, life would be intolerably boring. Sheer maintenance and well-worn routines are drags, especially if there is no relief from them." To settle for easy, unchanging day-to-dayness as a civic or social virtue was to her unthinkable. "The only way that dynamic systems can stay alive is constant self-renewal," said Jane. "That goes for a person, a city, a species, a biomass, whatever." Bob Dylan said it, not Jane, but she could have: He who's "not busy being born is busy dying."

Jane's ideal cities and civilizations were only those that could rival the freshness and vitality of her inner world.

Jane wrote most of the books not in New York, where she lived from age eighteen into her fifties, but in Toronto, Canada, to which she moved with her family in 1968. There she lived the last thirty-eight years of her life. At the time of her death, in 2006, wrote Barry Wellman, a University of Toronto sociologist, "Toronto grieved and remembered their Jane," upbraiding the New York–centeredness of some of the obituaries. Jane became a Canadian citizen, and Canadians made Jacobs one of their own. She wasn't long in Toronto before she, her husband, and her children were protesting the kinds of assaults to her new city and to common sense that she had faced back in New York. In no time she was thrust into the intellectual and political life of her city, involved in its civic discussion, friend to mayors; in her old age, people still beat a path to her door, wanting to absorb something of her wisdom.

"Wisdom," of course, is a fraught, old-fashioned word, but that's how many came to see her, as a font of wisdom; one book devoted to her, a compilation of scholarly articles, is titled *The Urban Wisdom of Jane Jacobs*. Once *Death and Life* and her second book, *The Economy of Cities*, had made her into a major public figure, she was often left to balance her writing time with a veritable procession of interviewers, scholars, economists, academics, politicians, planners, sometimes even schoolkids on class trips, there to meet with this famous old lady, wanting a piece of her. Strange fruit for a woman who'd had real trouble getting through high school.

Jane Jacobs was astonishingly well read, an intellectual by any definition you cared to use, a deep and determined thinker, but she got there by a decidedly unorthodox path. At age twenty-two, when many of her high school classmates were already college graduates, she started taking courses in Columbia University's continuing studies program. Two years later, she edited a book that grew out of one of her courses, and got it published by Columbia University Press. Yet she never got a college degree, never earned credits beyond those of a sophomore.

Back in Scranton, Jane would write, she'd gone to public school, where she'd "learned a great deal from the teachers in the first and second grades. Thereafter I think I mostly taught myself." One of her teachers, the story goes, asserted that towns and villages always grew up around waterfalls. Young Jane raised her hand: *Scranton hadn't*. And how was she so sure? Well, just look: their little city had a modest river running through it, but no waterfalls had played any role in its growth, so there you go. That's how she was: she looked, she read, she thought. With some preternatural gift of intellectual independence, she figured things out for herself, and said them.

At the height of the McCarthy years, Jane replied to an "interrogatory" implicitly questioning her loyalty with a response, barren of defensiveness, that in its buoyant brand of Jacobsean patriotism surely must have shamed her questioners. Her first major book toppled the canonical wisdom of a whole profession. She successfully battled some of the most powerful figures in New York. At the peak of her fame and influence she picked up and left New York and started all over again in Canada.

Now, here's the problem: Jane seemed to possess this independence, or eccentricity, or fearlessness, or whatever it was, right from the start.

(From the very start? As if it were written into her genes?) Certain,
she was more than ordinarily immune to pat nostrums handed down by
teachers, elders, peers, and credentialed experts, more comfortable challenging, questioning, thinking for herself, following her own star. If this
book aims to highlight any subject outside that of Jane Jacobs herself, it is
that of the independent mind in conflict with received opinion.

Everything Jane Jacobs did, both before she entered the public eye at the
age of forty-five and afterward, for the rest of her life, she did between
preparing meals, caring for her children, assembling Easter baskets, and
tending her garden. It was only a few hours into my first spell of research
in the Jane Jacobs archives at Boston College that I sensed that something
was, um, *different* about my new biographical subject. I'd spent the day
among the artifacts and correspondence of a person whose remarkable
gifts of insight and intelligence came out in all she did, in every letter she
wrote, every book she hammered out, every public meeting at which she
spoke. But it all played out against the backdrop of her life as girl, woman,
wife, and mother. Jane was no housewife; but hers was not a man's life,
either. The "women's work" she managed while writing *Death and Life,
The Economy of Cities,* and her other books made her for me, the author
of several biographies of "great men," something new to reckon with.

In capsule biographies and news accounts, Jane is not routinely
described as a feminist; at least, that's not the first thing we think of her.
And she didn't speak any of the various languages of feminism or address
specifically feminist issues. And yet, how *not* think of her as a feminist? She does periodically show up on Women's History Month reading
lists, women's history blogs, and the like. She has been listed among "300
Women Who Changed the World," along with Rachel Carson and Betty
Friedan, contemporary thinkers whose seminal works appeared around
the same time as *Death and Life* and who similarly helped shape the
age in which we live. When questioned by government authorities about
her union activities, Jane described her particular interest as the "equalization of pay between men and women for similar work." This was in
1949. A few years later, she wrote proudly of a relative who, "believing
in women's rights and women's brains," set up her own printing press to
publish her work "without a masculine nom de plume."

In *The Seasons of a Man's Life,* Daniel Levinson wrote of characteristic
arcs and patterns running through men's working lives that were pecu-

rly similar whether they were laborers, authors, or scientists. Women, has by now often been observed, are different, any otherwise "natural" arcs and patterns apt to be distorted by marriage, childbirth, family raising, and household running, or sometimes just the prospect of them. Once in the 1960s, New York mayor John Lindsay called Jane in the middle of the day. Her daughter Mary, about ten at the time, answered the phone, and advised the mayor that her mother "would not be available for conversation before 4 p.m."; the story would probably not have been told at all, ever, were Jane a man. She was not insulated by wealth or circumstances from most of the 101 distractions of everyday domestic life; like so many accomplished women, she did all she did by carving out space and time from among them. Inescapably, her life as a woman, navigating the shoals of domesticity, balancing, juggling, responding to the needs of others, largely unbuffered by the little props and perks that often support the professional lives of men, are part of this story, too.

Certainly it's not the case that there was no "trajectory" to Jane's career. She'd been on a trajectory, all right, but it wasn't the recognizably vaulting intellectual and professional arc that elite universities look for in their tenured faculty, or that literary and arts agents look for in their top young clients. It was a distinctly modest one—graduation from high school, a succession of low-paying secretarial jobs, a first decent white-collar job at age twenty-seven, ten years in the federal bureaucracy, then back to the private sphere as one of a dozen others like her at a mid-level professional magazine. The trajectory of someone we would have no cause to remember, who would live out a mostly unmemorable career, loved by family and respected by colleagues but otherwise making no great impact on the world. She did not, in the Jane Austen sense, "marry well"—though she did in the most important sense, of marrying someone by intellect and temperament supremely suited to her, whom she would love, respect, and enjoy all her life. She was not particularly ambitious. She'd never been singled out by an influential mentor as an up-and-comer and launched into the upper reaches of a national community. She hadn't had one of those early, explosive career successes at twenty-two or twenty-seven that propelled her into the ranks of the must-be-noticed. She had remained hidden, unknown, a married woman, mother of three, with a job she liked, living over a former candy store a few blocks from the warehouses and docks down by the Hudson River, who commuted to her job in Midtown Manhattan by bicycle.

And that should have been that.

Except that one day in 1956, four years into the last regular job s. would ever hold, her boss asked her to stand in for him at a conference Go up there and give a talk, would you, Jane? He couldn't go; he was going to be in Europe. No, she said, she didn't like to get up and talk in front of people. Please, he said, he needed her to. All right, she replied, but only if she could say whatever she wanted.

She did, which changed her life and, in time, the world.

The first part of this book tells of the curious, tangled path by which she got to that point.

The second, of what happened when she did.

The third, of the new life she made for herself afterward, in a new land.

PART I

An Uncredentialed Woman

1916–1954

CHAPTER 1

A GENEROUS PLACE TO LIVE

O N WINTER DAYS when she was a child, Jane's grandmother told her, they'd skate on the canal, along twenty miles of it frozen solid near their house. Back in the 1850s, before the railroad finally won out against it, the canal was how you got clean-burning anthracite coal from the mines of central Pennsylvania to big-city markets. It would be loaded on shallow-draft boats, maybe fifteen tons of it at a time, then towed down the canal that ran alongside the North Branch of the Susquehanna River, by mules on the adjacent towpath. A dollar a ton, you could figure, from Wilkes-Barre, in the heart of anthracite country, to Philadelphia. Making the boats, and repairing them, was its own little industry. And since the 1830s a key center of it was Espy, a town of a few hundred drawn out along the north bank of the canal, home to lock tenders and canal maintenance workers, as well as a tannery, a pottery, and a brickyard. From early spring, when the ice melted, until late fall, according to a 1936 memoir, the locals "set the tempo of their lives to the tireless plodding hoof beats of the mules." Boys in town looked with envy at those their own age driving the mules or else lolling on the decks of passing boats.

Espy, tucked away in mountainous ridge country that on topographic maps looks crumpled and crinkled, declined as the nineteenth century wore on. But it still carried some traffic in 1893 when Jane's grandmother, Jennie Breece Robison, and her husband, James Boyd Robison, bought a house on the north side of the main road running beside the canal. Both were central Pennsylvania natives of familiar Scots, Northern Irish, and English stock. They had four sons (another died when young) and four daughters. One of them was Bess Mary, or Bessie, born in 1879. She would become the mother of Jane Jacobs and live for 101 years.

Bess's father, Boyd, Jane's grandfather, was the son of a local merchant. Born in the adjacent, more substantial town of Bloomsburg, he attended Lafayette College and later fit in some legal studies. After the attack on Fort Sumter that launched the Civil War, he enlisted almost immediately, and was wounded in the hand at the Second Battle of Bull Run. "For purpose of labor," he wrote home, "my finger is just as useless as if it were cut off." In a second stint of service, in 1864, now an officer, Boyd was captured by Confederate guerillas and held in Libby Prison, a brick tobacco warehouse in Richmond into which Union officers, a thousand of them at a time, were infamously crowded. After the war, he returned to Bloomsburg, set up a law practice, and married Jennie Breece, a schoolteacher. For a few years he moved his young family to a place in the country, Esther Furnace Farm, a few miles outside of town. Then it was back to Bloomsburg, involvement in local politics, and, finally, the fine house in Espy. In the years Bessie was growing up, Captain J. Boyd Robison—lawyer, landowner, war veteran, member of the Presbyterian church, former candidate for Congress on the Greenback ticket, Knight Templar of the Masons—was a notable public figure.

In 1895, Bessie, sixteen, enrolled in the teacher's college in Bloomsburg, about two miles up the road from the family home in Espy, perhaps close enough, in those years before the trolley went in, for her to walk to school; there were dorms on campus, but she didn't live in one. Bloomsburg, population seven thousand, was where her father had grown up and where he maintained his legal practice. Its town center of two- and three-story brick commercial buildings along Main Street, plus a sprinkling of late Victorian Romanesque civic structures, together lent it an air of gentility and solidity evident even today.

At the head of Main Street stood the teacher's college, formally known as the Bloomsburg Literary Institute and State Normal School, a clutch of new brick buildings perched on a bluff along the Espy side of town that granted a view the school touted in its publications: "The river, like a ribbon, edges the plain on the south, and disappears through a bold gorge three miles to the southwest." Normal schools like Bloomsburg's represented the earnest efforts of high-minded nineteenth-century educators to raise standards in primary schools by making better teachers. A five-year burst of money and energy in the early 1890s had left the school with a new four-story dormitory, another dorm set aside for servants, an acoustically "perfect" thousand-seat auditorium, and that new boon, electricity. By Bessie's time, it included a model school, where in their second year she and her classmates could put in the twenty-one weeks of student teaching required by state law. Also required of students were algebra and geometry, English literature, Latin, American history, rhetoric, music, and geography. It's hard to be cynical about Bloomsburg's normal school. It seems to have taken its mission seriously and conferred on the state and its schoolchildren a genuine public good.

In 1897, at the age of eighteen, Bessie graduated with a BE degree— Bachelor of Elements, meaning the elements of teaching, which allowed her to teach in Pennsylvania. Three years later, in the 1900 census, she was recorded as living at home in Espy with her parents—occupation: teacher. This, of course, was just what she was supposed to be doing at this time of life, what most of her classmates did, and what her own mother, Jennie, had done before marrying Captain Boyd.

But here Bessie's story takes a turn. For in her early twenties, after six years of preparation and practice, she gave up teaching. What derailed her from it? Was she just bored with it, as one family member suggests she was? Was her move calm and well considered, or rash? Did family pressures of some kind intervene? Or did she simply feel a young adult's healthy urge to get as far away as possible from small-town Pennsylvania? What we do know is that by early 1904, four years after the census worker had come round to the house in Espy, Bessie wasn't a teacher anymore but a nurse. And she no longer lived in Espy at all, but in Philadelphia, population one and a half million.

Her mother figures in Jane's memories of her adolescence as a prim, provincial figure; what could you expect, Jane would as much as say, coming out of Bloomsburg and Espy? Bessie would become keeper of family scrapbooks, devoted gardener, serious churchgoer—not one you'd immediately figure for precipitously shifting gears, throwing over the past, leaving town, and hauling off for the big city. As we'll see, it was Bessie's elder sister, Martha, not she, who was the real dynamo among the Robison children and would go on to make a mark on the world. But just now, it was Bessie who was making changes.

In April 1904, at age twenty-five, Bessie received her diploma from the Polyclinic Hospital of Philadelphia's Training School for Nurses, located near Rittenhouse Square in downtown Philadelphia; Polyclinic would

Jane's mother, Bess Robison Butzner, in 1907, when she was a nurse. She lived to the age of 101.

later merge with the University of Pennsylvania. Nursing education was growing more professional, with first one- and then two-year programs at Polyclinic giving way to a three-year course that required anatomy and physiology, bacteriology and pharmacology, in addition to work on the wards. One of Bess's grandsons, a physician, would recall how, even as an old woman, she'd sometimes use medical terms left over from her nursing days—a *fracture* rather than a broken bone, a *carbuncle*, not a boil. In the years after 1904, Bess became supervising night nurse at Polyclinic, and met her future husband, Jane's father.

Around the time Bess joined the ranks of Polyclinic nurses, John Decker Butzner was receiving his MD degree from the University of Virginia and coming north to Polyclinic for a year-and-a-half-long residency. After that, perhaps in late 1905, he may have served briefly as physician in a West Virginia mining town. By 1907 he had joined an existing practice in Scranton, sharing an office on Wyoming Avenue, the city's Doctor's Row. Just how, during their overlapping years in Philadelphia, he and Bess met, and how their relationship deepened, we don't know. One family story tells how nurses often got stuck doing the personal laundry of the physicians, that Bess regularly got one pile of undergarments that stood out as particularly worn, shabby, and shredded, that she sewed them, mended them, fairly *rescued* them—and in this way came to the attention of young Dr. Butzner.

Dr. Butzner had come off a farm in the rural South. Not cotton country, not the Deep South of the great plantations, but still distinctly the South—Spotsylvania County, in the tidewater region of northern Virginia, midway between Richmond and Washington, D.C. All his life he spoke with a soft southern drawl. His father's side of the family, the Butzners of Virginia, had roots in Bavaria. His mother's side, the Deckers, were Yankees who had moved south from New Jersey in 1839. By 1846, John Decker had warmed enough to southern ways to own a dozen slaves: "All the field hands," a family history records, "were big women whom he had purchased at the Fredericksburg mart with the definite idea of raising his own negroes." At war's end, Mr. Decker owned seven parcels of Spotsylvania County real estate totaling 2,200 acres. In 1877, his daughter Lucy married. The groom was William Joseph Butzner. Their son, born the following year, was our Polyclinic physician, John Decker Butzner, known all his life as Decker.

All through the Civil War, hundreds of thousands of Union and Confederate troops marched, camped, and fought in the fields and woods of Spotsylvania County, as at bloody Chancellorsville or in Fredericksburg, the little trace of a town just over the county line from most of the Butzner holdings. After the war, nobody had much of anything; the well-off Decker family, it would be said, "never felt the pinching hand of want except in the cruel days toward the end and after the Civil War." But while Jane would picture them as poor, or at least cash starved, the Butzner side, too, was never much less than middlingly prosperous. During the years young Decker was growing up, his father owned, free and clear, four hundred acres rising up from the Rappahannock River that produced crops of hay, corn, wheat, and, notably, by family lore, Black Galloway cattle.

Meanwhile, Decker's prosperous uncle Marshall may already have been helping him and his brothers through school. Decker and his two brothers, Billy and Calvin, had attended a one-room farm school that brought them together with cousins from miles around. The teacher was ordinarily the family's eldest unmarried female; when she went off to have children, the next young woman in line got the job. Later, Decker put in a year at the Fredericksburg Academy, a recently founded Presbyterian-supported school. He and his younger brothers all did well there, Decker extraordinarily so. In 1894 he was one of only a handful of students to earn a gold medal for his grades, distinguishing himself in English literature, German, Latin, geometry, and physics. From there, with brother Billy, he attended the University of Virginia at Charlottesville, the two whip-smart Butzner boys for a while living next door to one another on campus. In 1901, Decker was awarded bachelor's and master's degrees, and in 1904 received his medical degree. Then it was off to Philadelphia, his Polyclinic residency—and Bess.

However their relationship evolved, it seems plain that for several years Dr. Butzner was establishing himself in his Scranton practice while Bessie was back in Philadelphia; as late as December 1908, Bessie was still getting mail there. During these years, with Philadelphia about three hours on the through train from Scranton, their relationship may have been something like what today we'd call a long-distance affair. When they finally married, on March 24, 1909, he was thirty, she twenty-nine—about seven years older than the average bride of those days. The ceremony took place at the home of her mother, across the road from the old canal in Espy. Just a few weeks before, her father, Captain Boyd, had died suddenly at age seventy-four. So the wedding, as the local paper noted, was "a quiet one, only members of the family and a few invited family being present." After a trip south, they returned to Scranton, where they would make their home.

Soon after they married, with Dr. Butzner still new to his practice, he

Jane's father, Dr. John Decker Butzner. He died when she was twenty-one.

bought an automobile—to more easily visit his patients, he said. Only trouble is, he never said a word about the big expense to Bess, just did it. The slight rankled. Then, another time early in their marriage, Decker's mother bestowed on Bess the recipe for his favorite pie. Well, young Mrs. Butzner so much as said, that might be well and good on the farm, with all the rich ingredients in hand, but money was tight—and for now, at least, she just wasn't going to make it, and didn't. To Bess, the Spotsylvania County embodied in her husband's Virginia drawl could seem like a mire of low, ribald humor and crude language. *Why, it's hot as seven bitches,* you'd hear a Spotsylvania man grouse; you didn't talk that way in Bloomsburg. There were small frictions, inevitable in any marriage, but hinting that any harmony of taste and sensibility Bess and Decker shared was not a perfect one.

And yet, out of their two dissimilar natures emerged, as if alchemically transmuted, a home of healthy, sometimes madcap exuberance, lively talk, free questioning, enjoyment, and encouragement that profoundly inspired the confidence and independence of their children.

The third child of Decker and Bess, Jane Isabel Butzner, was born on May 4, 1916, at 10:25 p.m., Dr. Butzner himself attending. The location was 815 Electric Street, the name honoring Scranton's claim as home of the first electric-powered streetcars. Dr. Butzner had bought the house in 1910, and would place it in Bess's name in August 1918 for one dollar "and love and affection." In this unprepossessing detached house in north Scranton, set on a slight slope down from the Dunmore hills to the east, Jane lived her first four years. She'd remember that they had two tricycles, or "velocipedes," as her mother mistakenly called them. "I learned to get out early to stake my claim," Jane would say.

Older by six years, her sister, Betty, was born in 1910; the age gap was enough, Jane's son Jim suggests, that Betty seemed "more part of the world of the adults, not a playmate of Jane's." Between the two of them came William, born in 1913; as late as spring 1915, on a visit to his grandparents in Virginia, he'd seemed fine, so it must have come as all the more a shock when on August 3 he died. Jane's birth nine months later, virtually to the day, hints at some deep compact between Decker and Bess to answer the loss of their son with new life.

In 1917 John was born. Jane, seventeen months older, remained especially close to him through most of her life; when, years later, a telephone call brought news of his death, she said, "He was my oldest friend." By 1920, the family was complete, Jane's youngest brother, Jim, having been born on November 10. Dr. Butzner's mother, Lucy, was living with them at the time, so the Electric Street house may by now have felt cramped. A few months later, in February 1921, Dr. Butzner bought a house at 1712 Monroe Avenue, a few streets east over the Scranton city line in a leafy suburb called Dunmore. There Jane lived for the next fourteen years and grew to young womanhood.

It was a house bigger than any Jane would live in later, a successful physician's house, biggest on the block. Their neighbors in 1930, when Jane was fourteen, included a plumbing supply company manager, a civil engineer, and the superintendent of a coal mine. There were grander houses a couple of blocks over on Washington Street, great sprawling affairs. But the Butzners' house was big enough—wide and deep, with porch columns supporting a second-floor terrace, with gables, cornices, shallow bay windows, a garden out back maybe thirty yards deep. Jane's son Jim, hearing about the house from his mother, came away imagining it "a wonderful, generous place to live."

You came in off the street, up past the front lawn, to the broad, columned porch, and stepped into the parlor. Jane's room was a few steps to a little landing, then up two more short flights to the second floor, then first door on your left—probably the smallest of the several bedrooms ranged around a little hall. Jane's window looked out past the balustraded terrace onto Monroe Avenue's quiet, residential harmony. Back on the first floor, kitchen, dining room, and Dr. Butzner's study branched off the broad expanse of parlor which, with its fireplace and passage to upstairs, lay at the center of things; it would have been hard to plant yourself there and not give yourself over to the life of the family. "It was a cheerful place," Jane would say of the house. "We did a lot of talking."

It must have been quite a scene when they all got together, the four Butzner kids, in, say, the early 1930s. They looked pretty much alike, actually—the same-shaped heads, the distinctive Butzner features juggled just a bit differently in each. All tall, strikingly so in youngest son Jim's case. All brainy, and encouraged from early on to use their brains. "Four amazing children," says Jane's niece, also named Jane, of the Butzner kids. When they'd get together later, by then older and married, it wasn't much different, except that then it was the eight of them—each spouse, it could seem, suited not just to one Butzner, but to all of them. All friends, discussing books, ideas, politics, the day's pressing problems, the crazy, funny, outrageous doings of the world. Years later, a family friend would speak of an almost preternatural Butzner-Jacobs optimism, a community of support that bound them together—not a simpy sweetness but a sense that life was too good, too interesting, to waste on wayward fits of ignorance and pettiness. They were "delightfully and acceptingly nonconformist," says another family friend of more than thirty years. "They had no mean streak." All of them, says Carol, sister Betty's daughter,

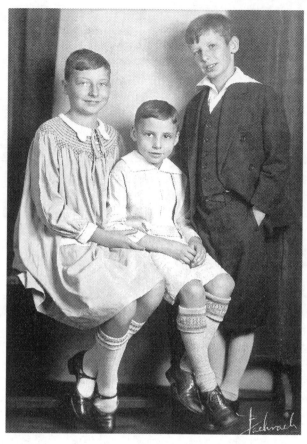

Jane, at left, in about 1927, age eleven, with brothers Jim and John

"reveled in life. Everything was celebratory. It was joyous. Every meal was joyous. Every walk was an adventure." It was a family of "no guilt, no regret, no shoulds, no should-nots."

Too good to be true, of course. And maybe there wasn't among them much latitude, or encouragement, to explore personal feelings or doubts, or to let boredom, annoyance, or futility have their day; this was part of the family culture, too. But allowing for memories sweetened by time and a streak of family boosterism, surely something healthy and productive was alive among them. Betty would become vice president of a major New York interior design firm and was later active in the Esperanto League. John would become a judge, for years a justice of the 4th District U.S. Circuit Court of Appeals, from which he'd issue important and controversial antisegregation decisions. Jim, most of his adult life spent in southern New Jersey, would have a successful career as a chemical engineer for a major oil company and, on the civic front, help transform a tiny local college into a major community asset. Jane would write books and change the world. Each remained married to the same spouse their whole lives—mostly, it seems, happily. The four of them found plenty to disagree about. Their voices could rise. But the way their children tell it, they had fun, and were determined to extract every last fresh nugget of pleasure and interest from the world.

One day when Jane was seven, sister Betty, by then a Girl Scout, took her on a hike. Jane remembered the toasted marshmallows that evening, but more vividly the moment when Betty bumped her foot on a rock. "That's puddingstone!" Betty cried out. *What a great word!* Jane thought, and what an interesting geological anomaly: a mass of rounded stones and pebbles embedded in a sandy, cement-like matrix. Here, at age seven, was something of the peculiar doubleness of Jane's intellect: her lifelong fascination with the world right in front of her nose—an explorer's fascination, a journalist's, a scientist's; and, right beside it, a delight in language and all its nuances of sound and meaning.

At six or seven, Jane was reading pretty much everything, sometimes trailing her mother around the house, book in hand, asking about words she didn't know. She liked nursery rhymes and traditional songs, thought about what they meant. "When Good King Arthur Ruled This Land" tells of pudding stuffed with "great lumps of fat as big as my two thumbs"; Jane saw in it a distaste for profligacy. She loved *The Three Musketeers*. She buried herself in *The Book of Knowledge*, a children's encyclopedia, popular and fun—if, in son Jim's words, "chock full of egregious misinformation, and racist." She discovered Dickens's compulsively readable *A Child's History of England:*

> So, Julius Caesar came sailing over to this Island of ours, with eighty vessels and twelve thousand men. And he came from the French coast between Calais and Boulogne, "because thence was the shortest pas-

sage into Britain"; just for the same reason as our steamboats now take the same track every day. He expected to conquer Britain easily; but it was not such easy work as he expected.

As a young girl Jane may not have talked of it so freely, but much later she'd often refer to the chats she'd have in her imagination with historical figures. "Since I was a little girl I've been carrying on dialogues with them in my head just to keep from being bored." First was Thomas Jefferson—until, that is, "I exhausted my meagre knowledge of what would interest Jefferson. He always wanted to get into abstractions." She turned to Benjamin Franklin, who, she advised an interviewer once, was interested in "nitty-gritty, down-to-earth details, such as why the alley we were walking through wasn't paved, and who would pave it if it were paved. He was interested in *everything*." She'd tell him how traffic lights worked, observe his surprise at how modern women dressed.

She set no limits to her imagination and apparently no one tried to do it for her. "Where I grew up in Pennsylvania," she'd write, "the children believed that on a night in August the lakes turned over." Later, she learned better, but just then "I imagined this marvel as a dark, whispered heaving and slipping of the waters with bright fish tumbling through. We knew when it had happened because we would find floating fragments of bottom weeds and in the top few feet of water, usually so clear, bits of fine muck and a rank smell."

Early on, Jane fell into poetry. In the 1950s, her mother gathered some of her youthful efforts and bound thirty or so of them into a little packet. Playfully or modestly, it's not clear which, they were "published" as the work of one Sabilla Bodine, a forebear, five generations back, on Bessie's side. Jane's poems bore names like "A Mouse" and "Washing" and "Winter," and look their age; they seem very much the juvenilia they are. Mostly, they rhyme: "I wonder if by any chance / Zebra babies like to dance." Mostly, too, they are sweet, sometimes cloyingly so. On the other hand, they are striking for their varied subject matter and style. They include Aesop-like fables involving flies, fleas, and mice; micro-histories of Abraham Lincoln, the pirate Blackbeard, and the French poet François Villon. And warm recollections of Girl Scout camp: "In the dusky moonlight / by the flickering fire / Listening to the whispering leaves / That never seem to tire . . ." And delight in silly wordplay: "The baby is crying 'cause puss caught a mouse / Dingsy, dangsy, dito . . ." Or: "One day the willowing Willow / Willowing like a willow / Saw a waddling / Wallowing / Dolphin / A-wallowing in the sea." A few, just a bit more sophisticated, draw young Jane closer to us: "Small puddles, token of a rainy day / Have always lured me from my schoolward way / I want the crash of thunder, and the rain / I want it beating on my head again! / How can I stay at home, a warm dry place / When I have felt wet hemlock cross my face?"

Whatever we might think of these youthful efforts, she kept at it. Several of her poems were published—later, as an adult, and then, as an adolescent: "Greetings to you from the office of *The American Girl*," the editor, Helen Ferris, wrote ten-year-old Jane in January 1927. "Miss Yost"—perhaps an assistant, perhaps Jane's teacher—"has just sent me some of the poetry you have written and I want to tell you how much I like it." She couldn't use it all, of course, "but you may be sure that I will use at least part of your poetry just as soon as we possibly can." Jane didn't write much poetry as an adult, but she would always read it, and recite it, from what one of her children calls her "endless store" of Shakespeare and Mother Goose, Longfellow, Lindsay, and Frost.

Between her parents, Jane was closer to her father. She'd remember him as "intellectually very curious, bright and independent. He was locally very famous as a diagnostician," a kind of Sherlock Holmes of bodily clues. He used his eyes and ears. "I loved to hear his stories about how he found out this and that." Dr. Butzner, bald and mustached, was forever reading the encyclopedia, not to idly amass informational factoids but to sink into its sometimes long, meaty essays, often discuss them with his family. Jane was about seven, she'd recall, when Poppa would ask her to retrieve for him one or another volume, like the one with *Gr* or *Ro*. "Then, while I looked at the drawings and plates, while he turned the pages, he would regale me with interesting bits" about the Greeks and the Romans. "The bit I liked best was how the barbarians demanded three hundred pounds of pepper from Rome, as part of a ransom payment. He said that as ransoms go, that was a pretty civilized demand."

Jane's relationship with her mother was more problematic. The old lady, hair up in a tidy bun, always neatly dressed and groomed, whom her grandchildren would remember warmly as storyteller and gardener, author of vast waffle breakfasts, likable, intelligent, principled, sometimes funny or wry, always a close and attentive listener, didn't entirely square with the much younger woman, not so long out of Espy, Pennsylvania, whom Jane, as an adolescent, knew as her mother. Bess would grow more tolerant over her 101 years; a staunch Republican, she'd resign from Daughters of the American Revolution when it condemned Jackie Kennedy for sending UNICEF Christmas cards from the White House. Jane, as an adult, recognized her virtues and was perfectly capable of painting a balanced portrait of her. Of how she would walk Jane around the garden each morning, pointing out this new growth or that. Or how, during a coal strike once, she tightly rolled up wet newspapers, one by one, to make artificial logs. "I can still see you in my mind's eye," Jane wrote her affectionately, "dipping them into a bucket of water and drying them in the back yard." Jane would tell how her mother "became the night supervising nurse at an important hospital in Philadelphia"; there's real pride there. She'd tell of her mother's compassion. As a nurse, most of her patients were poor. "She would tell me how limited their lives were," their poverty *eating* at her. In 1975, as her mother approached one hundred and grew more feeble, Jane would write that she still hadn't "come to grips with the idea of this wonderful old lady wearing out . . . I'm used to her being in existence [and] besides, in fact I love her."

But most of that came later and, as a young adult, and earlier in her adolescence, and maybe going back further still, her mother rankled her. She was "quite prissy," Jane wrote, "and particularly about anything to do with sex." Even later, in the 1950s, Jane could write an editor how her mother "to this day astonishes me by her capacity for disapproval of the earthy." A ditty making the rounds after World War I had somehow inspired Jane to recite it around the house:

> Kaiser Bill went up the hill
> To take a peek at France
> Kaiser Bill came down the hill
> With bullets in his pants.

Don't sing that, said her mother; "pants," of course, were underpants, and Jane was not to mention them. But of course Jane kept at it: . . . *with bullets in his . . . ,* whereupon Bess slung Jane over her knee and spanked her. "But I was going to say *trousers,*" Jane wailed.

Jane would picture her mother's mind as a veritable minefield of small-town narrow-mindedness. She remembered being ordered not to play with a Chinese girl in the neighborhood. She was advised that people from Sicily were slum dwellers—for the sole, if unassailable, reason that they were Sicilian. Politically, her mother was much more conservative than her father. When young, she'd been a strong Temperance advocate (as was enough of the country to get us Prohibition). Red wine was "Dago red," one strike against it, of course, being that it was Italian; when Dr. Butzner occasionally got a bottle of wine from a Sicilian coal miner he'd treated, Mrs. Butzner was known to turn it into vinegar if she got her hands on it, or else just pour it down the drain.

So, as many an adolescent before and since, Jane wrangled with her mother. Maybe worse, she felt "I had to shut up about things that I really would have liked to talk to her about." The detailed, pages-long, idea- and fact-filled missives Jane wrote to her mother much later—on farming practices in the Canary Islands, acupuncture, or the "micro-balance-of-nature" represented by ladybugs eating aphids—testified to her own need to *say*, to speak, to explain, and *also* to her mother's receptivity. But again, that came later. As a teenager, especially on more intimate subjects, she didn't feel she had her mother's ear.

This seems to have been about as troubled as Jane ever felt at home. Not that any hurts she did experience were trifling to her; how could they be? But set against the whole fabled, fraught landscape of children and parents, little in her life on Monroe Avenue hints at subterranean terrors or cries out for probing scrutiny.

Jane and her family inhabited the fat, happy middle of American economic and social life. They mostly had enough money, but not too much. Jane grew up in a nice house, on a pretty street of nice houses, in an upper-middle-class neighborhood; the house even had an early dishwasher. But she wasn't entirely cut off from the less lucky. She'd remember a down-at-the-heels area near their house, "the Patch," that had no sidewalks; "you just knew when you went into the Patch that this was a miserable place." She knew about the men who worked the mines; some of them were her father's patients. She heard from her mother about her nursing days and her poorer patients.

Her childhood was sprinkled with a full share of the familiar and the comfortably unremarkable. She went to church—Green Ridge Presbyterian, a few blocks away. (Jane was "never at war with the church," one of her children would say, "just bored.") She traded cards with her friends—of political figures, it seems, not baseball players. She played pirates, the loser walking the plank atop an old stump. She played cowboys and Indians. She sometimes roller-skated to school. She had a hiding place, in a cleft in a nearby cliffside, where she could secrete treasures. Like her sister, she joined the Girl Scouts, went to camp, enjoyed crafts. She'd remember the summer weeks when the Chautauqua came to Scranton, with its great children's programs. She loved listening to her parents and grandmothers talk about their childhoods—like her grandmother, on wash days, making soap from fat and wood ash, or her mother, when she was eight, flipping the switch on the town's first electric lights. She played pranks on her siblings, one time tricking brother John into giving up his favorite shirt. Come Christmas, the tree in the parlor was so cropped and positioned that it poked right up through the stairwell to the second floor, from where Jane and John, hidden, could pull on gossamer-thin threads tied to its branches, the neighbor children invited in to marvel at the tree wriggling and waving in the unseen breeze.

When Jane was about four, the family drove down to Virginia to visit their Butzner uncles, stopped to visit the White House, saw sheep grazing on the lawn, keeping it neatly cropped.

When she was eleven, she wrote in a cousin's autograph book, "Bite off more than you can chew—then chew it," apparently heedless of its unoriginality.

At least once as a child, she flew in an airplane.

But Jane Butzner's childhood was more and richer than any such litany of the everyday suggests. Daily life—especially, as we'll see, her life in school—was no match for what she read in books. And no match, either, for what she saw and heard around the dinner table or in the parlor at home. Her father's mother, Lucy, died when Jane was ten; her mother's mother, Jennie, when she was thirteen; she never knew her grandfathers. But somehow, the great stories and legends of her family reached into her, her head left full of times long past and larger-than-life characters. Not the Jeffersons and Franklins of her private dialogues, but members of her own family who had ventured to distant places, done wonderful things, held stoutly to their ideals.

She heard, of course, of her mother's father, Captain Boyd, who'd died years before she was born, and his Civil War exploits, his imprisonment in the South, his populist ideals, his run for Congress on the Greenback-Labor ticket. "I am pleased to see how many of that party's planks, 'outlandish' at the time, have since become respectable law and opinion," she would write, "and I am proud that my grandfather stuck his neck out for them."

Her father's younger brother, Uncle Billy, the famous one-eyed criminal defense lawyer, as wide as he was tall, all eloquence and cunning, would take up the cause of anybody—bootleggers, black people, scoundrels, and rogues, it didn't matter. In one celebrated case, he defended the husband of a Virginia socialite found hacked to death, successfully pushing the blame onto his client's spurned lover; the jury returned a not-guilty verdict in thirty-six minutes flat. Another time, during Prohibition, his client was prosecuted for two pints of bootleg booze. But when, in court, Uncle Billy opened the bottles and emptied them into a graduated flask borrowed from the town druggist, their contents came to a few drops short of a full quart—the threshold at which a stiff penalty kicked in. His client got off. How did he know they'd come up short? "Well," he said, "I've dealt with a lot of bootleggers in my time and believe me, they always cheat."

Jane's mother's aunt Hannah was another figure of family renown. At age forty-five, this outwardly proper and conventional woman hauled off to Alaska to teach Aleuts and Eskimos. Over a fourteen-year span, she camped out with Indians, clambered up cliffs in voluminous skirts and petticoats, traveled by kayak in garb made from bear intestines. Aunt Hannah was devoutly religious, and what Jane would term "an implacable, relentless prohibitionist"—yet in her own way a champion of women's rights, too. To Jane, growing up, "she had the glamour of a storybook heroine."

And then there was her mother's older sister, Martha, who after her own time at Bloomsburg Normal School and her years active in the Presbyterian church, at age forty-eight virtually vanished from civilization. In 1922, making an exploratory trip on behalf of the church to the mountainous backcountry of North Carolina, she had fallen in with the local people at a tiny, hopelessly backwater community called Higgins. Instead of returning after a few months, Aunt Martha stayed, and stayed, over the years bringing to it something of the light and warmth of modern life—books and learning, new buildings, a handicrafts center, a strengthened church. She was there all the years Jane was growing up on Monroe Avenue.

Jane's family included, of course, the requisite ciphers and nonentities, and plenty of solid if unremarkable mortals, too. You wouldn't hear much about her father's brother Calvin, a gruff figure in overalls who stayed back on the farm, beside his wood stove, with his dogs. Jane's mother was one of eight, and they didn't all work miracles in Appalachia like Aunt

Martha; around the time Jane started in school, Bessie's brother Irvin sold cars and her sister Emily was a school librarian, both of them back where they came from in Bloomsburg. Still, there were enough examples of family heroics and theatrics that Jane might reasonably have concluded that she came from quite a family.

Her life would prove rich in harmonies tuned to those of her family and her forebears. But if so, what—what, *exactly?*—should we make of this? That she came from "good stock," something rare and precious being passed down through her DNA? Or that whatever came down to her did so through the "culture" of the family? Certainly Jane was blessed with extraordinary intelligence; all she thought and said testifies to it. But we can say with equal assurance that she was blessed with an unusually nurturing family; and that of those social and family forces that crush so many children's spirits Jane was mercifully free. She couldn't have known at the time just how rare that was. She knew later, though: "Being in a family where I wasn't put down, that's luck."

Good luck, too, was that she grew up at the right time to be a woman, or a better time, anyway. A time that, more than the Victorian era preceding it or the post–World War II era of her own children, didn't discourage her as girl, woman, worker, thinker. Those years, she'd say, amounted to "an island of hope for women." A constitutional amendment brought women the vote in 1920, when Jane was four. The idea was alive, she'd say much later, "that women were equal to men and could do anything." In the Girl Scouts, she'd remember, "we had all sorts of merit badges, not just child care and being a hostess and those sorts of things, but for astronomy and tree finding and making things. All this was part of a liberating ideology for women. We were lucky." The world was a big place, where you could do great things. You had agency. You could become something. A *woman* could become something.

All in all, Jane Butzner didn't have much going against her. She seems never to have been hampered, or held back, or squeezed into something she wasn't. "I grew up with the idea that I could do anything," she'd say. "Nothing was going to be barred from me if I wanted."

CHAPTER 2

OUTLAW

IF THERE WAS A PROBLEM with this pretty picture it was that it was too special, too rare, and thus certain to butt up against the less forgiving realities of the world outside Monroe Avenue. In Jane's case, the conflict came early—in school, first at George Washington School in Dunmore, later at Scranton's Central High.

"In those days," Jane would recall, classrooms were "more regimented than they are now. For hours we would sit there doing this or that and we wouldn't be allowed to talk unless we were asked a question." Some of her classmates may have found this congenial enough, or at least tolerable. For Jane it was torture, so at odds with her life at home, so deadening, that it exacted its own peculiar price. She developed what she'd call a "misapprehension," a fear "that I couldn't talk anymore, that I didn't have a voice anymore." And out of that, in turn, developed "what you might call a little tic. I would make a little noise in my throat, a little voiced noise, just to be sure I could still talk." One day, finally, her parents asked her why she did that. She wouldn't answer, or couldn't, "because I had a feeling that if I did, it would open up the whole subject of how my teachers and I were at outs a good deal."

Her first two years at George Washington School, located a few blocks from home, at the corner of Green Ridge Street and Madison Avenue, were all right. But then things went downhill. As Jane told it, at numerous times and circumstances during her life, the ordeal of her school years could seem to apply to all of them without distinction—third grade, fifth grade, high school, it didn't much matter. Later, she'd sound downright jealous of her father's schooling in that one-room schoolhouse in Spotsylvania County, Virginia. She'd tell how as a schoolgirl she "didn't listen much in class. I would try to, but I would get bored with it." She always had some book hidden beneath her desk, maybe *Bulfinch's Mythology*, that was more interesting than anything the droning teacher had to say. She'd remember being subjected to "the most awful endless repetition," and years later could still recite all the countries of South America, in alphabetical order, pointing in the air at their locations on an invisible map. "To tell you the truth," she'd tell an interviewer once, "I thought that most of my teachers were rather stupid. They believed a lot of nonsense. I was always trying to educate them, so we would get into conflicts sometimes."

In third grade she managed to get herself expelled. And at least in Jane's adult telling, it was the great gulf between the vibrant, open air of home and the stiflement of school that led to it. A promise, her father told her one evening, was serious business; you never, ever make one unless you're sure you can keep it. Well, Jane would recall, the very next day at school, a man came in to talk to them about tooth care. In a scene redolent with the wholesome spirit of public health and do-goodery of Sinclair Lewis's 1920s, students were ushered into a common room to listen to the good gentleman. Of course, he exhorted them to brush their teeth. But he took things one step further, which is where he got into trouble with Jane: "He asked everybody to promise to brush their teeth every night and morning," for the rest of their lives, and that they raise their hands to affirm their promise.

No, whispered Jane to her schoolmates, they couldn't make a promise like that? *Don't do it.* And pretty soon, "they were putting up their hands and pulling them down," not at all as they were supposed to do.

Back in class, their teacher was mortified. What did they think they were *doing*? Someone pointed the finger at Jane and soon the teacher wormed the story out of her, going on to demand that she and the other miscreants now take the teeth-brushing-forever oath. Jane refused, urging her classmates not to do so, either; when she reenacted the scene years later, you could see her springy youthful energy restored, as she mimed begging her classmates not to comply: They couldn't *possibly* keep a promise like that. It was *wrong* to say they would. "Well," the teacher said, turning to Jane, trying to defuse the revolt. "I'll deal with you next."

The two met privately. "All she got from me was an argument. So, at her wits' end, she expelled me."

Expelled?! "I'd known of people suspended, but never knew anyone expelled." This was different. This was serious. "This was awful. It was like the end of everything." Her parents would be called in. "It came to me good and strong and fast that I was an outlaw"—a sense that would reach across the years into her old age, never entirely dissipating.

Her misbehavior seemed to feed on itself, and may not have been as discouraged at home as fully as school authorities might have wished. One time, Jane went off popping paper bags in the lunch room and was sent straight to the principal. The principal called her father. Dr. Butzner, according to family lore, replied, "I'm a busy man. You're a busy educator. I'll take care of my problems. You take care of yours."

"When we were kids," wrote a Scranton newspaperman who'd known Jane back then, "she was a free spirit, clever, hilariously funny and fearless." She'd spit on the stairway rail and slide down, which made for grand entertainment for the kindergarten children below. She'd run up the down escalator at Scranton Dry Goods, a major department store on Lackawanna Avenue. It was as if she sought trouble for the sheer delight of it.

In fourth or fifth grade, as one of Jane's children recounts the story, her teacher dispensed the wisdom that wearing rubber boots would make your eyes sore. Nonsense, Jane was sure. Nonsense, Dr. Butzner affirmed. Soon she was wearing rubber boots into school every day, parading them around. *See my eyes?* she'd taunt the teacher and anyone else who'd listen. *Look at 'em—they're just fine.*

Another time, a teacher kept her after school; she was to copy out two pages of the history book. "Which two pages?" Jane asked. Didn't matter, said the teacher. Jane selected the frontispiece, which had only an illustration caption: "Columbus Landing at San Salvador." No, said the teacher, that won't do, and gave her two more pages. Jane refused; she'd done precisely as asked. "So there I sat after school and there the teacher sat at her desk doing something, and we sat and sat." Finally, Jane just got up, gathered her coat, and left.

It was bad. The saga of Jane and her teachers mocks the more familiar script—of youthful bristling at classroom constraints, minor behavior problems, parents called into school, corrective action taken, surrender to adult authority, schoolhouse harmony restored. And certainly the story doesn't end with Jane emerging from her school years grateful for a routinized order she's finally learned to accept; she never accepted *that*. Rather, it was mistrust and rancor ranging across the years, a war interrupted by only temporary truces. "She was always afraid of teachers and teachers were always afraid of her," was the truth one of her children extracted from a lifetime of his mother's stories of school.

Years later, in the middle of a two-day university conference in 1987 devoted not to the childhood of Jane Jacobs but to her ideas, Jane would offer her own theory of those troubled years. In grade school, "the little girls who do best are the ones who take the teacher as a model," imagining themselves as teachers someday; in school, they're little apprentices, sopping up the tenets and values of their teachers. That, of course, wasn't her, not one bit. But other little girls "couldn't care less about being teachers," and didn't get "as meaningful an education either—[because] they're resisting it." *That*, she said was her. "I was *that* kind of little girl."

In early 1962, giving a public talk in New York City soon after publication of *The Death and Life of Great American Cities*, Jane Jacobs was telling how her book grew out of the discrepancy between how big housing projects were supposed to be and how they turned out. When she asked architects and planners why projects so often proved less lively and successful than promised, they'd all but call the people living in them stupid—unable or unwilling to do "what they're *supposed to do*." And then, as if the phrase itself caught on some raw tangle of neurons in her brain, leading her into a rhetorical riff, she said, "I didn't know why people weren't doing what they were *supposed* to do, but I did know this much"—here she slowed, laid on the weight of it, thickly—"that if people weren't behaving the way they were *supposed* to behave, then something was at fault with the theories about how they were *supposed* to behave." And knowing her adult waywardness, her lifelong resistance to authority, it was hard not to think of young Jane in school, squirming at all the ways she was supposed to behave but wouldn't or couldn't.

Her son Jim intimates that strategies Jane would later use against unthinking planners and city officials derived in part from those years of wrangling with her teachers. Certainly she came away stronger for them, as she did that day in third grade when she was expelled. Leaving school, she felt bereft, didn't know what to do, wandered off alone. Soon she found herself near the train tracks, which sat low, in a depression, verboten to everyone, certainly nine-year-old girls. On impulse, leaving her books and jacket on the heights above the tracks, she scuffled down the rock face that dropped to the tracks, then climbed back up. Up and down, repeatedly, she climbed, coal trains clattering by all the while, spewing smoke. Only when she heard kids going home for lunch did she clamber back up to the street one final time, gather her things, and trek home to Monroe Avenue for her own lunch, not knowing what would befall her.

Nothing befell her.

At home, with her mother, she tried to "rev myself up to tell her." But she never did, just ate her lunch.

"Better hurry up, Jane, you'll be late for school," said Mrs. Butzner finally.

So she walked back to school, hung her jacket in the cloakroom, and sat at her desk. The teacher never said a word. Jane theorized later that she may even have been relieved to see her. She "may have been terrified at what she had done," Jane's quiet reappearance averting any confrontation.

The incident left her with a feeling of independence. "I was an outlaw and I was accepting the fact that I was an outlaw . . . It really changed me. It was an important event in my life." She'd learned that "you can be afraid of something and the only way to overcome being afraid of it, or to lessen the fear, is to live through it."

In February 1929, Jane, finished at George Washington School, enrolled as a freshman at Central High School, downtown. While her grade school was just a few minutes' walk from home, Central High was a block's walk over to the trolley on Electric Street, then a two-mile ride on a clattering, brightly painted little vehicle with wood-slatted seats—south onto Adams Avenue, a little jog to the west, then almost a straight shot on Washington Avenue down to Vine Street. There, at the corner, was the great Gothic pile of stone that was Central High. Across the street was the central library. After eighth grade, she'd tell an interviewer, "we went downtown to school. Our life enlarged and we had a city life—going to plays, lectures and the larger libraries." Suddenly, all of Scranton lay within her reach, and with it resonances of a wider world.

SO FAR AS DISCONTENT IS EXPRESSED IN
CONSTRUCTIVE MOVEMENTS FOR HUMAN BETTERMENT,
IT IS NECESSARY AND TO BE ENCOURAGED.

These words of John Mitchell, the legendary mine union leader, were engraved on one flank of a monument to his memory erected in Courthouse Square, Scranton's municipal complex, in 1924. Standing before it, you needed no deep inborn appreciation for the rights of labor to feel

something for the men who toiled underground at their dark, dangerous work. A granite tableau, like a niche in a church, sheltered and surrounded the figure of Mitchell himself. It showed men in miners' caps
and high-laced boots emerging from a diagonally striated coal seam.
One of them wields a pickax. Another holds a horse's bridle as the animal
strains against a wheeled cart overflowing with black diamonds of coal.
The scene is cramped and, somehow, even in the light of day, dark—a
stirring monument to human labor. One day a year, Jane knew, miners'
children from a neighborhood near hers got the day off to march in the
John Mitchell Day parade. But who was this John Mitchell? she once
asked a classmate, the daughter of a miner. Oh, Jane recalled her simple
reply, he was "the greatest man in the world." And she would remember *that* right alongside all the boosterish talk she'd also imbibed about
Scranton's glory as anthracite capital of the world.

Black coal, hard coal, stone coal. *Black diamond*. Those were some of
the names given to anthracite, the gleaming-hard, clean-burning coal
that all through the nineteenth century heated millions of America's
homes. ("Bituminous" is the other kind—softer, smellier, more sulfu-
rous.) Most of it came from underground deposits found in an elongated
region of just a few hundred square miles in the mountains of north-
eastern Pennsylvania around Scranton. "Coal is the theme song of this
city in the hills," a Federal Writers' Project book would say of the city in
1940. "Coal brought prosperity and also despair. Coal built its mansions,
stores, banks, hotels, and hovels; it blackened the beautiful Lackawanna,
scarred the mountain sides, made artificial hills of unsightly coal refuse."
Anthracite built Scranton. It furnished jobs; a hundred thousand or more
miners worked those underground seams. It built fortunes.

Anthracite, and the industries that grew up around it, made for a city
that in the 1920s was home to almost 150,000 people. It was the third-
largest city in the state after Philadelphia and Pittsburgh, studded with
civic monuments erected over the past thirty or so years near Courthouse Square or along its downtown shopping district along Lackawanna
Avenue, alive with stores, thick with shoppers, brightly lit at night, plied
by trolleys. The city's electric trolleys were said to be the first in the
nation; "Scranton push, Scranton brains, and Scranton money" had
done it, an early-twentieth-century booster crowed. (Some trolleys were
routed to avoid miners coming home from work, lest a wealthy woman
wearing a light-colored dress soil it on a seat just vacated by one of them.)

The city had a zoo, a museum of natural history, a fine public reference library right across the street from Central High—all these, Jane would recall, "meant much to me as a child"—along with imposing hospitals and, as she remembered, "several stuffy but imposing clubs." The city had begun its long downward slide, owing to clean-burning anthracite no longer being required by law in New York City, ongoing labor troubles, and finally the Great Depression itself. But just now, Scranton was still vibrant, to Jane so interesting and exciting that, she'd say, she liked going to the dentist because it brought her into town. Now, in high school, she was there every day, and began to see the city close up, following her own nose, under her own power.

She was a bit younger than most of her classmates, enrolling at Central when she was not yet thirteen. Much of what comes down to us about her four years there suggests an adolescent girl, in time a young woman, a little lost in the clouds. This from a Central High student publication in December 1931:

There was some mixup or day-dreaming in Physics class last quarter. This example was used: If the current of water in a river makes beautiful scenery, what does the current in an electric wire do? A poetic student popped up and asked: "Does it make beautiful scenery?" I think the poetic student was Jane Butzner.

She was forever late for class. Her homeroom teacher her first year there, Henrietta Lettieri, kept scrupulous attendance records, most students recording untarnished streams of zeroes in the lateness column. Jane was absent rarely, but late seven times that first semester, nine the next. One time, Jane was on her way to being late again and begged her mother to write her a note. Mrs. Butzner obliged, explaining that "Jane sat too long at the edge of the bed with one shoe in her hand." Growing up, Jane's son Jim would recall her sitting like that many times: Jane was *thinking*, or, as he puts it, "figuring something out."

Maybe figuring out a poem, like "To Rupert Brooke," which laments trying "to write / The strange disturbing melodies I hear," but failing, and vowing not to try again.

> And then I read your poems; they give birth
> To glorious exultation, boundless dreams;

> I hope and strive again; you give me food.
> For man, they say, has conquered air and earth,
> But by a poet stars have been subdued.

Jane was still writing poems; this one got a modest prize. Like other alienated students for whom high school meant football or Saturday-night dances more than Latin or English literature, Jane found refuge outside class, in the school literary magazine. *Impressions* was presided over by an English teacher, Adelaide Hunt, who one of Jane's classmates would remember as "a merry person, with a melodious laugh that started somewhere near her solar plexus and gurgled its way upward, irrepressible, infectious." Jane became the journal's poetry editor. During at least her last two years at Central, few issues lacked a Jane Butzner byline, or just a J. B. attached to an essay or poem.

At age ten, her parents had given her a typewriter and a book on touch typing. In her teens, she was already a writer. Several of her poems were chosen for published anthologies, with names like *Saplings* and *Younger Poets,* devoted to student work. One of them earned an honorable mention—one of only ten, in a nationwide poetry contest judged by Joyce Kilmer and other poet notables, that attracted thousands of submissions. When it first appeared in *Impressions* in May 1932 it was simply "Sonnet." In its prize-submitted form, Jane called it "Of a Friend, Dead." It much suggests the preoccupation with life and health at war with death and decline that would run through Jane's adult work. "Fool!" she addresses an unknown figure too ready to accept a friend's death. Dead? When "he holds the concentrated red and golds of autumn afternoons, the flow of sun-warmed brooks in spring"? No, you

> never knew the groping beauty of his thoughts
> Like wing-beats of the night-birds in the dark.
> To say that he is cold is blasphemy,
> When you have seen him fling his arms in bliss
> And laugh, and kick his brown heels to the sky.
> And felt his ineradicable kiss.

In the December 1932 issue of *Impressions,* just before graduation, Jane brought Percival G. Tookey Jr. into the world, or at least, as a kind of fictional school mascot, into the collective mind of Central High. In

Jane's story, Percy laments his name to his father, who assures him that someday he'll have a son and name him Percival G. Tookey III. Thank you, no, replies Percy. But abruptly, now hopeful, he imagines a way out of his name problem. What of that middle initial, father, that G? Might it stand for, say, a nice, familiar, equable, *George*? No, Dad says, it stands for *Geschwindt*. This trifle might have been the end of it, except that the following year, Jane's brother John would bring Percy back to life in the same school journal: Percy's son gets into a scrap with a neighbor, which leads to a legal contretemps worthy of Jane's imagination and John's legal future.

Through *Impressions* Jane brushed up against the larger literary world. When *Cyrano de Bergerac* played in Scranton, a prominent drama critic, Clayton Hamilton, lectured about it at the Century Club. Jane Butzner, girl columnist, was there to ask him whether literary giants like those of old had a place in the modern world. Certainly, he assured her, as they had all through time. "And as he said it," Jane wrote, "I could fairly hear and visualize the centuries sweeping by."

A little later, Joseph Auslander, soon to be named the nation's first poet laureate, swept through town. Jane interviewed him, though not from any respectful journalistic distance: meeting Mr. Auslander, who could speak so beautifully, was like meeting Orpheus himself, Jane wrote, and to actually "exchange ideas" with him was "like speaking with Apollo." *Plus*, Auslander adored Rupert Brooke! At one point, the two of them commiserated about the world's dreamers. "It is those out of tune with the world who are called the dreamers," she had him adding, and they were society's only sure refuge. "Our hope is in the poets. It is the poets who see beauty in the machine age, and it is the poets who grant rescue from the machines."

If Jane was a little geeky, it didn't mean she stayed home all the time reading. Here she was, interviewing literary celebrities. She was on the swim team, too. She was getting something out of high school, just not in class. Accounts don't come down to us of any high school crushes, but she did make friends. One was Jeanne Madden, who enjoyed a brief career in Hollywood before returning home to manage her father's hotel in Scranton. Another was Gershon Legman, a butcher's son, who would go on to study origami, collect bawdy humor, and embark on the serious study of the dirty joke as a genre; Jane would marvel at how he'd made a career out of collecting dirty limericks. Then there was Carl Marzani, born in Rome, who immigrated to the United States in 1924. His family settling in Scranton, he'd entered Central High the year before Jane, speaking English with what he would admit was a "ludicrous" accent. But he took to America, Scranton, and Central High so readily that he graduated third in his class. Then he went to Williams College, fought in the Spanish Civil War, joined the British Communist Party, endured three years of prison for his trouble, and spent the rest of his life as a social activist, radical, and author. Jane would remember him as "a pleasant boy." He would remember her as "on the tall side, a bit gawky and socially shy, but very assertive in class"—and "a living witness to the quality of Scranton's public school system."

This last assertion seems indefensible; Jane was, rather, a living witness to all that can go wrong between school and student. Each semester, Central High listed students on the honor roll, which required grades averaging 90 percent or better. It was only a modestly select list; about one in seven in Jane's graduating class of January 1933 made it every single term. In her senior year Lena Charles made honor roll. So did Joe Scaramuzzo. Jane did not. She didn't make it even once in four years. She never came close. A story heard in Jane's family today probably dates to 1933. Someone, it seems, asked Mrs. Butzner what her biggest accomplishment of the year was. Oh, that was easy, she replied: "getting Jane through high school."

Well, her record doesn't seem *quite* that bad. Jane never actually failed a class, though she several times came close. One semester of sophomore year yielded grades of 74 in French and a barely passing 70 in Latin; she did no better in geometry, where she also got a 70. She did well enough in her eight semesters of English, even cresting over 90 once or twice. And, unaccountably—it flies in the face of her whole school record—she got a 98 in European history in her senior year.

Mrs. Butzner once called her big accomplishment of the year "getting Jane through high school." Proof of success: Jane's graduation photograph, January 1933.

Central High in the 1920s and 1930s was of at least locally high repute; it did not deify sports, did not downplay academics. Jane's classmates included Eastern European Jews, Irish, Poles, and Greeks, among others, who would go on to become librarians and FBI agents, chemists and priests. Statistics from a class a little before Jane's told of 126 graduates admitted to 41 colleges and universities, including Yale, Princeton, and Harvard, with Syracuse, Barnard, and Bucknell notable among the women. At Central, Jane did not inhabit an academic wasteland where the fashion was to reject effort and study. Rather, her problem seems to have come down to all those "stupid" teachers. Here in its entirety is one of her poems, which, once you learn its title, suggests something of her attitude:

> The moon, with all her brilliant light
> Illumines only space and night.
> The stars with but each other's aid
> Stand clearly out, all unafraid.
> Without a light to help explore,
> Some things seem clearer than before.

The poem's title? "To a Teacher." She didn't need teachers whose "light" illuminated nothing; she—presumably one of those stars standing out, unafraid—was better off on her own, without them. Jane would later insist that her dismal high school performance actually *spared* her the tedious college education she might otherwise have had to endure. Whether this was mere rationalization, snide potshot, or both, Jane's high school years fed an antipathy to the traditional classroom, and academic credentials generally, that she would express all her life.

Jane came out of Central High with her independence intact. "I'm not all that different as far as I can see from when I was 13 years old," she'd write *Whole Earth Catalog* founder Stewart Brand, when she was seventy-seven. "I was self-indulgent then about following my own interests and . . . still am. This didn't serve me awfully well in school, but it has ever since."

It must have been hard being Jane's parents during that last year of school. On the one hand, she was so obviously curious and clever. Yet as a student she wasn't any good at all. There was more to being a good student than being smart: you had to get out of bed and get to school on time, sit still, respect your teachers, do what you were supposed to do; at all these, Jane was a failure. "I was thoroughly sick of attending school," she'd say. So as graduation neared in early 1933, one thing was plain: she wasn't going to college. Her parents had put away college money for her, "if I wanted to," but made it clear she didn't *have* to want to. And Jane *didn't* want to.

For many intellectually agile young middle-class men and women, college meant a chance to stretch and explore, leave behind familiar circumstances, and push into new, more challenging ones. Jane's next two years would serve her in exactly this way—only no halls of ivy, no professors. During this time, she'd be ejected from the celestial gardens of Rupert Brooke and her rarefied life on Monroe Avenue into the modern workplace; from a life where it could seem not to matter much what she did into settings where she had to perform, on deadline; from the cozy and familiar middle-sized city where she'd spent her whole life to, first, the backwoods of Appalachia and then the streets of Depression-era New York City.

CHAPTER 3

LADIES' NEST OF OWLS,

and Other Milestones in the Education of Miss Jane Butzner

JANE GRADUATED from high school on January 26, 1933. Franklin Roosevelt took the oath of office as president on March 4, stepping into the most severe depression in anyone's memory. Twelve million were out of work, the unemployment rate at 24 percent. It wasn't just the chronically poor who suffered. Despair licked at the heels of the middle class, many of whom had prospered during the ebullient 1920s but now were jobless, hurting, and scared. Jane would one day picture the Depression's victims standing forever in line, for a job, for day-old bread, in "anxious rows of pinched faces."

Jane's parents had instilled in her and her siblings a memorable precept: pursue what you want in life, and also a practical skill or trade; not one or the other, but both. For Jane, it was not the best time to get lost in clouds of poetry or aim for a paying job as journalist that didn't exist; these days, dreams deferred to practicality and she would have had to be almost willfully oblivious not to see it that way.

All the time Jane attended Central High, *Impressions,* the school magazine she worked on more devotedly than she ever did her studies, carried big, full-page ads for the Powell School of Business. Housed in modest quarters on the third floor of a building a few steps down Washington Avenue from school, Powell doesn't figure much in the annals of higher education, or business education, or any education, really. It started up in the 1920s through the ministrations of its founder, Charles R. Powell, its principal; son Ellwood was vice principal. By the 1950s, it would be gone. But during this intervening epoch, and especially during the Depression, when young Scranton women, and some young men, chased scarce jobs, a lot of them signed on for classes at Powell.

An *Impressions* ad in November 1931, in Jane's junior year, promised the chance for "Building Success On Your High School Foundation." High school, it allowed, supplied a "splendid background." But in a long, explicatory block of text like you don't see much in ads today, it argued for how jobs now demanded specialized training. If graduates wanted a business career, they needed to take "intensive courses in business subjects" that would offer them "A Short Cut to Success." Through Powell's sharply focused programs, all "non-essential subjects" pruned away, you could "prepare yourself for the position of stenographer, private secretary, bookkeeper, accountant, or junior executive."

The stenographer is a fixture of old films and Edward Hopper paintings from the period, the pretty young thing called into the boss's office to take dictation (or, more darkly, *not* to), images filling our mental back pages today along with manual typewriters, carbon paper, and dial telephones. But for many the job was seen as a good one, a step up. Compared to those in factory, mill, or warehouse, it whispered etiquette and decorum. The workplace was clean. The skills it required were substantial. Purveyors of the most popular shorthand systems, Pitman and Gregg, boasted of the dictation speeds their users could attain. An able Gregg stenographer could take down 150 words per minute—fast enough, say, to transcribe a public lecture; the record for some types of material was upward of 250 words per minute. Gregg's was a complex vocabulary of flowing curves and dots. The most minute squiggles, or variations in line length, or location of lines and dots, conveyed meaning. To the unpracticed eye, the words "play," "plate," "plea," and "plead" all looked about the same. "Business" resembled a bird in flight. "Ransack" looked Chinese. Long lists of common forms and expressions had to be memorized and mastered. But with effort, you could get really good at it, and make yourself marketable.

OTHERS ARE SUCCEEDING

A great many high school graduates have attended our school during the past thirteen years. Many of them today hold splendid positions at good salaries. They capitalized on their High School foundation through business training.

Powell did pretty much as promised. In retirement notices and obituaries all through the 1980s and 1990s, aging Scrantonians of Jane's generation would tell remarkably similar stories: They'd graduated from this or that Scranton high school, gone on to Powell, come out knowing how to take dictation, type, compose business letters, and conduct themselves in accord with the starched expectations of the contemporary office. They got jobs with the telephone company, or the railroad, held on through the Depression, the war years, and afterward climbed the job ladder, sometimes to executive positions, and in the end could look back on their working lives with satisfaction.

In January 1933, around the time she received her high school diploma, Jane enrolled in one of Powell's programs, a specially accelerated secretarial course. She had a lot to learn. Writing a business letter meant taking notes on what the boss wanted, then expressing it in your own words later. To get your typing speed up, you had to learn *not* to understand what you were typing; to distract herself, Jane sometimes sang to herself as she typed. Then, of course, there was shorthand, with its endless drills. She took it all seriously, wanted to be the best typist and stenographer she could. And, reports her oldest son, Jim—her confidant across most of her later years and receptive listener to stories of her early life—she didn't begrudge her months at Powell, but found the work "interesting, challenging, necessary, and important."

Powell was enough of a fixture in Scranton that the local paper covered its graduations right alongside those of Central High. On June 23, 1933, *The Scranton Times* carried reports of the Babe's sixteenth home run of the season; of a rumrunner wanted for murder; and of 114 new Powell graduates, assembled in the Central High auditorium, treated to an orchestral procession, saxophone and trombone solos, singing "America," hearing Principal Powell's address, and accepting diplomas handed out by his son. It was rather a grand document, this diploma, one Jane kept all her life—on fancy paper, overlarge, with an engraved image of the school, 1920s-vintage cars and buses bustling by, all testifying to the graduate's "scholarly attainments."

We cannot dismiss Powell as some unlikely or irrelevant asterisk to Jane's life story, this towering figure somehow reduced to cramming humdrum office skills. Rather, it testifies to a groundedness that all her life tempered and redeemed her intellectualism. We don't know how much the decision to attend Powell followed from her own healthy, pragmatic nature, how much from her parents' urgings. What we do know is that for those times, and in that family, she acted reasonably, even wisely. Certainly it paid off. "If I do say so myself," she'd write, "[I] became a good stenographer. I am very glad I did [it], for I earned my living with it—and thus in a sense my independence—for many years."

But earning a living came later. For the next year or so, Jane worked at a newspaper, unpaid. Like many internships today, it proved invaluable, building up her skills, giving her a job credential, and leaving her with a taste for the world of writing and publishing, if only in the distant reaches of it. All through high school, it was writing that had sustained her—poetry, little essays, a stab at fiction, *words on paper*. Writers were her model, her dream. She knew she wanted to be one; nothing she said across her long life ever suggested otherwise. "Her ambition is to be a writer; first to be a newspaper reporter, and later to do writing of other kinds." This autobiographical snippet appeared in a book that published one of her poems, in 1932.

Jane's job, beginning in late summer 1933, was with *The Scranton Republican*, soon to be gobbled up by another local paper, *The Scranton Times*. One day in mid-October, maybe a month after she started there, the *Republican* ran a seven-column front-page headline, "Hitler Speech Wakes War Fear." Then came stories reporting that President Roosevelt was working to "thaw" funds trapped in the nation's closed and imperiled banks; that a tornado had struck Oklahoma, killing three; that the FBI had formed a special squad to track down the kidnapped son of a department store owner. By page 3, readers were deep into the local news, including a parachute jump gone wrong at a local airfield, along with ads for funeral parlors, wool coats, and $10.75 innerspring mattresses. Finally, on page 4, the paper opened up again to a kind of second page 1—a banner across the page, ornamented by silhouetted figures of women in social settings, heralding the Women's Society and Club News.

Here seventeen-year-old Jane Butzner earned her first journalistic spurs, "doing routine items about weddings, parties, and the meetings of the Women of the Moose and the Ladies' Nest of Owls No. 3." These, be it said, are Jane's words, written in 1961, and you might think she'd made them up. She hadn't. Both were real women's clubs of the era, offshoots of men's fraternal organizations. On a page dappled with photos of recent and future brides, readers learned that a baritone had been signed to sing in a musicale for the Lackawanna chapter of the Order of the Eastern Star. A week devoted to "The American Girl" had concluded at the Masonic Temple with a show depicting the seven ages in the life of a girl, based on Shakespeare's seven ages of man.

Some women's-page reporting got more room to breathe, as in a story appearing under this headline:

MOONLIGHT PICNIC
AT SCRANTON HOME
PROVES BIG SUCCESS
HUNDREDS OF REPUBLIC MEN
AND WOMEN ARE PRESENT
AT AFFAIR

The event had taken place on the "spacious grounds at 'Marworth,' the country estate of Mrs. Worthington Scranton," sponsored by the Lackawanna council of the Federal Republic Women—and, of course, was successful beyond expectation. There was a picnic, music, fortune-telling, booths devoted to national cuisines, and, "although there were plenty of candidates on the grounds," a happy absence of speech making. Meanwhile, "the weatherman provided the moonlight on schedule."

The paper rarely carried bylines, so we can't know whether this or any other *Republican* story was Jane's. For the most part, her time there is shrouded in legend—some of her own making. For example, she was known to make up recipes, like one for Normandy apple cake that couldn't possibly come out right; by one family member's account, Jane called for half a cup of baking powder instead of half a teaspoon. "It was preposterous and caused a huge outcry." Of course, she goes on, "Jane had never cooked anything." Jane's work sometimes took her off the women's pages, too. She covered civic meetings, and wrote film, book, and theater reviews. But it didn't matter, really; you learn the rudiments of journalism whatever your subject. Suddenly, facts count, spelling counts. Mrs. Worthington Scranton's bash had taken place just hours before the paper went to press for the morning edition: deadlines count.

One time, asked to revitalize the letters-to-the-editor section, Jane took to writing letters herself, on politics and local affairs. When her first efforts failed to prime the pump, she implored her father, "What in the world am I going to do?" He suggested she write a letter against dogs—that ought to rile up readers. She did, and it did. The section began generating interest. Jane never had to write another phony letter again.

How did she land the job in the first place? The way she told it later, the editor needed a reporter but had no money to hire one. "I can work for you for nothing," said Jane. The editor was taken aback, but agreed: "We can see how it works out, whether we like it and whether you like it." Later, on job applications, Jane would record her pay as $18 a week; it was just—and this was not uncommon during the Depression—that she never actually got it. Though the paper was unionized, Jane recalled, "nobody objected to my . . . make-do barter agreement." The paper assigned one of its reporters "to look after me and be my mentor. I wrote things and they put them in the paper. And I got a big bang out of that." The *Republican*, she'd say at another time, was "my 'journalism school,' and I think it was a good one."

During her time at the paper, she'd often sleep late, work into the evening, then drop by to see her father, who kept evening hours during much of the Depression. Around 1930, he had moved from his old office in the Dime Savings Bank building downtown to new ones, designed to his specifications, in the new Medical Arts Building, a brick- and stone-faced building fronting on Washington Avenue across the street from the *Republican*. The elevator operator would take Jane up to the ninth floor. Suite 909, at the end of a tiled stretch of corridor, had a long, skinny waiting room, Dr. Butzner's consulting room in the corner, and two small treatment rooms.

Sometimes, there were still patients waiting to be seen, in which case Jane would wait like everyone else for Dr. Butzner to be free. If she was restless, she could step over to the window and take in the view of Scranton to the north and east; the city was set in a bowl, hills rising around it. It was uncanny on how small a stage the last few years of her life had played out. Sighting down from her ninth-floor perch to Washington Avenue below, she could see, a few blocks north, the girls' entrance to Central High, poking out from the bulk of her old school building; across from it, the high, steeply pitched roof and dormer gables of the Albright, the library she loved; and then, just across the street, the Powell School and the offices of the *Republican*.

Once her father was free, she'd go in, he'd put down the medical journal he was likely reading, and they'd talk. Sometimes about weighty, even philosophical subjects. More often about patients he'd treated or stories she was covering for the paper. Did they go on from these, her early journalistic efforts, to what she might do next, to career goals, to grand plans for the future? If so, they were soon rendered moot. Because, by the late spring of 1934, her year at the *Republican* was over, Scranton was seven hundred miles behind her along the backbone of the Appalachians to the north, and Jane was in North Carolina, beginning the third "semester" of her post–high school education.

In the early years of the twentieth century, an ex-librarian and sometime adventurer named Horace Kephart dispatched his wife and six children back up north to Ithaca, New York, traveled through the Great Smoky Mountains, fell in with local backwoodsmen, and stayed. Later, he wrote a book about them, *Our Southern Highlanders,* which told of bear hunting and moonshining, of local people never getting around to chinking up their drafty wood-slatted cabins, of local accents so thick an outsider, a "furriner," could scarcely understand them, of people who wanted nothing but to be left alone. Where Jane found herself now, in the spring of 1934, in Higgins, North Carolina, was about the same distance through the dense hollows of the Pisgah mountains to the north and east of Asheville as Kephart had explored to the west. The locals here were not Scots-Irish, though, but mostly of English stock; the village had been founded by three Higgins brothers and their families in the early 1700s. Various and sundry Higginses—Dewey, Edith, Lizzie, Viola, Hoover, and Carrie were some of them—still lived here, virtually all Higgins residents tracing their lineage back to the three brothers.

Near Higgins, not far from Mount Mitchell, the highest peak east of the Mississippi, hills rose to five and six thousand feet. The whole mountain region was one of unspeakable beauty, range after range of peaks fading into one another in the distance, all enveloped in the mists that made the Smoky Mountains appear smoky and the Blue Ridge Mountains blue. Place-names like Bee Log, Bald Mountain, and Crooked Creek studded the map. But the roads were so rude or nonexistent, that, until recently, many people Jane met had never set foot in the county seat, Burnsville, population 866, just twelve miles away. The people were so poor, she'd write, "that the snapping of a pitchfork or the rusting of a plow posed a serious financial crisis." Jane's explanation for how she'd wound up here? "My parents," she would write, "thought I should get a good look at a very different and interesting kind of life." But maybe, you can hear it said among the family today, maybe it was as much Jane getting on her poor mother's nerves: *Well, now, Jane,* we hear Mrs. Butzner saying, *why don't you just go down and visit your aunt Martha . . .*

A local paper noted Jane's coming, as it did that of almost everyone else arriving in the mountain hamlet.

Higgins, May 17. (Special). Miss Jane Butzner of Scranton, Pa., has arrived at this place to spend the summer. Miss Butzner is the daughter of Dr. and Mrs. J. D. Butzner. Since her graduation from the Scranton High School and the Powell Business College she has been a reporter on the Scranton Republican. She expects to continue her writing while here, as well as assist in the various community activities being outlined for the summer. She is a niece of Miss Robison and is a member of the Sunshine Cottage family.

The news squib didn't need to say who Miss Robison was. Miss Robison was Jane's aunt Martha, her mother's sister, the big-bodied, round-faced fifty-nine-year-old ball of energy and devotion who, in important ways, *was* Higgins. She and Bess had grown up together in Espy and Bloomsburg and attended the Normal School there. But Martha, five years older, was the more driven of the two. She knew the alphabet at two years of age, was writing at three, could read at six. Her intelligence and personal force were of the kind that, by century's end, would yield a generation of high-powered women lawyers and executives; Martha became a high-powered missionary. When in 1930 the census taker came to her house in Higgins, that's just how she replied, plain and simple, when asked her occupation: *Missionary.*

"Bible study, a godly Sunday School teacher and other influences," she'd write, "led me to give my life to the Lord for fulltime service at 18 years of age." After leaving Bloomsburg, she'd taken short courses in religious education at Auburn Theological Seminary, worked for the Sunday School Association for fifteen years, and in 1920 she finally came to the Presbyterian Church's Board of National Missions. She "never thought seriously of any other work," she'd write, and by the time Jane reached Higgins in 1934, Martha had been the guiding light of the missionary center there for twelve years.

On a trip north in 1928, Martha told a gathering of church people how her great adventure had started. It was on "a wet, murky, gloomy January day" in 1922 after riding twelve miles along muddy roads to reach Higgins. Her assigned task was to use the scant money provided her to set up, over three months, a house for a permanent missionary worker, then move on. Instead, she remained for seventeen years, until shortly before her death. In the valley that reached a mile or two north and south of the blip on the map that was Higgins (though few maps noted it at all) and up the sides of the mountains flanking it, she found squalor, the local school rarely in session, a Sunday school that had never functioned for so much as a year at a time, a local preacher who boasted he hadn't learned to read until he learned to preach and who could not be persuaded that the world was round.

Early on, the story goes, Martha stumbled on some mechanical gear remarkably cleaner than anything else around—part of a still, naturally, that hardy staple of Appalachian moonshining lore. But Martha found others of her prejudices undercut. It was "most unfair," she'd tell her northern audience in 1928, "to describe extremes as though they were typical and to make general and sweeping assertions" of the mountain people. She found among them men and women stuck firmly in the past, but others forward looking; some intelligent, others "not only illiterate, but whose minds are closed to all that means growth and broadening of life."

One day, listening to an egregiously ignorant religious debate among some of the locals, she was seized by the "overwhelming conviction" to stay right where she was and try to better the community. She set about building up the Sunday school. She began men's bible classes, directed plays at the church, managed to prop up its finances. In the early days, sometimes forty or fifty children would crowd into her own modest house for bible school lessons. For seven years, with little support, she struggled.

Then, in the second week of November 1929, two weeks after the stock market crash, she received a letter from her cousin, John Markle, a wealthy Pennsylvania coal baron. Markle had learned of her work in Higgins, taken an interest in it, and wanted to help, with money. A few days later, in tones of mingled gratitude, astonishment, and hardheaded practicality, Martha wrote him back, sketching in some of what she'd done in Higgins, and outlining her needs: a school, a building to house it with room for craftwork, and an infirmary; recently, a little girl had almost died before they could get her to Asheville, forty miles away. The list went on. "You see, all these things for our work I've been dreaming about—but never dared think they would ever, any of them, come to pass. I think the heavenly Father," she added, "must have put in your heart the idea of helping some of these dreams to come true." Early the following year, Markle promised to give $25,000 toward Martha's work, an amount today worth half a million or more.

Soon the money was flowing south and a building was going up, with a mansard roof and great stone chimneys, like a chateau lifted intact from the French countryside. The first floor had a community library, a health unit, and a meeting room; the second floor was divided into three spaces, for woodwork, weaving, and pottery. "The spaces are all ample and yet hospitable and folksy," Markle heard in a letter from the Presbyterian Board of National Missions in 1931. Film footage shot probably around the same time shows a small level area in front of the Markle building and the adjacent minister's house, with a few automobiles; it's the only such area around, the rest of the site rising up toward the surrounding hills. We see movement and bustle, working men in overalls, suspenders, and caps, a little island of modernity conferring big-city grace notes on the otherwise isolated mountain community.

Soon, local people were making quilts, chairs, and brooms of tightly tufted straw, working the three looms on the second floor. And soon outsiders were coming to see what Martha (and cousin John) had wrought. "Welcome," declared a sign, in artfully inscribed letters, beside the road, to the

HIGGINS NEIGHBORHOOD CENTER
PRESBYTERIAN CHURCH
MARKLE HANDICRAFT BUILDING
LOCAL PRODUCTS WEAVING
WOODCRAFT BASKETRY, ETC.

That "etc." included wild honey and sorghum molasses. On July 3, 1934, while Jane was there, the first lady, Eleanor Roosevelt, visited, buying several "mountain jugs" at the little roadside stand they'd set up for the occasional tourist.

By the time Jane arrived in Higgins in May 1934, Aunt Martha—

Higgins's "inspiring genius," one account called her—had made great strides at dragging it into the twentieth century and bettering the social and, presumably, the religious life of the local people. Jane stayed with her and Martha's foster children at Sunshine Cottage, which sat on a knoll, up a steep slope from a stream that you could hear rustling and gurgling all around the little compound. The Markle building was substantial. It dominated the site. Yet it was wholly dwarfed by the mountain rising across the road from it, as if sited precisely in order to show off men's and women's insignificance in the face of God's grandeur.

Jane's sister, Betty, had come down for a visit in the summer of 1932, but stayed only about a week. Jane was up in the mountains for about six months and for at least some of that time put to work. In July, the center hosted a vacation bible school. "Girls' club work will be under the direction of Miss Jane Butzner," a local paper reported—noting what was apparently her chief credential, that in the Girl Scouts back in Scranton she'd been a Golden Eaglet, the highest rank. On July 29, Higgins briefly became a kind of rural metropolis, as "the largest gathering of people ever brought together in this neighborhood" converged on its Holland Memorial Church for a grand family reunion, 250 people from all over, dozens of Higginses among them, gathered on the lawn in front of the Markle building.

By early fall, just as the surrounding hills were erupting in fall color, Jane's father and younger brother Jim came down to pick her up, along with the brooms, chairs, and other craft mementos of Higgins she'd collected, and take her back to Scranton. In those first hours of her leave-taking, we can't say how Higgins inhabited her mind. But over time, it is plain, the place touched her profoundly. Fifty years later, she would devote to it a substantial chunk of one of her books.

In it, the mature Jane Jacobs did not view Higgins through a scrim of nostalgia or allow visions of a simpler rural past—of a Higgins perhaps poor, but more noble for all that—to distort her memories of the place. "We may mourn the disappearance of the old subsistence life with its bypassed, interesting ways," she would write. But, she all but said, she didn't indulge in that kind of thinking herself. Nor was Jane apt to remind you of Horace Kephart, that chronicler of the Smokies, in his love for the mountain people and fascination with their ways. Conceivably, her time in Higgins might have ignited in her a wish to return, renew old ties, immerse herself in the lives of those she'd met in 1934. But she seems never to have seen Higgins again, nor to have much corresponded with anyone she'd met there. The Asheville area became renowned for its artisans, craftspeople, and music makers and as a popular destination for tourists and retirees (including Jane's brother Jim and his wife, Kay, whom she did visit in 1988) as well as photographers who could never get enough of its mountain mists, of baby bears and great bounding bucks, of shimmering waterfalls and oaks in autumnal glow. Jane was not blind to these charms; she'd recall the area's "majestic folded hills, hardwood forests and loud, tumbling brooks." But they were not what made the deepest impression on her.

No, what stuck with Jane all those years later was something darker and bleaker: Higgins's poverty, its ignominious decline over the generations, the tragic disappearance of its old skills. Jane would write of how, before the coming of Aunt Martha, candles had disappeared from daily use, of families forced to "make do with firelight"; of an ancient relic of a sorghum mill, "powered by a circling, plodding mule"; of looms repaired so ineptly that the cloth they made was of inferior quality, "too fragile in some spots, too thick in others, lumpy and unraveling at the selvages." Jane would tell her son Ned how coffee in Higgins meant a pot of old grounds, hot water run through it again and again, stretched interminably; she tried it herself and "about died." Whatever the temptation to paint this backwoods world in a warmer glow, such loss of human craft, ingenuity, and economic vitality to her seemed a tragedy.

Read Martha Robison's accounts, public or private, read articles written about Higgins, and it is hard to avoid the truth that her little mountain outback depended on charity. When a writer for the *Presbyterian Advance* described her work there in September 1932, he billed it as "the thrilling story of Higgins Neighborhood Center and its enterprising executive Martha E. Robison." And it *was* a thrilling story, if you gave yourself over to it in the right spirit. But his account concluded by asking for help—for a radio, and "a phonograph with a lot of good records," and a Delco electric generator. Any letter to Miss Robison "proposing to send gifts," readers were assured, would "secure prompt response." And yet these hard times in Higgins, long predating the Depression, were not the product of a killer hurricane, spring floods, or racial oppression. Its people, from that same hardy English stock that first colonized America, worked hard, "were bright and full of curiosity, as intelligent as any of us," Jane would remember. "They were a far cry from the feckless and loutish hillbillies of the comic strips." Yet somehow, Higgins had descended to this sad state where it depended on the kindness of strangers.

Jane was neither unmindful nor unappreciative of Aunt Martha's efforts. On the contrary, she had seen with her own eyes all she had done, could contrast it with the Higgins of that wet January day back in 1922 when Martha Robison had first come to town. And, amid the depths of the Depression, Higgins was getting better—no question. But what gnawed at Jane was how it had descended so far in the first place. How had Higgins gotten to the point that all of Aunt Martha's dynamism and determination, and all of John Markle's money, were so necessary? A question began to form, if perhaps without words yet to put to it: *How could this have happened?*

CHAPTER 4

THE GREAT
BEWILDERING WORLD

I N NOVEMBER 1934, in the middle of the most malignant economic depression anyone could remember, eighteen-year-old Jane Butzner moved to New York City.

Nothing we know of her parents suggests that either of them discouraged her from doing so. They were both in "the helping professions," but hadn't tried to push her into nursing, teaching, or medicine. They had offered to put her through college; but Jane was not about to endure another day in class, and they were not about to make her. The spirit and energy of cantankerous Uncle Billy in Fredericksburg, the example of her adventurous aunts in Alaska and North Carolina, were alive in the family; in comparison, lighting out for New York was unspectacular, hardly apt to be discouraged—that is, if anything like discouragement was part of the Butzner family repertoire at all. Even Jane's straitlaced mother could be seen as a model, having thrown over one career for another and abandoning small-town life for big-city Philadelphia.

For Jane, high school was behind her. She had basic job skills, and a year of reporting experience with a serious paper. Her hometown, whose depressed coal economy had preceded the country into the Depression, offered scant reason, economic or otherwise, to remain. In moving to New York, she was doing what generations of ambitious and spirited young men, and sometimes women, had done before her—heading off to the city to become artists and writers. New York, Jane would write, was "where I came to seek my fortune." A cliché? Certainly, but true: "I was trying to be a writer."

By the time Jane arrived in New York, her sister, Betty, six years older, was already there. While Jane was painfully scraping through high school, Betty had been working hard, doing well, in Philadelphia. She'd graduated from the Pennsylvania Museum and School of Industrial Art in June 1933, completing a program in interior décor, her four years there brimful with furniture, fabrics, watercolor, and design; on the evidence of the several prizes and honors awarded her in her junior and senior years, she probably stood near the top of her class. But her career miscarried in Depression-sick New York. For a while she'd lived with other young women in a cheap rooming house on East Ninety-fourth Street. Finally, though, she got a job in Brooklyn, in the home furnishings department of the big Abraham & Straus department store downtown—one unworthy of her education, perhaps, but a job. Soon she moved to an apartment on the top floor of a walk-up on Orange Street, a fifteen-minute walk to A&S, where Jane now joined her.

Their building was on the edge of Brooklyn Heights, a neighborhood occupying a bluff rising sharply from the East River and looking across to Manhattan. The Heights had long been an aristocratic enclave of fine brownstones, a swank suburb of New York, really, though its luster dimmed a bit when the subway arrived in 1908 and with it less high-toned commuters. Just a few blocks from where the Butzner women lived, a street called Columbia Heights flanked the river; from it, the Lower Manhattan skyline could seem close enough to touch; on most days you could see the Statue of Liberty. Up Columbia Heights near the Brooklyn Bridge was Fulton Ferry, the stretch of riverside Walt Whitman had commemorated almost a century before in "Crossing Brooklyn Ferry," but now seedy, overgrown with flophouses and greasy restaurants; Jane and Betty lived a block from the print shop on Cranberry Street where Whitman had set type for *Leaves of Grass*. Their stretch of Orange Street was lined with both newer apartment buildings and grim "old-law" tenements that reformers had tried to root out but which still housed miserable hundreds of thousands all over the city. The street came to an end at Fulton Street, with its shops and clattering elevated trains.

From almost the beginning of that first year in Brooklyn and for most of her first two years in New York, Jane bounced between jobs—occasional jobs, part-time jobs, jobs that looked like regular jobs but vanished when her employer did, as happened more than once. Early on, she worked for a financial writer for the Hearst papers, Robert H. Hemphill, a former utilities executive, Federal Reserve Bank official, and sometime inventor who held decided views about the decidedly wobbly Depression-gripped banking system; she kept his clipping files, did his research, took his dictation. She helped a broker who thought he was writing a book about the stock market. She sought work at the Markle Foundation, Aunt Martha's benefactor—but came up empty. She worked for Westclox, makers of Big Ben, the "polite alarm clock," a mainstay of American bedsides, filing orders "from all the exotic places on Earth"—that's how Jane put it. For one heady moment, she felt "involved in this great enterprise, in which soon everybody in the world would be supplied with clocks." What she actually did all day, of course, was type and file, file and type. Ultimately, she realized that the great enterprise would never be done, "that the clocks would break down or get lost, and that the work was going to be interminable." The big Up, then the precipitous Down—played out across a single week, at the end of which she quit. Give her a break; she was eighteen years old.

It was the only time Jane actually quit a job during these years. Often she had no work at all. And jobs she did land might pay as little as $12 a week. "I could barely scrape by on it," she later wrote. She'd remember one that was particularly boring—working all alone, endlessly filing colored slips of paper. Coming to feel "hopeless and depressed," Miss Jane Butzner bought herself a $1.25 share of an Irish Sweepstakes ticket, which was illegal at the time. She'd been raised to disapprove of gambling "as stupid, feckless and in some way immoral . . . But in my mood of futility," she bought in. "I couldn't afford it. It meant postponing new soles for my shoes, making do instead with pieces of inserted cardboard." She didn't win, yet never regretted it: "Suddenly, and so easily, I had purchased suspense, anticipation, hope," she'd write. "I'm still grateful for the weeks of nutty anticipation when I needed it so badly. The daring and delicious illegality didn't hurt either."

Betty was doing a little better than she, making about $14 a week. When both of them were working they could sometimes even afford to get their apartment cleaned. But occasionally, too, they were reduced to eating Pablum, a bland, precooked baby food that, however unappetizing, was at least nutritious, or so their father said. More often, they'd chop up onions, tomatoes, and green pepper and mix in some beans and a little hamburger. And some garlic: "We thought we were really in the avant-garde," Jane would remember. "We'd never had garlic in Scranton." They called their concoction "catchabeano," because "it had lots of beans in it and we just thought it was a catchy name." Compared to Pablum, "it was our equivalent of a grand gourmet thing." At some point, Mrs. Butzner gave them a copy of *The Fanny Farmer Cookbook;* when once Jane complained to her that she'd never taught her how to cook, Mrs. Butzner shot back, "Well, I taught you how to read, didn't I?"

Later, Jane never made much fuss about the difficulties she faced in adapting to New York; it was adapting to the Depression she remembered with a shudder. "I think that's the hardest time I ever had," she'd say. And yet, it wasn't *as* hard for her as for many others. For people in their thirties who'd watched newly launched careers crash, or those in their forties or fifties flattened by rejection and idleness, the Depression was devastating. Back in 1929, the national unemployment rate had been 3 percent; in 1935, it was 20. But for Jane and some of her young friends, she'd write, they could still "make stories out of our rejections and frugalities and the strange people we met up with in our futile searches and could bask in the gasps or laughs we generated."

The short-lived, ill-paying jobs Jane held during these years might seem the most justly omitted element of a successful woman's résumé, the kind that, further along in your career, you simply forget to mention. Jane, though, was grateful for them. "It was not what I wanted," she'd write, "but it was interesting and I enjoyed myself." Indeed, they were just the jobs her Powell training had prepared her for; Jane could take shorthand at 110 words per minute and type 70—not extraordinary, but respectable—and she was proud of it. Jobs like hers gave her a peek into the underside of American business that many of her college-bound classmates probably lacked.

Many mornings, after scanning the classified ads for work, Jane took the subway into the city. Sometimes, though, she hiked into Manhattan across John Roebling's eternally glorious Brooklyn Bridge, along its wood-slatted promenade, under and through its great Gothic towers. The bridge's four muscular steel cables began their ascent from their moorings on either shore, climbed up to the towers, reached across the river. From the cables dropped steel suspenders, and from the towers diagonal stays; the two were clipped together where they met, shivering in the wind and traffic. At mid-span, the cables swung down to the roadway, then disappeared beneath it. So when Jane reached that spot, equidistant from either shore, high above the water, it was just her, and the river, and the great city below.

Sometimes Jane would be sent off for a shorthand or typing test. Sometimes she'd be turned down flat. But by late morning, in any case, there'd often be nothing left but to explore wherever she found herself, or else invest a nickel on the subway and take it to some random stop. There, she'd climb the stairs to the street, maybe pause for an instant as she emerged into an unfamiliar prospect of buildings, people, signs, and shops, then push off into the surrounding streets. "I didn't know where I was most of the time," she'd say. She had only the dimmest sense of the colossus that was New York. "But it fascinated me. It was wonderful. Every place I came out I was amazed."

Mornings scrounging for work, afternoons exploring the city—that was the pattern. It was toward the end of her first year in New York that one such voyage of exploration landed her in Manhattan's fur district, west of Sixth Avenue in the West Twenties, crowded with carts hauling pelts of mink, muskrat, and ermine, sometimes an errant tiger skin, on their way to becoming wraps and scarves. Jane's face must have betrayed her wonder, for at one point a man stepped from his shop, introduced himself, and soon was regaling the eager nineteen-year-old with tales of the fur district.

And just then, in the late summer or early fall of 1935, Jane Butzner took a giant step into her life's work. Back at Central High, being a writer mostly meant poetry. But a few times, something or someone capturing her interest, Jane had looked, listened, taken notes, and written of it not in poetry but in prose. Then, at the *Republican*, she'd taken her turn as unpaid cub reporter. Now, she would get paid by a national magazine, *Vogue*, for what in Scranton she'd given away free.

"Everyone in the New York fur district seems to know everyone else—but not everyone speaks to everyone else." That's how she began the article she'd write about it. Competition was intense. "Each packet of furs, in its journey from trapper to fur-farmer, to auctioneer to dresser, stirs up feuds." She was astonished by all she saw and heard. She wrote of racks and handcarts, heaped with furs, parading up and down Eighth Avenue; of an auction catalog promoting the sale of the hides of ten thousand mountain lions, seventeen thousand wolves; of fur theft so common that trucks had "hold-up horns" and shops had inner doors of iron bars. "Inside the barred doors and behind the wire grating back of the shop-windows," she wrote, "the shops are dark and eerie. Mounted heads of ferocious animals project from the walls. Mounds of furs cover crates and hand-carts, filling the shop with a rank, musty odour."

Jane would later minimize what she had done, would say her fur district account owed "practically word for word" to the gentleman, Mr. Edgar Lehman, who'd stepped from his shop to talk to her. But in her piece, you could see a real writer's sensibility at work, one alive to curious details. "Every Christmas," she concluded it, "thousands of white whiskers made of strips of Angora goat are sold for department store Santa Clauses. Just now, the district is hopeful that the hanging of red fox tails on radiator caps, a fad started by some taxi-drivers, will bring a boom to the fox-tail business."

In the November 15, 1935, issue of *Vogue*, fashion-conscious readers learned of the recent Paris collections, read about wool and fur pom-poms on hats, one-shouldered gladiator necklines, crocheted Spanish shawls, fringes dangling from tailored black dinner jackets. Modern women were advised that now they were free to "Dine in Suits" or "Dance in Pleats." A jeweler showed off rings with bands of alternating rubies and diamonds. Jane's one-thousand-word story, "Where the Fur Flies," fit right in.

It was quite a coup for a nineteen-year-old just out of high school. She'd written the piece, impressed an editor enough to have it accepted, and pocketed $40—two or three weeks' worth of typing and dictation in the uninspiring office jobs she had such trouble finding—and finally was pleased to see it appear in print, her name right there at the top of page 103. And her editor wanted more. Over the next year and a half, she delivered three more pieces to *Vogue*, each celebrating another of Manhattan's specialized wholesale districts: leather, flowers, and diamonds. Jane wrote of bullfrogs and sheep intestines made into novelty leathers. Of how on flower district sidewalks the "damp, sweet perfume [of cut flowers], blowing across the pavement, filters from hampers and crates piled beside doorways." Of how it took pawned diamonds thirteen months to reach the auction house; outside, meanwhile, on the Bowery, "the 'El' roars, trucks rumble, bums sprawl beside the curbstone, Chinamen from Mott Street mince by, snatches from foreign tongues are caught and lost in a reek of exotic and forbidding odors."

Each article offered a peek into the business of fashion; that's why they were in *Vogue* in the first place. Each delivered a streetside grittiness that could seem to foreshadow its author's life, forever linked to cities. But more than anything "urban" about them, each displayed a love of color and oddity, a curiosity about how the world worked, that reflected her deepest sympathies.

Living on Orange Street in Brooklyn Heights, Jane and Betty Butzner were New Yorkers—more or less, sort of.

Betty's daughter, Carol, would grow up hearing of the charming triplet of streets—Orange, Pineapple, Cranberry—that defined their Brooklyn neighborhood. Jane would adjudge it "delightful." Back in Walt Whitman's time, before 1898, when it relinquished its independence to become a mere "borough" of the City of New York, Brooklyn was its own city, sitting contentedly across the river from New York; until the Brooklyn Bridge went up in 1883 it was linked to New York only by ferry. When Jane moved there its population, at 2.6 million, was more, by 800,000, than that of Manhattan; just by itself, it was the third largest city in the United States, after only New York as a whole and Chicago. It had its own downtown core, its own stately blocks of brownstones, its own slums, its own shopping and industry; even in places like Flatbush or Midwood its own suburbs. On Orange Street, Jane lived closer to Lower Manhattan's luster, growl, and grit than most Manhattanites did. After a two-block walk to the Clark Street subway station and the elevator down to the tracks, she was fifteen minutes from Times Square, four from Wall Street.

But of course none of that counted; *Brooklyn wasn't New York.*

It couldn't have been long into her life there that Jane learned what every New Yorker knew, that "the city" was Manhattan, period. The fur district she'd stumbled upon so fortuitously was in Manhattan. So was the diamond district. *Vogue* itself, New York fashion personified, was in Manhattan. The jobs she got that first year were all in Manhattan, as were the better jobs she sought now. So were Broadway, Times Square, Fifth Avenue, the tall towers, the publishing houses, the galleries, and practically all the other iconic places of New York. It was hard not to feel the pull. Jane had only to glance down Henry Street, at the great stone arches that were the Brooklyn Bridge approaches, to take herself in her mind's eye to Manhattan. For Jane, as for any young person of curiosity and spunk, the city beckoned.

On one of her forays into Manhattan near the end of that first year, probably in late summer, Jane got out at the Christopher Street subway stop; she "liked the sound of the name," she'd say. She had no idea where she was, "but I was enchanted with this place . . . I spent the rest of the afternoon just walking these streets."

As she got off the train, she'd have seen the name of the station set in mosaic tile, as in most of New York's four hundred–odd subway stations:

CHRISTOPHER ST.
SHERIDAN SQ.

Sheridan Square was no "square" at all, of course. But out of its irregular and unlovely expanse radiated Seventh Avenue South and wide West Fourth Street. Stroll along them, or on Grove Street, Washington Place, or Waverly Place, which all converged there, and soon you found yourself among a warren of little streets south and west of the square, the clubs and bars lining West Fourth Street that drew revelers from the outer boroughs, art galleries, small shops, modest apartment buildings.

It was here, in a low-lying bowl of cityscape mostly off the tourist maps, far from the great employment centers, not grand, not rich, maybe a little ragtag, that Jane now found herself. No neatly defined shopping districts here in the streets near Sheridan Square, nothing like upscale Fifth Avenue or proletarian Fourteenth Street—no neatly defined anything. Blocks of handsome brownstones across Sixth Avenue that could have stepped out of a Henry James novel, musical Italian filling the shops and stoops of the tenements to the south, gritty warehouses and a sprinkling of small-scale industry to the west. Along Bleecker Street, a bakery selling Italian bread for a nickel a loaf, a cheese shop selling ricotta for twenty-five cents a pound. Peasant smocks, antique jewelry, and secondhand books for sale arrayed on one block. A drugstore selling cosmetics and contraceptives. An ice cream parlor where the neighborhood's young Italian men hung out. The scale was small, the range and variety stunning, the streetscape obeying nothing like cool Cartesian order. This wasn't New York in its bigness, its numbers, its densest crowds that Jane found here. If anything, it was New York in all its smallness, its irregularity, its turn-the-corner-and-what-do-you-find little shocks and surprises.

The Manhattan street grid fell apart here, as if by an abrupt, invasive fault in an otherwise orderly crystal matrix. West Fourth Street, obediently grid-bound just to the east, at Sheridan Square abruptly veered northwest and, after a few blocks, dared to run, against all sense and logic, into West Eleventh Street. Other streets, like Carmine, Cornelia, and Jones, simply disappeared after a block or two. A conscientious student of urban life, Professor Caroline Ware of Vassar College, had recently tallied the "contents" of one block of Jones Street. She counted old-law tenements and 1840s-vintage houses, an apartment house that went up only in 1929, factories that made feather mattresses, children's toys, and Italian ice cream; an old stable, a settlement house, two grocers, a tobacco and candy store, an ice dealer's cellar, a French hand laundry, a barber shop, a tea room, an "Italian men's café," a wrought iron workshop, and (it still being Prohibition at the time of her census) three speakeasies. All in a single block. Behind this line of five-story façades—inside, unseen, hidden—life played out each day and night, in all its struggles, pains, and pleasures; on the busy sidewalks outside, traces and whispers only of those silent stories, spilling out into the city's everyday jangle.

Spend an afternoon on streets like Jones Street, as Jane did, and any part of the brain habituated to easy order was bound to come away bruised. But Jane? She "liked the little streets," she'd remember. "I liked the variety of it and there were craft shops of hand-made things of ingenuity and artistry. I had never seen shops like those. I just thought it was great." The whole neighborhood was great. Could she have said why, exactly? Maybe not. She was nineteen. She was all enthusiasm. Toward evening she found her way back to Sheridan Square, took the subway back to Brooklyn, soon was trudging up the flights of stairs to her apartment. There she told Betty of her adventures and announced—in Jane's several tellings of this story, it sounds like a command—that where she'd been that day was where they would have to move. Across the next thirty-three years, Jane had only three homes in New York City, all within five hundred yards of where she'd emerged from the Christopher Street subway stop that day.

One weekend sometime later, Jane brought Betty back to the neighborhood and by around October they had moved into the first of the three. It was an apartment in an ordinary six-story building, a bank of fire escapes affixed to its face, on a stretch of Morton Street a block from Jones. Once a walk-up, it had been fitted with a small elevator. Here Jane and Betty, sometimes with other roommates, lived for the next eight years. The rent (in 1940) was $50 a month. Neighbors included a photographer, a teacher at neighboring New York University, a music teacher, an office manager at a law office, and a novelist and his illustrator wife. It's a little hard to credit, but Jane would insist "that we lived there quite a while before we knew we were in Greenwich Village."

Feminism, socialism, pacifism, Marxism, Freudianism, cubism, abstract expressionism: "Many major movements in American intellectual history began or were nurtured in the Village," Ross Wetzsteon observed in *Republic of Dreams,* his paean to Greenwich Village as bohemian icon. The Village had been home to the birth control pioneer Margaret Sanger, the poet E. E. Cummings, the playwright Eugene O'Neill, to hard drinkers, potheads, radicals, and troublemakers. All this was true. True from the perspective of 2002, when Wetzsteon's book appeared, and scarcely less true in 1935, when Jane moved there. And yet, for now, irrelevant: years later, Jane was asked, "Did you hang out with any of the Greenwich Village bohemians of the day?" Her reply was straightforward and unembellished: "No."

The same year Jane landed there, Professor Ware came out with her study of Greenwich Village, which she revealed as bigger and richer than its stereotype as "New York's Latin Quarter of 'long-haired men and short-haired women,' artists and pseudos." As city neighborhoods go, it was large. Home to fifty thousand people, it extended roughly from Broadway to the Hudson River, from Fourteenth Street down to Houston Street or a little south, and encompassed numerous subdistricts. Villagers worked in warehouses and small factories on the west side, spoke Italian in broad swaths of the South Village once mainly Irish. They studied and taught at New York University. They were shopkeepers, bartenders, physicians, clerks, and office managers, and, yes, even artists and bohemians. Village residents attended Catholic schools and public schools. Protestants worshipped at no fewer than eight churches. One could blithely record the history of Greenwich Village, recount its growth over the years, the coming of its waves of immigrants, tell of the literary lights who, by the 1930s, had already called it home, describe its impact on American political and cultural life, and yet still come up short, missing something vital. For it was the Village's infinite diversity more than its artsiness, or its political ardor, or its nineteenth-century streetfronts, or indeed any single strand winding through it, that Jane would embrace as her own and pronounce a virtue.

As it was for many newcomers from the hinterlands, New York could intimidate. Soon after she'd arrived in town—maybe while yet in Brooklyn or later on Morton Street—Jane and Betty took to playing a game they'd dreamed up. It was called "Messages," and went like this: They'd conjure up two people about as different as they could imagine—"say a headhunter in the Solomon Islands and a cobbler in Rock Island, Illinois," to use Jane's own example. Then each would try to figure how to get a message from one to the other: The headhunter talks to the village headman, who speaks to a copra-buying trader, who speaks to a visiting Australian naval officer . . . and so on to the Rock Island cobbler. Whoever came up with the shortest, reasonably plausible chain of messengers won. It was fun for a while, except that they found themselves relying too often on Eleanor Roosevelt as intermediary; "she knew the most unlikely people." But looking back at their game, Jane seemed to understand how it had figured in their new lives. "I suppose," she wrote, "we were trying, in a dim way, to get a grip on the great, bewildering world into which we had come from our cocoon."

With the passage of the years, however, Jane and Betty became seasoned New Yorkers and their great bewildering world became home. Sometimes Jane would go up to the roof of their building and just look down at the street, maybe at nothing much more than the garbage trucks making their rounds. "I would think, what a complicated, great place this is, and all these pieces of it that make it work."

In October 1936, Jane, still just twenty, got a new job, in Hell's Kitchen, whose lurid reputation went back to the Civil War but which these days was crowded with warehouses, garages, and factories. One of them was that of Scharf Brothers, a candymaker, located on a stretch of Fifty-first Street west of Tenth Avenue, not far from the Hudson piers. Jane would watch the production line fill chocolates with varieties of sweet goo. Her $22-a-week job was in the office, though, taking dictation, devising forms and charts, writing sales letters. She wrote to disgruntled customers, too: *No, there must be some mistake. There simply couldn't have been a snippet of steel wire in your chocolate,* she'd type as her boss sat *pin-ng-nging* the little spring the customer had mailed in as evidence. But by May 1937 she was out of this job, too, following a burglary she would come to suspect had been engineered internally, to put the company out of its Depression misery.

One Saturday evening in the fall or early winter of 1936, while Jane was visiting her parents in Scranton, her father sat her down and confided in her some of his own Depression miseries. Only seven years before, he had moved into his fine new offices in the Medical Arts Building. Then the market crashed. Now, many of his patients simply couldn't pay. What with office rent, the salary of Miss Eldridge, his nurse, subscriptions to medical journals, and the like, it took $48 a week in fees just to break even. Most days, after dinner, he was back in the office, staying till nine. He kept office hours Sunday afternoons, too. He struggled.

And the struggle, on top of a constitution weakened by childhood maladies, including a burst appendix—"It's a mess in there," he'd say—took its toll. Little more than a year after his sober-minded talk with Jane, Dr. Butzner was dead, of an intestinal obstruction, at age fifty-nine. The week before, he'd complained of not feeling well. He saw a doctor. He was admitted to the hospital, had an operation. He seemed to rally, but soon declined. "Miss Eldridge, is anybody else here?" he whispered near the end to his nursing assistant of fourteen years. All his children were beside him as he lay in an oxygen tent "dented by four little windows," as a Scranton news account had it. "No long faces," he told them. "If I get well, you don't need them. If I don't, long faces won't help me."

He died two days before Christmas, 1937. The will he'd written a few months after his wedding day in 1909 was admitted to probate early the following year. His wealth was modest. He left everything to Bessie—medical equipment valued at about $300, his five-year-old Dodge sedan, and about $1,000 in cash; the house was already in Bessie's name. A substantial life insurance policy cushioned the financial pain, leaving Jane, her siblings, and her widowed mother to absorb the emotional pain of their premature loss.

In the months between her heart-to-heart with her father and his death, soon after leaving Scharf, Jane had gotten a $25-a-week job with a steel distributor, Peter A. Frasse, based in Lower Manhattan, a fifteen-minute walk from her apartment. At first, it was just more dictation, more typing. One time, she took a letter in shorthand, typed it up, got it signed, stuck it in an envelope, and, after work, was about to drop it in the mailbox when something stayed her hand: *Thirty-eight curls of steel.* That's what she'd typed, but what was it supposed to *mean*? Then the truth dawned: in her boss's old-timey New York accent, steel *coils* came out as *curls*. Next morning at the office, she retyped it, had it signed, and sent it on its way.

After some months, Jane seemed poised for real success at the old New York company, whose roots in the city went back to 1816. A commemorative book Frasse published to mark its hundredth birthday showed off its executives and managers across the years, page after page of them—of course not a single woman. But now, was there the slightest crack in the glass ceiling? Jane had impressed at least one Frasse colleague as "a very intelligent person [who] could do the work of three girls," the "type of person who could talk on any subject." She was elevated to a newly created position, at $28 a week, that Jane would describe as " 'trouble shooting' secretary." Her job was "to step into any department which seemed to be bogging down and help devise ways for getting the work out faster."

This, however, was as far as Jane Butzner's career as Junior Efficiency Expert took her. In September 1938 she resigned. More than five years after the end of her ignominious academic career at Central High, about the time some of her high school classmates were graduating from college, Jane went back to school, enrolling in the continuing education division at Columbia University. The last time she'd been in school, at Powell, she'd learned how the slightest of curlicues changed "very truly yours" to "yours very truly." Now she was studying economic geography, psychology, geology, zoology, and constitutional law, and loving every minute of it.

CHAPTER 5

MORNINGSIDE HEIGHTS

W HAT MIGHT she have been if not a writer?

It was 1994, Jane was in her seventies, and the editors of a Canadian magazine, *Brick*, as a way to celebrate their fiftieth issue, were asking writers they admired to answer that question. Jane replied promptly. Telling the puddingstone story we heard earlier, she went on to describe other geological pleasures in her life: Scranton's anthracite, its slate sidewalks, the limestone that graced the exterior of the local library, the marble of the flooring inside. "All had their crunching, ancient stories," she wrote, then slipped into the "delicious sing-song," almost rhyming, of the classic geological periods: "Triassic, Jurassic . . . Paleocene, Eocene . . ." In short, she might have wound up a geologist.

Or maybe, had she gone on with the studies she'd begun at Columbia University in 1938, a paleontologist. "When I finally got over my grudges against school and took some university classes—whatever I pleased; what a luxury—of course I fixed first upon geology, which led into paleontology, which led into zoology, which led into chemistry and embryology."

Her geology course met Tuesday and Friday evenings in Schermerhorn 401, on the Columbia campus in Morningside Heights, a long subway ride uptown from the West Village. The subject, of course, was rocks, their origin and structure, how they weathered, the action of glaciers, volcanoes, and earthquakes. Class hours for this and a second course Jane took the following semester were supplemented by Saturday-afternoon field trips. One of them was to Croton Point, a peninsula projecting into the Hudson River north of New York City. There, on a stretch of beach about fifty feet long, she was introduced to a geological anomaly called "clay dogs." These were natural sculptures compacted into something like stone that Jane would remember for their wild shapes, from "subtle and simple curving forms to fantastic concoctions of more than Oriental splendor."

Unlike anything she had studied back in high school, her geology classes *took;* she got As in both. And this was pretty much the story of Jane's return to school. Administratively, she wasn't a student of Columbia College, the Ivy League school founded in 1754 that competed with Harvard and Princeton, but of Columbia's "University Extension," or school of general studies. Jane pored over the course catalog, picked whatever she wanted. Because she *could,* as it said right there in black and white: "All courses are open to both men and women. To students of adult age freedom is allowed as to selection of courses and study." Jane surely loved *that.*

Mostly, these were afternoon and evening classes, and thousands of New Yorkers took them. Jane had access to the university library in South Hall, open until 10 p.m. each weekday night, probably bought her books at the university bookstore at the corner of Broadway and 116th Street, next to the subway entrance. A student signing up for more than eight credits' worth of classes needed to consult the office of the school's director; Jane took fifteen her first semester, as she would through the next two years. The following year she took Development of Legal Institutions, which seems to have been the only course to give her trouble; an anthropology course under the name Prehistory of Europe; economics, zoology, more geography, and what was probably a grueling immersion in chemistry, with lectures Tuesday and Friday evenings, followed by hour-long recitations, plus a three-hour laboratory. Jane got an A+.

Actually, this was not quite Jane's first time back in the classroom since leaving Scranton. During the academic year 1935–36, while looking for work and writing for *Vogue,* she'd taken a few classes at New York University, blocks from her apartment, in magazine, feature, and editorial writing. But she'd never have much to say about them and they probably bore nothing like the intellectual heft of her Columbia courses, which left clear traces on her later thinking. Jane's studies were full-time and demanding. But now, pursuing her own interests, she was an eager student.

In the spring of 1940, Jane signed up for Vertebrate Zoology, another magnum course, like chemistry, with a big laboratory component.

Its informally bound lab notebook consisted of notes put together by Columbia faculty to guide students through required dissections. One page featured intricate line drawings showing the "Urinogenital System of Elasmobranch," the taxonomic category that includes the shark. Students were to label each anatomical feature—uterus, urinary papilla, dorsal aorta, and so on. From the neatness and clarity with which Jane did so, this may have been no soulless drudgery for her. The next focus of anatomical interest was the cat. On the back of one page, Jane made a detailed drawing showing the bones of the cat leg in all their interlocking detail: the great trochanter, the lesser trochanter, the patella, all the way up to the acetabulum and the ilium . . .

When Jane got interested in something she got *really* interested. During this period, the story goes within the Jacobs and Butzner clans, Jane and Betty visited the Museum of Natural History, where they saw a cat skeleton on exhibit. Primed by the zoology lab she was taking, or had recently completed, Jane decided she wanted one for herself. So the sisters—this is one version of a story shrouded in the musty past—caught a stray cat, took a crosstown bus to the river, drowned it, brought it back to the apartment, skinned it, and tossed it into a big pot in the kitchen, ultimately reducing it to a mess of bones and soupy gore. Then, Jane recovered the bones, tied them together with wire, glued as necessary, and mounted her specimen in a wood box she would keep for many years. The skinning itself probably posed no terror, as her lab book, which used the rabbit as model, supplied a welcoming how-to: "The skin should be removed with scissors around the middle of the body. Two persons can quickly pull the skin over the head and tail, cutting it at the bases of the ears and snout, tail and anus . . . The entire operation . . . should not require more than three or four minutes."

That was Jane in Vertebrate Zoology.

Here is Jane in American Constitutional Law . . .

This two-course sequence, which she took during the fall and spring semesters of her first year, was taught Tuesday and Thursday mornings by a regular law school professor, Neil T. Dowling, a tall, dignified, fifty-three-year-old Alabamian with a bent for the Socratic method. It was said of him when he retired many years later that he had a gift for conveying "the inherent grandeur of the human effort represented by the Constitution"; that his aim always was "to create a feeling of involvement in an exhilarating inquiry."

With Jane Butzner, it seems, he succeeded.

Jane was no lawyer and never aimed to become one. The course used Dowling's own thick text, *Cases on Constitutional Law*, which featured debates bearing on the regulatory powers of government going back to before the Constitution. What motivated her to take it, and why she was permitted to—it was normally an elective reserved for second-year law students—is murky; by any standard, she was unqualified for it.

But at some point, probably as part of a class project, Jane found herself rooting through old articles, editorials, and speeches citing ideas voiced at the Constitutional Convention of 1787. Soon she was poring through notes of the Convention proceedings themselves, as recorded by James Madison and others during those momentous days. And these, in turn, exposed her to a whole panoply of suggestions that had *not* made their way into the Constitution—that were rejected, seen as foolish or wrong-headed, or in the end simply voted down.

For example, the Constitution says legislative power is vested in a Senate and a House of Representatives. But Jane learned that William Paterson of New Jersey thought a single house would be quite enough and that Benjamin Franklin thought so, too. Of course, Rufus King of Massachusetts thought there ought to be *three* houses—"the second to check the first and to be proportionate to the population, the third to represent the states and have equal suffrage." The Constitution says Congress can overturn a presidential veto with a two-thirds vote. But someone back in 1787 argued that three-quarters would be better, more stabilizing, that "the danger to the public interest from the instability of laws is most to be guarded against."

Here is where Jane's story takes an improbable turn: somehow, in all those failed suggestions, those ideas that went nowhere, those thoughtful, or not so thoughtful, challenges to all we today take as Constitutional Truth, Jane Butzner found the material for her first book. Jane was a first-year college student, barely out of high school. She was new to constitutional law. Yet two decades before *The Death and Life of Great American Cities* made her famous, Columbia University Press in 1941 issued, under Jane's own name, *Constitutional Chaff—Rejected Suggestions of the Constitutional Convention of 1787*.

It is easy to see in the very idea of the book hints of her contrariness, of a deep-lying anti-authoritarian sensibility; she herself seems to have been alive to it. "It seems like a faithless thing," she wrote in the introduction,

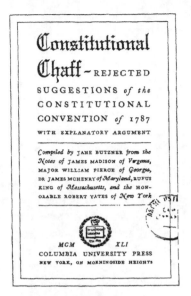

Constitutional Chaff ~ REJECTED SUGGESTIONS of the CONSTITUTIONAL CONVENTION of 1787 WITH EXPLANATORY ARGUMENT

Appearing twenty years before The Death and Life of Great American Cities *was Jane's first book,* Constitutional Chaff.

"to emphasize the differences of opinion, the plans which met disfavor." But no, she made it clear, those errant, futile, or misguided arguments needed no apology. Some of them were quite ingenious. More striking to her yet was the grit and determination with which, through them, their proponents sought a common goal—"a government calculated for man's, every man's happiness." Far from diminishing the achievement of the men of Philadelphia, she was saying, those "rejected suggestions" honored the American experiment.

In her preface, Jane expressed hope that her book might invite speculation on how a different Constitution could have led to a different America—if, to use her example, it had decreed that the Senate remain always in session, and that it, rather than the president, preside over foreign affairs. Her book, then, was in the spirit of what today is called "counterfactual history," the serious scholarly consideration of what might have unfolded had events turned out otherwise—if, say, Lee had won at Gettysburg.

She hoped her book would be enjoyed, she said, "by those who read for the best possible reason—entertainment." And there *was* a species of entertainment in *Constitutional Chaff*—in the brash conceit of its central idea; in the sheer perversity of some of the suggestions Jane dignified by her attention to them; in how the Framers cut and parried their way to the One True Constitution. And, of course, in her attached Appendix C—the delegate William Pierce's sometimes wicked *Character Sketches* of his Convention colleagues: "With an affected air of wisdom," said Pierce of Delaware's John Dickinson, for example, "he labors to produce a trifle."

Set against Jane's future work, *Constitutional Chaff* might be reckoned slight; it was merely a "compilation," Jane's own voice seemingly silent. But not entirely; it *did* reflect her sensibilities. It was contrary. It was serious; a "compendium of ideas," she called it. It expressly valued reading pleasure. By early spring of 1940 Jane had probably finished putting together the text and proposed it to Columbia University Press. By May the press's associate director, Charles G. Proffitt, wrote to Professor Dowling, then on sabbatical at the University of Virginia, for his views. Dowling wrote back that it was "a well done job by a very careful student" and that the manuscript would be useful to scholars. But not *many* scholars, he felt bound to admit—"a most limited market, if indeed it could be called a market at all."

On July 15, Jane learned that her manuscript was approved for publication, but that "finances" posed a problem. Some $350 beyond the press's own resources would be needed to go ahead with it. Did she know "of any source from which we might draw this amount . . . ?" If so, they'd be happy to place her under contract and schedule the book to appear the following year.

Three days later, Jane called Henry H. Wiggins, the Columbia Press officer who'd written her of this little wrinkle, peppering him with questions about how her book would be distributed, how much it would sell for, and the like. She admitted, as Higgins wrote in a memo, "that she would have some difficulty in raising the money, but would think the matter over and let us know."

Three hundred and fifty dollars was seven months' rent for Jane and her sister; or, when she was working, three months' pay. Think of it as at least $5,000 today. Where would she get such a sum? Could she?

Her father's death had begotten a substantial life insurance settlement, which would support Mrs. Butzner for the rest of her life and had probably loosened things up financially for the family. Soon after his death, Jane had stopped working and enrolled at Columbia. The following January, Mrs. Butzner sent her a check to help her visit Philadelphia; plainly, Jane had not cut the purse strings. Now, with opportunity beckoning, she doubtless turned to her family once more. She may also have turned to her first employer in New York, Robert Hemphill, who had become both her friend and, very much more, Betty's, and was often to be seen around the Morton Street apartment until his death the following year at age sixty-four. In any event, on July 22 Jane wrote Wiggins that she could come up with the money.

The book appeared, in an edition of about eleven hundred copies, at $2.25 each, in January 1941, early copies reaching her in time to hand out to her family at Christmas. "I am delighted with the appearance of the book," Jane wrote Proffitt on January 2, "and am very much impressed with the care and taste which the Press has given it in every respect." She liked the type used. She liked the binding. Even the book's eight-page index "fills me with awe."

The book was published by an important university press, the fourth-oldest in the United States and publisher of the works of two U.S. presidents. It found its way into libraries. It was reviewed here and there, cited in the literature. It bears reading even today—maybe especially today, when endless partisan infighting saps the nation's strength and confidence. Jane writes of Hamilton, Franklin, and Edmund Randolph of Virginia, each with reservations about the Constitution, yet urging its ratification, or in other instances acting counter to their own convictions; the country's good, in Jane's words, "could best be obtained by composing their own divergences, by compromising with one another."

It is tempting, and true, to see this book, by an undereducated twenty-four-year-old, contributing to questions plumbed since the very birth of the republic, as early evidence of genius. We may see it equally, however, through the lens of Jane's acknowledgment that her book "would not have been made without the encouragement and assistance of the members of my family." From what we know of her growing-up years, this seems heartfelt and entirely genuine, and reaching far beyond that $350. In a copy of the book she gave her brother John, probably that Christmas, she thanked him for the book's title and for his "helpful counsel." But the book's dedication is neither to him, nor her mother, nor her recently deceased father, but rather to something larger than any of them individually—"to 1712 Monroe Avenue," her Scranton home, and all, and everyone, who had nurtured her there.

Just before registering for her first classes at Columbia in 1938, Jane took a boat trip up the Atlantic coast to New England with Betty on something like a real vacation. Jane fell in love with Boston, at the time very much down on its economic luck. They visited Cape Cod, too, just missing the killer hurricane that swept through New England the following weekend.

In 1940, the two of them took a week-long bike trip in Quebec Province, where they visited, among other places, Sainte-Anne-de-Beaupré, a pilgrimage site whose Roman Catholic church had become a repository for crutches said to be discarded by the miraculously cured.

When, for six months each in 1939 and 1940, the New York World's Fair took over Flushing Meadows Park, Jane visited its iconic Futurama Exhibition, boarding one of the little cars that introduced her and millions of others to General Motors's modernist vision of fast and easy personal transportation, the superhighways of the future spread beneath them.

"I thought it was so cute," she'd tell an interviewer years later. "It was like watching an electric train display somewhere."

"Did you have an inkling that this was going to turn out to be Dallas in 1985?"

"No," she replied, "of course not."

Also before starting at Columbia, Jane heard from her aunt Hannah, her grandmother's seventy-seven-year-old sister, with a request she could not ignore.

After leaving Bloomsburg late in the last century, Hannah had gone on to study at the University of Chicago, teach Indians in the American West, then Aleuts and other natives for fourteen years in Alaska. Once back in Pennsylvania, where she regaled audiences with her adventures, she was won over to the idea of setting them down in print. Retrieving from her correspondents some of the letters she'd written from the wild, she put together a manuscript, "A Woman Blazes a Trail in Alaska."

Put together a manuscript? "It would be more accurate, though un-charitable," Jane would later write, "to say she threw together a manuscript." Aunt Hannah's years in Alaska were no doubt trailblazing, but her account didn't do them justice. "Reading it was a bit like contemplating a box of jigsaw-puzzle pieces," Jane wrote. "The fragments were fascinating but maddeningly unassembled." When Hannah first approached her, Jane said as much: the manuscript needed revision. At her age, though, Hannah was not about to tackle it herself. But *Jane* had written published magazine articles. *Jane* was a pro. Would *Jane* help her?

Jane tried. Hannah had had her manuscript typed up. Jane now worked up a new draft and, as she would write, sent it out over the next two years "to some admirers who liked it, and to publishers who did not." An awkward and belabored correspondence with a Philadelphia publisher, Dorrance, came to nothing. So did an approach to the University of Washington Press. So did all of Jane's other efforts on Hannah's behalf. "The book as a whole moves along too slowly and does not make dramatic enough use of the incidents as they occur," one publisher wrote back.

That was April 16, 1940. Aunt Hannah died a few days later. Jane put away the manuscript, not to take it up again for fifty years. "I lacked sufficient craftsmanship" to make it into a good book, she'd write, "and knew it."

By the spring of 1940, Jane had taken classes at Columbia for two years and was halfway toward a bachelor's degree. She had sampled the sciences, and decided she "passionately loved geology and zoology." She'd taken four courses in economic geography, the field in which much of her later work could be said to belong. "For the first time I liked school and for the first time I made good marks," mostly As.

But this late success, she'd say with humor and bitterness in approximately equal measure, "was almost my undoing." It seems that as a woman accumulating so many credits in the general studies arm of the university she had swung under the administrative scrutiny of Barnard College. Barnard was the women's college across Broadway from the main Columbia campus, variously linked with the university, but in other ways distinct from it. Until now, Jane had enjoyed rapturous intellectual freedom. No more. She was called in to meet with a Barnard administrator she would term "the Dragon Lady." *Now, Miss Butzner, you wish to take which courses? Oh, and with which prerequisites miss-ing? And with no college-level foreign language to your credit?* It only got worse. Turning to Jane's high school grades the Dragon Lady threw up her hands: How could Jane be admitted to Barnard at all with grades like those?

Jane managed to take a few more courses before she was through at Columbia. By fall 1940, with the publication of *Constitutional Chaff* imminent, she signed up for a single two-credit course in embryology, then went out looking for a job again.

She found one at a trade magazine called *Iron Age*, published weekly from offices near Grand Central Station, and serving the metals indus-try. "They hired me," Jane liked to say, "because I could spell molybde-num" (a key alloying metal). At first, despite her two years at Columbia, she was just a secretary again. And at $25 a week, she made less than she'd made at Frasse when she left. But with the magazine's top editors her immediate bosses, within a few months she had new responsibilities thrust upon her. Once a week she went down on the train to Philadelphia, to call at the offices of metals industry firms and scrap metal dealers, gathering news of market conditions. Or she'd get on the telephone to gather data on tonnage coming out of blast furnaces in Bethlehem or Baltimore. In time, she was editing and writing technical articles herself.

That year, 1941, Jane took a little Spanish at Columbia. Betty started taking courses there as well. Brother John graduated from the University of Virginia law school and joined Uncle Billy at his offices in a little brick building on Princess Anne Street across from the courthouse in Freder-icksburg. Aunt Martha, ill with breast cancer, came to live with Jane's mother in Scranton, but a few months later, on November 23, died there, at age sixty-seven. Two weeks later, the Japanese bombed Pearl Harbor and America was at war.

As a twelve-year-old, in 1928, on a trip with parents of friends, Jane had visited New York for the first time. "It was lunchtime in Wall Street in 1928 . . . and the city was just jumping," she'd say in an interview. "It was full of people." When, six years later, she moved to New York, things were different, the streets fairly exhaling the unemployed. "It was the difference between the high tide of the Twenties prosperity and depres-sion." And while she herself, a little cosseted, had managed all right, the times had been cruelly, inescapably hard for most—in families doubled up in shabby quarters, homes unbuilt, roofs unpatched, jobs never filled, opportunities quashed, hopes withered. The city, the country, everywhere and everyone felt poor, insufficient, dilapidated, and worn. The unemployed millions suffered, and their wretchedness seeped into the lives of everyone else, into the psyches of all who lived in uncertainty and constrained ambition.

With Pearl Harbor, the army of the unemployed vanished. In New York, the Brooklyn Army Terminal was soon processing servicemen bound for Europe. The Norden Company was making bombsights on Varick Street in Lower Manhattan. The city's garment industry was churning out millions of uniforms. The Brooklyn Navy Yard, just one of forty shipbuilding and repair facilities in the city, was building battleships. And as the men went off to war, women got jobs long closed to them. "Everyone knew it was ghoulish to delight in jobs and prosperity at the price of war," wrote Jane, looking back from a distance of six decades; "nevertheless, everyone I knew was grateful that suddenly good jobs and pay raises showered like rain after a drought. It seemed that the world did need us."

CHAPTER 6

WOMEN'S WORK

A T AGE TWENTY-FIVE, Jane Butzner had already sampled several sides of the world of writing, editing, and publishing—as high school poet, newspaper intern, research assistant to an established writer, freelancer, and published author (or "compiler," anyway) of a university press book. Now, for the past year at *Iron Age*, she'd inhabited yet another corner of it. *Iron Age*, poor thing, was never read just for the pleasure of being read, was of no interest to the larger literary world, was found rarely on newsstands, and was about as far from literature, on the one hand, or academic scholarship, on the other, as any publication could be. It was a trade magazine, its news, insights, and reportage valued by its niche readers, and by no one else.

Jane had started there as a secretary, was soon promoted to editorial assistant, would ultimately rise to the rank of associate editor. Just before that final promotion, in late 1942, she was working on a big article about nonferrous metals. Ferrous metals include iron and, especially, steel; nonferrous metals are all the others, like copper, tin, aluminum, zinc, magnesium, nickel, and lead. They are vital to modern life. And in 1942, that first full year after Pearl Harbor, they were vital to the war effort. To many of a literary bent, the subject itself might have seemed hopelessly utilitarian, barren of interest. To others, its technical ramparts stood forbiddingly high, the shops, factories, foundries, and dreary back-of-the-mill offices in which its industrial dramas took place rough and repellent.

Still, this was Jane's subject.

"All the common non-ferrous metals," she began her article, "have become precious metals, sought after and hunted down, cherished and pampered, aliens to thoughtless use and ordinary ends." Most of the world's tin supplies had fallen to the Japanese. Most other metals could be had, but the war-fed demand for them was insatiable, expanding wildly beyond even plentiful existing supplies. A bomber sent over Germany used a ton and a half of copper. Antiaircraft gun sights needed zinc die castings. Alloy steels needed nickel in vast quantities.

"To teeter these enormous, swift demands into balance with supply, everything has been used except transmutation"—Jane's coy reference to the alchemists of old. "Allocations, reclamations, requisitions, restrictions, prohibitions, substitutions, premiums, Indian giving, capacity building and manpower freezing have all clattered onto the scale."

Was Jane having *fun* with this?

A Cuban plant for making nickel from local ores, she reported, had been built from "a fabulous quantity of odds and ends, including steel from the World's Fair trylon," the iconic triangular pylon that had stood high over the fairgrounds, "an abandoned cement plant, an Indiana hotel, and a New Jersey factory. A complete Oklahoma machine shop was moved, like a Hearst monastery," down to the island.

In composing her long article, which took up fifteen pages in an early 1943 issue of the magazine, Jane was writing for readers hungry for industrial insider information; the technical details mattered: *To make magnesium, you mix calcined dolomite with pulverized ferrosilicon, and reduce it in a vacuum at 2100 degrees Fahrenheit.* In fact, Jane had recently completed a short course in physical metallurgy, receiving an "Engineering Science, and Management War Training" certificate attesting to it.

But it wasn't enough to collect raw information and slather it onto the page. Her task was to make it easy, even pleasurable, to take in. Among the nonferrous metals, she wrote now, "only lead is fat and happy." Lead was plentiful, restrictions on its use few: "While other metals must give way to substitutes," she went on, "lead moves into the manicured society where it never moved before. While other metals must skitter from hand to mouth, lead can rest peacefully and long in inventory." Jane, then, had to care about her readers *as* readers. *Not* caring explained why nine-tenths of the world's technical reports, legal briefs, and academic papers were scarcely readable at all. With sure command of her subject, stylish wordplay, and an occasional streak of merriment, even mischief, Jane made it almost fun to read about magnesium, aluminum, and lead.

At *Iron Age,* she seems never to have had people working for her, but she did enjoy substantial autonomy there, and in the end was making $45 a week, almost twice her starting salary. She often went down to Washington to meet with officials of the War Production Board, the Navy Department, the Department of Labor, and other agencies, her nose deep into the metals trade news, rounding up leads for stories. She visited refiners and metal fabricators around Philadelphia, New York, and up into New England. She attended scientific meetings. She met with metallurgists who had agreed to write articles for the magazine, edited their manuscripts, helped work out graphic and photographic treatments for them.

And, of course, she wrote. Was it the sort of writing she had in mind when she first came to New York in 1934 determined to become a writer? Hardly. But by now she had real skills she could turn to any subject she wished. And in 1943 she turned them to helping out her hometown.

Bylined simply as "a member of the *Iron Age* staff," Jane wrote for the March 1943 issue how Scranton, with its thirty thousand unemployed, had the resources of labor, electric power, and transportation for war factories—yet hadn't gotten any. Scrantonians by the thousands were decamping for jobs in war-boom cities like Baltimore. The year before, the Anthracite Coal Commission had judged Scranton well suited to making explosives, forgings, machine parts, and ammunition, but this determination had gotten Scranton exactly nowhere. Likewise, efforts by the city itself, working through *The Scranton Tribune,* successor to Jane's old paper, had failed. Their entreaties to the Army, Navy, and War Production Board, Jane wrote, had yielded only "a post-graduate course in the runaround." Jane's article got play around the country. She wrote other articles, too, in the *New York Herald Tribune* and elsewhere. She spoke at a rally in Scranton. By the end of the year, a factory for making B-29 bomber wings that would employ seven thousand people and run seven days a week was going up in Scranton. At one point, a letter of appreciation went out to the "gentlemen" at *Iron Age.* But many around town knew whom to really thank: "Ex-Scranton Girl Helps Home City," ran a local headline.

While Jane's regular salary came from *Iron Age,* she also got periodic checks from other publications, like the *Herald Tribune.* Her boss didn't much like it, but she'd sometimes take a subject researched for *Iron Age* and work it into a story with a different slant for ordinary readers. Remember her sidelong reference to World's Fair steel going into a new Cuban nickel plant? A week before the *Iron Age* article appeared, Jane had much more to say about it in the *Herald Tribune*. There she described the backbone of hills known as the Lengua de Pájaro (bird's tongue) where the new mills would rise, tin-roofed "pastel-colored cement houses" for thousands of new workers, and the "crumbly red-brown earth," thick with nickel ore, that made it all possible.

She wrote about women on the home front, too. The war had changed things for women. With men fighting in North Africa, Europe, and the Pacific, almost the entire world of work had opened up to them. It wasn't just Rosie the Riveter, though there were plenty like her. Jane's sister, Betty, worked as a draftswoman at an aircraft plant. "Women were everywhere," writes Lorraine B. Diehl in *Over Here!*, her account of New York City during the war.

> They sold you railroad tickets at ticket counters and took those tickets from you on the trains. At La Guardia Field they were part of the police patrol, controlling pedestrian traffic and watching for suspicious packages. They flew planes for the Civil Air Patrol. They drove trucks and taxis, tended bar, and operated elevators, and in the summer months you'd find them perched atop lifeguard chairs at the city's beaches.

In a 1942 article, Jane wrote about how the government had reviewed its roster of occupational categories and now deemed most of them open to women; previously, only 154 of almost 3,000 had any appreciable numbers of them—no electricians, no welders, no lathe operators. Now, she wrote in an article nationally syndicated among newspapers, "Wanted: Women to Fill 2795 Kinds of Jobs," women could work at all of them, though they usually earned less than men. At *Iron Age,* Jane belonged to the United Office Professional Workers of America International. She was no organizer, she'd later have cause to explain. But she did talk up the union, especially to lower-level clerical workers, asking, *If women are doing the same work, shouldn't they get the same pay?*

Her union efforts seemed to rub some of her coworkers the wrong way—in particular the managing editor, T. W. Lippert, a Carnegie Tech graduate in physics and veteran of almost ten years at the magazine when

Jane was hired. The two of them clashed. On her employment records, he'd insist on calling her a typist. He'd make "loose and untrue allegations about my morals," Jane would write. One time, he sent her off to a stag dinner "to which he was well aware no women were invited," determined to embarrass her. All this, at least, according to Jane, who had to defend herself against his accusations later. To her union sympathies, add what Lippert or others at *Iron Age* interpreted as a left-wing bent, a willfully anti-British streak, and her penchant for smoking a pipe, and you had the makings of "a troublemaker and an agitator," as an FBI report quoted one informant. After almost three years at the magazine, Jane was eased out.

She didn't formally apply for her next job until November 27, 1943, but it was apparently all but hers by the time she did. The day before, in Scranton, she'd seen her father's old colleague, Dr. Ernest Kiesel, and gotten the medical exam a government job required: blood pressure 104 over 82, no venereal disease, no deformities, normal in every respect—except for her nearsightedness, which was worse than 20–200 in both eyes but correctible to near normal with glasses. She set $2,600 as the lowest annual pay she'd accept—a bit more than what she made at *Iron Age*. She preferred work in New York, but said she'd consider an appointment outside the U.S., including Europe, Asia, Africa, Australia, or South and Central America; sounds like twenty-seven-year-old Jane was up for an adventure. But *not* in Washington, D.C.; she wouldn't move there. She signed the form. She swore to defend the Constitution and not to overthrow the government, and by the 29th was on the payroll of the U.S. Office of War Information.

Formed six months after Pearl Harbor, the OWI employed thousands. It designed posters, produced radio series, such as *This Is Our Enemy*, about Germany, Japan, and Italy. It showed off the country's war mobilization through newsreels on aircraft factories, women in the workforce. This was for the home front. Foreign audiences heard from the Overseas Branch. From it came documentaries and newsreels; radio broadcasts tied to the news; leaflets, newsletters, and booklets; a cartoon biography of FDR; *Victory* magazine—lavishly illustrated, slickly printed, which went to readers in neutral and friendly countries; matchbooks, with the Four Freedoms inscribed inside; "soap paper" bearing messages like "Wash off the Nazi dirt" that, dipped in water, became soap. "By the middle of 1943," according to one account, the New York staff "worked twenty-four hours a day on hundreds of productions in scores of different languages."

James Reston, the future star *New York Times* journalist, was part of the OWI. So were the photographer Gordon Parks and historian Arthur Schlesinger Jr. So was Milton Eisenhower, the general's older brother, the OWI's associate director. And the poet Archibald MacLeish, its assistant director. So was Jane Butzner, working out of offices of the Overseas Branch, in the stylishly ornate Argonaut Building, at the corner of West Fifty-seventh Street and Broadway, once used for automobile showrooms.

Jane wrote little biographies of American personalities in government, business, and culture. She prepared accounts showing off, as she'd write, "the magnitude of America's war production, and vignettes illustrating the achievements, efforts and way of life of the American people." At one point, for its Indian troops, the British needed a pamphlet about America, its history, the place of its women, its system of government. Jane did it. During her second year with the OWI, Portugal, Switzerland, Sweden, Iceland, and the Soviet Union became part of her beat.

In a way, her work was not unlike what she'd done at *Iron Age:* gather information, facts, and raw data, and, aiming at a particular readership, wrap it up in neat editorial parcels. Jane's title was feature writer. She was that, all right, but just as her aunt Martha matter-of-factly listed "missionary" as her occupation during the 1930 census, so Jane, if she'd cared to, could have set down "propagandist" as hers. The word itself, which goes back to a board of cardinals that a seventeenth-century pope founded to help propagate the faith, bears a stigma, of course. It's sinister and derogatory when it refers to an enemy, like Dr. Goebbels, the Nazi propaganda minister, spewing falsehood and hate. The stain vanishes when it's one of our guys doing it, offering American truth, countering the lies of enemy propagandists; this, certainly, is how the men and women at the OWI saw their jobs. Moreover, that Jane and her colleagues on West Fifty-seventh Street fashioned "propaganda" doesn't mean they made things up. Yes, noted a 1978 study of the OWI, American propagandists made selective use of the truth, shaping it to their own ends; but in their own eyes, they were "honest and forthright" about it. The playwright Robert Emmet Sherwood, director of the OWI during this period, testified before a House committee in 1942 that "the truth, coming from America, with unmistakable American sincerity, is by far the most effective form of propaganda." The "strategy of truth," you'd hear it called.

But twisted by the cruelties of war, "truth" needed special skills and sensibilities to convey forcefully. Whatever Jane wrote was being read (in translation) not by the sort of people with whom she'd grown up in Scranton, or by friends and colleagues, but by foreigners. She had to learn to see through their eyes, as well as her own, to think herself free of the myriad assumptions she held as an American, a Pennsylvanian, a Presbyterian, a Greenwich Villager, a middle-class white person.

> It was necessary for me to have gained an insight into misapprehensions concerning America current abroad; a basic understanding of which common facets of American life are totally unfamiliar abroad; facets of the American scene likely to elicit the greatest interest and admiration; and methods of giving foundation and background knowledge without becoming pedestrian.

She was describing this in uncharacteristically flat and abstract language (for a job application, later), but these were high-order skills that came easily to few. *Must I explain America's bicameral Congress? Does my reader know what a subway is? Do I need one more apt example to drive the idea home?* As at *Iron Age*, there was always a reader before her eyes, with his or her needs, prejudices, and blind spots as central to the writing as the information itself—the two, audience and subject, locked in intimate embrace, competing for Jane's attention—*that* was her work.

Ten months into the job Jane was tapped for what the government called "rapid promotion"— up a civil service grade, with a 23 percent bump in salary. "Miss Butzner has developed into one of the mainstays of the feature-writing staff," her boss Fritz Silber wrote in October 1944. He credited "her quick grasp of the propaganda job to be done, and her ability to do a fast, efficient and well-handled piece of work with any assignment given to her." In her efficiency ratings, the familiar one-page evaluations given government workers, she earned mostly "outstanding" marks, with only a few "adequate"s. "She now handles many of the top assignments, including special psychological warfare articles for European outposts, a weekly column which is air-pouched to Lisbon, and features requested particularly for use in Spain." Her work had received numerous plaudits. She was earnest, dug "hard and well for her stories," took suggestions willingly, and was "exceptionally easy to work with." The request went in on the third, and was approved by month's end.

In wartime, things happened fast. Whole factories shot up overnight. Officers ascended through the ranks. As Jane herself would realize, the wartime world gave her and other women opportunities they wouldn't have had otherwise. Social constraints on women, and the Depression's economic constraints on everyone, diminished. Much that might otherwise have hidden Jane's abilities or hindered their flowering during these years did not. Even one of the FBI's *Iron Age* informants had to admit that she was "a very brilliant, intelligent young lady." Her talents, her bristling intelligence, were plain to see.

Plain to see, at least, in her little world, at the office, or among her friends. Jane was twenty-eight. She worked for a government agency—doing fine, yes, but all within the context of an ordinary job, in an ordinary office, keeping ordinary hours for ordinarily good pay. She was still invisible to the great world of literature and ideas.

Later, while working for another magazine, Jane would be dragooned into service as a model for maternity clothes that, readers were assured, could be flattering—and on Jane were. More typically, though, she wasn't much caught up in clothes—or as her son Jim puts it, "sartorial exuberance." Her mother was forever and always trying to get her into prettier, more stylish outfits, to pay more attention to her appearance; Mrs. Butzner's surrogate, Betty, fretted over Jane's choices in hair, shoes, dresses. As Jim says, "they were right" to worry, Jane being devoid of fashion sense. Her hair was light brown with glints of red, perfectly thin and straight, and mostly she left it that way. How, then, to explain the letter that Jane, one day in 1939, wrote her mother in which she noted that, while she hadn't bought that new hat, she did "have a new permanent wave"? Jim's theory: "Her mother must have bribed her."

Back in high school, Jane Butzner had been a serious swimmer; Jim remembers her from the 1950s as a beautiful diver whose swan dives from the high board riveted onlookers with their grace. She was tall, about five-nine, a real presence—"so much taller than all the women and most of the men that the children here gawk at me," Jane observed years later on a trip to Denmark. During the 1940s and 1950s she was slim, even svelte, hovering around 140 pounds. Much later, especially when health problems slowed her down, she grew fat. But photos and accounts from her young and middle adulthood radiate a poised self-possession that, all by itself, can transform and elevate even ordinary looks.

Jane was not a beautiful woman, nor had she been when young. Most often, even among those who knew and loved her, the verdict was delivered as simple, straightforward fact—that, to use the formula I heard repeatedly, Jane was "not a beauty." One of her children described her face as like a bird's beak. She had prominent cheekbones, the unmistakably prominent Butzner nose, a receding chin, wide mouth, and eyes that, behind the glasses she always wore, were squinty and small. In a half smile masking some private joke, Jane's face could remind you of the Mona Lisa. With scant provocation, it could dissolve into a geeky teenager's giggle. It was a cruel fact that women were so reflexively judged by their looks, but fact it was, and the readiness with which both men and women commented on Jane's attests to the truth of it. Of course it didn't much matter. For once rendered, any unwelcome verdict would then almost instantly be submerged in other truths: her personality took over so immediately, her strength of intellect, her antic humor, her eloquence, that any failings of appearance were swept away—swamped, obliterated—by the proverbial "things that matter most," and that in the case of Jane really *did* matter most. "She was not what you'd call a beautiful dame," a friend and distant relative summed it up, "but she was a handsome, impressive woman."

Jane's recollections of her years with Betty in the Village bear no whiff of loneliness—emotional, social, sexual, or otherwise. She had a good job and, beginning in late 1943, a better one. She was ten years in the city by now; she knew lots of people—editors, Columbia professors, metallurgists from *Iron Age,* friends from work or whom she met through her sister, people she knew in the Village. She and Betty lived in one of the city's most flavorful neighborhoods, one known for relaxed social and sexual mores. Her son Jim won't precisely characterize the relationships she had with men during these years, except to say that both his parents had what he takes care to characterize, within spoken quotation marks, as "a variety of attachments."

One Saturday night in March 1944, Jane and Betty held a party at their new apartment at 82 Washington Place (where Willa Cather wrote her first novel in 1912). Betty was working at the huge Grumman Aircraft complex in Bethpage, Long Island, where thousands of men and women, in ten-hour shifts, seven days a week, turned out Wildcats, F6Fs, and whatever next generation of Navy fighter plane was in the works. For Jane, getting to work was easy—if she wasn't cycling, a straight shot on the subway up to Columbus Circle. For Betty, it was a haul out to the

Island, first the subway, then the Long Island Railroad. The lengthy commute and long work hours didn't leave much room for socializing. For Betty and her friends at Grumman, Saturday evenings were it.

On this particular evening, one of the guests was another of Betty's coworkers, Bob Jacobs. "I walked in the door," he said later, "and there she was," Jane, "in a beautiful green woolen evening dress, and I fell in love."

CHAPTER 7

AMERIKA

BOB—ROBERT HYDE JACOBS JR.—grew up in northern New Jersey, son of an engineer for the New York City subway system; at age ten, he got a chance to ride on a new subway line before it opened. In 1936, when he was nineteen, he took a bike trip through Europe, saw Nazi Germany up close. Just now, meeting Jane, he worked for Grumman, helping design aircraft components, and lived in a spare room in a house out on Long Island. It was the depths of the war. During one span of intense nonstop work—up before dawn, leaving work after dark—he never saw the sun.

He was a handsome fellow with a full head of curly dark hair and a winning smile. His father, a Cornell grad, was active in the local suburban church, and always careful to drive a fine car, which Bob was driving, sometimes too fast, by age sixteen. His first cousin, John Jacobs, who grew up on an apple farm in upstate New York, remembers Bob, in his tropical fiber suits, as effete, not sissyish, exactly, but somehow *pickier* compared to his, the gritty farmer side, of the family; he'd tease Bob, "a gentle boy," for learning French. He was later surprised to learn that, before Jane, Bob had been romantically involved with a young artist said to be "a regular hell on wheels," a source of consternation to Bob's conservative family.

Now, though, it was Jane with whom Bob was abruptly and irredeemably smitten. After meeting her at the party, he asked her out for the following weekend. They wound up on the roof deck of the Sutton Hotel on East Fifty-fifth Street east of Second Avenue, eighteen stories above the East River. There Bob proposed to her.

Robert Hyde Jacobs Jr., about the time he met Jane in 1944

They'd known each other a week.

"She said no," Bob would recall, "but very nicely."

The following Wednesday, she called him at work. "Have you changed your mind?" she asked. He hadn't.

"Because I have."

The engagement ring he bestowed on her, the story goes, was fashioned from a hose clamp, or *was* a hose clamp, probably from the Grumman shops. But the engagement wasn't long in any case, and would have been shorter still had Bob not felt Jane needed to meet his family; given the whirlwind courtship, they might have worried she was pregnant.

How long had he known her? they asked.

"Well," he replied, smoothly enough, "I've known her sister for almost a year." That, apparently, was good enough for Mom and Dad.

The small wedding took place in Jane's childhood home on Monroe Avenue in Scranton. The living room was decorated with lilacs and roses. Jane wore a white, street-length dress trimmed with turquoise and fuchsia.

MRS. JOHN DECKER BUTZNER
ANNOUNCES THE MARRIAGE OF HER DAUGHTER
JANE
TO
MR. ROBERT HYDE JACOBS, JUNIOR
ON SATURDAY, MAY THE TWENTY-SEVENTH
NINETEEN HUNDRED AND FORTY-FOUR
SCRANTON, PENNSYLVANIA

It was two weeks before D day, two months since they'd met. Their honeymoon took them on a bicycle trip into northern Pennsylvania and southern New York State.

"He was conventionally good-looking. She was conventionally not good-looking," says John Jacobs's wife, Katia, analyzing their marriage from a perch six decades into the future. "She was superior in brainpower and he admired that." He was from "a good family, good-looking, and this was flattering to her." That's one way to look at it. Another is that, through the fever of their romance, they could discern the deep harmony of spirit that would serve them so well and for so long. It must have helped that by this time, Jane was almost twenty-eight, had lived in New York for a decade, and knew something of herself and the world. "Their easy intimacy was the envy and wonder of people who knew them," one admiring obituary of Bob Jacobs asserted; and it seems to capture the largest truth of their marriage—the two of them, best friends, confidants, comfortable in one another, feeding ideas and fruitful insights to each other all their lives. Under other circumstances, Jane told her children later, she might have kept her maiden name. But given her weakness for alliteration, how could she *not* go through life as Jane Jacobs?

Bob was an architect by training. After two years at Bard College, he'd gone on to the Columbia University School of Architecture, where the normal run of courses included design, descriptive geometry, construction methods, architectural history, and strength of materials. Awarded a bachelor of architecture degree in June 1942, he did not immediately work as an architect. It took him until well into his thirties before he found a secure professional niche.

The war, first of all, directed Bob to serve its own stern strictures. At Grumman, he worked on a variety of design projects. In one, a test pilot's urine-release gizmo had to be redesigned so that bodily waste flowed out of the plane instead of back into the cockpit. Another was an auxiliary fuel tank. The prototype was supposed to be made of sheet metal but, unaccountably, the drawings went to the foundry, where they were used to make the heavy wooden pattern needed for metal casting. *Oops.* When they discovered the mistake, Bob was able to take the useless pattern home, where it became a doorstop.

After the war, Bob taught art appreciation at New York's City College. In an article he wrote for *College Art Journal,* he described an approach aimed at overcoming the slavish deference to word and symbol most students dragged into class with them. "We run the risk," Bob wrote, "of letting verbalized symbols overwhelm, smother and even negate the direct data actually supplied by our senses." His simple exercises—for example, using pairs of L-shaped cardboard as a collapsible frame around a scene—were designed to force students to simply see what lay before their eyes. They needed to push beyond "myths" linking, say, the color red to "blood, courage, war." They needed "to use their eyes as a direct instrument to the brain." In fact, this sounds like Jane in *The Death and Life of Great American Cities*. Did she influence Bob? Or did Bob influence her?

Bob would design many of the quirky clever features of their houses, from a kitchen that left the cook practically in the middle of the dinner conversation, to the public phone booth in their living room. He would be as much the community activist as she, in the Village and then later in Toronto. He was handy, a good draftsman and artist, a close student of human nature; he could meet people cold, his daughter remembers, make them feel special, learn from them. Friends would listen with interest as he declaimed on subjects close to him, including his work, but with perhaps greater interest when it was just him, alone; when Jane was around, says Katia Jacobs, he was apt to "slip back into the shadows." Jane, by every account, was the queen bee, Bob comparatively subdued. "Bob was wonderful," recalls Decker Butzner, son of Jane's brother John, whose earliest memories of Bob and Jane go back to the 1950s. He knew about everything, could talk about anything, was easy and calm. "And he was never bothered playing second fiddle to Jane."

Which, of course, he did.

To celebrate the Allied invasion of Europe on June 6, 1944, New York City mayor Fiorello La Guardia ordered the city's lights back on after years of wartime blackout. New Yorkers in tenements and brownstones trooped up to their rooftops to watch the spectacle. "Without warning, the entire skyline of New York erupted into glorious light," remembered the writer Pete Hamill, then a nine-year-old Brooklyn boy: "Dazzling, glittering, throbbing in triumph. And the crowds on the rooftops roared. They were roaring on roofs all over Brooklyn, on streets, on bridges, the whole city roaring for light."

With the race of Allied armies across Europe and the success of American arms in the Pacific, the war was drawing to a close. Near the end, Jane at one point had a dozen people reporting to her. Of course, some of them weren't very good and she wound up staying late trying to clean up their work. "They were so fast!" she would say. But "it took me so long to rewrite what they'd written." She tried farming some of them out to other departments, until she was down to just herself and one particularly adept researcher. She was a boss now, but apparently not a very good one. Says son Jim: "She was not a leader, not an organizer, not a manager."

But Jane did not have to endure this role for long. Soon, no one at OWI had much to do, since there wasn't much of a war left. People would show up late for work, gather together for the rest of the day discussing the postwar world ahead—"the PWW," they called it—talking hopes, dreams, and job prospects, thinking about the ad agency they'd start or the novel they'd write.

One day, probably in late 1945, the Washington Place apartment where Jane and Bob first met was the scene for another party, this one with many of the Butzner clan on hand. Jane's younger brother Jim and his wife, Kay, high school sweethearts who'd married in 1942, were there. So was John, newly demobilized after three and a half years with the army meteorological service in Alaska. And so were some of the Grumman people Bob and Betty liked to bring home. One of them was a tall, thin, stylish young Barnard College graduate from New York's Staten Island. She had enrolled in a graduate fine arts program at Yale, but the war had derailed that plan, bringing her to Grumman instead, where she worked as a draftsman. Her name was Viola Peterson but everyone called her Pete. Betty liked her. Jane liked her. Bob liked her. Everything they saw in Pete convinced them she was just right for John. Recalled Jane, "We wanted her in the family."

The two of them, John and Pete, had actually met at an earlier party but found little chance to talk. Well, then, how to promote a budding romance that hadn't budded? It was Bob who hatched the strategy. Uncle Billy Butzner's daughter Elizabeth was up from Virginia, visiting; of course they'd have to commemorate the occasion in a photo. So the whole party, all those Butzners, marched up to the roof, there to be artfully arranged for the camera: In front was Jane, in slacks and jacket, sitting on the roof, Bob squatting beside her. In the back, Elizabeth from Virginia; brother Jim, towering over everyone, with wife, Kay, in a pretty print dress; Betty in the center, looking regal; John in uniform, smoking a cigarette; and Pete, a great sweep of dark hair lofted behind her head, beside him. No hint of the hardships of war, everyone well dressed and groomed, looking great, lined up for the camera, *snap*. The scene recorded for posterity . . .

Clockwise, starting from Bob Jacobs crouched in the front row: Jane; Kay Butzner, brother Jim's wife; Jane's cousin Elizabeth Butzner, daughter of her uncle Billy; brother Jim; sister Betty; brother John; Viola ("Pete") Peterson, John's future wife. This was taken on the roof of the building where Jane and Betty were living at the end of World War II.

And now Bob's scheme swung into action. He guided John and Pete to the parapet by the side of the roof and started pointing out New York landmarks. But behind his back he was making hand signals to Jane and the others, shooing them off the roof. "And so we all beat it," Jane recalled. Bob got the couple fixed on some landmark, then quietly scooted away, too, locking the door to the roof behind him. Pete and John were stuck there, alone together, left to figure out how to get back down.

John urged Pete down the fire escape first; as a woman, she'd be less threatening to anyone seeing them swing gigantically into view at their window. Finally they found someone willing to buy into their story, open his window, and let them back inside. By this time, of course, they were fast friends, victims together of Bob's devilish ruse, intrepid adventurers.

On May 25, 1945, three months before the end of the war, they were married. Recalled Jane, "It all worked just the way Bob said it would."

. . .

In August, atomic bombs incinerated Hiroshima and Nagasaki. In September, Japan surrendered. Soldiers, sailors, and airmen began streaming home. The great belligerent apparatus of man, woman, and machine built to defeat Germany and Japan began to break up. Soon, paperwork progressing through the war-bloated federal bureaucracy was informing hundreds of thousands of government employees that they were out of a job. Jane was among them.

Like many a writer out of work before and since, Jane became a freelancer. The word sometimes just means a writer between jobs, or a wannabe who'll never make a nickel from writing. But it can also mean just what it sounds like: an independent writer for hire, paid by the article, essay, or book. It could be scary, weathering rejection, your income dependent on the vagaries of editors and the uncertain depths of your own wit, skill, and diligence. On the other hand, you were apt to meet people you wouldn't normally meet, go places—geographic, intellectual, and imagined—you might not normally go. One of Jane's early assignments took her to the South Pacific, if only in her head.

Even before Pearl Harbor, the Australian navy had put together a network of missionaries, planters, miners, and government workers that, all through the Pacific war, surrounded by Japanese army and naval units, funneled information on their movements to the Allies. Its head was Eric A. Feldt, an Australian naval officer, who wrote of their exploits in a book titled *The Coast Watchers:* "It is a story of damp, dimly lighted jungle camps, of hidden treetop lookouts; of silent submarines, landing a few intrepid men on hostile beaches, in the dead of night; of American airmen mysteriously rescued from enemy-held islands, surrounded by enemy-dominated seas."

That's from the first page of Feldt's book, but it's not certain he wrote this, or any other particular line. For in 1945, Jane was asked by Feldt's publisher, Oxford University Press, to take what she'd call "a huge, chaotic mass of data" and shape it into a book. "He was not," Jane would write of Feldt later, "a professional writer." She ought to know, because by now she was one. It was why she had landed this job, and why she'd have no trouble landing others.

The jobs Jane took on all through 1946 could scarcely have been more varied. She wrote press releases for a public relations firm about leather footwear. She wrote about Christmas customs. She edited a book of puzzles. She edited a textbook on powder metallurgy, a gig likely the product of her *Iron Age* contacts.

Jane wrote one article about the coastal islands of New England, Virginia, and North Carolina. "Some look like neatly cut Christmas cookies. Some are like drop cakes that spattered too much, and some are old-fashioned golden caramel sticks. They are dotted all along our Atlantic coast—the green and brown islands which are the fringes of a continent," like Tangier Island in Chesapeake Bay or Ocracoke off North Carolina. The article was for *Harper's Bazaar*, a fashion magazine; it almost had to be charming, and it was. But it was substantive, too; she selected the islands to highlight, researched their history, stepped into the lives of their inhabitants.

As was true all her life, she found herself drawn to invention, innovation, and ways of making a living: "For years," she wrote of Tangier Island,

> the crabbers have been making their own chicken-wire crab traps after a simple but ingenious design. A few years ago, a man from the mainland turned up with the news that he was the son of the trap's deceased inventor and was now asking an annual royalty of four dollars from each user. Each spring since, he has appeared and collected his fees. The crabbers see nothing remarkable in the fact that this homespun transaction takes place without benefit of agents, receipts, lawyers, or other mainland furbelows, and they cheerfully pay up every year. "It's the best trap," is their comment. "Good thing his father thought it up."

When Jane totted up her income at the end of nine months of freelancing, it averaged out to $88 a week—much more than she'd made at *Iron Age* or the OWI. Still, in October she applied for another federal job, as a writer for the magazine *Amerika*, published by the U.S. State Department for readers in the Soviet Union. Jane was a propagandist once more.

With the war over, so was its vast uniting impulse, the need to defeat Nazi Germany and Imperial Japan. But now the world split in two all over again, this time across the fault lines between the Soviet Union and the U.S., East and West, Communism and capitalism. During the war, the United States had been allied, if uneasily, with the Soviets. But the postwar division of Germany into Soviet and Western spheres, the Soviet takeover of Poland, Hungary, Romania, and other Eastern European countries, the brandishing of nuclear weapons, rhetorical feints, jabs, and angry mutual recriminations, all left the world on edge—sometimes, as in Berlin in 1948, Hungary in 1956, and Cuba in 1962, with cold war threatening to boil over into hot.

Amerika, the big, glossy publication for which Jane went to work late in 1946, and its dowdier counterpart, *Soviet Life*, embodied this geopolitical divide. Given the fractious relations between the two sides, it's a wonder an agreement to publish the paired magazines ever came off. But it did, through a deal worked out between the U.S. ambassador Averell Harriman and his Soviet counterpart, Foreign Minister Vyacheslav Molotov in 1944. The two countries maintained the arrangement, troubled but more or less intact, over the years Jane worked at *Amerika*. Certainly, both publications were peddling propaganda. But looked at through rose-colored-enough glasses, they were being a little more civilized about it, maybe making the world a little safer.

Between *Amerika*'s offices in New York and Moscow, ideas for articles shuttled back and forth, some of them destined for print, some not: an article on summer leisure in America; one on Robert Oppenheimer, the physicist; one devoted to a city high school. (This last was "a particularly fine job," the assistant cultural officer at the U.S. embassy in Moscow wrote to New York in early 1948, "and a lot of credit is due Jane Jacobs," its author.) There was a piece about a typical American small town. Others on the World Series, the American optical industry, the Kansas heartland, modern art. Jane suggested a piece on dictionaries, which shape-shifted into an idea for one on the American language. "We think it can be done without creating insurmountable translation problems," wrote the *Amerika* editor Marion Sanders; "the idea is to convey some notion of the wealth and flexibility of our language." Of course, words like "juke box," "short-order cook," and "swing band" were already causing trouble enough for the magazine's Moscow-based translators.

The logistics of putting out *Amerika* were formidable. It was written in one language for readers of another. Its two offices were halfway around the world from each other. Soviet censorship was always a concern. In June 1947, editor Sanders, a Wellesley graduate who'd studied also at the Columbia School of Journalism, "a dynamic, hell-for-leather New Yorker," as one colleague remembered her, tried to help the U.S. embassy in Moscow understand just how the New York side worked. In a four-page memo she told the "life history" of a single article, about American cafeterias, by Jane Jacobs.

Jane, one of three writers on staff, had submitted a written outline. At a Monday editorial meeting, she was told to go ahead with the idea. In a week she produced a manuscript, which was sent to the embassy in Moscow for review; a copy also went to a cafeteria manager, to catch any technical slip-ups. Jane had identified possible illustrations, and now she wrote captions for about two dozen of them. When translations of text and captions came back from Moscow, a Russian-language editor in the New York office went through them to pick out any infelicities of expression that had crept in. Soon the whole job was off to the typographer, and thence through the endless back-and-forth rigmarole the era's pre-digital technology required.

Amerika's writers and editors were acutely mindful of their Russian readers. "Reader comments," an in-house memo noted, "indicate that the magazine should not present too concentrated a dose of the more remarkable (to the Soviet reader) facets of the American standard of living. They simply aren't believed." Modern kitchens? Ordinary factory workers with their own wristwatches? Private *airplanes* for recreation? To write for *Amerika* meant seeing every word through the eyes of a reader in Moscow or Leningrad. An account of her duties Jane prepared in the late 1940s suggests she well understood this psychological side of her work. Her task, she wrote, was to "create the precise impression desired upon a Russian readership . . . much misinformed by its own press regarding America." Touchy subjects, like the American economic system, had to be "treated with discrimination and judgment, to convince rather than to antagonize." Here was the propagandist at work. Here, too, was a writer determined to reach her readers.

In September 1948, Bob Jacobs's first cousin, John, not long back from service in the South Pacific, dissatisfied by his flirtations with law school and advertising, came to work for *Amerika*. He recalls himself as "a personable young man," but footloose, living with his wife, Katia, in the Village near Jane and Bob. "Why don't you come here and work?" Jane suggested, referring to *Amerika*. He came for an interview and got the job; he could rightly say there were no Communists in his family because his brother, Edward, who *had* been a Communist, a member of the Abraham Lincoln Brigade, had been killed in the Spanish Civil War.

"It was the most marvelous job," John Jacobs says of his time with

Amerika, "with wonderful articles to write and a month to do them in." He did one on modern art, got to know one of the de Koonings. "I was happy as a clam." He and his colleagues "were doing God's work, giving the poor Russian people" information useful and true. As for Jane, she was "the best editor I ever had." One time he was supposed to be writing "a moody New York piece in the E. B. White mode, and I knew it wasn't working." He took it to Jane. By the time she was done with it, it was all he had wanted it to be but hadn't been able to bring off himself. "When Jane took something on," he says, "that something was dead," finished, you never had to worry about it again.

Back at the OWI, Jane had gotten a brief, unrewarding taste of being a supervisor. But by now, a few years older, she was better in that role. Government employee efficiency ratings were typically arranged in two columns—on the left for the work itself, on the right for any administrative or supervisory elements of it. Now, in August 1950, for the first time Jane was being rated—highly—on these administrative measures. She was still a writer, but now had five junior writers under her. Freelancers reported to her, too. All in all, she estimated, the supervisory side of her work took up three-quarters of her time.

Beginning in mid-1948, the geopolitical conflict that led to the founding of *Amerika* and *Soviet Life* in the first place touched down on Jane's personal life.

Communism had come to be seen in America as not only an external threat but also an internal one, with spies and "fellow-travelers" seen or imagined everywhere; patriotism and loyalty were to be proven, not assumed. Responding to the Republican sweep in the 1946 congressional elections and trying to counter criticism from the anticommunist right, President Truman in 1947 issued Executive Order 9835, requiring a loyalty review of most federal employees; should it yield "reasonable grounds" to believe you were disloyal to the government, you were out of a job.

Under Truman's order, Jane, a State Department employee, had to fill out what might have seemed a routine enough form, "Request for Investigation Data," giving the government the tools to investigate her loyalty and political correctness: list where you've worked, where you've lived for the past ten years, give names and addresses of friends, neighbors, and colleagues. This led to a series of FBI field investigations across three months in the late summer and early fall of 1948 that included reports about Jane—thirteen of them—from agents in Philadelphia, New York, Cincinnati, Washington, D.C., Newark, Boston, and other cities.

Most of those the FBI interviewed called Jane loyal, respectable, patriotic, or, in the language of one report, "of good character and reputation." But, inevitably, she had rubbed some people the wrong way. And some of her free-spiritedness had not escaped the eyes of neighborhood busybodies. The FBI learned that at one point Jane and Bob had put in for visas to visit Siberia. It cited one or more of Jane's ex-colleagues at *Iron Age* to the effect that she was a troublemaker. It pictured Jane's first employer in New York, Robert Hemphill, as a "sugar daddy," the Butzner women reputedly his mistresses, the three of them observed from nearby apartments sitting inside on hot summer days half naked. FBI informants describing Jane as "liberal" were sometimes further queried as to just what they meant by that. One said that "she had a complete mind of her own and would not be swayed by the opinion of others . . . [and] had no interest in the Communist Party or Communist front groups and that she was a person who would not have her thoughts dictated by any party whether it was a Communist or Fascist group." *Got that right.* Another said that to him "liberal" meant Communist leanings—though he admitted "he had no reason for making this statement" except that Jane lived in Greenwich Village, where Communists were said to live, and he'd heard her say things, though he couldn't remember what.

Years later, amid the acrimony of the Vietnam War, critics seeing the United States as behaving like a police state took to calling it—alive to the German spelling's totalitarian flavor—"Amerika."

On July 19, 1948, a letter from Carroll St. Claire, acting chairman of the State Department's Loyalty Review Board, went out to Jane, requesting answers to a number of specific questions. The letter probably reached her on Wednesday the 20th. By Friday, she had written a three-page reply. No, she'd not been a union organizer while at *Iron Age*, but simply a member of the union. She had indeed, with Bob, put in a request to visit Siberia. She hadn't followed the Communist line during the war.

She had never subscribed to *Daily Worker*, the Communist Party U.S. newspaper. And she'd never been a member of the Communist Party, nor ever been affiliated with it, nor ever been a member or participant in any "sympathetic associations" of the CP.

The final word on Jane, as of February 1, 1949, was that the FBI had uncovered some "unfavorable information relating to character or suitability of subject," but that she had been "cleared for loyalty and security." As most of the troubling information went back to before 1943, this was "not considered significant at this time."

And that seemed to be that.

Around the time Jane's loyalty to America was being investigated, she got hit hard, from the other side, by the Russians:

> It has long been known that the lying little magazine "Amerika," published in the Russian language, pursues the goal of deceiving readers, of creating in them a false impression about the contemporary situation in the United States, of disguising the imperialist policy of Wall Street, and of extolling in every way possible the "achievements" of America.

It was September 16, 1949, and V. Kusakov of the Academy of Architecture of the USSR was using the pages of *Izvestia*, which represented the views of the Soviet government, to tear into two recent issues of *Amerika*. Both featured articles about American architecture, and both were written by Jane Jacobs.

CHAPTER 8

TRUSHCHOBY

T HE COVER SHOWED two small girls in little dresses and black patent leather shoes, ribbons in their hair, faces aglow, squeezed close together, standing on the seat of a playground swing as it flew up against the deep indigo sky. Here was *Amerika*, issue number 29, reaching its Soviet readers probably in the summer of 1949, delivering its buoyant message of America. The issue's lead article was titled "New Horizons in the Architecture of the U.S.A." It was written by Jane Jacobs, and it was thick with images of American buildings and structures, set out on the broad American plain, all expressing American health and vitality: Cozy clapboarded houses. A southwestern pueblo. Dams, grain silos, and electric transmission towers. Chicago School architecture from the late 1800s. And, of course, that larger-than-life hero of American architecture, Frank Lloyd Wright, with "Fallingwater" and others among his architectural triumphs; one shot shows him beside an early model of the Guggenheim Museum, years before its iconic helix would rise over Fifth Avenue in New York. The following issue of *Amerika*, with part 2 of the article, showed a modern school, a modern hospital ward, open vistas and unobstructed views, an upper-middle-class suburban living room—all fireplace, sofas, great glass windows—inviting us to step through its sliding glass door and, cocktail in hand, settle down into the new postwar America.

But Comrade Kusakov, associate member of the Academy of Architecture of the USSR, was having none of it. In his *Izvestia* piece, Kusakov wrote off one building praised in Jane's article as "an ugly flat, steel box, architecturally dead and joyless," described Wright's school and experimental community, Taliesin, as "a monstrous variation of prehistoric cave dwellings and modern shacks." But it was not *architecture* so much that inspired his righteous Communist wrath. Rather, it was part of the built environment that Jane had hardly touched on at all—namely, American housing conditions, the facts surrounding which "expose completely the liars on the editorial staff of the magazine *Amerika*."

In American cities, he charged, six million apartments and houses were slums. In New York alone, half a million people lived in slums. "Poverty districts" consumed more than twelve square miles of Chicago. Out in the country, half a million people lived in trailers. There, for all the world to see, was "the ever increasing housing crisis which the cities of America are experiencing." American capitalism "dooms the majority of the population to a negative existence and death in ill-smelling cesspools, in slums deprived of air, sunlight, and trees or shrubs. The colossal, ever increasing death rate in the slums of American cities is a devastating verdict on the 'American way of life' and on that misanthropic 'culture' from which it is born."

America *did* have a housing crisis; for all the propaganda bluster of the *Izvestia* article, that much was true. A casualty of almost two decades of depression and war, much housing was in disrepair; a third of the nation's homes were said to lack complete plumbing systems. During the war, shipyard and war factory workers were content to simply find a place, any place, to live; no one was building or rebuilding. One critic would picture postwar slums as "a heritage of the building booms of the 1890s" and early twentieth century, the old properties decaying ever since. In 1949, American newspapers were reporting on a new federal bill that would provide for public housing and slum clearance; some of Kusakov's statistics were drawn from the debate surrounding it.

No matter that the Soviets were in worse shape. As the embassy cultural affairs officer Ralph Collins observed in commenting on the *Izvestia* attack, most housing in Moscow, shabby, old, and crowded, would be deemed slums by Americans. "It is obvious," he wrote, "that 'slums' means one thing to Americans and another to Russians." *A slum wasn't just a slum?* A hopeless mess of dark, dirty, dilapidated housing unfit for human habitation? That wasn't plain enough? Well, maybe not. In forwarding a translation of the *Izvestia* attack and Collins's analysis to Marion Sanders in New York a few days later, M. Gordon Knox, the American embassy in Moscow's first secretary, suggested that the Russian reaction to Jane's articles could be seen as "flattering" to *Amerika*—in that they had been noticed. Still, Kusakov warranted a response. "Let's see," he enjoined Sanders, "if we can't clear up what a slum is."

"Izvestia on our architecture piece really made us cringe," an *Amerika* staffer standing in for Sanders wrote Knox a few days later. "Jane, particularly, is unnerved by being tagged a mendacious capitalist writer. I'm used to it." But, he assured Knox, they would go ahead with what soon they were calling "the housing story," trying to cover points Knox had raised. Interview a housing authority official in New York, Knox had suggested. Perhaps set out,

> by cubic meter of space, by plumbing facilities, what lodgings are of minimum standards and what would be condemned. Factors such as fire risk and danger of collapse could be spelt out specifically . . . What are the regulations for how many people can sleep in one room, for how many people can use one toilet, etc. The result, I suspect, will be that Russian readers will think the condemned houses [in America] are luxury liners.

By early February, *Amerika* had a draft of the article they could send the embassy in Moscow. "The article on the Slum by Jane Jacobs is a courageous, careful, and, to me, highly successful" one, wrote Knox to John Jacobs, who was apparently standing in for Marion Sanders. "It packs a 'punch' and makes a point, and I congratulate Jane." Of course, then he went on to offer two pages of suggestions. For example, Jane had confused things by saying that housing might satisfy minimum standards yet be "slums anyway because they are ugly or discouraging to morale." He couldn't buy that: maybe the great Hearst estate in San Simeon, California, was ugly and, were he living there, it might damage his morale, "but it ain't no slum."

By March, following more back-and-forth between Moscow and New York, Knox had received the changes, which, he wrote back to Sanders, now back in the saddle in New York, were "acceptable here." The translation had worked out well, too. They'd worried, he explained, "that the article might contain the Russian word 'trushchoby' on every page, which is the word the Soviet press constantly uses in describing the horrible American slums." But though the translators hadn't been coached on the point, he went on, the dreaded word appeared only once. This, in cold war terms, was something of a triumph.

Jane's piece, appearing across ten pages of *Amerika* in August 1950, was titled "Planned Rebuilding of Run-Down Urban Areas": "The working day is done. In large and small cities people stream out the doors of offices, factories and shops and fill buses, trams and the subways that will take them home. Parking lots, filled during the day with private automobiles, empty out, and rush hour begins . . . Everyone is going home." But what kind of homes? Ninety-seven percent of Americans had electricity, 95 percent lived one family to a house or apartment, which averaged five rooms each, not including the bathroom. *But,* Jane allowed, "average" figures inevitably mean that "a lot are below average." A fifth of American houses needed rehabilitation, lacked bathrooms or proper ventilation, or otherwise failed to meet minimal standards. It was these, and what was being done about them, that her article was about. Comrade Kusakov had pointed up America's housing problems? Well, Jane was showing how America was tackling them.

It was a serious and factual piece, scant on color and rhetorical flavor with probably more meat and muscle than most American readers of *Life, Time,* or *Reader's Digest* would have swallowed, thick with facts and figures, case studies, history all the way up to the 1949 housing act. How did a "lagging district" or "run-down neighborhood" in America get that way? Some just grew old and worn with time. The decline of others, paradoxically, owed to periods of outsized prosperity during which aggrandizing industrial or shopping districts impinged on them. And just what were proper housing standards? In America these differed by locality; the city of Baltimore, for example, required that windows could come to no less than 10 percent of floor area, and that a bedroom could occupy no fewer than eleven cubic meters. Even the smallest apartments had to have plumbing with at least one sink.

Jane introduced her readers to the Danish social activist Jacob Riis, author of *How the Other Half Lives,* who in the late nineteenth century explored the slums of New York, campaigning against unsanitary housing. At one point, as she told the story, Riis set himself up at a crosswalk in the notorious Five Points neighborhood known as Mulberry Bend, flanked with back alleys with names like Bandit's Roost and Ragpickers Row. "Mulberry Bend," declared Riis, "must disappear"—which largely through his influence and publicity it did, becoming a park.

As might be expected, Jane's long article ended on a bright note. "Neglected, dilapidated houses, as residents of American cities now see, have started to disappear," though of course, she admitted, "they cannot disappear in a day." But the grim, too-familiar history of old neighborhoods filling with wave after wave of immigrants or other impoverished newcomers, was no more, she concluded. For example, "neglected Chicago districts, reconstructed today, will never be vacated and re-settled as before. They will disappear; they have already disappeared."

The article's illustrations contributed as much to the message as its text: futuristic apartment complexes, slums erased, a new American cityscape replacing them. It opened with a full-page photo of an "obsolete building" being dismantled by a crew of rugged workmen, the steel skeleton of a proud new high-rise towering above and behind it. In before-and-after illustrations of Baltimore, readers saw a decaying inner courtyard, littered with rubble, scraggly wooden fences falling apart, giving way to a cleaned-up ball court, the rear faces of the old buildings freshly painted and stuccoed.

In all this—in Jane's survey of the problem, her explanation of its roots, and her review of measures taken to remedy it—she expressed conventional strategies and sensibilities she would later question or disparage. One source of urban decline, as we've heard her say, was residential buildings left amid shopping and industrial districts; zoning laws to keep them apart had come too late to prevent this unhappy mixing—a mixing she'd come to celebrate. Better site layout and building practices had made it possible to use for the building itself only 10 to 15 percent of the site, the rest given over to sports facilities and open space; proportions like that, she'd later argue, represented a negation of the traditional city. And, she was saying now, bad neighborhoods had best be made to disappear, simply disappear. Jane's article on slum clearance was solid, thorough—and completely of its time.

Let's see if we can't clear up what a slum is? Knox had asked, and now, a year later, Jane had taken a shot at it. But for Jane, this seemingly narrow question would slip out of its original borders, become something big to chew on, broaden into one of the biggest questions of all: *What, really, was the Good Life?* After two decades of economic depression and wartime constraints, Jane, like many other middle-class Americans, now enjoyed the luxury of being able to settle back and consider new living choices and opportunities. Her choices would differ from those of many of her friends, many of her family members, many other Americans.

.   .   .

Jane and her brothers and sister were settling down, having kids, the first generation of baby boomers. The youngest of them, Jane's brother Jim, was the first to marry, and soon he and his wife, Kay, had a daughter, Jane, born in 1946. Betty, in an on-again off-again relationship with Jules Manson—a union mediator and academic, smart, handsome, a fine dresser—finally married him early in 1947, giving birth later that year to a daughter, Carol. John worked with Uncle Billy in Fredericksburg; their mother, Bessie, now almost seventy, had sold the family house in Scranton and moved down to Fredericksburg, where she lived in a nice house on Sunken Road and let out rooms for students at nearby Mary Washington College. Jane and Bob's first son, James Kedzie Jacobs—Jim—was born in 1948, a few months after she and Bob had moved from Washington Place to a dilapidated former candy store on Hudson Street, a broad north-south street a few blocks back from and parallel to the Hudson River.

A too-hasty glance might have suggested that Jane, Bob, and their young son had moved into a slum. Theirs was a three-story house, reputedly built by a sea captain for one of his two daughters in 1849, situated in one of the gnarliest areas of the West Village, the adjacent streets back from the Hudson piers full of decaying warehouses and light industry, a cacophony of noisy trucks, populated by rough-hewn seamen and longshoremen. The upper two floors had been an apartment, and into them the Jacobses moved while trying to resurrect what had been a first-floor candy store that sported Canada Dry and Phillies Cigars signs out front, rusted sheet-metal fittings, and a bullet hole in the frosted glass left over from some gang fight predating the Jacobses' arrival. What passed for a backyard was a garbage dump. The whole place was overrun by rats—"big ones," Jane would say many years later. Even later, in the mid- and late 1950s, with the house filled with Jane's children and sometimes visiting relatives, the place was often cold in winter, being heated largely by the fireplace in the living room, which was often banked by dawn, the house left cold; one visitor remembers needing seven blankets to keep warm. The house was loose-chinked enough that, even set back from a window, a magazine page could sometimes be seen fluttering in the draft. Of course, there was no air conditioning; they used wet washcloths to keep cool during the hot New York summers. The house demanded all their money, energy, and time. They rebuilt the foundation and installed new, industrial-grade windows. The street side of the house was in such bad shape that they had to tear down some of it and reface it. Bob's father kicked in some money to help with the repairs, but they ended up doing much of the work themselves. Jane and Bob had bought the house, son Jim estimates, for $7,000, which even in 1947 dollars wasn't much.

Its asking price in 2009 was $3.5 million.

In June 1950, a few months before the slum article appeared in *Amerika*, Jane's brother John and wife, Pete, had their only son, Decker. Five days later, Jane gave birth to her second son, Edward Decker, or Ned, as he would be known. For six weeks, she was on maternity leave, returning to *Amerika* early in August.

In March 1952, Jane heard from the Loyalty Board again.

Two and a half years had passed since she'd been judged, despite residues of "unfavorable information," loyal enough to keep her job. But all through the late 1940s and into the 1950s Red Fever spiked: the first Soviet atomic bomb, revelations of Soviet spying, the accusations against

The house at 555 Hudson Street, in New York's West Village, about 1950, a few years after Jane and Bob bought it

Alger Hiss, the "Pumpkin Papers" affair and the rise to prominence of Richard Nixon, the Hollywood blacklist, the Korean War, the investigations of the Senate Internal Security Subcommittee and the House Un-American Activities Committee, and, of course, that opening salvo of full-blown McCarthyism at the Republican Women's Club of Wheeling, West Virginia, on February 9, 1950. There, the zealous junior senator from Wisconsin, Joseph McCarthy, produced a paper he claimed was a list of known Communists working for the State Department: "I have here in my hand a list of 205— a list of names that were made known to the Secretary of State as being members of the Communist Party and who nevertheless are still working and shaping policy in the State Department." Sprung up from legitimate concerns—real enemies, real danger, real traitors—had grown, out of all reasonable bound, a new Red Scare, drenched in suspicion, accusation, and mistrust.

In April 1951, under intense partisan pressure, President Truman signed a new executive order lowering the bar to dismissal to mere "reasonable doubt" of loyalty. Of more than 9,000 government employees cleared under the earlier standard, the cases of more than 2,500 were reopened. Jane's was among them. In September, Conrad E. Snow, chairman of the State Department's Loyalty Review Board, requested that the FBI assess Jane's case; he wanted to know now about her voting registration, her union membership, and just when she'd changed her views about American entry into World War II. A report coming from the FBI's Baltimore office cited an informant who perceived "a degree of immorality and disloyalty about the applicant and her group." It was something "she could not put her finger on." She had "no concrete evidence that applicant is disloyal." Still, on March 14, 1952, Snow wrote Jane, demanding more answers to more questions.

This time, Jane rose up in righteous wrath. Her 1949 response had been confined to three single-spaced typed pages. This time, within a week or so, she had drafted an eight-thousand-word missive that constitutes as extraordinary a statement of one particular strain of patriotic feeling as you'll find anywhere.

"Enclosed are the notarized answers to your interrogatory," she wrote Snow on March 25. Her answers were going to be long, she explained, and she would not try to fit them into the limited space allotted to them. What was more, since she was "addicted to editor's notes and prefaces and the like," she'd taken the liberty of "enclosing a foreword to my

FEDERAL BUREAU OF INVESTIGATION

K

FORM No. 1
THIS CASE ORIGINATED AT BUREAU

NY FILE NO 123-252 chf

REPORT MADE AT	DATE WHEN MADE	PERIOD FOR WHICH MADE	REPORT MADE BY
NEW YORK	9/8/48	8/24;9/2/48	b7C

TITLE	CHARACTER OF CASE
JANE BUTZNER JACOBS, nee Butzner, aka Mrs. Robert H. Jacobs	SPECIAL INQUIRY—STATE DEPARTMENT Public Law 402, 80th Congress (VOICE OF AMERICA)

SYNOPSIS OF FACTS:

apartment house at 55 Morton Street, New York, New York, advised JANE ___ BUTZNER resided at this address from 1935 to 1943, sharing apartment with a Mr. ROBERTS. ROBERTS alleged to be girls' uncle, but this believed untrue.

JANE ___ studied and talked about Fascist Regimes in Europe, but could give no further information relative to loyalty.

— RUC — SEE REVERSE SIDE FOR ADD. DISSEMINATION.

REFERENCE: Bureau file 123-393.
Teletype from Washington Field dated 8/15/___
New York teletype to ___ dated 2/4/48.

DETAILS: the apartment house located at 55 Morton Street, New York City, New York, advised that JANE and ___ lived in an apartment at this address from approximately 1935 to 1943. This apartment house is located in a section of New York known as Greenwich Village. ___ stated that during the time the girls lived there, a man known as Mr. ROBERTS shared their apartment for several ___ keeping his clothes in the apartment, and sleeping there as well. He was introduced and

APPROVED AND FORWARDED   Edward Sch___

COPIES OF THIS REPORT
3 - Bureau
2 - New York

ALL INFORMATION CONTAINED HEREIN IS UNCLASSIFIED
DATE 06-24-2003 BY 60309 ___

A representative page from Jane's 180-page FBI file, 1948

answers"— *a foreword!*—even bothering to explain *why* she needed to do that: she had concluded that she was "probably suspected of being either a secret Communist sympathizer or a person susceptible to Communist influence." If Snow or others questioning her sympathies were to understand her answers, she would need to put herself, her life, her family, and her most deeply held values in context.

"It still shocks me," she wrote her inquisitor, "although we should all be used to it by this time, to realize that Americans can be officially questioned on their union membership, political beliefs, reading matter and the like. I do not like this, and I like still less the fear that arises from it." And yet, she understood that it might be necessary for some government employees. "I am not answering the enclosed questions in a spirit of sparring with you or trying to get away with anything. I want you to know how I feel." And so she began.

"First of all I was brought up to believe that there is no virtue in conforming meekly to the dominant opinion of the moment. I was encouraged to believe that simple conformity results in stagnation for a society, and that American progress has been largely owing to the opportunity for experimentation, the leeway given initiative, and to a gusto and a freedom for chewing over odd ideas."

She went on to talk about some of her freethinking forebears, on both sides of her family. Like some on her Virginia side who had opposed secession or slavery on the eve of the Civil War and became Republicans in the then staunchly Democratic South. She was proud, too, "of a remoter relative, a Quaker, who, believing in women's rights and women's brains, set up her own little printing press to publish her own works without a masculine nom de plume." The American tradition of freedom to deviate from accepted viewpoints, she declared, was no cliché to her. It was a lived and sacred value.

There were, she said, two great threats to the security of the American tradition. One was the power of the Soviet Union and its satellites. The other was "the current fear of radical ideas and of people who propound them." As to the first, she felt that in her work with the State Department, she had done her bit. "In the case of the second threat, that of McCarthy—or of the frame of mind of which McCarthy is an apt symbol—there is little practical that I could do other than take a stand in assertion of my own rights." That, of course, was precisely what she was doing now.

She believed, she said, in the right of Communists to speak and publish their ideas in the United States. But neither they nor anyone else had the right to spy or sabotage; those who did should be prosecuted.

As for herself, she had the right to criticize the government or Congress, but would never aid another country or act against the interests of the U.S. or for those of the Soviet Union.

All in all, she felt her views aligned best with those of Supreme Court Justice William O. Douglas, among the most committed civil libertarians ever to sit on the Court.

"This is how I stand," Jane came near to wrapping up, or at least to wrapping up her foreword; she hadn't gotten to Snow's questions yet. She realized that her views might represent a minority position, she wrote. "But the fact of being in a minority does not, in itself, trouble me . . . The only guide which I feel that I can follow is not the fluctuating dicta of those who are victors in the battle for popularity at a given moment, but my own understanding of the American tradition in which I was brought up."

And with that, Jane Jacobs, age thirty-six, finally turned to Snow's nine questions. Here, in its entirety, was the first of them:

1. Please discuss fully, for the information of the board, your membership and activities in the United Public Workers of America including (a) dates of membership and present membership status; (b) the nature and extent of your interest and activities and offices held, if any; (c) your attitude toward the Foreign Policy Resolution adopted by UPWA at the 1946 convention at Atlantic City, New Jersey, and other positions reportedly taken by the union leadership indicating adherence to the Communist Party line such as opposition to the American plan for the control of atomic energy, opposition to the Marshall Plan, support of Henry Wallace and the Progressive Party in 1948, opposition to the Atlantic Pact, support of the Communist dominated World Federation of Trade Unions, etc. and (d) your attitude toward UPWA's expulsion from the CIO in 1950.

She was asked, too, about any involvement she'd had with the American Labor Party; about delivery to her apartment of the *Daily Worker*, the Communist Party newspaper in America; whether she'd ever subscribed or received the *American Review on the Soviet Union*; whether she was acquainted with two particular people of apparently question-able political sympathies; and, in several forms, about any relationship she may have had with the Communist Party—in particular, of course, the classic question, the one that, in its indelible cadence, would come to define the era: *"Are you now or have you ever been . . ."* a member of the Communist Party, or a front group to it, or affiliated with, "or in sympa-thetic association" with such a group?

She was not, nor had she ever been, a Communist, she replied. Nor had she supported its ideologies. Nor had she "made a contribution of time, talent, or money," in the words of the loyalty board's question, to its activities. She believed that to the extent it engaged in espionage or sabotage, the American Communist Party was dangerous and needed to be thwarted; but that to the extent it was merely a purveyor of propa-ganda, it was not dangerous. As for the Communist Party of the Soviet Union, she saw it as "an apparatus for political tyranny. I abhor the Soviet system of government, for I fear and despise the whole concept of a gov-ernment which takes as its mission the molding of people into a specific 'kind of man,' i.e. 'Soviet Man'; that practices and extols a conception of the state as 'control from above and support from below'; that controls the work of artists, musicians, architects and scientists; that controls what people read and attempts to control what people think."

On all this, Jane was unambiguous, clear, and impassioned. On that long, detailed first question, however—her involvement with the United Public Workers of America—a sympathetic reader could watch the nuanced, shifting course of Jane's sympathies play out on the page, her personal conflict palpable. She had joined the union, then known as the Federal Workers Union, in the late fall of 1943, soon after she started at the Office of War Information. She'd paid her dues. She'd attended meet-ings of the OWI branch of the union. She'd written a few routine pieces for them, sold raffle tickets to raise funds. She believed in unionization and collective bargaining. She felt the union did a good job in settling grievances. This, at least, was how she felt until about 1947. She was not long in her new State Department job, however, "before I became aware that the union was now very politically minded," and concluded that it hewed to the Communist Party line and seemed unduly critical of the United States.

What to do? She didn't like the union's Communist leanings, differed with much of its political line, but still felt strongly "that it was a good thing to have a union"; and the union *did*, she felt, concern itself with "useful and legitimate functions." So she stayed. Her conviction to do so grew only stronger as public and congressional attacks on it mounted. "I resented the implication that it was dangerous to continue to belong to the union." She remained until the fall of 1951, at which time "I just became too unhappy about it. I had always been in conflict with myself over it, and my objections to the union in the concrete reached a point where they outweighed my feelings for a union in the abstract."

There was more like this, more thoughtful weighing of a difficult issue, more painful personal conflict exposed and expressed, pages of it, with regard to both the union and the American Labor Party, in which she was registered as a member until 1949. Early on, she admitted, she'd realized that the party had "a strong Communist element, as did virtually all liberal organizations of the time"—though, she emphasized, she "certainly and definitely did not think of it as tantamount to the Communist Party." She was attracted to it in part, she wrote, out of affinity for third parties generally, going back to her grandfather's participation in the Greenback Labor Party of the nineteenth century. "Third parties," she wrote, "have a valuable function in needling popular opinion and putting forward and familiarizing new ideas. It was a lively and militant third party which, I felt, a third party ought by rights to be."

It was a different time. The government could ask such questions. People like Jane were enjoined to answer them if they wished to keep their jobs. Of the specific figures in Snow's interrogatory, most are forgotten today—the United Public Workers of America, their Atlantic City convention, Henry Wallace, the Progressives, the World Federation of Trade Unions. They are the stuff of a particular moment in history. Only Senator McCarthy and his *-ism* remain in the consciousness of mainstream America.

Jane submitted her response and never heard anything further. She'd long wonder about this silence and would ask her brother John, a lawyer, on the brink of a distinguished legal career, what he made of it. Oh, the federal bureaucracy just doesn't know how to cope with you, he'd say. But years later, in 1998, after rereading Jane's "foreword," he changed his mind. No, he guessed, the loyalty board reviewer must have been won over by the sheer power and feeling of her ideas; Jane had "left the reviewer with no option but to agree."

Maybe so, but any judgment the government might have made was rendered moot when Jane submitted her resignation from *Amerika*.

.   .   .

It was a miracle *Amerika* held on as long as it did. As the cold war heated up, the Soviets reputedly did all they could to discourage its distribution, manipulating circulation numbers in order to claim their citizens just weren't interested, returning 25,000 unsold copies each month. "I think it's a safe conclusion that *Amerika* as we know it will shortly be throttled to death," Gordon Knox, the embassy's first secretary, had written Marion Sanders in the spring of 1950. Yes, it was good for *Amerika* to have a presence in Russia even if few Soviet citizens could get their hands on it; he understood that. But "my suggestion is that we quit quite soon," maybe once the British did—their publication, *British Ally*, was getting similarly hammered—"so that we keep a solid front and make it clear that the Soviets cannot tolerate Free World publications in the USSR . . . The cold war has become a good deal colder, and *Amerika* inevitably is one of the casualties."

The scuttling of the magazine didn't come right away. As late as early 1952, it was still given to soul searching over its mission, "presenting to the Soviet people the best in American civilization"; it was conjuring up article subjects apt to show off America to Russia's disadvantage, even weighing color palettes most likely to appeal to Russian readers: too many bright blue skies were "blinding to an inhabitant of the gray-brown Russian landscape." But in the end, Knox was right, the magazine folded later in 1952 and moved the vestiges of its operation to Washington, D.C., where it would be revived in 1956 under a different name.

Moving to Washington, of course, was nothing that Jane, her ties firmly to New York, with two kids, busy fixing up the house on Hudson Street, was about to do. So, effective May 2, 1952, she resigned. She was, at this point, a GS-13, fairly high in the U.S. civil service system, making $8,360 per year—something like $90,000 or $100,000 today. In writing to FBI Director J. Edgar Hoover about Jane's case on June 20, 1952, Hiram Bingham, the then chair of the Loyalty Review Board, simply checked a box: "Resigned or otherwise separated from Federal service prior to decision on loyalty."

When she left *Amerika*, she'd write, Jane was drawn to two magazines for her next job. One was *Natural History*, the magazine of the American Museum of Natural History, which went back to 1900, the whole natural world furnishing its subject matter. But it, too, was located in Washington, D.C., so that was out. The other candidate was *Architectural Forum*, a Time-Life publication that elbowed its way to the attention of American architects every month with oversized 250-page issues stuffed with accounts of new buildings coming down the pipeline, think pieces about the state of architecture, with lots of text but even more with photos and drawings, and, of course, pages of ads for stainless steel and masonry, aluminum curtain walls and folding doors. *Amerika* had used a number of *Forum* illustrations for its articles; Jane herself may have borrowed them from its editors. Bob read the magazine. Jane admired it. She was a good fit for it, her several ambitious articles on architecture and housing at *Amerika* strengthening her credentials. And it was likely to pay better, too. She did a trial run with the magazine, and by September was on the masthead as a *Forum* "associate," one of its dozen or so staff writers. From the beginning, she was left with a good feeling about her new employer. *Forum* had recently lost two editors, one whose beat was hospitals and schools, the other private homes. "They asked me—instead of automatically slotting me—which I would be more interested in. I said hospitals and schools, and they said fine." It was mutual respect from the beginning.

But now Jane had a new language to learn: recalling her first days at *Forum*, Jane would later tell how, in the evenings, once the kids were in bed, Bob taught her to read blueprints. Which sounds cozy and straightforward enough, but probably wasn't. Drawings, arranged in a hierarchy of set sizes, thick with symbols, cross-hatching, dimensions, and dotted lines, were the universal language of architectural practice. Through them, you presented ideas for individual buildings or whole projects and then conveyed detailed instructions for how they were to be built. They ranged from easy-to-read floor plans to intricate workings-out of window openings, or the complex junctures between floors and walls; site plans, elevations, and cross-sections; isometric projections and two-point perspectives, where lines leading off into the distance converge to a vanishing point. Each had its own purpose, each its own conventions. Ease with them normally came only with years of architectural education and practice. If you were writing about a new building for *Forum*, it didn't mean the building had gone up and you'd toured it from top to bottom; it meant that it *wasn't* up, you'd reviewed the drawings for it, and you had to imagine it. "I was utterly baffled at first," Jane would write, "being supposed to make sense out of great, indigestible rolls of working drawings and plans. My husband came to my rescue and every night for months"—*months*—"he gave me lessons in reading drawings, learning what to watch for as unusual," bestowing upon her new eyes.

Jane's first piece for *Forum*, about a mixed maternity and general hospital in Lima, Peru, appeared in June 1952, before she was scarcely loose from *Amerika* and not yet employed by *Forum*; this was her trial run. Though she asserted that "its planted entrance court and many patios are leisurely and welcoming," Jane had never seen them, never visited Lima, basing her account on interviews with the architects, and on plans, drawings, and models. But that was enough for her to be able to write that moving through the complex "is as pat and deceptively simple as a double crostic." Or this—that in Peru, childbirth was seen "as an exciting, wholesome event which has nothing to do with illness and should be kept strictly apart from arrangements for sick people."

In succeeding months, she wrote a succession of articles on her assigned beat, and off it. She wrote a long article on the hospital architect Isadore Rosenfield, and, in March 1953, a piece about shopping centers—air-conditioning them, anchor stores designed to pull in customers, what downtowns could learn from them—all full of bright energy and enthusiasm. Later that year, she did a piece on what was then a new phenomenon—self-service, not just in supermarkets but for clothing, perfume, or building supplies, and how stores needed to be redesigned with new fixtures, racks, and shelving systems. "Self-selection," as self-service was still called, "speeds things up for the fast-tempo customer and so increases turnover. It lets the dilly-dallier happily dilly-dally on his own. It gives the salesman a chance to concentrate on the power-tool or baby-carriage customers instead of the 25-cent screw-driver and dozen-diaper shoppers."

(Jane's initial beat, hospitals, ultimately became her husband's architectural specialty. Through her articles, by one account, he came to see "that hospitals presented design problems of such wondrous complexity that an architect might happily give a whole career to them," which is what he did. By 1953, he was working with Joseph "Munio" Neufeld on the Hadassah-Hebrew University Hospital in Jerusalem, the first of some two dozen hospitals overfilling his long career.)

As she scoped out subjects for future articles, recommended which buildings and which architects warranted editorial treatment, Jane seems almost from the beginning to have been taken seriously around the office. On August 25, 1953, less than a year after she first joined *Forum*, the longtime editor Douglas Haskell wrote his own boss, the publisher Perry Prentice, about what he imagined as a major editorial project for the magazine. In the distant reaches of British Columbia, the aluminum producer Alcoa of Canada was creating a new community. It would house, besides its manufacturing plant, forty thousand people. Kitimat, it was to be called. A bold project on a gargantuan scale, and one deserving commensurate treatment in *Forum*: "Every way you turn, this is a completely thought out town," wrote Haskell, worth maybe fifty pages in the magazine. One of the architects involved in the project himself wanted to write it. But Haskell saw the many interwoven aspects of the subject—architectural, geographic, economic, human—as extraordinarily challenging. And as he looked around at his staff, he wrote Prentice, "it seems to be the only writer we can assign to this is Jane Jacobs. She alone will have the capacity of giving it the human touch while digging into the details."

It didn't work out that way; the article was scaled back to twenty pages,

Jane, on a routine assignment for Architectural Forum, *October 26, 1956, not long past her fortieth birthday*

appearing about a year later, and Jane didn't get to write it. But still, it was striking how soon, and how completely, Jane had won Haskell's trust. Perhaps feeding off it, Jane grew increasingly free to express her opinions, often in strong language, about the many buildings and projects she reviewed. Of a prefabricated school, she wrote Haskell in 1955, "I heartily dislike the looks and the general tone of this school. It *looks* cheeseparing and niggling and no fun and no aiming high, and there is something wormy and pathetic about its little attempts at applied amenities." Of a shopping center in Yonkers, New York, she wrote him that it was "a spectacularly bad example of shopping center planning," then spent the next three pages, in close single-spaced text, explaining why: the two department stores were too far apart; the overall design only accentuated its forbidding length. "It is a monotonous succession of triangular planting beds (and ugly bituminous paving) with no variations, no enticement." The center's excellent site and large surrounding population might make it a success, but, if so, no thanks to its design.

With Jane's rhetoric always came fact, evidence. Back at *Amerika* her performance reviews had practically always come in at Excellent. For all the excesses of her personality, her need and determination to *express*, she inspired trust.

She was doing a good job.

But is there something a little watery and wanting in so homely an assertion?

In early 1955, Jane was thirty-eight years old. She was happily married, a mother of two, pregnant with a third. She had a house of her own. She had risen in the world, had achieved much of what she'd wanted in coming to New York; she was a writer paid well for her work. She had all the knowledge, experience, initiative, and talent she would ever need to do what she was going to do in the big world. But she had not yet done it; she wasn't one of those artists, thinkers, and precocious talents—mostly men, in a man's world, propped up by men's privileges—who, by age thirty-eight, had already made their mark. Hers was a more gradually unfolding story.

If you read her articles in *Amerika,* or in *Forum* during her first years there, you find little hint of the themes percolating up in *The Death and Life of Great American Cities*—except, that is, for her interest in the subject itself: cities. But her impatience with existing architectural and planning practice? Her rejection of the status quo? These are nowhere to be found. At least as she expressed them in the pages of *Forum,* and before that in *Amerika,* hers are conventional sensibilities. She attacks nothing, submits to what is, embraces the new suburban shopping centers. She accepts the postwar world without cavil or complaint.

Later, she'd say that in a way she *hadn't* been doing a good job at *Forum*—that as she'd listened to planners and architects, she'd too readily accepted what they had to say; did not question whether their lovely renderings and pretty models perhaps lacked something, or were misguided, or were just plain wrong. And that until she came to see it that way, *she* was wrong.

If we had to pin down a moment when that began to change, when Jane Jacobs began to see in a new way the streets and cities, buildings, plans, and architectural visions she had been writing about, it would probably be sometime in early 1955, in Philadelphia.

PART II

In the Big World

1954–1968

CHAPTER 9

DISENCHANTMENT

PHILADELPHIA, Jane wrote in a story about the city's redevelopment in July 1955, was perhaps the only American city really grappling with the stark contrasts of urban life. She saw "an atmosphere of hope" there, in the initiative of private citizenry "thriving in the little and the large." She marveled at the sheer scope of the city's efforts, scattered over more than a dozen sites and ten thousand acres. She wrote of sunken gardens; of a food distribution center that would eliminate squatters' shacks and burning dumps; of the architect Louis Kahn's "clever and practical devices" for improving a poor district called Mill Creek. She lauded an "embrace of the new" that in Philadelphia "has by some miracle not meant the usual rejection of whatever is old."

At intervals, Jane quoted the city's planning commission director, the already legendary Edmund Bacon, on his way to the cover of *Time* for his leadership of the city's redevelopment programs. A native Philadelphian, forty-five, born of a staunchly conservative publishing family, Bacon was a graduate of Cornell's school of architecture. He'd used an inheritance from his grandfather to travel the world, had wound up in Beijing, won a fellowship to study city planning at the University of Michigan, worked as a planner in Flint. By 1949, he was back in Philadelphia, pushing his ideas through the local bureaucracy, determined to clear away the debris of the city's industrial past and create gleaming new modernist vistas; the city had not seen a major new office building go up in almost twenty years. Bacon, it could seem, was not just Philadelphia's master planner, but America's.

Not everyone liked him. "Arrogant, arch, pompous, and wrong," an architect who knew him later, Alan Littlewood of Toronto, would blithely call him. To Bacon's enemies, an article in *Harper's* would say, "he had risen too fast, succeeded too soon . . . 'Lord Bacon,' they called him across the Schuylkill, at the University of Pennsylvania's School of Fine Arts, disliking his arrogance, theatrical manner and impresario air." Yet many appreciated that "he had accomplished more than any other town planner in the United States." And, of course, it was Bacon—thin, ascetic looking, driven—who had helped fill Jane's head with visions of Philadelphia's future and supplied the sketches, plans, photos, and maps she'd expertly folded into a coherent narrative heralding a city on the move.

And yet it's not clear how much—or even, just possibly, *whether*—Jane visited Philadelphia to research her story. A certain remove from the city runs through her ten-page article, which is subtitled "A Progress Report" but reads more like a preview. Early on, she laments of American cities generally that the urban deserts within them "have grown and still they are growing, the awful endless blocks, the endless miles of drabness and chaos." Yet she is moved to the brink of poetry by the thought of all "the work that went into this mess," the energy just below the surface, curdled into urban grit, which says "as much about the power and doggedness of life as the leaves of the forest in spring." Later pages, stocked with illustrations of the new Independence Mall, Penn Center, and Mill Center, tell of "what is happening" in Philadelphia, or "will be happening," or what "is going up," of projects "under construction," or "nearing completion." But not much of the real, under-the-skin city emerges.

At some point, certainly, Jane did visit Philadelphia. There she joined Bacon for a tour, letting him show off to her all he was proudest of. He was, of course, practiced at such showmanship, at one point treating Jane to a kind of before-and-after exercise in urban redevelopment. First they walked along a down-and-out street in a black neighborhood destined later for the Bacon treatment. It was crowded with people, people spilling out onto the sidewalk, sitting on stoops, running errands, leaning out of windows. Here was Before Street. Then it was off to After Street, the beneficiary of Bacon's vision—bulldozed, the unsavory mess of the old city swept away, a fine project replacing it, all pretty and new. *Jane,* Bacon urged her, *stand right here, look down this street, look what we've done here.*

She did. And certainly she could appreciate the vista Bacon offered her; *Yes, it's very nice.* But there was something missing: people. Especially so in contrast to that first street, which Jane recalled as lively and cheerful. Here, amid the new and rehabbed housing, what did she see? She saw one little boy—she'd remember him all her life—kicking a tire. Just him, alone on the deserted street.

Ed, she said, *nobody's here. Now, why is that? Where are the people? Why is no one here?*

The way Jane told the story, Bacon didn't offer a *Yes, but . . .* by way of explanation. He didn't say, *Well, in a few years, as the neighborhood matures, we'll see . . .* He offered no explanation at all. To Jane, he just wasn't interested in her question, which irritated the hell out of her. She was puzzled, he wasn't, and that was itself noteworthy. But more, for Jane the two streets seemed to point up some opposing lesson, or value, or idea, from that of Bacon—some sharply different sense of what mattered in a city and what did not, a divergent way of seeing. For Bacon, the new street exemplified all that was best in the new world that planners like him were making. For Jane, Bacon's perspective was narrowly aesthetic, a question mostly of how it *looked;* to her, the new street represented not entirely a gain over the old, maybe no gain at all, but a loss, one that mocked Bacon's plans and drawings and the glittering future they promised. "Not only did he and the people he directed not know how to make an interesting or a humane street," she'd say, "but they didn't even notice such things and didn't care." In time, scholars managed to find a measure of common ground between Bacon and Jacobs. But just now, they stood at the same spot, viewed the same streets, and saw them through different eyes.

Perhaps Bacon's Philadelphia diverged too far from the one Jane had heard about from her parents, who'd met and courted there; or the Philadelphia she'd seen herself in the 1930s visiting sister Betty at school; or on trips down from New York for *Iron Age* in the 1940s; or from some pure Platonic vision of City that had become part of her after twenty years in New York. Whatever the reason, the vehemence and frequency with which she'd later bring up the Bacon incident suggest no cool dissonance of values. Jane was angry—angry, it seems, at having been duped.

Jane's recollections of her early years at *Forum* hint at a still youthful naïveté on which she'd look back ruefully. She'd visited Philadelphia, she'd say,

> and found out what they had in mind and what they were planning to do and how it was going to look according to the drawings, what great

things it was going to accomplish . . . I came back and wrote enthusiastic articles about this, and subsequently about other [cities], and all was well. I was in very cozy with the planners and project builders. I suppose my readers . . . well, I must ask them to forgive me now, whoever they were.

For what she saw now in Philadelphia was that the new projects didn't look the way they were supposed to look and, more important, didn't *work* the way they were supposed to work. Not if the boy kicking the tire down the street was any indication. Not if projects she'd heard glowingly described, or had even written about, were turning out as they did: "They weren't delightful, they weren't fine, and they were obviously never going to work right," she wrote the Louisville writer Grady Clay in 1959. "Harrison Plaza and Mill Creek in Philadelphia were great shocks to me."

"The artists' drawings always looked so seductive," she'd all but shake her head in recalling. Yes, drawings specified the thickness of concrete walls and how air-handling systems were to be laid out. But they also *showed off*. They represented aesthetic vistas, how buildings, projects, and cities were to work. They showed people using them, trees and walkways, visions of the good life—often in bird's-eye views that left the viewer with a sense of promise and parade at the urban prospect before her. And, of course, they were the work of architects and planners with a cultivated sense of design, drama, and spectacle. What Jane found in Philadelphia was that these visions didn't match the city she met on the ground—not, at least, in ways that mattered to her.

The year or two before Jane's Philadelphia article appeared may have been a bit stale for her at *Forum;* she'd written, for example, about how self-service displays were influencing store architecture. She tried doing a little freelancing on the side. She tried to interest *Reader's Digest* in some slices of Americana that had come down to her through the Butzner side of the family. She tried science fiction, a retelling of the Adam and Eve story. She didn't get very far.

But after Philadelphia, Jane returned to the *Forum* offices on fire, began talking of her disenchantment. Her disenchantment, you might ask, with just what? Actually, she may not have been able to put it very articulately or profoundly as yet. At *Forum* she had imbibed the architectural and planning truths of her day as much as anyone; whatever

Doug Haskell, editor of Architectural Forum, *during the time Jane worked there*

bothered her was still new to her, something she probably didn't entirely understand herself.

In February 1955, about when Jane's Philadelphia article was making its way through editors and graphic artists to publication, Doug Haskell wrote to his staff about how, "in view of the terrific acceleration in the urban redevelopment picture," *Forum* now planned to treat the nation's cities more comprehensively. Philadelphia would get ten pages of the magazine in July; that was Jane's article. Cleveland would be next, and Jane—was she by now the magazine's resident urban expert?—got that one, too.

Cleveland had plenty going for it, she wrote in the article that appeared in August, but its future seemed to stop dead at the city line; suburbanites wanted nothing to do with it.

It is hard for an outsider to understand why Cleveland as an organism, as an idea, fails to captivate the suburban imagination in the immemorial way of big cities. For Cleveland has individuality, and visually it is a stirring sight. It deserves neither to be thought of as a mere facility, nor to be snubbed. Inherently, it is anything but monotonous; industry-lined river and creek valleys slash deeply through its hills. Bridges, ore-loaders, stacks put their peculiar zing into the humdrum commercial and residential scene. Maybe industry cutting through the city is not "nice," but from the freeway alongside or banks above, it makes a vista as exciting as the tumbled excesses of nature.

Jane went on to tell of the city's lakefront plans, news of freeways and rapid transit, as well as proposed redevelopment of Garden Valley, which, she wrote, would "transform a desolate industrial wasteland and an enormous, steep, barren ravine into a neighborhood" of low- and middle-income housing. If she had doubts about any of this—as she might well have, for Garden Valley became an awful slum—they didn't surface.

So whatever was going on in Jane's fecund brain, it didn't make for a wholesale break with the past. She had a good job. She was writing. Everything was fine. Except, everything wasn't: Bacon's Philadelphia remained a mental irritant, like a grain of sand in the eye that won't wash away.

If during the mid-1950s you came for dinner at the Jacobs house on Hudson Street, the first thing you'd see as you came in, parked just off the kitchen, was a bike, wicker basket suspended from its handlebars. Come 9:30 or 10 weekday mornings, garbed in respectable office dress, sometimes even pearls, Jane would pedal it up one of Manhattan's broad north-south avenues the two and a half miles to the *Forum* offices at Rockefeller Center. It was an era before bicycle lanes, helmets, and ten-speeds, much less messenger bags and fixies; navigating Midtown Manhattan by bike, especially for a middle-aged mother of three, was outlandish enough to earn Jane a place in her own magazine.

In 1956, *Forum* colleague William McQuade devoted the magazine's informal "Parentheses" column to a lady "who shall be nameless" but a photograph of whom, atop her steed, shows Jane. At workday's end, McQuade wrote, she'd round up her bike from "among the ranks of Cadillacs" in a nearby garage. Then she'd pedal "down Fifth Avenue, south through the crowded department store district . . . [and] the impossible press of the garment district, on through the fallen petals and broken blossoms of the wholesale flower zone, and then down through wicked Greenwich Village until she reaches home, her house on Hudson Street." McQuade's journalistic bibelot offered a sample of the jibes Jane absorbed on her commute. "Get a horse," she'd hear a lot. Or, "Watch out, girlie, you'll get hurt." More recently, back on the bike again after the birth of her daughter, Mary, in January 1955, New Yorkers seemed warmer to her. "That's a good idea," she'd sometimes hear. Or "Good for you," or "Take me with you." Of course, her street critics never tired of pointing out: "*Your back wheel's spinning.*"

Jane's marriage had all but begun on the bike, with a cycling honeymoon. After the war, she and Bob enjoyed what she'd call "hitch-hiking with the fish": they'd load their bikes on the train, get off somewhere within cycling distance of a fishing port, and, with their beat-up bags, hitch rides on fishing boats plying East Coast waterways. No reference to what Jane called this "intricate network of unofficial transport" appeared in any atlas or tourist map. They made no hotel reservations, yet always found someone to take them in. In a little town on Pamlico Sound in North Carolina, it was the owner of a local shrimp-packing plant. In Maine, it was the island butter maker and her lobsterman husband. One time, Jane would write, they feasted on lobster "direct from the sea into the galley cauldron, eaten on deck in a green and lavender twilight among the rock and evergreen islands of Penobscot Bay."

Back on Hudson Street, they got their boys onto bikes early on. When he was three and Jimmy was five, Ned recalls, their parents renewed the Sunday bike excursions around town they'd enjoyed before the children were born. The kids were taught to sit on the rear rack "with our feet in canvas saddlebags, our hands on the cyclist's waist." They never had an accident. They always had fun.

During this period, Jane made about $10,000 a year—about twice what a *Forum* secretary made and probably more than Bob, who, after a stretch as assistant architect with a New York City agency, was just finding his way into hospital design. With two incomes, the Jacobses were doing well enough, but with two, then three, children at home and the old house a money drain, they were far from well off. Around this time they bought an encyclopedia on the installment plan; Jane would remember the payments dragging on forever.

But during the 1950s and early 1960s, time was probably scarcer than money for them. Soon after son Jimmy's birth in 1948, Jane had hired a woman to take care of him while she was at work. Her name was Glennie Lenear, an African American woman who came in on the subway every day from Queens and who'd work for the family for a dozen years. Jane did what she needed to around the house, but never warmed to everyday domestic chores. From when he was five or six Jimmy remembers Aunt Betty, who lived across town in a new middle-income project called Stuyvesant Town, urging his mother to get a steam iron, to spiff up her clothes for work; it would be so much more efficient that way. But Jane saw nothing efficient about it; better just to take her clothes next door to the cleaners. She rarely shopped for groceries; more often, she made a list of what she needed and phoned it in to the local grocer, delivery coming a few hours later, a bill once a month.

Jane would become known for her first book's warm account of her neighborhood's shopkeepers—how she'd exchange a friendly nod each morning with Mr. Lofaro, the fruit dealer, how she'd leave a spare key with Joe Cornacchia, proprietor of the local deli. As a *New York Times* writer observed after the book came out, "Thornton Wilder's loving portrait of the leisurely life of Grover's Corners," in *Our Town*, was "no more romantic than Mrs. Jacobs's affectionate portrait of a day and night in Hudson Street." By 1955, she had lived there for seven years, in the Village for twenty—long enough, and stitched in enough, to feel protective of it. To outsiders, the wayward tracts of the Village, with tenement apartments atop hardware stores and trucks bebopping down crowded streets, might seem to offer little enough to protect. But by now the Village exerted a powerful hold on Jane. So when word got out that the city was bent on pushing a highway through Washington Square Park, she was among those who helped try to stop it.

Now, it so happens that this Washington Square Park—Waverly Place to West Fourth Street and MacDougal to University Place, ten acres shaded by pin oaks and yellow locust trees, benches lining its paths, the white marble Washington Arch looming over it—comes down to us as a cultural monument of the 1950s and 1960s; that its history went way back to the more genteel era of Henry James's *Washington Square*; that, even before Bob Dylan and Allen Ginsberg frequented it, it was already a tourist destination, suburbanites from Jersey and the Island descending on it to get their fix of folk singers, chess players, and *cool*.

But, please, forget all that: it wasn't folk singers, beat poets, or historic preservationists who battled back the threat to the park, it was mothers—mothers for whose children the park was their playground, open space in a crowded city. When Jane's brother Jim and his family came up to the city from South Jersey, the cousins would soon be trooping over to Washington Square, a ten- or fifteen-minute walk away. It was lovely, always full of people, and safe.

But, beginning in the early 1950s, it was threatened.

"I have heard with alarm and almost with disbelief," Jane wrote Mayor Robert F. Wagner Jr. and the Manhattan borough president, Hulan Jack, "the plans to run a sunken highway through the center of Washington Square." She went on to tell how she and Bob had transformed their home from a slum, were raising their three children in the city, doing their best to make the city a better place to live; this awful scheme would undo all that.

It was June 1, 1955. She had joined the fight late in the game; the campaign to save Washington Square Park had been going on for several years, and would for several more. Jane was only a foot soldier. But this wasn't the last time she would step into an urban turf war, and next time she'd be a general.

Early in 1955, Jane met William Kirk, who took her on another tour, of another city, and changed her life.

For the past six years, Kirk had worked in New York City's East Harlem at Union Settlement, which since the 1890s had provided health and social services to the neighborhood; Burt Lancaster of East 106th Street, the future actor, was one of its beneficiaries. The word "settlement" itself went back to the nineteenth century, when educated men and women in Victorian England settled in slums to live and work among the poor.

Kirk, whose official title was "headworker" but who functioned as executive director, had come out of Newcastle, Pennsylvania, an industrial town about fifty miles north of Pittsburgh. When Jane met him he was a big, lumbering, dark-haired man about seven years older than she who might have been mistaken for a longshoreman or union official except that he spoke with an accent more patrician than New York. He had graduated from Amherst College in 1931, attended the Virginia Seminary, was ordained an Episcopal priest in 1935. But as rector of a St. Louis church, he'd found that the social welfare side of his work meant more to him than the purely spiritual, and in 1949 he moved to New York to direct Union Settlement.

Now, six years later, Kirk saw the neighborhood reeling under new, disruptive forces no one could have foreseen. When he'd first moved into Union Settlement's offices on East 104th Street, both sides of the street looked about the same, each solidly lined with familiar walls of tenements, stores at street level, busy life sprouting up from among them.

William Kirk, director of Union Settlement in East Harlem, New York City

But now, in the mid-1950s, the south side of the street was gone, the tenements torn down, replaced by ranges of high-rise towers cascading off to the south—slab-sided structures of twelve or fourteen stories, each set amid park-like swaths of green, winding paths, and parking lots. They had been built to do good. But Kirk had come to feel that these big housing projects were doing less good than harm. He had no data, nothing like the hard evidence later studies would supply, maybe no words yet even to describe it. But he knew that storekeepers were disappearing from the neighborhood; friendships seemed discouraged, schools and churches weakened, the social fabric frayed. His daughter, Judy Kirk Fitzsimmons, recalls him from her youth as a man on a mission, the big projects all he could talk about. He'd come home in the evening to their apartment on Riverside Drive, sit down for dinner, "and that was the conversation every night," about what the projects were doing to East Harlem.

East Harlem, be it noted, wasn't Harlem, the great concentration of African American life and culture lying roughly between Columbia University on the west and the New York Central tracks along Park Avenue to the east. East Harlem lay on the other side of the tracks beside the East River, sprawling north from Ninety-sixth Street. In the mid-1950s, it was about a third each black, Puerto Rican, and white. The whites were mostly Italian; until the 1930s, East Harlem had been the largest Little Italy in America. In this one corner of Upper Manhattan lived 180,000 people, many more than in all of Jane's own Scranton. Spanish was the language of many streets, shops, and homes, as spoken by migrants from Puerto Rico (an American dependency since the Spanish-American War). And it was poor, not here and there, as in the Village, but in great swaths of tenements ranging over dozens of blocks. Many of these were old-law tenements built for the great waves of immigrants to New York in the late 1800s—cramped apartments, often four to a floor, back rooms giving onto dirty air shafts for their only light and air, several families sharing a common toilet in the hall. As recently as 1939, in what was then the most densely Italian part of East Harlem, four in five dwellings lacked central heating, two-thirds lacked tub or shower, more than half were without a private toilet. *What, exactly, was a slum?* Whatever it was, there were plenty of them in East Harlem. Crime was rampant. People were forever moving in and out. No bank, according to one neighborhood observer, had loaned a dollar of mortgage money in East Harlem since before 1940.

Of course, everybody knew all this, and after World War II, efforts were begun to remedy the neighborhood's housing evils; at a time when fifteen cents got you on the subway, $300 million in new housing had gone up since the 1940s, worth maybe $3 billion today. Beginning even earlier, in 1941, with East River Houses, and then with hurtling, unsettling rapidity after the war, blocks of tenements had been torn down, new eleven- and fourteen- and seventeen-story projects going up in their place. In time they would house a fifth of East Harlem. It wasn't just George Washington Houses, across 104th Street from Union Settlement. It was James Weldon Johnson Houses, ranging across six blocks between Third and Park Avenues, with more than 1,300 apartments. And Carver Houses, along Madison Avenue, with 1,246. And Lexington Houses, Taft Houses, Stephen Foster Houses . . . "Tear down the old," New York mayor Fiorello La Guardia, a son of East Harlem, had urged in a 1944 speech. "Build up the new. Down with rotten, antiquated rat holes. Down with hovels. Down with disease. Down with crime . . . Let in the sun. Let in the sky." And they had: clean, relatively spacious apartments, half a century newer than the tenements they'd displaced. They were "solid, institutional gigantic buildings," one social worker would write, that promised "the long-awaited and highly touted attributes of sunshine, fresh air, and modern plumbing."

And yet, from Bill Kirk's perch on East 104th Street, something was wrong with this fine picture. His friend Phil Will, he decided, needed to see what he saw in East Harlem. Will was a prominent Chicago architect who a few years later would become president of the American Institute of Architects. The specialty of his firm, Perkins & Will, was schools, but he'd earlier made a name for himself with Racine Courts, a model for low-rise public housing in Chicago. The two men had gotten to know each other through their wives, best friends in college, and across a span of twenty years had become close. So now, Kirk brought Will to East Harlem. "He wanted him to see how people worked, see the fabric of the community," recalls Kirk's daughter, and to see what the new construction—this new *kind* of construction, really—was doing to it. Afterward, Will suggested they approach Doug Haskell at *Architectural Forum*, whom he'd known since the 1940s.

It is just conceivable that Haskell had never set foot in East Harlem, though it was only three miles up the spine of Manhattan from Rockefeller Center. In any event, his in-basket was more typically piled with correspondence from famous architects like Walter Gropius and Frank Lloyd Wright; Kirk's letter to him didn't get a response. In March, he wrote Haskell again. This time, unwilling to wait for an answer that might never come, he announced his intention to call Haskell's office the following Monday and set up a time to meet.

It's unclear whether it was Haskell or one of his minions with whom Kirk eventually met. But in any case, Kirk was soon down in Rockefeller Center, hauling out maps, holding forth on East Harlem: it was, he doubtless pointed out, the biggest beneficiary of federal housing largesse in New York City and probably the country. The feds had torn down blocks of slums and replaced them with high-rises. The old slums were bad, but the new projects were bad, too, only in different ways. What *Forum* editors needed to understand was . . .

Well, the *Forum* editor apparently couldn't get all that worked up about Kirk's slum troubles, which didn't exactly sync with the magazine's more elite-minded editorial agenda. So, perhaps feeling trapped, he was glad to catch sight of Jane outside his office door and wave her in. Jane's Ed Bacon moment hadn't struck everyone around *Forum* the way it had her; she seemed troubled by things everyone else blithely accepted. But now, this Mr. Kirk seemed troubled by some of the same things: these fine new projects that were supposed to be the last word in low-cost housing, that looked great in the drawings, that expressed modernist social and architectural ideals, maybe *weren't* so fine . . . *Mrs. Jacobs*, Kirk said to her before he left *Forum*'s offices that day, *why don't you come up to East Harlem, and I'll show you around?*

East Harlem had been Kirk's turf since 1949, before most of the projects had gone up, his memory speckled with visions of kite fights waged from tenement roofs. Stickball games between boys from rival blocks. Rows of three- and four-story row houses, magnificent in their gingerbread detailing, their wide stoops climbing toward great windowed frontages. Produce markets, their wares sheltered by awnings that dropped

over the sidewalk. Tenement doors left open to catch the breeze on swel-
tering summer afternoons. And everywhere, on every street—front
parlor to their crowded apartments—*people*. People parading down wide
sidewalks. Tending clothes laid out to dry across steel-slatted fire escapes.
Stepping out onto the sidewalk from their stores, looking up to the sky to
check the day's weather.

"I can't imagine how he took the time" to show her the neighborhood,
Jane would recall, "but he did. Whenever I got a few hours that I could
take off from work I would call him up and he would walk me around . . .
He didn't seem to have any plan about what he was showing me. It all
seemed very aimless, in a way. We would just walk."

People who knew Bill Kirk remembered him for his wide web of
friends, acquaintances, connections. "Everybody knew him," recalls
Eugene Sklar, his successor at Union Settlement. "And he knew everybody . . . He was interested in all the local people, in the storekeepers, in
what was doing on the street." The overtly religious side of him surfaced
rarely—though Sklar did remember the big, colorful sign beside Kirk's
desk at Union Settlement: LET US REASON TOGETHER. He was warm, with
a ready smile, "a great listener . . . People admired him, and they trusted
him."

He was a public character. "We would stop every little while or somebody would stop him," Jane would tell of their times together. "I would
eavesdrop on the conversation. We would stop in at stores," at housing projects, a walk-up. Kirk would point out local landmarks. He knew
everybody. But while it was all interesting, she didn't at first see what he
was getting at, if he was getting at anything at all. "It was like a big basket of dry leaves being thrown up into the air. What would you make out
of that?" And yet, there *was* something, and she began to see it: behind
the seeming confusion of the East Harlem streets, a kind of order ran
through them, an endlessly intricate one. There, right beside the social
pathologies that were all too evident, behind the rattle of the trucks, the
young toughs, the jarring clash of old tenements and new projects, were
people of every color and shade, every species of vibrancy and decay,
together. Jane drank it all in.

You or me? Would we have drunk it all in? Might seeing East Harlem
with Kirk have left us cold? Might it have failed to tug at our imagina-
tions in the way it did at Jane's? Or maybe it would have seemed mildly
interesting, but only that—a briefly opened window on a world normally

closed to us, a peek at urban life's myriad variety, soon forgotten. Not Jane, though: somehow, she was *susceptible* to East Harlem's charms, qualities, peculiarities, and how together they made a living place.

When, years later, she was asked how she'd first gotten interested in cities, she said it all went back to the fourth grade in Scranton. It was a Friday, she remembered. A classmate, Elizabeth, was being told by the school librarian that since she'd returned her books late she owed a one-penny fee. Oh, said Elizabeth, "I'll bring it in when the bird's eye blows." And unaccountably, the librarian accepted this answer with perfect equanimity, as a full and satisfactory explanation—accepted it, as Jane told it, "with dignity." The Bird's Eye, Jane's mother explained to her later, was a nearby coal mine. If, come six in the morning, you heard the whistle blow, it meant there was work for you at the mine, money coming in. Elizabeth knew that. The school librarian knew it. Jane's mother knew it. And now Jane knew it as well—a network of knowledge reinforced with one more tendril of connection. The incident made her think about how, all over Scranton, people made their livings. Her father treated sick people. Elizabeth's father went down into the mine. Everybody working. Abruptly, "the whole city seemed so much more interesting to me. It became a web," tied together, with odd details, intricate links, patterns.

Jane's parents—one from a small town, the other from a farm, but who'd met and courted in Philadelphia—were "delighted to live in the city," she'd say. "They thought cities were far superior places to live, and they told us why." In New York, it had taken Jane no more than climbing up from the subway at Sheridan Square and a stroll through the surrounding streets to sell her on Greenwich Village. The fur district had captivated her. So had the other commercial areas she'd written about for *Vogue*. Now, beside Bill Kirk, she began to see beyond where even her lively curiosity had taken her, to an East Harlem that was much more than it first appeared, something interwoven, connected, whole.

Jane liked Kirk a lot. But not, says her son Jim, who first met him as a child, because of anything so fuzzy and indeterminate as his "personality." It was, rather, out of respect for how he saw and made sense of the world. He saw East Harlem in its entirety, as *all* it was, "not as something he had to fix. He would see in it its glories, its values, where most people just saw a mess." The piling up of detail and incident, the stream of insight, the snippets of conversation, that Jane absorbed at Kirk's elbow opened her eyes. "He was showing me a different way of looking at the city, the social aspect," the human ties that didn't show up in architectural drawings.

It was probably late in 1955 or early the next year that Jane learned of a study in the works, probably at Kirk's behest, conducted by a group called the East Harlem Small Business Survey and Planning Committee. The report it would later issue needed just three typed pages to hint at the havoc the projects inflicted on the neighborhood. Squeezed into the bottom of its first page was a crude, hand-drawn map of Franklin Houses, a 1,200-apartment project occupying five blocks between First and Third Avenues that had wiped out 169 businesses. Then, with page two, came an extraordinary list, an exercise in data collection and tabulation sure to make your eyes glaze over—that is, until you *got* it and allowed yourself to imagine what 169 businesses that weren't there meant, in their absence, to residents of Franklin Houses and adjacent blocks.

Across the top of the page ranged five columns, for the five blocks of Manhattan street grid that were the old neighborhood, labeled I through V. Running down the page were forty-four classes of business, from appliances and baby carriage storage to shoe stores, toys, and travel agencies. It was a Tabulation of the Lost: not long before, the streets circumscribing block I were home to three fruit stands; now there were none. There'd been three cleaners in block II, two meat markets in block III, five grocers in block IV, three barbers, a beauty parlor, and a radio-and-TV-repair shop in block V, and fourteen candy stores in the project area as a whole, among scores of others. All were gone. So were thirteen hole-in-the-wall manufacturers, two union offices, three churches, one political club, and eight social clubs.

All told, across East Harlem, the projects had eliminated more than fifteen hundred retail stores, with virtually none built in their place. Pity the poor capitalists? Maybe. But if you took your eyes off their troubles and looked instead at the neighborhood they served, you'd see not only entrepreneurial livelihoods lost, but social glue weakened—a community, as Jane would put it, replaced by a dormitory.

In early 1956, José Luis Sert, a Catalan architect who'd immigrated to the United States in 1939 and now was dean of the Harvard Graduate School of Design, proposed an urban design conference to be held at the university that April. *Urban design?* Sert saw it as a "design discipline" straddling the work of architect, landscape architect, and city planner, broader than each alone. As Andrés Duany, a chief proponent of the late twentieth century's New Urbanism movement, would put it, Sert's conference at Harvard could be seen as "a group of middle-aged gentlemen gathered in an attempt to mitigate the consequences of their youthful indiscretions"—as purveyors of city-bashing modernism. "Harvard must lead the correction," Sert had resolved.

Among distinguished figures from the planning, architectural, and design communities invited to the conference was the editor of *Architectural Forum*. On January 21, 1956, Doug Haskell wrote Sert that he would be delighted to attend.

But about two months later, when Sert's lieutenant, Jacqueline Tyrwhitt, phoned, he told her "a conflict had come up." The conflict was that "this is the one time I can get to Europe" that year. So he couldn't attend after all, "dearly as I would love to." Who, then, in his place? "If another woman [that is, other than Tyrwhitt, herself an accomplished architect] would not be out of place, might I suggest that a substitute be Mrs. Robert Jacobs—Jane Jacobs on our masthead." When it came to the urban redevelopment stories they were running in *Forum*, she was the most experienced.

It's not clear whether Haskell offered Jane's name to Tyrwhitt after he'd spoken with Jane or before; at this point, the conference lay only three weeks ahead. What is clear is that Jane first said she wouldn't do it.

Wouldn't do it because she was not going to stand up and speak in public—just wasn't going to torture herself again. A few years before she'd given a public talk. She'd written it out, scarcely giving a thought to actually delivering it. But when the time came, she'd remember, "my knees trembled and my voice trembled and I was terrified and I couldn't control this, and I just sort of ducked my head down and mumbled the speech from the paper and got through it."

Especially frightening was the way it had come over her out of the blue. She'd had no premonition, was heedless of any buried fears she might have had until the time came to actually do it. In print, Jane Jacobs was confident and authoritative. In person, in the right settings, among a few people, she voiced her views volubly, often was the dominant figure in the room. But give a talk publicly, in front of a roomful of people? This was sheer terror. She couldn't do it, wouldn't do it. After the earlier fiasco, "I said to myself I will never do this again . . . I wouldn't put myself through this for anything."

Yet now *Forum*'s managing editor was on the phone with her to say that's just what she had to do. Something about land banking for urban renewal—that was supposed to be her topic.

"I said no."

"Well," said the managing editor, "you have to. He is depending on you." "He" was Doug Haskell.

She said nothing. The phone must have seemed to have gone dead.

"Well, I'll do it," she said at last, "but it will be a subject of my own choosing." Land banking? No, no. "I'll talk about something that interests me."

TEN MINUTES AT HARVARD

JANE HAD ALREADY BEGUN to voice some of her contrarian ideas at *Forum*. Around the kitchen table at Hudson Street, Bob and some of their friends had heard her speak of them, too. But the Harvard conference would be different. This was public, and big. Among the two hundred attending would be many of the most notable figures in the worlds of architecture, planning, and design.

First of all, there was José Luis Sert, who had brought them to Cambridge in the first place. Sert, from Barcelona, had in his youth worked for Le Corbusier himself. "City planning has developed as a new science," he'd assert in his welcome speech. Planners now needed to think about the very "structure of the city, its process of growth and decay."

There was Ed Bacon from Philadelphia, whom Jane would call "the grand poobah" of American planning. And the Austrian American architect Richard Neutra, celebrated for the clean, crisp modernism of his California homes. And Lloyd Rodwin from MIT; David Lawrence, mayor of Pittsburgh; Charles Abrams, creator of the New York City Housing Authority; the Hungarian-born design theorist György Kepes; Hideo Sasaki, pioneering landscape architect. And, of course, Lewis Mumford, down briefly from his perch at *The New Yorker*, the grand eminence of American architectural criticism, author of more than a dozen books on art, architecture, technology, and culture—aloof, respected, proud. Virtually all of them were men—degreed and credentialed, with long résumés attesting to their distinguished careers, men who had designed important buildings, changed the face of cities. Jane needed no cheat

Jane, career woman, at Architectural Forum, *ca. 1960*

sheet for those she'd meet at Harvard; at least by name and reputation, she already knew many of them.

For months now, in the wake of her visits to Philadelphia and East Harlem, Jane had been troubled by the great gulf between how things were supposed to work in the new modernist city and how they really did. She needed to say something about it; that intellectual tickle, that writerly need to *express*, had grown. She had two, maybe three weeks to prepare her talk. As if composing any ordinary article, she wrote it out first. Not that she would simply read it out loud; that would be deadly.

On the other hand, notes or flash cards might leave too much room for a podium meltdown once she stepped up to speak. So she memorized her talk, all fifteen hundred words. Bob made her try it out on him first.

First my knees trembled and my voice trembled because I had to get through it. But he made me say it over and over to him so I could do it without that happening . . . So when the time came and I had to give the speech, I went into some kind of . . . I mesmerized myself. I have no memory of doing it. I just said it. I blanked out and said it without all this trembling and everything, and got away with it.

She began with East Harlem, and how, in the rehousing of fifty thousand people in the projects, more than a thousand stores had disappeared from the neighborhood. This was not just consumer goods and services made harder to come by; this was *community*. "A store," she said memorably, "is also a storekeeper. One supermarket can replace thirty neighborhood delicatessens, fruit stands, groceries and butchers . . . But it cannot replace thirty storekeepers or even one."

Candy stores, diners, and bars served as social centers. When sometimes they failed, social clubs, political clubs, and churches took over their empty storefronts. And if these, too, were gone? It was easy to joke about the poor ward heeler who'd lost his organization. But, Jane cautioned, "this is not really hilarious." She continued,

If you are a nobody, and you don't know anybody who isn't a nobody, the only way you can make yourself heard in a large city is through certain well-defined channels. These channels all begin in holes in the wall. They start in Mike's barbershop or the hole-in-the-wall office of a man called Judge, and they go on to the Thomas Jefferson Democratic Club where Councilman Favini holds court, and now you are started on up.

How all this worked couldn't be formalized. But by the whole weight of her argument, it *needed* the shabby, low-rent, leftover spaces of poor city neighborhoods. It didn't work so much in new buildings, in the secure, serenely ordered places of the world.

Places like Stuyvesant Town.

Jane had reason to know about Stuyvesant Town; her sister lived there.

All through the late 1940s, 1950s, and beyond, the two of them, their husbands, and their children were in and out of each other's homes, a half hour's walk or a ride on the crosstown bus away, their families off together to museums, free concerts, the zoo. Betty and Jules Manson and their three children (aged three through eight in 1955) lived in one of a great eruption of new thirteen-story apartment buildings named after Peter Stuyvesant, the last mayor of New Amsterdam before it became New York City. The complex was built after the war to help remedy the housing shortage faced by returning GIs. Stuyvesant Town wasn't a "project," in that it wasn't the work of federal housing agencies. It wasn't built to serve the poor. But "project" it was in every other sense—vast, covering sixty-two acres, its three dozen redbrick towers all but identical, home to twenty thousand people.

In 1942, from their perch six hundred feet above Madison Avenue in the headquarters of the Metropolitan Life Insurance Company, as Samuel Zipp tells the story in his masterful *Manhattan Projects*, the company's money men looked south and saw the whole East Side below the East Twenties as, weirdly, "vacant." That is, they saw crumbling tenements ripe for investment, demolition, and reconstruction. Eventually, work crews rendered the whole eighteen-block Gashouse District, as the neighborhood was known, indistinguishable from European cities laid waste by war. But before they did, Met Life went through it, block by block, photographing streetscapes that would soon be gone.

One corner of the site did look pretty bad. But some of the rest of the neighborhood, if not exactly bustling with life, could pass for prosperous, with four- and five-story tenements lining well-kept streets. There were theaters, two schools, numerous ornate churches. Lewis Mumford himself would write of the gasworks that gave the neighborhood its name, that the sight of its "tracery of iron, against an occasional clear lemon-green sky at sunrise" offered a memorably aesthetic moment. Journalists documenting the area's death throes found, in Zipp's words, "a living neighborhood . . . [whose] residents viewed the place with simple affection, despite poverty and a declining population . . . [It] was the setting for the great events of ordinary life and had become as precious to them as the people with whom they had shared their lives."

The Gashouse District was leveled. Stuyvesant Town rose in its place. By many measures it had to count as a success. Aimed squarely at the middle class, it boasted pretty landscaping, curving paths, relatively spa-

In her Harvard talk in 1956, Jane emphasized the similarities, more than the differences, between Stuyvesant Town, a middle-income development east of First Avenue in Lower Manhattan, and George Washington Houses, a low-income public housing project in New York's East Harlem.

cious rooms, and a careful tenant selection process—which for years excluded blacks and other minorities. In these ways, if not in every other, it mirrored the new suburbs going up around the same time. Betty Manson's daughter, Jane's niece Carol, would recall fondly how, from her bedroom window in apartment 10F of one of the buildings, she could look north to see the Empire State and Chrysler buildings. The window of her brother's room looked south, across Fourteenth Street, to the older tenement neighborhood where they could watch people flying pigeons from the rooftops. Stuyvesant Town, she'd think, was as different as could be from Aunt Jane's ramshackle Greenwich Village.

And, of course, it was as different as could be from East Harlem.

Only Jane thought it wasn't so different from East Harlem after all, which is what she wanted to tell her Harvard audience.

To her, Stuyvesant Town seemed a creature of the same postwar planning impulse. Like East Harlem, it had no stores, virtually nothing but apartments. Like East Harlem, it was huge, occupying a great swath of real estate along the eastern edge of Manhattan, from First Avenue almost to the East River. As with the East Harlem projects the street grid had been torn up, new buildings plopped down into a great superblock. Butting up against Stuyvesant Town, Fifteenth and Sixteenth Streets now simply vanished at First Avenue. In numerous visits to her sister's place, Jane had walked Stuyvesant Town's lawn-lined paths and apartment hallways, and didn't like what she saw.

"We all knew of Jane's dislike for Stuyvesant Town," says Carol, who recalls a breath of tension between the sisters about it. "I did not for a long time understand her antipathy to the place, since it was certainly cleaner, and less smelly, and with fewer rats and insects, than the buildings south of us. And the toilets and bathtubs I thought had nice lines, and the windows were larger, and I liked the parquet floors." Over the years Stuyvesant Town's hesitant early tufts of foliage and shafts of green would grow into a lush springtime canopy. To many among her listeners at Harvard, Stuyvesant Town had no business being mentioned in the same breath as East Harlem. It was middle income, not poor. It was private, not public. Maybe it wasn't up to the standards of the Upper East Side or Gramercy Park, but compared to the East Harlem projects, rooms were bigger, the level of finish and care higher. Certainly it was easy to list all the ways in which it and East Harlem differed.

But Jane was drawing out what she saw as their similarities, which she saw as more telling. And she did so, oddly enough, through a kind of "figure-ground" reversal, by looking *outside* Stuyvesant Town to the streets around it: Take the elevator down from your tower apartment, step out along a broad curving walkway to Fourteenth Street, cross it, and you were in another country. Now it was four- and five-story walk-ups, fire escapes parading down their streetside faces, basement grates poking up onto the sidewalks, streets crowded with people, small stores of every description. A feast for the senses (if for some an assault on them). Jane pictured "an unplanned, chaotic, prosperous belt of stores, the camp followers around the Stuyvesant [Town] barracks." And beyond, a yet more chaotic belt, of "the hand-to-mouth cooperative nursery schools, the ballet classes, the do-it-yourself workshops, the little exotic stores." All this, "among the great charms of a city," lay *outside* Stuyvesant Town.

"Do you see what this means?" Jane asked her audience. Some of the most essential and characteristic elements of city life had been extirpated from Stuyvesant Town and from East Harlem alike, "because there is literally no place for them in the new scheme of things."

It was this "new scheme of things" that was Jane's real subject. The architectural and planning notions of the postwar period wiped real neighborhoods clean away and supplanted them with places made uniform, inflexible, inhuman, and dull. *This* was the new scheme of things. It was "a ludicrous situation," said Jane, "and it ought to give planners the shivers."

At one point, as she told the story, Union Settlement had sought a spot in an East Harlem project where they could meet easily with adult residents. Well, there was no such place, anywhere—no place to meet and gather except maybe the laundry room in the basement. Did the project's architects realize that relegating the social and public realm to the bowels of the basement made for a "social poverty beyond anything the slums ever knew"?

Jane wasn't finished. She observed that some of the East Harlem projects were by now a decade old. Yet with enough time now elapsed to forge new social networks, residents still visited their old neighborhoods while few from outside came to visit them. Why? Because there was nothing for them there, *nothing to do*. Planners needed to learn from the stoops and sidewalks of the city's livelier old parts. The open space of most urban redevelopment was a "giant bore," whereas it "should be at least as vital as the slum sidewalk."

"We are greatly misled," she concluded, "by talk about bringing the suburb into the city." The city had its own, very different virtues, "and we will do it no service by trying to beat it into some inadequate imitation of the noncity."

When she emerged from the near-hypnotic state, or whatever it was that had gotten her through it, Jane learned her talk had been "a big hit, because nobody had heard anybody saying these things before, apparently." Lewis Mumford came up to her afterward, shook her hand, and "enthusiastically welcomed me," as if to throw an arm around her and admit her to the club. "Into the foggy atmosphere of professional jargon" of the conference, he'd write later, Jane "blew like a fresh, offshore breeze to present a picture, dramatic but not distorted," of the human cost of the projects. Her appearance had

> established her as a person to be reckoned with. Here was a new kind of "expert" . . . This able woman had used her eyes and, even more admirably, her heart to assay the human result of large-scale housing, and she was saying, in effect, that these toplofty barracks . . . were not fit for human habitation.

In later years, other urban design conferences would be held at Harvard. But this was the first, the one they'd talk about later, the one where Jane Jacobs first stood up to speak. A moment before, she had been invisible; now she was a name. She was like the understudy for a Broadway show brought in at the last minute to sub for the real star. Doug Haskell they'd wanted; they got Jane Jacobs instead. And a lot of them never forgot it.

The twenty-seven-year-old Japanese architect Fumihiko Maki, a future Pritzker Prize winner then studying at the Harvard School of Design, would recall Jane's "passionate plea" on behalf of endangered neighborhoods. But the passion didn't come out as broad emotion or through commanding stage presence; then and later, Jane Jacobs was not a galvanizing speaker. Rather, it was *what she said* that stuck with people, the actual words, the ideas themselves; *they* conveyed the passion. "I had hypnotized myself," she'd say in an interview later, "but I had apparently hypnotized them too."

This wasn't artful sleight-of-hand, either. Jane had been observing and writing about cities almost since she first came to New York—first in the pages of *Vogue*, then in *Amerika*, and now, since 1952, in *Forum*; she was no Janie-come-lately amateur. She had something to say because she'd thought deeply about things she'd seen and read; and because she'd been around long enough that she had plenty of city life to think *about*—plenty of buildings, plenty of streetscapes, plenty of architects, maps and drawings, books and articles, artistic statements and aesthetic principles, plenty of neighborhood characters, city officials and developers, storekeepers, moms and dads. When she stepped before her audience at Harvard, her stew of ideas had long been simmering.

A week after the conference, Doug Haskell heard from the architect Victor Gruen, whose work was the subject of one of Jane's *Forum* articles and who had attended the conference. Jane was "wonderful," he wrote.

Everyone was using the expressions "human scale" and "warmth" but Jane was the only one who really talked about it, without ever using any of the big words. She was like a fresh wind in the airless room . . . Her simplicity and sincerity and her thoughtfulness swept everybody off his feet. There's no doubt that she was the "star" of the show.

At Harvard, Jane stood among the giants of the field; you couldn't vault much higher into the urban design firmament than her audience there. It wasn't that everything she'd said in those ten minutes had never been said before. As Gruen intimated, modernist architecture and planning had begun to wear a little thin; intimacy of scale had become part of the conversation. Still, Jane made her mark. On the back of Gruen's letter, Haskell penciled, "The wisest thing I have done in a long time was to turn over that assignment to her!"

That Jane was independent, even fearless, doesn't mean she was immune to praise, that she didn't care what others thought of her. Certainly the plaudits that came her way now would help extinguish any vestigial self-doubt about the worth of her ideas or her ability to express them. Preparing her talk and enjoying the response to it plainly marked a turning point for her. In a letter to Catherine Bauer, the public housing expert, Jane would write that her ideas had "been stewing around in me for the past two years or so," taking care to add: "not before." The letter was dated April 29, 1958—two years, to the month, since Harvard. High-profile honors like Nobel Prizes often go to those toward the end of their careers. But a second-tier honor, coming earlier, can serve its own, perhaps greater social purpose, reinforcing the recipient's sense of worth, bolstering her ambitions, helping to propel her and her ideas into the world. Something like this had now happened to Jane.

Her Harvard showing strengthened her hand at *Forum*, landing her higher-profile assignments, many of them now anointed with her byline. Jim remembers his mother coming home with the news, the significance of which, at age nine, escaped him. Jane explained that her name would now appear on the articles she wrote; she was, quite literally, no longer anonymous. It was good for *Forum* to be publishing the work of the woman who'd electrified Cambridge. And good for Jane, too, left freer to stretch her intellectual and editorial muscles.

In September 1956, a substantial chunk of the magazine was devoted to the question "By 1976, What City Pattern?" Jane wrote the lead essay: "The last ten years have given us an unholy mess of land use, land coverage, congestion and ugliness. This is nothing to what the next twenty promise. Barring annihilation, deep depression, or a more tractable invention supplanting the automobile, we have no way to avert this crisis of growth."

In a March 1957 article, she surveyed the office boom in New York, which had seen sixty-four major office buildings go up since the war—Lever House, the Seagram Building, 430 Park Avenue. "What," she asked, "has happened to those sensible-sounding postwar catchwords, 'dispersal' and 'decentralization'? What has happened to the vision of the happy file clerks eating sandwiches on the grass far from the madding crowd?"

In May, she revisited that classic urban form, the row house: "The big rediscovery is that a basic scheme dating from pedestrian days in Pompeii, and carriage days in Philadelphia, turns out to be an excellent answer to the automobile."

In August, she turned from streets and alleys to regions. The problems of metropolitan government would be solved "not by abstract logic or elegance of structure, but in a combination of approaches, by trial, error and immense experimentation in a context of expediency and conflicting interests. Whatever we arrive at, we shall feel our way there."

All this energetic voicing-of-views appeared within Jane's longtime journalistic home. But *Forum* could not contain her forever. It was the littlest child in the Time-Life family. It had the smallest circulation. Bigger by far, with a broader reach and larger profile, was *Fortune*, Henry Luce's oversized business magazine, launched in 1930. In the first week of January 1957, nine months after Jane's Harvard talk, Doug Haskell received a brotherly memo from a *Fortune* editor, Holly Whyte, seeking help.

William Hollingsworth Whyte, a Princeton graduate and Marine Corps officer who'd served in the Pacific, had made a splash the year before with one of those era-capturing popular books, *The Organization Man*, about corporate life in the new American suburbs. Now, at *Fortune*, he was turning his attention to the problems of the cities. He had in mind a whole series of articles to come out later that year. He was looking for ideas, and for writers to take them on.

Jane was one of his finds. "I kept hearing about this Jane Jacobs," he'd recall. "I went to see her and I was mightily impressed. I thought she was a real genius."

CHAPTER 11

A PERSON WORTH TALKING TO

LATER, IN 1992, thinking back to the article he commissioned her to write for *Fortune* that would bring her such attention and acclaim, Whyte remembered deciding that Jane was "just the person" to do it. Nonetheless, the article, "Downtown Is for People," almost never happened at all.

At first, as Whyte told it, "she demurred and told me she wasn't up to it; she had never written anything longer than a few paragraphs." His colleagues at *Fortune* "felt she should not be entrusted" with so important a piece. "She was a female; she was untried." Why, she commuted to work on . . . a . . . *bicycle*. All in all, it seemed to them, Jane Jacobs was "a most inappropriate choice" and was actually taken off the story—which, to hear Whyte tell it, left her feeling relieved. But when a senior editor on the project fell ill, Jane was reinstated. And this time there was no stopping her. "She wrote and wrote and wrote, providing a first draft of 14,000 words with not a word, she believed, to be edited out. Our lamb had become a tigress."

Controversy lit up Jane's piece, not just potentially but right then, right there, within Time Life. When her draft was passed around, Whyte heard right off from the publisher, C. D. Jackson, who was "aghast." Just who, he demanded to know, was this "crazy dame" who, in the pages of *Fortune*, proposed to give "aid and comfort to critics of Lincoln Center?" That much-anticipated, gleaming new performing arts complex was all set to go up and transfigure the cultural life of the city's West Side. Yet Jane was painting it as an example of all that was wrong with modern planning.

A luncheon meeting was arranged. Jackson was there, along with a coterie of *Fortune* editors, and Jane. "The antagonists went at it," recalled Whyte. Jackson—Mr. Charles Douglas Jackson, a fifty-five-year-old Princeton grad, veteran of the Office of Strategic Services, the wartime predecessor to the CIA, expert in psychological warfare, speechwriter for President Eisenhower, trustee of the Metropolitan Opera and long-standing champion of Lincoln Center—questioned the accuracy of Jane's reporting. Jane defended her essay with "a screed of facts and first-hand observations." Whyte kept his head down; when it was over, Jane asked him why he hadn't stuck up for her. "No need," replied Whyte. "The poor man"—meaning Jackson—"thought he'd hit a buzz saw."

Now, there are discrepancies in Whyte's account, which may be a little more "colorful," and less accurate, than one might like. When he first encountered Jacobs, he'd assert in 1992, her work at *Forum* "consisted mainly of writing captions." This is untrue. Like other staffers, she wrote some of the captions a photo-stuffed magazine like *Forum* required. But this was the least of her work; her pages-long, research-heavy articles going back five years represented the magazine's last word on urban subjects. And in claiming that Jane demanded not a word of her article be cut, Whyte was imputing to her a stance more like that of a novice writer than of the seasoned pro she was; Jane knew better than anyone the value of an editor's blue pencil.

Because Jane's *Fortune* article led her directly to *The Death and Life of Great American Cities*, Whyte had legitimate reason to revisit those days in 1957 when, in retrospect, Jane stood at the threshold of fame and he, Whyte, was there to witness it. But just why he wrote so dismissively of her in 1992 remains a wonderment. He and Jacobs were friends. They lauded city life with equal ardency. They respected one another. Perhaps the passage of thirty-five years had clouded his memory. Perhaps depicting a callow Jane Jacobs made for a story more fun to tell. Perhaps he'd ingested more of the prejudices of his *Fortune* colleagues than he realized. Or maybe, back in 1957, he'd simply not known any better. As Jane's son Jim suggests, he may never have known that Jane's career as writer and editor reached back across two decades; "Jane wasn't one to toot her own horn."

Certainly, the article's passage into print was difficult; the fourteen-thousand-word draft of Whyte's memory got whittled down by more than half. Though he was only nine at the time, Jim remembers his mother working on it. "It was really hard; she worried she couldn't get it to work." But she did get it to work. And with it, the gate onto the big world that had inched open after her Harvard talk swung open wide.

The articles in the *Fortune* series began appearing in the fall of 1957. They stood out, Whyte would say in his introduction to *The Exploding Metropolis*, which carried them into book form, because they were written "by people who like cities"; in that era of Suburbia Ascendant, there weren't many of them around. Together the seven articles made for what Sam Bass Warner would call in his foreword to a later edition "a manifesto of cultural politics," one holding for the small-scale and the local as against the over-big.

Whyte himself introduced the series with a provocatively titled piece, "Are Cities Un-American?," though he didn't really ask, much less answer, the question. Then, month by month, came articles about cars and cities, slums, urban sprawl; this last was again by Whyte, who lamented how "huge patches of once green countryside have been turned into vast, smog-filled deserts that are neither city, suburb, nor country." Then, in April 1958, Jane's piece appeared.

Big cities, she began, were getting ready to build again; new downtown redevelopment projects were in the pipeline. What would they be like?

> They will be spacious, parklike, and uncrowded. They will feature long green vistas. They will be stable and symmetrical and orderly. They will be clean, impressive, and monumental. They will have all the attributes of a well-kept dignified cemetery.

She cited several of them by name—Golden Gateway in San Francisco, Lower Hill auditorium complex in Pittsburgh, the Convention Center in Cleveland. And a dreary business they would be: "The projects will not revitalize downtown; they will deaden it. For they work at cross-purposes to the city. They banish the street."

Jane's piece ran about six thousand words, about twenty-five double-spaced pages. It ranged over broad territory, referred to numerous cities, was accompanied by arresting illustrations. But at bottom, Jane was devoting a sizable swath of *Fortune*'s expensive editorial real estate to city *streets*. But just what were cities if *not* streets? Didn't the awful failures of city life all come down to streets that weren't safe, streets strangled with traffic, streets that were ugly, dirty, and depressing?

Maybe so, but any hope for cities, Jane said, lay in lively, interesting streets; streets were where the city *lived*. Taking readers by the hand, she deposited them on San Francisco's Maiden Lane, a "narrow, back-door alley" facing the backs of some nondescript downtown buildings. Local merchants had adorned it with redwood benches, trees, vines, and window boxes, making for "an oasis with an irresistible sense of intimacy, cheerfulness, and spontaneity." What you needed downtown, said Jane, was variety, contrast, and busyness, old buildings mixed with new, delightful focal points, like the steeple of Arlington Street Church suddenly hoving into view for shoppers on Boston's Newbury Street. Here was what the city could be and sometimes was. But the new projects coming down the pike? These, she groaned, turned their backs on the street—which, in the new way of planners, didn't matter anymore. Now what counted were superblocks, tracts of prime urban real estate set back from and ignoring the old streets.

The East Harlem housing projects lay within such superblocks. So did Stuyvesant Town. So did Lincoln Center. A bird's-eye view, a map even at the coarsest scale, revealed whatever might be of interest in these gargantuan geometries—overlarge modernist objects, apartment complexes, shopping malls, and hymns to *Kultur*, plunked down into the old city's tight fabric. Big and boring garnished with green.

"The smallness of big cities." This was the title Jane, or an editor, gave one section of her essay. "We are apt to think of big cities as equaling big enterprises, little towns as equaling little enterprises," Jane wrote. "Nothing could be less true." Rather: Think city, think small. The small, specialized, shoestring operation, like the storefronts now gone from East Harlem, "must draw on supplies and skills outside itself." It needed the breadth of the city market, needed other shoestring operations. The new downtown redevelopments, on the other hand, didn't think anything but big—great homogeneous blocks, dedicated to a single purpose.

Like Lincoln Center, which was what had gotten her into trouble with Mr. Jackson of *Fortune*. "This cultural superblock," Jane wrote of it, "is intended to be very grand"— coming from Jane this was no compliment—"and the focus of the whole music and dance world of New York." It was soon to go up west of Broadway in the West Sixties, the sort of cultural complex that would become the fashion for cities around the country. Step 1: Tear down whatever was there before. Step 2: Insert opera house, symphony hall, or arts center. But, insisted Jane, Lincoln Center simply did not fit the New York streetscape. It would neither profit from the surrounding urban texture nor contribute to it. Whatever cultural uplift it afforded New York, the city as a whole would suffer.

At least as they appeared in print—perhaps softened in the aftermath of that lunch with Jackson and Whyte—Jane's points verged on the technical, showing how, street by street, Lincoln Center would be severed from the rest of the city: "To the north, the street will be shared with a huge, and grim, high school. The south will be another superblock institution, a campus for Fordham." But Jane was talking about more than Lincoln Center—about how superblocks *generally* worked to undermine cities. The complex and intricate interplay of forces of city life, the visual and social variety of its streets, the diversity of its people, buildings, and parks, was yielding to a sterile new vision. Sacrificed to it was "the cheerful hurly-burly that makes people want to come into the city and to linger there." *That's* what was being lost.

At the time Jane wrote of Lincoln Center, its groundbreaking, with President Eisenhower at the dais to proclaim a great day for American culture and a "stimulating approach" to urban blight, was still a year away. But just then, before the first wrecking ball toppled the first of five hundred or so tenements in August 1959, people still *lived* in the blocks around Lincoln Square—fifteen thousand of them. They were mostly from the working and lower-middle classes. Largely white and native born, though with a growing Puerto Rican minority. To Lincoln Center supporters, of course, it was all a slum, period. The project's leading local proponent in 1959 predicted it would become "a symbol of victory in a great war—a war against disease, darkness, filth and vermin-infested homes. A fight to give children born and reared in basements the right to sunshine, fresh air, and beautiful surroundings."

Not everyone felt that way. "Save Our Homes" groups sprang up. "Shelter Before Culture," declared picket signs wielded by protesters, representing the Lincoln Square Residents Committee, in front of City Hall. It didn't get them very far. In the end, West Sixty-third Street was gone, West Sixty-fourth Street was gone, both displaced by the superblock that became Lincoln Center. The opening scenes of the film *West Side Story*, which pictured a Romeo-and-Juliet romance transplanted to New York City tenements, was filmed in and around the neighborhood;

when the movie was released in 1961, the streets where it was filmed were gone, become part of a great block of twenty-eight-story apartment buildings also part of the project.

On balance, many might count the transformation a good one. But, as in East Harlem and Stuyvesant Town, a world had been erased—not just individual buildings, not just especially run-down streets, not just notorious pockets of crime, but the whole thing. "The pain brought on by clearance and rebuilding," writes Samuel Zipp, in his study of the affair, "extended beyond the losses of individual homes and shops to the loss of a whole urban world, an informal system of connections that would disappear along with the tenements, factories, and corner stores." Maybe real slums were mercifully gone, along with real gang-war mayhem never so aesthetically choreographed as Jerome Robbins did for *West Side Story*. But *something* of worth had been swept away with them.

The architects, planners, and businessmen responsible for this wiped-clean vision, Jane wrote, were "seized with dreams of order," fascinated by scale models and bird's-eye views, the street-scale city lost to them. "The logic of the projects," she wrote, "is the logic of egocentric children, playing with pretty blocks and shouting, 'See what I made!'" The citizen, Jane wrote, needed to step in and exert his claim. "It is *his* city, after all."

Jane's article appeared in the April 1958 issue of *Fortune*, and soon letters were pouring in. "Look what your girl did for us!" Holly Whyte scrawled at the top of a seven-page collection of excerpts that went to Doug Haskell. "This is one of the best responses we've ever had!"

The letters came from planners, businesspeople, developers, mayors, consultants, architects, and ordinary citizens. *Delightful,* they said. *Fascinating, refreshing, provocative.* Jane's "plea for the human scale is a welcome note among so many faceless plans," a Washington, D.C., man wrote. György Kepes, the Hungarian-born MIT designer and art theorist, who'd probably heard Jane at the Harvard conference, wrote to say he'd read it "with great interest and great joy"; her article expressed not just knowledge and understanding "but a human warmth." In many letters, you could sense a personal connection, as if, somehow, Jane spoke for them, *channeled* them; as if what she said was what they felt but hadn't been able to express themselves.

An English journal, *Architectural Review*, editorialized about *The Exploding Metropolis* as a whole what could fairly be said of Jane's article in particular: it was "like the first blink of the fire-warning light in the aircraft cockpit," the nervous, insistent blinking that signals something wrong—in this case with the architectural and planning wisdom of the day.

"How enthusiastic we were in the young days of the 55's," Doug Haskell warmly reminisced to Jane a few years later when she was leaving *Forum*, "and how invaluable you were . . . as a cement, keeping the staff enthusiastically together on a high enterprise. I thought we had a very fine espirit." Jane would stay with Doug and the others for almost a decade, and they were good years. But *Forum* was quite the mainstream place, differing from its rivals, *Progressive Architecture* and *Architectural Record*, but not too much. When she was hired there, "the editor in chief gave me quickly to understand that I must shun critical comment," else lose access to the architects who were the magazine's lifeblood; this was pragmatic or self-interested, take your pick, but it was alive in every editorial decision. Any architectural "criticism" *Forum* offered didn't include the kind of harsh verdicts meted out to books or films; most of the time the magazine reported on buildings or projects "we could unreservedly admire, or that the editor in chief unreservedly admired." What they didn't like they'd ignore. *Forum* represented the center, not the periphery. The prevailing ethos mattered there. The big names in the field mattered. "We were attuned to reputations within the profession, and we bowed obsequiously to [architectural] fashion," dominated, as it was then, by the movement and spirit known as modernism.

Consider the Barcelona Pavilion, a smallish building of great horizontal planes, sumptuous expanses of marble, onyx, and tinted glass, virtually devoid of decoration. It is open, spare, and clean, its surfaces uncorrupted by intricate curves and curlicues, an exercise in simplicity, proportion, and broad, sweeping space. The wonder of it—what can make you gasp, really—is that, designed by the German architect Mies van der Rohe for an international exposition in Barcelona, it reaches back to 1929 and a world thick with baroque ornamentation and Victorian clutter. The exposition was temporary and the pavilion was torn down the following year. But so emblematic was it of the architectural style, modernism, it had helped usher in that, in 1986, it was reconstructed from the original plans, on the original site, with some of the original materials. The Barcelona Pavilion belongs comfortably in the modern world; it helped *make* the modern world.

You couldn't do much better if you were looking for an icon of modernism. But the movement's antecedents actually go back before 1929 to the late nineteenth century, when iron, steel, and glass began to displace age-old stone, brick, and wood as building materials; when builders and architects began to revolt against Victorian gimcrackery and turn to new building technologies, new visions of what a building, or a city, could be. In drawing after drawing, building after building, with the embrace of one new material, structural device, or idea after another, Mies van der Rohe, Le Corbusier, Frank Lloyd Wright, Walter Gropius, and the other modernist masters created the architectural style that dominates today's built world.

Modernism expressed itself, though, at not only the scale of the individual building but also that of the city, and of society as a whole, and was not solely a matter of aesthetics and design. A social vision ran through it, too: to fix the world and make it better. Good architecture, the idea went, *mattered,* made better cities, better lives. "What is the ideal city for the twentieth century, the city that best expresses the power and beauty of modern technology and the most enlightened ideas of social justice?" The historian Robert Fishman began his book, *Urban Utopias in the Twentieth Century,* by asking that question. Modernist planning can be seen as a century-long search for answers to it.

One day in 1930, one of the most influential of the creators of modernism, Charles-Édouard Jeanneret, the Swiss-French architect better known as Le Corbusier, stood before a map of the city of Paris and, as the camera rolled, drew a bold line from west to east, slashing across a broad swath of the city he wanted to see razed. Le Corbusier called for office skyscrapers to rise up against the flattened landscape of the city, one every four hundred yards in mathematical precision, each employing thousands, obliterating the harmony of five-story structures that made Paris what it was. More deliberate drawings he made of Paris and other French cities—no operatic slashes staged for the camera now but meticulously rendered in black ink on fine drawing paper—showed how serious he was. Le Corbusier would wipe out the intricate, small-scaled past, blighted as it often was, and replace it with skyscrapers set in spacious parks—*towers-in-the-park.* "The Radiant City," was what Le Corbusier called it.

That was one influential modernist vision. Another was one determined to bypass the city altogether, replacing it with small communities leapfrogging their way into the country—towns of thirty thousand or so, with adjacent agricultural belts, areas set aside for local industry. This late-nineteenth-century idea originated with an unassuming Englishman, Ebenezer Howard, a stenographer by trade—a "heroic simpleton," George Bernard Shaw once called him. Shamed and horrified by the damage wrought on cities by the Industrial Revolution—"ill-ventilated, unplanned, unwieldy, and unhealthy cities—ulcers on the very face of our beautiful island"—Howard conceived a city that wasn't a city at all but that re-created its functions in discrete, sharply demarcated areas: homes here, parks and gardens there, factories over here, all neat and tidy. "The Garden City," it was called, and it was progenitor to England's New Town movement.

In 1948, a British government information office produced a perky animated film pushing the idea, *Charley in New Town.* Charley looks like Stan Laurel of the old Laurel and Hardy movies. As a tune lilts away in the background, we see him pedaling his bike through town, red pompadour flopping and bouncing cheerfully, offering friendly "G'morning"s to passers-by. "My, this is a grand way to start the day," he says, turning to the viewer. "A bit different from what it used to be."

And as we step with Charley into a benighted recent past, the cartoon's palette shifts from pastel greens to angry blacks. Coal smoke obscures everything. The houses are drab, the factories ugly. The lilt's gone from the music now, the beat's become urgent, troubled. "Not even a bloomin' place for the kids to play," says Charley. A child's ball bounces out from a dark alley. "Poor little blighters." Insect-like, verminous hordes of workers are discharged from double-decker buses. Back then, Charley had been one of them. "I'll tell you, by the time I got to work I was all in."

Finally, though, Charley and his friends had enough of the old city and met with a bow-tied, waistcoated, and wise elder gentleman who showed them how cities had turned out so bad. How might they make their lives better? New skyscrapers, maybe? No, no, the townspeople objected, as we see their houses start to mushroom into high-rises. They wouldn't want to live in *them*. What about their gardens, their pubs?

Inevitably, it is made to seem, they converged on the idea of a new town, on a new site. "First thing we all agreed on was to separate industry from dwelling houses," Charley remembers. Yes, said their new leader: "Industry here . . . Residential areas there, with not more than five minutes travel from home to work." The great idea was realized. We see little factories sprout up; the wind, of course, always sweeps the smoke away. We see Charley himself running a bulldozer. Open spaces, parks, playing fields, flower gardens—paradise. "And so," Charley remembers, "we moved right in." In the end, we see him back on his bike, in the present. "I'm telling you, it works out fine." And as he cycles offscreen, he points to the viewer. "Just you try it."

In real English towns embodying Howard's ideas, like Letchworth in 1903 and Welwyn in 1920, and then in Radburn, New Jersey, and urban enclaves like Sunnyside Gardens in New York during the 1920s, thousands did try it, or something like it. Then, after World War II, in countless variations and permutations of the Garden City movement and inspired by similar impulses in suburbs across England and America, so did millions more.

Howard reached out into the countryside, Le Corbusier reached up for his towers-in-the-park. But both streams of modernist thought turned their backs on the confused jumble of the city street, the jangle, noise, and thrill of the city as generations knew it. Both redistributed its parts—homes, offices, factories, parks, stores—into discrete parcels, separate and distinct. Both echoed the lesson of a postwar world of bombed-out European and Japanese cities: Clear out the rubble. Build anew.

Certainly there was plenty of rubble to clear. Since she'd first visited New York in 1928, Jane had seen for herself the toll of years on the American city—in crumbling old-law tenements in New York; brownstones in Brooklyn and row houses in Baltimore and Philadelphia carved up into cramped apartments for war workers; poor blacks escaping the Jim Crow South crammed into overpriced, under-maintained slums. The Depression and the war made for two long, debilitating decades of stagnation and neglect during which no one, it seemed, had the time or money, or after a while the inclination, to fix up the old city.

All across these years, modernist dreams, too, had been placed on hold. But now, with the guns stilled after World War II and every sign of buoyant prosperity returning—automobiles taking on the Forward Look, air travel granting mile-high vistas—modernism reasserted itself. Something close to a social consensus emerged, one rejecting the old, ragged past, proposing to scrape it away, often literally, and replace it with a swept-clean, squared-away future: superblocks of Corbusian towers in town and great, green park-like tracts in the new suburbs. In both cases, the street, the heart of the old carcinogenic city and its evils, would be erased. And these sensibilities came on now with such ferocity, as if embracing the urgency, scale, and force of the war itself, that this New Truth could appear self-evident: no need to mend the postwar world's tattered social and physical fabric; best to obliterate it and start over.

To work at *Forum* during these heady midcentury years was to breathe in this intoxicating new modernist spirit. And, why not? What could be more natural, more seemingly inevitable? The slums Ed Bacon had presumably erased in Philadelphia meant a better world. So did Lincoln Center. So did housing projects going up in the cities of America. They were *good*, better than what they replaced. How else to see things? Since when was all that was shabby and old better than what was coming up new? Why, it was practically a contradiction in terms. Was any old horse-and-wagon better suited to us today, more desirable, than a new automobile? Then in what impossible, upside-down universe would you *not* want to tear down an aging slum of nineteenth-century tenements and put up a new apartment complex designed to make life easier, airier, and brighter? Under what topsy-turvy logic would you not want to leave behind the fetid streets of the old neighborhood for a new world of leafy green? These questions had such obvious answers they were silly even to ask.

And yet they were something like the questions Jane *was* asking. She was suggesting that modernist planning was not in all ways, certainly, and maybe not even in most ways, good for Philadelphia and East Harlem, that it hurt them; that the prevailing thinking of her day didn't work. She argued with her colleagues, but, she would admit, "I didn't bring them around to my way of thinking." Not right away, anyhow. "The editors of my magazine, of *Architectural Forum*, believed in all this urban renewal stuff. And I saw who their heroes were." Heroes like Ed Logue, urban renewal czar of New Haven, Connecticut, who, to listen to Jane, thought that "the best thing that could happen to San Francisco would be another earthquake and fire." Her editors *liked* Logue and his vision of cities wiped clean and rebuilt from scratch.

Peter Blake, who worked at *Forum* all through the 1950s and later became its editor, would observe that Jane Jacobs's message was "shattering to those of us brought up on various neat and seductive dogmas and diagrams of the Modern Movement." *Dogmas.* Like a religion.

But Jane had lost her faith, and was saying so to anyone who'd listen.

· · ·

One Saturday evening in February 1958, Doug Haskell attended a party with architects and other creative people. There he talked with a man named Chadbourne Gilpatric.

Gilpatric had a great job. His title at the Rockefeller Foundation was "associate director of humanities and social sciences," but really what he did was talk with smart, accomplished people about the things that mattered most to them and give some of them money. A Harvard graduate remembered by a classmate as "a philosophy student of flashing charm and audacity," he socialized, lunched, traveled, brought people into the office, talked, and listened, forever on the prowl for projects worthy and interesting. Then he'd write up memos in his professional diary, which ultimately filled book after book. And from time to time they led to grants of tens of thousands of dollars that changed people's lives. Gilpatric must have been very popular.

Among Gilpatric's own special interests was urban design, which he felt was unstudied with anything like the critical and reflective focus it needed. American cities were a mess. Barracks built during the war to house navy-yard workers had become housing warrens for the poor; slum clearance projects failed to eliminate slums; and on and on. These were many of the same issues, of course, that had led Holly Whyte into his *Fortune* series. Now Gilpatric was feeling his way into what the Rockefeller could do to bring light to these dark, unwieldy problems.

At the party, Haskell, too, deplored the almost unseemly lack of critical thinking about urban design, but added, as Gilpatric recorded, that "one of the few able and imaginative people concerned with this domain is Jane Jacobs, on his staff." She had just completed a big piece for *Fortune*. "She might be a person worth talking to soon."

Chadbourne Gilpatric of the Rockefeller Foundation

By this point, in late winter of 1958, Jane figured large at *Forum,* her ideas, like them or not, seeping into the intellectual air of the office. Back in November, Haskell had written to his top staff about how "Jane Jacobs has been talking about an approach to city pattern which I think we should discuss." Her approach disdained large-scale land acquisition, planning, and bureaucracy. It said no to the superblock, the greenbelt, and the satellite town—all staples of postwar thinking. In doing so, Jane was "dauntlessly going in the face of some 75 years of tradition in city planning." Haskell felt her ideas merited a serious look; perhaps they'd want to give her "a big hunk of space for exposition and debate. I can imagine it would make many an existing planner furious at first, just as my own temptation was to be furious."

On April 25, fresh from what someone at *Forum* had termed "Jane's blockbuster on the superblock" in *Fortune* and the hosannas it had inspired, Jane wrote Haskell with a suggestion for *Forum*'s January 1959 issue. How about an article—a sizable chunk of the issue, she made it sound—devoted to "What Is the City?"

What is it really made of, how does it really work, what has worked well in it in the past and what has not, how has the postwar rebuilding of it, both public and private as well as a mixture of the two, been working out and what does this tell us—and, from everything we can learn and put down about what the big city is, and does, what are the implications for its future planning?

I think there is no more important subject for us to do, if not in January, sometime soon.

"Wow!" Haskell wrote back three days later. But: "Could we not put this one down to more modest dimensions?"

Well, no, it would turn out, *we couldn't:* What Jane had to say about cities might be many things, but of modest dimension it was not.

Years later she would tell how she tried to interest *Forum* in a four-article series about city streets. As Gilpatric later summarized a version of this idea, or an evolution of it, one of the pieces would be devoted to how self-policing by street users minimized crime; a second was on neighborhood scale; a third on inter-group mixing; a fourth on the implications of the street for urban planning. Before writing even a word, simply in its declared focus, Jane was already running counter to the prevailing idea of her time, that "the street was an evil place, the street should be expunged in favor of superblocks and underground and above-ground things." Haskell respected Jane, had spoken glowingly of her to Gilpatric. But as for her colleagues generally at *Forum*, Jane would say, they were "kind of appalled that I wanted to do this."

Still, she'd add, "I would eventually have persuaded them to do those four articles."

Maybe yes, maybe no. But in the end she didn't have to persuade her colleagues because, as she went on to say, "in the meantime some [other] people got interested in these ideas." And soon she wasn't writing four articles for *Forum*, she was writing *The Death and Life of Great American Cities*.

It was April 20, 1958, a few days before she'd broached her "What Is the City?" idea to Haskell. Jane was giving a talk, devoted to New York's future, as part of a dinner panel at the New School for Social Research, an alternative university in the Village. She lambasted several of her sworn enemies, such as Lincoln Center—though now with a depth and detail missing from her *Fortune* article. And, of course, Robert Moses, New York's master planner, who was trying to run a highway through Greenwich Village.

But there was something new here, too. Her talk played out not alone in dark and muted colors, but in bright ones, expressing a dream and a hope for city life. Consider, she said, the interdependence of a great city, its networks of mutual support and—this in an almost hallucinogenic jazz riff—its bizarre, unexpected minglings:

This criss-cross of supporting relationships means, for instance, that a Russian tearoom and last year's minks and a place to rent English sports cars bloom well near Carnegie Hall, or that on the same block the Advanced Metaphysicians and the Dynamic Speakers and the Associates of Camp Moonbeam have all discovered they can fit sympathetically into the studios that do well for music too. It means that the Puerto Rican Orientation Club of East Harlem finds a place it can actually afford in a beat-up tenement basement—an unprepossessing place but a place of its own, beholden to no one, and thus it can flourish. This criss-cross network means that the textile companies of Worth Street move uptown from a quiet, uncrowded place into the maelstrom of the garment district because they see a higher logic in being closer to their customers.

New York was a mixed-up mess of a place, that was its glory. But let no one think there was an end to it. There never would be. Jane told a story we've heard before, of how when she first came to New York, at age eighteen, she'd worked for a clock manufacturer she believed would one day fit out the whole world with clocks; after a week or so, she realized it would never happen, it was an unending job. The same went for rebuilding a city. It was "tempting to want to fix it in such a way that things will get finished and stay put and that's that . . . But New York," she said, "is like the clock business; it is never going to get finished. This should not really be discouraging to anybody over the age of eighteen."

There was real energy to her talk, and love—love for the city. Lewis Mumford, *The New Yorker*'s haughty architecture critic, was there to appreciate it. Her talk, he wrote her in a letter on May 3, "gave me the deepest satisfaction." It asserted ideas few planners "even dimly understand." Her analysis of the ways cities worked "is sociologically of the first order." Her takedown "of the vast bungle called Lincoln Center is devastatingly just."

Lewis Mumford was a fan!

"None of the millions being squandered by the Ford Foundation for 'urban research' will produce anything that has a minute fraction of your insight and common sense." He offered a few practical suggestions for where she might publish her writing, but for Jane this was probably the least useful part of his letter. "Keep hammering," he told her. "Your worst opponents are the old fogies who imagine that Le Corbusier is the last word in urbanism."

As we've seen, Jane rarely suffered any great want of confidence. But coming off the *Fortune* article and the letter from Mumford, which she probably received around May 5, she could hardly have felt on professionally firmer ground, when, on May 9, she met with Chadbourne Gilpatric.

Gilpatric had just returned from Philadelphia, where, as part of his efforts to bring urban design under the scrutiny and guidance of the Rockefeller Foundation, he'd visited the University of Pennsylvania's Institute for Urban Research. He came back with a raft of interview notes, suggestions, books to read, and ideas about playgrounds, parks, gardens, and cities, page after page of them. Now, two days later, he was meeting with Jane, Doug Haskell's "person worth talking to."

So the two of them talked. They talked about the Charles Center project in Baltimore and why she thought it better than most other redevelopment projects. She approved of Ian McHarg's ideas for a series of books on civic design. She put in a good word for Ian Nairn, whom *Fortune* had brought to the United States for two weeks, urged that the Rockefeller give opportunities to first-rate architectural critics like Grady Clay, down in Louisville, whose work she much admired, or Nathan Glazer, who'd just written a perceptive piece for *Forum* on "The Great City and the City Planners."

Then, finally, the conversation swung around to what *she* wanted to do. "Mrs. Jacobs herself," Gilpatric recorded, wanted to take three months to pursue something like the city streets project she'd discussed with *Forum*, which might run parts of it but probably couldn't give her unbroken time to research and write it. So, "Mrs. J wonders" whether the Rockefeller would consider a grant, administered by the New School, to let her, and a researcher with whom she'd worked on the *Fortune* article, take leave to work on it.

Gilpatric told her that "this might well be a project of interest to the RF."

A month later, the two of them met again. Now Jane was talking about eight or nine months, not three, and a book rather than a series of articles. "In this conversation as before," Gilpatric wrote, "Mrs. J fairly bubbled with interesting ideas about how to interpret human needs in modern city life." They agreed that Jane would write him soon, laying out what she hoped to do in the book. For now, though, it came down to "'what is the city' or 'what should the city be for people'"; the first, of course, was the distinctly immodest subject she'd suggested to Haskell two months earlier. Jane thought $10,000—worth perhaps $80,000 or $90,000 today—would let her do it.

Ten days later, Gilpatric had her proposal in hand. Jane would look into "five factors of the city": streets, parks, scale, mixtures of people, and urban focal centers important out of all proportion to their size, like public squares. She would emphasize New York, especially East Harlem and Greenwich Village. She would aim for the "general interested citizen," not the specialist. She appreciated that nine months was a tight deadline, but felt she did her best work under pressure.

"I'm afraid this sounds very abstract," Jane apologized at one point.

She was right; it did. Maybe she had come back with her proposal too soon, hadn't thought it through enough. In any case, when she talked with Gilpatric on the phone two weeks later, he told her the Rockefeller was, yes, interested, but that "questions about the scope and content of her work remained." She, in turn, admitted dissatisfaction with what she'd submitted earlier. As Gilpatric set it down, she promised to "soon send in a clearer statement of the 'nub' of her study."

A few days later, he had it. And this time there was fire to it, and an ambition she made no effort to tamp down.

Two mental images, she began, dominated people's views of the city:

One is the image of the city in trouble, an inhuman mass of masonry, a chaos of happenstance growth, a place starved of the simple decencies and amenities of life, beset with so many accumulated problems it makes your head swim. The other powerful image is that of the rebuilt city, the antithesis of all that the unplanned city represents, a carefully planned panorama of projects and green spaces, a place where functions are sorted out instead of jumbled together, a place of light, air, sunshine, dignity and order for all.

You can guess where this was going: "Both of these conceptions are disastrously superficial."

Here, she wrote, was the sort of sloppy thinking that led you into crude abstraction, that overlooked how a city really worked, and from which emerged "hindrances and blocks to intelligent observation and action." She proposed to break through these calcified ideas. What she wished to do, she declared, "is to create for the reader another image of the city," one drawn not from the imagination, hers or anyone else's, but from real life, more compelling because truer. She was pushing far beyond those mechanical-sounding "five factors of the city" that had bogged down her first letter. And now she just came out and said it, unabashedly: she wanted her book to "open the reader's eyes to a different way of looking at the city."

The two letters to Gilpatric together expressed Jane's thinking. But they were business documents, too, sometimes explicitly so, talking dollars and cents. Toward the end of the first letter, Jane laid out how she expected to manage financially while writing the book—eight months living on the Rockefeller grant, plus an "advance which I hope to get from an interested publisher" for the final month. Gilpatric knew by now that this "interested" publisher was no mere hope or possibility. His name was Jason Epstein.

A Boston native and Columbia University graduate, Epstein, at age thirty, was already something of a publishing wunderkind as originator of the "quality paperback." Paperback books went back to the 1930s and before, but in the 1950s they were invariably known for their cheap paper and their affinity for bodice-rippers and adventure yarns. At the other end of publishing were handsomely produced hardcover books, like those Epstein's own house, Doubleday, produced. Into this gap stepped Epstein's Anchor Books, the first "quality paperback" imprint—good books, good paper, intermediate prices. In the spring of 1958, Epstein had heard from Nathan Glazer about Jane's article in *Fortune* and soon the whole series was a book, *The Exploding Metropolis*, first as Doubleday hardcover, then as Anchor paperback.

Whyte and Glazer both urged Jane to talk to Epstein about a book of her own based on ideas she'd expressed in "Downtown Is for People." She did so, and, as Gilpatric recorded in a June 26, 1958, memo, Epstein "expressed enthusiastic interest." He offered her an advance of $1,500—modest, certainly, but more than she had expected.

Jason Epstein, Jane's editor at Random House from 1958 on and a friend for the rest of her life

Things were heating up. The philanthropic gears were turning. On July 7, Gilpatric wrote Jane, thanking her for the "clearer and better composed picture of the book you want to write."

On July 13, Jane responded to Gilpatric's request for a professional biography with a single-page document, together with a one-page addendum listing the city-themed articles she'd written for *Forum*.

On July 23, *Forum* formally granted her a leave of absence to write the book.

On July 29, Gilpatric wrote

Lewis Mumford, asking for his frank assessment of Jane's project. Three days later, he heard back. "I first came across her at a conference a few years ago," he wrote, referring to her Harvard talk.

> She made a brief address so pointed and challenging and witty, so merciless to the accepted clichés and so packed with fresh ideas that I felt like cheering; and did in fact cheer when called upon to make a few remarks at the end of the conference. Her direct, first-hand method of attack, and her common-sense judgments are worth whole filing cases of what is sometimes too respectfully called research.

And, he concluded,

> I regard her purpose as important and her competence to carry it through indisputable; all the more because I am confident that her results will challenge a good deal of current practice. You will look far before you find a more worthy applicant in this field.

With that, and that alone, Jane's good graces at the Rockefeller were probably assured. But Gilpatric was taking no chances; he had written to others as well for responses to Jane's project. During August, he heard from Holly Whyte, who was, of course, "wholeheartedly enthusiastic." From Christopher Tunnard, of Yale, who was not; he dismissed Jane's project as "grandiose and vague." From Catherine Bauer, the public housing expert, whom Jane had edited at *Forum:* "I'd back Jane Jacobs if I were you," she led off her response. "She's a good writer, sensitive and imaginative." But Bauer did offer one caveat:

> Don't let her get bogged down with academic theorizing or too much would-be scientific research. That isn't her game and she probably knows it, but strange things sometimes happen to good creative popular writers when they get a Foundation grant!

In early September, Jane learned that her Rockefeller grant had been approved. She was grateful, she wrote Gilpatric on the 15th, for helping her do the book in the first place, but even more for helping her to understand what "I can do and want to do which might turn out to have some general usefulness."

CHAPTER 12

A MANUSCRIPT TO SHOW US

IT WAS JUNE 1959, nine months into her Rockefeller grant, and Jane was in trouble, running way behind, flirting with despair over time and money.

The Death and Life of Great American Cities could seem so much the product of Jane's distinctive intellect that one might forget that it was "researched"; she visited cities, talked to people, traded ideas with experts, gathered statistics, sought out pointed bits of knowledge. The previous October, Gilpatric noted that Jane had "completed plans for a series of discussions" with urban thinkers, including James Rouse, a shopping center developer in Baltimore; and William Slayton, involved in developing southeast Washington, D.C. She had recently attended a Rockefeller-sponsored conference in Rye, New York, on urban design criticism that had also drawn Louis Kahn, Kevin Lynch, Ian McHarg, and Lewis Mumford, among other notables. In a memo about six weeks later, Gilpatric observed that Jane had plenty of "opinions and critical comments about Los Angeles and San Francisco," yet had never been to either city; she hoped soon to correct that lapse. In St. Louis, the Washington University architecture professor Roger Montgomery showed her around a fifty-seven-acre housing complex of Corbusian buildings—much celebrated in the architectural press when it went up a few years earlier—known as Pruitt-Igoe.

It was all interesting. It was all worthwhile. And it all took time.

While in Boston, Jane met Harvard and MIT faculty who had learned of her grant and suggested she drop by for lunch. Turns out, as Jane recounted, they knew exactly how she needed to proceed:

They had it all figured out—how I should use that grant, how I should use my time. They had decided what they wanted done and they were treating me as if I was a graduate student. What they actually wanted me to do was make up a questionnaire and give it to people in some middle-income sterile project somewhere, to find out what they didn't like. Then I was to make tables of it. They had it all worked out, what I should do. So I listened to them and remained polite, but I couldn't wait to get out of there.

Years later, the memory of that lunch could move her to fury. "Disgusting!," she'd call the intellectually banal project they had in mind for her. "That's what their interest in cities was, just junk like that."

Boston also introduced her to the young sociologist Herbert Gans. The previous October, Gans had moved with his wife into a $42-a-month apartment in Boston's West End. It was the last days of that Italian working-class neighborhood before it was cut down for new modernist apartment buildings with fine views of the State House dome on Beacon Hill. Gans, thirty, had done some of his earliest studies in a Chicago suburb known as Park Forest, where Holly Whyte, Jane's champion at *Fortune*, had done research for *The Organization Man*. So when one day Whyte called to tell him "about how this woman wanted to see the North End," he obliged.

In fact, though Gans knew the West End intimately—his field work there would culminate in his classic, *The Urban Villagers*—he was less familiar with the North End, the next neighborhood over, a jumble of tenements and chockablock old buildings that went back to the American Revolution, including Paul Revere's house; to many an eye, it looked exactly the way a slum ought to look. He doesn't remember much of the tour he gave Jane except that it was superficial; "I must have shown her the settlement houses, the restaurants." As for the West End, Jane didn't seem interested; only the North End seemed to be on her agenda, maybe because she recalled it from her New England trip of 1938, when it impressed her as "a district taking a terrible physical beating and certainly desperately poor."

Now, though, she came away "amazed at the change" there, with dozens of buildings rehabbed, crowding reduced, apartments warmed with fresh paint and pretty Venetian blinds. "I looked down a narrow alley," she'd write later of her trip, thinking to find there the old, squalid North End of her memories. "But no: more neatly repointed brickwork, new blinds, and a burst of music as a door opened . . . The streets were alive with children playing, people shopping, people strolling, people sitting." The North End would emerge from *Death and Life* as urban folk hero in old brick. Even by late 1958, just back from her Boston trip and advising Gilpatric of her progress, she was all aglow over it. Recorded Gilpatric: "Mrs. J's most exciting discovery was in the north end of Boston, essentially in the Italian area, which continues to be regarded as a 'slum.' In fact, Mrs. J finds it one of the most attractive, animated and interesting sections she has come upon in a long time."

All this early research was crucial, supplying just the texture of fact and impression Jane needed. But it took time, more than she'd allowed. The writing itself had progressed but fitfully. After lunch with Jane in June, nine months out, Gilpatric concluded that she "has run into a lot of unexpected problems and that she has finished less writing than [he, Gilpatric] had expected." In a letter about a month later Jane enlarged on her difficulties: Three months of research had stretched to four and a half. Then, another month and a half to sift through all she'd gathered. Every time she talked with someone, she was left awash in ideas, about aspects of city life she'd not considered or had previously written off as insignificant: What happens when a city "unslums"? Is a densely built city automatically overcrowded or unsafe? "On almost everything I had thought about I found relationships I had not taken into account." Everything was harder to make sense of than she'd bargained for, full of fascinating, but time-eating, "discoveries."

Never having attempted to write a book of this sort before, I did not anticipate the difficulties I was going to get into in organizing and writing. It is far different from writing and organizing articles, and how different I had no conception until I waded in. In retrospect, how over-optimistic I was about the writing!

In her letter, Jane didn't include among her difficulties the siren call of East Harlem—a project she'd become involved with there, that contributed to her time crunch.

Back in 1955, Union Settlement had been invited to run a community center in one of the big new projects, George Washington Houses, across 104th Street from the row of brownstones that was its headquarters. It wasn't long, however, before Kirk and his colleagues realized they knew little about these new objects in their midst, the big housing projects. To them, whose institutional life had since the late nineteenth century been built around East Harlem's familiar five-story tenements and the life bubbling up from them, these new alien things represented terra incognita. With a grant from a local foundation, they undertook a study of the project. At its helm, under Bill Kirk, was a social worker named Ellen Lurie.

A 1951 graduate, summa cum laude and Phi Beta Kappa, of New York University, Lurie, then just twenty-five, would go on to a flame-bright career as community organizer and champion of integrated schools in East Harlem and around the city; a New York City public school is named for her today. She was deeply ethical, charismatic, exacting. "If you're working on behalf of poor people," a colleague, Ron Shiffman, would remember her saying, "you can't be slipshod in anything you do." Indeed, even the earliest outline of her study plan for George Washington Houses in January 1956 showed a seriousness and depth of engagement beyond her years. Through interviews with residents, Lurie proposed to explore the communities they had come from, child-parent relationships in the project, how the project influenced friendships. She asked such questions as, "Are there restrictions to community life inherent in project living?" "Are we trying to employ middle-class concepts of community life in an economically low-class neighborhood?"

In the end, Lurie's study served like a medical probe set into the necrotic tissue of the project, putting numbers, data, and insight into the concerns Kirk had intuited from the street. Its depiction of social disconnection was, as Union Settlement would admit, "sobering"—indeed, too much so to publish: "Urban rot is more than merely a physical deterioration," Lurie's report concluded. "The morale and spirit of the people in the project have not been emancipated from the slums."

It was probably early in 1956 that Lurie met Jane. The two women were fourteen years apart in age. Lurie was more caught up in people and their needs, Jane in broad ideas. But they got to know and respect one another. Some of Lurie's early insights had flavored Jane's Harvard talk. Lurie would explicitly acknowledge Jane's help on the Washington Houses study. Jane encouraged Lurie to write a piece for *Forum* and would quote her at length in *Death and Life*. Now, in late 1958, the two women had a chance, just possibly, to remedy some of the pathologies Lurie's study had laid bare.

Two years before, yet another huge housing project, DeWitt Clinton Houses, had been earmarked for the neighborhood. It was to encompass 104th to 106th Street, Park Avenue to Lexington, and house 750 families in eighteen-story buildings—more of the same, in other words, for East Harlem. But in December 1958, three months into Jane's Rockefeller grant, the New York Housing Authority, responding to an "urgent request" that summer from Union Settlement, agreed to briefly put its plans on hold and consider design alternatives to it. "We realize," Bill Kirk wrote the housing authority, "that our request to proceed in this way is unusual," as indeed it was, a rare halt to the bureaucratic clock. The group behind Union Settlement's petition consisted of Kirk, the longtime neighborhood activist Mildred Zucker, Ellen Lurie, and Jane Jacobs.

On January 15, 1959, Jane and the rest of the group met with architects from Perkins & Will, the firm presided over by Kirk's old friend Phil Will, which had agreed to work up, pro bono, an alternative design. In early February, plans and drawings in hand, they made their plea to the New York Housing Authority. Jane was at the helm, making their case.

"We are convinced," they said, that much of the social pathology of East Harlem's projects owed to "the physical design of the buildings themselves and their grounds. They are ill suited . . . to the needs of the families who must live in them and to the neighborhoods of which they are a part." The projects disregarded the communal and cooperative elements of city neighborhoods, and undermined "the constant, casual and varied human contacts" that enriched life in the old slums. As planned, DeWitt Clinton represented a "bankrupt stereotype." That the housing authority should "continue to travel the path of social erosion" seen in Washington Houses was "unthinkable."

In their alternative proposal, most of the site would be given over to low-rise courtyard structures that let parents keep an eye on their children. It encouraged interplay with surrounding East Harlem streets. It provided for open space, but avoided "meaningless and isolated malls and lawns which experience shows will be shunned." It didn't try to mimic the classic tenement streetscape but did hold to one unlikely feature of it: half a century after the last generation of walk-ups in New York, Perkins & Will proposed four- and five-story walk-ups for families with children; that is, *no elevators*, in disregard of the federal housing code, which the group saw as "unrealistic" and insensitive to New York City experience. Climbing stairs, while not ideal, was better than the well-documented blight of vandalized, crime-ridden, breakdown-plagued elevators afflicting most high-rise public housing projects.

No way was such a design going to be built, of course, and it wasn't; the New York Housing Authority promptly turned it down. Something close to the original design went up, and it was as if this brief East Harlem Spring had never happened. But it had, and Zucker wrote Phil Will with thanks. For this neighborhood "dominated by tall, angular, monotonous and massive public housing projects, withdrawn and separated from the rest of the community by broad, untouched lawns, your fresh approach offers new hope."

It was a noble experiment. And yet, from the narrow, necessary perspective of Jane's grant deadline, it was a distraction. The meetings she'd attended on behalf of the alternative design, the documents, press releases, and correspondence she'd helped prepare, the presentations she made, all took time that didn't go toward her book. All her working life, Jane had been an employee, subject to office discipline that, whatever its annoyances, helped shape and structure her workday; her children would recall how she kept reliably to a ten-to-six schedule. Right now, though, Jane was more the independent artist, freelancer, or entrepreneur—on her own clock, hers to decide how to use her time. And in late 1958 and early 1959, across at least three key early months of her Rockefeller grant, her time and energy were drawn off by East Harlem. The DeWitt Clinton alternative brought her close to some of the themes of her book. But it was *not* the book. And though she didn't mention it in her correspondence with Gilpatric, it contributed to her angst in the summer of 1959.

Jane had not one patron to whom she was accountable, but two: Gilpatric, and Jason Epstein, who had signed up her book when he was still at Doubleday, then brought her with him to Random House. In his correspondence with her, Epstein was less formal and more supportive than the man from the Rockefeller. In her first few letters to him, Jane signed herself Jane Jacobs, over a typewritten Mrs. Robert H. Jacobs Jr. But that soon gave way to just Jane; and then, "love, Jane." The two of them would develop a personal and professional relationship spanning almost half a century, ending only with Jane's death. They'd travel together, would be in and out of each other's houses. "I just liked being with her," Epstein would say. "I never had a closer friend." They talked about everything—politics, books, ideas. But not much of personal things. And certainly nothing of, say, sports, which "would be like hanging out with Darwin and talking about football." It was a friendship almost "frozen in time," says Epstein, little changing with the years. And it was there from almost the beginning.

So in early summer of 1959, it was Epstein, more than Gilpatric, who got the clearest signals from Jane about how troubled she really was. He'd not heard from her, he wrote on June 22, "since your last rather unhappy phone call." A week later, she sent him the latest version of the book's outline. Oh, just glance at it and throw it away, she suggested, "and think no more about it until I have something to show you," meaning actual manuscript—not *about* the book, but the book itself. Why this gesture at all? "Well, I have a vague idea you ought to have some notion of what I think I am doing anyway. Also I do get an overwhelming feeling, on occasion, of being a hermit and wishing to break through with some communication, however fragmentary, to the outer world."

Epstein wrote back promptly, and in probably just the way Jane needed most. Yes, the outline was what she'd led him to expect. "I have every confidence that you will turn out a book that we will both be proud of and I think I know exactly how black your moments of despair must at various times be. But it is out of such despair that great books are written."

Jane's understanding of her own book was still fluid and uncertain; just three weeks after submitting a fifteen-chapter outline to Epstein, she sent a twenty-chapter outline to Gilpatric with a whole new Part II and unfamiliar chapter titles like "Incubation of Enterprises and Culture," and "The Pitfalls of Too Much Success"; she was still foundering. In a letter to Gilpatric on July 17, she reported she was "now coming toward the end of Part I," though she knew it needed rewriting. She'd written some fifty thousand words, but planned to winnow it down to thirty thousand, the difference a measure of how far she had to go with it.

Jane was originally supposed to be almost finished by now; she wasn't even close, maybe a quarter the way through. She'd gone through much "trial, error, and bafflement," she wrote Gilpatric, but now seemed to be "working myself clear of it. I have been learning by doing, I guess." But now she needed money. In the same letter, she submitted a statement of expenses; assured Gilpatric that Epstein had told her not to worry, that she should just keep writing; and noted that Doug Haskell was okay about extending her leave. Still, her unease was palpable:

I am rather dismayed at requesting from you more money, after your initial and generous grant, and am chagrinned that I have consumed some of this money and time in trial and error that I should somehow have been bright enough to avoid, and yet was not able to avoid. I hope you will be able to give sympathetic consideration to my request, and both for this consideration and for all the help you have already given me, I am very deeply grateful.

Gilpatric apparently read into Jane's letter that she was thinking of abandoning the project altogether. No, under no circumstances, she wrote him back. But she might have to postpone it, go back to *Forum* for a year, save up money, take out a loan. She didn't want to do that. "Without wishing to sound immodest about it," she went on, "I feel very deeply that it [is] important for this book to get finished and published." City rebuilding, which was taking place so fast, was "based on faulty thinking and misguided notions . . . We are copying failure."

Caught up in her ideas, alone with her typewriter, worried she hadn't the resources to finish this book that had become her life, Jane could seem in the grip of a religious fervor, possessed of a new urban Truth it was her duty to confer on the world. "In my book, I am not rehashing old material on cities and city planning. I am working with new concepts about the city and its behavior. Many of these concepts are quite radically opposed to those accepted in orthodox and conventional planning theory." If the old ways persisted, ahead lay only "the social, economic and visual disintegration of the city."

And no, her ideas weren't the outpourings of an over-fertile imagination, she assured Gilpatric. She'd tried them on others. The times, intellectually speaking, were ripe for them. Most ideas of urban blight were "based on symptoms, not causes, with demonstrably foolish myths invoked to explain the symptoms . . . This is the kind of thing I am up to, and it is hard work, but I cannot think of anything I could do which might be more useful to my times."

Her plea won Gilpatric over. He agreed to her request that she need not prematurely submit to him unfinished drafts, that she just continue in her own way. And he agreed to consider her request for more money.

Around July 29 he called Jane, told her as much, but asked for some names to corroborate her story. Jane came back with Whyte, Haskell, Bill Kirk, Eric Larrabee, the editor of *Horizon*, and a few others.

Haskell wrote Gilpatric, "I guess we'll have to give her what she needs in order to create a book that will be really incisive and probably quite wonderful," though he suspected he'd probably disagree with much of it.

Whyte wrote that he believed Jane's was "a *great* and influential book" in the making.

On September 28, Gilpatric wrote Jane that they were giving her another $8,000. She had a second chance. Thank you, she wrote him back, she was doing better now.

> I'm averaging a chapter a week, instead of the slow and discouraging chapter a month of the spring and summer, and doing better writing to boot. This is a satisfying feeling, and sometimes exciting. I look forward to the day, which now begins to seem in sight and to be real to me, when I'll have a manuscript to show you. There's still a lot of work to do, but it is a pleasure to be doing it. I just could hardly bear not to be doing it.

Although for a while, Gilpatric worried Jane might abandon her book, there was never a chance of that: Jane could *hardly bear not to be doing it.* Words and ideas, expressing them, shaping them—that's what Jane Jacobs did, and had done, for most of her working life. And now she was favored by the most fortunate of circumstances, one every writer dreams of: she had the time and money to charge ahead with a big, fat book on what seemed to her the most important subject in the world. "She knows," Holly Whyte wrote Gilpatric, "that this is her big chance to hammer out what she has so long wanted to say."

Later, some would call *Death and Life* the work of an amateur. Jane had never gone to architecture school, never studied planning, had no degrees. She had designed no buildings, planned no urban districts, conceivably never once wielded T square and triangle to scribe a straight line. She hadn't come to professional maturity at the elbow of a Mies van der Rohe or a Louis Kahn. She hadn't redrawn the streetscape of Philadelphia like Ed Bacon, or of New York like Robert Moses. In the 1950s she'd learned to read drawings from her architect husband; *that,* you could say, was the extent of her "studies."

Of course, by the time Jane gave her Harvard talk in 1956 she *did* have credentials of a sort: She had lived in the middle of New York City for a quarter century. *Iron Age* had sent her, while still in her twenties, to Philadelphia, Washington, and other cities. Her articles for *Amerika* on architecture and slum clearance had forced her to confront some of the same issues she would face in *Death and Life*. At *Forum*, she had visited city after city to file her long, detailed reports; she read drawings, visited construction sites, absorbed planning documents, interviewed architects and every sort of urban expert. All this had been her professional duty.

But the whole preceding paragraph, with its recital of Jane's "credentials," while true enough, supposes that her fitness for writing *Death and Life* rested on her experience of cities, period, and pays no heed to her abilities as a writer. And yet it was as writer that she identified herself all along, and always would. As she began *Death and Life* it was twenty-four years since she'd come to New York and written her first articles for *Vogue*. Since then, she'd done every sort of editorial work, work demanding clarity, accuracy, deep understanding, compositional finesse, and sometimes rhetorical flair. She was no Hemingway or Robert Frost; hers was a different sort of writing, nourished and constrained by the facts of the world, every word aligned with what she'd learned or knew to be true. Everybody understood, or thought they understood, what novelists and poets did. And everyone knew of professors ready to propound at a moment's notice on their credentialed area of expertise. But Jane was like neither of these more familiar classes of men and women who put words to paper professionally. She was a writer, but of a different kind, one that scarcely had a name.

Certainly grammar and spelling—Jane was an almost preternaturally perfect speller—were the least of her skills. She could frame ideas and express them, as she wished, in fifty words or five thousand. With every writing problem, she looked three ways at once: Toward a body of knowledge and fact. Toward her reader and what he or she "needed" in order to keep turning the pages. And toward her own inner self and its expressive needs. Without a firm grip on the first, the subject matter, she'd be spouting nonsense. Without regard for the second, her reader, she could write sentences, paragraphs, *tomes*, that were perfectly accurate—and perfectly boring. Without the third, without mining her inner landscape for diamonds of meaning or feeling, she'd deny herself her whole reason for writing in the first place. Jane had learned (though not, as we'll see, infallibly) to review her own work at every stage with hard, cold, critical eyes that spotted infelicities of expression and sloppiness of thought, and go back and make them right; at one point she'd write Gilpatric about the "good, cold-blooded mood" she looked forward to bringing to the final manuscript.

At *Forum*, she had stepped onto new intellectual terrain. But she had been doing that all her working life—moving from ignorance of a subject to confident insight, absorbing new bodies of fact, ideas, and contexts, commanding them so well she could write about them gracefully. She had delved into economics with Robert Hemphill; the legal and philosophical currents of the American constitutional system with *Constitutional Chaff*; high-temperature brazing and powder metallurgy at *Iron Age*; every sort of subject, cities among them, at *Amerika*. Unlike her Columbia professors, who staked out one or two corners of intellectual life, no single territory, no one *subject area*, was Jane's own; architecture and planning were simply the latest in a long line. To take almost anything in the great universe of people, places, and ideas, scientific and human, current and historical, and make fresh, lively sense of it—*this* was Jane's theater of expertise. She may not have conceived her art, or craft, or whatever it was, in quite these terms, but she would doubtless have recognized herself in them.

By January 1960, she seems to have hit her stride, her desperation of six months earlier now mostly gone. "I am working away quite happily," she wrote Epstein, "with intermittent bafflements and problems." She was on the nineteenth of what she now supposed would work out to twenty-two chapters. Much rewriting lay ahead, and "this is still going to take time, but nothing is as bad as those blank sheets of paper."

Four months later, Jane finally got to Gilpatric the first five chapters of *Death and Life*. He had some quibbles, he replied on May 19, but "if the remainder of the book has this richness and vigor, it should have very important effects. More power to you."

Jane didn't normally write about herself. And yet, peppering *Death and Life* were tidbits of her life's experience that, while supporting her ideas, were also apt to connect with readers. Read it and you learned, for example, that Jane had gone to the same West Eighty-sixth Street dentist for fifteen years; that a favorite art gallery stood near the fish market she patronized; that she'd once had a friend who thought babies were born through their mothers' navels; that after her Harvard talk, where she stressed the need for small neighborhood shops, she'd begun getting mail filled with plans for corner grocery stores—"sweetly meant inanities," she'd call them—as if that's all she'd said at Harvard. *Death and Life* could be challenging. It dealt with ideas, sometimes formidable ones. But these glimpses of her personal life gave it a sometimes warming intimacy.

One particular first-person stretch of *Death and Life* would linger in readers' memories, *attach* itself to them. It came near the beginning. Jane was talking about how busy sidewalks, crowded with people, enhanced safety and performed other functions by furnishing "eyes on the street."

Under the seeming disorder of the old city, wherever the old city is working successfully, is a marvelous order for maintaining the safety of the streets and the freedom of the city. It is a complex order. Its essence is intricacy of sidewalk use, bringing with it a constant succession of eyes. The order is all composed of movement and change, and although it is life, not art, we may fancifully call it the art form of the city and liken it to the dance—not to a simpleminded precision dance with everyone kicking up at the same time, twirling in unison and bowing off en masse, but to an intricate ballet in which the individual dancers and ensembles all have distinctive parts which miraculously reinforce each other and compose an orderly whole. The ballet of the good city sidewalk never repeats itself from place to place, and in any one place is always replete with new improvisations.

The stretch of Hudson Street where I live is each day the scene of an intricate sidewalk ballet. I make my own first entrance into it a little after eight when I put out the garbage can, surely a prosaic occupation, but I enjoy my part, my little clang, as the droves of junior high school students walk by the center of the stage dropping candy wrappers.

Jane sweeps up the wrappers. The hardware store opens. Longshoremen off for the day gather at the White Horse Tavern or the Ideal. "Character dancers come on, a strange old man with strings of old shoes over his shoulders, motor scooter riders with big beards and girl friends who bounce on the back of the scooters and wear their hair long in front of their faces as well as behind." Across several pages, the day winds down. "The night workers stop now at the delicatessen to pick up salami and a container of milk."

Then, finally, "the deep night ballet," which Jane knew best "from waking long after midnight to tend a baby and sitting in the dark, seeing the shadows and hearing the sounds of the sidewalk." Finally, the sound of a bagpipe skirls in the February night, "and as if it were a signal the random, dwindled movements of the sidewalk took on direction," a crowd developing around the music maker.

When she started on *Death and Life* in 1958, she'd write years later, "I expected merely to describe the civilizing and enjoyable services that good city street life casually provides—and to deplore planning fads and architectural fashions" that undermined it. That wound up as Part I of her book, "The Peculiar Nature of Cities." Following an introductory first chapter and representing about a third of the book, it ranged across five chapters:

2. The Uses of Sidewalks: Safety
3. The Uses of Sidewalks: Contact
4. The Uses of Sidewalks: Assimilating Children
5. The Uses of Neighborhood Parks
6. The Uses of City Neighborhoods

The uses of this, the uses of that, first one subject, then the next. Three chapters on *sidewalks*? Just what sort of book was really winding through Jane's typewriter? In one letter to Gilpatric, she'd said it was aimed at "the general interested citizen," not the specialist. But what might such a creature, this good citizen, want or expect from it? In what sense, if any, was Jane writing a "popular" book? It was not some heartfelt memoir. It did not boast scenes studded with brisk, slangy dialogue. There were no gang wars. No glittering soirees. No erotic couplings in fifth-floor tenements, city lights sparkling through the windows. But if it didn't have elements like these going for it, what *did* it have?

What it had going for it, in the first place, were good guys and, especially, bad guys. Among the intellectual villains were Ebenezer Howard of the Garden City movement; and Daniel Burnham of City Beautiful, which grew out of the 1893 Columbian Exposition in Chicago; and especially that towering evil genius of modernity, Le Corbusier, and his Radiant City. Jane lumped their ideas together, emphasizing their kindred elements rather than their differences—Radiant Garden City Beautiful—as the product of thinkers who couldn't think about a city without imposing neatness, order, and sterility.

There were villains-of-place, too—streets, neighborhoods, and districts that Jane saw as failures. For example, Benjamin Franklin Parkway, in Philadelphia, with its lineup of grand cultural monuments—"impressive" but bland, all but dead on arrival. Or Chatham Village, a Pittsburgh neighborhood, which she wrote off as hopelessly homogenous, lacking anything like a healthy public life; or the Elm Hill Avenue section of Roxbury, in Boston, which suffered from the Great Blight of Dullness, Jane's most damning epithet.

Then, there were the black-hatted city planners as a gang, barren of ideas, purveyors of the "pseudoscience" of urban planning, stuck "in the same stage of elaborately learned superstition as medical science was early in the last century, when physicians put their faith in bloodletting, to draw out the evil humors . . . believed to cause disease," an analogy Jane developed at impressive length.

Of Ebenezer Howard, Jane wrote, "His aim was the creation of self-sufficient small towns, really very nice towns if you were docile and had no plans of your own and did not mind spending your life among others with no plans of their own." This was not the only time Jane was acerbic or unforgiving. "You were pretty ticked off at American culture" while writing *Death and Life*, James Howard Kunstler once said to her: "What was it that was getting under your skin in those days?"

"What was getting immediately under my skin," she replied,

was this mad spree of deceptions and vandalism and waste that was called urban renewal. And the way it had been adopted like a fad. And people were so mindless about it and so dishonest about what was being done. That's what ticked me off, because I was working for an architectural magazine and I saw all this first hand and I saw how the most awful things were being excused.

Herbert Gans may have been wrong to think that Boston's West End, a neighborhood soon to be wiped off the map, had failed to interest her. She did visit it, talked to shopkeepers there, found in its sad story examples of just the kind of dishonesty that made her livid. In 1958, she talked to two architects who had helped justify its destruction. One said of its homes that they were built so well its displaced residents would never again live in anything so structurally sound. Another told of having to get down "on his hands and knees with a photographer through utility crawl spaces so that they could get pictures of sufficient dark and noisome spaces" to label it a slum. Here was duplicity justified as serving a greater good—the elimination of a slum that, from all Jane (and Gans) could see, was no slum at all.

As a girl, on a trip to Fredericksburg, Virginia, near where her father had grown up, Jane visited a museum featuring machines and tools brightly painted "to show you how they worked"—wheels and housings, rotors and ratchets, showing themselves off as they whirred in front of you or as you imagined them whirring. At the Scranton railroad station, too, she liked "the locomotives and those pistons that moved the wheels," the cams and connecting rods transferring the steam's hot pressured power into forward motion, so visceral and direct. But then, beginning in the 1930s, locomotives began to sport *skirts*—sheet metal shaped and positioned to suggest modernity and motion, but hiding the real works behind them. Now, said Jane, "you couldn't see how the wheels moved, and that disturbed me." Likewise for cities, so much more complex than any locomotive, a similar incuriosity: Billions went into housing projects. Neighborhoods were torn down. Towers went up. Streets were widened, or eliminated. Zoning laws prescribed mathematical ratios of this to that. And yet, it seemed to her, no one stopped to ask how the cities thus affected actually worked. "It may be that we have become so feckless as a people that we no longer care how things do work, but only what kind of quick, easy outer impression they give," she wrote in *Death and Life*.

What made cities work, and work well, was the overarching theme of her book. Cities required "exuberant diversity," the endless mixing of every kind of everything. And that demanded the satisfaction of four conditions: 1) mixed primary uses; 2) short blocks; 3) buildings of varied ages, including old ones; and 4) dense concentrations of people. To each, in Part II, she devoted a substantial chapter.

"Mixed primary uses" was Jane's name for an urban texture in which commercial areas were not segregated in one place, residences in another, and warehouses and factories in a barren third, but were all mixed up. In any one stretch of street, divergent uses and needs—shops, bars, houses, grocery stores, little factories—fed off one another, drawing people at every hour of the day, and sometimes night, helping to keep the area lively and safe.

Short blocks encouraged varied walking paths, the chance to encounter different people, businesses, activities—more choices, more corners for small shops, more liveliness; long, self-isolating blocks led to stagnation. "It is fluidity of use, and the mixing of paths, not homogeneity of architecture, that ties together city neighborhoods into pools of city use."

Ramshackle old buildings, with their low rents, encouraged new business start-ups and fledgling neighborhood institutions. "Among the most admirable and enjoyable sights to be found along the sidewalks of big cities are the ingenious adaptations of old quarters to new uses," like the stable that becomes a house, the basement that becomes an immigrants' club, the brewery that becomes a theater. "Old ideas can sometimes use new buildings," she wrote. "New ideas must use old buildings."

Finally, Jane devoted a chapter to how great cities depended on dense concentrations of people—not just downtown, but in residential neighborhoods. "The overcrowded slums of planning literature are teeming areas with a high density of dwellings. [But the seemingly] over-crowded slums of American real life are, more and more typically, dull areas with a low density of dwellings." Witness Oakland, or Roxbury in Boston, or Detroit, with its "seemingly endless square miles of low-density failure."

This sort of cartoonish summary of some of its key ideas is not the best way to appreciate *Death and Life*. Like other books almost unbearably rich with fresh ideas, it loses much in the translation to outline and overview, is left vulnerable to unthinking adulation or lazy distortion. Its memorable catchphrases, which have become fixtures in the literature of cities and planning, do help bring the book to mind: *border vacuums; mixed primary uses; unslumming; cataclysmic money; eyes on the street.* But once *Death and Life* became a kind of urban gospel, developers and others sometimes took to invoking them with scarcely a nod to what Jane actually meant. Then, too, the book's aphoristic flavor makes it tempting to reduce it to the likes of study guide or catechism:

- "In cities, liveliness and variety attract more liveliness; deadness and monotony repel life."
- "In orthodox city planning, neighborhood open spaces are venerated . . . much as savages venerate magical fetishes."
- "Why are there so often no people where the parks are and no parks where the people are?"
- "Corruption grows more inventive, rather than less so, the longer it has an object to play with."

- "People are rightly suspicious of programs that give them nothing for something."
- "Cities have the capability of providing something for everybody, only because, and only when, they are created by everybody."

To paraphrase Walt Whitman, *Death and Life* contains multitudes. It can be abridged and digested, but not without irremediable loss. Not just Jane's artfulness but her loving attention to each facet of city-ness, detailed and nuanced (if occasionally tedious), made the book what it was.

Even the likes of parking lots and windowless industrial frontages were eligible for that sort of treatment from her. Consider a later chapter, "The Curse of Border Vacuums," Jane's term for certain lifeless tracts deadening to the eye and destructive to pedestrian life. She showed how a railroad *station* could tie in to its surroundings, but not a railroad *track;* a single government *building*, but not normally a large government *complex*. In both cases, the former could unite and strengthen a city district while the latter tore it up. "Frequent borders, whether formed by arterial highways, institutions, projects, campuses, industrial parks, or any other massive uses of special land, can in this way tear a city to tatters."

Railroad tracks, of course, are the classic example of a border vacuum. "The other side of the tracks," after all, is shorthand for a social border one side of which is poorer or slummier than the other. Jane didn't mean social borders here but physical and functional ones. The "blight-proneness" of areas beside railroad tracks was sometimes explained by the noise and soot thrown off by passing trains. But that was a secondary factor—*had* to be, really, because you could see the same deadness adjacent to a high-way, or hospital complex, or featureless parking lot, or high-rise housing project, or over-scaled college campus, or even a park ineptly integrated into the rest of the city. The root cause was not noise and soot; rather, border vacuums served as unlovely barriers to movement and interaction. The streets abutting them were the "end of the line," attracting few pedestrians; it was discouraging or difficult to cross a broad highway or parking lot, much less a warehouse's blank wall. They "fail to get a by-the-way circulation of people going beyond them in the direction of the border, because few are going to that Beyond." With the adjoining streets shunned, the vitality of the whole area suffers.

But it *didn't have to,* said Jane. Borrowing a principle from Kevin Lynch, an MIT professor whose *The Image of the City* she much admired, a *bor-*

der could be made into a *seam*, "a line of exchange along which two areas are sewn together." For example, waterfronts, blocked off from neighboring streets and often serving as border vacuums, "should be penetrated by small, and even casual, public openings calculated for glimpsing or watching work and water traffic." She continued:

> Near where I live is an old open dock, the only one for miles, next to a huge Department of Sanitation incinerator and scow anchorage. The dock is used for eel fishing, sunbathing, kite flying, car tinkering, picnicking, bicycle riding, ice-cream and hot-dog vending, waving at passing boats, and general kibitzing . . . You could not find a happier place on a hot summer evening or a lazy summer Sunday. From time to time, a great slushing and clanking fills the air as a sanitation truck dumps its load into a waiting garbage scow. This is not pretty-pretty, but it is an event greatly enjoyed on the dock. It fascinates everybody.

And so, a troublesome border metamorphoses into a "seam," the city stitched whole.

I cite at somewhat greater length Jane's treatment of this one unattractive urban phenomenon—she devotes seventeen pages to border vacuums—to suggest something of her method. The book's abiding worth lay not in her ideas alone but in the richness of insight, detail, and observation with which she developed each of them—often, as in the preceding passage, from her own life and experience.

In arguing that cities need old buildings to nourish economically precarious businesses, Jane describes the shabby old building on Sheridan Square that housed her writing studio:

> The floor of the building in which this book is being written is occupied also by a health club with a gym, a firm of ecclesiastical decorators, an insurgent Democratic party reform club, a Liberal party political club, a music society, an accordionists' association, a retired importer who sells maté by mail, a man who sells paper and who also takes care of shipping the maté, a dental laboratory, a studio for watercolor lessons, and a maker of costume jewelry.

And then, as if to throw in her lot with her Sheridan Square friends, she adds, "There is no place for the likes of us in new construction."

·   ·   ·

A little after her book came out, a Cleveland man wrote Jane for advice on how he might track down housing and crime statistics for New York housing projects. At the city housing authority, she wrote back, he could expect little help on crime statistics. "They are extremely touchy on this matter. They may even deny that they have such a thing." At police precincts, they probably couldn't break down the stats the way he'd want. Still, it was "possible to get a pretty good idea by going in person to police precincts" and interviewing officers; likewise, schoolteachers serving the project. "In short, you have to see many people and do a great deal of detective work."

In 1959, Ellen Perry, a recently divorced twenty-eight-year-old who had studied at the Harvard School of Design, was advised by a friend that a Mrs. Jacobs needed help in researching a book. Soon, she was fielding Jane's requests, feeding facts back to her. On Chloetheil Smith, a modernist architect; on population density figures for Georgetown, in Washington, D.C.; on the union pay scale for elevator operators. The modest checks Perry received, for the equivalent of $100 or $200 in today's money, came through Jane's Rockefeller grant. "There is something more you could do now," Jane wrote Perry in October 1959: She needed crime statistics on the ten or fifteen largest cities. And juvenile crime and delinquency rates, too, if Perry could get them. And something on what London was like before the automobile. Perry would report back to Jane with little executive summaries she recalls Jane appreciating. "The subjects she asked me to follow were those on which she had hunches but no firm numbers." Sometimes, Jane would have Perry wander through neighborhoods, counting mom-and-pop stores, or people sitting out on stoops or hanging out of windows.

Jane's hard facts stood out sharply from the artful sketches and bird's-eye vistas that were the stock-in-trade of design studios and planning departments. "People who are interested only in how a city 'ought' to look and uninterested in how it works will be disappointed by this book," she wrote in its introduction. "To seek for the look of things as a primary purpose or as the main drama is apt to make nothing but trouble." Here, her anger welling up, she told of a pretty patch of green in an East Harlem project. A social worker was "astonished" by how often, and with how much vehemence, it was derided, though no one could say just why. Then, finally, one tenant did:

Nobody cared what we wanted when they built this place. They threw our houses down and pushed us here and pushed our friends somewhere else. We don't have a place around here to get a cup of coffee or a newspaper even, or borrow fifty cents. Nobody cared what we need. But the big men come and look at that grass and say, "Isn't it wonderful! Now the poor have everything."

"There is a quality even meaner than outright ugliness or disorder," wrote Jane in one of her most quoted passages, "and this meaner quality is the dishonest mask of pretended order, achieved by ignoring or suppressing the real order that is struggling to exist and be served."

Death and Life was not the work of a day. It was "much more difficult than I imagined it to be," Jane would say. "I was filled with anxiety the whole time I was doing it," occasionally tempted "to put everything into a garbage bag" and set it out for pickup. It was packed tight with ideas many of which traced back not to the few years of the book's actual composition but, as we've seen, to 1955 and long before; some of Jane's thinking harked back to her Columbia days. Set against the articles she wrote for *Forum*, the book was virtually unrecognizable, its flavor markedly different even from that of her 1958 *Fortune* article. For most of her career, an article meant a few days or weeks of work, then on to the next one. Now, in late 1960, she was concluding a project that dwarfed by a factor of twenty or thirty anything she'd done before. "This is the fourth draft of this damn chapter," she wrote Jason Epstein on December 15, "and it probably needs a fifth and a sixth. I have forgotten how to write & this makes me very worried. Four more to go seems like forty more to go." Just now, approaching the end, she was showing portions of the manuscript to Epstein, his assistant Nathan Glazer, and Chadbourne Gilpatric, each of whom responded with opinions, objections, and last-minute questions.

One editorial interchange concerned her last chapter, "The Kind of Problem a City Is," the very strangeness of its title calling attention to itself as a separate species, set apart from the rest of the book. Jane took as inspiration an essay (appearing in the same 1958 report of the Rockefeller Foundation that listed her original grant) by retiring vice president Warren Weaver, a mathematician who had helped develop the philosophical implications of Claude Shannon's famous 1947 paper on information theory, a founding document of the digital age. Weaver's focus was mostly on the biological sciences; Jane would apply his thinking to an intellectual regime, cities, which he'd probably never thought about at all. It seemed to her that Weaver's breakdown of the types of problems with which scientists grapple summed up, "in an oblique way, virtually the intellectual history of city planning."

Weaver described, first, a class of simple scientific problems: you strike one billiard ball with another, at a particular spot, from a particular angle, and with a particular force, and you can predict in some detail what will happen. This was old-hat physics, explored before the twentieth century, relatively straightforward, mathematically navigable.

A second category of problem was one of "disorganized complexity," which you might find on a giant billiard table cluttered with not one, or fifteen, balls but millions of them; no way, even in principle, could you trace the path of any one ball amid all that clacking chaos. On the other hand, you could probably come up with useful averages and broad patterns; you could approach statistically and probabilistically, for great numbers of balls, what you couldn't for any one of them. This approach was applicable to a welter of real-world problems, from life expectancy tables to thermodynamics.

The study of living systems, Weaver observed, yielded to neither approach but rather fit a third category. "What makes an evening primrose open when it does? Why does salt water fail to satisfy thirst?" These, Weaver's own examples, were more complex by far than plunking billiard balls together. But they were by no means "disorganized," and weren't much illuminated by statistics. Rather, they were problems of "organized complexity"—in Weaver's words, marked by "a sizable number of factors which are interrelated into an organic whole."

Like, Jane now argued, a city.

How to understand, she offered as example, a neighborhood park, with its slew of interacting forces? The physical design of the park itself figures in. So does its sheer size. So do its users, who they are, when they use it, the pattern of the surrounding streets, and much else. You might wind up with a fine, well-used park, happy and safe; or one that proved barren and dangerous, unappealing to adults and children alike. Either way, the outcome didn't depend on any one single factor; it wasn't one of Weaver's simple problems. Nor could statistics, maybe some crude ratio of open space to local population, shed much light. Rather, the problem occupied

Weaver's third category, where, as with the evening primrose, numerous interrelated factors figured in. There was "nothing accidental or irrational about the ways in which these factors affect each other," wrote Jane. But understanding it required close-in, almost microscopic study that resisted, as she wrote in relation to a related problem, "easier, all-purpose analyses, and . . . simpler, magical, all-purpose cures."

This was the *kind* of problem the city represented, the kind that the Ebenezer Howards and Le Corbusiers of the world didn't see. For Howard, the city reduced to housing and jobs. For Le Corbusier, as Jane wrote, "his towers in the park were a celebration, in art, of the potency of statistics and the triumph of the mathematical average." With statistical techniques, the relocation of people uprooted by the planners "could be dealt with intellectually like grains of sand, or electrons or billiard balls." But so crude an approach fell woefully short of real understanding.

Jane's final chapter didn't read much like the rest of the book. It read suspiciously like science. And Nathan Glazer, for one, was little sympathetic to it. "I am somewhat allergic to talking about science in situations where a general intelligence and sensitivity are demanded," he wrote Jane. She'd made too much of Weaver's distinctions. He saw little value in them. Stick to more concrete arguments, he advised her. Maybe, he allowed, his was "an over-personal reaction to abstract and theoretical points," but still, he hoped Jane would reconsider.

In retrospect, it shouldn't be surprising that Jane turned now to science. Back at Columbia she'd relished her dips into biology, psychology, geology, and zoology. And what was her "method" generally in *Death and Life* but a careful, fine-grained *seeing* common to much of science? She emphasized less what cities were than how they worked; not the nature of a slum but how it got that way; process more than product. (In a note I found among her papers, she takes issue with a scholar's assertion that "the task of science is to lessen the pain of encountering the future by anticipating its problems." No, it was not, she insisted. "The task of science is to understand how things work.") She was not, of course, a scientist herself; she didn't count galaxies or trace metabolic pathways for a living. But as a leading Jacobs scholar, the architectural historian Peter Laurence, would observe, even her earliest New York essays from the 1930s reveal a "deeper, protoscientific curiosity about the city's underlying processes." *Death and Life,* meanwhile, retained "the freshness and immutability of scientific principle."

We don't know how much thought Jane gave Glazer's suggestions. We do know that two days later, she fired back a reply: "I very strongly disagree with you about the last chapter." For one thing, she wasn't making analogies to science, as Glazer had implied, but was discussing "methods of thinking and analyzing that are *common* to science and various other kinds of thinking, not analogous." No, "that last chapter may take a while to sink in, but if and when it does, it will change planning more than any other idea" in the book.

The chapter stayed.

Of course, at this point it little mattered. By now, any issues Glazer and Epstein were raising (and on which they mostly deferred to Jane) could be seen as narrow, even technical. For the manuscript, all 150,000 or so words of it, was now all but done; whatever tweaks it would require over the coming months, its nature was fixed. *The Death and Life of Great American Cities* was, Epstein weighed in, "the most exciting book on city planning that I have ever read—and one of the most exciting books on any subject I have ever seen. I'm delighted with it and proud of you and I eagerly await the manuscript in its final version."

On January 24, Jane wrote Nathan Glazer, saying, "Here is chapter 22, the *last*! Now I am going out and getting two martinis. Maybe three."

CHAPTER 13

MOTHER JACOBS
OF HUDSON STREET

IN 1961, A BLISTERING REVIEW of *The Death and Life of Great American Cities* would dismiss its author, in its very title, as "Mother Jacobs." Later, when Jane led the fight to block a highway backed by Robert Moses, he would declaim in a fit of pique that the only people who opposed it were "a bunch of mothers." Now, whatever else Jane was when she left her job at *Forum* in 1958 and set to work on the cities book, she was indeed a mother. Her three children, Jim, Ned, and Mary, were ten, eight, and three respectively. By the time the family left Hudson Street for Toronto in 1968—with *Death and Life* published to much acclaim and Jane a public intellectual and community figure of note—Mary was an adolescent, the two boys were men, and Jane had been a Greenwich Village mother for two decades.

In the fall of 1958, Jane was forty-two years old. It was the first time she hadn't reported to work at a Midtown office since 1946, when she'd briefly freelanced from home. Actually, she didn't work from home now, either, but in a rented office. Early on she'd realized, as she wrote to Chadbourne Gilpatric the following July, that she needed "a room to work in, where I am uninterrupted by people, telephone, etc." She found one on Bethune Street, a five-minute walk from home, on the second floor of an old 1830s-vintage rooming house that shook to the rumble of trucks bound for the West Side Highway. It was Bob who arranged it, for $45 a month, and when Jane moved in, rumors spread that, as son Jim would tell the story, she was "a kept woman." Later, the building was sold out from under her (to a literary agent), so she had to find another place, and

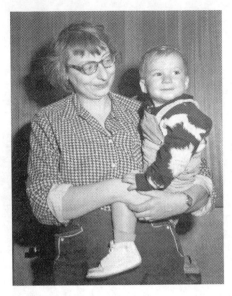

Jane and her son Ned, about 1952

she wound up in the Sheridan Square building she mentioned in *Death and Life*. Mary would remember that "stark little room" of an office, with its shouts and thumps of boxing from the gym next door.

Meanwhile, Jane paid for the help she needed at home. During these years, up until 1960 when she died, Glennie Lenear, the woman whom Jane had hired after Jimmy's birth, was a conspicuous figure in all their lives. When she was still at *Forum*, Jane's routine was to wait until Glennie arrived in the morning, then haul off on her bike for Rockefeller Center. Glennie cared for the kids when they got home from school and prepared their meals, staying until Jane got home at around six. "She looked after me in the nicest way," says Mary, who, groping for words, opens her arms wide, hugging Glennie's remembered girth fifty years later. "She was wonderfully capable. I just loved her. She was like another mother." Ned walked Mary to kindergarten, Glennie picked her up. With school about to let out for the boys, she might be heard to groan, "Oh, it's time for those devils to come home." Jimmy and Ned could be a handful; their cousin Jane, Jim Butzner's girl, remembers them as "wild, rambunctious, mischievous," her own visits to the house welcomed by Glennie as those of, finally, "a girlie girl." The rented office and Glennie's ministrations over many years (which Jane acknowledged in *Death and Life*) let her keep her writing time sacrosanct.

Jane cooked for Bob. She read to her children before putting them to bed. She could be counted on to get what the kids needed for school or play, to head up to Macy's to buy ankle straps for the kids' ice skates or a corduroy jumper for Mary. Sundays, she and Bob took the children to church, St. Luke's Episcopal, a few blocks down Hudson Street. Jane wasn't religious. She felt scant attachment to the Presbyterian church of her childhood. She saw people of a spiritual bent as misguided. And yet, she wrote one correspondent, services at St. Luke's "gave me the satisfying, in fact inspiring feeling that I was a link in a long, sinewy, living human tradition of being." This worked for Jane, anyway; for the kids, who attended Sunday school, not so much. A "vaccine to stave off religion," is how Jim came to see their Sundays at St. Luke's. In the end, seen through a liberal-minded enough lens, Jane was just another American mother, doing her parental best.

Still, if she was a mother of the 1950s, she managed to sidestep most of its tyrannies and would rank as one of somewhat unorthodox style—as were she and Bob, together, as parents. "There was something weird about us," allows Jim, speaking of the family. To the children, all through their lives, their parents were never Mom and Dad, but Jane and Bob. From early on, Jane treated her children as adults; for his parents, says Jim, the children were "not small versions of you. They were their own people." *Hey, listen to this,* she'd say, rounding them up to read aloud what had caught her attention in some book she was reading, about archaeology or politics or who knows what else. She and Bob included them almost automatically in their adult activities. An acquaintance from one community battle, Pierre Tonachel, remembers Jane bringing them to protests and neighborhood meetings; the kids—"happy, sweet kids," he calls them—were "always listening in" to whatever was going on. "It must have been fun for them to come along." Mary remembers being with the adults at the Lion's Head, a local tavern, where a round table in the window served as neighborhood meeting place.

Death and Life devoted a whole chapter to the role of city streets in "assimilating" children. The streets and sidewalks granted them an "outdoor home base from which to play, to hang around in, and to help form their notions of the world"—in short, she all but says, become civilized.

Jane's boys, Jimmy and Ned

The tone is one of clear-eyed acknowledgment of what young people are really like. "Little tots are decorative and relatively docile," she writes, "but older children are noisy and energetic, and they act on their environment instead of just letting it act on them," which is what gets them into trouble. As they grow older, they leave their jump ropes and roller skates behind, and flirt, talk, push, shove, and indulge in horseplay. "Adolescents are always being criticized for this kind of loitering, but they can hardly grow up without it." Mary was too young while Jane worked on *Death and Life* to figure much in it, but glimpses of the boys do appear—darting out into the street, finding secret hiding places in the subways, contriving to avoid getting beat up by other kids.

A photograph of Jimmy and Ned, ages maybe seven and five, shows two ragamuffins, the bigger boy with his arms tightly twined around his younger brother, devilish glee written across his face, Ned looking plaintively off to the side. Ned, in his sixties, recalls that one of his parents' regrets is that they seemed unable to restore peace between them, intervening perhaps a bit too little or too late. *Oh, they'll be friends someday*, Jane's own mother assured her, and they are. "But it was certainly hard to believe" at the time, Jane would say, "when they were such fighters." They were *always* fighting. A friend of Jane's from later years theorizes that they'd ratchet up the conflict to gain her attention. Ned tells how he and Jim exploited Jane's tendency to get lost in what she was thinking, counting on a distracted "Yeah, yeah" when asking permission for this or that. But they got into trouble often enough that eventually Jane rewrote the rules: "Not only do I have to say yes, I have to know I'm saying it."

There was plenty of intellectual challenge in the family, less room for the emotions, navel gazing, or overt criticism. "It wasn't part of the family dynamic to raise voices," the way you'd see in some families, says Mary.

"There were no heavy trips," no histrionics, no yelling and screaming. The emphasis was on thinking things through, the children left to learn from experience, free from too heavy and oppressive an adult hand. "Permissive" is the word that can bubble up. Indeed, Jane and Bob's relaxed parenting style could raise the eyebrows of some, even among friends and family, who felt their brand of permissiveness, if that's what it was, went too far. "Some of their shenanigans would not have been acceptable" in her own family, says cousin Jane, Jane Henderson today, speaking of the Jacobs kids. Her second husband, Riley, who joined the family in the late 1960s, speaks of the Jacobses' "unorthodox way of rearing kids." Still, he adds, "no matter what they did or didn't do, Jane always praised them."

Katia Jacobs, whose husband, John, Bob's cousin, had worked with Jane at *Amerika*—the four of them close friends who would vacation together on Nantucket in a house in Sconset near the beach—says of her that "Jane had a wonderful, vivid personality, but not much of a maternal instinct." It bothered her the time Jane and Bob came over with baby Mary, and Jane "didn't seem to care where she was going to sleep." *Oh, we'll find a place to tuck her in.* "I was shocked with her casual approach," Katia says.

A letter in the Jane Jacobs archives, from Mary to her grandmother when she was twelve, in block printing mixed with cursive, is littered with misspellings, like "gooing" for "going" and "rember" for "remember"; Mary was dyslexic. At home, among her parents and brothers, life was stimulating, educational, with lots going on, and she soaked it right up. She was bright, even gifted. Like her father, she could do almost anything with her hands. But, she says, she "had a hard time in school." Her reading problems had slipped through whatever there was at school to help her, as well as right by her parents; no one, it seems, ever asked whether she'd done her homework. Jane "didn't pay a lot of attention" to her school problems, she recollects—*until,* she says in a carefully neutral way, "at age nine it came to her attention that I hadn't learned to read." Her brothers had been teasing her about it for a while "before Jane finally got wind of it."

When she did, Jane pounced on the problem. She tracked down a special kit of color-coordinated books, with stories and questions, that someone had recommended to her and that she purchased by mail order. It was perfect for her, Mary remembers, something she could use on her own;

maybe Ned and Jim could block out all the distractions of home, street, and school, but she couldn't. Using the reading kit Jane found for her, she "progressed by myself and learned to read in jig time." The first book she remembers reading was Robert Heinlein's *Stranger in a Strange Land.*

Something similar happened with Jim. In high school, taking the Preliminary Scholastic Aptitude Test, he did poorly on the math part. Around the house, Jimmy was the Little Professor, obviously very smart (he would wind up with a PhD in solid-state physics), so why had he done so miserably on this standardized test? Belatedly, Jane and Bob realized, it wasn't mathematical concepts hanging him up, it was basic arithmetic—times tables and the like. Jane began drilling him in these fundamentals and, the following year, when he took the college-qualifying SATs, he did well.

Their parents, the children agree, didn't tamp down or crimp their natural instincts. No need to micromanage, intervene, or unduly fret over your children; trust in them and they'd do fine. Something like this was the Jacobs credo. On the other hand, you could miss things that way, as Jane and Bob occasionally did. "Benign neglect"? The children themselves, reflecting back, don't see it that way. The hands-off stance that let Mary's reading problems and Jim's in arithmetic slip by could seem a blessing. Jane "had a sense that we were *all right*," says Mary. When one of the kids got into trouble in school, Jim recalls, Jane or Bob—more typically Jane, at least while she was still at *Forum*—showed up at school "and supported us totally," he says, "no matter who was right or wrong." One time, the boys wanted cowboy boots, which Jane bought for them and they wore to school. But the teacher said no, that for whatever reason they couldn't wear them in her class. Jane went in and remonstrated with her. *She* was the parent. *She* had bought boots for *her* sons. They were perfectly good boots. There was nothing wrong with the boots, or with them. The teacher gave in.

It was a moral and practical education the Jacobs kids received at home. When Glennie was dying, Jane gave blood, taking Mary with her to the hospital, which was "a total hell hole, all black people, terribly sick people, very crowded"; Mary never forgot it. Jane taught her about scams, the kind that came through junk mail, and about book clubs that suck you in and charge you for books you don't want. She was lucky to get an education like that, she says, one that inoculated her against being manipulated as an adult. One time, around 1961, in the cold war days of nuclear posturing and real nuclear threat, the air raid sirens went off while she and Jane were out walking; the wailing sirens meant they were to "duck and cover," and, sure enough, everyone disappeared from the street. But not them. It was silly and pointless, Jane told her six-year-old. "We're not ducking and covering."

Reminiscences of Jane's children and their cousins often come tinged with the flavor of extended family, of one big clan of Butzner cousins. Jim and Kay Butzner's family and their children, Jane, Ann, and William, lived in southern New Jersey, in a suburb called Woodbury. John, his wife, "Pete" Butzner, and their son, Decker, lived in Virginia. Of course, Betty and Julie, and their children, Carol, Paul, and David, were over in Stuyvesant Town. As several of them tell it, they were cousins, yes, but closer than cousins, more like brothers and sisters.

Decker Butzner, today a physician living in Calgary, Alberta, holds memories of the Jacobs household going all the way back to 1953, when he was three. On family trips to New York they'd also visit his mother's family in Staten Island, and Aunt Betty and Uncle Jules in Stuyvesant Town. But it was Jane and Bob's Hudson Street house he remembered best. As you came in from the street, there was a galley kitchen to your left, with open shelves separating it from the dining room; Bob had designed it that way so whoever was working in the kitchen wasn't cut off from conversation around the dinner table.

On Thanksgiving, the men would take the kids to the Macy's parade, finding a spot along the west side of Central Park near the Museum of Natural History at Seventy-ninth Street. Most often, it was Jane's three kids, Betty's three, and him, Decker, but sometimes also the South Jersey contingent. They'd get around by subway or, more often, on foot—the better to burn off youthful energy before dinner, as Decker later reckoned the grown-ups' strategy. Meanwhile, the women would be cooking—turkey, green peas, creamed onions, three or four kinds of pies. The big meal would come around three. Then the cousins would go out and play, the food left out for "grazing." He loved those trips up to New York. "We were all so excited to see each other."

To the cousins, Hudson Street could seem an isle of liberation. Decker and the Jacobs boys would ride the train down to the South Ferry station, there to briskly make their way down the bank of pay phones, collecting coins left by frazzled Staten Island Ferry commuters rushing for the boat. Jane Butzner, sometimes known as Little Jane to distinguish her from her aunt, after whom she was named, was the eldest of the cousins. Growing up in New Jersey, she "couldn't wait to visit my cousins in New York," the Jacobs kids and the Mansons. When she was old enough, she'd be dropped off at the bus station in Philadelphia and arrive at the Port Authority in New York, where Betty would pick her up and ferry her over to Stuyvesant Town or to Jane's. She'd arrive at Hudson Street wearing her pretty patent leather shoes and soon head off with the boys to Washington Square. Fun, apparently, was planting her on one end of the seesaw, then jumping precipitously off the other, slamming her end down. She'd return with the boys hours later hopelessly "dirty and disheveled," her nice shoes sorely scuffed; her own mother would never countenance *that*. In the house, she played on the jungle gym in the boys' bedrooms, a horizontal ladder that let you walk across the room with your hands. She ate raw clams and artichokes, things she'd never get at home. They'd take the storied subways; she was still small enough to duck under the turnstiles. Once or twice her mom invited the Jacobs kids to their house in New Jersey, doing them a kindness, presumably, by getting them out of the city; of course, says cousin Jane, "they were bored out of their minds" in leafy Leave-It-to-Beaverville. Hudson Street was more interesting, though it didn't adhere to the highest standards of suburban spit and polish. Lucia Jacobs, Katia and John's daughter, second cousin to Jane's children, remembers walking barefoot around the old house, the soles of her feet in no time turning black.

Jane's West Village was as much a place of business, warehousing, and small-scale manufacturing as of homes. A former stable at the corner of Hudson and Perry dealt in industrial fasteners. The Fisher Chemical warehouse was just down Hudson Street; Jimmy, not much older than twelve at the time, would walk there for a liter of potassium chromate, some sulfuric acid, potassium hydroxide pellets, and purple dye, pay for it with a little pocket money, and head home to concoct crazy "experiments." Decker recalls visits where they'd play under the old West Side Highway, a few blocks from the house, and spy longshoremen, with their iconic, scary-looking steel hooks, pilfering from broken-open crates.

Christmas at the Jacobs house had its own rhythms. Christmas cookies meant not just the cookies themselves but the family ritual of producing them in the hundreds, the kitchen littered with trays of them, shapes stamped out with cookie cutters, in countless sizes, styles, and recipes; as Jane herself would say, "We would go crazy." And, of course, there was the annual ham to prepare. Each year, Jane would buy a new datebook to record doctors' appointments, social events, and the like, one small enough to stick in her own Christmas stocking. And first thing each year she'd open it to the back and enter, as almost ritual incantation, the same words: December 22: soak ham . . . December 23: boil ham . . . December 24: bake ham.

Come vacations they'd pile into the car, if you want to call it that. It was one of those evolutionary dead ends in the history of the automobile that, like evolutionary dead ends in the natural world, was more interesting than most. It was called a Multipla, made by Fiat, a miniature van introduced in 1956, smaller than a VW Beetle, that looked about the same coming or going, powered by a tiny, four-cylinder engine that took most of a minute to get the car up to highway speed; they bought it new in 1958. "A delightful lemon," Jim calls the car. In family lore, its fuel pump was forever going on the fritz, which meant frequent, seemingly endless waits in service stations. When that happened, or just on long drives out to Shelter Island, on the eastern tip of Long Island, the children needing to be entertained, Jane would make up stories. One of her characters was an industrious little boy named Peanut, so tiny he could fit into a hat, who was always getting into scrapes. Jane could spin out these stories—maybe kid photographer Peanut sliding down the weasel hole, or Peanut escaping from the evil carnival barker—as long as it took to fix that damned fuel pump, or traverse those endless tracts of Long Island, or until the children fell asleep.

CHAPTER 14

THE PHYSICAL FALLACY

B Y T H E T I M E her book came out, Jane Butzner Jacobs of Scranton, Pennsylvania, had lived in New York for twenty-seven years, virtually all of it in Greenwich Village. Her jobs had typically taken her up to Midtown. Her familiarity with East Harlem was of recent vintage. Of vast tracts of Brooklyn and the Bronx and the other outer boroughs, she was ignorant. Yet with publication of *Death and Life*, all her insights and impressions of New York, about how it worked and what it meant, her opinions and prejudices, would stand beside all those who'd ever tried to say something fresh about the city: E. B. White's love letter to the city, *Here Is New York*, in 1948. Alfred Kazin's Jewish Brownsville, in *A Walker in the City*, from the late 1940s. Joseph Mitchell's cast of outlandish neighborhood characters in *The New Yorker*. Novels, essays, poetry: "How funny you are today New York / like Ginger Rogers in *Swingtime* / and St. Bridget's steeple leaning a little to the left." Dark or bright, gritty or grand, the Manhattan skyline inimitable, the poorer quarters seen with affection, horror, or shame. The city squeezed into a character or elevated to a symbol, each a way to see New York. And now Jane's own strong feelings for the city, long sublimated in her magazine articles, or surfacing only in table talk with friends, were to join the great conversation. With publication of her book, she would step from an almost entirely private life onto a larger public stage, to be seen, appraised, and judged.

.   .   .

January 1961. Jane was cutting it pretty close. She had all of a week before she was supposed to return to her job at *Architectural Forum*. "I want to get as much as I can done on clearing up points, rearranging some chapters, cutting excess adjectives, sentences & paragraphs," she wrote Epstein's assistant Nathan Glazer on the 24th, in the same letter in which she looked ahead to her martinis. She appreciated his upbeat response to an earlier submission, she said, "because I have a very hard time knowing how it is coming off, & vary from exhilaration to despair and dejection."

Soon after she'd finished it, she showed the manuscript to Elias Wilentz, longtime proprietor of that Beat nexus, the Eighth Street Bookshop. "It is truly a great, important and impressive book," Wilentz wrote Epstein. It would sell well, he predicted, and not just to planners and architects; there was something *big* about it. "It should hit the same audience that bought Paul Goodman's *Growing Up Absurd*," a surprise best seller about young people lost in a repressive society. Jane's book would draw a broader audience yet, Wilentz was saying, "if it is promoted not as a technical work but as an exciting revelation of city life and what makes it tick."

Naturally, Chadbourne Gilpatric got an early copy, too, but his response, in a letter to Jane in March, was more measured than she might have liked. He judged it "thoughtful and thought-provoking, vividly and constructively concrete . . . powerful in its effect, and most timely." *But.* But the chapter on parks "could be deleted entirely without much loss." So could the one on traffic and cars. All told, the book's 669 mimeographed pages could be reduced "by almost half." That could hardly have cheered poor Jane, who'd sweated and strained over every one of them. Even his closing comment—that Jane had "many reasons to feel pleased with this contribution"—seems lukewarm and too careful.

As a publishing venture, however, Jason Epstein was pleased as could be. By early June he could report that magazines were lining up to run excerpts from it: *The Saturday Evening Post, Harper's, Architectural Forum, The Reporter,* and *Mademoiselle.* Here was the kind of kickoff every publisher dreamed of. In mid-September, prepublication copies went out to Murray Kempton, Max Lerner, J. Kenneth Galbraith, Oscar Lewis, Dwight Macdonald, Edmund Wilson, and Gore Vidal, all intellectual and cultural heavyweights of their day. Also getting an advance copy was Holly Whyte, who, in a fevered scrawl of a handwritten letter, wrote Jane in October, "Jane—TERRIFIC! *You did it* and I can't wait to hear the [??] and yells and churlish comments of the fraternity. I'm only part way through it but I can see that it's going to be one of the most remarkable books *ever* written about the city and probably the best in this century." In parentheses, he added, "And it's fun to read!"

But all this, gratifying as most of it must have been, came from Jane's own tribe, from a narrow, sympathetic inner circle. For the past three years, it had been just her, with Bob and the kids, and Jason, and Nat Glazer, and, near the end, a few others who'd gotten their hands on the manuscript, all FRIENDS OF JANE. But after a launch party in October and the book's formal publication, and then across the next year—during which, as we'll see, she was caught up in tumultuous fights on behalf of the West Village and against the Lower Manhattan Expressway—Jane and her book were at last rocketed into the big world.

"Hers is a huge, a fascinating, a dogmatically controversial book," wrote Orville Prescott in the *The New York Times*, "and I am convinced, an important one." He thought it was overlong, "but much of it snaps like a flag in the fresh wind of her new ideas and challenging statements." That was November 3.

Two days later, the *New York Herald Tribune* weighed in: "It is a considerable achievement to have written a book that will irresistibly overturn the preconceptions of generations of city-planners, as Mrs. Jacobs's book will surely do."

On the 10th, Jane was featured in *Time* magazine, *Death and Life* described as a passionate, well-documented book that was already shaking up the planners. Imitation being the sincerest form of flattery, the writer conjured up his own *Time*-inflected Jacobsean city, down to "the shriek of children scooting in the streets, the clamor of crowded living; the neighborhood butcher's, where the housewife can leave her door key . . . and the strangely silent Sunday morning sweet with the smell of freshly washed streets."

In *Commonweal* on December 22, Edward T. Chase led off his review, "How seldom one comes upon a new book of unmistakably seminal importance like this one . . . This is a dangerous book. Dangerous to vested interests: to all our city planners, to almost all our architects."

Declared *The Wall Street Journal*, "In another age, the author's enormous intellectual temerity would have ensured her destruction as a witch."

Those who loved the book reached for superlatives. Edwin Weeks, editor of *The Atlantic Monthly*, wrote to Jane on January 29, 1962: "Reading it is like opening a window of January air in a room laid heavy with academic discussion . . . It is the best package of fresh, vigorous thinking that I have come across in a long, long time."

Almost overnight, Jane was a hot ticket. Everyone wanted her to write for them. Something on the new architecture in Midtown Manhattan? *Partisan Review* queried her. No, she replied. She got a telegram from *The New York Times Book Review* wondering whether she'd do a seven-hundred-word review of *The Intellectual vs. the City:* CAN SEND GALLEYS NOW FINISHED BOOK WILL FOLLOW PLEASE REPLY SOONEST. She replied that same day: No, she couldn't do it. "Now that you have foiled the bulldozer invasion of the Village," John Fischer wrote her from *Harper's,* referring to a civic battle she'd led, "do you have the time and inclination for some writing? If so, I have a couple of ideas I would like to discuss with you." On December 27, William F. Buckley, the young editor of *National Review,* wrote her, attaching the favorable review of Jane's book it would soon carry, and wondering whether she'd do a piece on Lincoln Center for him. Sorry, she couldn't; by now she was back at *Forum,* she explained, and "all my writing on cities or on architecture is committed to my own magazine." Mostly, then, she was saying no. But surely it was nice being asked. The whole world of New York publishing had suddenly opened up to her—suddenly, that is, after twenty-seven years in New York.

Early February found her at the Museum of Modern Art for a panel called "The Laws of the Asphalt Jungle," a reference to the novel and noir movie of a few years before. Jane faced two of her longtime antagonists, Edmund Bacon from Philadelphia and Boston's chief planner, Ed Logue, who was "as cautiously caustic as Bacon is cheery," in the words of Jane's former colleague at *Forum,* Walter McQuade, who covered the event for *The Nation.* "Mrs. Jacobs is understandably a little tired of making speeches," McQuade noted; she declined the rostrum, preferring to sit at a table by the side. But when it was her turn, he wrote, Jane "butchered both professional planners." She dismissed a vaunted Bacon project as "dull and droopy." She called Logue's claim that no bulldozers were aimed at the North End simply false. As McQuade reported, she "soon had the audience laughing sardonically."

But Bacon and Logue came back at her. What, exactly, was Mrs. Jacobs *for*? Bacon wanted to know, earning "a wave of nervous clapping" in the auditorium. Logue castigated Jane for wrongly picturing his redevelopment proposal as an assault on the North End. Not so, he said; the proposal actually took in a much wider swath of Boston. Then he turned personal. The evening before, he'd ventured into the West Village himself and found it not at all the urban paradise Jane had portrayed. He saw few "eyes on the street," most stores closed by 8 p.m., paper littering the street, buildings ugly and unkempt. If you wanted a model for the next urban America, this wasn't it.

But she'd not picked the Village as a model, or as anything exceptional at all, Jane shot back, but rather "because it was a good average area of no outstanding quality" that happened to embody her values of diversity and urbanity. That it was *not* a model was just the point.

Valid riposte or not, notable now was that a few months after publication of *Death and Life,* Jane was not just firing arrows but was the target of them. Her "ballet of Hudson Street" was on its way to becoming a classic, yes—but now she could be fairly labeled, as she in fact was by one reviewer, "the enchanted ballerina of Hudson Street, with a chip on her shoulder." Thrust into the larger world, she would have to live with the attention, misunderstanding, and hostility public figures face. Some critics made fun of her for loving Greenwich Village too much. Some leveled heavy, thoughtful intellectual artillery at her. Some took easy potshots. Some twisted her ideas out of shape. Some faulted her for being too dramatic or categorical. Some allowed that in *Death and Life* she'd made something fine and good, only to fault her for not making it finer and better.

Early in 1962, Jane was on the road, visiting Pittsburgh, Miami, and Milwaukee, touring neighborhoods, giving interviews, batting out *bons mots,* recounting experiences she'd had with the host city while researching her book—and sometimes, as in Pittsburgh, getting into trouble with the hometown faithful.

In late January, press releases announced Jane's forthcoming arrival in Pittsburgh for a week of lectures and tours beginning in mid-February. She was to speak at luncheons, talk to students, sign copies of her book. "An invigorating week was anticipated," community organizer James V. Cunningham wrote after it was over: "fresh ideas, stimulating discussion, bracing debate, constructive controversy, a shot-in-the-arm for the [city's] renaissance effort." Arriving at the airport "buoyed [and] confident," Jane "was whisked off on a tour of the city." To a medical center, to rehabbed row houses on the South Side, housing projects in the northern section of the city, neighborhood renewal projects in the East End.

And what did Pittsburgh get for its hospitality? Well, reported Cunningham, "many a sniff and snort." Middle-income apartments known as Spring Hill Gardens, the product of an earnest effort to integrate an all-white neighborhood, were, said Jane, "disorganized, as bad as can be, a highly suburban box development." The Northview Heights public housing project was "bleak, miserable, and mean." Another neighborhood plan she'd seen was "homogenized, dull, unimaginative," certain to do nothing for the community but lead it downhill.

These opinions did not unfailingly please her hosts. "The lady is unenlightened," a Spring Hill Gardens resident was quoted as saying. "Why didn't she come inside and see our attractive homes?" A local citizens' renewal council came away "stunned, confused, and angry" at Jane's charges. In an open letter to her in *The Pittsburgh Press*, the city housing administrator gave Jane a little of her own medicine. "You must have heard of the old adage that a half-truth is similar to a half-brick, because it can be hurled further." Well, Jane's book—he called it "a novel"—proved the point. Mrs. Jacobs called Northview Heights bleak? Well, of course—they hadn't even landscaped it yet! She should return once they were finished, when pretty walks would "lead from home to home through lovely resident-maintained lawns and gardens, under shady trees, to pleasant playlots and community recreation rooms." Besides, compared to "the crowded, narrow, dangerous, dirty, rodent- and bar-infested streets in Downtown New York—and the Greenwich Village area in particular, which you call more ideal—Northview Heights, to many thoughtful citizens, would seem a veritable paradise." Jane didn't *get* the social costs of disease, poverty, and crime—and never would "by star-gazing from the second floor window of a Greenwich Village flat."

The lectures she gave that week in Pittsburgh didn't earn huzzahs, either. After one, "The Citizen in Urban Renewal: Participation or Manipulation," the lobby bubbled over with disgruntled listeners. Sure, as Mrs. Jacobs said, you shouldn't allow yourself to be manipulated by the city or anyone else. But that was a little thin. People wanted specifics. And two ex-Chicagoans were there to point out that the packinghouse neighborhoods in Chicago that Jane extolled were known to exclude black people.

At lunch the next day, Jane backtracked, said she'd been misquoted about one neighborhood she'd brushed off. Maybe, she was asked, the neighborhood should hire an independent planning consultant? No, she replied, there wasn't a decent planner in the whole country. They all got "the same bad training."

Well, said a Pittsburgh urban renewal leader once Jane was back in New York, local bookstores having sold out of her book, "it wasn't a clean fight, but she made 'em mad and she made 'em think."

In time, a new round of reviews of *Death and Life* began coming out, not from newspapers now but from professional journals, including those of planners and architects. Some were buoyant: "I am filled with delighted admiration for her skill and courage," wrote Eugene Raskin, professor of architecture at Columbia University. "The appearance of her book should be the occasion for the only urban function she fails to mention—dancing in the streets." Some reviews, though, were downright wicked in a way I suspect Jane, were she not their target, might have appreciated. A reviewer for *American City* made Jane's enthusiasm for Boston's North End sound silly: "Here, apparently, is the full flowering of the American Way of Life," where European tourists could come to learn about American democracy. "Let [Soviet premier Nikita] Khrushchev see the North End and he would immediately stop that nonsense that communism will bury us." He also mocked a scene in *Death and Life* where a child falls through a glass storefront, severing an artery, but is rescued by concerned Villagers. For Jane, this was "eyes-on-the-street" in action. For the reviewer it was about that "mysterious, unidentified stranger [who] emerges from the circle of peering eyes" to save the child, then disappear.

"What a dear, sweet character she isn't," Roger Starr once said of Jane. When *Death and Life* came out, this outspoken future New York City housing commissioner and editorial writer for *The New York Times*, whose views placed him squarely in the Robert Moses camp, reviewed it for a planning newsletter. He began with his own boyhood memories of an early Hollywood star named Grace Moore. Her films, as Starr remembered them, were set in idealized cities "noted for the quaintness and charm of their older buildings and for the absence of dirt, poverty, noxious fumes, and political or racial turmoil." He'd long forgotten this Mooritania, as he called it, until he read *Death and Life*. "Jane Jacobs, I discovered, lives there. In her part of Mooritania, people dance instead of sing . . . but she describes her folksy urban place on Hudson Street (Manhattan) with such spirit and womanly verve that she has made a considerable number of readers believe it really exists." How, in Jane's vision, he asked more seriously, could we "find our way back" to Mooritania? "We must forswear any serious interest in sunlight, clear air, quiet streets, open space, and give obeisance to the good fairies by bending the knee to no other gods before diversity, noise, and crowding."

Jane was getting beaten up. But fair is fair: her book's vivid colors made it memorable, but also easy to lampoon.

Just as Jane was finishing the book, in December 1960, Jason Epstein had written her that Lewis Mumford's *The City in History* was in galleys; "your book and his, when they are both published, will approach each other like two Japanese wrestlers." Mumford won the first round; his book beat out *Death and Life*, also nominated, for the National Book Award. That, however, wasn't the end of their bout.

Since hearing Jane at Harvard, Mumford had been one of her most influential admirers, helping to get her taken seriously by those who mattered, including the Rockefeller Foundation. But five years later, toward the end of 1961, when he finally read the book he'd helped into the world, he was livid. She had called his *The Culture of Cities* "a morbid and biased catalog of [urban] ills. The great city was Megalopolis, Tyrannopolis, Nekropolis, a monstrosity, a tyranny, a living death. It must go." Mumford, said Jane, was so far gone as to see well-off people who chose to live in high-density urban enclaves as inhabiting slums, but "too insensitive to know it or resent it." The very afternoon he finished reading *Death and Life*, Mumford began composing a rebuttal. But then months passed, nothing yet appearing in print. "I held my fire . . . for a whole year," he wrote a friend, "but when I got down to write I discovered that the paper burned." He felt, wrote Donald L. Miller, Mumford's biographer, that Jane "had gone at him with hate in her heart."

Finally, Mumford let loose. He'd hoped to take three long articles to mount his attack, but his editors at *The New Yorker* prevailed on him to limit it to one and tone it down a bit. *Tone it down?* "Mother Jacobs' Home Remedies for Urban Cancer" began on page 148 of the December 1, 1962, issue, amid Christmas-season ads for panettone and gin, went on for page after page, columns of text flanked by ads all through the fullness of the magazine, for eight thousand words; read it out loud and you'd be at it for an hour.

Lewis Mumford, at first Jane's enthusiastic champion, later her vituperative critic

Mumford started out reasonably enough. He offered some history, told of Jane's emergence at Harvard, gave her her due. Then he reached the book itself: "From a mind so big with fresh insights and pertinent ideas, one naturally expected a book of equally large dimensions." And yes, Jane Jacobs, that "shrewd critic of dehumanized housing and faulty design," was still there. But joining her now was "a more dubious character who has patched together out of the bits and pieces of her personal observation nothing less than a universal theory" of big cities. Much of it rested on "faulty data, inadequate evidence, and startling miscomprehensions of views contrary to hers."

She sentimentally overvalued Greenwich Village. She overlooked the endless square miles of nearly identical houses spread across New York's outer boroughs that lacked the diversity she valued in the Village. How to credit her ideas when they were contradicted at every turn? A single walk through Harlem ought to have been enough to correct her pet notions, since most of her urban ideals were fulfilled there. The same went for eighteenth-century London, which likewise satisfied them yet was a "nest of violence and delinquency."

Mumford, who wore his city roots proudly—"like a chestful of combat ribbons," writes his biographer—was infuriated that Jacobs dared try to wrest from him the more-urban-than-thou mantle. "I speak as a born and bred New Yorker," Mumford wrote. He'd lived in all sorts of neighborhoods and all sorts of housing, which he proceeded to list, right there in the review, down to a "two-room flat over a lunchroom" in Brooklyn Heights, "with the odor of stale fat filtering through the windows." No, he hadn't much liked that, though the area had laundries, florists, and groceries enough to qualify for the Jacobsean urban pantheon.

For most of the decade before 1936, Mumford had lived in an out-of-the-way corner of New York City known as Sunnyside Gardens, in Queens. This was a community of starkly simple two- and three-story row houses, set off from the surrounding street grid, reached by greenery-lined walkways, making for a superblock all its own. While different in detail, it couldn't help but remind you, even down to its name, of all the suburban garden apartment developments that would come later—leafy, graceless, and squat. At the time, though, it made for an ambitious experiment, a piece of Garden City in the spirit of Ebenezer Howard just a subway ride from Manhattan. It was Jane's portrayal of the Garden City movement—crude, distorted, and almost comical, in Mumford's view—that was one reason her book incensed him so. Now, in *The New Yorker*, he noted his time in Sunnyside Gardens. It was "not utopia," he allowed, "but better than any existing New York neighborhood, even Mrs. Jacobs' backwater in Greenwich Village."

In her distaste for planned communities like Sunnyside, it seemed to him, Jane abhorred any wisp of order. No wonder she opposed those gifted pioneer planners, Clarence Stein and Henry Wright, who bestowed on Sunnyside its harmonious homogeneity. In holding up diversity and dynamism as supreme good her thinking was sadly myopic.

> Her simple formula does not suggest that her eyes have ever been hurt by ugliness, sordor, confusion, or her ears offended by the roar of trucks smashing through a once quiet residential neighborhood, or her nose assaulted by the chronic odors of ill-ventilated, unsunned housing.

Jane Jacobs simply couldn't see the ecological disaster the modern city had become. And that was "something worse than oversight," Mumford declared; "it is willful blindness."

When his review appeared, an acquaintance at *The New Yorker* reassured Jane, "Your book seems to have driven Mumford into schizophrenia—Father Mum's Sweet and Sour Pickles. I haven't checked his critique with your book but my impression is that I'm on your side more than his." How did Jane herself feel when she saw Mumford's piece? Years later, any wounds having had a chance to scar over, she told one interviewer, "I laughed at a lot of it. I have a fairly thick skin." Jane knew her book "would make people angry, perhaps especially Mumford," says Jim Jacobs. "I remember her saying so, with regret, before it was published. She certainly didn't want to offend, but . . . she was realistic enough to expect tirades."

"Mumford was quite a sexist," Jane would tell another interviewer. "He talked about my 'schoolgirl silliness,' and I was in my 40s!" Two decades her senior, Mumford did bear the baggage of his generation. But dip into the writings of the two of them and they are not, always and automatically, far apart. Neither had much use for Robert Moses, for example. Both realized how much cars harmed city life. And after all, wasn't it what Mumford had heard straight from Jane herself at Harvard, and later at the New School, that had first won him to her side? "When two people are so close together in their thinking, and so eager for influence," observes Mumford's biographer, they're apt to "magnify their differences to the point of outright caricature." They were alike in another way, too. They had both come up as writers first. Both brought to their language a distinct rhetorical stamp. Both threw verbal brickbats, and aimed well.

Among Jane's intellectual antagonists, Herb Gans was different. He was a perfectly capable writer but a sociologist by trade, people and community his concern, and his review in *Commentary* in February 1962 raised a whole other range of objections to Jane's book. "I'm not sure whether you'll like the review," he wrote Jane on January 19, with an advance copy of it, "I'd be surprised if you did—but I hope you will think it a fair one, which I have tried to make it. I agree with many of your observations, but not with your explanations—because you have not considered the sociological factors."

Gans, recall, was the University of Chicago–educated sociologist, eleven years younger than Jane, who'd gone into Boston's West End to record its final days. He had reached some conclusions similar to hers, especially that working-class neighborhoods that looked a little ragtag were not necessarily slums. Jane had quoted from his work, appreciatively so. Gans was sure her book would be influential, he wrote her, and got his editor to assign him twice the usual space to review it.

In notes Gans took while reading it, he got to the heart of *Death and Life:* "What is lively is what is good . . . If it is alive, it is working." Here was Jane's bedrock belief. Vitality and diversity trumped everything else. Of course, Gans knew, not everyone felt that way. Other satisfactions counted, too—harmony, natural beauty, order, quiet family life, for just a few—and these, Gans all but said, didn't figure for much in Jane's universe. "No child of enterprise or spirit will willingly stay in such a boring place after he reaches the age of six," Jane wrote of Garden City–style developments in Pittsburgh, Los Angeles, New York, and Baltimore that she deemed wanting. There was no room in her city, it could seem, for those lacking the personal qualities she prized.

Just such blind spots, or narrowness of vision, were what most troubled Jane's critics. "She doesn't accept the existence or desirability of other styles of urbanity as well as her own and, therefore, falls into the same pattern of single-minded thinking that she loves to condemn," noted one review in the *Journal of the American Institute of Planners*.

Another, in the same issue, pictured Jane as scarcely able to believe that "anyone would choose a life style different from the one she has chosen. She imposes her tastes and values on the city more narrowly than any planner would dare to do." Her views of parks, for example, were hopelessly narrow. Why didn't she "risk a trip" in Fairmount Park in Philadelphia, along the Wissahickon Creek valley, and meet "people of all ages getting away from watchful eyes in the city. She would see children exploring the trails above the creek or feeding the swans."

Catherine Bauer Wurster, among those supporting Jane's Rockefeller grant, called *Death and Life* "a brilliant personal diatribe," perceptive and illuminating "within her narrow range of concern." But—and it was a big *but*—she "simply disregards the entire gamut of middle class values related to home and family life."

Kevin Lynch, whom Jane had quoted admiringly in *Death and Life*, called hers "a brilliant and distorted book," one holding out for "a very restricted kind of urban environment." And, he went on, it "assumes that buildings and streets have a very singular power to change people's lives."

This point would recur in objections to *Death and Life*. After a *Saturday Evening Post* excerpt from the book appeared in October 1961, the Boston planner Donald M. Graham suggested that Jane was forever "mixing apples with battleships, confusing the social environment with the physical environment." They were *two different things*. Ironically, Jane had made a similar point in *Death and Life:* "There is no direct, simple relationship between good housing and good behavior." Good shelter was good, period; you didn't need to justify it on the grounds "that it will work social or family miracles"—a self-deception someone had called "salvation by bricks."

But it was just such self-deception that Herb Gans saw in her book now, too. *Death and Life* was grounded, he wrote, in three assumptions: that people want diversity; that diversity makes cities live and the lack of it makes them die; and that buildings, streets, and the like shape human behavior. "The last assumption . . . might be called the physical fallacy, and it leads [Jacobs] to ignore the social, cultural, and economic factors that contribute to vitality or dullness," blinding her to the deeper roots of urban problems.

The vibrant street life of some neighborhoods "stems not so much from their physical character as from the working-class culture of their inhabitants." Gans was speaking of Boston's North End, and of Italian and Irish sections of Greenwich Village. In such districts, "the home is reserved for the family," with much social life taking place outdoors. Also, children were less kept home, and less closely supervised in their play generally, than middle-class kids, and so naturally more apt to be out on the street. Throw in a few café-haunting artists and bohemians, pepper the mix with tourists, and you were on your way toward the "highly visible kind of vitality" Jane celebrated. But it grew out of how particular people lived, not population density and the other factors Jane highlighted. Then, too, wasn't "vitality" itself really in the eye of the beholder? Some neighborhoods might *look* less vital to a visitor but be quite as vital to those who lived in them. Here, in any case, were some of "the sociological factors" Gans felt that Jane had missed.

A few days after Gans sent her a copy of the coming review, Jane wrote him a note decrying what she called its "old-hat stereotypes . . . about ethnic behavior and city life," insisting that she'd carefully weighed the points he claimed she'd ignored. She thanked him anyway, for granting so much attention to her book, but apparently still came away wounded; Gans would report that "she broke off relations" with him for a time. After Jane died, Gans would suggest that as a middle-class resident of the largely working-class West Village, Jane romanticized it, coming away "blinded . . . to the economic insecurity and the resulting personal and social problems that some of her Hudson Street neighbors" experienced. An "innocent" from Scranton, Jane "missed the dark sides of life below the middle income."

Ellen Lurie, the young social worker who'd studied George Washington Houses for Union Settlement, and from whose work Jane drew, didn't miss them. Some of her project residents, she'd reported, had been relocated from their homes in the old neighborhood, some moved from other projects. Still others were "volunteers," who'd applied for a place there, like Mr. and Mrs. McLean and their two small children. He worked as a presser in a clothing factory. They had friends on the floor with whom they visited, played poker, watched TV. For George Washington Houses, all in all, theirs ranked as a success story.

Then there were the Larkins, who'd lived in East Harlem all their lives, grown up with Negroes, Chinese, Jews, Germans, and Irish, but whose home at 101st Street and Third Avenue had been torn down four years before. They'd been moved temporarily to another project and now found themselves at Washington Houses, mostly with Puerto Ricans and blacks for neighbors. Their kids were constantly fighting. The project was no place for them.

Among blacks who had moved from a middle-income Harlem project, the Wilsons liked their old neighborhood better. The stores were more convenient, the people seemed more intelligent. Their new neighbors, black and Puerto Rican alike, struck them as somehow lower class. The Wilsons were itching to get out as soon as possible.

And Mrs. Acosta? Why, she loved George Washington Houses. Her husband played basketball at the local community center. They had lots of friends in the neighborhood. In Lurie's words, she "wants to live here always."

After reading *Death and Life*, accounts like these somehow *jar*. Not for the facts they represent, or for any arguments they might bolster or undermine. It's just that you don't find much close attention to real people in Jane's book. One can admire how Jane draws important truths from Lurie's study; the trains of logic are there, certainly. But, viewed through a less obliging lens, it isn't hard to see the ordinary people of East Harlem as less interesting to her than the insights she extracts from their lives.

Just weeks before she submitted the final manuscript, Epstein had written to her with "a question to put before your argument: Negroes. Nat, I know, has asked you to comment on ethnic groups in general and I hope you will, but I think it's urgent that you include, perhaps in an appendix, the Negro question, since so much of your argument depends on a solution to it." Epstein's reasoning was plain enough: some of the most atrocious slums were those of African Americans who'd emigrated up from the Jim Crow South. Surely a book presuming to address the problems of cities needed to address the especially urgent problems of black people in cities. Epstein appreciated that this would "take you out-side your argument somewhat," but still . . .

Jane wrote back after Christmas saying that from the time she'd started her project, she'd thought about the issue; but no, it was "a poor idea for my book." She had reasons for this, but couldn't just then, in the throes of completing the manuscript, take time to explain. "In the meantime," she added, "do not cherish a hope that I will change my mind because I am very convinced and firm about this." He might, she suggested, want to talk to Ellen Lurie, who was thinking about writing a book about East Harlem.

The next day—he'd probably not yet received her letter—Epstein wrote Jane once more. He "was more firmly convinced than ever that the Negro question must be one of the main obstacles to your propos-als." Certainly she needed to acknowledge it. "I don't think that you can proceed as though the question didn't exist." A month later, Nat Glazer wrote her, mostly on another matter, but noting, "Jason is very worried about the fact you don't talk about Negroes. I am convinced the character and background of the social groups making up a city contribute as much to the things you are interested in as any physical factors"—there it was, again, the physical fallacy—"and consequently I feel Jason has a point." But maybe by then Glazer had figured that he and Epstein had lost the battle, for he added, "On the other hand, you can't do everything."

In a chapter on "Unslumming and Slumming," Jane wrote that "the discrimination which operates most drastically today is, of course, dis-crimination against Negroes. But it is an injustice with which all our major slum populations have had to contend to some degree." And that was about it, so far as Epstein's Negro question was concerned. She was not about to be waylaid by what seemed to her a distraction from the book's main line of argument. People occupying unique social and cul-tural niches—well, they were simply not her subject.

Here, then, was what much criticism of *Death and Life* came down to: that what Jane focused on was brilliant; but that she was sometimes *missing* something, her focus too narrow; that the very blinders needed to avoid distraction by the inconsequential or irrelevant left her blind to other truths. Jane, in short, didn't see what she didn't see. And what she didn't see, at least not with the same urgency others did, was the trou-bling impact on cities of race, class, and ethnicity.

·   ·   ·

A persistent feature of the critical response to *Death and Life* was a peculiar doubleness—voluble praise and severe misgivings set close, side by side, and hard to tease apart, like those ghost images seen on old TV sets. Think not of blandly "mixed reviews," good and bad blended into a gray soup. No, more typically you'd have a reviewer busily pointing out the book's failings—yet who, as if he couldn't quite help it, or as if he'd be dishonest with himself not to acknowledge it, felt moved to comment on its passion, insight, and intelligence. A generally negative review in *The Yale Law Journal* castigated *Death and Life* for all manner of sins, yet concluded that Jane had "touched some sensitive chords and her point of view cannot be sloughed off." A reviewer for the *Antioch Review* lamented Jane's "inept introspective scholarship," yet admitted that the book "proves one thing: Mrs. Jacobs has within her the capacity to produce a very great book, a very important book"; for him, *Death and Life* wasn't it—yet *Death and Life* itself had made him think so! A reviewer for the *Journal of the American Institute of Planners* observed that in Jane's analysis of Philadelphia's rejuvenated Rittenhouse Square she "conveniently overlooks the massive dislocation of low-income Negroes by high-income whites." Yet he anointed *Death and Life* as "a challenge to complacency and smugness," to "every formula and slogan of city building." Herbert Gans's critiques embodied this doubleness, too. A *Commentary* reader marveled at his "remarkable appraisal" of Jane's book—in which, having asserted that her assumptions were wrong and broadly faulting them, he could still call the work a "path-breaking achievement."

The world had reached no settled verdict on Jane's book; it represented too sharp a break with the past. But unlike most books published in 1961, or any year, it was not going to be forgotten.

CHAPTER 15

WEST VILLAGE WARRIOR

I. STREET FIGHTER

In 1963, two years after publication of *The Death and Life of Great American Cities*, Jane Kramer wrote about Jane Jacobs in *The Village Voice*:

> People who have seen her in action at the Board of Estimate or down on Broome Street rarely forget that clomping, sandaled stride and that straight gray hair flying every which way around a sharp, quizzical face. And she can magnetize a populace into action as well as any of her archetypes . . . She has turned her causes into hot-potato issues, and is lately the terror of every politico in town. She has mustered public support and sympathy to the extent that now even the mayor bends to a Jacobs decree or completely loses face.

If we didn't know any better and recalled her only as a writer, Kramer's account of Jane Jacobs as public figure might seem unrecognizable. But since 1955, Jane had drifted into new work for which she would become as well known as for her books. It wasn't paying work. It was not of her choosing. But, despite herself, she had become a community activist. So significant were the string of battles in which she played a major hand, and so effective was she at leading them, that together they make for an alternative portrait of her, like a photo snapped from a surprising angle, that complements, or even competes with, that formed by her life as a writer.

What did Jane do? She helped ensure that today children splash in the fountain at Washington Square Park untroubled by the roar of traffic; that the broad sidewalks around her house were not ignominiously narrowed; that the West Village avoided the heavy hand of urban renewal. She addressed some of the neighborhood's housing problems through a project architecturally more at home in the nineteenth century than the twentieth and helped actually get it built. And she blocked an enormous expressway that would have all but sliced off the tip of Lower Manhattan and changed the face of the city forever and for the worse. Probably only the last of these civic battles would figure in any general history of New York City. The others, to anyone who didn't live in the Village, might today seem trifling or remote; we live here and now, not there and then. But it was just Jane's fierce focus on the intimate, the nearby, and the small that was her most lasting contribution to the culture of civic activism: not just the Big Picture counted, but *your* street, *your* house. In each of these confrontations with civic authority, powerful public figures failed to get what they wanted; their aims were thwarted, their say-so challenged,. Tides of traffic, demolition, and faceless new construction *didn't* (back then) wash over Greenwich Village. And because they didn't, the species of urban life Jane Jacobs championed was better preserved.

It might seem self-evident that the aims of her activism were of a piece with what she preached in *Death and Life*. For example, she had illuminated the abuses of urban renewal and the ravaging of old neighborhoods in East Harlem; what, then, could be more natural than to oppose the same malignant forces in the West Village? Moreover, her exploits on the civic front lines exhibit the same orneriness, the same sweet outlaw streak, that runs through *Death and Life*. We discover in Jane, as activist, scant dissonance between actions and ideas. We find little to parse or rationalize away.

True enough, yet not wholly true.

For in fighting city hall, Jane was confronted with new, quite different parts of herself with which, at first, she could not have been entirely familiar or comfortable. Jane the scrappy street fighter—sitting through public meetings of mind-numbing tedium, head resting in hands, looking out through her black-framed glasses, rising to make public statements, launching into vituperative debate, working through friends and enemies alike, making backroom deals—needed different skills than did Jane the writer. Dispatching your children onto the streets to gather signatures required quite a different mental stance than blue-penciling a recalcitrant paragraph.

To her friends from those West Village years of the 1950s and 1960s, she was master strategist, the brains, wit, and spirit behind their most inspired victories. But some, like Claire Tankel, who, with her husband, Stanley, worked with Jane in those days, could recall her as needlessly abrasive. One time, a press release they'd drafted came out too long. Jane hectored Tankel's husband about it, almost reducing him to tears: "If you write a press release you've got to do it this way, this way, and this way. You didn't write it right." Tankel was not alone to remember her like this. Jane could irritate and annoy, though mostly it was her foes who bore the brunt of it. Later, Jane would be asked whether the civic activism that occupied her during those years came naturally to her. No, she replied. "I wanted to be learning things and writing. I resented that I had to stop and devote myself to fighting what was basically an absurdity that had been foisted on me and my neighbours."

II. MR. AND MRS. MACHIAVELLI

As a child growing up in the Village, the author Roberta Brandes Gratz remembers Washington Square Park as "the focus of every activity from regular chess games to political speeches to guitar fests around the steps of 'the circle,' a massive fountain with spacious steps useful for seating. My grandfather and his cronies met on a park bench. My contemporaries met in the playground."

Beginning in 1952, this urban oasis was threatened by a scheme to funnel the traffic coming down Fifth Avenue from the north through the park in a wide sweeping arc to West Broadway (today's La Guardia Place) at the south end. A Chicago-born actress and mother of four named Shirley Hayes was the first, most adamant force against the park roadway. In 1955, as we've seen, Jane did her bit, in a letter to city officials protesting it.

In 1958, the threat remained and Villagers came together in the Joint Emergency Committee to Close Washington Square to Traffic. That, Jane would acknowledge, might seem "to outsiders like a cumbersome kind of name . . . Why couldn't you have something catchier?" But it was just this targeted specificity that defined their strategy. The park was their *sole* concern. They had no interest in uniting the fractious political views in the Village under one banner; that would have been impossible anyway. They had but one sharply defined object.

In Jane's telling, the winning strategy for this last battle of a long civic war emerged one night when she and Bob were in bed. She'd fallen off to sleep. But Bob was still up, troubled by the endless park imbroglio. When, abruptly, he hit upon it, he woke her up to tell about it, and it wasn't pretty. These were the days of tightly controlled machine politics, and Bill Passannante, a protégé of the patronage- and favor-dispensing Tammany political machine of Carmine DeSapio, was up for reelection as assemblyman. DeSapio, who lived in the Village, was "the personification of a boss, you know, the backroom boss," Norman Redlich, one of Jane's allies, would remember. "Whatever he told you he would do, he would do." And he could do pretty much as he pleased, by simply picking up the phone. Passannante's challenger was Whitney North Seymour Jr., a white knight in the Jacobs circle, who'd favored closing the park to traffic all along and who, as Jane would admit, "had every reason to expect" their support in the upcoming election. He wouldn't get it. He'd never get it. Because "he was not in power. The people who were in power were DeSapio's machine." Whatever Seymour's virtues, Bob's Machiavellian scheme sacrificed him to their larger aim.

As Jane told the story, they went to DeSapio, saying, *If anyone can get the park closed to traffic, you can.* "We expect you do it, and if you don't do it we're going to consider you rascals and throw you out," by coming out for Seymour and working for him. To demonstrate their muscle, the mothers' group put together an almost instant rally. Overnight, posters went up around the neighborhood. Inexplicably, many of them appeared on walls, lampposts, and storefronts just a little lower, closer to the ground, than you might expect. It seems that Jane's and other neighborhood children, armed with paste pots, had been enlisted to put them up. "We had all these little elves," Jane said later, smiling at the memory, "all these kids putting the posters up." And collecting signatures, too—some 35,000 of them. It was a performance whose significance was not lost on DeSapio—who, as a *New York Times* obituary of Hayes would put it, simply "passed the word that he wanted them out," meaning the cars.

Seymour was outraged. But DeSapio, sworn the support of the mothers' group in the election, and set to be hailed as their hero, was as good as his word; the stanchions went up and the park was cut off to cars and buses. The traffic jams ominously predicted by the city failed to materialize. The experiment was pronounced a success, and the park was liberated; it has remained so to this day. On June 26, 1958, the *Daily Mirror* immortalized one early success in the struggle with a photo of Jane's daughter—three-year-old Mary, round-faced, blond-tressed, and adorable—with another child holding aloft a ceremonial ribbon; the moment merited not a ribbon-cutting ceremony but, as a symbolic bar to traffic, a ribbon-*tying* ceremony.

"Rather tough political pressure," Jane would term their successful strategy, her language veering uncharacteristically toward euphemism. But, as she'd frame it at another time, "[w]hat we were inventing was issue-oriented politics," focused not on individuals or parties, but on the daily life of one's community.

Behind the threat to Washington Square Park, of course, was Robert Moses, the city's master builder, who had pushed plans for moving traffic through the Village since the 1930s. Moses erected housing projects, spanned rivers with tunnels and bridges, built expressways, created public beaches, threw up world's fairs. He seemed to care little how he did it, nor worry much about the tens of thousands of people dis-

Robert Moses

placed by his urban pawn-pushing. In an article for *Architectural Forum* in 1942, ten years before Jane Jacobs joined its staff, Moses wrote a long, admiring article about Baron Georges-Eugène Haussmann, the fabled late-nineteenth-century planner of Paris. "All new work," he quoted Haussmann's retort to his critics, "makes an unfavorable impression because it is a change that upsets settled ways of life. But this first impression is fleeting; it soon gives way to a juster and more generous appreciation." The article was profusely illustrated with maps, drawings, and photographs of Paris, many of them tellingly paired with promenades and parkways Moses had pushed through New York.

Moses was never mayor, never governor, never held elected office, but wielded power through banal-sounding positions like parks commissioner and chair of the mayor's anti-slum committee. Behind the scenes, however, he had his hands on everything. He blustered and bludgeoned. He delighted in putting his opponents in their place; he referred to one group of them as "partisans, enthusiasts, crackpots, fanatics, or other horned cattle." He was a bully; what other word could you use? Jane would say years later that Moses "did more harm to New York City than any other hundred men you can imagine put together. One of his favorite sayings was, 'You cannot make an omelet without breaking eggs,' and the omelet was the common good, and the eggs were the people who were broken." Viewed more charitably, Moses got things done; he was *effective*—if by now, during his late sixties and early seventies, when he clashed with Citizen Jane and her friends, less so. His defeat at Washington Square would come to be seen as a mark of his slackening power.

That battle, and his subsequent rout at the hands of Jane and her allies over the Lower Manhattan Expressway, would leave the two of them, in the minds of many, indissolubly linked—as they are in the titles of at least two recent books—Anthony Flint's *Wrestling with Moses: How Jane Jacobs Took on New York's Master Builder and Transformed the American City*; and *The Battle for Gotham: New York in the Shadow of Robert Moses and Jane Jacobs*, by Roberta Brandes Gratz. In fact, Jane may have met Moses only once, at a meeting of the city's board of estimate. "There is nobody against this," Jane has Moses bellowing, incredulous at the defeat of his park roadway, "NOBODY, NOBODY, NOBODY, but a bunch of, a bunch of MOTHERS!"—whereupon he stomped out. But if face-to-face encounters between the two of them were few, their pairing does seem inevitable and apt: two memorable figures, tied to diametrically opposing visions of New York. Moses, the man of plans, maps, and models, the reshuffling of whole urban landscapes, the destruction of neighborhoods, wielder of the marionette strings of power; Jane Jacobs, all by herself in her writing studio, lured onto the urban battlefield only by existential challenges to her home, protective of her streets and sidewalks against the dark forces of unbridled power.

Grist for an opera? At this writing, there's one in the making.

III. SAVE OUR SIDEWALKS

One evening in 1960 while Jane was putting him to bed, son Jimmy said to her: *We're going to lose our tree.* He meant the tree the family had planted on Hudson Street in front of their house in 1956, almost the only one on the block. No, said Jane, the tree was doing fine, no need to worry. *Yes, there is,* insisted Jimmy. "They're going to cut off our sidewalks and the tree is on that part of it."

Coming home from school, Jimmy had seen men marking up the sidewalk in paint and chalk. He had gone up to them and asked about their work. Jane had seen them, too, but couldn't get a straight answer about what they were up to: *Oh, just a routine survey.* But, as Jane proudly noted when she told the story later, eleven-year-old Jimmy was *really* interested in what they were doing. "And they saw that and told him—showed him—this brave, inquiring little boy, how surveying was done." Along the way, of course, they spilled the beans: the plan, courtesy of the Manhattan borough president's office, was to lop off five-foot strips of sidewalk on both sides of Hudson Street, to create another lane for cars.

In 1960, as now, "the sidewalks of New York" of the old song were nothing like the skinny cement strips of most suburban subdivisions, with barely enough room for a single pedestrian, much less an amiably chattering group of friends. In *Death and Life*, as we have seen, Jane gave over three chapters to the "uses of sidewalks" in all their variety. The last of them, devoted to "assimilating children," offered a typology of sidewalks by width: thirty-foot sidewalks could "accommodate virtually any demand of incidental play put upon them"; twenty-footers, like those on Hudson Street, precluded rope jumping but left room for almost anything else. To Jane, sidewalks were the very basis of city life.

And now, as "part of a mindless, routinized city program of vehicular road widening," as she'd describe it in *Death and Life*, the city wanted to emasculate theirs.

Next morning, Jane wrote a petition and, children in tow, marched off to the local printer to have it run off. Forget it, the printer told her; he had too many restaurant menus to set in type and print up; it would be weeks before he could get to it. "That'll be too late," said Jane, the sidewalks would be gone by then. "Which sidewalks?" he said; of course, they included the one right outside his store. An hour later Jane had her petitions. Jimmy began taking them around. Ned and little Mary, bundled up in hats and hoods and heavy coats, gathered signatures in front of the house. They sat at a little table, under a sign tacked to the front door that looked like this:

SAVE

THE

SIDEWALKS

ON HUDSON STREET

Local parochial schools sent petitions home with their children. Jane approached influential Village figures she'd met in the park fight, especially the well-connected Tony Dapolito, a baker by trade, who'd go down in Village lore as its honorary mayor. Jane was among a delegation that made their plea before the borough president, but, Dapolito told Bob Jacobs later, the outcome had been decided before they went in to see him. The sidewalk-snipping scheme was stopped in its tracks.

Early on, Jane would recall, some of her neighbors had concluded that, petitions and signatures notwithstanding, they'd lose: "You can't fight city hall." But the realization that they *could* fight city hall, and win, would serve them well next time around.

IV. NIBBLED TO DEATH BY DUCKS

In February 1961, a month after submitting the manuscript for *Death and Life*, Jane opened the newspaper to learn that part of the West Village had been named an urban renewal area. Its slums were coming down, *The New York Times* declared. New housing was going up. "I knew at once what that meant," Jane would recount—"that we were going to be designated to be wiped out." The designated fourteen-block stretch ran from Hudson Street to the Hudson River. It included her own block. It included her own house. Any sweet, peaceful interlude she might have anticipated for the months leading to her book's publication was abruptly cut short.

The stakes were much bigger than a few stunted sidewalks; yet this early in the story it all seemed to come down to $300,000. This was the amount, according to the city's housing and redevelopment board, successor to Robert Moses's slum clearance board, that would go into a planning study for West Village urban renewal. Even back in 1961, $300,000 wasn't that much. But to Jane, this little pot of money was just the first step toward bulldozing her neighborhood into anonymity, unaffordability, or both. This "advance of planning funds," which the board of estimate had formally to request from the feds, would set in motion events Jane had seen play out time and again, signaling that urban renewal, in all its malignancy, was on the way: amid the uncertainty, businesses pull back on their investments; landlords stop maintaining their properties; residents move out. The result? A downward spiral of deterioration that accelerates neighborhood decline. Just before the announcement in the paper, a woman named Elizabeth Squire was offered $50,000 for her house; a few days later, after the announcement, but before she'd thought to accept it, the offer was rescinded. Let that pot of planning-study money go through, Jane was certain, and such painful stories would recur daily.

So Jane got on the phone.

The battle would play out over almost a year. Jane's days and those of her friends grew thick with calls to make, letters to solicit or write, hearings to attend, legal papers to file, presentations to prepare, petitions to draw up, rallies to organize, church basement penny sales to orchestrate, puppet "citizens' committees" to expose. The fight became so frenetic, Jane would report, "that we just disconnected the doorbell and left the door open at night so we could work and people could come and go." These were the days of the fabled West Village Martini, gin and a few drops of vermouth in any handy glass, an olive or a pickled onion, an ice cube, and then, by Jane's recipe, "you put your finger in it, and go swish, swish, swish"; no time for niceties. The battle for the West Village, Jane's son Ned recalls, "totally consumed the lives of my parents and their neighbours." But in the beginning, everything happened all at once—*had* to, because the city had left only two days before a board of

This photo of a West Village strategy session, from about 1961, was taken for an article about Jane that never appeared. That's Jane's son Ned at far left.

estimate hearing intended to set the whole process in motion. When Jane and thirty of her neighbors trooped downtown to see the commissioner of housing and redevelopment, they succeeded in postponing the hearing for a month.

Three days after the postponement, on February 26, three hundred people crowded into the St. Luke's School auditorium, a few blocks from Jane's house, and set up the Committee to Save the West Village. They elected Jane, who in the wake of the sidewalk battle had something of a reputation, as one of two co-chairpersons. "The aim of the committee," Jane was quoted as saying, "is to kill this project entirely because if it goes through it can mean only the destruction of the community." She and the other Villagers were angry: the rationale for designating the West Village as suitable for urban renewal was simple—that it was a slum. And they knew it wasn't.

But what if it *was*? That is, if the West Village were really the sort of hopeless mess that federal urban renewal laws and the whole spirit of modernism had in mind to wipe clean and start over with, then tearing it down and replacing it with new housing, as the city planned to do, might be a good thing. The West Village fight can be seen as a succession of public hearings and presentations, charges and countercharges, set against a backdrop of the sheer day-to-day work of waging civic war. But in the end it came down to just what the West Village really was: A slum unworthy of life, to be put out of its misery and made into something better? Or a community to be preserved much as it was?

The facts themselves were there for anyone to see, there on the streets and in the homes of the West Village; the threatened area ran from West Eleventh Street down past Christopher to Morton Street, back from the Hudson River piers east to Washington, Greenwich, and, finally, Hudson Street. About eighteen hundred people lived in those blocks—home owners, renters, longshoremen, teachers. Thousands more from outside worked in the neighborhood's warehouses, factories, retail stores, and other small businesses. Its urban palette ranged from blackened brick and rutted concrete to cobblestone and oil-slicked asphalt. West Village houses were almost never like the iconic ones kindergarten children crayon in, with front door, windows, chimney, and lawn. Rather, they were new or gussied-up apartment buildings, firetrap tenements, the occasional frame house going back to the early nineteenth century, stunningly rehabbed row houses, and shabby single-room-occupancy hotels near the piers. There were parking lots and warehouses, St. Veronica's Church and a Western Electric research laboratory. All jumbled together within an area of less than a twentieth of a square mile. The question was, how to *see* all that.

How to see cities, of course, was what Jane's book, just then on its way to publication, was all about. Every chapter offered alternative ways to see: tottering old buildings could be sources of anarchic creativity; new housing could mean a brutal wiping-clean of old, familiar social connections; a factory near your house need not be unwholesome, but instead a nexus of economic and social renewal. And now, just as Jane's book would challenge conventional urban thinking, so did the battles of 1961 playing out in her neighborhood. Oversimplify just a bit and you could dub the yearlong drama *Death or Life: The West Village*. Jane's committee printed up index-card-sized handbills that read, simply, "SAVE THE WEST VILLAGE." Save it from what? Save it from extinction, from its transformation into the sort of place in which its residents either wouldn't be able, or wouldn't want, to live. The neighborhood was just fine the way it was.

But *no*, not true, *that* wasn't it either: Jane and her neighbors didn't see the neighborhood as just fine the way it was. They weren't blind, could hardly miss its failings, the raucous truck traffic, the decaying warehouses. Cobbled streets could sing of charm and nostalgia, but they also warbled of the worn and the decrepit. Compared to today, there were few trees, the streets were more littered and dirty, the façades of tene-

ments and industrial lofts bore scant sign of today's proud infusions of
new paint, new windows, and new money. There wasn't much money in
the West Village, hadn't been for years, and it showed. "We are 100%
for improvement and we know our neighborhood can stand some," an
early Committee to Save the West Village newsletter emphasized. They
did want to see new middle-income housing, welcomed the "opportunity
to work with officials of the city's conservation program to make our
neighborhood a still happier place to live." *Like, say, a stretch of new
park beside the river?* Other improvements would come from "building
up what we have instead of destroying the existing neighborhood. *Our*
best efforts would be aimed at saving and improving, not destroying."
They already had so much: low crime, little overcrowding, much liveliness, even an old farmhouse or two, lovingly restored, that went back
practically to colonial times.

When, in May, the department of city planning's newsletter made the
case for urban renewal, it acknowledged that the West Village included
some decent housing and showed signs of rehabilitation. But it emphasized
the "blighting influence" of an elevated New York Central freight line
spur that ran to an abandoned terminal along its west side. It bemoaned
the "indiscriminate mixture of warehousing, truck terminals, garages
and loft buildings" along Washington Street, the many tenements and
nonresidential structures that were "run down and deteriorated."

They weren't making things up. A few years later, when she moved
into an apartment at the corner of Horatio and Washington streets, a bit
north of the contested blocks, longtime Villager Patricia Fieldsteel would
remember the West Village as a

> less-than-desirable area, tucked away ... in a faraway inaccessible
> pocket bordered by the Meat Market and the shipping docks, massive
> crumbling carapaces that had leeched themselves to the Lower West
> Side, obliterating the river from view. Across the piers, from West to
> Greenwich streets, was a dank warren of small factories, meat pack-
> ers, printing plants and light industry. Enormous trucks blocked the
> streets, spewing fumes into already fetid air, blackened by free-flowing
> soot from unregulated building incinerators. There were no trees, no
> gardens, no parks.

What later became a row of fine restored townhouses along Jane Street
was then still "broken up into seven- and ten-family tenements, or

boarding houses renting out single-occupancy rooms to single, often 'wayward' men."

For the city planning department, it was the neighborhood's "mixture of land uses," including bad housing, heavy commercial traffic, and the freight line, that left the neighborhood blighted. No matter that just such a mixture—residential, commercial, and industrial all together—was what Jane said could make for a healthy, interesting, vital area. *No,* insisted the planners, it was *just that* which generated blight, all but *made* it a slum. How could a neighborhood exhibiting such a disparate mess of uses, which the planning wisdom of half a century, reaching back to Ebenezer Howard and beyond, had ordained as ill-befitting a modern city, be a good, healthy, respectable way to live? That was one essential question.

Of course, the other essential question was, *Who was to say?*

This was not long after the end of World War II, when trust in generals, government officials, scientists, and experts was not wholly unknown, before the Vietnam War sowed doubt about "the best and the brightest" and authority in general. The default position was still to trust the people who knew their technical disciplines and possessed knowledge most people didn't. But already Jane didn't buy it. She had seen the work of the planners across America and how, presumably with the best of intentions, they had done harm. Academically uncredentialed herself, with an outlaw streak going back to her school days and an abiding faith in her own vision, she and the rest of her committee were inclined *not* to trust the experts, but to see in them corruption, incuriosity, and ignorance. When, early the following year, Jane reflected on what they'd learned from the West Village war, she painted a picture of behind-the-scenes skullduggery and incompetence on the part of the authorities. No, not the vaunted "experts" but only the residents themselves could properly decide a neighborhood's future. A few weeks after the battle was joined, the columnist John Crosby wrote an essay for the *New York Herald Tribune* with the apt and challenging title "Who Says What Is a Slum?" And no, it wasn't necessarily the blinkered experts. What Crosby called "the psychological beauties of a neighborhood, where people live together in their own harmonies, is far more precious than the paint job on the houses." Score one for Jane and her friends.

From their offices down on Lafayette Street, the city planners were saying it just couldn't be—that so topsy-turvy a mix of new and old, residential and grittily industrial, charming and unlovely, *necessarily* made for a slum. To prove the contrary, Jane and her neighbors invited journalists and others to visit West Villagers in their homes. However awful the neighborhood was supposed to be, went the strategy, it wouldn't square with what you'd see right in front of your nose. A building at 661 Washington Street? Well, yes, a bit run-down—yet with clean hallways, tidy apartments. The borough president came through in March and, according to a *New York Times* reporter, was "impressed by the generally high standards of the living quarters he saw within outwardly shabby buildings," and "by the intensity of feeling among tenants who were clearly not slum dwellers."

During March, the West Village committee surveyed all fourteen blocks in the threatened area, systematically reporting on renovations made to homes in recent years: A new roof at 739 Greenwich in 1951, new wiring in 1953, new bathrooms in 1956. At Jane's neighbors' at 561 Hudson, new plumbing and oil burner, windows repaired, new paint inside and out, new kitchen fixtures. Over on West Eleventh, a whole row of houses completely renovated. At 115 Perry, the halls painted the previous year, along with new pipes, plumbing, and windows. Page after

"During the West Village neighborhood fight, we had a penny sale at St. Luke's Church,"
Jane wrote of this photo. "Penny sales were not part of the Anglican tradition, but
they were a part of the Catholic tradition in the neighborhood, so they ran the sale and
St. Luke's gave the space. This was the first ecumenical thing I know of that had ever
occurred in the area. It was a great success."

page it went on like this. As for West Village businesses, 140 of them, they included a uniform maker, a dance studio, a bookstore, a cabinet maker, a motor scooter shop, a clothing store, a locksmith, a tax consultant, bars, sculptors, artists, printers, importers. They employed 1,950 men and women. If the cheek-by-jowl quality of homes and businesses in the West Village's twentieth of a square mile was supposed to be so bad, virtually the definition of blight, it didn't come out that way in the survey.

In late April, the committee distributed a letter to the planning commission by two members of the Municipal Art Society's Historic Architecture Committee. "The 14-block area of West Greenwich Village that has been proposed for urban renewal," these experts led off, "is fundamentally as attractive as other portions of Greenwich Village, and in some ways more unusual in much of its architecture," some of which dated to the early 1800s, when a section of it was a river landing. They referred to its "waterfront town architecture"; pointed up "a rare group of early workaday structures" on Greenwich and West Eleventh; Greek Revival interiors on Charles Street; some bright, many-windowed tenements that showed off a "surprising exuberance of decorative masonry treatment." This was 1961, before the demolition of Penn Station had sparked the historic preservation movement, but the writers were anticipating what today is called "adaptive re-use": some "inherently messy or unattractive [uses], such as paper baling, exist like hermit crabs in buildings which might quite easily be put to other uses—and if the natural history of the structures is not cut short by urban renewal," they added, "undoubtedly will be."

Much the same, different in detail but identical in principle, could have been said of East Harlem before the projects went up, or of Boston's West End before it was razed. This time it was being said *before* the damage was done.

Bruno Zevi, a distinguished Italian architect, historian, and former Village resident, author of an influential book called *Towards an Organic Architecture*, weighed in: "I have no romantic attitude toward slums," but no part of Greenwich Village, he declared, was a slum. Cities, he went on, had a "natural texture" that needed respect; to tamper with it was to destroy it.

In a community such as the west Village, where residential and industrial uses are mixed, one can never know if the community has created its own pattern and architecture, or if the architecture creates the community. Where the result is admirable, as it is in the west Village—that is, where integration is complete and viable—it should not be questioned. Yet I understand that your city planners have stated that they will segregate residential and non-residential uses. What can be considered bad about industry if it does not pollute the air and soil of the community?

Save the West Village's campaign was a relentlessly negative one—by design. It said *No*. It asked for nothing but a reversal of the city's plans. It sought no compromise.

The West Village was no slum, went its drumbeat of a message. Don't mess with it.

No slum; block its designation as one.

No slum; don't let urban renewal get its mitts on it.

This tack, Jane would explain, had its roots in their group's efforts to bring influential outsiders to the neighborhood. One was a federal housing official whose tour of the West Village surprised him with its range of incomes and convinced him it was not a slum. Along the way he bestowed on Jane what became a central tenet of their strategy—a "secret" she'd reveal numerous times over the years: "Never ever tell anyone in state or city government what you want for improvements because then you're considered a 'participating citizen.' Then they can say they have citizen participation and do whatever they want. He told us not to be afraid of being considered 'merely negative.' " And *that*, to the endless annoyance of city officials, was exactly what they were: first overturn that damning slum designation, went the idea. Only then come back with positive and constructive plans—which, as we'll see, is just what Citizen Jane and her friends later did.

"We've had to become experts in everything from how to run torchlight parades to how to analyze typewriter type and collect legal evidence," Jane wrote while in the thick of the fight. At one point they sent an audio engineer around town to record sound levels; of course, he found the West Village quieter, presumably more peaceful, than some of New York's tonier districts. Pierre Tonachel, a young lawyer enlisted early in the fight, remembers Jane saying of their opponents, "You have to make them feel they're being nibbled to death by ducks." Fresh out of Cornell, Tonachel was living in a nineteenth-century house on a busy block of Bethune Street not far from Jane's place when he was introduced to her.

Inside of fifteen minutes, he concluded that he stood in the presence of some odd breed of genius. She was smart, but much more. She *always* knew what she was talking about. She possessed capacious warmth yet, faced with duplicity or stupidity, could express withering contempt. "She didn't suffer fools gladly," Tonachel says. "She got impatient with drivel." Under Jane's leadership, it seemed to him, the West Village war was being waged not by some ragtag community militia but by real pros; everything was more professional than it had any right to be. Even "the quality of the paperwork" the committee put out, he marvels, "was stunning; Jane inspired that."

Another veteran of the West Village, Nate Silver, who met Jane in November 1961, would conjure up a bad movie of those years, down to "an action-packed montage of calendar pages flipping," people marching with placards, fund-raising parties, "now a medium shot of Jane Jacobs speaking at a public hearing in the balustraded Old-Bailey-style municipal council chamber of New York and the shot should take in Italian laps with babies, black faces, defensive-looking city officials."

Jane, as chairman of the Committee to Save the West Village, presents evidence at a press conference at the Lion's Head restaurant, New York, 1961.

A public meeting on June 8 dragged on until four in the morning, fresh speakers summoned by telephone to testify into the night. Planning commission head James Felt would remember the meeting's "unreal and almost dreamlike quality."

On the eve of a key primary election, Mayor Wagner asked the planning commission to withdraw its proposal, "so as not to leave an integral portion of Greenwich Village in a state of limbo." But affirming its own independence, the commission ruled at its October 18 meeting that the neighborhood was indeed blighted and thus eligible for urban renewal. "The villagers, led by Mrs. Jane Jacobs," *The New York Times* reported, "leaped from their seats and rushed forward," shouting that a deal had been made with a builder, that the mayor had been double-crossed, that the commission's action was illegal. Chairman Felt pounded his gavel, demanding that order be restored, called in police. Shouted protests only increased. Felt called a recess, sent for more police, and, with the other commissioners, left the room. The West Villagers stayed where they were, chanting "Down with Felt!" When later chastised for their behavior Jane coolly replied, "We were not violent. We were only vocal . . . We had been ladies and gentlemen and only got pushed around. So yesterday we protested loudly."

Early the following year, responding to the neighborhood's relentless pressure, Mayor Wagner finally prevailed on the planning commission to see things his way, which was Jane's way; a newsletter of the Citizens' Housing and Planning Council, a group supporting the commission, described the mayor as like "a weary father asking his son to drop a young lady of dubious repute." The neighborhood had won, as Jane would calculate, "eleven months and ten days after our ordeal began."

The victors, it is said, write the history books. But this time, the losers got their say, too. In his October 18 ruling, soon to be reversed by the mayor, Chairman Felt, troubled and resentful after what for him had been an ordeal, too, set out a long, measured, even philosophical defense of the commission's action. The stance of the "highly sophisticated and articulate opposition leadership," he wrote, was rooted in "two premises," with both of which he disagreed. First, that neither the planning commission nor public officials generally "mean what they say, can be believed, or can be trusted to do what they say they intend to do." Second, that urban renewal and housing programs were inherently destructive, "and that only local residents, if left to their own efforts without the interference of government," can renew the city. This he called "the *laissez faire* theory of urban renewal." He was right; this *was*, more or less, what Jane and her friends were saying. Today, for better and for worse—perhaps equally so—versions of both premises are deeply ingrained in American public life.

When it was all over, a friend from the United Housing Foundation, which had helped bring cooperative housing to poor areas of the city, wrote Felt a letter of sympathy and lament. It was fortunate, he wrote, that people like the West Villagers had never tried to block cooperative housing projects like those successfully brought to the Lower East Side: "They would have discovered beauty in the colored drapes of the stores behind which the gypsies lived and in the old clothes shops that lined both sides of Grand Street from the East River to Third Avenue. The capacity of these people to find beauty in the cold water flats and the belly stove never ceases to amaze me."

At a public lecture around this same time—she was back at *Forum* now and *Death and Life* was in print—Jane told of a rumor "that I had somehow whipped up this book during the fight as a campaign document." In a way, this was flattering. "I would love to be able to carry on a job, and a fight against the city, and whip up a book at the same time," she said, but it was a long and lonely job to write a book, one that meant talking to herself interminably. Just now, she said, she was happy to be talking again with others besides herself.

Clearly, she enjoyed the victory. "She loves the game . . . of wheeling and dealing for a cause," *The Village Voice*'s Jane Kramer reported in 1963. "She manipulates, though she thinks that's a nasty word." Maybe Jane enjoyed her life on the urban front lines more than she let on; if she didn't relish these time-crunching civic battles, maybe they weren't unalloyed misery, either. "As long as it couldn't be avoided, which it couldn't be if you were a responsible person, you had to fight," she'd tell another interviewer. But "as long as you're doing it, you might as well decide to have a good time.

"Of course, what makes it a really good time is if you win."

v. "NOT A SINGLE SPARROW"

It was good when you won, yes, but it would be a dozen years before Jane and her West Village committee could chalk up anything like a win for their radically old-fashioned housing plan. Over the years, West Village Houses, as their plan was known, would face resistance and delay, and run smack into the realities of the New York City housing market and the New York City housing code. When it finally materialized, Jane would be long gone from the Village and the bricks-and-mortar incarnation of their idea could be counted only a partial victory.

West Village Houses took one early step on its rocky, eleven-year ride to realization in a 1963 brochure designed to make its quirky case: a row of stylized city houses march, block-printed, across a blue cover. Inside, on its first page, is a line drawing of a bird, fragile in its stick-figure simplicity, venerable—like city dwellers, snared by urban renewal, facing loss of their homes and neighborhoods. But not this time, vowed Jane and her co-conspirators, not with West Village Houses: "Not a single person—not a single sparrow—shall be displaced."

Jane's group had blocked urban renewal by being relentlessly negative, unwilling to so much as entertain the city's plan. Now, with West Village Houses, they were rebutting the charge that they stood in the way of needed improvement. "This will show that we have a constructive side," said Rachele Wall, one of those instrumental in the scheme and a longtime friend of Jane's. Of course, what they came up with was so different, so new—and so weird and so *old*—that when it finally came before city officials it would be ridiculed as a throwback to a primordial urban past. Which, in a sense, it was. An ad in *The SoHo Weekly News* in 1974 would herald

WEST VILLAGE HOUSES
. . . WHERE PROGRESS IS OUR *LEAST* IMPORTANT PRODUCT.

A *New York Herald Tribune* writer observed that "although Mrs. Jacobs disowns impressing her ideas on the plan . . . [West Village Houses] meets most of her published objections to renewal plans in other neighborhoods." You tear down most of the neighborhood so you can start over with a clean slate? No, said Jane, you pick and choose, preserving what's worth preserving, razing only where necessary. You lavish on a neighborhood great buckets of what she called "cataclysmic" cash? No, she'd said in *Death and Life*, you keep things small. You tear down nineteenth-century tenements, put up modernist high-rises? No, any new buildings should respect the scale and flavor of the surrounding neighborhood. Most of all, you don't kick anyone out of their houses: *Not a single sparrow.* "Revolutionary in its modesty," Mary Perot Nichols, a *Village Voice* writer, called West Village Houses in 1969. It was surely that, in its conception and in how it turned out.

It was to include 475 dwelling units, which was not so small, as urban projects go. It included no efficiency, or "studio," apartments—the Village had enough of those—but, rather, one- to three-bedroom units suitable for families. At which corner, or between which two streets, would West Village Houses go? There was no simple answer to that. Rather, forty-two individual buildings were to be arrayed on seven small sites, along six blocks of Washington Street from Morton to Bank—a Monopoly set of unassuming structures stuck into the corners of lots, replacing truck parking here, a rattletrap of an old factory there. The new housing would restore the balance between residential and commercial that had existed before the overhead rail track (which, farther north, became today's High Line linear park) had gone in to serve the adjacent warehouse district. The architects devised three simple building plans and arranged them, in different combinations, to fit oddments of underused land, leaving room for gardens, courtyards, and plazas, first floors sometimes given over to small shops. No stretch of Washington Street would look just like any other, but no stretch of it, either, would look so different from the rest of the Village.

The plans called for five-story buildings, two apartments to a floor, with no elevators. "The dangers of unattended elevators to children—and adults—are already too well known to require retelling here," said the blue brochure, referring to the new high-rise projects. West Village Houses would all be walk-ups. Walk-ups, like the one Nathan Glazer had grown up in on East 103rd Street in East Harlem. Or the one Jane and Betty had inhabited in Brooklyn Heights. West Village Houses was radical, in a nineteenth-century sort of way. Ranging up the avenues and down the crosstown streets of Manhattan and in swaths of the other boroughs as well, the walk-up was a veritable icon of old New York. Besides, you'd hear it argued, walk-ups were perfect for Greenwich Villagers, for whom "walking upstairs is considered a sound and healthy diversion."

Were they serious?

The reaction to West Village Houses among city officials was incomprehension, curdled with rage at what Jane and her friends had the effrontery to offer the city of New York. And yes, it was Jane herself—Jane Jacobs of Hudson Street—who was seen as the instigator of this insult to the city and to the most elementary precepts of modern planning. What, asked the anonymous author of one internal planning commission document, were the chief influences behind this nutty idea? One was the "well-publicized 'victory'" of the West Village committee in blocking urban renewal. A second was the assumption that the sole way to better a neighborhood was to fight city hall. A third was "the philosophical point of view of its most vocal member, Jane Jacobs," who opposed the prevailing planning troika of urban renewal, residential relocation, and high-rise construction.

This commission author saw West Village Houses for what it was—a model for inserting new housing into slivers and specks of underused or vacant land; here was Jane's "in-fill," not just for Greenwich Village but for the city at large. And it advanced a breed of community planning that was neighborhood focused and so, presumably, more trust inspiring than anything government could do. But while he (or she) could more or less fairly outline the thinking behind the project, he was hostile to it. It required no residential relocation, true, but it did demand *nonresidential* relocation. Maybe the local truckers made a ramshackle mess of their river-fronting blocks. But, as later documents would point up, their little companies, with names like Empire Transfer and Arjay Consolidators, were a going industry, moving goods twenty-four hours a day, seven days a week, up and down the East Coast. And they had no wish to move; their handy access to the West Side Highway gave them what might be the last suitable site on Manhattan Island. With West Village Houses, they'd *have* to move, which risked forcing many of them out of business. Didn't they count, too?

The West Village plan, according to another anonymous foe, had been "conceived in utmost secrecy," and was pushed with "not even vaguely disguised attempts at blackmail and retribution." It promised no fresh cityscape at all, just "a simple-minded repetition of a basically antiquated housing type—the five-story walk-up." Its "avant-garde trappings of 'human scale' and 'mixed land use'" made it no less regressive.

These criticisms rank as among the more measured ones. A local newsletter writer, Jeanne Godwin, termed the West Village Houses plan ("through which the fine hand of Jane Jacobs may be discerned") "startling and frightening." It was "appalling" that anyone should propose anything like it. When the housing and redevelopment board's Frank S. Kristof weighed in on June 25, 1963, he termed it "the most incredible proposal for housing that we have met since the adoption in 1879" of the old-law "dumbbell" tenement. Arguments in its favor added up to "absurd allegations, assertions masquerading as fact, attempts to make virtues of obvious deficiencies, and false and misleading misrepresentations."

The architect of the West Village scheme was thirty-seven-year-old Ray Matz, who worked out of the White Plains, New York, offices of Perkins & Will, the Chicago firm that had worked on the DeWitt Clinton alternative; that scheme also proposed walk-ups, and was also decried. Now, in November, Philip Will wrote William Ballard, the planning commission head, trying to explain to him what the West Villagers were about. Back in Chicago, Will was a planning commissioner, too; let's try to see this, he seemed to say, commissioner to commissioner. Before them lay a "classic example of conflict between established rules and the pragmatic proposals of local citizenry." Here was "a rare opportunity to be experimental and daring." Ballard needed to realize he was "dealing with a unique community populated with concerned and determined people," who knew what they wanted and were willing to push for it; who wanted "not only to preserve but to enhance a way of life which they find to be complete and rewarding." He and Ballard—*we planners, we commissioners*—might not see it that way, he all but said, but *they* did. If cities were to retain the middle class, "we must listen respectfully to the wishes of the very families we wish to keep." He hoped Ballard could find a way to support the West Village plan. "The result might well be a breakthrough in the art of city planning."

Will's letter ranged over a single-spaced page and a half. Ballard's reply was three sentences. Yes, the West Villagers were "a determined lot." There were, however, "problems to consider" with their idea. He'd distribute Will's letter to other commission members. The following month, Ballard wrote the housing and redevelopment board that the West Village proposal was simply "unacceptable."

That was 1963. Years passed. The neighborhood pushed. Politics intervened. A new mayor, John Lindsay, was elected. Holdovers from the previous administration first blocked the project. But when Lindsay's appointees consolidated their power, it finally won approval, warranting an article in the August 3, 1969, *New York Times:* " 'Village' Group Wins 8-Year Battle to Build 5-Story Walk-up Apartments." Jane's arrival at a city planning commission meeting a week later was welcomed with "a thunderous, standing ovation."

The buildings went up. But the mansard roofs of one early sketch, floor-to-ceiling sliding windows, pretty landscaping? These and other features of the original design had largely vanished. The years of fighting had taken their toll. Politics, steep inflation, opposition by the city—*principled* opposition, it should be said—and the passage of years hacked away at some of the design features and flourishes. The result, as one account had it, was "plain brick buildings punctured by small windows, topped by flat roofs, and unadorned by anything other than an occasional window box of flowers." That was the bad news.

The good news was that, socially speaking, West Village Houses worked.

Pearl Broder, who moved in with her daughter in 1978, remembers how, hard by the city's West Side, pushed up against the river, it felt like "the end of the earth"; she speaks from a Manhattanite's perspective that makes a ten-minute walk to the grocery a trek across Siberia. Mostly gay men lived in her building in those days. The surrounding area was "run-down, yet exciting"; the gentrification so ubiquitous today—new high-rises, expensive condos—came later. She loved being there. "I couldn't have lived in Manhattan if it weren't for this," she says.

And whatever their aesthetic failings, the West Village Houses worked pretty well as places to live, with bright, decently sized rooms, some of them garden apartments directly off courtyards, just one other apartment to the floor, only ten or twelve per building; you got to know your neighbors that way. "The people who live on the top floors are in great shape and live longer than the rest of us!" says Katy Bordonaro, another long-timer, who lives with her husband in one of the garden apartments. Those were pretty, but they could be a little dark, whereas top-floor apartments, up tidy, well-lit stairs, were flooded with light, with fine views of the West Side and the river.

Walk along Washington Street today and you might not notice West Village Houses at all; they're precisely the opposite of "starchitecture." Maybe you couldn't celebrate their dowdy, bare-bones appearance. But for their thousand and more residents, and for their neighbors, they embodied many of Jane's ideas for moderately priced in-fill housing. No housing torn down. Nobody shooed away. A masterpiece of sorts—if you dare use the word for something so modest.

And a victory.

CHAPTER 16

LUNCHEON
AT THE WHITE HOUSE

I. A NICE, NINE-MINUTE TALK, HONEY

In the aftermath of *Death and Life*, Jane's friends and acquaintances, her experiences both personal and professional, the very rhythms of her days and weeks, all took a turn. About a year after returning in early 1961 to *Architectural Forum*—"their patience (and my money) both having thoroughly run out," as she wrote Epstein—she advised the new editor, Peter Blake, that she planned to leave for good at the end of May. Now, and for the rest of her life, Jane would be self-employed, on her own clock, responsible primarily to herself. In one sense, her everyday life became narrower, no longer nourished by her colleagues at the magazine; in another sense, it became broader, beyond Hudson Street, beyond Rockefeller Center. Her 1964 date book mentioned dinner parties with old friends, like the Kirks and the Haskells, but also a Hillman Award dinner at the Windsor Ballroom in the Hotel Commodore; an appointment with the feminist writer Betty Friedan; in the back, phone numbers for the radical organizer Saul Alinsky and Mayor John Lindsay. She met John Holt, whose 1964 best-selling book, *How Children Fail*, must have resonated with her. Jane was stepping onto the stage of the nation and the world, her attention drawn off from her writing not just by battles in the West Village but by opportunities and life experiences she might scarcely have imagined a few years before.

.   .   .

In 1963, the architect Noriaki Kurokawa, who had begun work on a Japanese translation of *Death and Life* the year before, wrote Jane from Tokyo. Her writing, he said deferentially, was "so clear even for us Japanese to understand," but on a few points he did need clarification. For example, Jane had pointed out that street lighting could discourage crime only so much. "Street lights," she had written, "can be like that famous stone that falls in the desert where there are no ears to hear." In other words, she was asking rhetorically, without eyes on the street to see, did street lighting cast light at all? "What means 'famous stone'?" Kurokawa asked. "Has it any special meanings? Or [is it] a proverb?" He also wanted to know what a bocce court was, and who the "perverts" were who'd taken over Philadelphia's Washington Square.

Jane replied with suggestions for how Kurokawa might get around the cultural gaps between the languages. As for the "perverts," she explained in her July 1963 letter, these were "people who are abnormal, usually in a sexual way; and when it is used as I have used it, it is understood to mean homosexuals who are aggressive and brazen, and seem unpleasant or even frightening, perhaps, to normal people."

Of course, Kurokawa's final translation didn't entirely escape error. The street crime Americans call a "mugging" came out as "overacting," the "frosted pastry" you could get at Rockefeller Center as a "frozen pie shell."

The British publisher of *The Death and Life of Great American Cities* didn't much like that title for its readers and appealed to Jane for alternatives. "I keep thinking of things like 'Plans Agley' or 'Secrets of the Streets,' " Jane wrote back in March 1962. "Kind of awful. Maybe the best thing is to stick to the American title by default, if for no other reason."

They did.

As early as spring 1962, *Death and Life* was being used in studio courses at the Harvard Graduate School of Design. In spring 1963, the midterm for one Harvard seminar, "Visual Evaluation of the Urban Environment," was based on Jane's book.

·   ·   ·

"I have some real news for you," Jane wrote her mother in 1964. She'd gotten a call, and then a formal invitation, from Liz Carpenter at the White House, inviting her to a luncheon with Lady Bird Johnson, the first lady. "I told Bob your first thought will be 'What will she wear?' Right? It was mine. I guess I will have to get a dress, which I need anyhow."

The way the story was told some years later, Jane was advised that "Mrs. Johnson would really appreciate, honey, a nice, nine-minute talk on beautification." Jane said she'd be glad to talk for nine minutes, but not on beautification. On June 16, 1964, in the East Wing of the White House, at the Fifth Monthly Women Doers Luncheon—that's what it was called—Jane spoke of "the profound need we have for character, convenience, visual pleasure and vitality." These she lumped together as "amenity," which required *keeping things up*. Amenity required people to clean, repair, and garden—maintenance, not capital spending. These days, however, cities found it easier to let things disintegrate, then pour in money to make something new and grand—which swept away "the good with the bad, the beautiful with the ugly, and the productive with the unproductive." Cities, she declared, were impoverishing themselves with capital improvements!

"I wanted to talk sense to those women," Jane would say later, "not a lot of inspirational stuff about tulips."

It was late winter of 1964, at the Lion's Head, the neighborhood bar that had served as headquarters for the battle against urban renewal, and Jane was being "buttonholed" by Leon Seidel, its owner. A photographer friend of his was on assignment from *Esquire* to take pictures of mothers and sons. The photographer was forty-one-year-old Diane Arbus, then still on her way up; she'd won a Guggenheim, taught at local colleges, but was still a couple of years from her first big solo exhibition at the Museum of Modern Art. It was quite a deal for her to land this assignment from *Esquire*, Seidel told Jane. Would she agree to let Arbus photograph her? Sure, she said.

Big mistake.

Arbus was not exactly your garden-variety "objective" recorder of the visual world. She would become famous for her photographs of giants, dwarfs, and freaks, elaborately arranged in odd compositions she felt revealed more than her subjects, or her viewers, might have imagined.

Her portrait of Jane and her son Ned proved no exception. "She was so concentrated and so deliberate," Jane remembered, "and put so much effort into exactly how she wanted it." At one point, Arbus ordered Jane back into the house to get a raincoat and "told me how I had to button it all up. Then she looked at us both for a while and she decided she wanted me to have gloves on." Didn't matter that it wasn't cold enough for gloves.

Arbus posed the two of them in the little yard at the back of the house on Hudson Street. "This was quite an arduous thing. Our feet had to be exactly so. Our arms had to be exactly so." Finally, Arbus started firing away with the camera.

If you're looking for *flattering,* don't. Jane remembered feeling manipulated and exploited, "buttoned up and covered up." She was pointed squarely at the camera, practically trussed up in her raincoat, looking dowdy and awkward, Ned angled toward her, his arm around her shoulder, the two of them set in front of a wooden fence. By family-snapshot standards, it was a disaster.

But, of course, this was no family snapshot; it was Art.

II. OBSIDIAN DAYS

"As you know," Jane wrote *Forum*'s new editor, Peter Blake, at the time she left it, her decision to do so reflected not dissatisfaction with the magazine, "but rather that I am anxious to get to work on some other writing, particularly another book I want to do on cities."

The book turned out to be *The Economy of Cities,* published in 1969.

But there was apparently a brief period during which her next project was still uncertain. When she talked with Chadbourne Gilpatric in early 1962, the Rockefeller man came away thinking she was interested in finishing a book for children the following summer, then devoting "all of her best energies to a study of . . . citizen action." A children's book did materialize, many years later. The citizen action "study," whatever it was, never did.

Jane told of the origins of *The Economy of Cities* this way, in talking with a friend, Roberta Brandes Gratz, years later:

It became evident to me while I was doing *Death and Life of Great American Cities* that if the city's economy declines, that's the end of it.

It doesn't matter what else cities have, what grand temples they have, what beautiful scenery, wonderful people, or anything else—if their economy doesn't work. If a settlement does have a lively economy and is able to maintain that, almost everything else becomes possible.

If it doesn't, nothing is possible.

What, then, accounted for healthy city economies?

It could seem that Jane was turning away from the streets and sidewalks that had nurtured her and made her first book so memorable, giving herself over instead to the soft-sided field of economics, the notoriously Dismal Science, stepping onto its dreary landscape of supply-and-demand curves and marginal returns.

In fact, the new book might better be seen as a sequel to *Death and Life*—in its very focus on death and life, on the fall and rise, decay and bursting-forth, of human society generally. Why did some cities decline while others prospered? As she'd one day put it, "This question of, you might say, 'the death and life' was what puzzled me." That's what had *always* puzzled her, really, all the way back to her father's insistence that she look, look really hard, at that living tree. "Life is an end in itself," she'd quoted Oliver Wendell Holmes Jr. in *Death and Life*. For a while she called the new book *Cities and Work: The Economic Principles of City Growth*. Its inspiration lay in her

cheerful and respectful curiosity about the persistence of big cities. They are, after all, the most durable of settlements. They endure longer than the nations and governments of which they form a part. They outlast whole series of the institutions, the businesses and the people, that seem to compose them. They survive invasion, revolution, physical destruction, and misery.

Even Hiroshima and Dresden, she might have noted, had made their way back to life. On the other hand, she'd watched Scranton wither, seen up close the pitiful little fragment of economic life that was Higgins, North Carolina. She'd experienced the street life, economic life, public life, and every other kind of blustery, triumphant life, of New York City. These examples haunted her, held her.

In an early draft of the new book, Jane wrote, "The most elementary point is the most startling: There are no causes of stagnation. There are no causes of poverty. There are only causes of growth." She could have been talking physics, one of its most cherished and firmly established principles, the Second Law of Thermodynamics: left alone, everything runs down, falls apart. It doesn't *have* to run down, doesn't *always* run down, but without an infusion of outside energy it will for sure. Decline was natural, whereas germination and growth needed fresh energy. Scranton stagnation and Higgins poverty were in the nature of things. The real question was, what explained those moments in space and time—seventeenth-century Amsterdam, Chicago during the 1880s, London for much of the nineteenth century, Silicon Valley, parts of China today—that sprouted and gushed into prosperity?

She made little progress on the new book at first. Her West Village battles, she'd later estimate, had cost her two years. And *Death and Life's* success brought opportunities, seductions, and demands that were always threatening to pull her away from the writing. No, she wrote Brown University vice president John Elmendorf in August 1962, she couldn't accept his invitation to become a Convocation Fellow for the coming academic year. "I have to stop talking and start working." She had two talks to prepare that she "would give anything to be able to extricate" herself from. "Until I apply myself to learning and thinking some more, I'm only repeating myself and this has become just intolerably tiresome to me."

The following September, she wrote to her Japanese translator, Noriaki Kurokawa. He'd suggested that, for Japanese readers, photographs might be a useful adjunct to the text. No problem, Jane wrote back, but if he wanted her to collect the photos, she couldn't do it. "I am already so badly delayed and behind my schedule in working on another book that I must finish, that it would be impossible for me to take the time required to hunt for the right ones." Over the years, she would write dozens of letters begging leave *not* to serve on a panel, give a lecture, write a foreword, or do some other chore she deemed tedious—or, in some cases, not tedious at all, but nonetheless apt to draw her away from her writing.

In the same 1964 letter to her mother in which she wrote of her invitation to the White House, she added, "I'm still plugging away at my book, making some progress I hope but having *such a hard time* with it. I sometimes wonder how I ever got into this mess!"

At least in part, the "mess" could be laid at the door of *Death and Life*, whose success had shot her into a new life. Back in October 1961, after a party celebrating that book's publication, Chadbourne Gilpatric wrote

Jane that he and his wife had had a good time. "I certainly enjoyed the party too," Jane wrote back. "I'll never forget it." How could she forget any of what had descended on her during those months? One might track Jane's writing life by what she wrote *about*—from her adolescent poems about Girl Scouts and Blackbeard the pirate, to glimpses of American life in her propaganda work, to hospital and school architecture at *Forum*, and so on. But *Death and Life* represented a more seismic shift—not of subject but of genre. She was writing *books* now, and pretty much only books. Once, whatever she had to say would come out in modest articles like those she'd written for *Vogue* or *Forum*. But now, and for the rest of her life, any subject Jane Jacobs took the trouble to think much about was apt to emerge as a book. After that last year at *Forum* her whole previous life's work was, to all intents, finished. She worked only on big canvases now. In a foreword to a 1992 edition of *Death and Life*, she wrote that whatever the book's influence on the world, it "exerted an influence on me, and lured me into my subsequent life's work."

She worked on a longer time cycle now, too—years instead of days or weeks, digging in for the long haul, dedicating herself to big ideas—groping, struggling, and then, after five years, or ten, delivering a book. Anything else—a brief essay, a letter to the editor, a public statement—however much it might strike an outsider as just more "writing," was to Jane mostly unwelcome interruption now. In September 1963, she wrote David Gurin, a young planner she'd befriended, in response to his suggestion that she submit pieces of her book as articles for a journal he edited. No, thank you, she said, "I have to think of it and work at it as a total knit-together book." Writing books—big and all-together, one after another, year by year—*this* was her "subsequent life's work."

On the book destined to become *The Economy of Cities*, Jane's progress was unsure and intermittent. "I am still distressingly and maddeningly slow," she wrote Jason Epstein on March 3, 1966, "but the thing will get done. I have reached a point where new ideas click into place and make older ones click into place, instead of boiling up the pot of confusion into more confusion—that long misery." Now, four years or more since she'd conceived the book, it bore "little resemblance to what I thought it was going to be when I first lightheartedly explained it to you and to myself." She enclosed the book's table of contents of twelve chapters in three parts. "I don't *think* it will change further, so you can get some idea of what to expect."

It did change, of course, but by now Jane had reached a remarkable conclusion, one she'd stick with to the end and had developed enough to try out, as an excerpt, on Jason and his wife, Barbara, editor of *The New York Review of Books*. Barbara Epstein wrote back saying it was "marvelous" and that she might want to run it in the *Review*. It was called "Cities First; Rural Development Later" and it became part of chapter 1. In it, Jane breathed a new, invented city into the world, "New Obsidian."

Once, long ago, humans were hunter-gatherers. Living in small bands, they killed animals, gathered nuts and berries, surviving on what they could collect in the wild. That was human existence for eons. Then, ten or twelve thousand years ago—on this figure, at least, there is not too much scholarly disagreement—people began to domesticate animals and to plant and harvest crops. With the resulting agricultural bounty, the story went, stable and settled communities developed, and with them crafts, division of labor, complex social organization, and, ultimately, cities. In short: *Agriculture first, urban development later.*

Jane didn't think so. "Our understanding of cities, and also of economic development generally, has been distorted by the dogma of agricultural primacy. I plan to argue," she wrote in *The Economy of Cities*, "that this dogma is as quaint as the theory of spontaneous generation," the idea that, for example, maggots festering in rotten meat come to life out of nothing. Here was "a vestige of pre-Darwinian intellectual history that has hung on past its time." Jane wished to advance quite a contrary notion, one that might seem "radical and disturbing" to some—that cities came first and from them, agriculture.

To illustrate the idea, she created first in her mind's eye, then for her readers, New Obsidian, located on the Anatolian plateau of Turkey near a real city, Çatal Hüyük, the ruins of which had been discovered by the British archaeologist James Mellaart some years before. Obsidian, of course, was real enough—a tough, black glass produced in volcanoes, in some ways the nearest thing to steel, used to make early man's sharpest cutting tools, knives, arrowheads, and spearheads; yet, gleaming and glossy as it was, it was used for mirrors, too. Trade in it was known to go back to at least 9000 BC, among and between hunting groups, in small settlements. One of them, in Jane's reconstruction, becomes New Obsidian, a nascent city.

Over the course of twenty manuscript pages, we watch it grow. Its population climbs. Its people become skilled at crafts. Traders from afar visit, bartering for obsidian with goods from their own hunting territories. Likewise, traders fan out from New Obsidian, the volcanic mineral in hand to barter, trading for copper, shells, and pigment. In both directions, commerce includes nonperishable food, especially live animals and hard seeds. In time, some of the animals are domesticated. Some of the seeds, not immediately consumed, are sown, at first haphazardly, in time with patience and care. Under the watchful eyes of local inhabitants, hybrids, crosses, and mutants lead to better, more bountiful food, superior to wild strains. All this takes place in the budding city's relatively safe, protected precincts. "Prosperity is a prerequisite. Although time is necessary, time by itself does not bestow cultivated grains." But the two together do. Agriculture, as we know it, comes to New Obsidian.

But New Obsidian had been there first.

Copper in the Caucasus, Jane allowed, or the trade in seashells from any coastal settlement, could have served as well to tell her story. But this, anyway—cities as the basis for agriculture—was what Jane was getting at. Of course, she was writing about more than agriculture, more than cities. She was writing about the tides of economic growth.

III. TECHNICOLOR DREAMING

Early in 1967, invitations to give talks in Hannover, West Germany, and in London took Jane, at age fifty, out of North America for the first time. In her almost monthlong travels through Europe, she proved an eager tourist and, in her letters home, a gifted raconteur. And maybe more: she seems liberated, as if being off in Europe, away from her book's demands, left her freer to declaim on anything at all that caught her eye. These were not vapid postcard jottings, but small gems of reportage and memoir that together make for a fresh and lively picture of Jane in a new setting.

She wrote of her struggle with unfamiliar foreign currencies; of the short skirts the English girls wore; of a large hospital with projecting sunporches designed by Finnish architects, commending it to the attention of her husband, the hospital architect; of a Denmark that was clean, neat, and manicured: "When our living room is all cleaned up it looks very much like Denmark." At a club, she saw how the Danes loved jazz. "But the dancers," she lamented, "are much too sedate and uninventive and self-conscious. I kept wishing they could see some Americans doing the monkey." She visited many places and met many people, but plainly she missed home. "I hope you get my letters," she wrote from Amsterdam, to Bob, Ned, and Mary (Jimmy was away in college). "I think of you so often." Once she reached London, she noted with evident pleasure, she'd be on a clock only five hours off, not six, from that of her family in New York.

On January 25, about a week into her trip, Jane wrote a long letter home from her Venice-bound train. She'd given her talk in Hannover, a city she found nicely rebuilt after the war's devastation. Frankfurt, by contrast, had come as a shock—"dirty, garish, ugly and just plain mean looking," redeemed only by Goethe's rebuilt house, in whose music and game room she saw early pianos, clocks, and chessboards. "You could play chess in that house almost anywhere the fit took you!" On the plane from Frankfurt to Milan, she caught her first sight of the Alps. "Snow covered, wild, beautiful and incredible: peaks, valleys, glaciers and finally the lake bordering Switzerland and Italy." But Milan had been shut in by fog, so they'd had to land in Genoa instead, and now she was sprawled across three seats of a nearly empty first-class train carriage bound for Venice.

The following morning, installed at her hotel, drinking her coffee after breakfast in her room, she thought back to her arrival early the previous morning. She'd come in the fog—"just enough to enhance the mystery and beauty." Getting off at the Rialto, a porter had escorted her across Venice to the hotel, Jane's bag atop his head. "This walk through the streets was enchanting, in the quiet and the fog; through a maze of astounding alleys, steps, bridges, squares, hidden corners, populated only by cats."

She'd enjoyed her day in the city. "I spent most of yesterday walking the streets," which she liked more than the fabled canals, "and could hardly stop." And then, on into the night, "when the city had returned to the cats and the fog, and a few people were left, most of them singing as they walked. This city is so beautiful it almost breaks your heart."

Two days later, she was in Paris, writing just to Mary this time, thanking her for her "dear, lovely letter. I was so glad to get it, and have read it about ten times." She told Mary about a street along the river where they sold birds, goldfish, and turtles. "The whole street for blocks was like a big, cheerful pet store. I also saw a church with stained glass so beautiful it was like standing inside a jewel." She promised to save a coin from each country she visited; she'd ask Jimmy to drill a hole in each so she could make a necklace or bracelet from them.

A week later she was finally in London. She went on a walking tour of the city, visited the Tower of London, was later taken to "one of those great and famous London clubs for a drink." This was a men's club, but one that opened its great gates to women "for about an hour on Fridays. This radical move is a 5-year experiment!" Well, she did see the rooms of the club—"what a palace, what a refuge"—but she saw no club members. "Evidently they all clear out while the weekly experiment occurs. Bill & I were the only souls to be seen except for the servants."

On February 7, at a meeting of the Royal Institute of British Architects, Jane gave the last of her scheduled talks, which was like a work in progress, a foretaste, of *The Economy of Cities:* How did some cities come to prosper? One way was when a product or service "produced for a market within [the city slips] into supplying people outside." Case in point: London's Carnaby Street clothing makers, for years serving only the locals, had in the early 1960s become an icon of hip and cool in world fashion. This kind of transformation, a "slippage" from purely local to export markets, represented one path toward economic vibrancy.

This was her last talk, she wrote the night after it was over, and she was "so relieved that that is done. Now I feel truly on vacation. NO MORE SPEECHES." Jane appended a PS: "In answer to your question, Bob, I hardly *can* stand it. I dream about you, in full technicolor, if you know what I mean."

From Chester, near the border of Wales, after a bit of sightseeing and tea with the mayor, Jane wrote home grousing about another dull evening with the planners. "These people are tiresome beyond belief about their new towns, etc. I wish they would just leave me alone." By now this was a vexing problem for her and, on the train to Edinburgh the next day, she set her mind to solving it. That evening, the chill of the house where she was staying relieved by a roaring fire and a hot water bottle in bed, she wrote home with her solution, which was simply "to enjoy my own company instead." The following evening, inaugurating her strategy, she "took charge of the conversation and never let it get on the subject of planning for more than 30 seconds." She pulled off this feat right there, in front of the great Sir Robert Matthew, eminent Scottish modernist architect, who "came absolutely hating me . . . and determined to do me in," needling her, goading her. She responded by simply laps-ing into "funny stories about Higgins, North Carolina." Worked like a charm. "Sir Robert left madder than ever, I suspect, but I for one had a good time. This will be my policy henceforth. I get a bang out of my own stories, fortunately."

She'd largely succeeded, she continued, at avoiding tours of dreary projects and reviewing student work. She still owed an appearance at several cocktail parties and dinners, but she'd managed to see something of Edinburgh on her own—especially its glorious castle, "complicated and wonderful, with keeps within keeps, and strategic points superimposed upon strategic points," the whole edifice "intricately incorporated into and upon the great rocky outcropping on which it rises." She'd visited a bagpipe shop, too, talking for an hour with the instrument maker about the wood used for the pipes, a bagpipe lesson from the next room sounding all the while.

It was February 9. Soon she'd be off to Glasgow, then Belfast on the 13th, Dublin on the 14th, and, after close to a month away from her family in the great cities of Europe, a 6:45 p.m. arrival on the 16th in New York.

CHAPTER 17

GAS MASKS
AT THE PENTAGON

O N APRIL 10, 1968, after a noisy disturbance at a public hearing, Jane was arrested, packed into a squad car, and driven to the
local precinct house. Later she would be fingerprinted, photographed
for mug shots, and charged with riot, inciting to riot, criminal mischief,
and obstructing government administration; each alone could get her a
year in jail. It was not the first time Jane had been arrested. The earlier
incident stemmed from her opposition to the war in Vietnam; this one
from her opposition to a highway. No napalm and carpet bombing here,
just off-ramps and asphalt, jobs for construction workers, a few minutes
lost or gained in getting to New Jersey—*infrastructure*, for goodness'
sake.

It was called the Lower Manhattan Expressway. It was to have been
two and a half miles long, connecting two East River bridges at the lower
tip of Manhattan to one Hudson River tunnel. Today, it doesn't exist. If it
did exist, reminisced Jane's editor, Jason Epstein,

> the building I live in would be gone. There would be no mozzarella in
> the morning, no Chinatown, no garment industry with its thousands
> of entry-level jobs, no grandmothers taking their children to school, no
> De Sica films on warm summer evenings and no SoHo with its lovely
> cast iron buildings, its cobbled streets, its restaurants, its galleries and
> shops and its millions, indeed billions of dollars of taxable property.

At least in broad brushstrokes, the Lower Manhattan streets the expressway meant to erase look today much as they did then, only better.

We speak today of habitat preservation, of protecting natural resources, virgin forest, and family farms against the ravages of sprawl, each properly seen as precious, worthy of strong feeling. For those who opposed the Lower Manhattan Expressway, there was also a precious habitat at risk, only not a natural one. It was a product of human hands, a patch of tightly textured city. Someone encountering it for the first time, newly arrived from, say, a Phoenix suburb or a Kansas farm, might be hard-pressed to see it as a distinct *thing* at all, much less one inspiring nurture or affection. But this crowded urban landscape harbored homes, whole communities, businesses representing many lifetimes' work, and, more broadly yet, a way of life.

In *Death and Life* Jane had much to say about highways and cars, especially in the chapter "Erosion of Cities or Attrition of Automobiles":

> Today everyone who values cities is disturbed by automobiles.
> Traffic arteries, along with parking lots, gas stations and drive-ins, are powerful and insistent instruments of city destruction. To accommodate them, city streets are broken down into loose sprawls, incoherent and vacuous for anyone afoot.

And so on, a litany of sins that today can seem overfamiliar or self-evident. But then, Jane, being Jane, had the nerve to take an abrupt turn: "But we blame automobiles for too much." Soon she was taking us back to London, circa 1890, a hell of horse manure, mud, and stench, of metal-rimmed wheels grating on granite, "the creaking and groaning and chirping and rattling of vehicles, light and heavy," all raising a din beyond imagining. This, noted Jane, was Ebenezer Howard's London; small wonder he saw city streets as unfit for human beings. "Stop telling ourselves fairy tales," wrote Jane, "about the suitability and charm of nineteenth century streets for horse-and-buggy traffic." The automobile, with its internal combustion engine, could even be seen as a force "for liberating cities from one of their noxious liabilities." Jane herself didn't drive, normally getting around New York on foot, by bike, on the subway, or by cab. But Bob did drive and the family did have a car, kept in a garage on Greenwich Street and used mostly for vacations.

The car, in itself, then, was not the problem. However, "we went awry," Jane wrote, by replacing each horse "with half a dozen or so mechanized vehicles, instead of using each mechanized vehicle to replace half a dozen or so horses." *Too many* cars was the problem, cars with every provision made for them, cars taking up space, crowding out everything else. Cars *eroded* cities; this was the word Jane used, with its intimations of a good thing worn away: a street widened here, roaring one-way traffic there, parking lots, more and bigger parking lots, a bridge double-decked. And finally, as Jane wrote, "an expressway is cut through yonder, and finally whole webs of expressways." So that in the end there was nothing left *but* highways, cars, and parking lots, once-bustling city centers worn down into nothing, reduced to "a great, thin smear."

But in the 1960s, Manhattan remained the exception to all this.

A trio of early-twentieth-century suspension bridges linked Manhattan Island to Brooklyn. Several more modest spans across the Harlem River tied it to the Bronx and beyond. Two tunnels had, since about the time Jane moved to New York, connected it, beneath the Hudson, to New Jersey, supplanting a network of ferries. The George Washington Bridge, opened in 1931, at the northern end of the borough, made for a third trans-Hudson link. Traffic circulated up and down Manhattan's spine along west- and east-side highways.

But, and here was the difference, little of this network actually penetrated Manhattan's interior. That is, cars coming in through the bridges and tunnels didn't feed into expressways but rather perfused into the city's dense capillary street grid, leaving its twenty-three square miles, in a sense, *pristine,* the city's fine-textured tissue relatively intact.

Since the war and on into the 1960s, car ownership had climbed in New York, as elsewhere in America. But once your car or truck got onto Manhattan Island—bound for New Jersey, say, or for a delivery in Lower Manhattan—it all but stopped, its speed through streets clogged with people, buses, cabs, trucks, and carts dropping to single digits. For Robert Moses, Jane's antagonist intellectually, socially, politically, and every other way, the Lower Manhattan Expressway would cure all that. It *needed* to be built, if movement and commerce in the great metropolis were to be preserved. All this was obvious to Moses; so much was so obvious to Robert Moses.

The expressway, which would run mostly along Broome Street, skirting Greenwich Village to the north and Little Italy to the south, had a long history in Moses's plans for leaving the nineteenth-century city behind. Over the past thirty years, he had built the Belt Parkway around the perimeter of Brooklyn, pushed the Brooklyn-Queens Expressway and the Cross-Bronx Expressway through once-intact neighborhoods of those outer boroughs, linked the city to Long Island through the Long Island Expressway, Manhattan to Brooklyn through the Brooklyn-Battery Tunnel. But several cross-Manhattan expressways bruited about since as early as the 1920s, including the Lower Manhattan Expressway, had so far come to nothing.

At various times, the new expressway was imagined to pass behind the buildings fronting Broome Street, or at various heights above it, as a skyway. In some schemes it was tied to housing, or maybe a school, in some even dropped beneath the street, there to be slipped in, around, and through the existing tangle of subway tracks, pipes, conduits, steam lines, and water mains. In its details, the design was forever changing. But by the time Jane got involved, it was established that LOMEX, as it was sometimes called, would be a Y-forking, eight-lane thoroughfare channeling traffic from the East River bridges across Lower Manhattan to the Holland Tunnel and New Jersey. Established, too, was that it would take with it the homes of two thousand people and ten thousand jobs—and these were the estimates of its proponents.

In October 1961, a local real estate man, Stephen Freidus, wrote the owners of buildings along the expressway's right-of-way. Demolition and relocation being inevitable, he advised them, they'd need to "consider [their] present space requirements." If, as he expected, they planned to relocate soon, he'd be glad to help. Call him at the office, he urged them, or call him at home: "[I] prefer to offer my services on a 168-hour per week basis." Mr. Freidus, it seems, was a high-energy fellow, if maybe too much so for his own good. He wrote Jane's old nemesis, New York Department of City Planning head James Felt, of his plans, adding, "Please do not regard me as being too forward." That was just how Felt regarded him: "The methods that you have used distress me and do not reflect creditably upon you." But the expressway was inevitable, anyway, Freidus might have replied.

Certainly it seemed inevitable when, in 1962, Jane was dragged into the fight against it. For the moment, she was still at *Forum*. Her book was out. She had helped hold off the urban renewal octopus in the West Village; locally, she was famous for it. "Now," she remembers, "I could get along only with my job and with my domestic duties and interests as a wife and mother. My, wasn't life calming down?" And then—this was probably early spring—Father La Mountain showed up at her door. Could she help?

Father Gerard La Mountain was the young pastor of the Church of the Most Holy Crucifix, which served a poor parish at the edge of Little Italy. The church itself, with its ornate, brick-fronted exterior tucked in between residential and commercial neighbors, fronted on Broome Street, directly in the crosshairs of the expressway. Father La Mountain faced the loss of his home, his church, and his parishioners, who by now had mostly surrendered to lethargy and fatalism. Parts of the neighborhood had already been condemned, including the church itself. People like Stephen Freidus were busy trying to make a buck out of the situation. It was a classic case of a neighborhood's vitality sapped long before the first wrecking ball crashes down on some antique treasure of a building.

Could Jane help?

Her first reaction was no, she couldn't.

Oh, she *wanted* to help. The expressway would be every bit the disaster Father La Mountain said it would be—for the church, for his parishioners, for Broome Street, for all of Lower Manhattan. It would all but destroy Little Italy. Its ramps and interchanges would slice through the west and east sides alike. The Village, too, was threatened; Broome Street was just seven blocks south of Washington Square. Still, "I felt very resistant to getting into another fight. I wanted to work on my work," the city economics book. The expressway was *not* her work.

But she relented. "Oh well," she'd tell an interviewer years later. "Couldn't be helped." In the earliest stages of the expressway fight, she was uninvolved, Father La Mountain being the key figure. Likewise at the tail end, by which time she'd left New York. But during the vital middle period, from about 1962 to 1968, Jane was in the thick of it.

Was the Lower Manhattan Expressway by now just more of the same for Jane Jacobs, like an orthopedic surgeon's 17th hip replacement operation? After all, as she'd say later, Father La Mountain approached her hoping that "some of these seasoned fighters" from the West Village wars could help him. And he was right—Jane *was* by now a seasoned street fighter, a pro, with established methods, worked-out ideas. In a sense LOMEX would be second nature to her; there'd be hearings to attend, strategies to devise, supporters to mobilize, media to cultivate, morale to keep up. And, it seems, songs to write: "Listen, Robert Moses" spoke out against Moses's bulldozers and highways. Its author was Bob

Dylan, living in the Village since early 1961 and still largely unknown, his first album not yet released.

Jane and the joint committee, of which she was co-chair, faced opposition from Moses, but also from much of the city's political and planning establishment. James Felt liked to call the neighborhood broken up by the expressway Hell's Hundred Acres—"making us sound," recalled Jane, "as if we believed in fire traps and dilapidation."

Jane and other local residents showed up for one hearing in gas masks; how better to represent the soot, dirt, and filthy exhaust that would accompany the expressway?

At a rally, she got a chance to tell the popular local television reporter Gabe Pressman, "The expressway would Los Angelize New York." *That* got attention around New York City.

She approached Lewis Mumford for help. His coruscating recent review of her book in *The New Yorker* was being used to discredit her and, by association, the anti-expressway cause. She got him on the line and, before he could object, briskly said, "This isn't about *The New Yorker.*" The expressway was more important than wounded pride, his or hers. Would he write a letter of opposition that could be read at an upcoming hearing? Yes, certainly, Mumford replied. He did. It was good. It helped.

On December 12, 1962, the city's board of estimate unanimously rejected the latest plan for the expressway. Mayor Robert F. Wagner's announcement touched off "an outburst of cheering, hugging and kissing." It was "the best Christmas present the people could have gotten," said the local politico Louis DeSalvio, Jane's co-chair. On a newspaper account of the victory that she sent her mother in Virginia, Jane scribbled, "We won! Isn't it marvelous!" The expressway had been defeated.

Of course, it had not been defeated; what they'd won was breathing room. The backers of the expressway would regroup. Like so many civic battles in which Jane participated, the great, sapping struggle went on and on, across the years. It wore you down, twisted up your life, made you angry; it made *Jane* angry—which she was a lot during the mid- and late 1960s.

In July 1965, asked for permission to include her *Fortune* article in an urban renewal reader, Jane scrawled at the bottom of the original letter that no, she wouldn't allow it. "Indeed, the idea dismays me greatly. To include *that* piece, in *this* context, quite falsifies my position and ideas concerning urban renewal. Please leave me out of the book." In the end, she seems to have let *Fortune* say no for her, no doubt more temperately.

A little earlier, Jane served on a Washington, D.C., panel devoted to "the city and the freeway." Speaking just ahead of her was Harold Gray, who had worked in highway transportation, his capsule biography said, "throughout his adult life," since 1934 with the National Highway Users Conference. Gray saw in the new interstates a transportation ideal of safe, nonstop driving, unimpeded by red lights and congestion, pulling traffic off local streets, giving jobs to construction workers, paid for by those they benefited, through vehicle and fuel taxes. "In America," said Gray, "every mother's son aspires to own, operate and tinker with his own automobile. Motor vehicles typify the American way of life."

"I'm going to be very ungracious," said Jane when it was her turn. "I'm very angry. I couldn't disagree more with the things I just heard Mr. Gray say." Just one cliché after another. It was untrue that highway users paid the whole cost of highways. Who paid for the medical care of people mangled in accidents? And for the courts? And policemen ministering to traffic when they ought to have more important things to worry about? And air pollution? Gasoline taxes didn't pay for any of that.

Look at the Lower Manhattan Expressway: "In New York, where I live, there's one highway that we're fighting that is going to wipe out 10,000 jobs . . . about 6000 of which are held by Negroes and Puerto Ricans who have a hard time finding jobs." Highways benefited cities? What about Newark, which had plenty of highways, but which could hardly be said to benefit from them? As for Gray's notion that economic development depended on "more and more automobiles—all this is a terrible, terrible idea . . . a colonial idea"; she likened it to sad one-crop countries that fed the mother country coffee, oil, or peanuts but enjoyed no lasting benefit. "There's no faster way of becoming a backward city or a backward country than that." No, she'd say, using language reminiscent of *The Economy of Cities* (still far from finished), "you have to keep developing; you have to keep adding new things," not cling to a single crop or product, certainly not to automobiles.

The long struggle to protect the Village against sidewalk snippers, urban renewalists, and expressway builders had left Jane exquisitely sensitive, run through by a streak of dark, toxic anger. Used to be, she said now in Washington, you could debate pedestrians, cars, mass transit, whatever, you could talk "about ideas, philosophy, honest differences of opinion." No longer. Highway advocates, said Jane, "are not doing it honestly any more. There's a great deal of skullduggery; I think this highway program is probably the most corrupting thing we've had since Prohibition." Later, looking to the many New York civic groups that backed LOMEX, Jane would assert that some of them—she cited by name the venerable Municipal Art Society—had grown "corrupted and decayed."

After the tentative victory of 1962, the LOMEX fight did settle down for a while. But in time, the expressway found new champions in the New York State Department of Transportation and Governor Nelson Rockefeller. It faced new opponents, too, including artists and historic preservationists.

Ranging along Broome Street and the area around it stood block after block of five- and six-story buildings, many going back to the mid-nineteenth century, their fancy façades made not from the usual brick, concrete, or stone but cast iron. For years they'd housed factories, their thick wooden floors bearing the weight of sewing machines, printing presses, and lathes. Built before electric lighting, they had broad banks of tall arched windows to admit light to otherwise dim interiors, high ceilings to accommodate tangles of steam-powered overhead drive belts.

"Lofts," they were called in New York. And now, with the decline of manufacturing in the city and their abandonment by industry, a new breed of New Yorkers took an interest in them. Artists and sculptors were drawn to their wide unobstructed bays, abundant natural light, and high ceilings with room for large canvases and sculpture. Ideal as studios, some artists took to *living* in them, too. This was illegal; zoning codes didn't look kindly on people living in factories. But the artists did it anyway, and by the mid-1960s, championed by the sculptor Harry Jackson, a spirited depicter of cowboys, Pony Express riders, and other Old West icons, whose studio occupied one of the Broome Street lofts and whom Jane befriended, they made for a vocal new enemy of the expressway.

Then there was Margot Gayle, an apostle of historic preservation, and a friend of Jane's. The artists stood to lose their studios. But the irreplaceable cast iron–fronted buildings that housed them would be lost altogether. Jane, in white gloves and pearls, had unsuccessfully protested the

1963 razing of Penn Station, the calamity that had sparked the historic preservation movement. Avoiding a new calamity and saving the glorious old buildings of Broome, Mercer, and Grand streets meant stopping the expressway.

On the evening of April 10, 1968, another hearing, a crucial one in the LOMEX saga, was being held in the auditorium of Seward Park High School on the Lower East Side: the expressway was back, this time being pushed by the New York State Department of Transportation. Jane was among several hundred people on hand. On the stage in front stood large, colorful depictions of the great project. John Toth, the department's planning engineer, presided over the hearing from a table onstage. At one end of the same table sat a stenotypist, there to furnish the official record of the proceedings. This woman would figure centrally in the whole affair.

Each speaker approached the microphone set up at the foot of the stage and, his or her back to the officials, addressed the audience; this arrangement Jane took to signify a lack of real interest on the part of the officials, their minds already made up. Supporters of the expressway were soon being shouted down with questions from the floor. Time limits were being imposed without rhyme or reason. It was "bedlam," in Jane's telling. "The chairman gave the impression of indulging the disorder, like someone whose mission was to allow people to let off steam, rather than like someone conducting a serious public hearing." After a recess, many people went home, but perhaps a hundred stayed. "The incredible shenanigans then resumed."

At one point someone shouted for Jane to speak; someone else passed a microphone to her. "I turned to the audience, as all speakers did, and said that we were only talking to ourselves." The officials were making no pretense of listening to them. They were just "errand boys" anyway, who needed to be sent "back to their bosses" with word that the people didn't want the expressway. And to convey this message with a force beyond words, Jane suggested that they march, those who wished to, onto the stage in protest.

"You can't come up here," Toth said to Jane. "Go back, get off the stage."

"We are going to march right across the stage and down the other side," she replied.

"Arrest this woman," Toth told an officer on duty.

Amid the ruckus, the stenotypist, a seemingly gentle soul, became flustered. She got up, clutching her stenotype machine to her bosom with one hand and, in Jane's recollection, waving away the intrusive tumult around her with the other. It was a brand-new machine, she was heard to say, her personal property. She felt protective of it. She felt threatened. "As she danced around like a one armed prizefighter," Jane wrote, the machine's paper tape began to "unroll like a long streamer of confetti," spreading out over the stage. "People began picking it up from the floor and tossing it in the air as if they were dancers . . . It was so surrealistic."

But that tape, its stenotype symbols parading down its length like ancient hieroglyphics, was the only record of the hearing, or so it abruptly struck Jane. A hearing required an official record. Without it, well, it hadn't really occurred. "Listen to this!" she'd remember calling out to the crowd. "There is no record! There is no hearing! We are through with this phony, fink hearing!"

On her way out, a police captain waylaid her and, at Toth's behest, arrested her, hauling her off in a squad car to the precinct house.

Later, at the courthouse for a subsequent hearing in connection with the affair, Jane was asked to identify herself.

"I'm the prisoner," she replied.

A police officer tapped her on the shoulder. "Don't say that, dear. Say, I'm the accused."

Back in December, Jane had been arrested at an antiwar protest along with that most high-profile of social critics, Susan Sontag. A photo taken of them that day at the Criminal Court Building in Lower Manhattan showed Sontag, twenty-eight, looking stylish as ever, jeans tucked into calf-high leather boots. "Flanking her," a close student of this photo, William Bole, would write, was a "woman who doesn't seem to belong in the picture. That's Jacobs with her silver bangs, wearing a wool coat that might have been fashionable a decade earlier during the Eisenhower administration, and thick, round, black eyeglasses." Jane had plunked herself down on the sidewalk in front of the Whitehall induction center, where draftees were absorbed into the army. She pled guilty to a minor charge and was released.

So now, the day after her arrest at Seward Park, Jane wrote her eighty-nine-year-old mother, "Well, here I have been arrested again! I'm afraid you will have a jailbird daughter, or anyway one whose conduct is disorderly."

Jane's conduct, of course, had always been a bit disorderly, if cheerfully so: levity, not shame or regret, spiced her letter to Mrs. Butzner. But the Seward Park incident proved no laughing matter. At a later hearing, Jane would recall, "the prosecutor made such a case of what a monster I was," the judge seemed to buy into it, and for the first time she worried about what might yet befall her. She left for home that afternoon "feeling pretty depressed about it. Scared, too. When I got home, the children were all in school and my husband was at work. I went inside and I sat down gloomily at the dining table, feeling pretty hopeless. I could practically hear those jail doors slamming behind me."

Then, Ned came home, threw his books on the table, listened to how things had gone in court, sat down, and said to his mother, "You know, for a woman of fifty-three, you lead a very exciting life."

Jane brightened. "All of a sudden I felt about a thousand percent better."

In the end, several months later, the charges were plea-bargained down to a single count of disorderly conduct. Consigning the expressway to oblivion would take a little longer; but the events playing out at Seward Park that evening—the trappings of democracy questioned, the workings of government descending into tumult and protest—could stand for America all through the troubled late 1960s.

Even by November 1966, when Jane served on a panel at the New School devoted to "The Social Uses of Power," it was plain the times had taken a toll on her equanimity, leaving her angrier, more cynical. "In this America of 1966, I tell you, the only way you learn about power is to learn by doing. You learn by being frustrated, mostly, and finding out where the frustrations are coming from." She told of her mother teaching her as a child, " 'When a boy gets a stick in his hand, his brains run out the other end of it.' Power," Jane continued, "is a stick in the hand," and America held it. "As a nation, our brains are running out the other end."

Back in 1962, James Felt complained that Jane and her West Village cronies acted as if public officials could not be trusted to say what they meant, or do what they said they'd do. That was before the assassination of President John F. Kennedy, when such a stance was still uncommon. But the intervening six years had wrought a sea change in attitudes toward authority. The trust was gone. Lies and corruption seemed everywhere in the American air. The assassination of Martin Luther King Jr. prompted angry riots in cities around the country. Nothing made sense anymore. Black and white stood apart. Government and the people, young and old, scarcely spoke the same language. American society sat on cracked and shaky pillars. Just a few years before, when Jane was invited to the White House, the country might still be thought to act in ethical, or at least lawful, ways. Now, though, as the poison of Vietnam seeped through American society—with its body counts and burning villages, with the despised "Establishment" in their white shirts and skinny ties sending young men to die in Southeast Asia—the social bonds of the country were left twisted and frayed. At this time, and in these circumstances, speaking truth to power and getting arrested would for Jane and many of her friends be seen as necessary, noble, even a badge of honor.

In April 1967, Jane and Mary, by then twelve, and Bob, a flower in his lapel, attended a peace march at United Nations Plaza in New York. Jane publicly signed on with other prominent figures to hold back the fraction of her federal taxes that financed the war. She and her family signed petitions, attended vigils and rallies, against the powers-that-be in New York, against the hated war. One time during this period, near Christmas, Jane went shopping at Macy's for long winter underwear for Bob and the boys. "Is it for hunting or fishing?" the sporting-goods salesman asked. " 'It's for picketing,' I said, smiling sweetly."

In October 1967, a huge antiwar demonstration took place in Washington, D.C. A hundred thousand protesters massed on the Mall at the Lincoln Memorial and from there walked across Memorial Bridge, over the Potomac, to the Pentagon, where the orders for waging the war originated. Revolution was in the air; for some, that idea was so much social blather, for others utterly serious and urgent. But when the size and scope of the demonstration became clear, the government mobilized, ranging armed troops around the Pentagon building itself.

For many massed outside the Pentagon it was—to slip into the language of the day—a "radicalizing experience," a crystallizing moment that left you convinced that well-meaning appeals to reform and moderation were not enough, that the System was corrupt through and through, that something larger, more committed, or more final was required. Jane was at the Pentagon that day. She confronted lines of armed soldiers—there were said to be 2,500 of them—arrayed in helmets and gas masks. "They looked like some horrible insect, the whole bunch of them together, not human beings at all." The soldiers pushed back against the demonstrators, arresting more than six hundred of them. "I was outraged that they should be marching on me, on me, an American!"

At a peace march at United Nations Plaza in New York, April 15, 1967: Mary, Jane, and Bob

A few days back from the Pentagon, Jane got a telegram from an editor at *The New York Times*.

CAN YOU CONTRIBUTE 500 WORDS TO SYMPOSIUM NEW YORK TIMES MAGAZINE WILL PUBLISH ON CIVIL DISOBEDIENCE? . . . DOMESTIC CRITICS OF U.S. VIETNAM POLICY INCREASINGLY ADVOCATE ABANDONING QUOTE MERE QUOTE DISSENT FOR RESISTANCE—SPECIFICALLY, CIVIL DISOBEDIENCE.

What did she have to say about this? She had plenty to say. "Vietnam demands disobedience," she wrote. America had all but lost the war and, having done so, now engaged "in an enterprise sicker and uglier than war itself: an enterprise of slaughtering, starving, destroying and uprooting," to no end but to postpone the acknowledgment of failure.

The war, she went on, "was an enterprise that feeds directly and insatiably upon the bodies of our own young men."

Eight months later—two months after her arrest at Seward Park—Jane's twenty-two-year-old niece, Jane Butzner, brother Jim's daughter, was getting married. She had grown up in a suburb of Philadelphia, Woodbury, New Jersey, attended the local high school, graduating in 1964. Later, as a student at Adelphi College in Garden City, Long Island, she'd sometimes call Aunt Jane, ask whether she could come in on the train and visit. "She always had a bed for me to sleep in," she'd remember. "Sometimes I'd bring my friends." Young Jane Butzner had been in and out of the Hudson Street house all her life. She was close to Jimmy and Ned. She was close to Aunt Jane. And now she was getting married.

The invitations went out. The Jacobses, of course, were invited.

But Jane and Bob wrote back that they weren't coming.

PART III

On Albany Avenue
1968–2006

CHAPTER 18

A CIRCLE OF THEIR OWN

THEY TOLD no one.

Jane was still under indictment from the stenotype episode and couldn't be seen as trying to elude the authorities. So it had to be a secret. And how is it a secret, Jim Jacobs asks today, if you *tell* people? Then it's no secret. So they didn't tell niece Jane Butzner, who was getting married the next day. They didn't tell Pat Broms, Jim's girlfriend and future wife. Didn't tell family. Didn't tell friends. Secrets didn't come naturally to them. But this time the kids really had to keep their mouths shut, and so did Bob and Jane.

They packed up the car, closed up the house, gathered their documents, and drove north. Jane immortalized the day, June 21, 1968, in her day-book: "GTC."

Go to Canada.

They didn't much trust their old Fiat Multipla, which, Jim says, was "breaking down every 40 minutes." But some friends of Jane's from her State Department days had an old VW bus—shipped to them at each new duty station from Cambodia to Copenhagen, family lore had it—and the Jacobses had bought it from them. It had no heater, it had a gazillion miles on it, and it was on its third engine, but it was more reliable than the Fiat, so that's what they piled into for the trip.

They aimed north for Lake Ontario, its eastern end, because it was closest. Mary and Ned sat in the back, singing the Bob Dylan song "Just Like Tom Thumb's Blues," collapsing in hysterics when they'd get to the last line: *"I'm going back to New York City / I do believe I've had enough.*" Neither of them had ever lived anywhere but New York City, and now they were leaving it, maybe forever. Was it especially hard for Mary, the youngest of them, just thirteen, leaving her adolescent social circle behind? Jim, for one, didn't think so: "We were a circle of our own."

After four hundred miles through mostly rural upstate New York, they crossed the International Bridge spanning the St. Lawrence River, entering Canada at Ivy Lea, Ontario. Jane, Mary, and Ned, who for a few more days was still a minor, stayed in the car. Bob and Jim submitted their documents, applying for "landed immigrant" status, which is what Canada called permanent residents who were not Canadian citizens; one "landed," as the Jacobses were doing, at an official point of entry. They were in and out in half an hour. No customs official or police officer so much as poked his head into the car. Soon they were on the road again to Kingston, thirty miles west along the north bank of the river, where they put up in a downtown hotel for the night. Next day it was on to Toronto, another three hours west.

That night, Ned's eighteenth birthday, they stayed at a campground outside the city. Bob and Jane slept in the car. The kids huddled in the tent, trying to keep dry in the ceaseless downpour that greeted their first days in Canada.

A year earlier, in 1967, Bob Jacobs had been in Toronto for a convention, staying at the venerable Park Plaza Hotel. At one point, he took time to look out over the city from the hotel's famous eighteenth-floor rooftop patio, in those days a gathering spot for literary figures and bohemians; "If we think kindly of Toronto," someone once said, "the Plaza roof confirms our opinions." From there, below him, Bob would have been able to see the traffic splitting off around Queen's Park, seat of the Ontario provincial legislature; to the east were the peaked and gabled halls of the University of Toronto; to the west, green swaths of playing field; two miles to the south, Lake Ontario—"the lake zinc in the distance," as a character in a Margaret Atwood novel sees it from the roof's balustrade. To a New Yorker, anyplace not New York could seem like the sticks, and thus unworthy of interest. But it didn't seem that way to Bob now. He was due back in New York the next day, Jane would recount, but "he phoned me up and he said this looks like such an interesting city. Is it OK with you if I stay until tomorrow and see a little bit of it?"

After walking around Yorkville, near the hotel, Bob took a bus downtown. By the waterfront, he bought a ticket for the ferry that took commuters and tourists to the Toronto Islands, several tiny rural enclaves located on small islands in the lake, less than two miles offshore. The ferry groaned away from the docks and gray industrial infrastructure of the Toronto waterfront, soon escaping its urban gravitational pull. Fifteen minutes later, it slid up to an island dock, clumps of cottages bordered by low wood fences swinging into view, country lanes, greenery . . .

This was Toronto?

This was Toronto.

Early the following year, as Bob's son Ned moved inexorably toward his eighteenth birthday and, with it, vulnerability to the military draft, that day in Toronto stuck with him.

Ned would soon be graduating from New York's High School of Music & Art and had no particular interest in college (which would have "horrified" Aunt Betty and her husband, Jules, says his brother, Jim, but little troubled their parents). Mary was a sixth grader at Intermediate School 70, which she'd remember as a vast, awful, chaotic place, with two thousand students at a time crammed into the lunchroom and a "dean of discipline" who'd drag students through the halls screaming. As for Jim, after exhausting the science offerings at Bard College he'd transferred to Oberlin, where he'd be graduating in June. His adviser figured him for a doctoral program at Michigan State; but these days, physics research typically meant defense industry work, which he wouldn't do. Without a student deferment, of course, he, too, would be liable to the draft.

At the height of the war, America had more than half a million men under arms in Vietnam—more than it ever had in Korea, Iraq, or Afghanistan. The black stone walls of the Vietnam Memorial in Washington would be engraved with the names of the 58,000 Americans who died in the war. Deep inequities figured in who fought and who didn't. College students and young men who snared occupational deferments (including me) avoided service. But unlike today, when all servicemen and servicewomen are volunteers, conscription touched everyone. At age eighteen, you had to register with the Selective Service System; this was "signing up for the draft," and it was the law. Then, if health, educational, occupational, or other factors didn't intervene, you'd be rated 1A, fit for service, inducted, and very likely shipped off to Vietnam.

The Jacobs boys vowed they'd go to jail before they'd serve in a war that they, and much of the country, saw as immoral, senseless, and cruel.

One evening, reading the paper, Bob thought, "A year from now I'll be sitting in this chair and my boys will be in jail." How would they survive it, locked up, vulnerable to unspeakable jailhouse cruelties? He couldn't let it happen. "There's a beautiful big country up north of us," he said to Jane, "and I think we ought to go there." He regaled her with what he'd seen that day in Toronto and was so enthusiastic she came around to the idea.

Later, some wondered why Jane Jacobs, so long and deeply a New Yorker, had moved to Toronto. Or rather, why *exactly*, for there seemed no dearth of reasons. Jane and the family were exhausted from years of battling city hall; this was true. And with the war raging and soldiers in gas masks at the Pentagon, Jane saw America through a darker lens, her patriotism shaken; this was true, also. Meanwhile, American cities endured dark nights and days of racial tension and riot. All these and other factors could be heard to explain the flight of the Jacobs family, leaving one to conclude that maybe all of them—mixed all together, somehow, vaguely—were responsible.

But no, that *wasn't* it. It was simpler: the Jacobses left for Canada because Jane and Bob didn't want to see their children go to Vietnam or, more likely, to jail.

June 1968, their third day in Canada.

What do you do if you're a New Yorker looking for an apartment in your city's competitive housing market? Well, late in the evening you head for the nearest newsstand, pick up the next morning's papers, leaf through the classified ads for Apartments to Rent, circle the best prospects, and, early next morning, sit down at a phone and start calling. This was the only strategy the Jacobses knew and the first thing they did in Toronto was adapt it to their new circumstances. At a Kresge's, which was not exactly a New York City newsstand, they bought papers, and set to work, having first stopped at the offices of the War Resisters League, a pacifist organization, for some rudimentary grounding in Toronto's residential neighborhoods.

The place they liked best, a ground-floor flat of a bow-fronted three-story house with a pitched roof at 58 Spadina Road, was vacant. But it couldn't be rented right away, said one of the owners; he'd have to check with his sisters first. *C'mon*, Jim recalls his father insinuating, *what kind of a man are you* that you need to ask your sisters? Oh, all right, but there *does* need to be a lease. Bob helped him write one, a few sentences on a scrap of paper, so they could move right in. It was a little tight for the five of them. But they had a pocket-sized garden out back, complete with crabapple tree, insulated a bit from the traffic whizzing down Spadina Road. Next door was a nursery school, from which they could hear the shouts of children playing. Three days after leaving Hudson Street, they had a new home.

Aside from this modest triumph, however, they got off to a wobbly start in their adoptive city: Toronto was tidier, and *tighter,* than the New York that had formed their habits and values. Jane, who in her plucky long-stridededness could be daunting as she crossed a busy street, was stopped for jaywalking. Bob was pulled over to the side for driving with his rearview mirror obstructed by furniture piled in the backseat. And Mary . . . well, Mary had the gall to step out at six o'clock one morning to explore the neighborhood; maybe that was a little too early, or maybe she was a little too young, but she caught the eye of two cops, who picked her up, brought her back to Spadina Road, and delivered a stern warning to her parents. All this within their first week in Toronto. "I don't think we're suited to this place," Jane worried. At the least, it was going to be a big adjustment. "If you come from New York, Toronto doesn't look like a city," Jim recalls them feeling at first. It was a far cry from the ragged but familiar precincts of Hudson Street.

From almost the moment they'd landed in Toronto, Bob had gone prospecting for jobs. He soon got an offer from the Toronto architect Eberhard Zeidler, whose firm had embarked on a big hospital project, the McMaster University Health Sciences Centre, in Hamilton, Ontario; seeking senior architects for it, Zeidler had heard about Bob from a trusted friend. By this point, Bob Jacobs was known as an expert in the design of surgical suites, was established enough to comment on "The Future of the American Hospital" for *Architectural and Engineering News.* Bob knew hospitals, knew everything that went into them. A doctor's examination room needs space for an exam table, a sink, a cupboard, and so on; well, Bob knew the requirements for every arcane, out-of-the-way hospital space you could imagine, or couldn't imagine. "He had an encyclopedic brain," says a colleague from a few years later. Brought in as one of five or six top people on the McMaster job, Zeidler recalls Bob as "a great guy, funny, very clever, a good architect."

After Bob's four-week "vacation" in Toronto, he had first to get back to his job in New York and give notice. But by summer's end, he was working for Zeidler. Soon enough, he and Jane and Zeidler, an ex–German navy submariner who'd migrated to Canada after the war, and his wife, also named Jane, became good friends. Based on all he'd heard of Jane Jacobs, whose book he'd read, Zeidler figured her for something of a firebrand. But soon they were in and out of each other's homes, trading recipes, Jane drawing particularly close to Zeidler's daughter Margie.

Soon after Jane's arrival, probably late in 1968, Marshall McLuhan, the University of Toronto media critic, famous for his maxim "The medium is the message," learned she was in Toronto. He asked her to lunch at the faculty club, then at one point visited her on Spadina Road. "You need a cleaning lady," McLuhan pronounced. Well, yeah, maybe so, allows Jim, who tells this story. They'd just moved in, were exploring Toronto, getting used to things. "No one was thinking about cleaning. We were none of us clean-freaks." McLuhan proposed his own housekeeper for the job, a Calabrian woman with limited English, Mary Malfara. "No, too dirty," she said when she first saw the Spadina Road place. But she wound up working for the family for many years. In talking with her, Jane leaned toward vocabulary from the Latinate, "Italian," side of English, and soon Mary could understand her. In time, built on their ongoingly imperfect conversation about children and other matters domestic, they became friendly, baby showers and weddings bringing the families together.

Early in 1969, Jane sent her old editor at *Forum*, Doug Haskell, now retired, a kind of progress report:

Bob is working on a large new teaching hospital, full of exciting new architectural ideas and procedures that I think would fascinate you, Doug. Jimmy . . . is working as a laboratory technician in the physics department at the University of Toronto, and says he is learning more than he would as a graduate student . . . Ned is writing a novel (!) in the mornings and has just gotten a job, about which he is very pleased and excited, in the afternoons as a kindergarten teacher to ten little boys whose energy and wildness were evidently too much for the regular, "elderly" (his report) kindergarten teachers. Mary is in the eighth grade at the same public school where Ned is working . . . My book is *finally* finished and will be out in May.

In moving to Canada, the Jacobses were reenacting a scenario repeated thousands of times during the Vietnam War by draft dodgers, deserters, conscientious objectors, and others who judged America's war in Southeast Asia immoral and unjust. Facing prison for resisting the draft or leaving their units, antiwar émigrés to Canada numbered at least fifty thousand. Many of them highly principled and well educated, they contributed much to their new country. Inevitably, some of them found their way to the Jacobs house.

One was Cliff Esler, who'd been drafted around the time the Jacobses moved to Canada; he had spent the summer in basic training in New Jersey, then in advanced infantry training in Louisiana. Along the way he met veterans of the fighting back from 'Nam, "scary guys, telling scary stories" of killing and being killed, senselessly, brutally. For the first time, he thought, "Whoa, I'm not going to do this." In October, he got his orders, for Long Binh, Vietnam, a big American base. But he wasn't going. In his thirty-day leave before shipping out, he got the name of a Toronto contact, wrote a rant to be forwarded to the Army once he was gone, dumped a duffel bag full of uniforms into a trash can, boarded a plane for Toronto, entered the country with a visitor's visa, and arranged to meet his Canadian contact at Rochdale College, a new experimental school near the University of Toronto. His contact's name was Hester and she was a friend of the Jacobses'.

The Jacobs family, he'd recall in an unpublished memoir, "welcomed me with open arms," and soon he was a regular at the house, which softened his landing in Canada. "I was kind of surprised that they treated me as an equal," he recalls. "It was, 'Come on in and sit down.' I loved going over there." He often hung out with Ned, whom he thought voluble, enthusiastic, and cheerful; and Mary; and sometimes Jane's nephew Paul Manson, Betty's son, also much around the house during this period. One time, Cliff visited Jimmy at the physics lab where he worked and found himself agog—right there in front of him, Real Science! Ned and Mary, on the other hand, "were still in the teenage zone, not knowing what they were going to be, full of Love-is-in-the-air and Flower Power." But always at the Jacobses there was the dinner table, the undisputed center of family life, gladiatorial arena for intellectual battle. Jane was forever challenging him: " 'You're jumping to too big a conclusion there, Cliff,' and invariably she was dead on."

He'd remember Jane, at fifty-two, as "a large haystack of a woman . . . with a thick, beaky nose and shoulder-length hair, dressed in the green mechanic's coveralls which the whole family (particularly she and Jimmy) had adopted as their workaday uniform." He'd remember her "owlish round tortoise-shell glasses"; her wry, ready laugh, her salt-of-the-earth mien, her approachability; her "drink of choice," dry sherry, as well as the eggnog, spiked with apple brandy, that she'd make from scratch come Christmas. And he'd remember her traipsing down the street, "with two gigantic shopping bags, sagging," stuffed with books, which for the next few days she'd retreat to her study to devour.

One other impression stuck with him across the years: "She was not afraid of anything in the world"; it rubbed off on the children, too, "who tended to see things as exciting, as an adventure," not scary. Jane, he says, was "genuinely fearless."

Jane and the rest of the family had much to learn and absorb; spelling it "colour," not "color," was the least of their worries. They hadn't immigrated to Somalia or Peru; Canada was different, but not *very* different—just different enough to catch you up. Local politicians ran for office in "ridings," not districts. America's "life, liberty, and the pursuit of happiness" was Canada's "peace, order, and good government." City, provincial, and federal relationships differed from their American counterparts just enough to leave you perplexed. Then there was the country's French-English divide, with Quebec forever in tension with English-speaking Canada. And the peculiar relationship of Canada to the United Kingdom, with the queen of England the country's head of state and the governor general her representative. From an American perspective, history could look quite upside down; those who'd fled the new United States for Canada after the American Revolution were now good guys, not unpatriotic Tories. Canadian dollars were normally worth roughly that of American dollars, but never exactly so. Canadians celebrated Thanksgiving, but not on the same day as Americans. Other holidays bore names like Victoria Day and Dominion Day. Then there was the first Monday in August, which, Jane wrote her mother, "is a holiday here, but Canadians don't know what to call it." None of this was intellectually daunting; unfamiliar street names, new maps to master, were the necessary work of every traveler. But still, it was all a little strange and new for a woman of fifty-two who'd spent her whole life in America, her adult life solely in New York City.

What helped them adapt was the Spadina fight, into which they were thrust soon after their arrival. Pronounced *spah-DY-nah* and named for a local estate, Spadina wasn't just the street where they lived (a "road" north of Bloor Street, an "avenue" south), but, for provincial traffic engineers going back to the 1940s, a future expressway. The campaign to block its construction split Toronto for more than three years. "Where local politicians stood on the Spadina Expressway," wrote John Sewell, a friend and collaborator of Jane's for most of her time in Toronto, "was the defining issue of the day. Two opposing visions of the city had rarely been presented in such a powerful, volatile and bitter way." Jane was drawn into the controversy through another transplanted American, Bobbi Speck.

Speck had moved from New York in 1966 and was living in the neighborhood known as the Annex when one day she read of an expressway, already being built, that was to barrel down from the northern suburbs in wide swaths of asphalt, in tunnels and trenches, and ultimately right down Spadina Road, to mate up with planned crosstown expressways. "We are not experts, but we know a monster when we see one," Speck would say of the Spadina. Teaming up with another young mother, they formed a Committee of Concerned Citizens. When Speck spoke up at a public meeting, the local papers covered it, and soon her phone was ringing nonstop. She became virtually shackled to the phone, her career as a freelance editor derailed.

At one meeting, she'd recall, a woman "with this familiar New York voice" spoke up forcibly about tactics and strategies to defeat the Spadina. Speck thought, "This woman is incredible! She has everything down pat! Her thoughts came out in paragraph form, and put our instincts into broader context." "I hope you'll get involved," said Speck, going up to her after the meeting.

"That's why I'm here, dearie," said Jane Jacobs.

The Spadina was supposed to slash down through the heart of the city from Highway 401, which had been built in the early 1950s as a modest intercity highway but would morph into a commuter artery at some points eighteen lanes wide. "Those who lived in the suburbs had difficulty understanding why anyone would want to save older neighborhoods," wrote John Sewell, in his book *The Shape of the City.* "Suburbanites thought it entirely reasonable that the existing city be demolished to make way for the new city," which required highways to link their suburban homes to the downtown towers where they worked. "City residents didn't quite see it that way."

Opposition had already stiffened by the time Jane got involved; no one, least of all she, would claim she alone was responsible for the expressway's defeat. But by early 1969, still new in town, she was already a voice in a civic debate that would extend over the next two years. "My understanding," said Speck many years later, "was that she had not yet unpacked." Early that year, Jane was featured in a Canadian television program about urban design. At one point, we see her stride across University Avenue, uncharacteristically regal, in a dark matching winter outfit, skirt to just above the knees, and heels. "Toronto's a very refreshing city to come to from the States," she says. But "probably the biggest single menace to Toronto is the Spadina Expressway. The minute you take an expressway into—not up to, but into—the dense part of the city," then you start doing damage, exchanging parks for parking lots, narrowing sidewalks, deadening street life.

Later that year, Jane wrote a blistering attack in *The Globe and Mail,* "A City Getting Hooked on the Expressway Drug." In it, she looked in seeming wonder at how Canadians, faced with direct evidence for how American cities like Boston, Buffalo, and Los Angeles had bungled so much, could possibly consider following their example. As a transplant from New York, she was often asked whether she found Toronto exciting enough for herself. "I find it almost too exciting. The suspense is scary. Here is the most hopeful and healthy city in North America, still unmangled, still with options." Maybe Toronto would go down the road of its wrongheaded American cousins, but still she was grateful to have at least "enjoyed this great city before its destruction."

The whole Jacobs family got involved—though *not,* Jane insisted to an interviewer later, because they wanted to. "I did not, and neither did the rest of my family, react with joy when we heard we had another expressway to fight." Here, she lapsed into a juvenile voice: *"Oh, we can do it here, we did it in a bigger city.* No, no," it wasn't like that. Still, plunge into the fight they did.

On New Year's Day 1970 a group of "minstrels," as a news account had it the next day, protested the Spadina at the mayor's New Year's Day "levee," a Canadian word, a Canadian tradition, where an officeholder hosts a celebratory open house, this one at a new performing arts center. But as soon as the singers, who called themselves the Provocative Street Players and whose chief writer and singer was Ned Jacobs, began to belt out the first chorus of "The Bad Trip," they were shut down. A newspaper showed long-haired Ned, wearing a paisley outfit Jim had made for him for Christmas, being peacefully, but firmly, ushered off the premises by a guard. The chorus went like this:

> And it's a bad trip, yeah it's a bad trip—
> That Spadina Expressway
> While the highway boys are playing with their toys
> The people are the ones who pay.

Among other foes of the Spadina Expressway was Marshall McLuhan, who suggested to Jane that they collaborate on a movie about it. "You and I can do the script."

"But I don't know a thing about scriptwriting," she said. No worries, he didn't either. They'd do it together.

The two of them convened at his University of Toronto office, where McLuhan called in his secretary to record everything they said. After an hour of throwing around ideas, they were finished. "Got it all down?" McLuhan asked his secretary. "Well, that's it," he said, turning to Jane. "We've got the script."

Jane was horrified. They had no script at all, just a collection of variants of "Hey, what about this?" When she finally saw the transcript, that's all it was, words and ideas jumping around, "without beginning or end," the flimsiest of threads holding it together. "This did not bother McLuhan," she said, "but it did bother me."

Yet miraculously, they wound up with a fourteen-minute film called *The Burning Would* (apologies to James Joyce), thick with noisy construction scenes, jackhammers, and demolition derbies, awful screeching sounds, ruthless destruction, all set against the peaceful humanity the expressway would erase—a burbling brook, a little boy playing with his plastic pail in a spot of greenery. Nothing subtle here, voice-over scarcely required, yet oddly effective. "I couldn't have been more astonished,"

Jane recalled. McLuhan had really worked it over. "There was a shape to it" now. "It had music. It did have a thread, and raised a lot of important issues." In Toronto, *The Burning Would* made its mark against the Spadina, and ended up being shown all over the U.S. and Canada, too. "It's a mystery to me," Jane reminisced, "that something tangible, coherent and constructive could come out of that mess."

In Jane's daybook that year, for January 14, she noted "Expressway meeting at Convocation Hall," the great domed ceremonial auditorium at the University of Toronto, and beside it, simply: "Speak."

"Do Spadina brief," she reminded herself for March 25.

"Get copies of Spadina brief," for the 27th.

"The Spadina fight is coming to a head," Jane wrote Jason Epstein on March 29. "People here are so innocent, which is nice but also exasperating. I have privately made up a strategy that would shock them, I fear, but will just try it on my own."

"It started quietly enough," *The Toronto Telegram* reported the day after the key April 6 hearing. For seven hours the Metro transportation committee moved smoothly through sixteen speakers at the opening session of hearings into the William Allen (Spadina) Expressway. "Then urban expert Jane Jacobs shattered the lull."

> My name is Jane Jacobs. I reside at 58 Spadina Road, Toronto. I am the author of several works on cities and I first involved myself in the Spadina Expressway controversy with the hope that such knowledge as I may have about cities and their dynamics would prove helpful.

At this point, setting aside her measured, ladylike tone, Jane went on to attack not just the expressway itself but its backers. She impugned their honesty, called the hearing a "charade." She charged that the planners behind it lacked integrity, choosing data "selectively and even contradictorily to prove a case rather than to illuminate realities." One account described Jane that day as "a gray-haired lady with grown children and a very pleasant smile, and she comes on with a soft, clear voice that has just a trace of acid in it, a voice as cool as non-alcoholic cider."

They tried to cut her off, to which Jane replied, "If a citizen cannot speak of a politician's official capacity without being charged with being personal, we might as well have robots in these jobs."

She was charged with being a rabble-rouser. One councillor asked her how, voicing such attacks, she could expect a sympathetic response from them. "I'm not asking you to be sympathetic with me," she said. "I don't give a damn."

Another councillor shot back, "You don't give a damn about anything."

In the end, this board, and all the others that needed to give their assent to the expressway, did so. But it was too late; the ground had shifted under them, public opinion turning against the road. Even with the project seemingly cleared by every board and council, the provincial governor, Bill Davis, quashed it, famously declaring to the Ontario legislature, "If we are building a transportation system to serve the automobile, the Spadina Expressway would be a good place to start. But if we are building a transportation system to serve people, the Spadina Expressway is a good place to stop."

For the Jacobs family, there was a hidden payoff to their work over the two years: it helped them acclimate to their home. "I think the 1969–70 Spadina Expressway fight was a blessing for all of us," Ned Jacobs would say. "We met many interesting people and got involved in Toronto civic life, which made us feel less like exiles."

It had been no gradual transition. It was more like they'd jumped into a cold, northern lake, the whole Jacobs clan, each of them swimming and paddling like crazy, trying to keep warm, making new lives for themselves. "When we came," Jane would later tell an interviewer, "we made up our minds we were not exiles, we were immigrants. It was a great adventure for us." The house on Spadina Road always bustled. They had new friends, new jobs, new activities. They'd drop by en masse at Cineforum, a former porn house, now an art movie center on Bloor Street, to see Buster Keaton and Marx Brothers movies. Jane would rummage through the offerings of Bloor Street fruit and vegetable merchants, just as she had back in the Village. She'd dig into her two or three daily newspapers, along with *The New York Review of Books*, *Scientific American*, *I. F. Stone's Weekly*, *Esquire*, and some of the Toronto underground papers, reading always.

"What's it like there?" the Jacobses had started to hear back from friends in New York once the plea bargain on the steno-tape incident had been hammered out and they began getting the word out to their friends about their new home in Canada. *Are there igloos in the street?* To their

New York friends, Canada mainly meant those feared winter weather advisories, the ones warning of "a massive cold front coming down from Canada." Jane didn't like the dark of winter—she loved the sun, fairly charting its progress all winter long—but didn't mind the cold. Toronto, she decided, was just like the U.S., only with an extra February and no July.

CHAPTER 19

SETTLING IN

A MONG BELONGINGS crowded into the VW bus the Jacobs family drove to Toronto were Jane's typewriter and the manuscript of the book she'd worked on through much of the 1960s, no doubt extracted from the freezer chest in their Hudson Street basement where she safeguarded it. On Spadina Road, a sheet of plywood, legs screwed into it, served for a desk. That, together with a file cabinet, and she was in business. It wasn't more than a week on Spadina Road, figures Jim Jacobs, before she was at work on the remaining editorial chores for *The Economy of Cities*. Its acknowledgments page was dated August 1968, two months after their arrival. The book was published the following May.

"I will [tell] the story as I go along of small cities no less than of great," Jane quoted the fifth century BCE Greek historian Herodotus in the book's epigraph. "Most of those which were great once are small today; and those which in my own lifetime have grown to greatness were small enough in the old days." The rise and fall, death and life, of cities and economies—this is what she had been thinking about for much of her adult life. And in *The Economy of Cities*, she had answers: for one, cities prospered by creating new work out of old. Doing the same old thing didn't cut it. Maybe you had a big, productive coal mine or sprawling steel mill to show off, but digging coal or churning out steel ingots year after year led nowhere but to stagnation and decline. Cities withered when they stopped generating new work—as she saw occurring, even then, in the car monoculture that was Detroit.

Like *Death and Life,* the new book had a way of insinuating itself into a reader's mind with what she had to say—with what she *dared* say. For starters, as we saw earlier, she asserted that cities predated agriculture, not the other way around—that agriculture was the product of nascent cities that had grown up around earlier hunter-gatherer settlements; this was the idea she'd illustrated with her imagined early city, New Obsidian. Yet as arresting as that was, it was but prologue to her more abiding question: Why did one city or country blossom into ruddy growth while another stagnated?

Ideas ran all through *The Economy of Cities*—big ideas, little ideas, import replacement, and captive division of labor, diversification, and differentiation. But mostly, Jane illustrated them through story, anecdote, and example. Consider Los Angeles: in the years just after World War II, the city saw a loss of 150,000 jobs in aircraft manufacturing and 70,000 in shipbuilding, along with a steep decline in Hollywood filmmaking. Yet impossibly, it boasted a big increase in jobs overall, its economy exploding after the war. What could explain so counterintuitive a result? Los Angeles, Jane argued, was successfully replacing "imports," by which she meant not just foreign imports from Mexico, say, but everything Los Angeles needed to bring in from outside. Angelinos were producing much more of these imports, then turning around and selling them to the world.

> The new enterprises started in corners of old loft buildings, in Quonset huts and in backyard garages. But they multiplied swiftly ... And many grew rapidly. They poured forth furnaces, sliding doors, mechanical saws, shoes, bathing suits, underwear, china, furniture, cameras, hand tools, hospital equipment, scientific instruments, engineering services and hundreds of other things. One-eighth of all the new businesses started in the United States during the latter half of the 1940s were started in Los Angeles.

Not all replaced imports, but many did. A young engineer formerly working in the materials lab at Douglas Aircraft started making sliding glass doors for local housebuilders. Succeeding locally, he was soon the largest manufacturer of them in the United States.

Jane memorably compared and contrasted the English cities of Manchester and Birmingham. In the 1840s, as she told the story, Manchester, the great textiles city, seemed the city of the future. Friedrich Engels, who lived there then, indicted it for the degradation of the men and women who worked in its ranks of smoke-belching factories; "Cottonopolis," some called it, the world's first truly industrialized city. Birmingham was nothing so dramatic. It made saddles and harnesses, shoe buckles, buttons, glass, and, later, guns, jewelry, and everything in between. Nothing on the scale of Manchester, nothing to imprint itself on the mind of the world the way Manchester did. But, Jane delivered the verdict, "Manchester was not the city of the future and Birmingham was." Once others had learned to spin and weave cotton, Manchester was bound for decline. Multi-skilled Birmingham, on the other hand, crucible of trial and error, adapted and grew. "Its fragmented and inefficient little industries kept adding new work, and splitting off new organizations," some of which, in time, grew large themselves.

Maidenform, the bra manufacturer, wasn't always big, either. Ida Rosenthal, a New York City dressmaker dissatisfied with how her dresses hung on her customers, designed an early brassiere (though not, as Jane suggests, the *first* brassiere), which she gave to customers with each new dress. We know how *that* worked out. Dressmaking, in Jane's terminology, was "old work." Brassieres were "new work." Here was the true wellspring of economic health, one most often billowing up from the small in scale, particularly in the bustling precincts of big, diverse cities, where experts and entrepreneurs, the creative and the ambitious, were thrown together in unpredictable, mutually beneficial, ways.

And what of that icon of efficiency and economy, the division of labor, exemplified in the famous pin factory described by Adam Smith in *The Wealth of Nations*? Well, Jane didn't buy it. "*Division of labor, in itself, creates nothing. It is only a way of organizing work that has already been created.*" Besides, it was a fixture of stagnant economies, too,

> where men and women spend their entire working lives at very specialized tasks: tapping rubber trees, or herding goats, or loading bananas, or twisting fibers, or dancing in temples, or mining salt, or crushing ore, or carrying baskets of dirt for public works, or cultivating corn and beans.

You can hear Jane's revulsion groaning up from the page. Whatever it had in its favor, division of labor did not embody or explain economic health.

What did was Jane's heroic mantra of "one sort of work leads to another," which she developed and enriched through numerous examples: Sandpaper leads to masking tape, Scotch tape, and sound-recording magnetic tape. A hospital's outpatient department grows into a new home care department. Police officers, building on their own "old work," demand bribes from illegal enterprises, organizing to collect and dole out the take; criminal, certainly, but this, too, was new work. "New goods and services, whether criminal or benign, do not come out of thin air. New work arises upon existing work."

Everything in *The Economy of Cities* conjured up innovators, entrepreneurs, small-scale genius bursting forth, never settling into ruts, a bazaar of little companies forever taking skills, trades, and expertise they already possessed and putting them to new use. Here was vitality triumphant, embodied in new products and ideas. The enemy was stagnation, ineptitude, minds on automatic pilot, economic death.

Much in the book was provocative—and not alone Jane's precept that, as Jason Epstein put it, economic life "does not begin in a garden but in a city," as in Jane's New Obsidian. Some months before publication, Epstein sent copies to outside experts, not for three-sentence blurbs but, with due prudence, to see what credentialed authorities had to say about some of Jane's outlandish claims. One went to the Columbia University economist Robert Lekachman, who wrote back, "As always, Jane Jacobs is a pleasure to read. The ideas are fresh and the opinions are firm. Now whether she has produced a whole new theory or not, I am less certain." Some of it, he said, wasn't really so new, having been "foreshadowed" by economists like Colin Clark and Joseph Schumpeter. What he thought "important and different" about the book was "the boldness of [her] claim that innovation, growth, and progress can come only from small, almost casual beginnings."

The University of Chicago anthropologist Robert McCormick Adams was harsher. He applauded some of what he read in *The Economy of Cities,* and said he was glad Epstein was going to publish it. But he didn't buy all her arguments. "I think she both oversystematizes and overgeneralizes, under the mistaken impression that the very comprehensiveness of her attack is a point in its favor." Academics, he worried, might not lash out at the book at all but simply ignore it, issuing only "bland disclaimers that anything in her work is relevant to *them.*" Then, turning to New Obsidian, he gave it four pages of detailed criticism, citing both the particulars of her arguments and the scant scholarly superstructure underlying them. He concluded on a friendlier note, observing that "an argumentative—and stimulating—work provokes an argument. Jacobs is surely tough-minded . . . enough as an author not to let any of this seriously undermine her basic conception . . . You are surely knowledgeable and tough-minded enough as a publisher to know a good thing when you see it."

Asked in 1970 which of her opinions she deemed most unconventional, Jane allowed that it was her cities-before-agriculture idea. "But I think it will have become conventional opinion 20 years from now." It didn't, and hasn't. At a Boston College conference devoted to Jane's ideas in 1987, Carroll Keeley briefly disposed of cities-first as still "an open issue," suggesting that in any case it would "permanently nuance one's idea of the primacy of agriculture into a much more sophisticated" model. If we peek ahead we see that scholars continue to quarrel over it today. One defense of cities-first, by Peter J. Taylor, a British geographer, came out in the *International Journal of Urban and Regional Research* in 2012. His attention to it, following that of others similarly sympathetic, infuriated a trio of American archaeologists led by Michael E. Smith of Arizona State University. Jacobs's argument was all but nonsense, they wrote in a long refutation of it, "Jane Jacobs' 'Cities First' Model and Archaeological Reality." It appeared in 2014, in the same journal that had carried Taylor's article. For them, there was an unbridgeably wide chronological gap, thousands of years, between the first agriculture and the first cities. They weren't challenging Jacobs's overall contribution, they said, just this one in particular: "We cannot . . . envision any scenario in which we [would need to] debate the chronological priority of cities over agricultural origins." Others, of course, would say it all comes down to just what you mean by "city."

But all that, as inconclusive as it remains, came much later. When it was published in May 1969, *The Economy of Cities* often stirred reviewers to their rhetorical best, as if aping Jane herself. "Bless Jane Jacobs," a *Time* review led off. "Lively, lucid, blunt, original, she triumphs by being mostly wrong."

For the *New York Times* reviewer Christopher Lehmann-Haupt, writing under the wholly apt headline "The Death and Life of Economies," the new book was "astonishing . . . It blows cobwebs from the mind, and challenges assumptions one hadn't even realized one had made. It should prove of major importance."

In *The Village Voice*, Michael Harrington, whose recent *The Other*

America had done much to alert the country to its forgotten poor, described himself as "provoked, stimulated, and charmed by her insights almost as much as I disagree with her basic theory and conclusions." All told, the book was "bad economics and good values."

In *The Hudson Review*, Roger Sale seemed as intrigued by how the book worked on him as by what it actually said: its impact was "mysterious, in a way that makes you want to look around, to reflect on what you know of elsewhere, to read the Yellow Pages and the U.S. Census and see it all different, as if for the first time . . . It's like having a whole new world to think about." And then (as first quoted in the Introduction), he said one of the truer things to be said of her: "There are ways to disagree with Jane Jacobs, but not as many as you might think, because on her own terms she is almost invariably right and the real questions arise when you start to consider what she has left out."

Pointing to some of what she'd left out was, again, Herbert Gans, who had seized on what he saw as the "physical fallacy" in *Death and Life*. "In her new book," he began his *New Republic* review, "Mrs. Jacobs continues the search for vitality, this time to discover what makes urban economies live or die." Again she'd written "an exciting book . . . But once more, I find her analysis skewed." Jane had largely ignored the role of big corporations, or simply written them off as exemplars of stagnation. Getting too much credit, on the other hand, was the innovative entrepreneur. "Sometimes the book reads like a tract on behalf of 19th-century rugged individualism."

As in *Death and Life*, wrote Gans, "Mrs. Jacobs places a higher value on vitality than on well-being. But . . . imagine a one-or-two-industry city producing 'old work' for which demand is stable and permanent, paying high wages and taxes." Think tires in Akron, or country music in Nashville. That might make for scant vitality but much community well-being. Single-industry towns might lack the diversity and economic *oomph* of great cities, but at least while they prospered many residents managed to lead contented lives. And wasn't a good life . . . a good life? Gans, who since he'd written of Boston's West End had written a long, ambitious study of tract-house contentment in Levittown, New York, seemed to see around and within ranges of American life for which Jane had little sympathy. For Jane, boredom was bad, stagnation was bad, always and forever, both a kind of death.

Still, Gans rounded out his long review, "What Mrs. Jacobs has done in this book and in her earlier one is to begin to formulate a badly needed urban myth for our now almost entirely urbanized society. In the long run, this may well be her most important contribution."

After Lehmann-Haupt's review in *The New York Times*, an archaeologist, Patricia Daly, wrote Jane, faulting her on some of her points, mostly about ancient Çatal Hüyük, what it really meant to be a city, and several technical issues. At one point in her lengthy reply, Jane had this to say:

> Anthropologists make a terrible mistake in looking at the most stagnant (that is, the most primitive) economies *now* in existence in the world, and attempting to draw conclusions from these concerning prehistoric processes of development. That can't work; one simply cannot extrapolate from stagnation.

There was little to learn from stagnation and decline, she was saying. The lessons were all in life and health.

"Back when I came to Toronto in 1968," Jane would report, "there was not a single outdoor café . . . In fact you couldn't sit in your own back yard and legally take a drink of alcohol. Or on your front porch . . . Because a child might see it . . . That was the thing. I'm not making that up."

At the time, Toronto was a city of about 2 million people, 350 miles from Montreal, 500 from Quebec City, 250 from Detroit. It was a famously sleepy town for much of its history, certainly up to 1968, lying in the shadow of older, more cosmopolitan, French-influenced Montreal; and maybe even, for that matter, of Buffalo, New York. If you wanted a night on the town, you'd hear it said, drive a hundred miles around the western lip of Lake Ontario to Buffalo, with its beautiful Olmsted parks and hint of urban bustle.

In its Great Lakes–flavored English stolidity, Toronto might have seemed to a midwesterner from the U.S. comfortably familiar, laid out on roughly orthogonal lines, unprepossessing, flat. Of course, it *wasn't* flat, not really, but furrowed, right down into the city, by dozens of what Torontonians called "ravines," shallow valleys left over from the glaciers that gave it topographical richness, sylvan streambeds, bits of untended forest, even seeming wilderness. New Yorkers might see Toronto as the end of the world, but even in his brief 1967 visit, Bob found in it redemptive features. The city was growing, beginning the surge in population and influence that would let it soon overtake Montreal as Canada's premier city. During the late 1960s and early 1970s, English-speaking Montrealers, scared off by the political tumult in Quebec, began moving to Toronto, tens of thousands of them, laden with money and talent. Energetic, increasingly Asian newcomers, 75,000 of them a year, were moving in, too. A new city hall had gone up a couple of years before Jane's arrival—"two boomerangs over half a grapefruit," as someone called Viljo Revell's striking modernist structure—that was neither universally loved nor reviled; but certainly, as Robert Fulford wrote in *Accidental City*, "it transformed Toronto by cracking open the city's prejudices about how buildings should look; the public idea of what was acceptable in architecture seemed to change overnight." Toronto's gray was blossoming into color.

By the time Jane arrived, hints of pink, blooming health were enlivening Toronto's doughy face, just when most American cities were in decline, hemorrhaging population. Canadian banks, Jane would hazard as one reason, had never "redlined" neighborhoods into destruction. Racial ghettos were almost unknown. Though Canada's local and provincial authorities could still do damage, at least the federal government wasn't pushing highways through cities. Finally, Canada's version of urban renewal had intruded less, and destroyed less. These virtues of omission, Jane would point out, were enough to make Toronto more hopeful than most of its American counterparts. The city had fine old neighborhoods, a decent subway system, three daily papers, a top university. It was the provincial capital. Its localities bore English place-names like York and Scarborough, Glencairn and Runnymede. Its old Kensington Market district could remind you of New York's Lower East Side, with crowded streets and tiny shops, live chickens in cages, a welter of foreign languages, a bit decrepit, yet charming, more like Hudson Street back in the 1940s. House hunting soon after they got to Toronto, the Jacobses did tour Kensington Market but couldn't find just the right place among its thin residential offerings. "It looked a little desolate," Jim recalls, "but so what, it didn't *feel* desolate."

It must have been late in their second year in Toronto that they began to look for a more permanent home; the Spadina Road house was being sold, so they *had* to move. And besides, it was way too small. They wound up a few blocks away, near the western end of the same neighborhood, the Annex (for its annexation by the city back in 1887).

The Annex was a rectangle of real estate sitting just north of the University of Toronto across Bloor Street, two miles from city hall, marked by large brick and sandstone houses arrayed along tree-lined streets; some of its Victorian mansions went back to the 1880s. Bobbi Speck, the woman who'd helped draw Jane into the Stop Spadina fight, recalled the Annex of the late 1960s as mostly absentee owned, the Depression having broken up many old houses into apartments. But it was busy, with lots of foot traffic, safe, kids out on the street at all hours, and, as one resident would recall, spectacularly diverse:

> We had one or two of the original inhabitants going back to 1903, 1905 or their descendants. We had a large Eastern European community. We had Holocaust survivors. We had a genuine Nazi. This is on one block. We had communists. We had rooming houses. Chinese rooming houses . . . We had drug drops. We had unsavory people. We had three brothels. They were part of the community, actually. My son played with the son of the madam. And then there were young professionals like us who were renovating. It was a completely mixed community.

Here in the Annex, at 69 Albany Avenue, the Jacobses found a home.

"We think we have bought a house, four blocks from here," Jane wrote Jason Epstein in July 1970. "I hope so. It has space enough in it for a room for me just to work in!" It was a three-story, semidetached, redbrick affair dating to about 1910, built for the University of Toronto dinosaur expert, William Arthur Park. Two large rooms on the third floor; Jane and Bob's bedroom second floor front, Jane's office in the rear; dining room, living room, and kitchen on the first. Albany Avenue was no broad "avenue" at all, but a modest street, with room enough for a single lane of traffic and two of parking. The houses lining it were packed close, narrow spaces between them, making for mostly uninterrupted street frontage. Each had a little garden out front, a more extensive yard reaching out back. Jane's daybook recorded their planned move: they were to measure rooms on August 1st, close on September 10th, get the phone installed on November 13th, move in on the 21st, clean out Spadina Road the next day.

"We are going to have more room," Jane wrote her young planner friend, David Gurin, not long after the move. "I say 'going to' because at present the first floor, where we demolished walls, is kind of a half-plastered welter." Bob was putting his design mark on the place, opening up the ground floor, kitchen shelves facing the living room, a lawn glider covered in imitation leather the new living room couch. Son Jim remembered it, for all its quirks, as "a very elegant-looking place." Some months after the move, Jane wrote her mother, "The carpenter yesterday finished a balcony—or as they say here, a veranda," on a roof extension at the back of the house above Jane's work room, practically in the treetops. "We are still in a mess," Jane wrote Epstein early the following year. "The painters are at work; what a relief after the plasterers. Hey, this is going to be a nifty place." In time, the house would be covered by thick vines. Towering maples would rise from the front yard.

Of course, with Jane it was never just the house itself that mattered, but the street. And not just the street, either, but its ties to the rest of the neighborhood and the city. From Albany Avenue, Jane was a couple of minutes' walk to the subway, the Bathurst station on Bloor Street, where trains pulling out every three or four minutes brought her, with transfers to the Yonge Street line, virtually anywhere downtown. Bloor Street's array of shops and businesses changed over the years. Early on it was mostly local, studded with grocers and butcher shops, little clothing stores, a yarn shop. Jane would take her "bundle buggy," a small shopping cart, to pick up provisions, sometimes take the subway down to the city's old St. Lawrence Market. In time, as the Annex gentrified, Bloor Street became a shopping destination for outsiders and students, the more neighborhood-oriented shops thinning out.

Jane would live on Albany Avenue for the rest of her life—for the first quarter century or so with Bob and then, for ten years more, alone.

The house gloried in that first flurry of Bob's design wittiness. But with the passage of time, it settled into its old age just as he and Jane did, grown familiar and friendly, if inevitably a bit shabby, with its stained-glass windows, African sculpture, oil portrait of Jane's great-aunt, a clothes-and-wire scarecrow over the staircase, endless shelves of books. The children, settling into their own lives, were frequently in and out. When Jane's brothers and sister and their families visited, they stayed with Jane and Bob at 69 Albany Avenue, or across the street with their friends Toshiko and Sid at 74, or down the street with son Jim and his wife, Pat, at 31.

Jane became a fixture of the neighborhood. She'd sit out on the front porch watching children rattle and whiz down the sidewalk on their skateboards. She'd sell jam at the neighborhood's fall fair. She could be seen walking chummily along with Bob; sometimes they held hands. At neighborhood meetings she might show up without having registered to speak beforehand, but someone always would give her his time; as one neighbor said, "You can't say no to Jane Jacobs." Another neighbor told of having a sick tree removed from in front of his house, only to encounter Jane on the street, angry, labeling him a "white painter," the local term for those who'd buy a house, slap on a coat of white paint, and sell it for a quick profit. Later, it seems, after digging around in the root bed and discovering the tree was really dead, she apologized.

Another Annex neighbor, Katherine Gildner, told of the time Jane rescued her. She was a doctoral student and young mother, up near dawn that day in the local park, a toddler in tow and infant twins in the stroller, and having a hard time of it: "You know, you're feeding one, the other's screaming, right?" And the older kid is carrying on, "Mommy, Mommy, I want to show you my hockey cards." Her husband was out of town, she was on her own, exhausted, having trouble keeping it together. Then, an older woman approached her. "She didn't say, 'Would you like some help?' Because I'm the type who would say, 'No, I'm fine, thank you very much.'" Instead, she just stopped, picked up a [baby] bottle, picked up one of the twins, and started feeding him, meanwhile talking softly with the toddler about his hockey cards:

> *Oh, I know Gordie Howe* . . . She seemed really interested in them. She turned them over while she was feeding one baby, read all the statistics. *These are amazing cards. Let's organize them.* And he loved that. He was just thrilled to have the attention. I remember this so clearly. Because I saw the sun come up and it was the first time since the babies were born . . . the first time that I had silence. It was like *velvet.*

Of course, the woman was Jane Jacobs, though it was a year before Gildner realized it, her husband pointing her out one day while shopping on Bloor Street.

Never itself celebrated in any of her books, as 555 Hudson Street was in *Death and Life*, the Albany Avenue house became a place of pilgrimage; Jane would have abhorred the word, but it wasn't far wrong. Mayors and other civic leaders, journalists and scholars, would come to work out political strategies, try out ideas, settle in to the bouts of intellectual combat she relished. "She had a droll, dry way of speaking," remembers

Bobbi Speck. "She never showed emotion . . . She was expressionless, like an ancient tortoise."

Meanwhile, Canada *took* with Jane. "I find all the threshing around that goes on here about a Canadian identity absolutely bewildering," she told an interviewer as early as 1970. "When you come here from outside, as I did, you know immediately what 'Canadian' means." To her, it meant common sense and less suspicion of government; Jane was much impressed with how calmly Canada opened its arms that summer to a threatened "hippie invasion." She developed "faith in the Canadian character, in [its] whole lack of hysteria as a people, in [its] refusal to be caught up in what I call 'righteous manias.' "

In September 1974, six years after immigrating, Jane became a citizen. She went to a special court in Toronto, paid a $12 fee, filled out an application, submitted passport and birth certificate, and, a few weeks later, was summoned to appear before a federal judge. The judge was a woman about as old as Jane who had herself emigrated from Poland a quarter century before. At one point Jane volunteered that she liked Canada's "mosaic" idea: immigrants and their descendants did not need to wholly assimilate but could retain their ethnic and linguistic roots, like brightly colored tiles contributing to the whole. That was better, it seemed to her, than the American "melting pot" idea, which looked to erase such differences. At this, the judge laughed. *Wasn't always like that.* After first coming to Canada she'd worked in a factory where the manager forbade her to speak Polish with other Poles, warning she'd be fired if she did. She did, and she was. Sometimes, said the judge, Canadian women would say to her, "Oh yes, my mother had a Polish maid." To this, she'd reply, "So did my mother, four or five" of them.

A few weeks later, Jane appeared for her swearing-in and, with eighty-nine others from around the world, became a Canadian citizen. Each in turn approached the bench, placed their hands on the Bible, and vowed to "bear true allegiance to Her Majesty Queen Elizabeth the Second, her heirs and successors." The judge "listened with close attention to each one of the 89, not a sign of boredom or of his mind wandering, as if it were all just as important to him as to the person making the oath," then shook hands with each and handed them the certificate of citizenship.

·   ·   ·

We know just how Jane became a Canadian because she wrote a long letter describing it. Its recipient was Bessie Robison Butzner, her mother, since 1946 living in Virginia, near her son John, and who, in her nineties now, was still in passably good health.

In another letter to her mother, in 1971, Jane wrote about the vacation she'd just spent with Bob in the Canary Islands, off the coast of Morocco: they'd spent time with old friends, a prosperous farmer and his family whose company shipped bananas, strawberries, and vegetables all over Europe. Jane told of their experimental bulb breeding, how the pigs lived mainly on rejected tomatoes, cattle on the cores of chopped-down banana plants. She described the farm's water supply, how water ran from deep wells in the mountains, through rough country into aqueducts, reservoirs, and irrigation pipes; how the family planned to cultivate a wild-growing breed of cactus that required no irrigation and harbored a particular insect—cochineal, from which a valuable red dye could be extracted. The plan was to pick off insects from the plants by vacuum cleaner. Jane went into the family's whole business and social philosophy, as well as the island's extraordinary scenery—"wild mountains and great gorges with tiny valleys and here and there little, almost isolated, villages"—contrasting its tourist economy with those of the Caribbean.

This and Jane's many other letters to her mother from the 1970s, now housed at the Burns Library at Boston College, of course say something of Jane herself. In their number and frequency, they reflect, at least, a good daughter's dutifulness. And they suggest she is not indifferent to earning her mother's pride and respect—not when, seemingly in passing, she mentions being offered $2,000 to give the Dunning Trust lectures at Queen's University, or that *Death and Life* had been named a "core book" for the American Association of University Women's continuing education program: "Just thought you might be interested to see this," she writes of that announcement. "Don't bother to return it." But that Jane could write to her mother letters so rich in ideas, insights, and personal experiences, in sometimes astonishing detail, reflects, in the first place, her confidence that Bess Butzner would care to *hear* them, would be *interested* in them. Plainly, this went back a long way.

On May 1, 1973, Jane wrote her mother about her son's ambitious bike project. At a Chinese export fair, Jimmy, then twenty-five, had inquired about whether he might import bicycles to Canada. Soon he'd bought thirty of them—Flying Pigeon was the brand name—for $19 each, planning to sell them for $60. The bikes dutifully arrived, in pieces. Actually, in *many* pieces. Putting them together was no matter of merely attaching wheels to the frame, or even building up wheels from hub, spoke, and rim. No, the hubs themselves had to be assembled. They came with bags of ball bearings that had each to be inserted in thick grease to hold them in place. Jim's assembly team included his parents, who, he asserts, didn't have to be begged or otherwise dragooned into service. "They were enthusiastic to do it." The bikes arrived just before Easter, Jane wrote her mother. Jim had

> rented a little garage around the corner where he puts them together, weekends and at night. Bob and I spent the whole Easter weekend, just about, assembling wheels. It is quite wonderful to see a beautiful bicycle wheel form in your hand from a rim, a hub, a handful of wires [spokes] and a little pile of screws. They are quite tricky to put together properly, and Jimmy wrote out the directions for us, which he figured out from analyzing the wheel on his bike. Each bike has 408 parts which have to be assembled! No directions. Names of things in Chinese . . . The bikes are really beautiful, everything of such high quality and so well made. Beautifully machined, solid parts. Splendid seats, of thick, real leather.

A few months later, on November 6, 1973, back from a trip to Kyoto, the old imperial capital of Japan, and Tokyo, where she appeared at an international congress on industrial design, Jane wrote her mother:

> The inn in Kyoto was so beautiful. Very simple, but serene and lovely. My rooms consisted of an entrance room; a main room in which a low table was set for my breakfast and dinner, then put aside at night when my bed was brought out of the closet (a thick pad on the floor, very comfortable), a little alcove, all glass, with a table and dressing table and a cushion on the floor in front of it; and a Japanese bath with a wooden tub always full of hot water, kept hot by a heating system around the tub. All the rooms except the bath were floored with thick, comfortable and beautiful straw matting, and the walls were sliding paper; on the outside, sliding glass. All this looked out into a small but beautiful garden. I was waited on by a very tiny lady in a blue kimono who could speak no English. We got along very well with pantomime.

Among regular features of Jane's letters during these years were gardening news; odd real-time snippets, as when she broke in to tell of "three black squirrels, all racing around the yard, chasing each other like crazy"; and, of course, news of the grandchildren. During the early to mid-1970s, with America and Canada caught up in baby boom–fueled youth rebellion, this made for an especially rich vein of interest. In 1971, to pick a year, Jim was twenty-three and a graduate student in physics at the University of Toronto. Ned was twenty-one and all over the world, traveling in Europe, Asia, and western Canada. Mary was sixteen, embarked on adventures of young life and spirit.

Just thirteen when the family arrived in Toronto, Mary was enrolled in Jesse Ketchum School, a public school within walking distance of the Spadina Road house. But school—she'd only recently escaped the untender mercies of the New York City schools—had always been trouble for her. "I was behind already," she remembers back to that time. And it was so wildly different from New York; Canadians "did odd things, like field hockey." Ultimately, she dropped out of high school. For a while she enrolled in a local "free school" inspired by A. S. Neill's Summerhill ideology; she need take no particular courses but, somehow, was responsible for her own education. "We deprogrammed ourselves," is what she says today. She put together some course, or experience, or *something*, in art, but soon, by age sixteen, feeling a little lost, drifted out west.

Any drifting by Mary or the other Jacobs children didn't seem to much worry their parents; whatever they wanted to explore was fine with Jane and Bob. When Mary wound up in a tiny town in western Canada, she says today, that was all right with them; the author of *The Death and Life of Great American Cities* had "nothing against rural areas or small towns." Jane wrote to her own mother in July 1972 about how Mary "went to a country fair run by a farmers cooperative, and they served up two roast pigs each weighing 200 pounds, and 200 pounds of baked potatoes and carrots. Guess who carved the pigs? Mary!! . . . She says, 'a truly excellent weekend.' "

But even Jane could fret about her youngest child most of the way across the continent. Or so concluded Jane's friend and neighbor, Toshiko Adilman, whom she'd met at a neighbor's tea soon after arriving on Albany Avenue. A Japanese-English interpreter married to a local journalist and herself a new mother, Toshiko was sometimes left slack-jawed by Jane's laid-back parenting style. But then one day, as they spoke of

Mary's cross-country wanderings, Jane blurted out, "She's too young, don't you think?" You might expect to hear that from any parent of a teenager who'd left home. But hearing it from Jane, who "accepted everybody" just as they were, encouraging them in any direction they wanted to go, in whatever they wanted to do, this, to Toshiko, was actually comforting. "It was the only time Jane showed concern in a normal parental way." Finally, she could conclude, "After all, she's normal!" On one trip, Mary hitchhiked across Canada in the middle of winter, wearing a coat she'd made from a heavy sheepskin rug. "Jane was worried until she saw how bulky that coat made her look," recalls Ned. "No one was going to mess with her."

For a while, Mary lived on Texada Island, up the Strait of Georgia from Vancouver. Ned, who'd missed his New York friends, found Toronto "socially cold," and had earlier hitchhiked to Vancouver himself, visited her, and reported back, as Jane wrote to her mother, that Mary lived "in a little log cabin, with permission of the family that owns it, and she is really entranced with life in the wilderness . . . She reproved Ned for chattering too much; she told him that all that talking is a city trait." She'd "fed Ned on clams, mussels, mushrooms, wild onions, huckleberries, all of which she had gathered, bread and porridge that she made, and bacon and eggs and potatoes that she bought."

Then, December: "Day before yesterday we had a grand surprise. Mary returned. She looks strong and healthy and beautiful, and is full of life and good spirits . . . You can imagine how happy we are to see her, and what a good time we have been having listening to her adventures." Mary was with her boyfriend, Doug, with whom, it seemed to Jane, she was happily in love. Would they marry? Doug, at twenty-seven, was old enough to know his own mind. But Mary, it seemed to her, "is still awfully young for marriage."

Soon she wasn't "Mary" at all.

Her name, it seems, had long bothered her. It carried New Testament baggage and bore as blandly feminine a stamp as any name you could imagine, while she saw herself as almost beyond gender. So she cast about for a new name, one that better reflected who she really was. She chose Burgin, the maiden name of a relative of her father. "I really love that family connection," she says; growing up, she'd heard it around the house, though she didn't even know how to spell it. ("I'm not that big on spelling," she says.) But she decided to try it; soon everyone was calling her Burgin, and Burgin she has remained.

To one family friend, Burgin was going about as far as she could to slip from Jane's shadow. Heading west at so young an age perhaps also reflected that impulse—or so another family friend, Toshiko Adilman, had heard it conjectured. For Riley Henderson, the husband of Jane's niece, Jane Butzner, the switch to Burgin reminded him of how some black people rejected their old slave names and stared over with unusual new ones. As for Jane herself, she had some trouble adapting, occasionally slipping back into "Mary," or, on a few occasions, misspelling it as "Bergin" or "Bergen."

"Day after tomorrow," Jane wrote Jason Epstein—this was June 1975—"Bob and I are off to Vancouver and the wilderness beyond to see our West Coast contingent. Mary and Doug will put us up in their second tipi, which fortunately they haven't sold yet. We'll be back July 7, and then, to work with a will."

To work, that is, on her third book, unfinished after five years.

CHAPTER 20

OUR JANE

"B E REGULAR AND ORDERLY in your life, like a bourgeois," Flaubert once wrote, "so that you may be violent and original in your work."

Something like that goes for Jane Jacobs. Her life on Albany Avenue might seem all middle-class solidity. She maintained family traditions. Right there in her daybook you find her Thanksgiving grocery list: turkey, cranberries, stuffing, onions. Each year, like clockwork, she prepared the Christmas ham according to the same set schedule. Christmas cookies, too. And cookie *cutters* to *make* Christmas cookies. "We made a lot of new cutters," she wrote David Gurin in December 1971, "including a (recognizable!) Venus de Milo, because the arms were always breaking off our cookie people anyway." Only when she escaped to her study could she set her mind entirely free. There she read, indulged the play of her intellect, hammered out her ideas—crude, unformed ideas at first, caught up in wayward tangles of fact, theory, observation, and memory—into sentences, paragraphs, and books.

Well, in principle, anyway. Because all through the 1970s and beyond a new book she wanted to call *Free Cities*, planned since at least 1970, hadn't materialized. In June of that year, she'd written Jason Epstein, "At last I'm down to serious work . . . and am not going to get diverted any more. All this time I've really been sort of figuring things out." Certainly she'd been thinking big. Jane's son Ned recalls the two of them in a crowded Toronto subway car when "out of the blue she blurted out that she had plans for three more books." *Free Cities*, she wrote Jason Epstein, was to be, with *Death and Life* and *Economy of Cities*, the third book in what she called "one coherent thing on the City."

The first signs of trouble, however, showed early on. In October 1971, responding to a preliminary draft of part of it, Epstein made it clear he didn't like it. The pages she'd sent him would

> work well enough as an outline or précis for a book yet to be written, but I don't think that they work quite well enough to serve as the beginning of the book itself. The argument is too abstract, too simply asserted and not sufficiently argued or demonstrated. For faithful converts like myself it will seem thin, obvious and repetitive; for the uninitiated it will seem obscure and willful.

A week later, Jane wrote back. "You are absolutely right; your letter and marginal comments were wonderfully helpful; they set me on a different tack which I might otherwise have groped for for a long time."

Two weeks later, Jane signed a contract for the new book. Now it was called *Cities and Countries;* it would later be published as *Cities and the Wealth of Nations.* In it, Jane would lay out a vision for the wealth of the world riding on the backs of innovative cities, economic decline the sad lot of places cut off from them. It was supposed to be fifty thousand words—short compared to Jane's first two books—and was due at Random House on October 1, 1972. Needless to say, it didn't get there.

Back in July, Jane had written her mother:

> I'm working hard on my book these days, but there is a long way to go. If I think about the whole thing I'm appalled, and so mostly think about the part I'm at work on—which is enough to cudjel [a rare misspelling] my brains over. I'm not going to let anything more interfere with it, now that we're moved, etc., and the expressway has been stopped.

But she *did* let things interfere—or, rather, let us say, *things interfered,* whether Jane "let" them or not. *Death and Life* had, together with her activist notoriety, made her a public figure. *The Economy of Cities* only solidified her standing; she was no one-book wonder. In 1969, *Vogue* ran an interview with her that included a photo. "Mother," she reputedly said to Mrs. Butzner, who had long lamented Jane's lack of fashion savvy, "when was the last time *your* picture was in *Vogue*?" She wouldn't have to put up with *that* nonsense anymore! Now, and all through the 1970s, Jane grew into the role of public citizen, and public intellectual, even as the times affirmed her ideas and ratified her sensibilities.

·   ·   ·

In the dozen years after publication of *Death and Life*, in schools of planning and architecture around the world, ideas were changing about cities. Years later, Nikolai Roskamm, an urban researcher at the Technical University of Berlin, would give it a name. He'd call it "the density turn," referring to population density, as in so many dwelling units per acre, or people per square mile. Before *Death and Life*, high density was bad, period; you didn't even need to think about it, you just reflexively imagined overcrowded slums. Then Jane Jacobs came along to say that density could be benign, a positive good; that cities *needed* high enough density to be vibrant places; that good neighborhoods like Greenwich Village and Boston's North End had higher densities, while some of the worst slums were low-density wastelands.

In a thirty-page chapter, "The Need for Concentration," she'd made a sustained, nuanced argument that unquestionably helped bring about a "paradigm shift"—an unsettling new way to see a subject that leaves you either holding on, futilely, to old truths or else forever and fundamentally changed. With *Death and Life*, Roskamm writes, "it became possible to swap the position 'high density is evil' with the position 'density is urbanity.'" If you wanted lively streets, or a mass transit system that worked, or economic vibrancy, you needed people thronging together. This thinking, Roskamm allowed, hadn't always made its way into urban planning *regulations*, which represented the old thinking. But among designers, planners, and architects all through the 1960s and into the 1970s, the great "turn" was evident. Jane's arguments were taking hold and becoming part of what sophisticated people knew to be true. As the *New York Times* architecture critic Paul Goldberger would write a little later, Jane had become "standard urban theory."

In St. Louis, the great experiment was over.

A vast housing project—twelve thousand people, in thirty-three eleven-story buildings towering over fifty-seven acres on the north side of the city, acclaimed at the time of its construction in the early 1950s as a marvel of modernism, sure to benefit the poor people it would pluck from the slums—was, beginning one day in 1972, unceremoniously blown up. Designed by Minoru Yamasaki, future architect of the New York World

Trade Center's Twin Towers, it had degenerated, with stunning swiftness, into a grim tableau of crime, vandalism, and despair. By the end it housed only the poorest of the poor.

It was called Pruitt-Igoe and the footage of its last moments became a species of creepy urban porn: We see emptied buildings lined up, standing there, awaiting the firing squad, yet already lifeless. A moment of stillness. Then, in one building, on a lower floor, the first white puffs of the engineered explosions. And then, in rapid sequence, a succession of puffs, finally the whole building toppling to the ground in a paroxysm of smoke, thunder, dust, and debris. "Modern architecture died in St. Louis, Missouri, on July 15, 1972, at 3.32 pm," the architecture critic Charles Jencks wrote of Pruitt-Igoe.

Of course, things weren't so simple. Modern architecture survived. And besides, Pruitt-Igoe did have its virtues. Its first residents had new apartments that were all anyone could want; "A poor man's penthouse," one of them called hers. Jane herself would write of Pruitt-Igoe, "I don't think things should be blown up. I don't think we can afford to be that wasteful. Instead of destroying them, we must learn to knit them back and make them part of the fabric of the city." Still, for Jane, who had condemned New York's own Pruitt-Igoes and the architectural and planning nostrums behind them, the dynamiting had to be an intellectually redeeming moment.

In a June 1974 letter to her mother, Jane apologized for not having written in a while. She excused herself because, first, "it is planting and weeding time and I have to hop to it to keep up with Nature, who has been giving us a glorious and incredibly beautiful spring"; and, second, because work on her book had left her so exhausted she could "hardly bring myself to hit those typewriter keys again until after a night's sleep." She went on to tell of the tomato plants on the roof, of tulips and lilacs past their prime, of how high and fast the bean plants had grown.

Then, abruptly, the next paragraph: "A stupendous book has been written about Robert Moses." The publisher had sent her a prepublication copy of Robert Caro's *The Power Broker,* all twelve hundred pages of it, so big that the prepub edition had to be bound in two volumes. She and Bob lay "in bed at night, propped up under the reading light with our twin volumes," she wrote. "Jimmy says the sight is hilarious. Well, we always knew Moses was an awful man, doing awful things, but even so this book is a shocking revelation. He was much worse than we had even imagined." Moses, long seen as the Goliath to Jane's David, was now revealed, in damning detail, as bully and liar, destroyer of communities and lives.

One more strike for Jane's own more intimate and humane vision of city life.

In Toronto, you probably didn't need to be aware of all these particulars to know that ideas about cities were changing and that Jane Jacobs had something to do with it. Over the years, Torontonians would lay claim to her, with friendly, familiar warmth, as "Our Jane"—as if to emphasize that she was no longer "Their Jane," the Jane Jacobs of Hudson Street, New York City, USA. More and more she belonged to Toronto. She tried to keep her writing time sacrosanct, but that was hard when she was so often solicited for her advice, probed for her ideas, or sought out for her imprimatur on a project or petition.

Soon after arriving in town, her husband's employer, Eb Zeidler, who'd read *Death and Life* early on, consulted with Jane on a number of his projects. Like Eaton Centre, his firm's vaulted, more-than-a-mall galleria in the middle of downtown Toronto and how it might better be stitched into the surrounding city, not walled off from it. Or his ambitious plan, never realized, for a complex of sixty thousand people sitting out on land reclaimed from Lake Ontario. Harbour City, it was called, and it represented, declared Jane at a press conference in May 1970, perhaps "the most important advance in planning for cities that has been made in this century."

Privately—and probably more comfortably—she prepared a memo on zoning principles to guide Harbour City. "Prohibitory" zoning forbade certain practices but left you free to do anything else. "Permissive" zoning allowed a few activities but barred everything else. Jane looked into noise and air pollution, inharmonious scale, ugly signs: The idea was to avoid "nasty, tacky collections of signs" but not standardize them or bar them outright. One strategy was to limit their area in square feet, another was to require approval of each one individually; neither approach was ideal. In any case, Jane wasn't skating lightly over these tricky questions but digging down into them: *nineteen pages* on zoning.

Partly through the Spadina Expressway fight, Jane drew close to a generation of young political figures who would grant her an entrée to city government she'd never had in New York. At the end of December 1972, she wrote Jason of the "fantastic election" just held in Toronto: "Many rascals out. Many unbelievably good people in." The new mayor was David Crombie, who, as a young professor at Ryerson University, had actually taught *Death and Life*. Later, he'd be dubbed, in homage to his diminutive stature and immense popularity, Toronto's "tiny, perfect mayor." The new "reform" council included the community organizer and future mayor John Sewell, who, long before Jane arrived in Toronto, had battled, Jane-style, on behalf of a poor community. Both became Jane's friends. Both brought energy, talent, and a dollop of '6os idealism to the new Toronto.

Before Jane arrived, Crombie says, Toronto still looked too much to the U.S.: *"We need urban renewal and expressways, we need to learn from the U.S.,"* was the attitude. Of course, when you looked across the border you might see Detroit in flames. But either way, "America was the constantly reminding background." What Jane did for Torontonians of a certain urban bent "was not [so much] deliver her wisdom as legitimize our instincts . . . She gave a moral legitimacy to us."

To the suggestion, sometimes heard, that Jane's personal influence on the city, apart from that of her books, was slight, Crombie doesn't buy it: "If you could be any wronger than that," he doesn't know how. Alan Broadbent, a Vancouver-born philanthropist who came to Toronto in 1972, and a longtime admirer of Jane's, allows that maybe you couldn't draw an absolutely "straight line from her to any particular planning process" in Toronto, but "the power of her ideas was there," and those ideas "became central tenets of Toronto planning." Not just through her books but behind the scenes, in conversation, reviewing plans, recommending people, at public forums. And sometimes she was right there on the front lines.

"This morning at 6:30 am," Jane wrote Jason Epstein on April 5, 1973, "I helped knock down a lot of fences around some houses that were to be wrecked for a horrid apartment tower, thus staving off the wreckers, because they aren't allowed to wreck without a fence up. Very satisfying." Orchestrated by John Sewell, neighborhood groups had rallied at the corner of Dundas and Sherbourne streets, a shabby corner of the city just east of downtown. The day before, a high wooden fence—"hoardings," in Canadian parlance—had been erected around the twenty old houses to be demolished. The houses were run-down, no question. But, fixed up, they'd be a lot better than the six identical apartment houses set to go up in their place; the province, the demonstrators felt, was imposing on the city something vacuous and impersonal. Those "gathered in the predawn dark that morning," wrote Jane, didn't at first know what to do. "But as they stood talking together and stomping their feet in the cold," someone remembered that key regulation: no demolition without a fence.

The remark was repeated from person to person, and group to group, and without another word everyone began taking action. You would be amazed at how rapidly and purposefully several hundred men, women, and children, with no one directing them, can dismantle a sturdily built fence and turn it back to neatly stacked piles of lumber.

Their act of civil disobedience, Jane wrote, had left her almost giddy, primed for round two early the next morning. Of course, she added, "The schedule has its advantages. One can knock down fences and be back home, ready to go to work, at 8:30. Better than usual. Of course it makes you dreadfully sleepy by 10 at night." The old houses were saved. Two days of fence whacking, together with Mayor Crombie's pull, and they had the promise of a provincial loan that would permit building near the site without destruction of the old buildings.

One of the first things Crombie did as mayor was set up a housing department to spearhead a new low- and middle-income housing project for downtown Toronto. A *project*? For *poor* people? Near *downtown*? Why, Toronto had one of those already. It was called Regent Park and, as *Farewell Oak Street*, an artful black-and-white film produced by the Film Board of Canada, attests, it was in 1953 still being offered as an example of modernist planning at its best.

In the film we see an adolescent boy happily tossing a ball with his buddies in the new Regent Park; then, the grim past, as the same boys play amid slum rubble, the music's disarming lilt yielding to dark, disturbing jazz notes. "This is how it used to be," intones the narrator, "one of Toronto's oldest streets, and not one of its best . . . Aged houses, crowded quarters, squalor. Not quite a slum, but close. Call it substandard. Life was unavoidably substandard, too." Even around the supper table we see it—parents and children trading dark, menacing looks, only the clicking of utensils to break up the silence, the very air on edge. It's the street's fault, the film all but says, the street that bears the full load of slum pathology. In the new Regent Park, where "everything's sparkling and new and tidy," there is no street. No Oak Street or any other. The old blocks of two-story peaked-roof row houses have been torn down. In their place are mid-rise cruciform-shaped apartment buildings set in a superblock of lawns cut off from neighboring streets.

Sound familiar? Altogether, a more modest, maybe more *Canadian,* version of George Washington Houses in East Harlem, built around the same time, in the same spirit—and a failure in the same degree. Just twenty years after it went up, Regent Park was on its way to becoming what some would call "the largest Anglo-Saxon slum in North America." Ryan James, an anthropologist raised there, would observe at a Toronto urban history conference years later that it was perfectly possible to live a decent life in Regent Park. Certainly it was no Pruitt-Igoe. Still, in the early 1970s, Crombie and his housing head, Michael Dennis, wanted nothing like it for their new project.

The plan was to house ten thousand people on fifty-six acres of under-used industrial wasteland east of downtown and north of the railroad tracks paralleling the lakefront. But best to think of St. Lawrence, as it was named, as no "development" at all but as a skein of new cityscape knitted into the old, seamlessly worked into the existing street grid; in John Sewell's words, it was "the new community downtown that felt like it has always been there." Its central spine, Crombie Park, is lined by seven- to ten-story apartment buildings, their ground floors occupied by restaurants, grocery stores, hairdressers, schools. Behind them sit rows of traditional three-story townhouses. Mixed in are a few old buildings, vestiges of the area's earlier industrial past. Well-off people live there, and not-so-well-off, in co-ops, condos, and private townhouses. New development has arisen spontaneously along its invisible edges. Thirty-five years after it went up, the local paper, *The Globe and Mail,* returned for an affectionate look back, taking the opportunity to pronounce St. Lawrence "the best example of a mixed-income, mixed-use, pedestrian-friendly, sensitively-scaled, densely-populated community ever built in the province." Altogether, the sort of neighborhood a Jane Jacobs could like.

Christopher Klemek, a scholar of Jacobs and her work, calls St. Lawrence "a district-scale experiment inspired by Jane Jacobs' urbanistic principles—and influenced by Jacobs' presence as a Toronto citizen." Yet

Jane herself did not bring it into being. She didn't put together the reform council whose energy ignited it. She was not herself a planner. She had designed none of the buildings. She had apparently not even attended most of the civic meetings leading up to its approval by the city. Yet in Klemek's assessment, and as a walk through the neighborhood attests, her stamp lies upon it.

Across Albany Avenue from Jane in 1973 lived Michael Dennis, Crombie's housing adviser, who sought an architect for St. Lawrence. Dennis went to Jane, who suggested a young man named Alan Littlewood. Did he know anything about planning? Dennis asked her. "I certainly hope not!" Jane famously replied. Littlewood got the job, which soon morphed into that of St. Lawrence's de facto chief planner.

An Irish architect in his thirties, Littlewood had recently worked for Eb Zeidler, where he was teamed with Bob Jacobs on a hospital project in Detroit. (Zeidler had a branch office and apartment in the old Ford Hotel building there. The two of them roomed together; Littlewood did most of the cooking, he recalls, Bob most of the smoking, offering up "perverse arguments about why smoking was not bad for you.") Bound

Jane lived in this house on Albany Avenue, in Toronto's Annex neighborhood, from 1970 to her death.

for the airport in a cab, Littlewood would pick up Bob on Albany Avenue, where Jane, on the porch, invariably saw him off with a zestful goodbye hug. But one time, as the cab pulled up, Bob wasn't there, so Littlewood rang the doorbell. "Jane answered and embraced me, saying how nice it was to meet me at last." She was so demonstrative! Soon the Jacobses and Littlewood and his wife were friends, getting together frequently for dinner. And that might have been that, a cozy friendship kept up over the years . . . except that big things were brewing in Toronto.

Early in his new job with St. Lawrence, Littlewood found himself trying to navigate his way through competing visions of what, as a "facilitator," much concerned with process, he was actually to do. *Typical bureaucrat*, Jane upbraided him one evening over dinner at the Littlewood place. Why didn't he, he remembers Jane telling him, "get off my ass and get on with making a plan." Another thing: he needed to stop calling St. Lawrence a "project," she said, or rather "yelled," as Littlewood recalls it; it was a neighborhood. "What you call a thing," he absorbed the lesson, "determines how you think about it." He went to bed that night "mentally exhausted."

The next day, he stayed home from work, went back to his copy of *Death and Life*. "Like a recalcitrant sinner," he recalls, "I knew exactly what to do. I didn't even have to open the book," but sat down and disgorged onto paper the site planning principles that ought to govern St. Lawrence. Homes would have normal street addresses. Public streets would run right through the community, which would thoroughly intermix housing types. Shops, schools, parks, and community facilities would be part of the mix, as would varied incomes, different developers, a royal mix of everything. He presented his proposal to Dennis, who "grilled me for an hour, as a lawyer might a hostile witness . . . during which I unashamedly cited Jane to bolster my [her] position." He got Dennis's support. St. Lawrence was on its way to making Toronto a better city.

Jane helped change Toronto in small ways and large and plainly relished the chance to do so. She "liked the accessibility to power," says David Crombie. As in New York, it wasn't just drudgery for her. "She was just as happy hatching plots against powerful people" as thinking and writing. "She really enjoyed the activist part. The strategy, the being on the streets."

Still, it would be hopeless to insist that it hadn't deflected her from her writing. On December 15, 1974, Jane talked on the phone with Jason Epstein about her book. She was so badly stuck, she wrote him later that day,

> I realize I have been inflicting myself with the straitjacket magazine editors used to inflict on me when I had to write captions of so many lines, so many characters per line—and all because I have been arbitrarily thinking in chapters that over-compress some things and over-inflate others, the genesis of that being an original outline which was not really suitable and which I have been measly adapting instead of overturning.

In any case, she hoped to deliver the promised book the following year. She didn't.

A year and a half later, Jane wrote brother John and his wife,

> I write a little way, and then I rewrite and rewrite, then write a little way and rewrite and rewrite, achieving a snail's pace with a quantity of paper that would do credit to an elephant, if elephants ate paper. Anyhow, in this inefficient way I am making progress (I guess).

> Love from all,
> Jane

CHAPTER 21

FLUMMOXED

Family and friends saw the trouble Jane was having but were, of course, powerless to help her. In July 1976, Jane's nephew Decker came to stay with Jane and Bob while doing his residency at the Hospital for Sick Children in Toronto, remaining until June 1978. Later, in the early 1980s, he stayed with them again. During both periods he got to see close-up Jane's problems with the book. "She was so flummoxed and frustrated."

All the while, of course, she had Jason Epstein to account to. For how long could he be so patient? In August 1976, Jane wrote to him, "When you ask about my book, you must feel somewhat as if you are making inquiries about an idiot child. I sometimes feel that way about it myself." She'd not written to him recently, she explained, first, because she didn't have much manuscript to show him, and second, because she came away from each day's work "too damn tired, and when tomorrow comes I get drawn into the book again as if it were some irresistible magnet."

This was not a pretty picture.

"I always hit some point when I am really discouraged," Jane would tell an interviewer later. A point where she'd realize, "I would never have gotten into this if I knew what I was getting into. And I am tempted, really seriously . . . to put all my research and all my awful writing I can't bear to read myself at this stage into a big green garbage bag and put it out and be done with it."

Jim Jacobs would recall his mother's "huge impatience" with her slow progress. What made it worse was that, since *Death and Life*, she'd come to define herself as a writer of books almost exclusively—yet now seemed unable to write one. "I've forgotten how to write," she'd say on a bad day. "I'm remembering how to write," she'd say on a good one. She had her tricks. "You've done this before," she'd tell herself. Jim recalls her trying to all but sweet-talk her way into writerly optimism. Or, she'd dismiss herself as "silly for having this despairing pathology." But for too long now, all the tricks and sweet talk weren't working. Her frustrations gnawed at her. "One of her other remedies," admits Jim, "was getting into bed and pulling the covers over her head. She did that, too."

At one point a little later, Riley Henderson, niece Jane Butzner's husband, noticed that the ivy growing up the back wall of the house on Albany Avenue obstructed Jane's window, blocking the light. Too little natural light, he'd heard, could play on the emotions, and he suggested they cut back the ivy. Jane went along with the suggestion, reporting back that yes, well, it did seem to have some effect.

Early in 1977, Jane sent Epstein about fifty pages. "I feel strongly that you're off to a good start this time," Epstein wrote back. "The material is full of good, strong ideas and the only real problem is your tendency to state your conclusion before you demonstrate it concretely." He followed up with four pages of suggestions and pointed questions: "Why is Palermo impotent and what happened to make it so?"

"You should begin with the example of Uruguay rather than with the generalization about supply regions."

"What are Bardou's people doing after 1870?" he asked in reference to a French town whose tribulations Jane had described.

"Why is Soviet productivity low?"

"It would be good to know more about Ethiopia. How and why did it collapse economically?"

In the end, Jane's book was finished. She would dedicate it to Epstein, "who has waited so long for it with good humor and good counsel." It was a 232-page book perhaps better appreciated as 500 or 600 *paragraphs*, each long and intricate, densely argued, richly textured, thick with fact—and a struggle to get it right. It took her more than a dozen years, a period shot through with her adjustment to Canada, the distractions she faced from her unaccustomed perch close to power in Toronto, the growing-up of her children, their travels and adventures, and the death of her mother in 1981. Much of that time, she was mired in an intellectual and emotional swamp, muddled as to just what she wanted to say or how she wanted to say it.

Which, in varying degree, in fact, is how she was with all her books.

Depending on how you count, *Cities and the Wealth of Nations* was Jane's third, fourth, or fifth book. It was her third major work conceived afresh. But it was her fourth, if you included her compilation, *Constitutional Chaff,* from back in 1940. Or her fifth, if you included a short book, *The Question of Separatism,* that grew out of lectures Jane delivered in 1979 and was published the following year. After the separatism book, and then *Cities and the Wealth of Nations,* Jane wrote a deeply serious book titled *Systems of Survival,* which took the form of conversations among friends; in it she developed the idea of two distinct moral systems working in tandem to keep civilization civilized. Next, Jane took her great-aunt Hannah's manuscript from a half century before, about her adventures in Alaska, and brought it back to life, with reworked text and added commentary, as *A Schoolteacher in Old Alaska.* In *The Nature of Economies,* she returned to the dialogue form to explore nature as a source of principles for economic development. In *Dark Age Ahead,* published two years before her death, Jane warned of some of the malignant directions in which modern society was headed. Along the way, she also wrote a slip of a children's book, *The Girl on the Hat,* a collection of stories adapted from ones she'd told her own children years earlier.

None of these books left the lasting mark or enjoyed the commercial success of *Death and Life,* with which, inevitably, they'd be compared and in whose shadow they stood. But mostly, they sold well enough, got respectful attention, earned good reviews, are still in print, and sometimes won literary prizes. *Cities and the Wealth of Nations* won the Los Angeles Times Book Prize. *Dark Age Ahead* proved a best seller in Canada. Just as some Jane Austen fans champion *Emma,* say, or *Mansfield Park,* over *Pride and Prejudice,* each of Jane Jacobs's books had its adherents. "There is a fight to be had," reports Mary Rowe, a friend of Jane's from later in her life, over "which of her volumes is the most important." One of Rowe's colleagues picked "*Dark Age Ahead,* hands down." Rowe's own favorite was *Systems of Survival.* Each book had its own history, its own role in Jane's intellectual development. And as she came to be recognized for books that weren't pop sociology, weren't academic treatises, weren't in every way "literary," but were, indisputably, like no one else's, she was sometimes asked to reflect on just how she made them and how, more broadly, she worked.

In the beginning (in the beginning, that is, after much reading, observing, and thinking) came the idea, in all its temporarily delicious clarity. Then, immediately, came a questioning of it. Jane once offered this example: "Islands seem to be wonderful places for building great cities." Think New York or Hong Kong. But "then you think of all the islands that don't have great cities and then you think of all the great cities that aren't on islands and then you say, 'Wait a minute.' " As soon as she'd hit on an idea, confusion and doubt followed.

Progress normally came only with fitful slowness. *Death and Life* might seem the exception—less than three years from start to finish. Except that the start didn't really come in 1958, when she got the Rockefeller grant, but in 1954 or 1955, when she began to harbor doubts about urban renewal in Philadelphia and East Harlem; or else in 1952, when she was first thrust into the professional world of buildings and cities as an editor at *Architectural Forum;* or maybe in 1949, when she first wrote about city planning for *Amerika;* or perhaps in 1935, when the New York cityscape first swung under her microscope in those four articles for *Vogue.*

Even with *Death and Life,* then, it all came slowly, so much needing to marinate and stew. And yet to listen to her over the years, Jane never quite accepted this; it seemed always to bother her how long it took. "I'm very slow and full of trial and error and plodding and I wish I knew some faster, more efficient way to work but experience hasn't taught me any."

She was forever taking on ambitious subjects from new directions, marching imperturbably into all she didn't know. She'd never understand, she told an interviewer once, how other authors could "stand the boredom of just writing down everything [they] already knew." But she paid the price for indulging her insatiable curiosity. With each new book, she would tell Bob's niece Lucia Jacobs, "I always get scared to death." Caught up in complexities of a new field not at first fully apparent, "I realize it's too deep for me, but I have to keep on with it." Until she gets it.

The same went for getting the words right. In 1965, a letter from Jane to a New York poet, Ned O'Gorman, included this assertion: The new architecture and planning were "tightly imprisoned in the old paternalistic visions, and at the bottom of them is a simple-minded notion of people as passive domestic animals, who will flourish like well-kept domestic animals if their environment is well kept." A little more than a year later, she returned from a trip to Europe to find that O'Gorman planned to publish part of her letter. She was incensed. When she'd earlier written to him, she wrote him now, she'd given no thought to it being published. She "would not have written as I did, if I had," and did not wish to see it published now. She'd just thrown out an idea, one perhaps useful to him as he worked on his own book, but that was all. "It is badly written. It makes assertions that I would never make for publication without attempting to support them and to explain them." She went on: "I do not like to lay myself open gratuitously to being misunderstood, and I would take it very hard if that letter . . . saw print." Actually, you can see why O'Gorman wanted to use her plucky letter. But still, who would want one's half-cocked ideas made public? Jane certainly didn't. As much as anyone, she knew the difference. Much of her working life was spent refining or eliminating language that, in early form, was awkward, crude, silly, or just plain wrong.

As it is, examples of clumsy language did sometimes make it into print under Jane's name. As much as *Death and Life* was lauded for its literary virtues, it had its lapses, plenty of them, the reader sometimes caught up in thick undergrowths of abstraction. One snarky online review of an audio edition of the book made fun of sentences "all around 200 words or more comprising a multitude of phrases and clauses, remarking on several feelings, digressing, couching her terms, and presenting 'on the other hand' arguments . . . always adding exceptions and exceptions to the exceptions." Laughing at Jane at her worst (exacerbated in the spoken word), he wasn't being entirely fair. But he wasn't entirely wrong, either. Working on *Death and Life,* Jane was no longer moored by the restraining hand of a good magazine editor, normally more tightfisted with editorial space than a book editor and more bent on eliminating windy excess.

How could a mind like Jane's, known for delivering rhetorical flourishes that lingered in the mind—*cities-before-agriculture, eyes-on-the-street*—spew out so much that was fuzzy or embarrassingly awkward? Well, she could. "Oh, I'm so chaotic," she'd tell one interviewer, regarding her writing process. "I just scramble as best I can." Her mind might recognize a departure from clarity, yet actually *achieve* clarity only with enormous effort. As a boy and later, Jim Jacobs remembers hearing his mother work, periods of silence punctuated by rat-a-tat machine-gun bursts from her manual typewriter. But those bursts, as propulsive as they sounded, didn't always produce great prose. They were part of Jane's *process* of writing. They expressed an almost physical need to *utter.* But that didn't mean they expressed her point—even if, just then, she knew what her point was. Given Jane's reports of how much paper, in an age before word processors, she crumpled up in the course of writing, it's safe to conclude that much of it wasn't very good. Before the pungency and clarity readers admired came the muddle.

Muddle borne not alone in the errant vagaries of her brain but in all the perplexities and confusions of the world. If there was a common denominator to her books it was, *How does the world work?* How do cities or successful economies work? What explained why greengrocers and Mafia dons, say, held to such wildly different values? When she looked out at the world, the evidence often seemed contradictory, threatening to overturn any fragmentary idea she might hold. Yet she sought such evidence compulsively. She looked, she observed, she listened, she read voluminously, she took in popular articles and scholarly ones. In the Jacobs Papers at Boston College stand folder upon folder, stuffed with yellowed clippings, all labeled with the distinctly unromantic heading "material used," giving evidence for the case histories she developed, the stories she told, the conclusions she reached.

In *Death and Life* and *The Economy of Cities*, Jane included no notes, no bibliography, no scholarly apparatus—maybe an occasional lonely footnote. But in the early 1970s, Jim Jacobs recalls, she came upon a book with notes in the back but nothing about them in the body of the book to undercut reading pleasure or involvement. She liked that. Perhaps by now more mindful of her role as public intellectual, in *Cities and the Wealth of Nations* she included such a section, as she would in her subsequent books. And from them, we can draw insights into what Jane read, to whom she listened, the broad gamut of those influences-of-fact upon which she relied.

She read *The Wall Street Journal, Scientific American, Natural History, The New York Times, The Globe and Mail.* But these and other such mainstream publications were just the overlay atop her deep reading and fact gathering. She read *Shinohata: A Portrait of a Japanese Village*, by Ronald P. Dore, published in 1978. A memoir of Catherine the Great. Henri Pirenne's book, from her student days at Columbia, *Medieval Cities*. Stories of pirated software supplied by a visiting scientist at a conference. A New York City agency's list of white-collar crimes. A book about chivalry. The Code of Hammurabi. Jane read of James Lovelock's Gaia hypothesis, of biomimicry, the efficiency expert Frederick Winslow Taylor, viruses, cybernetics, fractals, and the obsolescence of recording technology. As she'd one day describe herself, she was like "a caterpillar munching, munching, munching, munching away in a forest, digesting all kinds of leaves, and in the process being informed of what's there."

Her family could be counted on for stray, intriguing bits of information, too. For *Cities and the Wealth of Nations,* her niece Carol, Betty's daughter, drew her attention to an Arabic-language book, *The Muqaddimah,* dating to 1381. To confirm her recollections of Higgins, the remote mountain town where she'd lived in 1934, she turned to brother Jim, then living with his wife in North Carolina. In April 1974, she wrote brother John about what she suspected was a well-known quotation she just couldn't lay her hands on. It was from the turn of the century and was

in the form of a funeral description summarizing the economic paradox of the South at that time. The corpse, the speaker says, was buried in cotton land but his shroud was woven in New England, near a pine forest, but his coffin was made somewhere else in the north—this is the gist—and so on and so on.

Could John help?

Ten years later, there it was on page 36 of *Cities and the Wealth of Nations,* exactly on point to her theme—how poor regions, bereft of vital cities, were reduced to importing most of what they needed: "The grave was dug through solid marble, but the marble headstone came from Vermont," said Henry Grady of Pickens County, Georgia. "It was in a pine wilderness but the pine coffin came from Cincinnati. An iron mountain over-shadowed it but the coffin nails and the screws and the shovel came from Pittsburgh."

Jane's personal experience figured in her book research as well: A tour of the jade market in Hong Kong. An old boss at *Iron Age* who'd dismissed the prospects for plastics. A pet store in San Francisco founded by a distant relative. Making it into one of her books was, of all things, Bob's trouble extracting from the clergyman who performed their wedding just how much he was owed. All this supplied grist for developing her ideas or even inspiring them in the first place. "People say, 'You use such wonderful examples to illustrate what you're saying—how do you find them?' It's just the opposite. The examples come first. I think from the concrete. I can't think from the abstract."

In 1985, Richard Carroll Keeley lured Jane to a conference at Boston

College built around her work. In the conference's published proceedings, he wrote of his attempt to characterize her "method." He started from her assertion near the end of *Death and Life* that understanding best came from working inductively, from particulars to the general, not vice versa; in particular, one sought " 'unaverage' clues involving very small quantities, which reveal the way larger and more 'average' quantities are operating."

What, pray tell, was an "unaverage" clue?

In a 1994 letter to Stewart Brand, founder of the *Whole Earth Catalog*, Jane would observe that the usual division between "solid statistical evidence," on the one hand, and "random, highly suspect anecdotal evidence," on the other, was too wide and too crude. Left out was a third species of evidence, "systematically illuminating cases" that shed especially revealing light on a topic. *Death and Life* was littered with them. But how, Keeley wondered now, did she find the clues that would ultimately come to seem so illuminating? "I am left with an admiring puzzlement: How *did* she do that?"

Keeley's questions inspired a long response from Jane: "When I start exploring some subject, I hardly know what I think." Again she referred to what sounds like a kind of intellectual pain as she wandered through the misshapen byways of her own confusion. It was all "very messy," she wrote, and "very uncomfortable. I don't like all this confusion." But she endured it, pushing through it, only to finally reach the patterns, ideas, and conclusions that held up.

"If I wanted, I could go on and on and on," she concluded her letter to Keeley, "but that would only be tiresome and repetitive and perhaps self-indulgent in displaying my industriousness and labor!" There was, however, "a different type of self-indulgence" to which she succumbed: "While I'm not an artist, I do feel bound to try, as far as I'm able, to produce a work of art as well as a piece of truth."

Two-thirds of the way through this difficult period, as she struggled to complete *Cities and the Wealth of Nations*, Jane was pulled away by another project. Coming when it did, when she was already so late with the book, is it best seen as a distraction to which, unfortunately, she gave in? Or as a welcome and refreshing detour, an opportunity too good to refuse?

It came in 1979, when Jane was approached by Max Allen, a prominent Canadian broadcaster representing a group charged with selecting that year's Massey Lecturer. The Massey Lectures—radio lectures without, in fact, a live audience, broadcast by the Canadian Broadcasting Corporation—were named for former governor general Vincent Massey and were immensely prestigious; past lecturers included Paul Goodman, Martin Luther King Jr., Willy Brandt, and John Kenneth Galbraith. Jane could speak on any subject she pleased. Architecture or planning, for sure, Allen figured. But no, Jane wanted to talk about Quebec separatism.

Canada was just then embroiled in a great national dialogue about the fate of French-speaking Quebec, whether it should remain within Canada or define its national destiny outside it. The British defeat of the French on the Plains of Abraham in Quebec in 1759 had hardly resolved the question once and for all. Recently, the leader of the separatist Parti Québécois, René Lévesque, had issued an impassioned argument for Quebec independence—which, duly translated into English, could scarcely be found in Toronto bookstores. A few months hence, a referendum was to be held in Quebec, presumably to settle the issue. And now Jane, a Canadian citizen for barely five years, was determined to weigh in on it, too, in a series of five half-hour radio addresses she would later flesh out in book form as *The Question of Separatism: Quebec and the Struggle over Sovereignty*, published in 1980.

In fact, her lecture topic wasn't entirely remote from the book she'd been working on for so long, whose original title was *Cities and Countries*. In her Massey Lectures, Toronto and Montreal, the great cities of English- and French-speaking Canada, respectively, figured prominently. So did *the size of things*, which had interested Jane all the way back to *Death and Life*—the size of neighborhoods, buildings, and cities, the relationship of small things to big. In the separatism book, she'd devote a chapter to "National Size and Economic Development," another to "Paradoxes of Size." Over the years, she'd mostly favored small entities free from the corrosive bullying of the big; little Quebec versus big Canada was a natural. And so were the "city regions," set against whole nations, that would figure in *Cities and the Wealth of Nations*.

In the Massey Lectures Jane didn't quite say Quebec should split from Canada. What she did say was that, if it did, no terrible fate would befall either English-speaking Canada or Quebec. Given the success of small countries like Switzerland and Norway, Quebec was not too small to

thrive. Canada would not disintegrate with Quebec's secession; its slim-
ming in size and population would not prove crippling. In fact, there was
a charming historical parallel for the sort of split Quebec might engineer,
namely that of Norway from Sweden in 1905. That, Jane showed, was
achieved peaceably and respectfully, at no loss to the two countries even
a century later—a model of civilized behavior on both sides.

> Here in Toronto, where I live, in two different office buildings about
> a mile apart, are to be found two trade commissions, one Norwegian,
> one Swedish. To me, the two establishments seem more than busy,
> competently run commercial offices, staffed by cheerful, helpful peo-
> ple. To me, they seem the concrete evidence of a miracle—a secession
> achieved without armed rebellion, without terrorism, without the mil-
> itary defeat of a former ruler.

Canada and Quebec, she as much as said, could do the same.

It was a nuanced response to a nagging national problem, and when
her lectures came out in book form the following year, its extraordinary
finesse was recognized. Writing in *The New York Review of Books,* Edgar
Z. Friedenberg called it "a *tour de force,* the kind of force that expresses
itself through restraint and precision, like a laser beam used with such
exquisite care as not to insult the distressed body it is intended to relieve."
In it, she brought insight and lucidity to "the most inflamed social question of a very touchy people, her fellow-citizens in her adopted country.
She does so with a tact so fine that it's scary."

Max Allen, who had invited Jane to do the Massey Lectures and became
a friend, would say that Jane had produced "perfect lectures"—but that,
on the other hand, she "was not a great lecturer. It was not a compelling
performance." Not fiery, not dramatic, not the work of a gifted performer;
you can hear the schoolmarm in her speaking. In the national dialogue
over separatism, admits Allen, her lectures "made no difference at all."
They were rarely cited, little influenced public debate. Among English
speakers, Jane would recall in 2005, "there was practically no reaction."
In part, perhaps, because as one critic, Alex Mazer, has cogently written,
Jane had refuted "some of the weaker arguments against secession" while
failing to address some of the stronger.

In a *New York Times* review of the book, John Leonard concluded of
Jane that "about Canada, including Quebec, she is shrewd; about Quebec,
excluding Canada, she merely dreams in very good prose."

CHAPTER 22

ADAM, KARL, AND JANE

A ND THEN, FINALLY, there was *Cities and the Wealth of Nations.* Jane pictured it as "a kind of overhaul of macro-economics." It began like this:

> For a little while in the middle of this century it seemed that the wild, intractable, dismal science of economics had yielded up something we all want: instructions for getting or keeping prosperity. Economists and the rulers they advise had thought up so many ideas for ridding national and international economies of chanciness and disaster, the ideas had such an air of rationality, predictability and informed statistical analysis, that governments took to supposing they need only muster up commitment, expertise and money to make economic life do their bidding.

But, it seems, economic life wasn't doing *anyone's* bidding. Jane cataloged economic failure and its consequences in Poland and Uruguay, southern Italy and India, the Soviet Union and China, Britain and the United States. In America, she wrote, "the manufacturing economy has gradually but steadily been eroding, and much of what remains has been slipping into technological backwardness," compared to Japan and parts of Europe. For failing to predict or forestall economic stagnation around the world, she pronounced macroeconomics, devoted to explaining economics at a national and international scale, "a shambles."

Jane began by taking on a seemingly unlikely target, the Marshall Plan, almost universally credited with rescuing Europe, then in ruins, from its post–World War II economic afflictions. Yes, Jane allowed, its billions in bulldozers, tractors, trucks, pumps, pipes, and machine tools had helped heal the continent. But if you really wanted to make a healthy economy from a sick one, a Marshall Plan wouldn't do it—*hadn't* done it: southern Italy, poor before the war, remained so despite all the development aid thrown at it, was still losing workers to Italy's prosperous north. Backward regions of Europe remained backward. The Marshall Plan's outsized claims, and those of the international development agencies grown up around it, were unjustified. "The consequences of such groundless promises are appalling: angry disillusioned populations in countries that have remained stagnant and poor after hopes were raised so high; cynicism about the worth of aiding others, and worse, about the worth of people who have gotten aid," backward countries bowed down under the weight of unpayable debt.

One clue to the failure of conventional macroeconomic thinking, Jane argued, was "stagflation," an economic malediction combining high unemployment and high prices—stagnation and inflation, together. The two miseries weren't "supposed" to go together, but in 1975, for example, the United States recorded 8.5 percent unemployment and 9.1 percent inflation, both painfully high. "The puzzle of stagflation," according to Jane, had destroyed the intellectual foundations upon which most macroeconomic theory rested. Thinkers from Adam Smith and John Stuart Mill to Karl Marx and John Maynard Keynes, and on to the latest lights in the field, had failed to predict the phenomenon, or account for it, or were left baffled by it in the first place. "Fool's Paradise," Jane titled the chapter.

While treated as new and troubling, stagflation—the word itself was a 1964 coinage—wasn't new at all, argued Jane. Prices too high? Too few jobs? Why, that was the lot of most of the world. Jane told of a visit to Portugal in 1974, where, as a middle-class American, she found the prices for bus fares, fish, and restaurant meals all enticingly cheap. "But to the Portuguese the prices were very high." For most Portuguese, middle-class comforts were beyond reach and jobs were hard to come by. In this sense, then, stagflation was not odd or newfangled, but, rather, "the normal and ordinary condition to be found in poor and backward economies the world over." It was new only in that now it threatened advanced economies with "profound economic decline." And conventional macroeconomics couldn't explain it.

"One thing we do know," she concluded this provocative first chapter, because events have rubbed our faces in it: it would be rash to suppose that macro-economics, as it stands today, has useful guidance for us. Several centuries of hard, ingenious thought about supply and demand chasing each other around, tails in their mouths, have told us almost nothing about the rise and decline of wealth.

There was no future, she declared, in choosing among existing lines of economic thought. "We are on our own."

Which meant, of course, that for the next two hundred pages, Jane was on *her* own.

Conventional macroeconomics. she felt, hewed to faulty premises. You want to understand the causes of prosperity, the dynamics of decline? Well, said economists from Adam Smith on, you look to national economies as the "salient entities"—England, not London; Russia, not St. Petersburg. Smith had titled his pathbreaking book of 1776 *The Wealth of Nations,* and nations, big and small, had remained the focus of economists since.

But the nation, said Jane, was too large a unit of study, obscuring insight rightly gained only at smaller scale. Nations comprised cities, rural districts, poor regions and rich; at this larger scale, telling details of economic life were lost in numbers and facts bundled up for measuring whole countries, like "gross national product." The focus needed to be on where economies really developed, in cities and the regions they enriched. At their best, cities were the high-revving engines responsible for economic development, hothouses of innovation, forever inventing and reinventing themselves, creating new work; this, for Jane, was what *made* them cities. Cities, not nations, were the "salient entity" through which you could come to understand growth.

Look to the small, advised Jane. Look, for example, to Bardou, a hamlet situated high in the Cévennes Mountains of south-central France. Two thousand years ago, when Gaul was a Roman province, iron was mined there. Iron reached the cities, where it was fabricated into swords, chisels, and hinges, by a network of roads that, when Jane wrote, still served as hikers' trails. But, probably in the fourth century, the iron gave out and the mines were abandoned. The area reverted to wilderness. Then, in the sixteenth century, landless peasants from the valley below began building stone houses in Bardou. "They scratched out little garden plots among the rocks, gathered chestnuts," caught local game, "and on their poor and rocky soil pursued as well as they could the subsistence arts they had inherited from economies of the distant past more creative than their own." For centuries, nothing much changed. Then, after the Franco-Prussian War of 1870, a few venturesome souls from Bardou began leaving for Paris and richer lives. By 1940, only three families remained. In the 1960s, vacationers from the city transformed some of the old stone houses into summer rentals. A hint of prosperity returned to the old village.

Jane's history of Bardou made for a charming little story, but it was not for its local color that she told it. "Bardou is an example, in microcosm, of what I am going to call passive economies," which, initiating nothing themselves, merely respond "to forces unloosed in distant cities." In Bardou's case, it was Rome, Nîmes, Lyon, and Paris that, over the years, had shaped and reshaped it.

> We could beat our brains out trying to explain Bardou's economic history in terms of its own attributes, right down to compiling statistics on the probable average yield of chestnuts, the tools used there, the amount and quality of iron taken out and that remaining, the man-hours required to build a house, the nature of the soil, the annual rainfall, and so on—and none of this would enlighten us at all as to why and how Bardou's economy took the twists and turns it actually did.

For that, the clues would all be found in distant cities, with their technologies, expertise, money, jobs, and markets.

Cities, wrote Jane, "shape stunted and bizarre economies in distant regions," such as "supply regions" like her hometown of Scranton, or, for that matter, the whole country of Uruguay. Scranton produced coal; Uruguay, meat, wool, and leather. They had done this year in and year out, attaining notable prosperity. Until, that is, the coal was gone and the markets for meat, wool, and leather were undercut by events on the other side of the world. Then their economies crashed.

Midway through the book appeared a ghost from Jane's youth, from half a century before: it was most of a lifetime since Jane's six months in Higgins, North Carolina, the hills rising around that tiny enclave into which Aunt Martha had tried to breathe hope and progress. Stunning scenery and warm appreciation for the folkways of the mountain men and women she met there may, possibly, have figured in Jane's memories. But figuring more was the economic desolation of the place. And now, in a chapter called "Bypassed Places," she took her readers there. To preserve its anonymity, she called it "Henry"—as in *My Fair Lady*'s Henry Higgins—but Higgins it was.

When local economies lost their links to cities, Jane wrote, "their people sink into lives of rural subsistence," often losing know-how they once possessed. By the time of the Roman Empire, Egypt had lost its papyrus industry and with it the skills of making paper. So it was in Higgins: "Crafts that had been their heritage were decaying, and some were being lost . . . People had long since stopped making looms," and no one any longer knew how to make them. Weaving had become a lost art. *These* were the memories that left their imprint on Jane. Over the course of a century and a half, "Henry had been retrogressing economically in perfect peace and tranquility."

Chapter by chapter, Jane chomped away at widely held notions of economic truth. Like, for example, that it made sense, as a development tool, to bring new factories or military bases to barren rural tracts in return for tax credits or other perks. No, Jane said, not if you wanted to breathe real life into an economy that would survive the next swings in the market. Yes, you might get a few jobs for a while. But such strategies didn't create new work, and so contributed nothing to long-term prosperity. Only real cities did that.

Jane punctuated her arguments with audacious assertions and aphoristic take-home lessons: the subsistence life of Higgins "was not a demonstration, as romantics like to think, of how economic life begins, but rather of how it decays and peters out."

Or, again referring to Uruguay and its superficially prosperous economy: "The difference between a rich backward economy and a poor backward economy is not all that great."

Like all of her books, *Cities and the Wealth of Nations* was thickly stocked with ideas, insights, anecdotes, and argument— and also with a flavor of science. "I am going to argue," Jane wrote in a long chapter called "Faulty Feedback to Cities," that national currencies "give faulty and destructive feedback to city economies and that this in turn leads to profound structural economic flaws." Feedback: You're keeping to the 60 mph speed limit, you look to the speedometer, which tells you you're doing 65, so you take your foot off the gas; the speedometer supplies feedback that lets you correct the error of your ways. Likewise the thermostat in your air-conditioning or heating system, which senses the actual temperature, compares it to the desired and turns the system on or off to make things right. Similarly, Jane pointed out now, economies. The rise and fall of a nation's currency in international markets supplies essential feedback, the information that helps "correct" or reset the economy: the dollar weakens, American goods are cheaper in world markets, spurring production here at home.

In principle, very pretty. *But*, said Jane, much too coarse. A nation is an "economic grab bag," with different parts of its economy—Illinois farms and big-city Chicago—needing precisely tailored feedback corrections of their own. But, since all are tied to the same national currency, swinging back and forth in response to broad geopolitical and economic forces, they don't get the fine-tuned signals they need to slow down or speed up. They get feedback not useful and pertinent but "faulty."

"Jane Jacobs has done a great service with her new book," wrote Bernard Levin in an *Economist* review. "She has slain many dangerous myths, exposed many ruinous follies, demonstrated beyond argument that many eagerly-embraced remedies for our economic difficulties are certain to make those difficulties worse." For Richard J. Barnet, in *The New York Times*, the book was a "learned, iconoclastic and exciting study of the causes of economic stagnation and decline [that challenges] . . . ideas, schemes and pieties all across the political spectrum." One economist objected to Jane's take on stagflation, saying it wasn't high prices that typified it but *rising* prices, which was not the same thing. Generally, though, the book was lauded. In 1984, as we've noted, it received the Los Angeles Times Book Prize. At the 1987 Boston College conference on Jane's work, it was studied respectfully along with her two previous books. So long in the making, *Cities and the Wealth of Nations* largely lived up to its promise, passing into the Jane Jacobs canon.

But in the mind's eye of almost everyone, Jane remained an urban visionary; she was still, primarily, the author of *Death and Life*—no matter that her last two books were about economics. Writing to a friend, Roberta Brandes Gratz, soon after publication, Jane reported that her book was "hated" by economists; "ignored" might be the better word. But that was in 1984. And in 1988 things began to change.

It seems that professional economists, in their own ways and using their own methods, had come to take an interest in problems broadly similar to those so interesting to Jane: Why were some places more prosperous than others? Why were some able to break out from their subsistence past and grow wealthy while others remained economically backward?

Malthus had grimly seen population growth, with its swelling tide of hungry bellies, always outpacing economic growth; to Malthus we owe economics' epithet as "the dismal science." Adam Smith, more optimistic, found clues in his pin factory for how economic wealth emerged from the factory floor. Karl Marx fretted less about the production of wealth than its distribution, gross inequities between worker and capitalist leading unavoidably to crisis. Among more recent economists, economic growth, as a distinct subject, had begun to work its way into their thinking. And as David Warsh writes in his captivating intellectual adventure story, *Knowledge and the Wealth of Nations: A Story of Economic Discovery*, they were talking about something they'd not much talked about before, *knowledge*. And along the way they stumbled on Jane.

Traditionally, when economists spoke of the "factors of production," they meant capital, labor, and land; making automobiles might require a billion-dollar capital investment, put three thousand people to work, in a factory erected on a hundred acres wrested from former farmland. Of course, as any reasoning mind could see, other factors besides capital, labor, and land figured in industrial success or failure. One of them was the knowledge that led to the design of new machinery, or new materials, or new ways of putting them together. In 1890, Alfred Marshall, of Cambridge University in England, described as necessary for understanding economic growth "the general development of the industry." By this he meant brain work. In an industry benefiting from it,

> the mysteries of the trade become no mysteries; but are as it were in the air, and children learn many of them unconsciously. Good work is rightly appreciated, inventions and improvements in machinery, in processes and the general organization of the business have their merits promptly discussed: if one man starts a new idea, it is taken up with others and combined with suggestions of their own; and thus it becomes the source of further new ideas.

Knowledge spills over to the benefit of all.

But, as Warsh writes, "Marshall didn't inquire too deeply into exactly how this spillover process might work." Nor, for a long time, did anyone else. Somehow, knowledge and its workings seemed to lie outside the realm of economic study: knowledge increased, principles were discovered, processes were improved, inventions were devised—all as simply the product of "noneconomic background forces" that you could pretty much take for granted, like the air you breathed. What, after all, was there to study?

After World War II, however, the sources and diffusion of knowledge *itself* fell under the economist's gaze. It was no longer something "out there" that no one could influence or affect, but a key element of any economic system, amenable to study like anything else. Where did the new products and processes that fueled economic growth come from? What was the role of entrepreneurs and universities? Or of think tanks and private research labs? Or of trade secrets? Could government do anything to foster the growth of such knowledge, and should it?

In 1985, the University of Chicago's Robert Lucas, at forty-eight one of the most respected theoreticians of economics in the world, gave that year's Marshall Lecture, named for Alfred Marshall, in Cambridge, England. His subject was economic growth, or, more specifically, "On the Mechanics of Economic Development." Not far into his lecture, he directed his audience to some arresting statistics of wildly unequal growth. Japan had recently been growing at 7.1 percent a year, the United States at 2.3 percent, India 1.4 percent. These were numbers, but not *just* numbers: behind their cold face, they represented human happiness and human suffering. For they meant prosperity, possibility, and choice for some; demeaning poverty for others. And this brought Lucas to the next big question: "Is there some action a government of India could take that would lead the Indian economy to grow" as fast as countries then enjoying robust growth? And, "if so, *what* exactly?"

That is, what could you do, in real life, to lead India's desperately poor hundreds of millions to fuller, more prosperous lives? Or if, sadly, nothing, why not? "The consequences for human welfare involved in questions like these are simply staggering. Once one starts to think about them, it is hard to think about anything else."

Lucas was trying to pin down why the rich get richer and the poor stay poor, why the split had widened rather than, as some had expected, shrunk, and how knowledge and ideas figured in the answers. And toward the end of his Marshall Lecture—which, wandering a bit, had not always followed the clearest of paths—he turned to the ideas of Jane Jacobs.

Lucas, as he'd later tell the story, had long admired Jane's work—if not, it seems, through the usual gateway: he was perhaps the only person in the world, he'd say, who'd read *The Economy of Cities* before *Death and Life*. Jane's imagined city, New Obsidian, which some critics wrote off as fabulist fantasy, he saw as the work of a sound and sober intellect; here was a natural theorist at work, keeping her theoretical vision and her well of evidence scrupulously separate and distinct. "She's crystal clear as to what she's making up and what she's getting from archaeological data." And at some point while struggling to understand growth discrepancies around the world, Lucas said, he landed back in Jane's second book.

Ideas—knowledge, science, technology, innovation, invention—were responsible for much of the West's growth since the earliest days of the Industrial Revolution; that much was plain enough by now. "So," Lucas would recount, "you might think that economists interested in growth theory would put ideas at the centre of their work. How do ideas get produced? Where do they get generated? How do they get diffused and passed on to other people?" Yet growth theory had largely neglected such questions. Ideas were simply in the air? That just wouldn't do.

"What I found exciting about Jacobs's work was that this question is at the centre of everything. What are cities good for? They're good for ideas. Ideas get put into use, they arise from different cultures and bodies of knowledge meeting each other." In 1993, responding to a Columbia University economist interested in her ideas, Jane would wonder why most economists scanted the study of innovation. "Is it because innovations are so unpredictable?" True, specific innovations *are* unpredictable. But "the conditions that permit them are not." The conditions that encouraged innovation, incited it, practically pulled it out of people, said Jane, bubbled up from close-packed, diverse cities.

To switch back now to the language of Lucas's Marshall Lecture, Jane was seeing deeply into the "external" effects of human capital. Go to school, work beside an expert or inspiring mentor, develop intimate knowledge of an exciting new industrial process, and you gain "human capital." Your productivity shoots up, your income likely climbs, maybe you start a new company and make a million bucks. These are "internal" effects; they benefit *you*, possessor of that human capital. But human capital also benefits your company, university, think tank, city, or country; your hard-won body of expertise, your new product, idea, or method, profits your employer, which hires workers, maybe soon stands at the nexus of a cluster of new companies; these are "external" effects, or—spillovers. *Win-win*, big-time.

In pursuing how this powerful economic driver worked, Lucas said in Cambridge,

> I will be following very closely the lead of Jane Jacobs, whose remark-able book *The Economy of Cities* seems to me mainly and convinc-ingly concerned (though she does not use this terminology) with the external effects of human capital . . . [As Jacobs had illustrated] with hundreds of concrete examples, much of economic life is "creative" in much the same way as is "art" and "science." New York City's gar-ment district, financial district, diamond district, advertising district and many more are as much intellectual centers as is Columbia or New York University. The specific ideas exchanged in these centers differ, of course, from those exchanged in academic circles, but the process is much the same.

And wasn't there, Lucas added, an implicit "proof" of all this? Land was normally cheaper outside cities than within them. So why don't com-panies invariably set up shop there for the cheaper rents? Many times they do, especially for their "back office," or more routine functions. But often they do not, because they are *getting* something from it—a cre-ative human environment that nurtures new ideas and practices. "What can people be paying Manhattan or downtown Chicago rents *for*," asked Lucas, "if not for being near other people?"

Jane, her son Ned reports, was "gratified" by the acceptance Lucas's talk brought her, which was only underlined when Lucas won the Nobel Prize in Economics in 1995. In succeeding years the attention grew. People started talking about "Jacobs singularities," economist-speak for innova-tive leaps occurring not within, but *across*, industries in close physical proximity. One research group compared Jane's predictions about growth and innovation to those of two other, more mainstream lines of economic thinking and found hers more predictive. Another went looking for "Jacobs Spillovers" among Canadian inventors. As a newspaper headline put it in the 1990s, Jane was now something of an "economic guru."

But not really an economist, not in the narrow, professional sense, anyway. Lucas himself would say how you could never turn to Jane's work and pull out an equation. Her work was astonishingly fertile and

Jane at her ease, age eighty-one, in a photo taken for an article in The Globe and Mail, *headed, "Jacobs Embraced as Economic Guru"*

fruitful. But that didn't make her an economist, either. When, in 1997, the University of Toronto economist David Nowlan reviewed Jane's contribution, he titled his essay "Jane Jacobs Among the Economists," which gets it about right—Jane usefully *among* them but not *of* their particular species.

This, of course, wouldn't have troubled Jane one bit.

A few years after winning the Nobel, Robert Lucas came out with a volume of essays devoted to economic growth. In one of them he made much of a 1961 novel, set in Trinidad, *A House for Mr. Biswas*, terming it V. S. Naipaul's "great novel of economic development."

Mr. Biswas is the grandson of indentured servants come to Trinidad from India. His ambition as a child is nothing more than to become a cattle herder. But by novel's end he's managed to carve out—painfully, insecurely, tentatively—a middle-class existence for himself and his family in Trinidad's capital city, Port-of-Spain. "His talents are modest," writes Lucas, "but his unwillingness to accept the limits of each current situa-

tion as permanent, to make the best of it, turns out to be his strength."
Crucially, Mr. Biswas lives in a place and time that offers him options,
where

> a man with a little literacy could move from rural to small town to
> Port-of-Spain jobs, jobs where he could interact with people who could
> teach him a little more. Somehow Biswas survives, marries, supports a
> family after a fashion, and succeeds in passing on to some of his chil-
> dren this sense of living in a world with possibilities.

Reading *Cities and the Wealth of Nations*, I was struck by similarities
between Higgins, North Carolina, and a small island of my acquaintance
off the west coast of Ireland, the Great Blasket. The book I wrote before
this one, *On an Irish Island*, told the story of this island and the tiny,
Gaelic-speaking community inhabiting it. The island lived off fishing and
a few fields of potatoes and oats. For several hundred years it changed
little. But beginning before World War I, its reputation as a haven for the
Irish language, and as a culturally vibrant community, rich with speech
and song, began to draw linguists and writers from London, Dublin,
Oslo, Paris. These urban intellectuals instilled in the islanders a sense
of their own cultural worth and encouraged them to record their stories,
which emerged in a group of books known as "the Blasket Library."

Around the same time, however, the island, never home to more than
about two hundred, began losing its young people. Increasingly, they
left for the mainland or, more often, for America, where they settled
in Massachusetts. The islanders heard regularly from their brothers and
sisters of the economic opportunities in America; the island offered them
none, nothing but the rude, constrained existence they and their forebears had lived for centuries. The coming of commercial fishing trawlers
to their traditional fishing grounds only made things worse. "We have
determined at last to leave this lovely Island," one native islander wrote
in 1942. Visitors "would never believe the misfortune on this Island no
school nor comfort, no road to success . . . everything so dear and so far
away." By 1953, the last islander was gone and the tiny village of stone
houses on the slope of hill facing the mainland was on its way to ruin.

The Great Blasket was cut off by a narrow, navigationally tricky strait
from the mainland, by three hundred miles from Dublin, and by three

thousand miles from America. Higgins, North Carolina, was cut off by mountains, bad roads, and poverty even from nearby Asheville, much less larger cities. Both inhabited astonishingly beautiful natural settings. Both had their interesting folkways, their unique charms. But in the end, both were places that people left, wanted to leave, or had to leave.

From the ruins of the Great Blasket one might pause a moment and, as I wrote in my earlier book, contemplate pleasures the villagers enjoyed and that modern lives—too fevered, insubstantial, or inauthentic—deny us. But if clear-eyed Jane told the Blasket story, I suspect, she'd lay quite different emphasis—on the island's want of opportunity, on how it failed so cruelly to offer "a world with possibilities."

CHAPTER 23

WEBS OF TRUST

I. JANE AND COMPANY

It might be natural to imagine Jane as wholly independent, a woman all her own, off in her study by herself, reading, thinking, and writing. And yet, she was no recluse. She had plenty of friends. People were always in and out of the house—which, for all Mary Malfara's efforts to keep it tidy, was never overbearingly immaculate. Family meant a great deal to her. She was not oblivious to what people thought of her. She'd achieved much, in New York and Toronto, working with and through others. Intellectually, she was similarly stitched in. The notes and acknowledgments in her books are thick with names. She could be reached, she could be influenced, in person and in print. She was a social animal. Sipping a cocktail, sharing her thoughts, enjoying the attention of her friends, she could be very happy.

Alan Littlewood, the architect whom Jane befriended in the 1970s and who played so key a role in the St. Lawrence project, tells of parties at Albany Avenue in the 1980s and 1990s: arrive at seven, Gibson's gin and onion martinis soon flowing, son Jim the bartender. The drinkware was what Littlewood, who was partial to crystal, calls "odds and ends," nothing elegant, maybe picked up at Honest Ed's, the local discount emporium; "she took pride in being unaffected." There'd be cheese and pâté, small talk over drinks, Jane sometimes reminiscing about New York. "Then Jane would disappear to finish off dinner," which Littlewood recalls as (too) often pork.

By the time everyone sat down to eat, it might be 8:30 or 9, an air of expectancy in the room: "People would be waiting for Jane to start." Who would draw her into conversation? Or else, *"What is Jane going to say next?"* Some provocative question might get her going, or some story. And then she'd be off. "You can't deny being in the presence of a great personality," Littlewood says today, shaking his head. "You can't deny your own awe."

She could talk about anything, and did. Only religion seemed to stymie her or leave her cold. "Jane was visibly agitated by references to the Bible . . . I never found a way to talk about it" with her. "I never found a way to penetrate her defenses." Any other subject, though, was fair game. She'd never retreat. About all you might exact from her was the admission that, yes, she might "need to consider that point of view." Jane could seem egoless—but never, says Littlewood, when it came to debate. "She certainly had an ego, a pride, when it came to her point."

For a time in the late 1980s, Lucia Jacobs, daughter of Bob's cousin John Jacobs and his wife, Katia, lived with Jane and Bob. Doing a postdoc at the University of Toronto, she shared the top floor with Burgin, who was in from British Columbia just then, helping brother Jim with the high-tech battery business he was starting up. For Jane, says Lucia, argument was "pure blood sport"; the culture of the family revolved around it. The idea was "to come up with something original and then argue for it." One time she and Jane got into a dandy fight over, of all things, the word "sibling," which Jane viewed as hopeless jargon. "That word should be expunged from the dictionary," Jane said; you're better off using "brother" and "sister." For five hours, in Lucia's recollection, it went on like that. "It was a great fight. We both wanted to get to the bottom of it. It was fun."

It wasn't always fun, but it was always spirited. Jane was "a no-holds-barred fighter." She never made anything up, yet "she never had to do any research," it seemed to Lucia. "She just knew things." She'd introduce some line of argument saying, "In ancient China . . ." and you'd be confident that's how it was in ancient China. Jane's friend from across the street, Toshiko Adilman, reports that Jane knew all about hockey pads and how they were made. "She had knowledge of obscure things."

Jane, by then in her seventies, didn't talk much about sex, recalls Lucia, but Uncle Bob did. He relished the occasional risqué joke, seemed to enjoy indulging his appetites generally. Once, she remembers, he sat down to a quiche larded up with maybe a half pound of butter, devoured it, then pleaded for more. It was Bob who'd made the Jacobs house the original and memorable place it was, stocked with his design flourishes; "Jane didn't have a bone of that." They were a perfect match, devoted to one another. Women, it seemed to Lucia, sometimes need a brother more than the more clichéd father figure. "And that's exactly what Jane and Bob had" in each other. Sometimes Lucia would catch them in the morning, making each other roar with laughter.

None of this is to say that Jane and Bob, or Jane and anyone else, for that matter, were evenly matched in those kitchen-table debates. "No one else in that family," observes Lucia, "had intuitions [like hers, even as] they had no shortage of opinions." The brutal truth was that the others were "pale imitations of Jane." She was the "hearthfire" of their extraordinary family, "the only genius." Still groping for the apt metaphor, Lucia describes the household as "a beehive, with Jane the queen bee." In some ways, it made life tough for the rest of the family. "It was like living with Zeus."

Ultimately, says Lucia, "I needed oxygen." She was embarked on a conventional academic trajectory — today she is a professor of psychology at the University of California, Berkeley—and Jane "was a little dismissive of the path I was taking: *If you had any guts you wouldn't need that,*" meaning colleagues, conferences, campus ivy. Plus, the family had its kitchen-table-centered ways to which Lucia, working long hours at the lab, couldn't entirely adapt. "I wanted to come home at 11 p.m. and eat peanut butter sandwiches." When she announced she was moving out, Jane put on "a very brave face: '*Oh. Of course. Too bad.*'" But Lucia's antennae told her Jane was hurt.

Jane *hurt*? Whether she was or not, they'd probably never have talked about it. Feelings were not something Jane was inclined to discuss or explore, weren't part of the otherwise vast, all-encompassing universe of discourse she made her own. And her own social antennae were not finely attuned. Alan Littlewood tells how, at a public event, two architects trying to represent Jane's ideas got them all wrong. "That's not me at all," she rose to challenge them. "That's silly." And they just couldn't go on. They were crestfallen; they just slunk away. Afterward, Jane turned to Littlewood. "Do you think I hurt those people?" she asked.

"Yes, Jane," he replied, "you did."

She hadn't meant to. She felt bad about it. In this way, she seemed to him "like a little girl." Sometimes, she just "blundered into things." She was *not* the stage actor adept at picking up on cues, knowing when to keep silent, when to move on. "Jane didn't pick up. She was so interested in the subject matter," whatever it was, "that she suppressed her natural instincts to be kinder."

Jane's friendships don't seem to have included much trading of intimate or introspective revelations; hers was not the "sharing" style of a later generation. "I never heard her reflecting upon herself," says Lucia Jacobs. Jane wasn't apt to stew over the past, friend Toshiko reports, nor to air old grievances. When another friend, having just read William Styron's *Darkness Visible*, his memoir about depression, opened up to Jane about her own frequent depressive episodes, she came away disappointed, even a little hurt: Jane just didn't seem to understand.

The realm of the personal and the intimate? "None of that ever appeared in any of the Jacobses," says Littlewood. "She never talked about herself in a personal way. It was never individual." Always, with family and friends, it was about ideas, about the great world of making, doing, and thinking. With the planner Ken Greenberg, she would argue about the merits of this Toronto project or that. Anne Collins, Jane's editor at Random House Canada from about 1998 on, remembers her "huge, catholic tastes in books and ideas," remembers talking with her about medical research, the author Jared Diamond, not much about children. "If you got engaged with Jane she wanted to know what you were thinking." And invariably, you'd come away from conversations with her feeling "way more interesting than you were before." Just to talk with her somehow reflected well on you.

Design in white: Jane reviewing design entries for the Toronto Main Streets Competition in 1990

Jane's friend Alan Broadbent tells how, after a visit to China, he brought back some photos he thought might interest her. "You want to see these pictures?" he asked. They were from Xi'an, the capital of Shaanxi province. Yes, of course she did. But oh, *how* she looked at them! The photos showed a Muslim area of low buildings, narrow laneways, streets filled with hand- and animal-drawn carts, street markets; the barber shop was a man on a stool, out in the open, with a pair of scissors. "She was hugely interested." She peered at each one—or was it *into* each one?—way longer than you'd expect. The moment stuck with him. Nobody focused the way Jane did.

To be the object of that focus could seem the highest compliment. In 1978, Jane met Roberta Brandes Gratz, then a reporter for the *New York Post*, who'd received a grant to pursue her first book, which became *The Living City*, a collection of urban success stories. At the time, Gratz's editor was Jason Epstein. "You have to go up to Toronto and meet Jane," he told her. Jane invited her to stay at the house. "She was so welcoming, so warm. She put me at ease" right away. Gratz remembers the big jigsaw puzzle spread across the table; how when it was time for coffee, Jane spilled out some raw beans and pan-roasted them, then ground them, right on the spot. She was there two or three days that first time. But Jane made sure the visit didn't crowd out her own work. Daytimes, Gratz was sent out into Toronto, exploring. In the evenings, "we sat at her dining room table and just talked." She was getting an education, and knew it. "I was in awe at the attention she was giving me."

In coming years, Jane and Roberta Gratz, then in her late thirties, became friends. They realized they already had a connection; Roberta's husband had a metal-fabricating business in New York that used to buy materials from Frasse, one of Jane's earliest employers. They both had kids, but seldom spoke of them. Rather, they talked about Roberta's work. She was finding the transition from newspapers to books difficult. Jane sat her down, worked with her through drafts of the troubled manuscript.

At one session, in 1978, Jane began by affirming an element of Roberta's writing strategy: "I think it's *brilliant* to start with the South Bronx." But then, well, yes, this one part did need some attention. "I hope you don't mind my marking this." Soon, they were delving into the "urban homesteading" of that era and its roots in America's original Homestead Act of the late 1800s—except that Jane thought the links tenuous. "Forget that '40 acres and a mule,'" she said to Roberta. "That's a red herring." Gently, she directed Roberta toward the history of homesteading, serving up a disquisition on William Jennings Bryan, the Cross of Gold speech, and land grants—solid facts and fine distinctions to undergird

Roberta's account: back then, "it was the government giving the pioneers land . . . You can't say that now PDC [People's Development Corporation] wanted the same thing. They wanted something *analogous*."

At another point, Jane told her, "I have a quarrel with a word, but it's symbolic of what you do every once in a while." She read from Roberta's draft: *"They had targeted the completion . . . ,"* and explained her problem with it: " 'Targeted' is a present-day bureaucratic fashionable jargon word," downright "barbarous." (Maybe, to Jane's ear, like "sibling"?) "It just means you've been reading too many reports and memos."

It could be hard to take, this pointed critique of her budding manuscript. But Roberta was tough-skinned enough to take it, grateful for the attention she got at Jane's side. "That was part of her nurturing . . . She was interested in what I was doing," even if it amounted to a kind of editorial tough love.

Alan Littlewood also basked in Jane's deep interest. In the years after his St. Lawrence success, he went through a bad period, was discouraged and depressed. Jane offered him a stipend, "to get me over a hump," which he declined. At another low point, she inscribed one of her books and gave it to him. He took it home, opened it up, and all it said was, "I love you. Jane." She just *knew*, says Littlewood, that nothing else from her, no great words of wisdom or inspiration, could have lifted him as much as that did. Jane, says her friend Toshiko, seemed able to accept everyone and find "something unique and individual" in them, fairly stripping away their particular craziness to see them as they were, give them what they needed.

In such ways, certainly, she was the best of friends. One time, Toshiko was slated to interpret at an event where she needed to know specialized botanical terms, and soon Jane was marshaling her intellectual forces to help her. Jane's nephew Decker, staying at the house just then, remembers coming home to find them hunched over the table, dictionaries and books strewn around them, deep into a crash course on fruit trees, blossoms, the qualities of good pears, and the like. (Jane loved fruit, was bothered by how groceries would stock only three or four varieties of apple, kept a running list of the hundred or so varieties she had tasted over the years.)

Summers, Jane and Bob often vacationed with Toshiko and her husband, Sid, on Prince Edward Island. PEI was the smallest of Canada's ten provinces, a real island, heavily agricultural, thick with farms and gardens spewing out vegetables you'd never see in city supermarkets. Soon

after Jane and Bob moved to Albany Avenue, the Adilmans invited them
to join them there. Over the years, they'd go often with the kids, sometimes with brother John and wife, Pete. It was a few weeks or a month
in a modest cabin, part of a cozy summertime community of about fifty
families on half-acre lots a few miles from Charlottetown, the island's
chief town. Sid, a journalist, liked to lie out on the island's red sand
beach, down the grassy path leading to it from the cabin—no news, no
TV. Jane, who needed to protect her body from the sun, typically wore a
hat with a big, wide brim. They'd dig clams, eat giant lobsters, visit light-
houses, make jam together. Eating and reading and talking and laughing
with good company in an idyllic spot far from the cares of the world:
wasn't bad.

Actually, we know of one other visitor to PEI during those years: Spicy,
the pet hamster of Jane's granddaughter, Caitlin, Jim and Pat's daughter.
In a story hatched by Caitlin, maybe nine at the time, and Jane, who was
caring for her that day, and Lucia Jacobs, who immortalized it on film,
Spicy escapes and heads for PEI on his own. Jane shows us the miniature
ladder, probably dollhouse furniture, with which he's made his getaway.
"Oh, I'd better let Caitlin know the bad news," she says into the camera,

Jane, family, and friends at Prince Edward Island, ca. 1990

a little woodenly; she's no actor. She steps into the red phone closet that is a fixture of the Jacobs living room to make the call. Now the action shifts to Spicy, trying to find his way across a thousand miles of eastern Canada. "How do you get to PEI?" he asks. A bird—in Caitlin's voice, of course—replies, "Just bear east." This becomes the mantra for the rest of the journey: *Just bear east.* Finally, in a ferocious storm, Spicy skitters onto an island-bound boat. Lucia's Oscar-worthy camera work, all pitching and heaving, conveys the storm's primal force—and grants us a peek at Jane's new role as grandmother.

For four years, until she was about eight, Caitlin would get dropped off in the afternoon at Jane's. They'd play games, like Ambulance, or Loose Door Knobs, or Protect the Fruit; the idea of that one was to protect Jane's fruit bowl from marauding monkeys and tigers. Periodically, Jane would turn back to her work and, saying so, leave Caitlin on her own for a while. "I loved time at her house," Caitlin recalls today. Whatever one might say of Jane's parenting style, notes Lucia Jacobs, who saw Jane and Caitlin up close while living on Albany Avenue, she "totally redeemed herself . . . by being the world's best grandmother."

In 1989, at the ripe old age of six, Caitlin got a book dedicated to her (as did her cousin Larissa, Ned and Mary Ann's daughter, and the three Jacobs children). It was Jane's children's book, *The Girl on the Hat.*

One summer day in 1987, an editor at Oxford University Press Canada, Richard Teleky, received a call from Jane, who'd gotten his name from a neighbor. On long drives with the children out to Long Island in the 1950s, Jane told stories of Peanut, the doughty, literally peanut-sized boy forever getting into trouble. Now, Peanut had become Peanutina, and little Tina had become the heroine of one of Jane's books. Teleky's colleagues hoped they might become Jane's regular publisher. No such luck; all she wanted was a home for the children's book. Teleky signed her up, along with the artist Karen Reczuch for the illustrations. "I was thrilled!" says Reczuch, for whom this was her first book. "And then to find out that the author you were illustrating was so illustrious: 'You're doing a book with *Jane Jacobs*?!'"

The pictures were lovely. Tina in her Jane-like pageboy haircut, in mittens, scarf, and earmuffs, was adorable. The story was charming.

Thinking about a useful life for herself, Tina's first idea was to make little Easter baskets, starting a long time ahead to have plenty to sell by next Easter. She put ten empty peanut shells out in a row. She lined them with sweet-smelling dried basil and filled them with red cranberries, blueberries and green peas. They looked like darling little nests of tiny colored eggs. But in a few days the berries spoiled and the peas began to shrivel.

When the book was published, a friend wrote Jane to say he found it "enchanting." But it didn't do well, was scarcely reviewed, and soon disappeared. "The feedback I got from other illustrators and authors," says Reczuch, "was that the book was already a little dated." Maybe it would have done better in the 1950s or 1960s—to which, of course, it owed its birth. But by then, as Reczuch says, "children's literature had moved on."

As in Jane's adult books, the things of this world are much part of Tina's life—caves and carnivals, cameras and canoes. And certainly there is plenty of Jane in tiny Tina, who is industrious, resourceful, and always ready for adventure. Why, someday, she declares, she'd take her camera out to the mountains of British Columbia and photograph Sasquatch.

"But the Sasquatch is imaginary," says her father.

"How do you know?" Tina pushes back. "Remember the man at the Bureau of Missing Persons?"

Her parents had called him when Tina was kidnapped, reporting that she was two inches tall.

"He said *I* was imaginary."

II. HONESTY OR HONOR

The Girl on the Hat appeared in 1989. Jane's next book, *Systems of Survival,* published the following year, was inspired by the events of a single day many years earlier, Monday, January 24, 1967.

Jane, on her first trip to Europe, was in Hannover, West Germany, and in fine spirits. Earlier that day she'd given the first of her European lectures, and was taking in the city's sights. At some point, she stopped at a bank to transfer into her New York account the proceeds of the sizable check she'd received for her lecture. She handed someone the check, which was in deutschmarks, the German currency predating the euro. She gave them her account number. They gave her a receipt. And that was that. She felt "like an international merchant transacting my business." Of the bank itself, she'd remember little except for its expanses of "polished brass, marble and inlaid wood." But then, out on the street, she just stood there for a moment, happy, marveling "at how extraordinary this was—that I could feel so secure and protected within a great web of responsibility and trust." She'd completed similar transactions back home, of course. But here, just a few days into her trip, knowing no one, the foreign surroundings perhaps batting away the blinders of home, it jumped out at her: what made economic life work was this "fantastic web of trust" between strangers.

She experienced a similar jolt of pleasured insight while working on *The Economy of Cities,* as she looked back to the emergence of European cities in the Middle Ages. "Those were times of terrible piracy," she would say. Maybe trading Spanish leather, or Scandinavian fur, you couldn't help but fear robbers, ready to take everything you had. And yet during these years trade fairs sprang up across Europe.

> I thought how extraordinary it was, that in these barbarous times, when the line between raiding and trading didn't seem very clear, that trading ships could meet at certain places and actually exchange things and not take from each other, and do it in a civilized way . . . Those early European fair-sites were, in this sense, sacred sites where the mayhem was halted and the piracy held at bay, and people did this amazing, civilized, mutually helpful thing.

This all sounds very nice, inspiring in its way. But the book emerging from these insights was no simpleminded tribute to international banking or medieval trade fairs. For there was a wrinkle to the pretty picture, a surprising departure from what we'd expect, and from what *Jane* had expected.

Systems of Survival had its roots in Jane's fascination with the morality of the market, the honesty and industry that everyday trade required. In time, she got downright systematic about it, "jotting down precepts people are taught or that law prescribes for how business is carried on." From business histories, biographies, scandals, and bits of cultural anthropology she'd note behavior extolled as admirable. "If a businessman was praised because his handshake was as good as his bond, I cast it as the precept, 'Respect contracts.'" She did the same for despised or discouraged behaviors, too. And she kept it up for fifteen or twenty years. "I didn't know why I was doing this except to help myself better understand how the world works."

All along, then, there'd been a prim, white-hatted figure in the room: trade, it should be plain by now, was a good and beautiful thing to Jane Jacobs. Whereas if you bludgeoned or connived your way to what you wanted, if you tricked or cheated, relied on force, or exacted vengeance, your hat was black indeed. Jane long resisted the idea that there could be anything morally virtuous in the actions of soldiers and spies, czars and cops, and others resorting to such behavior. But in time—in very great time, she'd make it sound—she began to conclude just that.

A hunter can't be aboveboard as he tracks his prey. A spy eavesdrops and otherwise deceives; she wouldn't be much of a spy if she didn't. A diplomat's ability to lie convincingly is a job requirement. A Roman emperor has little use for the cobbler's timid prudence and thrift; his tastes are more for lavish and unseemly entertainments. None of them could be mistaken for an honest, hardworking tradesman. Theirs was a different world, with its own rules.

"Guardians," Jane dubbed them. They believed in loyalty, hierarchy, vengeance, and deceit. Policemen owe loyalty to the force, soldiers to their platoon. Political parties demand obedience from their members. So do churches to the tenets of their faith. And much of this, Jane concluded, was, in its own way, *good*, necessary to the workings of the world. Society needs protection from criminals, invading armies, religious heretics, and unruly mobs. Guardians, abiding by their own rules, provide it. Their rules, Jane decided, are "as morally valid as [those of] 'traders,'" and are grounded in concerns just as legitimate: learn of a vermin-infested restaurant and you want a city inspector with toughness and fight to shut it the hell down, now, no negotiation, no discussion. That's the guardian spirit at work.

Over the years, Jane refined these ideas, ultimately concluding that society rests on two broad sets of rules, expectations and moral precepts that are not a little different from one another, but fundamentally so, speak different languages, inhabit opposing universes. Roughly, the first group's emphasis is honesty, industry, collaboration, and thrift; the other's is tradition, loyalty, obedience, and force. Each represents what Jane called a "moral syndrome"; that medical-sounding word, "syndrome," just refers to the gathering of these precepts into clusters.

As Jane summed it up at Boston College in 1989, while still working on the book, society required "not one over-riding system of everyday right and wrong," as might be more comfortable to believe, and not many systems either, as moral relativists might suppose, but just two, which had arisen and endured for good reasons. In her book, she would use this split to explore honor and loyalty among soldiers, the practices governing Wall Street, species of corruption that follow when one moral system butts up against the other, and much else by way of puzzles and muddles clarified.

Jane opened one line of argument this way:

> As Machiavelli understood so well, the indispensability of loyalty infuses all the work of ruling and its derivatives. It is a moral buttress against all manner of guardian betrayals, military or not. It is not for nothing that officials swear fealty to a constitution or a crown.

But, actually, Jane *didn't* open this line of argument, not in her own name, anyway. These were the words of a character she'd created, a crime novelist by trade, named Jasper. For in *Systems of Survival: A Dialogue on the Moral Foundations of Commerce and Politics*, to give it its full title, Jane not only took on a new subject and a raft of new ideas, but chose to write about them in a different form, one akin to fiction. "Didactic dialogue," this genre was called, and it went back two millennia to the Platonic dialogues of ancient Greece, which feature Socrates wrangling with his philosopher friends in Athens. Except that in Jane's version, there is no one intellectual leader of infallible wisdom—no Socrates. "My characters," Jane wrote, "are equals, struggling together to make moral sense of working life."

One of her characters was Armbruster, a retired publisher who summons a few serious-minded friends and colleagues to his home in Manhattan. "I've become disturbed about dishonesty in workplaces," he leads off once they're introduced to one another and settled in with drinks. Like his creator, Jane, he'd once had a revelation in Hannover, West Germany, where he stopped at a local bank to have a consulting fee credited to his account, "a great web of trust" showering him with its blessing. These days, however, he feels the web is tattered. Corruption is everywhere. At a recent symposium, he saw computer science students shamelessly steal copyrighted software and peddle it for profit. Returning home, his senses newly alive to white-collar chicanery, all he sees around him are embezzlement, false advertising, fraudulent labeling, dishonest accounting, collusive bids, kickbacks, and insider trading. He decides he must better understand this breakdown of "morality in practical working life." That's why he's gathered them here. Their imagined conversations constitute *Systems of Survival*.

Jane, it seems, had grown frustrated and bored at the prospect of writing another conventionally long essay of a book. The dialogue form, with its "questions, answers, second thoughts, digressions, amended answers, speculations and disagreements," struck her as ideally suited to philosophical sparring. She'd had little use for philosophy in school, she told an interviewer once. "It went over my head and I just forgot about it." Now she was "astounded" to realize that in her didactic dialogues she was reinventing the wheel. "I could have saved myself a lot of work if I had read Plato" beforehand, she'd say.

Armbruster's apartment, where the conversations take place, lies in the middle of New York City. This represented a late authorial change of heart. Originally, Jane's five characters—Armbruster and the crime writer, Jasper, a lawyer, an environmental activist, and Kate, a young scientist Jane imagined as a blend of Burgin and two of her nieces—had been Torontonians. But that was just not going to work. "Talking to Canadians," she'd explain, was "like talking to a pillow." They were too damned polite. The moment she made them New Yorkers, they "were happy to seize the argumentative bit in their teeth and say what they wanted, no matter how uncivil. Since these fictional people came out of my head and so are really me, no doubt this says something about my own impatient and uncivil impulses."

Normally, by Jane's breakdown, trade was conducted according to Commercial precepts. Government, the military, and other such hierarchical institutions adhered to the Guardian syndrome. Commerce flourished. States, armies, and religions endured. It was only when the two syndromes collided in a single person or institution that you faced problems. For example, cops assigned arrest quotas and paid for meeting them. Or government fecklessly trying to run an energy utility. Or, as one more example of such an unhappy collision of values, Jane wrote in a chapter called "Trading, Taking, and Monstrous Hybrids," how about the Mafia?

With rituals worthy of the British Crown and loyalty the highest good, the Mafia might seem to embody classic Guardian sensibilities. "Where the Mafia most resembles legitimate guardians," Jasper tells the others, "is in its protection of city or suburban neighborhoods where important members live"; look for scant robbery, purse snatching, or sale of street drugs on their turf. "A tight Mafia neighborhood is a wonderfully safe place to live as long as you remain uncurious why." But, Jasper goes on, the Mafia doesn't just protect the neighborhood; theirs is a business. They extort from legitimate companies, run illegal businesses like pimping, gambling, bootlegging, smuggling, drug dealing, and money laundering; in the Mafia, the two realms—Guardian and Commercial, guns and money—lie wickedly entwined.

Jane had once chanced to observe a Mafia conclave at a Caribbean resort. It was February 1970 and the Jacobses were halfway through their second winter in Toronto. Jane and Bob flew to St. Maarten, the Dutch side of a Caribbean island shared with French St. Martin. "Dear Mother," she wrote a few days into the trip. "Well, it is all true: turquoise water, flowering vines & trees, trade winds, goats & pelicans, velvety tropical night that descends incredibly swiftly at sunset, & all the characters one has glimpsed in novels. In short, we are having a wonderful time indeed."

Their travel agent had booked them into a grand, casino-strutting hotel right on the water, beyond their budget but apparently all that was available. They signed on for the two-day minimum, figuring to find a cheaper, more congenial place later, which they did. But in the meantime, they were in for a surprise—a meeting of two Mob families; once they realized what was going on, she and Bob were fascinated by every minute of it. From breakfast to nightfall, they acted the part of "two exhausted dopes just sitting in chairs," or else strolling innocently around the waterfront. At one point, they saw two dons, stationed out in the warm, chest-deep water, who from time to time would summon subordinates. The lapping of the waves made electronic bugging impossible. The only women were the wives of the two dons and "one young beauty" who "not only looked like an inanimate fashion mannequin, but literally behaved like one," shifting her position, even just to move, only when permitted; apparently, Jane learned later, she was being punished. On the last day, an all-morning shopping spree seemed to Jane "as if sultans were in town and everybody was showing their wares and bowing and scraping and entourages were following them with packages." So here, nourishing *Systems of Survival*, was the Mafia up close, Jane a "discreet but fascinated observer."

"A brilliant exploration of the meaning of justice," *The Globe and Mail* reviewer called the book. "The evidence of a voracious mind, an active devourer of libraries and reading rooms, is impressive and reassuring." Not everybody thought so highly of it. Jane's friend Toshiko Adilman reports that "a lot of people felt it didn't work." The broadcaster Max

Allen, an admirer of Jane's who had helped put together Jane's Massey Lecture on Quebec separatism, was one of them; he'd spent his life with the spoken word and felt that Jane didn't appreciate dialogue as its own subtle art. He told her so after the book came out, but by then she was onto the next one and, he says, didn't much care. But not everyone rendered so harsh a verdict. Alan Ryan, writing in *The New York Review of Books*, saw the book offering "a very cold look at the depressive state of American politics and commerce, and an even colder look at what went wrong in the Soviet Union." For him, it was "wonderfully lively and readable." Of course, like Jacobs's other books it was "so different from run-of-the-mill social science that it is hard to decide quite where its insights fit in."

Ryan referred to Armbruster, Jasper, and the others as "lightly sketched characters," which smacks of euphemism. Jane's five characters were supposed to be different yet managed to sound alike. Their conversations, which should have marched right along, stumbled over themselves. Jane's little novelistic touches—"Armbruster clinked his ice for attention . . ."—mostly didn't succeed in lifting the book beyond what it really was, a philosophical discourse among the warring sides of Jane's intellect. As for Jason Epstein, it didn't entirely take with him, not, at least, the way her three earlier books did; it was "didactic, rather than a living thing." And certainly, "fiction" or not, it was no novel. "She didn't have that gift. She couldn't have been a novelist."

In the end, Jane herself seems to have agreed.

I don't think I was successful at changing prose rhythms for my different speakers.

I tried to differentiate my characters' speech, but I was unable to do it in the fundamental way I would have liked to. It would have been better to give each character his own idiosyncratic prose rhythm. That is what masters of dialogue do.

III. ON THE ILIAMNA PORTAGE

With the early 1990s, and Jane well into her seventies, the Early Days were upon her: *Systems of Survival* had its roots in the 1960s; her children's book in the 1950s. Now, her aunt Hannah's Alaska book from the late 1930s led her into her next big project.

Hannah, Jane's grandmother's younger sister, had attended the same teacher training school in Bloomsburg as had both Jane's mother and her aunt Martha. But after twenty years teaching in Pennsylvania, she had veered onto a new path. She began taking summer courses in anthropology at the University of Chicago. Soon she was being dispatched by the U.S. Department of the Interior to teach on Indian reservations in the Rockies and the Southwest. After four years of this, in 1904, at age forty-five, she went off to teach in Alaska. There she lived and worked among Aleuts, Kenais, and other natives in places with names like Afognak, Nondalton, and Iliamna. Some villages still testified to the long Russian presence in Alaska, the walls of their houses bearing images of the czar. Hannah traveled on horseback and by dogsled. From the deck of a pitching steamer, she clambered down the side by rope ladder. She endured winters deemed mild when the temperature stayed above ten below. Mainly, Hannah Breece set up schools, taught young native boys and girls, brought her notions of civilization to the inhabitants of remote Alaskan villages.

When, after fourteen years, she returned to the States, her mind was stocked with scenes and stories of backcountry adventures, and she was encouraged to work them into a memoir. Collecting letters she'd written while in Alaska, she patched them together into a manuscript and sent it off to publishers—only to have it turned down. This was the manuscript that, in 1938, she brought to Jane, seeking her help. Jane reworked it within the limits of her ability at the time and sent it to other publishers. Again, no interest. In 1940, Aunt Hannah died. Jane laid the manuscript aside, finished up her studies at Columbia, got her first real editorial job at *Iron Age,* and set off on her career.

But during the next half century, Aunt Hannah's manuscript never entirely relaxed its grip on her. Jane had grown up hearing Hannah's stories. "She was a great heroine to us all through my childhood." A birch-bark basket the native women of Nondalton made for Hannah was part of Jane's life growing up; her mother used it to hold letters and keys. Hannah's manuscript "had hooked me; so I had the notion that some time I should try to do it justice."

One day, probably in 1993, after Burgin asked to see it, Jane started reading it again and "got such a bang out of it, I just decided it should be published." This despite reservations about some of what good Aunt Hannah actually had to say, including what Jane termed "white man's burden ideas." Her task, Hannah Breece wrote in all earnestness, was to help the natives "overcome ignorance, poverty, disease, and superstition. [It] was to bring them benefits now available to them from civilization and from Uncle Sam's care for his less fortunate children." Jane was as bothered by such notions as she'd been half a century before. But then again, how could you understand Hannah's time in Alaska *without* confronting them? A more sophisticated modern public, Jane felt sure, would be able to read Hannah without undue judgment.

When the book came out, Jane wrote that she had done what Aunt Hannah expected of her, that she'd "improved organization, removed repetition and digressions that interrupt the flow, fact-checked distances, names, spelling, vegetation—the customary assistance an editor can give an inexperienced writer." But that wasn't all she did. For in July 1994, she and Bob, together with Ned's wife, Mary Ann, joined a week later by Ned, flew to Alaska to see for themselves something of Aunt Hannah's world.

They'd gathered brochures that showed off Alaska's placid blue waters, tree-topped islands, and sun-dappled mountain peaks; marked up old U.S. Geological Survey maps, retracing Hannah's travels; worked out their itinerary for the two-week trip. As their departure date neared, Jane's date book recorded their preparations:

> July 4: Get travelers' checks; get emergency food; pack; get
>   Mary's money.
> July 5: Money for Mary M: $210; call Limo for morning. 8:30.
> July 6: Leave 10:05 am [for] Anchorage.

They were to arrive there, gaining several hours on a flight mostly due west, at 5:30 that evening.

Until 1967, when she visited Europe for the first time, Jane had traveled little. In the years since, she'd made up for it some with vacations in the Caribbean; with a trip to Japan, where she'd stayed at the inn in Kyoto; Hamburg in 1981; the Netherlands in 1984, where she gave a speech at the royal palace and met the queen; Hong Kong in 1992, from which she came back with new ideas about high-rises as incubators of diversity. She'd come a long way since her first travels, when foreign currencies left her flustered.

Now, in 1994, Jane and family took floatplanes across the Kodiak Archipelago, set down at remote villages figuring in Hannah's life. They met natives in whose families tales of Miss Breece had been passed down. At one point they flew over a dozen-mile stretch of rough country from Iliamna Bay, on the Gulf of Alaska, navigating, as Jane wrote, "along a crooked airpath between awesome mountain peaks and glaciers to both sides of us." Beneath them lay the Iliamna Portage, which Hannah had crossed with a guide, variously on foot and by horseback. "I had lived in the Rocky Mountains and crossed the continent several times," wrote Hannah, "but never before had I been in such a wild grandeur of chasms, valleys and mountain peaks." She and her guide tramped along the edge of a mountain, looking down into a valley cut by streams from glacial ice fields. From there it was "into a valley where grass was higher than our heads and fireweed blazed everywhere."

Back home, Jane wrote John and Pete of their adventures—of the obscure, out-of-the-way museums, the "treasure trove of Aunt Hannah's correspondence" on microfilm they'd unearthed at a university library. "Mary Ann and I spent most of two days with it." In the same letter, Jane outlined her ideas for the book's complex structure, which she'd tried out earlier on Jason Epstein. It would have a foreword giving context; Hannah's memoir itself; a section, "Puzzles, Tangles, and Clarifications," about historical questions intriguing to Jane—like reindeer herds and Herman, the first Alaskan saint; an epilogue, on how the villages had fared since Hannah's time; finally, a lengthy notes section. All told, these came to more than a hundred pages beyond the memoir itself, a third of the book. The result was an intricate palimpsest—Jane and Hannah, Hannah's time and Jane's, memoir and history, reportage and travelogue, each talking back and forth to one another across the years.

An early draft of the book's epilogue tells how Afognak, part of the Kodiak Archipelago, where Hannah had worked from 1904 to 1906, was "demolished by the tidal wave that accompanied the terrible earthquake of 1964." In Jane's final edit, the earthquake is no longer "terrible"; earthquakes usually are. But *A Schoolteacher in Old Alaska*, as Jane titled it, proved much more than a routine exercise in editorial craft for her; it made for what she would call "probably the three happiest months of my working life. And when I did the research in Alaska I found myself wishing I had a whole extra life to live to be a historian," to work with raw materials, original documents.

It was Hannah who, fording the Chinkelyes River in knee-high boots, had had her poor feet frozen blue-black; who'd met mountain men and native villagers, lived with them, taught their children. That was *her* experience. But now it was *Jane's* experience, too—deliciously imagining Hannah's life, retracing her steps, laboring over each word—and finally, depositing the whole story, neatly wrapped, on the threshold of the twenty-first century. It was Jane's book, too, part of her life, layered in family: her childhood soaking up Hannah's stories; as a young woman trying to find a home for the manuscript; her mother urging her to go back to it; Burgin's interest triggering her own; brothers Jim and John helping in practical ways; the trip to Alaska with Bob, Ned, and Mary Ann; a life come full circle. "Every generation," Jane would say of Hannah, "had their part in valuing her story."

In Hannah's story, enacted far from any city, Jane plainly found value, interest, and worth. To one acute reviewer of *Schoolteacher*, this was itself notable. In an essay in *The New York Times Book Review,* Paul Goldberger, the paper's longtime architectural and urban critic, used the book to comment on Jane's intellectual evolution. A frank admirer of her work, he nonetheless recalled the criticism that, as in *Death and Life,* "she has always tended to fall prey to the fallacy of physical determinism," the overvaluing of a physical form. Yet now, chasing down Hannah's life in the ragged, nondescript villages of rural Alaska, visiting them, taking them seriously, Jane was making an "implicit concession" to the contrary. "I have always wanted Jane Jacobs, iconoclastic, wide-ranging thinker that she is, to see the world in still broader terms, and with this book she truly has." Hannah Breece, he suggested, would probably not have been happy in a Jacobsean big city, and Jane's "willingness to see her as hero in spite of this both deepens and softens our view of Ms. Jacobs herself."

To her adversaries, and maybe some of her friends, too, Jane could seem harshly outspoken, single-minded, even narrow-minded: *What a dear, sweet grandmother she isn't.* Well, now Goldberger was seeing in *Schoolteacher* evidence of a softening. It was a lovely, touching take, and one hard not to see as true. Approaching eighty, Jane was looking back, reflecting on the past, not so angry as she'd sometimes been.

Besides, she was now a grandmother after all, and a loving one at that.

IV. INFIRMITIES OF AGE

On June 21, 1994, a few weeks before setting off for Alaska, Jane had written of her upcoming trip to John Branson, a historian at one of the

Alaskan national parks. "I have my doubts about the trail to the falls," she said, referring to a possible side trip.

> I'm seventy-eight years old, and although in good health suffer some disadvantages of age, mainly difficulty in walking more than short distances and then slowly. My knees, a weakness Hannah also suffered when she had reached my age, catches up with us in our seventies, alas.

It would be a few years before Jane would blame her need to decline a speaking engagement in the Netherlands on "the infirmities of age." But gradually, they had begun to accumulate, the inevitable pains and frailties and calamities. Back in 1973, after her return from Japan, a bad fall had broken her left hand, menacing an important nerve. "That was one hell of an operation," she wrote Jason Epstein from the hospital. "Last week is all a (mercifully) doped blur to me." Without the operation, "I would certainly have lost the use of my arm & hand." The letter was handwritten; she'd not be able to type for months. As it was, she could "move only in a sort of sliding, slither-pivot fashion—I think, actually, it is an old Charleston step—and just managing this now takes about what energy I can muster."

In 1981 or early the next year Jane stumbled over a pile of bricks in her backyard, broke her right arm and nose, and bashed up her lip. Such a "stupid, stupid lady" she was, she wrote Roberta Gratz with the news.

In 1985, it was something quite similar. "I did such a stupid careless thing," she wrote Gratz again. "In a hurry & neglecting to turn on the light, I slipped on the stair & broke my collar-bone. Not serious, & it's healing well, but it has held me back from work"; she couldn't type.

Jane seems to have measured these mishaps against a backdrop of generally good health—good, at least, for her age, which was ticking ahead, like everyone's around her. Her brother John, appointed fifteen years earlier to the U.S. Court of Appeals, in 1982 took "senior" status, at age sixty-five, which allowed him a lighter caseload. Around the same time, brother Jim retired, moving with his wife, Kay, from New Jersey to North Carolina. In 1993, on March 12, Betty died, aged eighty-three. A memorial service held at the New York Society for Ethical Culture eight days later brought Butzners together from all over. A few months later, a *Boston Globe* reporter wrote Jane that "white hair and a marked stoop remind a visitor of Jacobs's age" but that otherwise she seemed just fine. "Internally, I'm not any different from when I was younger," Jane told him. "It's always a surprise to me that I don't get out of bed so easily, and I can't run up and down those stairs . . . It doesn't seem natural to be physically old."

Back in her late thirties, renting a cottage with John and Katia Jacobs on Sconset in Nantucket — collecting rose hips on the beach, a whole wonderful week of laughing, talking, and playing—Jane had made a mutual vow with Katia: when they were eighty—"which to us," says Katia, "then seemed an unreasonable distance"—with the relatives gathered around the Thanksgiving table set for The Moment when it was time to serve the turkey, they'd exhibit instead, the two of them cackling crazily, a bird and a pig sewn up together, a chimerical creature. "In subsequent years," Katia says, "we reminded one another of our pledge," though they never did it. But now, impossibly, that "unreasonable distance" had been bridged, and Jane was eighty.

But however old Jane was, Bob was much older.

While working on the Alaska book in 1994—it was before the trip, the manuscript still "quite disjointed"— Jane wrote to a Dutch friend that she and Bob were "aware we're aging—creakier." Bob's, though, was more than a benign creakiness. He was actually a few months younger

Siblings and spouses, 1988: Compare this photo with the one on page 100, from 1945— same family members forty-three years later (except for Elizabeth Butzner). The family, left to right, are Bob, John, Betty, Jane, Pete, Jim, and Kay. A newcomer is Jules Manson, who married Betty in 1947, at extreme right.

than Jane, but had already been retired from Zeidler for several years. Then came a succession of blows. "Bob has lost the sight of his right eye from a burst blood vessel," Jane wrote Ellen Perry, her sometime research assistant from *Death and Life* days, "but minimizes the loss and keeps on working, now at machinery design for our son Jim."

That was early in 1996. In April, Bob was able to accompany Jane to Charlottesville, Virginia, where the University of Virginia was giving her a medal. Someone snapped a picture of them as they sat together on a bench, their heads two matching puffs of white hair. The stately columns of Thomas Jefferson's campus behind them, they sat, Jane in a fringed jumper, gripping her cane, Bob in tuxedo, bow tie, and dress shoes (forsaking the sneakers he usually wore), one hand on Jane's shoulder, a drink in the other. He looked okay. He wasn't.

A few months later, Jane wrote John Branson, the Alaska historian, "Our news is not so great, because Bob is ill with inoperable cancer." After most of a lifetime's smoking, lung cancer. He'd gotten a course of radiation treatment at Princess Margaret Hospital, which he'd helped design. "He actually liked going for the treatments," Jane would say, "and I did, too, because he liked seeing how his hospital worked." He handled the treatments well. Between then and the next round they were bound for Prince Edward Island.

They had "a happy month" on PEI, Jane wrote Branson in October, "which is good to remember." But in the end, the cancer took him fast. Early in September, he'd begun "to weaken and decline rapidly." The children gathered, nursing him at home. He died on the 17th. "An interesting, loveable, good and irreplaceable man," one obituary called him.

Jane wrote with the news to Ellen Perry, who had approached her for memories of her grandmother back in Bloomsburg, for a book Perry was preparing on family recipes.

> I am kind of useless at the moment, as you may imagine. You had better not count on my contribution to the cookbook. It's ridiculous, but I feel so blank and distracted that just the idea of hunting up a photo of my grandmother, getting it copied, and doing the small revision . . . that you need seems so formidable.

At the funeral, Jane didn't cry. "I never cry," she once told Toshiko Adilman. But the sadness washed over her whenever she'd think, *I want to tell Bob something.*

CHAPTER 24

IDEAS THAT MATTER

I. THE LIFE OF *Death and Life*

The citation for Jane's Jefferson Medal, received that day in Charlottesville, Virginia, Bob still by her side, declared that *The Death and Life of
Great American Cities* was

> firmly ensconced on the list of the most influential books of our cen-
> tury. It is hard to identify a single work that has influenced more the
> thinking and strategies in the field of American urban planning and
> design.
>
> From the publication of this book, one can date the rethinking of
> U.S. urban renewal policies, the eclipse of modern architecture, the
> rise of historic preservation, the invigoration of neighborhood involve-
> ment, and even vigorous and principled public opposition to large-scale
> public projects that threaten to destroy the texture and vitality of
> urban places.
>
> She created a mood that has influenced urban planning and archi-
> tectural concepts for over 40 years.

Across those forty years, Jane had explored new subjects in new
books, but all the while *Death and Life* was sinking its roots deep into
the earth of intellect and culture, finding new readers, inspiring scholars, architects, and planners, influencing the shape of real cities. Jane
could escape the book no more than anyone else. Inevitably, she was cel-

ebrated for it, forced to think back to its origins, respond to criticisms of it—and surely, in spare moments, drink deep drafts of pride that she had created it.

Bustle and surprise, bountiful variety, human energy, and sheer, vital messiness: might these trump the suburban troika of light, air, and green? Hundreds of thousands, probably millions, had read the book whole or in part and absorbed the idea that maybe they did. Among planners and architects who had grown up on the tenets of modernism, *Death and Life* asked, *Are you sure?* "I still cannot walk down a city street without Jane Jacobs rushing up to me and shouting: 'Look at that . . .'" wrote the British journalist Simon Jenkins. "She saw in streets the crooked timber of mankind on vibrant display." An urban consultant grown up in London, Richard Gilbert, wrote Jane that *Death and Life* had "made sense of my life." A Stanford University student, Nick Grossman, feeling cut off from the energy of his New York roots, read it during his sophomore year and abruptly *got* it, understanding how he felt about where he'd lived before and where he lived now. Michael Kimmelman, art critic of *The New York Times*, wrote that on reading the book, "it was with a jolt of recognition . . . It said what I knew instinctively to be true but had never articulated, which is the quality of great literature."

No need to dwell on testimonials like these; I've heard or read dozens of them and so perhaps have you. The book that on publication had faced both derision and praise had become enshrined, early criticism mostly drowned out by a sustained chorus of attachment, loyalty, and love — for the book and for the kind of city it championed. By the time of the thirtieth, then the fortieth anniversary of the book's publication—and then later, after Jane's death, with the fiftieth anniversary in 2011—critics and scholars of every stripe were exploring its origins, its impact on the U.S., Canada, and the world, its literary and intellectual qualities, and whether its insights even still applied.

"Is There Still Life in *Death and Life?*" asked Roger Montgomery, a University of California, Berkeley, professor of city and regional planning. For Jane Jacobs, he went on to observe, the city was a kind of "vernacular utopia. . . And that is what the book is really about: teaching us how to love big cities . . . Jacobs taught her readers city love." It let readers 'fess up, during those long decades of suburban night, that it might actually be among the stately row houses of Baltimore's Mount Vernon Place that they felt more at home than in Cockeysville, or Towson, or any of the city's other sprawling suburbs; or in San Francisco's still-ragtag Castro District more than some perfect little town up in Marin.

In 1961, when the book came out, the postwar suburbs, their modernist style, their vision of the good life, were so entrenched it could be hard to recognize any other. But in a way reminiscent of the "liberation" struggles of black people, ethnics, women, gays, and other marginalized groups during roughly the same years, Jane's book helped legitimize the heretical sensibilities of the confirmed city dweller. It helped its readers think about neighbors and strangers, anonymity and privacy, security and adventure, ugliness and prettiness, the very shape of daily life, in new ways.

At the time of Jane's death, a Canadian writer, Sandra Martin, observed that *Death and Life* "connected with a generation of young adults who were trying to make sense of the post-war world." But not that *whole* generation, Jane realized, only part of it. Writing in 1992, she distinguished between "car people" and "foot people," those seeking "the camaraderie, bustle, and promises of surprise and adventure" of the street. They *got* her book, which gave "legitimacy to what they already knew for themselves."

The city, *Death and Life* emphasized, throws you up against strangers, whereas the suburbs insulate you from them, leave you snug in a cocoon of familiarity and comfortable sameness. One scholar, Jamin Creed Rowan, has pictured Jane as part of a literary tradition, epitomized by certain *New Yorker* profiles of the 1940s and 1950s, that abjured sweet togetherness (a "nauseating name for an old ideal," Jane called it); city dwellers were "*interconnected*, not *interrelated*." That is, the city wasn't a place where most people knew your name; on the other hand, it tied you by invisible threads to everyone else, and to the larger organism that was Chicago or LA. Urbanites, Rowan wrote, were bound by "the involuntary accumulation of public contacts rather than the purposeful cultivation of private intimacies." A good thing? Bad? You could debate that all day and night. But it was *different*—and different, *Death and Life* declared on every page, was *okay*.

Of course, the long decades during which the book became a back-to-the-city bible also allowed time for a reaction to set in against it, for new rounds of reappraisal and revisionism. Early critiques of the book had pictured Jane as antagonistic to visions of the city other than her own; as unmoved by sides of city life unrelated to physical form, including the social and, especially, the racial. Now, with the stark improvement of many city neighborhoods, also laid at Jane's door has been gentrification—that unwelcome consequence, or exaggeration, of the "unslumming" Jane hailed as a route to urban health: the new gentry snatch up marginal properties, make them glisten and shine, attract glittering boutiques, new high-end gyms, and high-rise condos. Prices rise. Taxes climb. Ordinary people can't afford to live there and soon move out. Just tour broad square miles of Brooklyn, Boston, and San Francisco to see the social damage. Not that it *looks* like damage; at first it seems seductive, bright, and appealing. But it exacts a price. "I have lived in the West Village since 1964, and I can attest to the fact that gentrification has destroyed this area," wrote one respondent, "Joyce," to an online article by Michael Powell titled "An Urban Theorist Questions the Gospel of St. Jane":

> Gone is any semblance or authenticity of a vibrant, creative, economically mixed area. I am sickened by the influx of unbelievable wealth . . . I can barely afford to buy a hamburger in my neighborhood anymore. I mourn the death of this once vibrant community.

Another example of a good thing gone wrong, thanks, presumably, to Jane's book, was the planning profession as a whole. Or so said Thomas J. Campanella, professor of urban planning and design at the University of North Carolina at Chapel Hill. He pictured Jane as a latter-day Martin Luther, *Death and Life* like the manifesto he nailed to the Wittenberg church that sparked the Protestant Reformation.

> So thoroughly internalized was the Jacobs critique that planners could see only folly and failure in the work of their own professional forebears. Burnham's grand dictum, "Make no little plans," went from a battle cry to an embarrassment in less than a decade.

Things had gone too far, Campanella asserted. The planning profession had become emasculated. *Death and Life* was to blame.

And speaking of planners, why had Jane directed her animus at them in the first place? They were too easy a target, wrote Sharon Zukin, looking back at *Death and Life* in *The Architectural Review* in 2011, "compared to developers who build, and banks and insurance companies who finance, the building that rips out a city's heart"; of them, Jane's book stood largely mute. In her West Village battles, she had failed to "attack the nexus of economic and state power" behind Robert Moses, instead picking on the relatively powerless planners.

Jane did sometimes bother to answer charges leveled at *Death and Life*. Gentrification? It attested to how much people really *wanted* diverse and vibrant neighborhoods. Unfortunately, she said in 2005, with the growth of the automobile "we stopped building places worth gentrifying," so demand "increasingly outstrips supply," forcing up prices in the few potentially good neighborhoods. So-o-o, make more such places!

Some of her critics said that the good life wasn't "possible in the [high density] situations I recommend. Well, I don't say 'I recommend.' I say 'This exists.' " This was Jane in 1963, and it would remain her most abiding defense, that she didn't prescribe, merely described. To test her ideas, Jane held, you needed only to look at how they worked, or didn't, in real cities. "I hope any reader of this book," she wrote in *Death and Life*, "will constantly and skeptically test what I say against his own knowledge of cities and their behavior. If I have been inaccurate in observations or mistaken in inferences and conclusions, I hope these faults will be quickly corrected." In fact, her book had many assertions you *could* test, like an *Origin of Species* set against the observed facts of nature.

For example, did older, smaller buildings of the kind Jane said contributed to urban vitality really do so? A report by the National Trust for Historic Preservation, based on the experience of San Francisco, Washington, D.C., and Seattle, concluded that they did.

Did "eyes on the street" reduce crime, as Jane argued in the book? Maybe not, a *University of Pennsylvania Law Review* study suggested; pedestrian-dense mixed-use development in Los Angeles neighborhoods did record lower crime than those exclusively commercial; but purely residential areas had crime rates lower than either. A "meta-study" of research drawn from the broad discipline of environmental criminology came away similarly skeptical.

Was gradual and piecemeal development of a neighborhood, as opposed to broad-scale redevelopment all at once, with piles of big money behind it, more apt to promote a sense of community, as Jane said? Looking to Chicago, the Duke University sociologist Katherine King found evidence that it did.

These and other such studies didn't always yield scientifically ironclad results. And, as in science generally, most of them raised as many questions as they answered. But in trying to test the book's conclusions they hinted at the singular status it had achieved: *Death and Life*, the measure.

It became the measure not alone in the United States and Canada but around the world, in Berlin and Vienna, Abu Dhabi and Buenos Aires. Two Egyptian scholars, for example, reported that the Beirut, Lebanon, central business district was being redeveloped with an eye to principles laid out in *Death and Life*, but that so far the city's built fabric lacked "true diversity and vitality." In the Netherlands, observed Gert-Jan Hospers, the name of Jane Jacobs had become "a warranty of urban quality." In Spain, where *Death and Life* was first published in 1967, her thinking had by the 1970s already become part of the city planning curriculum, wrote the Spanish historian of architecture José Luis Sáinz Guerra. Her "message in favor of the dense, diverse city" was helping to bring "vitality, intensity of use, and quality of life to Spanish city centers."

Was *Death and Life* worthy of being the one measure of all things urban? Was Jane right in all she preached, correct in all she saw? Obviously not. On the other hand, the book's influence didn't hang on the validity of any one specific claim. It was more than a collection of insights and assertions; it was a manifesto, one that looked at the city from a fresh, deeply sympathetic point of view. Jane took Le Corbusier, Ebenezer Howard, and many others and corralled them into a single pen; all were, by her lights, anti-city. Whereas she alone, *Death and Life* could seem to say, was the city's last, best champion. And though you could chip away at this or that of her claims, it didn't *matter* in the end; because the book's sweeping, irreducible essence remained and you could never see cities the same way again.

In 1962, a year after *Death and Life* first appeared, Thomas S. Kuhn introduced the concept of a paradigm shift. Kuhn was a historian of science who thought about how scientific ideas are shaped and changed—how, for example, the Copernican revolution reshaped the heavens from that of the old Ptolemaic view. His book, *The Structure of Scientific Revolutions*, had nothing to say about cities, or about the social sciences generally. But its ideas were so seductive that scholars in numerous other disciplines—in economics, political science, and sociology as well as the hard sciences—began to apply them to their own fields.

Science doesn't happen by the slow accumulation of neutral facts gradually worked into theories, Kuhn said. Rather, at any moment in a science's evolution, some particular theory is the prevailing one, forms the "paradigm" that guides the sorts of questions scientists ask and into which experimental evidence is made to fit. With new knowledge, glitches, anomalies, and surprising errors crop up. At first, and routinely so, they're explained away. But with time, the anomalies accumulate. The old pretty picture grows tattered. Alternative theories contend. And out of it, finally, comes a new way of looking at the facts of nature, a new paradigm—a revolution in form not so different from a political one, that all but die-hard champions of the old paradigm come to accept. What *really* happens, then, in science, said Kuhn, is that some long-prevailing view of nature undergoes, often disconcertingly, a paradigm shift, and the world is never the same again. Think Darwin's evolution. Think Einstein's relativity.

And think, with but few apologies to *Death and Life*'s incompletely scientific roots, Jane's transcendent vision of cities and city life. Her book, observed the historian Mike Wallace in an episode of a Ken Burns video series devoted to New York City, served as "a counternarrative, a counterargument, a countervision of what the city is." And the counternarrative has taken hold.

Attitudes toward city living have changed; *cities* have changed, and for the better. These days, the virtues of density and walkability are widely enough shared that real estate listings increasingly cite a property's, or a neighborhood's, "Walkscore." This is a database-generated numerical index between 1 and 100 that estimates the ease of buying a quart of milk, say, or doing other everyday chores, on foot; a 90 attracts the *Death and Life* crowd, while a 30 or 40 turns them away. In 2013, real estate researchers meeting in Atlanta declared that America had crossed a threshold—"peak sprawl," they called it—meaning that most new construction was now in higher-density, walkable districts.

Meanwhile, walkability, street life, diversity, mixed use, and other words and ideas associated with *Death and Life* now verge on catchphrases, sometimes so thoughtlessly invoked as to mean nothing. "Mixed use" had become "a developer's mantra," Paul Goldberger marveled after Jane's death.

Who could have envisioned the day when politicians and developers trying to sell New York on a gigantic football stadium beside the Hudson River would propose surrounding it with shops and cafes so that they could promote it as an asset to the city's street life? When that happened in 2004 . . . I knew the age of Jane Jacobs had entered a new phase, the phase that comes when radical ideas move into the mainstream, and can be corrupted by those who claim to follow them. In the twenty-first century, the danger is not with those who oppose Jane Jacobs, but with those who claim to follow her.

Recent years have seen the rise of a New Urbanism, which outwardly embraces some Jacobsean ideas. New Urbanist communities, known for their pretty front porches, nineteenth-century scale, and nod to walkability, normally lack much socioeconomic mix. And built all at once, at relatively low density, under tight regulatory and zoning controls, they rarely include the old, low-rent buildings Jane saw as incubators of urban vitality. Jane "didn't have much patience with the New Urbanists, whose very philosophy of returning to pedestrian-oriented cities would seem to owe a lot to Jacobs," Paul Goldberger would report. "She found them hopelessly suburban, and once said to me, with a rhyming cadence worthy of Muhammad Ali, 'They only create what they say they hate.'" More charitably, the New Urbanism could be seen as a small, halting step away from orthodox sprawling suburbs. In it, UC Berkeley's Roger Montgomery has pointed out, "the influence of Jane Jacobs lives, misused perhaps, but very much alive in today's practice environment."

The preservationist James Marston Fitch once observed that Jane "wrote as if the urban tissue which she was defending was programmed for automatic repair and renewal, like organic living tissue with its miraculous capacities for regeneration." So it is happening: in wide swaths of San Francisco, Boston, Toronto, and New York, in smaller but growing patches of Baltimore, Chicago, Cincinnati, and Sacramento, and really everywhere in America and Canada, in-town districts reflecting Jane's sensibilities have come back to life as bustling, walkable, delightful, and diverse urban places. In his book of the same name, Alan Ehrenhalt describes what he calls a "great inversion," in which the old postwar pattern of well-off suburbs and poor city centers has begun to turn inside out, with dead, dying, and abandoned malls and decrepit suburban ranch houses flanking cities of rebirth and rejuvenation.

But by now we are getting ahead of ourselves, looking back to *Death and Life* from our time, today, as if Jane had already passed on. In fact, when we left her last, near the turn of the century, she was alive and active, chugging away at her writing. In September 2000, when she was eighty-four, she was interviewed by James Howard Kunstler for a feature to appear the following spring in *Metropolis* magazine. "You spent really the prime of your life living in Manhattan and Greenwich Village . . ." he began to frame his question.

"I wouldn't say that," Jane interrupted him.

"No?"

No, she chuckled, "I am still in the prime of life."

In 1997, the year after Bob died, Jane joined the board of Ecotrust, an environmental group with offices in the American West. Across five days that July, Ecotrust's strategic planning meeting was built around a raft trip down the Salmon River in Idaho. As boulders on the far shore reared up behind roiling white waters, there, nestled in one of the rafts, bundled into a life vest, was Jane, a happy smile planted on her eighty-one-year-old face. "We'd strap her on the front of the raft every day and she'd go bouncing down the river," remembered the group's president. She was chubby and stooped, and she worried she'd hurt herself getting out of the boat or stumbling on a rock, but she managed, a banged-up shin the only price she paid for the adventure. "She was an unbelievable font of ideas, and funny as a hoot."

II. ACOLYTES AND APOSTATES

As Jane moved into old age, and even more so after her death in 2006, the respect accorded her sometimes slipped over into veneration, hero worship, or worse. Honorary degrees were offered her, streets named for her, her name invoked as talisman, *Death and Life* and her other books cited as if holy writ.

She was not wholly immune to blandishments of attention or praise, nor was she above honors, nor averse to accepting awards; she received many. Sometimes these were for specific books, like the Sidney Hillman Prize in 1962 for *Death and Life;* or the Los Angeles Times Book Prize in 1984 for *Cities and the Wealth of Nations;* or, for the same book, the Mencken Award in 1985, named for H. L. Mencken, the cantankerous, libertarian-spirited critic. In 1998, she received a life award from the American Institute of Architects. The awards formula normally included ceremony, citation, dinner, maybe an address of some kind required of her. At the University of Virginia, a five-day round of events included tours, seminars, meetings with students, the Founder's Day Luncheon

Jane, with Queen Elizabeth's representative, Hilary Weston, on being awarded the Order of Ontario in 2000. Four years earlier, she had become an officer of the Order of Canada.

on Friday at the Rotunda (pan-seared chicken with shrimp and farfel; toasted meringue shell with strawberries and rhubarb compote for dessert) and a black-tie dinner at Monticello, Thomas Jefferson's home, on his birthday.

Honors like these seemed neither to roll off Jane's back, leaving her unmoved, nor to go to her head. But by now she had a history going back to the early 1960s, when *Death and Life* and the West Village wars first thrust her into the glary floodlights, of public distractions that pulled her away from writing. These years later, she wasn't often leading neighborhood battles anymore. But she'd deeply internalized the need to protect her writing time and she often just said no. Back in 1986, named recipient of a $5,000 honorarium for a prestigious lecture in Jerusalem, she replied that, though honored, she just couldn't accept:

> While I can always use more money, really my problem isn't buying time to work, but rather protecting and taking advantage of the time I do have to get a book written, as well as avoiding the (to me) severely

energy-sapping business of switching to something else, then getting all geared up again to concentrate on the difficulties and complexities of my book.

She drew the line altogether at honorary degrees. Someone once totted up the number of them offered her over the years, about thirty. During one span flanking the new millennium, offers came from the University of Toronto, Clark University in Massachusetts, University of Victoria, California College of Arts and Crafts, and Columbia University. She declined them all as false credentials. Besides, she wasn't much at home with academic ways generally; she rarely attended events at the University of Toronto, just blocks from her house. "Much as I feel fondly attached to Columbia—which I do," Jane wrote in reply to Columbia president George Rupp, on December 31, 2000, "it would be awkward and difficult" to alter her stance on honorary degrees. She accepted the Jefferson Medal because it was *not* an honorary degree, but an honor of real substance; past recipients included Mies van der Rohe, Lewis Mumford, and Frank Gehry. Besides, she'd note with satisfaction, her father and brothers all had attended UVA.

By the mid-1990s, scholars and would-be biographers interested in Jane and her work began introducing themselves to her. "About a year and a half ago I began a journey of research and discovery," a Harvard graduate student, Peter Laurence, opened his appeal to her in 1999. He was working on a project, "The Jacobs Effect." He outlined his ideas for it and wondered whether they might meet. They did meet, his work ultimately leading to several serious and original articles and, recently, two books. In 2002, another graduate student, Christopher Klemek, wrote Jane expressing his wish to write "a comprehensive intellectual biography" of her. He concluded, "If you would have me as a biographer, I welcome your participation to whatever extent you are willing." He was about the age Jane was, he noted, when, during the 1940s, she'd offered to help a woman named Tania Cosman with her memoir. "I pray this project gets further." It didn't, not as a biography, but they did meet, and Klemek went on to write an ambitious, Jane-rich study about the postwar collapse of urban renewal in Europe and North America.

To Klemek and Laurence, both serious scholars, Jane accorded respectful treatment. But to the parade of those approaching her with requests to submit to this, contribute that, or appear here or there, she was not always so patient. Normally, she found a gracious way to turn down potential time wasters. But sometimes, an inquiry risked liberating her inner crankiness. A woman named Vanda Sendzimir, whose biographer's chops seemed to extend only as far as a book about her inventor father, wrote a three-page letter that presumed to educate Jane about her own cultural significance: "Anyone with this amount of sway has a place in history, and that place needs to be given shape, color, shading and voice," which she volunteered to supply. "I'm ready to jump on a plane and come up and meet you anytime you say." Don't bother, Jane wrote back. "My answer is an unequivocal No." Her own book project occupied her fully. The last thing she was going to get involved in was "somebody else's writing project, especially one that doesn't interest me the way my own project does. To tell you the truth, I even churlishly begrudge the time it takes to answer letters."

A few years later, in June 2001, Michael Illuzzi, executive director of a Scranton museum, wrote Jane that he was working on a book, "Cityscapes, Sidewalks and Scranton: Jane Jacobs and the New Urbanism," for which he wished to interview her. No, Jane wrote back, if he wanted to know how the New Urbanists viewed her, talk to them, not her. As for Scranton, he didn't need her for that, either, "except possibly as a gimmick and that I will not be." When, a few weeks later, Illuzzi wrote again, pressing his suit, Jane shot back, "I have no interest in a book about my work and no time or inclination to become interested. If you persist in undertaking it, it will be without any cooperation from me."

But while Jane could be dismissive, a thoughtful letter from out of the blue could sometimes excite her interest, luring her into lengthy correspondence. Early in 2000, she received a long letter from a PhD student, Timothy Patitsas. "These past six months," it began,

> I have been considering the question you pose at the end of *The Death and Life of Great American Cities,* about the kind of problem a city is, in connection with a doctoral thesis I am undertaking for the department of Theology at the Catholic University of America. I am trying to place the New Urbanism in a broader philosophical and theological context through a study of the modern antipathy toward liturgy.

From this not entirely promising start, Patitsas launched his argument. For the Le Corbusiers and Ebenezer Howards of the world, he wrote, "the City is dead matter to be manipulated by the reasoned plans of a single will, for the benefit of a unitary gaze, while nature is a dumb garden to be manipulated cutely." Jane's approach, on the other hand, could be seen as "liturgical." In this provocatively unfamiliar sense, the city could be appreciated for its "openness to the unknown, built around recurrent cycles of death, rebirth and risk," the product of "many actors freely relating and contributing their own dreams and vision."

If maybe a bit of a stretch, still it must have flattered Jane to see her work of four decades earlier the object of such fresh thinking. Thoughtful engagement was what she lived for. Patitsas's ideas were so surprising and original—which was what it took to get Jane in gear with you intellectually. "Thanks so much for your astonishing and enlightening letter," she replied. She'd never thought much about liturgy, she said, owning up to her own almost nonexistent religious feeling. And with at least one of Patitsas's key arguments, she agreed entirely: conventional city planning didn't worry much about the passage of *time*, and that went as well for the New Urbanism. Its communities didn't develop organically but were built whole, from scratch: you planned your charming little town, you realized your plans, whatever they were, and that was that—done, finished. But this indifference to the workings of time, Jane wrote Patitsas now, "means almost everything important is left out: trial and error, risk and dreams, birth, death, success, failure, celebration, regret, relationship . . . the whole chain of being. You've put it beautifully." Not surprisingly, this was not the end of their intellectual relationship, which stretched across Jane's remaining years.

The attention to Jane during this period came to her as a Canadian. While her first two books were conceived and written in the United States, she wrote more books, over a longer time, in Canada than she did in the U.S. She'd come to love Canada and seems never to have seriously considered leaving it. Her three U.S.-born children and their families, spread out across the breadth of the country—Jim in Toronto, Burgin in rural British Columbia, Ned in Vancouver—all lived as Canadians.

In the cases of the Spadina Expressway and the St. Lawrence project, as we've seen, Jane exerted a marked influence on Toronto. Later, the resurgent health of two former industrial districts along east and west King Street in downtown Toronto, together known as "the Kings," also owed much to her. Out of meetings between Jane and local planners and architects in the mid-1990s emerged a plan to free these two loft districts from most zoning restrictions; within their four hundred acres, you could do pretty much as you pleased, so long as you didn't raze sound old buildings. It would "allow the city to organically define itself," says Ken Greenberg, a friend of Jane's and one of the scheme's champions. The experiment spewed forth new businesses, bustling entrepreneurial laboratories, new residences. In 1996, virtually no one lived in the Kings; today, thousands do. Over the years, it's been estimated, the Kings downzoning injected $7 billion into the city, 38,000 jobs. "It's magical, it's wondrous," Jane told an interviewer in 2001, "how fast those areas have been blossoming and coming to life again." Barry Wellman, a University of Toronto sociologist and another transplanted American, noted that whereas Jane "saved one neighbourhood in Manhattan she saved many more in Toronto by word, deed, and inspiration."

Take the elevator up to the observation deck of Toronto's signature CN Tower, look out over the city from a thousand feet up, and you see Corbusian towers, hundreds of them, condos and offices, parading north along Yonge Street as far as the eye can see. Below, the elevated Gardiner Expressway, slipping around and through the downtown lakefront, pulsing with traffic, reminds you of nothing so much as the Futurama exhibition at the New York World's Fair. In short, Jane Jacobs didn't singlehandedly transform Toronto into a twenty-first-century Greenwich Village. Still, in its vitality, Toronto stands as an affront to struggling American cities like Buffalo and Detroit on the other side of the border. It is dense with new immigrants, its streets bustle with life, it boasts enormous cultural vitality. "The mere fact Jane Jacobs chose to live in Toronto," wrote the local journalist Kelvin Brown at the time of her death, "came to be an endorsement for the city's brand. She was synonymous with the notion of a livable city and her Toronto residency was proof that we, in Toronto, inhabited a special place."

During the thirty-three years she'd lived in Toronto, Jane said in 2001, "so many parking lots and gas stations in valuable locations have been replaced by dwellings, working places, and cultural institutions that it's hard to buy gasoline or park on the surface in the center of the city." She meant this to celebrate the flowering of a more vital, less car-oriented—yes, more Jacobsean—city. But some Torontonians never wanted that at all. "The first hit our city took was the arrival of Jane Jacobs," declared one eighty-year-old blogger and self-described former "repairman, mister-fix-it and mechanic" made livid by the daily gridlock of Toronto traffic. For this he blamed Jane, who, once in Toronto, "started selling her snake oil. Which amounted to her proclamation that cities are for people not cars. It is a grossly stupid idea and appeals to dreamers." The master plan for new highways in Toronto, he pointed out, went back to 1948; stopping the Spadina unraveled it, "twenty years of work went down the drain," and it was Jane's fault and that of the cabal around her.

John Downing, a longtime local journalist, also faults Jane, whom he labels a classic "shit disturber." Years ago, Downing took an urban geography course at the University of Toronto; "they might as well have had a statue of Jane in the front of the room," so closely did it track her ideas. Those ideas, he says, did the city grievous harm. The Spadina would have benefited more people than it would have hurt. So would the enlargement of the little airport on Toronto Island, which Jane successfully opposed in part for its air and noise pollution. John Downing knows his Jane Jacobs: "I don't believe in 'eyes on the street,'" he says, "but I'll never forget that imagery" from her book. And he's glad for people like her "who express strident views." Even so, he reckons Toronto worse for her influence: Traffic inhibited. Truck suspensions bashed up and gas wasted by traffic-impeding speed bumps installed at the behest of Jane's anti-car cronies. Jane a guru? No, he wrote in a 2006 column, she was more "a sentry outside the urban camp, challenging everyone from generals to privates, insisting only she knew the password. The tragedy in her adopted city is that many of us liked it the way it was before she came."

True, Jane's friend Max Allen sums it up, some in Toronto did see her as "an old fogy, standing in the way of progress. And they said it was hard to argue with her." (Because, he adds, "she was right.") And yes, he allows, a kind of cult did form around her, where to criticize her made you practically an apostate. But, blame or praise, it was "immaterial to her. She was absolutely sure of herself and absolutely not full of herself."

Mostly, Jane's affection for Canada was abundantly reciprocated. Her friend Toshiko Adilman tells of Jane on the eve of a trip to Japan, realizing at the last minute that she had no visa, at which point the whole Canadian government, so it seemed, was enlisted to get her one. In 1991, Toronto held a Jane Jacobs Day of public appreciation, with an afternoon symposium and a formal dinner that evening. "Through it all," the Toronto author Robert Fulford would recall, Jane "smiled benignly, a tall, stooped woman with the look of an ancient hawk." In 1996 Jane was awarded the Order of Canada. "You are now entitled to use the initials O.C. after your name, and to wear the lapel pin," an official of the order's council advised Jane that July, enclosing two pins together with guidance on "the Order of Precedence for the Wearing of Orders, Decorations and Medals."

All this was just a preview for the conference, celebration, lovefest, or whatever it was, held in Jane's honor across five days in October 1997— lectures, debates, and tours going on into the night on subjects dear to Jane's heart. Conceived by Alan Broadbent, John Sewell, and others among her friends, the earliest discussions bloomed into an advisory committee, the hiring of staff, and the selection of speakers. "Ideas That Matter" is what they called it, and it was probably the only thing they *could* have called it: for Jane, ideas were most of what mattered to her. And it was her ideas that mattered most about her to Canada and the world.

At first, Jane had mixed feelings. But once the program, listing its substance-stuffed phantasmagoria of events, came out, she sent it to her brother John, taking care to assure him and his wife that they needn't feel obliged to come. "I agreed they could do this, with three stipulations," she explained, maybe a little defensively—"that I wouldn't have to be involved in organizing it, wouldn't have to make a speech, and that they wouldn't invite any windbags."

Eighteen months and half a million dollars in the planning, Ideas That Matter was all a-bubble with intellectual ferment: Livable cities, human ecology, and self-organizing systems. The future of Toronto's Yonge Street. The Magic of Local Currencies. Biomimicry. "So bedazzling were the array of ideas presented here," wrote one attendee, *The Globe and Mail's* Don Cayo, "so rapid-fire did they fly, my head still spins." Inevitably, *Death and Life* was well represented, as in a session on "Why We Love Density, Congestion and Crowding." Each afternoon at 5 p.m., Jane held forth in a one-hour public conversation with one or another prominent interviewer. With one of them, Peter Gzowski, she told of her visit to Hong Kong, marveled at how its residents started up tiny hotels by combining apartments, how with a washing machine or two they'd start up a laundry. "They have all kinds of improvisations on how to make a living . . . all kinds of little manufacturing things going on that are ostensibly just residences." Onstage, sitting back in an armchair, she enjoyed herself, a laugh sometimes sweeping through her whole body, gleeful eyes scrinching into slits, cheeks alive with color.

Soon after Ideas That Matter, Jane was treated to a hot air balloon ascension. "Have you ever been?" she wrote Ellen Perry afterward. "Do,

Jane at the Ideas That Matter conference in Toronto in 1997

if you get a chance. Absolutely the only sounds coming from earth were the barking of dogs, and they were as clear as could be." This was her news—along with word that her latest book, *The Nature of Economies*, was coming out soon.

III. OBEDIENCE TO NATURE

The last chapter of *Death and Life*, "The Kind of Problem a City Is," had looked at cities in a way bordering on the biological. "At some point along the trail," Jane wrote in a new 1992 foreword to it, "I realized I was engaged in studying the ecology of cities. Offhand, this sounds like taking note that raccoons nourish themselves from backyard gardens and garbage bags," as apparently they did in Toronto. That's not quite what she was getting at. The ties between natural and urban ecosystems, however, were myriad. Both featured intricate webs of connection. In both, diversity developed organically. Both are "easily disrupted or destroyed." This, in brief, was Jane's thinking about urban ecology around 1992. Now, with *The Nature of Economies*, she was developing these ideas, particularly in relation to healthy economies. Economies grew, or didn't, said Jane, largely in obedience to laws of nature like those governing biological systems.

Early in 1999, Jason Epstein, now past seventy, invited a younger colleague, David Ebershoff, to become involved in Jane's latest book project. Just twenty-nine at the time, he was still "pretty green," he says today. At that point, he'd not yet even read Jane's *Systems of Survival*, nor much of Plato—both confessions of a sort because for the new book Jane had reprised her Platonic dialogue technique from *Systems of Survival:* Armbruster and the rest of the gang were back for new bouts of intellectual repartee.

Ebershoff didn't at this point become Jane's new editor. But that's how it worked out. "Read this," Epstein said to him one day, referring to a draft of Jane's new book, "and tell me what you think." What he thought was, "I kind of loved it. Because it was so original to me." It was hard to write about ideas, and Jane did that so well. But he wasn't won over by the "characters" she had brought over from the earlier book. "They weren't like five characters you'd see in a novel." On the other hand, in how ideas were volleyed back and forth among them, amended, revised, and polished smooth, it was a book that "literally embodied the writing process." That in itself made it a coup of sorts. "I knew I'd never seen anything like that coming across my desk."

Said Epstein: "Let's go to Toronto and meet Jane."

CHAPTER 25

CIVILIZATION'S CHILD

EPSTEIN AND EBERSHOFF flew up to Toronto and met Jane at Canoe, a restaurant on the fifty-fourth floor of a downtown tower with fine views of the city, patronized by bankers, businesspeople, and others comfortably well off. In came Jane wearing her customary shapeless poncho and carrying a papier-mâché ear trumpet Burgin had made to help her hear better. "Almost every head in the restaurant turned as she made her way to the table," Ebershoff recalls; the last time he'd seen that was with Norman Mailer.

It was June 9, 1999. Jane's manuscript was all but done; they had it there in front of them. Ebershoff told her how much he liked it. They talked about the publishing schedule, went over the dust jacket design. Any anxiety he might have felt about meeting Jane fell away. They ate. They spent a couple of pleasant hours together. Then, the same day, the two men flew back to New York.

At lunch they'd brought up no misgivings with Jane's dialogue technique. "The form was really Jane being herself," says Ebershoff; they weren't going to mess with it at this point. As for Jane's "characters," they'd evolved little since *Systems of Survival*, their speech patterns grown no more distinctive. On the other hand, if you gave them their head, as Jane had, they had plenty to say. One of them, the sole newcomer to the group, Hiram, an ecologist, declares that his personal project "is to learn economics from nature." Indeed, the whole book bears just this stamp. "I'm convinced," Hiram says a little later, "that economic life is ruled by processes and principles we didn't invent and can't transcend whether we like that or not."

Take, say, embryonic development, where you could see up close what Jane took as a cardinal principle, "differentiation emerging from generality." A fertilized egg divides, "forming a blob of multiplied generality"; that is, the cells, though more numerous, are still identical. But then, depending on their locations in the blob, they differentiate into distinct *types* of cells. Those differences morph further into the animal's tissues—intestines, heart muscle, fur, and so on. Jane argued that the branching rivulets of a river delta or the proliferating clauses and subclauses of a legal code exhibit the same overarching principle. So do many facets of economic life. "Our remote ancestors," says Hiram, "started developing tools and weapons with nothing that was of their own making"; the sticks, stones, and bones they found around them became spears, scrapers, pokers, and hammers. And across the long tide of human history, each became a new "generality" that could potentially—and usually did—differentiate further into hammers, say, of a hundred different kinds, each expressing human ingenuity and economic drive.

This, broadly, was Jane's strategy—through her conversations among Armbruster, Hiram, and their friends, to venture back and forth across the divide separating nature from economic life, learning from thermodynamics, control theory, fractal geometry, evolution, and other sciences. And always, at the root, the book's central premise—that "human beings exist wholly within nature as part of a natural order."

The book didn't work for everybody, just as *Systems of Survival* didn't, and for kindred reasons; the dialogue technique, however satisfying it was for Jane to write, left some readers cold, or bothered. One critic was annoyed enough to aim a full, hilarious broadside at the book. "Those insufferable yuppies Armbruster, Hortense, and Kate are back: slicing kumquats into their Perrier as they pretentiously discourse about bifurcation, feedback controls, and bonobo chimpanzees," Mike Davis began a review in *The Village Voice* in 2000.

No, this is not a *Saturday Night Live* skit or a new Doug Coupland novel. It is Jane Jacobs—the Mother Teresa of neighborhoods—writing about the ecology of wealth . . . Jacobs, as usual, is intent on intellectual heavy lifting and obviously thinks [the dialogue technique] lightens the load for her readers. I wonder. Staggering through the pompous dinner conversations (in which the women, as in real life, seldom get a word in edgewise) that make up *The Nature of Economies*, I kept hoping that someone would toss hemlock with Armbruster's radicchio.

Others, less distracted by Jane's technique than warmed or exhilarated, praised the book as, for example, "fresh and provocative." A British champion of Jane's work, Peter J. Taylor, guessed it would "come to be seen as her most important work." Another observed that, beyond having so much to say, Jane's characters embodied an almost forgotten standard of civilized discourse. They actually *listened* to one another.

She was sorry to be so slow to respond to his letter, Jane wrote one correspondent in February 2000, but she'd suffered a serious accident. She'd caught her foot in a telephone cord, slipped, broken her hip, and ever since had been "learning to walk again." More than ever now, she resorted to language like *must reluctantly decline.* Her life, fuller of doctors, was more constrained, more dependent on others, pulled this way and that by the vicissitudes of age. "I'm taking the glucosamine," she wrote a friend who'd recommended an arthritis book, "and while I'm not yet in shape for skateboarding (the book does say to be optimistic) I have a distinct feeling that it is making the joint and leg stronger." She would soon see a specialist to determine whether some muscle or blood vessel "has fallen down on the job."

The following month, Jane managed to make an appearance at the New York Public Library. "You were as poised as a queen when the auditorium gave you several minutes of applause when you came on stage," Margot Gayle, one of her West Village friends, wrote her. She added, "It was good to see your son looking after you so well."

A year later and it was Jane's knee that was the problem. She could walk well enough with the help of "a nice wheeled walker on the level, and a cane and railing on stairs." She was in no pain when standing or sitting still. But while no worse recently, she was no better, either. She'd been advised against surgery: "This would be very chancy and could leave matters worse."

Jane needed help to travel, make public appearances, just get around. She often had dinner with Jim and Pat, at their house a few doors down Albany Avenue, Caitlin sometimes delegated to walk her grandmother back home. Or else Jim and Pat would go over to Jane's, bearing a cooked meal; "Meals on Feet," Jane liked to call it. During these years, too, neighbors would drive her around parts of Toronto she'd not much seen; Jane dedicated her last book to two of them—"merry leading-edge explorers" who bore her on "discovery jaunts" to such exotic locales as Toronto's industrial suburbs or the Hong Kong–flavored malls on the edge of the city.

On November 26, 2003, Jane wrote David Ebershoff to say she'd sent the corrected page proofs for her latest book, *Dark Age Ahead*, about troubling symptoms of cultural collapse, to the Random House production editor. She'd "worked day and night" to meet her deadline, in part so "I could have the luxury of thinking for a few days about the next book." At age eighty-seven, the *next* book. Indeed, she was including a preliminary table of contents for it, which she proposed to call *A Brief Biography of the Human Race*. Of course, she couldn't get to it right away. There was the book tour for *Dark Age Ahead*, a Toronto civic battle in which she was embroiled, and "the speech for City College which has been a great trouble because I confused my book-writing mode with my speech-writing mode." City College was City College of New York, and the speech was the Lewis Mumford Lecture she'd agreed to give in May 2004, four days after her eighty-eighth birthday.

That was the second paragraph of her letter to Ebershoff. The third began, "Now (don't scream!) I am also seeing my way to the next book after *A Brief Biography* . . . a sort of self-anthology" of her economics writings, "with some added introductory and interstitial material. This," she added brightly, "ought to be quick and easy!"

Jane seems to have been entirely serious about these plans. *Dark Age Ahead*, though not Jane at her best, showed glimmers of the Jane who was. "Crisp, entertaining, scholarly, scary," one early review called it. And when the book came out in May 2004, she was game for the promotional tour on its behalf. It wasn't quite Jane's last hurrah, but it was getting there: New York for a couple of days, including the Mumford Lecture. Back to Toronto for three days of interviews and photo shoots with *Time*, *The Globe and Mail*, and *Maclean's* at her home. Taped interviews with CBC at their broadcast center. Then off to San Francisco and Vancouver with Ned; and Powell's Bookstore in Portland, Oregon, with Alana Probst. Roberta Gratz picked her up in Portland to bring her back to Toronto. At a college in Portland, Gratz recalls, they entered a campus building, Jane in flowing scarf, hobbling along with her walker down the corridor and into a crowded room where Roberta heard someone whisper,

"Oh, it's Jane Jacobs. This is better than a rock star!" When Jane gave a talk at UC Berkeley, niece Lucia Jacobs visited her in her hotel room. A chance *Whaddya think about this . . . ?* and they were lost in what Lucia recalls as "another marathon discussion" like those she remembered from Albany Avenue years before.

As for the new books Jane had in mind, according to Anne Collins, her Random House Canada editor, she meant the title, *A Brief Biography of the Human Race,* without the slightest irony. "It was dead straight. A title very descriptive as opposed to a joke." In the Mumford lecture she delivered on May 8 before a packed auditorium at City College, and in a *New York Times* essay based on her talk a week later, she offered a preview: humankind had lived through, and needed to transcend, what she called its long Plantation Age, with its "serfs, feudal tenants, indentured servants, outright slaves, or sharecroppers shackled by discrimination and debt," along with bankrupt notions of industrial, spatial, and political order. What, after all, were modern American suburbs but "grotesque parodies of plantations. Look at them: Monocultural residential tracts on ever-larger scales, like so many endless fields of cabbages. Standardized shopping centers, multiplying like so many flocks of identically pedigreed sheep."

While in New York, a talk with Adam Gopnik for a piece in *The New Yorker* gave Jane the opportunity to tell a favorite story. New York, she said, still had its old pizzazz, for it changed every day—unlike neatly designed New Urbanist communities, everything built in from the get-go. It reminded her of the preacher who warned children that in Hell there would be much "wailing and weeping and gnashing of teeth." But what if, as a child wonders, you have no teeth? Then teeth, too, would be provided: No way out. Everything thought out from the beginning. *This,* said Jane, was the overdesigned city—all done, just so, with none of a vital city's inner messiness.

As for Jane's *other* new book, the economics anthology, she was perfectly serious about it, too. By late 2004, she'd sent Ebershoff in New York and Collins in Toronto a chunk of it that promised "the first theoretical explanation for normal expansion of economic life"—in particular, those sudden, sporadic growth spurts she saw as the essential marker of great cities everywhere. The book had started out more modestly, Jim Jacobs recalls, as a kind of best-of anthology. Once she began going through it, however, she was "appalled. Some of her explanations missed so much.

How," she lamented, "was anyone to understand them?" Now, in full cry, she'd remedy those old lapses, advance new ideas.

Did she figure to just go on and on?

She was old now and had medical problems too numerous to count. But it is hard to discern in her plans, ideas, and proposals any doubt about completing them. And why not? Her mother had lived to 101. If you were the least bit susceptible to magical thinking, you could read her correspondence, survey the evidence of this time in her life, and doubt death would *ever* take her. Indeed, Anne Collins had chosen to act as if this were almost literally so; call it a gesture, but it was a gesture in lawyerly black and white—formal contracts drawn up for the two books, submission dates extending three years into the future that would leave Jane pounding away at her typewriter well into her ninety-first year. Says Collins, "I thought she would be with us forever."

"Thank you very much for the first terrific pages of *Uncovering the Economy: A New Hypothesis*," Ebershoff wrote Jane in response to her twenty-eight-page piece of it.

> If the rest of the book reads as Part 1 does—and why shouldn't it!— you'd have done just what I was hoping for; and what your many readers will want. I'm very pleased that this isn't merely an anthology of your greatest hits. You've hit on a new but profound idea about cities and economies . . . Please keep writing. Please keep sending me pages. I hope you're healing swiftly and that you have many long hours to write and think.

Jane's decline in her later years, before 2005 or so, did not extend to her mind. If it did, we might expect to find it in her correspondence, closer to her raw, unmediated self. But it's not there. Not in her spelling. Not in the organization of her thoughts. Nor in their characteristic energy and spirit. In 2005, she apologized to a correspondent for not replying earlier: "You must think that I was swept silently into the Grand Canyon." She'd had another accident, fallen and broken her leg "badly enough that I've had to try to relearn how to walk . . . This is a boring tale of woe—but what is upsetting, rather than boring, is that no, I haven't done the blurb you were expecting for your U. of Michigan Press book on development."

"Don't send me a Get Well card," she added. "I am getting well; it's just slow."

Back in 2002 Jane had suffered a serious stroke. It happened in the middle of the night. She called Jim, who got her to the hospital, where she stayed for a couple of weeks before entering a rehab unit. Half her body was paralyzed. She had trouble swallowing. She couldn't type, couldn't write. But she could think just fine. It was there, as Jim tells it, that she conceived *Dark Age Ahead*. She was in a hurry, "determined to get as much done as she could, before the deadline." After leaving the hospital, "from outward appearance unscathed," she wrote with uncharacteristic nervous energy, rushing it through. "It was the only book she wrote out of her head, without notes."

Ned, in from the coast, helped Jane with the index and entered her text into the digital form her publisher required. The two of them sat "at the screen together," as he remembers, going over a word choice here, an idea there. "It was a wonderful learning experience for me," he says. As Jane acknowledged, he contributed to the "Unwinding Vicious Spirals" chapter, pushing her for ideas about "how to get out of this mess," the sad, cultural decline that was her subject. Otherwise, the book was her own. But it came slowly, at great cost. Jane relied on family and friends in ways she hadn't before. Her signature, normally rounded and clear, was now jagged, angular, and scratchy. Every little thing came harder.

Until near the very end, at least, her mind remained clear. More than clear—*engaged*, eager for any bit of life she could still grab hold of. But finally, sometime late in 2004, maybe around Christmas, David Ebershoff began to realize that the hope he'd voiced for Jane "healing swiftly" was unrealistic; the seesaw battle between recovery and decline was settling in one direction only. After the Mumford Lecture in May, he recalls, she seemed to be struggling. As the months went by and he checked in with her, "she'd say she was trying to write, but I could see how hard it was for her." In some of their later phone calls, "I couldn't have the same kind of conversation with her." Ebershoff's counterpart in Toronto, Anne Collins, noticed much the same: what had seemed almost regular cycles of weakening and renewal now ebbed permanently into decline. Sometimes Anne would drop by the house for tea. But now there were no "So, how's the writing?" questions for Jane. It was just tea.

Jim Jacobs, of course, had seen it coming earlier, following his mother's return from the *Dark Age Ahead* tour: "Pat and I noticed that something was seriously wrong." This woman who spoke in perfect paragraphs now could hardly speak at all. Sentences drifted. Jane realized it, too. "She knew there was trouble." Her doctors found evidence of mental slippage now but, to Jim's taste, were too inclined to say, *Well, it's about what you'd expect for a woman her age, we have to let nature take its course.* Looking for a way out, he thought he saw improvement when she happened to be on an antibiotic regimen and suspected infection was worsening her mental condition.

In late summer of 2005, Jim took a leave of absence from the company he'd cofounded to care for Jane himself. "But it was more than I could do," so they brought in round-the-clock nursing care. Late that year and early the next was the worst of it. Jane would slide into unpredictable outbreaks of anger, affection, and despair. "What was I thinking?" she'd say as she came out of one of them. It was hard for her, hard for everyone.

It was not a happy time for those who loved Jane Jacobs. She had broken her hip the year before, was confined to the house, increasingly isolated. There were times, relates Jim, when "she was in no condition to see people," which upset some of her friends, who felt that maybe she was being kept more isolated than need be. It seemed to Roberta Gratz that Jane "hungered for company." When friends did visit, they honored Jane's voracious sweet tooth. Margie Zeidler would come by with butter tarts. John Sewell and his wife, Liz Rykert, started bringing her Saturday meals. They'd show up, march into the kitchen, get things organized, lay out a meal, break out the Basque tarts that were one of Jane's favorites, and sit down and talk. "She had lots of opinions about the world," says Sewell. But rarely did she reminisce; this was one old-timer who took no refuge in the past, at least in public; who knows what she whispered to Ben Franklin or one of her other old friends?

Jim, his daughter Caitlin recalls, was desperate for "a solution that would make her well," delving into medical science, looking "for what he could do to save her." Early in 2006, with Jane on a regimen of antibiotics Jim had prevailed on her doctors to prescribe for her, Jane seemed to rally, her mental acuity, speech, and emotional stability improving. For a time she found her way back to work again, mainly on the economics book. She'd never much talked about work in progress, but now she seemed eager to tell Jim about it. Up until March, maybe April, she was still at the typewriter.

Finally came the sudden turn for the worse; Jim took her to the hospital, stayed with her almost nonstop until, three days later, on April 25, 2006, she died. The family issued a statement: "What's important is not that she died but that she lived, and that her life's work has greatly influenced the way we think. Please remember her by reading her books and implementing her ideas."

And if you don't, Ned Jacobs was supposed to have joked, "there's a Dark Age Ahead."

Jane was cremated, her ashes laid to rest in Creveling Cemetery, down the Old Berwick Road from where her mother had grown up in Espy, in the Butzner family plot, beside Bob, their common stone recording their names, dates, and nothing else.

"When someone like that dies, she doesn't go anywhere," says Jason Epstein. "She's not dead. She's so vivid, you can't imagine her dead, like Shakespeare." Maybe so, but we are enjoined to consider her legacy, what the example of her life holds for us. The word itself carries some stuffy baggage, but I don't think Jane would have dismissed the question or, with false modesty, scolded us for raising it.

Jane's legacy was, first of all, more than *The Death and Life of Great American Cities*, more than any of her individual books. This might seem heretical to assert for a woman who was author first of all and who said so time and again. "I am quite an ordinary person, I assure you," she wrote in 1997, "who has led a happy ordinary life, the only perhaps notable things about it having occurred in my head as I sit undramatically at a typewriter; and those things are already in my books." Still, Jane was wife, mother, and friend, too. She was social activist, gadfly, rogue, and rebel. She was an economist of sorts, and something of a philosopher, and, one hears it said, an expert on cities, too.

These clumsy qualifiers nod to Jane's uncredentialed relationships to the very fields and disciplines to which she contributed most. Similar reservations might apply to Jane-as-scientist, which she was, too, in a way. "She was a great theoretician," says Lucia Jacobs, tenured professor of psychology at UC Berkeley. "She identified with Darwin." When people complained about the absence of hard data in her work, Jane would reply, "Darwin didn't have data either." Professor Jacobs deems Darwin quite the creditable comparison for her. "Darwin went his own way, knew he was right, and had unbelievable intuition." Like Jane.

Professor Jacobs means "theoretician" as praise, certainly when uttered in the same breath as Charles Darwin; so did Robert Lucas, the Nobel-winning economist, in applying the word "theorist" to her. And yet, the more Jane was theoretician, the less she was the kind of writer she'd arrived in New York to become. In those early articles she wrote for *Vogue*, Jane was rooted in fact, datum, and incident, in sidewalk and street, leather, flowers, and furs. But in the years after *Death and Life*, lauded as an important thinker, she might be excused for slipping back from the rough-and-tumble of the world and into the cosseted realm of ideas: Economics. Morals. Ecology. As age and physical frailty kept her more at home, retreat to the abstract and theoretical probably became easier, even inevitable. She became less the maker of vivid images and scenes, more the intrepid explorer of ideas. Of course, the two were always in her, locked in creative tension; *Death and Life* is stocked to the brim with ideas. But as the years passed and the public intellectual in her bloomed, Jane did find it harder, or maybe less important, to rid her prose of generalization and abstraction—leaving more of it behind to sometimes thwart or entangle her readers.

In the years leading up to her death, and then after it, critics began to notice that within the space of a few years in the early 1960s, three women wrote three classic books, launching three social movements that changed the world: Betty Friedan's *The Feminine Mystique*, Rachel Carson's *Silent Spring*, and Jane's *The Death and Life of Great American Cities*. All three women identified primarily as writers, not as credentialed experts in the fields about which they wrote; Carson, with a master's degree in zoology, was a partial exception, but by age thirty, long before she wrote *Silent Spring*, she was making a living as a writer, her childhood dream. All three were popularizers; that is, just as they were not themselves traditional scholars or scientists, they did not write *for* scholars but for ordinary, nonexpert readers. Mostly, they avoided specialized vocabulary, used language intended to draw in, not exclude. And, rather than hide their deepest convictions beneath a patina of objectivity, they expressed themselves with intensity and feeling.

Friedan, Carson, and Jacobs had something else in common, of course, which is that they were women. However much or little their books might be judged expressions of "women's thinking," or "women's sensibilities," they surely reflected women's *experience*. In the 1940s and 1950s, when the three of them came up, that normally meant working lives not so tied to professional discipline or traditional career arc as men's were; more often bound to steno pad and typewriter, or to the bearing and care of children; and routinely undercut by the sort of crude sexist barbs Lewis Mumford aimed at Jane in "Mother Jacobs' Home Remedies." ("Mr. Mumford," Jane got back at him in her Mumford Lecture at City College, "seemed to think of women as a ladies' auxiliary of the human race.")

Even as recently as 2011, critics who should have known better were still calling Jane a housewife. Veronica Horwell, writing in *The Guardian*, pictured her as pushing a baby carriage after she married Bob. Sir Peter Hall termed her "a middle-class housewife who found her voice." Well, Jane was *never* a housewife, not if by that we mean someone who sees her primary role as at home, who is "just" a housewife. Jane was a good wife, and tended the house as best she could, which wasn't all that great, turning to paid outside help when she could. Aside from brief maternity leaves, she *always* worked, viewed the great world of ideas and action, of politics, buildings, and books as her natural and settled domain.

Back in 1971 Jane read *Man's World, Women's Place,* an influential early feminist book by Elizabeth Janeway that took on myths of women's weakness and women's power, and had plenty to say about both. In a

Jane sometimes wound up in the most unlikely places. Here she dances with Gertrude Vanderbilt Whitney and Willa Cather, in a mural by Edward Sorel installed at the Waverly Inn, a restaurant in Greenwich Village.

letter to Jason Epstein around the time her family was moving into the Albany Avenue house, she called it "the first book on the subject of women's fix that has not just depressed and enraged me, but has enlightened me." She appreciated Janeway's ideas about why sex occupied the place it did in advertising and art. "Also a very nice treatment of that bugaboo about women fucking men into limbo if given the chance, and the best (because it is so true) put-down of penis envy."

In 1980, Jane shared a platform at Faneuil Hall in Boston with James Rouse, developer of the planned suburban community of Columbia, Maryland. At one point, Rouse invoked the famous dictum of Daniel Burnham, "Make no little plans; they have no magic to stir men's blood." But "Jane brought down the house," recalled somebody there that day, "when she quietly announced, 'I'm not sure big plans ever did have the magic to stir women's blood.'"

In the 1990s, as Jane sat for an interview with a Canadian magazine, her interviewer referred to "man's fundamental propensity to do harm." Jane interrupted him: "I wish you wouldn't just say 'man' all the time. This is a human thing and it applied to women as much as men."

"Believe me," her interlocutor put in, "I know it applies to women. I use the word 'man' in the traditional inclusive way."

"Yes, and I don't like it, because we get a distorted view of who has been doing all these things. Women have been doing them, too, and they're just as important." For Jane, women were always central to the working of the world; she liked to imagine the "market mamas" who tended market stalls and oversaw local trade across Africa as "bossy and self-confident, which is all to the good."

She didn't assert herself as a feminist; she just was one. That she had started out as a stenographer, right there with teacher and nurse as a stereotypically woman's occupation, is immaterial. So is it that for a time she applied a cosmetic cream, "leg paint," in a shade darker than her natural skin, to mimic nylon stockings, which she despised; or that she whipped up cookies for Christmas; or shopped for her children's clothes; or that she was this kind of mother or that. The fact is, she was an uncommonly strong and self-confident woman never afraid to air her views or exhibit her reliably superior intellect. Even had she never come to the attention of the world through *Death and Life* and her Village activism, had she remained "merely" an accomplished editor and mid-level publishing figure, that she was able to establish herself so securely among the Doug Haskells and Ed Bacons, the Lewis Mumfords and Chadbourne Gilpatrics, of This Man's World of 1958 in itself ranks as an achievement.

Toward the end of her life, in 2005, Jane wrote,

> Like other women who are neither dolts nor masochists I have always recognized that sociology is based on a tissue of outright lies about the inferiority of women (and others who are not men of Western European descent) and the natural superiority of men. I have not made this an overt cause, but have simply acted as if it is not true, trusting that falsity destroys itself eventually.

Another way to view Jane Jacobs, unlikely though it might seem, is as gentleman amateur. Think, say, of the Victorian-era English aristocrat of our imagination who, wealth and station liberating his enthusiasms, pursues at leisure his interests in science, literature, or statecraft, holding idiosyncratic views he needs little encouragement to express. Jane might seem to share nothing with him. She was not a man, much less a gentleman. She was never rich. For much of her life, she enjoyed nothing remotely like leisure. Besides, as a writer she was no amateur at all, but a thoroughgoing professional, her family dependent in part on her earnings.

And yet, she *acted* in something like this tradition: She read what she liked, in every corner of human knowledge, without letup, as deeply as she wished, *as if* she had all the time and money in the world. She indulged an astonishingly wide range of interests that she *made* her own. She fretted that she worked too slowly, that her books took too long to write; but in the end, she *gave herself* the time she needed or wanted, as if she were a Darwin, that other gentleman amateur, who took twenty years to shepherd *On the Origin of Species* into print. And when it came time to say what she thought, Jane likewise partook of this tradition. Her writing was never in debt to some governing discipline; astonishingly often, it read as unapologetic, forthright, and fresh. Unblinkered by assumptions and constraints borne of four years at Harvard or a doctorate from Stanford, she felt free to ignore the professionals and academics in urban planning, economics, and philosophy, hewing only to her own ideas. In *Death and Life* she launched an "attack on current city planning and rebuilding"; even city parks, oases of green seemingly beyond criticism, could not escape Jane's plain talk. In *Economy of Cities*, she claimed, counter to almost everyone else, that cities preceded agriculture. In *Cities and the Wealth of Nations*, she debunked two hundred years of received economic thinking.

The English geographer Peter J. Taylor has called Jane "an amateur in the professional's den." As we've seen, this often got her into trouble. After all, "unapologetic, forthright and fresh" can be cranky, uninformed, and wrong, as Jane sometimes seemed to her critics. Her disdain for high-handed nostrums, at times for whole professions, like sociology and planning, could seem simplistic. She could sometimes seem a little too eager to write off conventional scholarship or professional practice as worthless or worse. In some degree, she was still the outlaw she was back in Scranton, speaking a little "too" honestly, heedless of the tender feelings of her listeners. Ready to measure all things by her own moral and intellectual compass, she could seem antisocial, or out of touch, or as just not giving a damn. "Ever since I was a little kid," Jane once told her niece Lucia Jacobs, "I didn't worry about being thought a fool."

But in the end, Jane stands as icon of unfettered, incorruptible intelligence. Formally uneducated, virtually any field she stepped into would have at first seemed unfamiliar and alien to her. Yet by the time she was through with it, it was as if she had rediscovered the world, seen it fresh and for the first time, the dark side of the moon cast in new light. "She is a revolutionary writer in the full sense of the word," Peter Taylor once said of her. "She does not enter a field of study to revise or reform it; she turns it upside down"; by his count, she had done that at least three times. "When reading her books I always have a most unprofessional thought lurking at the back of my mind: 'Sock it to 'em, Jane!'"

If in some ways "revolutionary," Jane Jacobs was in others surprisingly old-fashioned, even conservative. For all her antiwar, anti-Establishment 1960s credentials, political conservatives and libertarians often embraced her; *Death and Life* was hailed by the conservative critic William F. Buckley Jr. and listed as one of a hundred favored books by the Conservative Book Club. Her words, as Alex Mazer summed them up after her death, "were more about restoration than revolution." She admired innovators and entrepreneurs. Many saw in her economic thought strains of the "Austrian" school of free-market economics. Not herself religious, she took her children to church because, as we've heard her say, it gave her "the satisfying, in fact inspiring feeling that I was a link in a long,

sinewy, living human tradition of being." Long making her home in a
Greenwich Village notorious for one or another breed of naughtiness, she
seems to have abstained from most of them. Jane herself embodied the
Victorian virtues. She worked hard; she finished what she started. When
she berated her opponents in the Village or Toronto, it was often because
they'd failed, in her opinion, to live up to entirely conventional precepts
of honesty, fairness, and good common sense. "She had the moral authority of an Old Testament prophet," David Crombie once said of her.

A charge sometimes laid against her was that, middle-class to her toes,
she didn't acutely feel the weight of injustice that bore down on so many.
"She was blind to issues of class and race," says Herbert Gans. Jane did
have populist leanings. She mistrusted the airy pronouncements of the
powerful. "If planning is good for human beings," she said in 1962, "it
shouldn't keep hurting them in the concrete and helping them in the
abstract." She felt wisdom flowed up as often as down, from the many
as reliably as from the few. She understood that many people didn't get
a fair deal. She asserted true, right, and good things: "Any child is more
important than any idea." *She* was good, thoroughly decent. Bigness
riled her. So did brute authority, stupidly exerted by the world's bullies
and simpletons. Still, her empathy for the unlucky and oppressed was
probably not as urgent as it is among some; she'd been too lucky, too
favored by fortune and circumstances.

Once, Ned Jacobs reports, while in a public hospital to give birth Jane
listened to one story after another of hopelessness and pain, money problems and spousal abuse, from women she might not otherwise have met.
She lamented, "I couldn't have survived those things. They would have
destroyed me." And maybe she was right. She had her share of disap-
pointments and frustrations, certainly. But the kinds of trauma, tragedy, and defeat that destroy the soul? No. It wasn't as if Jane had been
coddled, but she'd made it through without suffering life's most ruinous
calamities.

"Really, I've had a very easy life," she said. "By 'easy' I don't mean
just lying around, but I haven't been put upon, really. And it's been luck
mostly." This was no pat remark; she seems to have given it plenty of
thought. "Being brought up in a time when women weren't put down,
that's luck. Being in a family where I wasn't put down, that's luck. Finding the right man to marry, that's the best luck! Having nice children,
healthy children, that's luck.

"All these lucky things."

Jane's family in America went back at least to the mid-eighteenth century; Sabilla Bodine, the pseudonym Jane adopted for her collection of youthful verses, was a real person who lived four generations before Jane's mother (who, into her eighties, belonged to the Daughters of the American Revolution). Jane herself made no fetish of such genealogical links. But in the early 1950s, responding to McCarthy-era probers of her patriotism, she did write freely of forebears who'd belonged to unpopular political parties, fought in America's wars, suffered in enemy prisons, or through their backbone and industry otherwise helped make the country what it became. Though not preoccupied with her own past, she was proud of her links to the American past, and especially to the deep past of our culture and civilization. To know what Jane really stood for, we'd best turn off the scratchy old LP that squawks of cities and sidewalks and think instead of civilization at its best and most precious.

In his introduction to its Modern Library edition, Jason Epstein said of *Death and Life* that it "and especially her subsequent books are . . . about the dynamics of civilization, how vital economies and their societies are formed, elaborated, and sustained, and the forces that thwart and ruin them." Jane's final published book, *Dark Age Ahead,* confronted the subject explicitly. We all know of the "original" dark age that followed the collapse of the Roman Empire, she says in its first chapter; this was one instance of what she feared, but only one. "In North America," for example, "we live in a graveyard of lost aboriginal culture," she begins a sad litany. And "whatever happened to the culture whose people produced the splendid Lascaux cave paintings some seventeen thousand years ago?" All lost. "How and why can a people so totally discard a formerly vital culture that it becomes literally lost?" Now we were threatened by similarly destructive forces. Her purpose in writing, she tells us, is

to help our culture avoid sliding into a dead end, by understanding how such a tragedy comes about, and thereby what can be done to ward it off and thus retain and further develop our living, functioning, culture, which contains so much of value, so hard won by our forebears.

Jane identified five pillars of culture she saw as "dangerously close to the brink of lost memory and cultural uselessness": family and community "rigged to fail"; higher education corrupted by its emphasis on credentials, not real learning; science and technology rendered impotent; government out of touch with its citizens; and the learned professions failing to police themselves. Pretty grim, and easy to satirize: here's your street-corner purveyor of doom and gloom, wailing that the end is near. Then, too, *Dark Age Ahead* veered toward the generalities Jane had once decried, got caught up in intellectual hobby horses Jane had already ridden to exhaustion. One critic, Bruce Fisher, briskly summed it up as "not the book for which we should remember Jane Jacobs."

Still, as Jane made clear right off, her book expressed hope, too, in that she thought threatened cultures could be "rescued." And that was what her book set out to help do, its source of urgency. Even in some bleak ruined future, she told *The New Yorker*'s Adam Gopnik, people would one day want to know "how these ruins were made. . . . It sounds very conceited to say it, but I hope that what I wrote will help people start back."

Jane realized that modern civilization at its sunniest and best had smiled on her. She enjoyed a long, full life, earned a goodly share of the world's plaudits. Within herself she reconciled seemingly opposing tenets of rebel and outlaw on the one hand, and pillar of society, guardian of civilization, on the other. She believed, says son Ned, "that civilization was a remarkable phenomenon," and that people had responsibilities to preserve it, "that we're here to work really hard to not slip back into a dark age." She wasn't a spiritual person in the conventional sense. And yet, he says, "certainly she had a sense of awe." For the great pine forests of New Hampshire, yes, but for all of human creation, too. "What a waste," Ned conjures up her spirit, to see it disappear.

"Jacobs began by writing about sidewalks," observed Alex Mazer in the Canadian magazine *The Walrus*, "and finished with an account of Western civilization itself." But actually, kindred themes run all through Jane's books. Try making a list of them, categorizing each by subject— like CITIES, or ECONOMICS, or DIDACTIC DIALOGUES, or MORALS. I did this, listing Jane's books and assigning each to every category it fit. At first my little exercise seemed silly and sterile—until, in one startling moment of illumination, it wasn't: for one of my categories I hadn't even a name at first, just a vague sense of prosperity, growth, and the secure, steady tick of hearty, healthy CIVILIZATION. But when I went through each of Jane's books in turn, beginning with *Constitutional Chaff* and all the way down to *Dark Age Ahead*, and then, for good measure, the two books she never finished, each of them (whatever the other categories it might also fit) snugly fit this one as well: each, in substantial measure, was about what civilization needed to survive and prosper, what a culture needed to be vigorous, what human society needed in order to thrive. Jane's great-aunt Hannah's tale of Alaska was an adventure story, yes—but also the story of a middle-aged woman trying to bring the light of civilization, as she saw it, to a part of the world that needed more of it. Jane's account of Quebec set against English-speaking Canada came down to how two national identities could resolve their tensions in a sane and civilized way. Even little Peanutina could seem to epitomize civilization, one species of it, anyway, at its industrious best. In her books, Jane was standard-bearer for those healthy, constructive forces that keep the whole untidy mess of humankind from sinking into chaos and ignorance. With enough close looking and clear thinking, she was convinced, the world could be made a better place. At the end of *Systems of Survival,* Armbruster hauls out another bottle of champagne, pops the cork, fills the glasses of his friends, raises his own, and offers a toast: "To civilization!"

Dark Age Ahead was deeply personal for her. While civilization and its shaky pillars can seem a "big" subject, it turns repeatedly to the small, to events in Jane's own life. It takes us back to her first jobs in Manhattan; to her father's struggles during the Depression; to Higgins, the little town in that bypassed Appalachian pocket whose handful of residents had forgotten much their forebears once had known.

In this, her last book, Jane didn't make her arguments as deftly as she had before. And yet, if its execution was flawed, its urgency calls out to us. It is as if here, near the end of her life, she sheds a tear for the world that has been so good to her but from which she must soon take leave. That human world, with its many cultures, its cities, its achievements in the arts and sciences, was civilization's child—ours to nurture, lead toward healthier, more vibrant, more abundant life.

ACKNOWLEDGMENTS AND SOURCES

PEOPLE AND PLACES

First, many thanks are owed the following members of the Butzner and Jacobs families for their recollections of, and insights about, Jane: Carol Manson Bier, Decker Butzner and Deborah Sword, Ned Jacobs and Mary Ann Code, Burgin Jacobs, the late John Jacobs, Katia Jacobs, Lucia Jacobs, Jim Jacobs, Pat Broms, Caitlin Broms-Jacobs, Jane and Riley Henderson, Annie Butzner, and the late Kay Butzner, all of whom were unfailingly generous with their time, often as well with their personal papers and other artifacts of their lives with Jane.

Thanks to David Ebershoff, Jason Epstein, Anne Collins, Mary Rowe, Max Allen, David Gurin, Herbert Gans, Nathan Glazer, Roberta Brandes Gratz, Karen Reczuch, and Alan Littlewood for their memories of working with or collaborating with Jane.

For helping me to draw a picture of Jane's life in Scranton, I wish to thank Arthur Magida for his leads to his old hometown; Louis Danzico for showing me around the Medical Arts Building in Scranton and furnishing the architectural drawings for Dr. Butzner's office in the 1930s; Jean Harrington for admitting me to Jane's first house on Electric Street; Connie Brown for showing me around Jane's house on Monroe Avenue; Esther Keisling for her recollections of the Powell School of Business of long ago; Jim Dilts and Herb Harwood for key tidbits about the realities of early-twentieth-century rail travel.

For help with Jane's Virginia roots, I would like to thank the indefatigable genealogists Betsy Butzner Greene and her husband, James C. Greene, especially for their guided tour of Fredericksburg and environs.

Jane lived only about six months in Higgins, North Carolina, but her time there came at an impressionable age, represented her first substantial exposure to a place outside her hometown, and introduced her to lives and life stories very different from her own. For help on this North Carolina side of Jane's life, as well as that of her aunt Martha at the Higgins Neighborhood Center, I would like to thank Kay Butzner, now deceased, her daughter Jane Henderson and Jane's husband, Riley, for their hospitality in North Carolina and their memories of Jane; as well as Diana Ruby Sanderson at Warren Wilson College, for tracking down the Higgins Neighborhood Center footage; and the staff of the Rush Wray Museum of Yancey History, in Burnsville, North Carolina. I wish especially to thank Annie Butzner, for showing me around the area and furnishing me with a 150-page trove of clippings bearing on Higgins from local publications like the *Burnsville Eagle* and *Asheville Citizen*, church publications, and those of the Higgins Neighborhood Center itself. These may originally have been part of a scrapbook and appear in something like chronological order, but often lack complete bibliographical information. I have kept this cache intact, as received from Ms. Butzner in 2012, citing it in the Notes simply as the "Ann Butzner papers."

In New York City, where Jane lived from 1934 to 1968, I would like to thank Katy Bordonaro and Pearl Brower for introducing me to West Village Houses; Kathy Goldman, Judy Kirk Fitzsimmons, Rebecca Lurie, Eugene Sklar, Sara Stuart, and Sam Hall Kaplan for helping me to bridge the years back to the East Harlem of the 1950s. Likewise, thanks to Pierre Tonachel for his recollections of the West Village wars and for the cache of documents he so graciously provided (and to his brother Dick for leading me to him); to Ellen Perry Berkeley and Ron Shiffman, for their memories of Jane from her New York years and for access to some of their personal correspondence. A warm and sustained round of thanks goes to Robin Henig and her husband, Jeff, for their easy warmth and lively hospitality on my frequent visits to New York. (And thanks, too, Robin, for being my date at the Jacobs/Moses opera preview!) Barbara Garson at Westbeth, Ryan and Jamie Webb in Brooklyn, and Joel and Patty Schaindlin in Ossining were also kind enough to put me up on some of my New York visits; thanks to you all.

I am grateful to this book project for bringing me back to the New York City I lived in as a child and teenager. Through it, I renewed my ties to the streets of New York, and saw a lot I'd never seen before, from

East Harlem to Sunnyside, Queens. As a student at Stuyvesant High School from 1959 to 1962, I looked across First Avenue to Stuyvesant Town, or passed it on the way to the Canarsie Line subway, almost every day, without once venturing within it. Writing about Jane gave me the chance to atone for this lapse.

Finally, Toronto, where Jane lived from 1968 to the end of her life: For remembrances of Jane drawn primarily from her life in Toronto and for introductions to various places within the city, I would like to thank, in addition to family members mentioned previously: Megan Ogilvie, for my earliest car tour of the city; Max Allen, for taking me around through "the Kings"; and Alan Broadbent, Diane and Robert Brown, Anne Collins, David Crombie, John Downing, Cliff Esler, Ken Greenberg, Alan Littlewood, Liz Rykert, John Sewell, Bobbi Speck, Richard White, Eb Zeidler, and Margie Zeidler. A special thanks, on many counts both within and outside Jane's orbit, to Toshiko Adilman, for her kindness, helpfulness, generosity of spirit, and access to some of her personal papers; thanks to Toshiko, too, for introducing me to "Heron Maiden."

Though Jane never lived there, Boston figures in the making of this biography, too. The Jane Jacobs Papers, which brought me to the city repeatedly, are located at the Burns Library of Boston College; my first foray into the Burns collection came in late 2010, when I still lived in Cambridge, before moving back to Baltimore the following year. For their kind hospitality in Boston and environs, I wish to thank Ann and Dick Tonachel; Roz Williams and her late husband, Gary; and Jessie Arista and Duncan Webb.

Thanks go to the following scholars and writers who have made city planning, architecture, or Jane Jacobs herself among their areas of special interest: Lizabeth Cohen, Pierre Desrochers, Richard Florida, Paul Goldberger, Roberta Brandes Gratz, Chris Klemek, Glenna Lang, Timothy Mennel, Jamin Creed Rowan, Dirk Schubert, David Warsh, Sandy Zipp, and Peter Laurence (whose early work on Jane Jacobs, going back to the late 1990s, threw up signposts alerting me to promising leads I later pursued on my own). Thanks, too, to the Society for American City and Regional Planning History for their enormously worthwhile conferences in Baltimore and Toronto.

I would also like to thank Bill Dedman, for his help and encouragement at a crucial moment in pursuit of Jane's FBI file; Anne-Marie Corley, a former student of mine in MIT's Graduate Program in Science

Writing, for her translations of some of Jane's work for *Amerika* from the Russian back into English; Arthur Magida for a stream of leads, human and digital, clippings, online references, and good humor; Jane Entwistle Shipley for her help in pursuing Mr. Frank; Neil Kleinman, for helping to get school records of Jane's sister, Betty; Khanh Hoang, Dwight B. Waldo Library, Western Michigan University, for supplying the Robert Hemphill materials; and Martin Perschler, for his enlightening evening course at Johns Hopkins University, "Modernism & Postmodernism in Architecture."

The Alfred P. Sloan Foundation gave me a substantial grant in support of this book, which permitted me to follow leads, research avenues, and travel that would have been beyond my means otherwise, and thereby helped make this book a better one: Thank you. Along with Doron Weber, vice president, who shepherded my application through Sloan's deliberations, I wish to thank Delia Di Biasi and Sonia Epstein, for their much appreciated administrative help and advice.

I also wish to thank Michael Carlisle, my agent, and the whole crew at Knopf for their help in bringing this book into being. Ann Close presided over the whole business with insightful editing and good, measured advice. Maggie Hinders designed the book; Kevin Bourke oversaw its march toward production; Jessica Purcell has set about telling the world about it. Annie Eggers, Marisa Melendez, and Todd Portnowitz handled numerous recalcitrant editorial chores; they were patient, persistent, intelligent, and kind.

My thanks and love go out to Rachele, who gave the book its title; to David, Harry, Jessie, and Duncan; to my late father, Charles Kanigel, and my mother, Beatrice Wolshine Kanigel, who died while I was finishing this book; and every day and always, to my beloved Sarah.

ARCHIVES AND PERSONAL PAPERS

I've made use of manuscript and other archival resources at the following listed institutions, whose staffs I wish to sincerely thank for their help, patience, and professionalism. In the excitement of the chase surrounding archival research, it is too easy to misplace the names of those, at the front desk and in the stacks, who have helped you. But the debt is huge, one that I, and all those who do this sort of work, owe. I am writing this at a time when barbaric forces in the Mideast have been destroying precious icons of our cultural heritage. Working within a great library or archive reminds us of all that, in an instant, can be lost forever.

Bloomsburg University, Bloomsburg, Pennsylvania
  Early historical materials about the Normal School, courtesy of Robert Dunkelberger, archivist, Andruss Library

Brooklyn Historical Society, Brooklyn, New York
  Brooklyn, ca. 1934

Burns Library, Boston College, Boston, Massachusetts
  Jane Jacobs Papers; a special thanks to Justine Sundaram, who helped me at the beginning, back in 2010, and, with her colleagues, all across the years since

Centre de Estudios Puertorriqueños, Hunter College, New York
  Ellen Lurie Papers

Columbia County Historical and Genealogical Society, Bloomsburg, Pennsylvania
  Bloomsburg and Espy

Columbia University Rare Book and Manuscript Library, New York, New York
  Columbia University Press Papers
  Herbert Gans Papers
  Union Settlement Papers
  Random House Papers, especially those of Jason Epstein; Box 535 covers his papers from 1959 to 1962; Box 1365 from 1962 to 1984

Columbia University, Avery Architectural and Fine Arts Library, New York, New York
  Douglas Haskell Papers
  James Marston Fitch Papers

Federal Bureau of Investigation, Washington, D.C.
  228-page file on Jane Jacobs requested under provisions of the Freedom of Information/Privacy Act

Greenwich Village Society for Historic Preservation, New York, New York

Lackawanna Historical Society, Scranton, Pennsylvania
  Scranton history, street directories, newspaper archives

Museum of Modern Art, New York, New York
  Le Corbusier exhibit, "An Atlas of Modern Landscapes," 2013

National Archives, College Park, Maryland
  Amerika magazine, mostly RG 59, P 316

National Archives, St. Louis, Missouri
  Jane's federal employment records from her jobs at the Office of War
    Information and *Amerika,* including job applications, efficiency ratings,
    detailed job descriptions, leave requests, references to FBI reports, notes of
    personnel actions, pay records, memos, etc.; in all, these papers add up to
    about 180 pages

New-York Historical Society, New York, New York
  Peter Frasse & Co. Papers
  "WWII & NYC" exhibit, 2013

Municipal Archives, New York, New York
  Goldstone Papers
  City Planning Commission Papers

Rockefeller Archive Center, Sleepy Hollow, New York
  Chadbourne Gilpatric Papers
  John Markle Papers

Scranton Central High School, Scranton, Pennsylvania, Donna Zaleski, librarian
  Jane's school records

Toronto Reference Library

*Personal papers of Toshiko Adilman, Ellen Perry Berkeley, Annie Butzner, Decker
Butzner, Anne Collins, David Ebershoff, Cliff Esler, Roberta Brandes Gratz, Betsy
Butzner Greene and James C. Greene, David Gurin, Jim Jacobs, Lucia Jacobs, and
Pierre Tonachel*

NOTES

KEY TO ABBREVIATIONS IN THE NOTES

To save space in the Notes, the following frequently cited sources have been abbreviated as follows:

ARCHIVES

Burns—Jane Jacobs Papers, MS 1995–29, John J. Burns Library, Boston College
CollPark—National Archives and Records Administration, College Park, Maryland
ColumbiaRare—Columbia University Rare Book and Manuscript Library, New York, New York
FBI—FBI file on Jane Jacobs
HaskellPap—Douglas Haskell Papers, Columbia University, Avery Architectural and Fine Arts Library, New York, New York
Rockefeller—Rockefeller Archive Center, Sleepy Hollow, New York
StL—National Archives and Records Administration, St. Louis, Missouri

BOOKS BY JANE JACOBS
(full citations located in the Bibliography)
Alaska—A Schoolteacher in Old Alaska
Chaff—Constitutional Chaff
CityWealth—Cities and the Wealth of Nations
Dark—Dark Age Ahead
D&L—The Death and Life of Great American Cities
EofC—The Economy of Cities
Girl—The Girl on the Hat
Nature—The Nature of Economies
QofS—The Question of Separatism
Systems—Systems of Survival

OTHER BOOKS
Ethics—Ethics in Making a Living: The Jane Jacobs Conference,
ed. by Fred Lawrence. Atlanta: Scholars Press, 1989.

KentVillage—Leticia Kent, oral history interview conducted for Greenwich Village Society for Historic Preservation, October 1997.

LaurenceDiss—Peter L. Laurence, "Jane Jacobs, American Architectural Criticism and Urban Design Theory, 1935–1965," University of Pennsylvania dissertation, 2009.

Matter—Ideas That Matter, ed. Max Allen. Owen Sound, Ontario: Ginger Press, 1997.

Projects—Samuel Zipp, *Manhattan Projects: The Rise and Fall of Urban Renewal in Cold War New York.* New York: Oxford University Press, 2010.

Transatlantic—Christopher Klemek, *The Transatlantic Collapse of Urban Renewal: Postwar Urbanism from New York to Berlin.* Chicago: University of Chicago Press, 2011.

Wisdom— Sonia Hirt, ed., *The Urban Wisdom of Jane Jacobs.* New York: Routledge, 2012.

WPA—The WPA Guide to New York City. New York: Pantheon, 1982 (originally published 1939).

INTRODUCTION

3 "a screed of facts": Dillon, p. 41.

3 "There are ways to disagree": Roger Sale, "Thinking About Cities," *Hudson Review* (spring 1970): 178.

4 "What a dear, sweet grandmother": *Matter,* p. 15.

4 "you really should not have sounded off": Memo, Doug Haskell to JJ, July 2, 1959, HaskellPap.

5 "the most influential urban thinker": "The most influential urban thinker of all time"—2009 Planetizen, ahead of Frederick Law Olmsted, Lewis Mumford, Robert Moses, Le Corbusier, Richard Florida, James Rouse, and Thomas Jefferson.

5 "genius of common sense": Lang and Wunsch.

6 "godmother of urban America": Bole, p. 22.

6 "the Rachel Carson of the economic world": *Matter,* p. 205.

6 "bitchily observant": Her *Systems of Survival* described as "a Platonic dialogue as bitchily observant as a Woody Allen film," *Matter,* p.166.

6 "channeling Jane Jacobs": Christopher Hawthorne, "How Woody Allen and Terence Malick Gave Their Summer Movies a Nostalgic Glow," *Los Angeles Times,* July 23, 2011.

6 "Luther nailed": Campanella, p. 143.

6 "like a trip to Graceland": Dave Cieslewicz, "Citizen Dave": Stalking Jane Jacobs," http://www.isthmus.com, accessed April 9, 2012.

6 "Society of Saint Jane": Mariana Mogilevich, "Society of Saint Jane," review of *Block by Block": Jane Jacobs and the Future of New York,* book and museum exhibit, *Next American City,* spring 2008.

6 "What would Jane Jacobs do": Sandy Ikeda, "Know Thine Enemy, Know Thyself": What Would Jane Jacobs Do?," *Freeman,* posted October 4, 2011.

6 "one-lady Venice": *Matter,* p. 201.

6 "Mrs. Insight": Harvey, p. 41.

8 "must move in different circles": Interview with Hannah Gartner, CBC, October 15, 1997, Burns, VHS03.

9 "Barbara Fritchie of the Slums": Article about JJ, *New York Herald Tribune*, January 31, 1965, scrapbook, Burns, 23:6.

9 "Madame Defarge leading an aroused populace": *Matter*, p. 50.

10 "What is its purpose": Wachtel, p. 42.

10 "I just wanted to know": *Matter*, p. 17.

10 "finest Girl Scout troop": *Ethics*, p. 294.

11 "The most elementary point": From December 1964 draft of *EofC*, Burns, 8.

11 "Think for a minute": *Ethics*, p. 306.

11 "The only way": Fred Kaplan article about JJ, *Boston Globe*, April 12, 2000.

11 "Toronto grieved": Wellman, p. 2.

12 "learned a great deal": *Matter*, p. 3.

12 grew up around waterfalls: *Matter*, p. 26.

13 "equalization of pay": "Answers to Interrogatory for Jane Butzner Jacobs," responding to question #1, accompanying letter of JJ to Carroll St. Claire, July 22, 1949, Burns, 5:4.

14 "would not be available": *Matter*, p. 22.

CHAPTER 1: A GENEROUS PLACE TO LIVE

19 Back in the 1850s: Columbia County Historical & Genealogical Society, library, museum, and *Newsletter*, for maps, old photos, clippings, and other background on the life of Espy and Bloomsburg; WPA Project 5175, 1936, includes "Espy Notes" scrapbook, with "History of the North Branch Canal, 1828–1901"; articles about Espy from *Berwick Enterprise*, December 22, 1900; *Morning Press*, June 25, 1938; *Morning Press*, February 1937; "The Passing Throng," newspaper article, November 4, 1936; *Walk Bloomsburg: Self-guided Tours of the Historic District*; William M. Baillie, ed., *Discovering Bloomsburg: A Bicentennial History* (Bloomsburg, PA: Bloomsburg Bicentennial Commission, 2002).

19 Both were central Pennsylvania natives: See JJ, "Reading, Writing, and Love-Apples"; "Captain James Boyd Robison Found Dead," *Democratic Sentinel*, March 5, 1909; federal censuses from 1870–1920; *Historical and Biographical Annals of Columbia and Montour Counties, Pennsylvania* (Columbia County, PA: J. H. Beers & Co., 1915); *Book of Biographies of the Seventeenth Congressional District* (Chicago: Biographical Publishing Company, 1899); Marc Fritz, "Robison Family Endured Un-Civil War," http://www.robisonsuncivilwar .blogspot.com, distilled from Gertrude Keller Johnston, *Dear Pa . . . And So It Goes* (Harrisburg, PA: Business Service Company, 1971); genealogical chart of Robisons and Butzners compiled by Bess Robison Butzner, Burns, 4/7; *Souvenir Views of the State Normal School, Bloomsburg, PA,* and school catalogs from the period; thanks to Robert Dunkelberger, Bloomsburg University archivist, for supplying these and other information from the Normal School archives on the Robisons.

21 Bessie wasn't a teacher anymore: *American Journal of Nursing* (1904), p. 555,

records "Miss Bessie Robison admitted to membership" in the Philadelphia
Polyclinic Alumnae Association on March 3, 1904; "The Philadelphia Polyclinic
and College for Graduates in Medicine," *Trained Nurse and Hospital Review*
32 (1904): 419: "The graduating exercises of the Polyclinic School for Nurses
was held April 29 at the hospital," diplomas presented to fifteen young women,
including Bessie M. Robison; Roberta Mayhew West, *History of Nursing in
Pennsylvania* (Pennsylvania State Nurses' Association, 1938), pp. 623–27. In
an interview, the late Kay Butzner, Jane's sister-in-law, says Bessie was simply bored with teaching in rural Pennsylvania and wanted to try life in the big
city.

21 what could you expect: Wachtel, p. 426.

22 West Virginia mining town: Chavez, Duer, and Fang, p. 46.

22 pile of undergarments: Interview, Jim Jacobs.

22 Dr. Butzner had come: Greene and Greene, Butzner Family History; see also
Matter, p. 150; Wachtel, p. 44; (Fredericksburg) *Free Lance,* April 27, 1915, on
death of William J. Butzner; Garrett Epps, "The Fourth Circuit Court of Appeals
Is Losing a Star: Uncle Billy's Boy," (Richmond) *Style Weekly,* January 1, 1980;
"Office of Commonwealth's Attorney to be Filled by Billy Butzner," *Daily Star,*
December 31, 1909; young Dr. Butzner's early whereabouts in Scranton traced
through city directories of those years; *Philadelphia Medical Journal,* May 28,
1904, p. 1049.

23 "All the field hands": Greene and Greene, Butzner Family History, p. 79.

24 still getting mail: President's Office, American National Red Cross, Pennsylvania State Branch to Bessie M. Robinson [sic], at 1622 Summer Street, Philadelphia, December 12, 1908, Burns, 24:1.

24 three hours on the through train: Email, rail expert Herb Harwood, who reports
"at least two through-trips a day each way, each taking roughly three hours,"
between Scranton and Philadelphia.

24 "a quiet one": (Bloomsburg, PA) *Columbian* March 25, 1909.

24 Soon after they married: Interview, Jim Jacobs.

24 his favorite pie: Interview, Jim Jacobs; see also Sandra Martin, "An Urban Legend," p. 84.

25 "and love and affection": Indenture, August 6, 1918, John D. Butzner to Bess
Robison Butzner, DBK no. 294, p. 228, Lackawanna County deedbook.

25 "I learned to get out early": Wachtel, p. 41.

25 he'd seemed fine: "He was the picture of health and brightness," (Fredericksburg) *Free Lance,* August 10, 1951.

25 a house at 1712 Monroe Avenue: *Matter,* p. 33. From the sidewalk, the house
can seem as if it had a real third floor. But despite pediment, elaborated window
treatment, and vestigial porch suggesting otherwise, it was really just an attic.

26 "a cheerful place": Wachtel, p. 41. Years later, a Jewish friend, David Gurin, told
Jane how the sole surviving remnant of his Orthodox childhood was that, on
Friday nights in his house as an adult, there were no television, no electronics, no
distractions, that they were all just there with each other. Replied Jane: "That's
how I spent every night."

26 "no mean streak": Interview, Toshiko Adilman.

28 "That's puddingstone!": Jane Jacobs, "What Would I Have Been if I Hadn't Been
a Writer," response to editor's query, 1994, Burns, 6:5.

28 a distaste for profligacy: Interview, Jim Jacobs.

29 "carrying on dialogues": Warren, p. 16; Fulford, "Radical Dreamer."

29 "the lakes turned over": Early draft, *EofC*, Burns, 8:6.

29 Sabilla Bodine: Thanks to Decker Butzner and Burgin Jacobs for letting me see the Sabilla Bodine compilation.

30 "Greetings to you": Burns, 2:1.

30 "endless store": Interview, Jim Jacobs.

30 "intellectually very curious": Wachtel, p. 42.

31 resign from Daughters of the American Revolution: Interview, Jane Henderson.

31 artificial logs: JJ to her mother, December 30, 1974, Burns, 4.

31 "the night supervising nurse": *Matter*, p. 11.

31 "how limited their lives were": Wachtel, p. 44.

31 hadn't "come to grips": JJ to Jason Epstein, January 8, 1975, Random House Papers, ColumbiaRare.

31 "quite prissy": Wachtel, p. 44.

31 "to this day astonishes me": JJ to John S. Zinsser, December 22, 1950, Burns, 22:9.

31 *Don't sing that*: Interview, Jim Jacobs.

31 minefield of small-town narrow-mindeness: Interview, Jim Jacobs.

32 "I had to shut up": Wachtel, p. 44.

32 "the Patch": Chavez, Duer, and Fang, p. 10.

32 She traded cards . . . played pirates: Warren, p. 10.

33 secrete treasures: *D&L*, p. 112.

33 Chatauqua: JJ to Susan Wynn, September 18, 1997, Burns, 1:6.

33 his favorite shirt: Decker Butzner's remarks in "Memorial Ceremony and Portrait Unveiling in Honor of Honorable John D. Butzner, Jr.," *West's Federal Reporter*, vol. 464, F.3d, pp. XXXIX–XLI.

33 tree in the parlor: Interviews, Jim Jacobs, Decker Butzner, Kay Butzner.

33 "Bite off more": Mary Robison Fawcett to JJ, 1996, Burns, 44:2.

33 "I am pleased to see": *Matter*, p. 170.

34 "I've known a lot of bootleggers": Interview, Decker Butzner.

34 "relentless prohibitionist": *Alaska*, p. 10.

35 "Being in a family": *Matter*, p. 13.

35 "an island of hope": Wachtel, p. 45.

35 "could do anything": *Matter*, p. 11. Jane's sister, Betty, on the other hand, at least once did feel stymied. She wanted to become an architect, but Dr. Butzner discouraged her, seeing the field as inappropriate for a woman. "She thought it was ridiculous," Betty's daughter Carol Bier reports. But Betty yielded, turning instead to interior design.

CHAPTER 2: OUTLAW

36 "In those days": Wachtel, p. 46.

36 "misapprehension": Wachtel, p. 46.

36 downright jealous: *Matter*, p. 150.

37 "didn't listen much": *Matter*, p. 11.

37 book hidden beneath her desk: *Matter*, p. 15.

37 "rather stupid": Wachtel, p. 46.

37 managed to get herself expelled: Lucia Jacobs, taped interview of JJ, 1992, courtesy of Prof. Jacobs; Wachtel, p. 46; *Matter*, p. 16.

38 "I'm a busy man": Interview, Kay Butzner.

38 rubber boots: Interview, Jim Jacobs.

38 "Which two pages?": Harvey, p. 36.

39 "She was always afraid of teachers": Interview, Jim Jacobs.

39 "the little girls who do best": *Ethics*, p. 9.

39 "what they're *supposed to do*": Books and Authors Luncheon, March 10, 1962, audio, New York City Municipal Archives, wnyc_LT9522.

40 "I was an outlaw": Lucia Jacobs, taped interview of JJ, 1992.

40 "we went downtown to school": Penny Fox, "Suburbs Do Not Suit Citified Author," 1961, Burns.

40 all of Scranton: Local history, including Anthracite's role, drawn from "Scranton" in Writers' Program, *Pennsylvania: A Guide to the Keystone State* (New York: Oxford University Press, 1940), pp. 322–29; David Crosby, *Scranton Then and Now* (Charleston, S.C.: Arcadia Publishing, 2011); Benson W. Rohrbeck, *Scranton's Trolleys* (Ben Rohrbeck Traction Publications, 1999); Fred J. Lauver, "A Walk Through the Rise and Fall of Anthracite Might," *Pennsylvania Heritage Magazine* (winter 2001); "History of the Green Ridge Presbyterian Church" and "50th Anniversary of the Present Church Building, 1893–1943, Green Ridge Presbyterian Church," both reviewed at Lackawanna Historical Society, Scranton.

41 "the greatest man in the world": Wachtel, p. 45.

42 "meant much to me as a child": *EofC*, p. 160.

42 "There was some mixup": *Impressions* (December 1931): 22.

42 forever late to class: Grade book, 1929–30, Scranton Central High School, records furnished by Donna Zaleski. Jane may have been getting mixed messages at home. "Early risers," Mr. Butzner liked to say, according to Jim Jacobs, "are conceited all morning and sleepy all afternoon."

42 "To Rupert Brooke": *Impressions* (December 1931): 18.

43 "a melodious laugh": Carl Marzani, *The Education of a Reluctant Radical, Book 2—Growing Up American* (New York: Topical Books, 1993), pp. 78–79.

43 "Of a Friend, Dead": "Sonnet," *Impressions* (May 1932): 19.

44 Auslander: Jane Butzner, "Joseph Auslander," *Impressions* (December 1932): 14.

44 Carl Marzani: "Leftists in the Wilderness," *U.S. News & World Report*, March 19, 1990, pp. 26–27.

45 "on the tall side": Carl Marzani, *The Education of a Reluctant Radical, Book 2—Growing Up American* (New York: Topical Books, 1993), p. 77.

45 the honor roll: *Impressions* (June 1933).

45 "getting Jane through high school": Interviews, Jim Jacobs, Kay Butzner.

46 Jane's classmates included: Booklet, 50th Scranton High School reunion, May 14, 1983, with short biographical sketches of attendees, Burns, 38:5.

46 "The moon": "To a Teacher," *Impressions*, ca. 1932.

46 "I'm not all that different": JJ to Stewart Brand, January 31, 1994, Burns.

CHAPTER 3: LADIES' NEST OF OWLS AND OTHER MILESTONES
IN THE EDUCATION OF MISS JANE BUTZNER

48 "rows of pinched faces": *Dark*, p. 52.
48 Powell doesn't figure much: Margery W. Davies, *Woman's Place Is at the Type-writer* (Philadelphia: Temple University Press, 1982); "Early Office Museum" website; Powell School of Business ads from the period; John Robert Gregg, *Gregg Shorthand* (New York: Gregg Publishing Company, ca. 1930), and other Gregg-related materials; interviews, Jim Jacobs, Esther Keisling.
50 high school diploma: Burns, FF1D17.
51 "Her ambition": Nellie B. Sergent, *Younger Poets: An Anthology of American Secondary School Verse* (New York: D. Appleton, 1932), p. 377.
51 gobbled up: *The Scranton Times* bought the *Republican* in February 1934, while Jane was still working there.
51 "doing routine items": *Matter*, p. 3.
52 "It was preposterous": Interview, Katia Jacobs.
53 "work for you for nothing": JJ interview with Peter Gzowski, Ideas That Matter conference, 1997, videotape, Toronto Reference Library, no. 2345212.
53 $18 a week: StL, Application for Federal Employment, November 27, 1943, and September 8, 1949; in email to author, March 18, 2013, Ned Jacobs sheds light on Jane's arrangement with the paper.
53 "nobody objected": *Dark*, p. 53.
53 "be my mentor": JJ interview with Peter Gzowski, Ideas That Matter conference, 1997, videotape, Toronto Reference Library, no. 2345212. The mentor may have been an editor named Gordon Williams. See "Bess Butzner, Ex-Teacher-Nurse, Celebrates 90th Birthday Saturday," *Scrantonian*, June 15, 1969.
53 "my 'journalism school'": JJ to Hakim Hasan, February 28, 2001, Burns, 3:6. See also *Matter*, p. 189.
53 see her father: Wachtel, p. 42.
53 Medical Arts Building: Architectural plans of the office, and access to the premises, graciously provided by Lou Danzico, president, Management Enterprises, Scranton.
54 mostly of English stock: *CityWealth*, p. 125.
54 "snapping of a pitchfork": *CityWealth*, p. 126.
55 "different and interesting kind of life": *Matter*, p. 3; Wachtel, p. 42.
55 *Well, now, Jane*: Interview, Jane Henderson.
55 noted Jane's coming: Ann Butzner papers.
55 The news squib didn't need: *CityWealth*, chapter 9, pp. 124–34; *Dark*, p. 168; Denny Moore, "Sunshine Spread Between States," *Presbyterian Advance*, September 15, 1932; "History of Markle School at Higgins," *Asheville Citizen*, July 26, 1936; correspondence bearing on Higgins and Martha Robison, Markle Papers, RG 3, Series 5, Box 4, Folder 28, Rockefeller; see also partly illegible account about Martha Robison, probably September 1936, Burns; Gerald W. Gillette to J. I. Butzner, June 11, 1965, Burns, 12:10; "Miss Martha Robison Dies," *Morning Press* (Bloomsburg), November 24, 1941; my account profits from a visit to the Higgins site, and from correspondence and interview with Annie Butzner, and from her papers; see also notes to chapter 1, on the Robisons.

56 "wet, murky": "Miss Robison Tells of Work in North Carolina Mountains," no publication, no date, but from internal evidence about 1928, Burns.

56 part of a still: Interview, Kay Butzner.

56 "overwhelming conviction": "Miss Robison Tells of Work in North Carolina Mountains," no publication, no date, but from internal evidence about 1928, Burns.

56 received a letter: Chronology established in Florence E. Quick [John Markle's assistant] to A. S. Woods, July 29, 1930, Markle Papers, RG 3, Series 5, Box 4, Folder 28, Rockefeller. Markle was an uncle by marriage to Jane's mother.

57 "never dared think": Martha E. Robison to Cousin John (Markle), November 14, 1929, Markle Papers, RG 3, Series 5, Box 4, Folder 28, Rockefeller.

57 promised to give $25,000: John Markle to Martha E. Robison, January 14, 1930, Markle Papers, RG 3, Series 5, Box 4, Folder 28, Rockefeller.

57 "The spaces are all ample": C. T. Greenway to John Markle, May 9, 1931, Markle Papers, RG 3, Series 5, Box 4, Folder 28, Rockefeller.

57 Film footage: Untitled Board of National Missions film, twelve minutes. Thanks to Diana Ruby Sanderson, Warren Wilson College.

57 tightly tufted straw: Thanks to Annie Butzner for letting me see one of those brooms.

57 On July 3, 1934: Martha E. Robison to Florence E. Quick, July 4, 1934, Markle Papers, RG 3, Series 5, Box 4, Folder 28, Rockefeller.

58 Jane's sister, Betty: Ann Butzner papers.

58 "Girls' club work": Ann Butzner papers.

58 "the largest gathering": Ann Butzner papers.

58 "We may mourn": *CityWealth*, p. 129.

59 never to have seen Higgins again: Interview, Jim Jacobs.

59 "majestic folded hills": *CityWealth*, p. 125.

59 "make do with firelight": *CityWealth*, p. 127.

59 "the thrilling story": Denny Moore, "Sunshine Spread Between States," *Presbyterian Advance*, September 15, 1932.

59 "bright and full of curiosity": *CityWealth*, p. 128.

CHAPTER 4: THE GREAT BEWILDERING WORLD

61 "came to seek my fortune": *D&L*, dedication.

62 Pennsylvania Museum and School: See the school's *Circular of the Art Department*, beginning in 1931–32, for curricula and some of Betty's awards; interviews and correspondence with Betty's daughter, Carol Bier.

62 cheap rooming house: Kunstler, I, p. 3.

62 Orange Street: JJ to Myrna Katz Frommer and Harvey Frommer, June 26, 2000, Burns. The building itself is gone but maps at the Brooklyn Historical Society give some sense of the street.

62 Brooklyn Heights: Whyte, *The WPA Guide*, pp. 441–47.

62 bounced between jobs: See JJ's federal employment records, StL; interview, Jim Jacobs.

63 Robert H. Hemphill: StL, Application for Federal Appointment, September 8, 1949, Attachment F; Hemphill obituary, *New York Times*, April 24, 1941. Later

in the 1930s, Hemphill wrote for *Social Justice,* Father Coughlin's extreme right-wing publication. The Dwight B. Waldo Library at Western Michigan University has a small cache of Hemphill materials, including a "pencil sketch done by a neighbor on yellow copy paper at 55 Morton St., New York City, NY, about 1937–38"; Betty seems a better guess for the artist than Jane.

63 helped a broker: Request for Investigation Data, April 10, 1948, StL.

63 sought work at the Markle Foundation: Florence E. Quick to Martha Robison, April 1, 1935, Markle Papers, RG 3, Series 5, Box 4, Folders 28 and 29, Rockefeller: "I am sorry I was not able to be of any assistance to your niece and hope she was successful in locating a position here in New York." In her reply (Martha E. Robison to Florence E. Quick, April 12, 1935), Martha expresses uncertainty as to whether it was Jane or Betty who approached Markle. But Betty already had the job at A&S—and kept it (correspondence with Carol Bier) for a couple of years. This, and Jane's early employment history generally, argue persuasively for Jane.

63 "all the exotic places": Noah Richler, "Wealth in Diversity," *Weekend Books,* March 18, 2000.

63 turned to gambling: JJ, "Futility vs. Taking Chances," lecture manuscript, no date, no place, Burns, 13.

63 apartment cleaned: Interview, Burgin Jacobs.

63 Pablum: Kunstler, I, 4. Jane adds, "I don't want to give you the impression that we lived for long periods like this. Maybe toward the end of the week."

64 "catchabeano": See video, *Think Again: Jane Jacobs on Urban Living,* TVO, Ontario Public Television, 1997.

64 "taught you how to read": Interview, Jim Jacobs.

64 "rejections and frugalities": *Dark,* p. 53.

64 110 words per minute: Application for Federal Employment, November 27, 1943, item 42, StL.

65 "didn't know where I was": Alexander and Weadick.

65 a man stepped from: Amateau, "Jane Jacobs, Urban Legend, Returns Downtown." For fur district, see also *The WPA Guide,* p. 163.

65 "know everyone else": Jane Butzner, "Where the Fur Flies," p. 103.

66 "damp, sweet perfume": *Matter,* p. 35. See also Alexander and Weadick.

66 thirteen months: *Matter,* pp. 36–37. The original manuscript can be found at Burns, 13:1.

68 "sound of the name": Kunstler, I, 3.

68 Sheridan Square: Whyte, *The WPA Guide,* pp. 140–42.

69 Jones Street: Ware, p. 44.

69 "liked the little streets": Alexander and Weadick.

69 a small elevator: JJ to Myrna Katz Frommer and Harvey Frommer, July 12, 2000, Burns.

69 $50 a month: 1940 U.S. Census, which also tells us something of Jane's neighbors.

70 "lived there quite a while": Alexander and Weadick.

70 "Did you hang out?": Kunstler, I, p. 4.

70 "'long-haired men'": Ware, p. 3.

71 "Messages": *D&L,* p. 175.

71 "complicated great place": *Matter,* p. 15.

71 Scharf Brothers: Application for Federal Appointment, November 27, 1943, StL.

71 She wrote to: Interview, Burgin Jacobs.

72 father sat her down: *Dark*, p. 54. Jane remembered her father's break-even point as $48 per day, but figures on typical physicians' expenses from the period point to $48 per week as the more likely figure.

72 "a mess in there": Interview, Jim Jacobs.

72 "Miss Eldridge": Joe Polakoff, "About a Man's Man," *Scranton Tribune*, 1937.

72 "dented by four little windows": "Dr. J. D. Butzner Dies in Hospital," *Scranton Tribune*, December 23, 1937.

72 admitted to probate: Lackawanna County, PA, Register of Wills, January 6, 1938.

72 Peter A. Frasse: Application for Federal Appointment, September 8, 1949, Attachment F, StL; records of Peter A. Frasse & Co., 1818–1977, at the New-York Historical Society, make no reference to Jane Butzner.

72 *curls of steel*: Interview, Jim Jacobs.

73 "do the work of three girls": FBI, Jane Butzner Jacobs, File No. 123–252, July 20, 1948, p. 6.

73 "'trouble shooting' secretary": Application for Federal Appointment, September 8, 1949, Attachment F, StL. "Junior Efficiency Engineer" is my conceit, not her title.

CHAPTER 5: MORNINGSIDE HEIGHTS

74 if not a writer: M. Ondaatje to Jane Jacobs, September 26, 1994, and undated reply, Burns, 6:5.

74 geology course: Information on this and others of Jane's courses at Columbia comes from *Bulletin of University Extension*, 1938–1939.

75 "clay dogs": *D&L*, p. 582.

75 Jane Butzner, grade transcript, Columbia University School of General Studies.

75 New York University: "Information Required to Complete Application," response to question, "Have you taken any courses in English or journalism?," January 5, 1950, StL.

76 lab notebook: It was called *Laboratory Directions in Elementary Vertebrate Zoology*. Furnished by Jim Jacobs.

76 one version of a story: The story, in similar form, related by three family members.

76 Neil T. Dowling: Group of articles about Dowling in *Columbia Law Review* 58, no. 5 (May 1958): 589–612, by Herbert Wechsler, Stanley Reed, William T. Bossett, Thomas I. Parkinson, Frederic P. Lee; Louis Luskey, "In Memoriam Noel T. Dowling," *Columbia Law Review* 69, no. 3 (March 1969): 351–52. See also *Columbia University Bulletin of Information*, 1938–1939, for information on Jane's law courses.

77 a single house: *Chaff*, p. 5.

77 "the second to check": *Chaff*, p. 7.

77 "danger to the public interest": *Chaff*, p. 57.

77 "a faithless thing": *Chaff*, p. 1.

79 "best possible reason": *Chaff*, preface.

79 "affected air of wisdom": *Chaff*, p. 160.

79 "a well done job": Noel T. Dowling to Charles G. Proffitt, June 3, 1940, Columbia University Press Papers, ColumbiaRare.

79 "of any source": Henry H. Wiggins to Jane Butzner, July 15, 1940, Columbia University Press Papers, ColumbiaRare.

79 "some difficulty": H.H.W., Memo for the File, July 24, 1940, Columbia University Press Papers, ColumbiaRare.

79 life insurance settlement: Interview, Jim Jacobs, who also suggests Jane may have received some help from Hemphill, who was romantically involved with Betty at this time. In Jane's preface to *Chaff*, she acknowledges "the enthusiasm and wisdom of Robert H. Hemphill."

80 Mrs. Butzner sent her a check: JJ to her mother, penciled onto bottom of Jane Butzner to R. F. Price, Dorrance & Co., January 18, 1939, Columbia University Press Papers, ColumbiaRare.

80 "I am delighted": Jane Butzner to Charles G. Proffitt, January 2, 1941, Columbia University Press Papers, ColumbiaRare.

80 "composing their own divergences": *Chaff*, p. 1.

80 "helpful counsel": Note of thanks on typescript of *Chaff* given to John Butzner, courtesy Decker Butzner.

81 boat trip up the Atlantic coast: *Ethics*, p. 229.

81 "thought it was so cute": Kunstler, II, p. 9.

82 "A Woman Blazes a Trail": Jane Butzner to Fleming H. Revell Co., December 7, 1939, Burns, 17.

82 "threw together a manuscript": *Alaska*, p. xiv.

82 "some admirers who liked it": *Alaska*, p. xv. The story of Hannah Breece and her Alaska manuscript is taken up again in chapter 23.

82 "moves along too slowly": Elizabeth M. Morrow to Jane Butzner, April 16, 1940, Burns, 17.

82 "lacked sufficient craftsmanship": *Alaska*, p. xv.

82 "loved geology and zoology": *Matter*, p. 3.

82 "was almost my undoing": *Matter*, p. 3.

82 "the Dragon Lady": Account drawn from Harvey, p. 37, and video interview of JJ by Lucy Jacobs, 1992.

83 "I could spell molybdenum": *Matter*, p. 12.

83 $25 a week: Application for Federal Employment, September 8, 1949, Attachment E, StL.

83 train to Philadelphia: Application for Federal Employment, October 26, 1946, StL.

83 "lunchtime in Wall Street": Kunstler, I, p. 2.

84 processing servicemen: For New York City during the war, see Diehl; Jackson, *WWII & NYC*; exhibition of the same name, at New-York Historical Society, 2012, provided further details.

84 "Everyone knew it was ghoulish": *Dark*, p. 55.

CHAPTER 6: WOMEN'S WORK

85 in late 1942: Application for Federal Employment, September 8, 1949, Attachment E, StL. "Shortly before I had completed two years" at *Iron Age*, she was promoted, which would make it about late 1942.

86 "All the common non-ferrous metals": J. I. Butzner, "Non-Ferrous Metals," *Iron Age*, January 7, 1943.

86 course in physical metallurgy: The certificate is dated May 20, 1943. The course comprised sixty-three class hours and was conducted through Columbia University, Burns, 23:3.

87 substantial autonomy: Application for Federal Employment, September 8, 1949, Attachment E, StL.

87 helping out her hometown: The Scranton story is nicely told in Lang and Wunsch, pp. 31–33. See also Jane Butzner, "Daily's Effort Saves City from 'Ghost Town' Fate," *Editor & Publisher* (1943); "30,000 Unemployed and 7,000 Empty Houses in Scranton, Neglected City," *Iron Age*, March 25, 1943.

87 boss didn't much like it: For one take, see LaurenceDiss, pp. 93–95.

88 A week before: Jane Butzner, "Trylon's Steel Helps to Build Big New Nickel Plant in Cuba," *New York Herald Tribune*, December 27, 1942.

88 women on the home front: Jane Butzner, "Women Wanted . . ." *Washington Post*, October 26, 1942.

88 *same pay*: Jane Jacobs to Carroll St. Claire, July 22, 1949, Answers to Interrogatory for Jane Butzner Jacobs, paragraph 1, Burns.

88 T. W. Lippert: See *Carnegie Alumnus*, unknown date, class notes, '32.

89 "loose and untrue": JJ to Carroll St. Claire, July 22, 1949, Answers to Interrogatory for Jane Butzner Jacobs, paragraph 1, Burns.

89 "a troublemaker and an agitator": FBI File 123–252, July 20, 1948, p. 5.

89 all but hers: Application for Federal Employment, November 27, 1943, StL; Certificate of Medical Examination, November 26, 1943, StL.

89 Office of War Information: See Winkler; Application for Federal Employment, September 8, 1949, Attachment D, StL; interview, Jim Jacobs.

90 "with unmistakable American sincerity": Winkler, p. 76.

90 "the strategy of truth": Winkler, p. 13.

91 "necessary for me": Application for Federal Employment, September 8, 1949, Attachment D, StL.

91 "rapid promotion": "Justification for 'Rapid Promotion,'" prepared by Frederick Silber, October 3, 1944, StL.

92 "a very brilliant": LaurenceDiss, p. 74.

92 dragooned into service: *Matter*, p. 44.

92 "a new permanent wave": JJ to her mother, penciled onto bottom of JJ to R. F. Price, Dorrance & Co., January 18, 1939, Columbia University Press Papers, ColumbiaRare.

92 "the children here gawk": JJ to her family, January 21, 1967, Burns, 4:7.

93 "a handsome, impressive woman": Interview, John Jacobs.

93 Grumman Aircraft: See Diehl, pp. 172–74.

94 "I walked in the door": *Matter*, p. 12.

CHAPTER 7: AMERIKA

95 Robert Hyde Jacobs Jr.: Interviews with Bob's children, his cousin John, and his wife, Katia, and other family and friends; informal timeline by his granddaughter Caitlin, Burns, 22; biographical listings including *American Architects Journal*, 2nd edition, 1962; obituary, *Villager*, September 25, 1996; Robert Fulford, "Lives Lived": Robert Hyde Jacobs," *Globe and Mail*, September 24, 1996;

Sid Adilman, "Robert H. Jacobs, 79, Hospital Architect," *Toronto Star,* September 19, 1996.

95 Sutton Hotel: Harvey, p. 36.

96 a hose clamp: Interview, Jim Jacobs.

96 "known her sister": Interview, Jim Jacobs.

96 The small wedding: *Matter,* pp. 42–43.

96 announces the marriage: Burns, 38:4.

97 "conventionally not good-looking": Telephone interview, Katia Jacobs.

97 "easy intimacy": Robert Fulford, "Lives Lived": Robert Hyde Jacobs," *Globe and Mail,* September 24, 1996.

97 weakness for alliteration: Interview, Jim Jacobs.

97 design, descriptive geometry: Columbia University School of Architecture, program description, 1930s.

97 urine-release gizmo: Interview, Jim Jacobs.

97 "We run the risk": Robert Hyde Jacobs Jr., p. 107.

98 "playing second fiddle": See also Sid Adilman, "Robert H. Jacobs, 79, Hospital Architect," *Toronto Star,* September 19, 1996": "He preferred to be in the background, especially where his wife's writings and fame were concerned. 'I know that my wife is more eminent than I am,' he told a friend this summer. 'I'm proud of that and I am so proud of her.'"

98 "Without warning": Pete Hamill, *A Drinking Life: A Memoir* (Boston: Little, Brown, 1994), p. 50.

98 "They were so fast": Harvey, p. 37.

99 no one at the OWI: Interview, Jim Jacobs.

99 another party: This account drawn from *Matter,* p. 45.

101 Jane became a freelancer: In Jane's Application for Federal Employment, September 8, 1949, Attachment C, StL, she recounts her freelance period.

101 "damp, dimly lighted": Eric A. Feldt, *The Coast Watchers* (New York: Ballantine Books, 1959), p. 7. Originally published by Oxford University Press, 1946.

102 "Christmas cookies": *Matter,* p. 38.

102 "chicken-wire crab traps": Jane Jacobs, "Island the Boats Pass By," *Harper's Bazaar* (July 1947): 79.

102 $88 a week: Application for Federal Employment, September 8, 1949, Attachment A, StL.

102 *Amerika:* Account drawn from visual review of Russian-language issues from period Jane worked at the magazine; select translations from the Russian by Anne-Marie Corley; correspondence and other documents, CollPark, mostly RG 9 P 316, Boxes 3 and 4; Application for Federal Employment, September 8, 1949, Attachment A, StL; Elise Crane, "The Full-Format American Dream: *Amerika* as a Key Tool of Cold War Public Diplomacy," *American Diplomacy* (January 2010); Creighton Peet, "Russian 'Amerika,' a Magazine About U.S. for Soviet Citizens," *College Art Journal* (Autumn, 1951): 17–21; Andrew L. Yarrow, "Selling a Vision of American to the World: Changing Messages in Early U.S. Cold War Print Propaganda," *Journal of Cold War Studies* (fall 2009): 3–45.

103 "a particularly fine job": Joseph O. Hanson Jr. to Marion Sanders, March 12, 1948, RG 59, P 316 Box 3, CollPark.

103 "translation problems": Marion K. Sanders to George A. Morgan, December 3, 1948, RG 59, P 316, Box 3, CollPark.

103 "juke box": Peet, p. 19.

103 "hell-for-leather New Yorker": Telephone interview, John Jacobs.

104 "life history" of a single article: Marion K. Sanders to Melville J. Ruggles, June 27, 1947, RG 59, P 316, Box 3, CollPark.

104 "Reader comments": Memo, "Reader Reaction—Regarding the Problem of Credibility," March 11, 1949, RG 59, P 316, Box 2, CollPark.

104 "create the precise impression": Application for Federal Employment, September 8, 1949, Attachment A, p. 2, StL.

104 "Why don't you come": Telephone interview, John Jacobs.

105 three-quarters of her time: Application for Federal Employment, September 8, 1949, Attachment A, p. 6, StL.

106 those the FBI interviewed: Account drawn from 258-page file on Jane Butzner Jacobs obtained through Freedom of Information Act request, June 2014. Subsequent specific citations normally given by file no., field office, and date.

106 "sugar daddy": FBI file no. 123–252, New York, September 8, 1948. The "Mr. Roberts" cited in the report, according to Jim Jacobs, is Robert Hemphill. See also FBI File no. 123–245, Cincinnati, September 13, 1948, for reference to Hemphill.

106 half naked: FBI File no. 123–252, New York, September 8, 1948.

106 "he had no reason": FBI File no. 123–252, New York, September 8, 1948.

106 a three-page reply: JJ to Carroll St. Claire, July 22, 1949, with attached "Answers to Interrogatory for Jane Butzner Jacobs," Burns, 5:4.

107 "lying little magazine": V. Kusakov, "American 'Horizons,'" *Izvestia*, September 16, 1949, with appended "Analysis of Criticism," by R. S. Collins, in memorandum, American Embassy, September 27, 1949, RG 59, P 316, Box 3, CollPark.

CHAPTER 8: *Trushchoby*

108 "an ugly flat, steel box": V. Kusakov, "American 'Horizons,'" *Izvestia*, September 16, 1949, with appended "Analysis of Criticism," by R. S. Collins, in memorandum, American Embassy, September 27, 1949, RG 59, P 316, Box 3, CollPark.

109 "'slums' means one thing to Americans": R. S. Collins, in memorandum, American Embassy, September 27, 1949, RG 59, P 316, Box 3, CollPark.

110 "flattering": M. Gordon Knox to Marion Sanders, September 30, 1949, RG 59, P 316, Box 3, CollPark.

110 "made us cringe": To Gordon Knox from unidentified *Amerika* staffer, perhaps John Jacobs, October 12, 1949, RG 59, P 316, Box 3, CollPark.

110 "by cubic meter": M. Gordon Knox to Marion Sanders, September 30, 1949, RG 59, P 316, Box 3, CollPark.

110 "courageous, careful": Gordon Knox to John Jacobs, February 11, 1950, no. 53., RG 59, P 316, Box 3, CollPark. Knox's comment actually appears as part of a letter under the signature of Ralph Collins who, on p. 2, writes, "Gordon drafted the present letter up to this point."

110 "'trushchoby' on every page": Gordon Knox to Marion Sanders, March 13, 1960, no. 56, RG 59, P 316, Box 3, CollPark.

111 "Planned Rebuilding": I am indebted to Anne-Marie Corley for her translation of this article and the illustration captions accompanying it.

113 settling down: About Bessie's move to Fredericksburg (probably in early 1948)

and that she let out rooms for students at Mary Washington College is drawn from "Results of Investigation," June 7, 1948, Richmond, VA, Jane Butzner Jacobs, FBI. Other details drawn from interviews with numerous family members.

113 three-story house: 555 Hudson Street has, of course, emerged as legendary. This account is built up from interviews with family members and other visitors to the house; the Canada Dry detail owes to *Matter*, pp. 64–65; Jane's recollection of the big rats is from *Matter*, p. 213.

115 assess Jane's case: Conrad E. Snow to James E. Hatcher, September 19, 1951, FBI.

115 "a degree of immorality": December 10, 1951, Ba. 123–1256, FBI.

115 eight-thousand-word missive: *Matter*, pp. 169–79.

120 "no option but to agree": John Butzner to JJ, January 4, 1998, Burns, 20.

121 "a safe conclusion": M. Gordon Knox to Marion Sanders, April 4, 1950, RG 59, P 315, Box 3, CollPark.

121 soul searching over its mission: For example, Tobe Brunner to Marion Sanders and John Jacobs, January 30, 1952, RG 59, P 316, Box 1, CollPark.

121 "prior to decision on loyalty": Hiram Bingham to J. Edgar Hoover, June 20, 1952, 123–393, FBI.

121 drawn to two magazines: *Matter*, p. 4.

122 "They asked me": JJ to Roberta Brandes Gratz, March 20, 1979, Gratz papers.

122 taught her to read blueprints: *Matter*, p. 4. See also Lucile Preuss, quoting JJ, *Sunday Milwaukee Journal*, July 8, 1962: "I'd work days. Nights, after the children were in bed, my husband gave me lessons in reading plans so I'd know enough to do the stories."

123 "its planted entrance court": "Big Double Hospital," *Architectural Forum* (June 1952): 138–45. (In this same issue, *Forum* welcomed Lever House, a modernist icon: "From across Park Avenue, Lever House is a horizontal streak of stainless steel and green glass suspended on rows of tall columns, whose metal skins have a cool wavering sheen.")

123 "speeds things up": "Self-Selection," *Architectural Forum* (November 1953): 156–68. When the story came out, *American Druggist* sent someone out to interview her, Burns, 4:1.

123 "wondrous complexity": Robert Fulford, "Lives Lived: Robert Hyde Jacobs," *Globe and Mail*, September 24, 1996.

124 "Every way you turn": Memo, Douglas Haskell to Perry Prentice, August 25, 1953, HaskellPap, 38:11.

125 "I heartily dislike": Memo, JJ to Douglas Haskell, October 4, 1955, HaskellPap, 14:6.

125 "a spectacularly bad example": Memo, JJ to Douglas Haskell, April 27, 1954, HaskellPap, 6:4.

126 *hadn't* been doing a good job: Jane says as much in JJ to Grady Clay, March 1959, LaurenceDiss, p. 195.

CHAPTER 9: DISENCHANTMENT

129 Edmund Bacon: See, for example, Klemek, "Bacon's Rebellion"; Izzy Kornblatt, "Planning Philadelphia," review of Gregory L. Heller, *Ed Bacon: Planning, Poli-*

tics, and the Building of Modern Philadelphia, Swarthmore Phoenix, January 20, 2014; Amateau, "Jane Jacobs, Urban Legend"; Inga Saffron, "An Appreciation: Flaws and All, Edmund N. Bacon Molded a Modern Philadelphia," *Philadelphia Inquirer,* October 16, 2005; James Reichley, "Philadelphia Does It: The Battle for Penn Center," *Harper's* (February 1957), in HaskellPap, 36:10.

130 "Arrogant, arch": Interview, Alan Littlewood.

130 or even, just possibly, *whether*: The possibility that Jane did not see the Philadelphia projects before she wrote about them for *Forum* draws support from three sources: First, an editor's note to a June 24, 1962, article about Jane in the *Philadelphia Sunday Bulletin Magazine* quotes her: "My initial skepticism that urban renewal was on the right track occurred as a result of comparing the city planning department's sketches and verbal rationalizations of things-to-be for Philadelphia with the results." Second, the excerpt of the letter to Grady Clay quoted at the end of the previous chapter (March 1959, LaurenceDiss, p. 195) is preceded by: "Then I began to see some of these things built." Finally, in their summary of a 1962 panel discussion at the Museum of Modern Art in New York, Frigand and Lapham summarize JJ's comments as follows: "Bacon showed her sketches of their concepts and projects, and she wrote the articles praising their work. When she visited the completed projects later on she felt that she had been tricked—that what looked nice on paper was horrible in reality."

130 "awful endless blocks": Jane Jacobs, "Philadelphia's Redevelopment," *Architectural Forum* (July 1955).

130 she joined Bacon: Account distilled from some of Jane's many tellings of the incident, including: Saunders; Dillon, p. 41; Wachtel, pp. 47–48; Alexander and Weadick, p. 15; *Matter,* p. 126; Frigand and Lapham; Books and Authors Luncheon, March 19, 1962.

131 visiting sister Betty: *Philadelphia Sunday Bulletin Magazine,* editor's note to article about Jane, June 24, 1962.

131 "found out what they had in mind": Books and Authors Luncheon.

132 "looked so seductive": *Matter,* p. 126.

132 slices of Americana: See correspondence with John S. Zinsser Jr., Burns, 22:9.

132 science fiction: Burns, 22:10.

133 "the terrific acceleration": Doug Haskell to colleagues, February 4, 1955, HaskellPap, 58:3.

133 "hard for an outsider": "Cleveland: City with a Deadline," *Architectural Forum* (August 1955), unbylined.

134 "Parentheses" column: William McQuade, "Get a Bike!," *Architectural Forum* (April 1956).

135 "hitch-hiking with the fish": "Hitch-Hiking with the Fish," typescript, with appended note dating it to 1954, Burns, 22:8.

135 sit on the rear rack: Ned Jacobs, Jane's Walk description, "Cycle Cambie Corridor-Vancouver," May 2, 2010, online tour description, for Jane's Walk 2010; Ned Jacobs to author, October 19, 2013.

135 $10,000: Memo, Chadbourne Gilpatric, June 4, 1958, Rockefeller: "Her present salary on the staff of Forum is $13,750." But that was two years after the events of April 1956 that, as we'll see in chapter 10, dramatically elevated Jane's profile. In Joe Hazen to R. D. Paine Jr., February 24, 1961, HaskellPap, 2:1, we learn that a *Forum* secretary averaged a little under $6,000 a year, a researcher about $8,300, a writer about $11,750.

135 Glennie Lenear: Interviews, Jim Jacobs, Carol Bier, Jane Henderson, Burgin Jacobs. *D&L* included Lenear in the acknowledgments.

136 "no more romantic": *Matter*, p. 52.

137 "almost with disbelief": Flint, p. 65.

137 transformed their home from a slum: *Matter*, p. 65; see also Lucie Preuss, Sunday *Milwaukee Journal*, July 8, 1962: "The back yard had been a dump and Bob had to reinforce the foundation . . . We did a lot of the work ourselves. We did it as we could afford it. That's different from urban renewal, which is done all at once."

137 William Kirk: Interviews, Judy Kirk Fitzsimmons, Eugene Sklar, David Gurin; "Metro North: Death of a Slum," WNBC-TV broadcast, February 25, 1967, viewed at Paley Center for Media, New York City; obituary, *New York Times*, October 24, 2001; Union Settlement Papers, ColumbiaRare.

138 great swaths of tenements: For a taste, visit the Tenement Museum on New York's Lower East Side.

139 As recently as 1939: Gerald Meyer, "Italian Harlem: America's Largest and Most Italian Little Italy," http://www.vitomarcantonio.com.

139 No bank: Lurie, "Community Action in East Harlem," p. 247.

139 a fifth of East Harlem: See *Projects*, part IV.

139 Phil Will: Obituary, *Chicago Tribune*, October 24, 1979; R. Randall Vosbeck, *A Legacy of Leadership: The Presidents of the American Institute of Architects* (Washington, D.C.: American Institute of Architects, 2008), pp. 98–100. In 1961, Rev. William Kirk conducted the marriage of Will's daughter Elizabeth.

140 approach Doug Haskell: Kirk to Haskell, November 19, 1954, HaskellPap. See also William Kirk to Chadbourne Gilpatric, August 11, 1959, RF 1.2, 200 R, Box 390, Folder 3381, Rockefeller.

140 wrote Haskell again: Kirk to Haskell, March 17, 1955, HaskellPap.

140 hauling out maps: Books and Authors Luncheon, from which much about Jane and her experience with Bill Kirk is distilled, and probably the most vivid and complete of the several accounts Jane offered over the years. See also Alexander and Weadick, p. 15.

140 Kirk's turf: See Gerald Meyer, "Italian Harlem: America's Largest and Most Italian Little Italy," http://www.vitomarcantonio.com; Lurie, "Community Action in East Harlem"; *The WPA Guide*, pp. 265–70; New York City Housing Authority photos from the period, La Guardia and Wagner Archives.

141 "can't imagine how he took the time": Books and Authors Luncheon.

141 "We would stop every little while": Books and Authors Luncheon.

141 see what he was getting at: JJ to Chadbourne Gilpatric, July 1, 1958, Rockefeller.

141 "a big basket of dry leaves": Books and Authors Luncheon.

142 "when the bird's eye blows": Edwin J. Slipek Jr., "An Urban Planning Expert Shares Her View of Richmond," *Style Weekly* (Richmond, VA), January 1, 1980.

142 "delighted to live in the city": Kunstler, II, 14.

142 Jane liked Kirk: "He wasn't just a one-trick pony of East Harlem," says Jim Jacobs.

142 "He was showing me": Lucile Preuss, Sunday *Milwaukee Journal*, July 8, 1962.

143 study in the works: "Fact Sheet, East Harlem Small Business Survey & Planning Committee," January 16, 1956, Union Settlement Papers, RB 35/7, ColumbiaRare. See also "Shops a Problem in East Harlem," *New York Times*, May 8, 1955.

144 "mitigate the consequences": Krieger and Saunders, p. xviii.

144 delighted to attend: Haskell to Sert, January 21, 1956, HaskellPap, 20:5.

144 "a conflict had come up": Haskell to Sert, March 19, 1956, HaskellPap, 20:5.

144 she wouldn't do it: Account drawn primarily from Kunstler, II, p. 13; Alexander and Weadick, p. 15.

145 "depending on you": Alexander and Weadick, p. 15.

CHAPTER 10: TEN MINUTES AT HARVARD

146 Harvard conference: See Krieger and Saunders.

146 "developed as a new science": Krieger and Saunders, p. 3.

148 "First my knees trembled": Alexander and Weadick, p. 16.

148 She began with East Harlem: The text of Jane's talk, from which the quotes over the next few pages are drawn, can be found in *Architectural Forum* (June 1956), as "The Missing Link in City Redevelopment"; in *Matter*, pp. 39–40; excerpted also in *Progressive Architecture* (August 1956): 102–03; and Krieger and Saunders, pp. 9–11.

148 Stuyvesant Town: See *Projects*, part II; Jane's references to it in her Harvard lecture and later in *D&L*; interview, Carol Bier.

149 from their perch: *Projects*, p. 73.

149 "tracery of iron": *Projects*, p. 85.

149 "a living neighborhood": *Projects*, p. 95.

152 "posperous belt of stores": *Matter*, p. 39.

153 "a big hit": Kunstler, II, p. 13.

153 "the foggy atmosphere": Lewis Mumford, *The Urban Prospect*, p. 185.

153 "passionate plea": Fumihiko Maki, "Fragmentation and Friction as Urban Threats: The Post-1956 City," in Krieger and Saunders, p. 88.

154 "wonderful": Victor Gruen to Douglas Haskell, April 16, 1956, HaskellPap.

154 "stewing around in me": Jane Jacobs to Catherine Bauer, April 29, 1958, in LaurenceDiss, p. 348.

155 "The last ten years": Jane Jacobs, "By 1976 What City Pattern?," *Architectural Forum* (September 1956): 103.

155 "sensible-sounding postwar catchwords": Jane Jacobs, "New York's Office Boom," *Architectural Forum* (March 1957): 106.

155 "The big rediscovery": Jane Jacobs, "Row Houses for Cities," *Architectural Forum* (May 1957): 149.

155 "not by abstract logic": Jane Jacobs, "Metropolitan Government," *Architectural Forum* (August 1957): 125.

156 a brotherly memo: Holly Whyte to Doug Haskell, January 17, 1957, HaskellPap, 78:6.

156 "I kept hearing": *Matter*, p. 16.

CHAPTER 11: A PERSON WORTH TALKING TO

157 "just the person": William H. Whyte Jr., "C. D. Jackson Meets Jane Jacobs," preface to Whyte, *The Exploding Metropolis*, p. xv.

158 "a screed of facts": Dillon, p. 41.

158 "mainly of writing captions": William H. Whyte Jr., "C. D. Jackson Meets Jane Jacobs," preface to Whyte, *The Exploding Metropolis*, p. xv.

158 They respected one another: On two occasions, for example (see below and next chapter), Whyte supported Jane's grants with the Rockefeller Foundation.

159 "a manifesto of cultural politics": Sam Bass Warner Jr., foreword to Whyte, *The Exploding Metropolis*, p. iv.

159 "huge patches": William H. Whyte Jr., "Urban Sprawl," in Whyte, *The Exploding Metropolis*, p. 133.

159 "They will be spacious": Jane Jacobs, "Downtown Is for People," in Whyte, *The Exploding Metropolis*, p. 157. In what follows, I use the page numbering of the 1993 University of California Press reprint, which differs from the 1957 edition (which is credited to "The Editors of *Fortune*").

160 "narrow, back-door alley": Jacobs, "Downtown Is for People," p. 162.

160 "*The smallness of big cities*": Jacobs, "Downtown Is for People," p. 163.

160 "This cultural superblock": Jacobs, "Downtown Is for People," p. 173.

161 "To the north": Jacobs, "Downtown Is for People," p. 173.

161 "the cheerful hurly-burly": Jacobs, "Downtown Is for People," p. 158.

161 Lincoln Square: My account largely follows *Projects*, part III.

162 "The pain brought on": *Projects*, p. 200.

162 "the logic of egocentric children": Jacobs, "Downtown Is for People," p. 158.

162 "Look what your girl did": "Comments on Downtown Is For People," Ruth Kammler, *Fortune* Letters Dept., RF, RG 1.2, Ser. 200R, Box 390, Folder 3380, Rockefeller.

163 "the first blink": Gillian Darley, "Ian Nairn and Jane Jacobs, the Lessons from Britain and America," *Journal of Architecture* 17, no. 5 (2012): 738.

163 the mainstream place: My account of *Forum* during this period derives in part from Blake, *No Place Like Utopia*; LaurenceDiss; see also David A. Crane, "Working Paper for the University of Pennsylvania Conference on Urban Design Criticism," University of Pennsylvania, Institute of Urban Studies, 1958, p. 11. Crane could be harsh: "These magazines seem to defer to a real or imaginary demand for easy entertainment: 'slick' pictures and glib captions which never intentionally show faults in a building. The level of discourse is rarely of real professional caliber; indeed it compares unfavorably with some newspaper writing on art or drama." (But, he noted, "Jane Jacobs's recent comprehensive and thoughtful treatment of urbanism in *Forum* comes as a very welcome change.")

163 "quickly to understand": *Dark*, p. 127.

163 Barcelona Pavilion: This brief survey of modernist architecture and planning has been drawn from, among others, Fishman, *Urban Utopias in the Twentieth Century*; Blake, *No Place Like Utopia*; Goldberger, *Why Architecture Matters*; the Le Corbusier exhibition at New York's Museum of Modern Art, 2013; Martin Perschler, through his course "Modernism & Postmodernism in Architecture," Johns Hopkins University, 2013; and, inevitably, *D&L* itself.

164 "What is the ideal city?": Fishman, *Urban Utopias in the Twentieth Century*, p. 3.

164 stood before a map: I saw the footage at the Le Corbusier exhibition at the Museum of Modern Art, 2013.

165 "The Garden City": Fishman, *Urban Utopias in the Twentieth Century*, part I; Miller.

165 *Charley in New Town*: Halas & Batchelor Cartoon Film Production, Central Office of Information, U.K., 1948.

167 "didn't bring them around": Kunstler, II, p. 9.

167 "shattering to those of us": Blake, *No Place Like Utopia*, p. 290.

168 party with architects: Chadbourne Gilpatric diary, February 22, 1958, RF, RG 12, Box 168, Rockefeller.

168 "flashing charm and audacity": Arthur Meier Schlesinger, *A Life in the Twentieth Century: Innocent Beginnings, 1917–1950* (Boston: Houghton Mifflin, 2000), p. 115.

169 "approach to city pattern": Douglas Haskell to Messrs. Hazen, Lessing, Grotz, November 21, 1957, HaskellPap.

169 "Jane's blockbuster": Laurence, "Jane Jacobs Before Death and Life," note 46.

169 "What Is the City?": JJ to Doug Haskell, April 25, 1958, HaskellPap.

169 "Wow!": Douglas Haskell to JJ, April 28, 1958, HaskellPap.

170 "I would eventually": I wasn't there when she said this, which was during an interview in 1994 for a television station in Texas; rather, I watched a video recording of it. But what she said didn't sound the way the words read on the page. I must have played back the clip a dozen times, trying to read into Jane's peculiar mix of shyness and self-assurance. As she said, ". . . *eventually have persuaded* them," her eyes closed and her eyebrows lifted, and abruptly she seemed like some geeky high school student telling us, sweetly and demurely, "Oh, and I won the school science fair prize"—except with an implicit "Of course, what would you expect, *certainly* I won it, how could I not?" The interview was by Lee Cullum, May 4, 1994, VHS recording, Burns.

    In a letter to Peter Newman, January 20, 1997, Burns, Jane uses similar, if more qualified, language: "My editors were very orthodox in their beliefs about city planning and related architecture and not receptive to this iconoclasm. Eventually, I think, I might have persuaded them—maybe—but in any event I got a contract with Random House to write a book instead."

170 "The criss-cross of supporting relationships": Typescript, "Talk given April 20, 1958, at a dinner panel of the New School Associates," Box 37, Folder 380, Rockefeller.

171 "the deepest satisfaction": Lewis Mumford to JJ, May 3, 1958, Kunstler, II, p. 22.

172 "Mrs. Jacobs herself": Chadbourne Gilpatric diary, May 9, 1958, Rockefeller.

172 "fairly bubbled": Chadbourne Gilpatric diary, June 4, 1958, Rockefeller.

172 "sounds very abstract": JJ to Chadbourne Gilpatric, June 14, 1958, Rockefeller.

173 "questions about the scope": Chadbourne Gilpatric diary, June 26, 1958, Rockefeller.

173 "One is the image": JJ to Chadbourne Gilpatric, July 1, 1958, Rockefeller.

173 "an interested publisher": JJ to Chadbourne Gilpatric, June 14, 1958, Rockefeller.

174 His name was Jason Epstein: See Jason Epstein, *Book Business: Publishing, Past Present and Future* (New York: Norton, 2001); introduction to 50th anniversary edition of *D&L*, Modern Library, 2011.

174 both urged Jane: Chadbourne Gilpatric diary, June 26, 1958, Rockefeller.

174 "clearer and better composed": Chadbourne Gilpatric to JJ, July 13, 1958, Rockefeller.

174 a professional biography: JJ to Chadbourne Gilpatric, July 13, 1958, Rockefeller.

175 "She made a brief address": Lewis Mumford to Chadbourne Gilpatric, August 1, 1958, Rockefeller.

175 "wholeheartedly enthusiastic": William H. Whyte to Chadbourne Gilpatric, August 4, 1958, Rockefeller.

175 "grandiose and vague": Christopher Tunnard to Chadbourne Gilpatric, August 18, 1958, Rockefeller.

175 "I'd back Jane Jacobs": Catherine Bauer to Chadbourne Gilpatric, August 5, 1958, Rockefeller.

175 "some general usefulness": JJ to Chadbourne Gilpatric, September 15, 1958, Rockefeller.

CHAPTER 12: A MANUSCRIPT TO SHOW US

176 "completed plans": Chadbourne Gilpatric, October 17, 1958, Rockefeller.

176 "opinions and critical comments": Chadbourne Gilpatric, December 2, 1958, Rockefeller.

177 "had it all figured out": Lucy Jacobs video interview; see also Claire Perrin interview of JJ, May 1999, Burns, 23:32.

177 "woman wanted to see the North End": Interview, Herbert Gans.

177 didn't seem interested: Herbert Gans, "Remembering *The Urban Villagers* and Its Location in Intellectual Time: A Response to Zukin," *City & Community* (September 2007): 231–36.

177 "district taking a terrible beating": *D&L*, p. 12.

177 "I looked down a narrow alley": *D&L*, p. 13.

178 "Mrs. J's most exciting discovery": Chadbourne Gilpatric, December 2, 1958, Rockefeller.

178 "a lot of unexpected problems": Chadbourne Gilpatric, June 10, 1959, Rockefeller.

178 "On almost everything I had thought about": JJ to Chadbourne Gilpatric, July 17, 1959, Rockefeller.

179 realized they knew little: Union Settlement brochure, January 31, 1961, p. 14, Burns, 2:4.

179 Ellen Lurie: Interviews, Ron Shiffman, Kathy Goldman, Rebecca Lurie, Jim Jacobs; Zipp, "Superblock Stories."

179 George Washington Houses: Statement of General Purpose of George Washington Houses Study Project, January 9, 1956, Union Settlement Papers, ColumbiaRare.

179 "sobering": Union Settlement brochure, January 31, 1961, p. 14, Burns, 2:4.

180 DeWitt Clinton Houses: See *Projects*, pp. 327–32.

180 "We realize": William Kirk to William Reid, December 30, 1958, Union Settlement Papers, Box 35, Folder 8, ColumbiaRare.

180 "We are convinced": See, especially, typescript presentation, February 3, 1959, Union Settlement Papers, Box 35, Folder 8, ColumbiaRare.

181 close to the original design: *Projects*, p. 332.

181 "tall, angular, monotonous": Mildred Zucker to Will, February 6, 1959, Union Settlement Papers, Box 35, Folder 7, ColumbiaRare.

181 time and energy were drawn off: See William Kirk to Chadbourne Gilpatric,

August 11, 1959, where he comments on Jane's role in East Harlem over the preceding five years, RF 1.2, 200R, Box 390, Folder 3381, Rockefeller: She, along with her husband, "was indefatigable in attendance at all manner of large and small neighborhood meetings . . . In all of these her interest was unfailing and her discernment was sensitive, perceptive, and deeply imaginative."

181 "I never had a closer friend": "We were as intimate as you can be without . . ." He pauses. "Without being intimate?" *Yes.*

182 "rather unhappy phone call": Jason Epstein to JJ, June 22, 1959, Random House Papers, Box 535, ColumbiaRare.

182 "think no more about it": JJ to Jason Epstein, June 30, 1959, Random House Papers, Box 535, ColumbiaRare.

182 "I have every confidence": Jason Epstein to JJ, July 2, 1959, Random House Papers, Box 535, ColumbiaRare.

182 twenty-chapter outline: Compare JJ to Jason Epstein, June 30, 1959, Random House Papers, Box 535, ColumbiaRare, to JJ to Chadbourne Gilpatric, July 17, 1959, Rockefeller.

183 under no circumstances: JJ to Chadbourne Gilpatric, July 23, 1959, Rockefeller.

183 "I am not rehashing old material": Compare Jane's words, and even their cadence, to those of another formally uneducated genius. In my book *The Man Who Knew Infinity* I tell of an Indian mathematician, Srinivasa Ramanujan, who appeals to the distinguished English mathematician G. H. Hardy this way: "I have not trodden through the conventional regular course which is followed in a University course, but I am striking out a new path for myself." Jane: "I am not rehashing old material on cities and city planning. I am working with new concepts about the city and its behavior."

184 "have to give her what she needs": Douglas Haskell to Chadbourne Gilpatric, August 5, 1959, Rockefeller.

184 "a great and influential book": William H. Whyte to Chadbourne Gilpatric, August 1, 1959, Rockefeller.

184 "I'm averaging a chapter a week": JJ to Chadbourne Gilpatric, October 29, 1959, Rockefeller.

184 "her big chance": William H. Whyte to Chadbourne Gilpatric, August 1, 1959, Rockefeller.

186 "good, cold-blooded mood": JJ to Chadbourne Gilpatric, August 2, 1960, Rockefeller.

186 "working away quite happily": JJ to Jason Epstein, January 11, 1960, Random House Papers, Box 535, Columbia Rare.

186 "if the remainder of the book": Chadbourne Gilpatric to JJ, May 19, 1961, Rockefeller.

187 "sweetly meant inanities": *D&L*, p. 248.

187 "Under the seeming disorder": *D&L*, p. 65.

188 "I expected merely to describe": Foreword, *D&L*, p. xxi.

189 "elaborately learned superstition": *D&L*, p. 17.

189 "His aim was": *D&L*, p. 24.

189 "pretty ticked off": Kunstler, I, p. 5.

189 She did visit it: JJ to Herbert Gans, November 24, 1958, Herbert Gans Papers, ColumbiaRare.

189 "on his hands and knees": Kunstler, II, p. 1.

190 "show you how they worked": Kunstler, I, p. 6.

190 "so feckless as a people": *D&L*, p. 11.

191 "It is fluidity of use": *D&L*, p. 238.

191 "Old ideas": *D&L*, p. 245.

191 "The overcrowded slums": *D&L*, p. 265.

191 "In cities, liveliness and variety": This and the next five quotes appear on these pages, respectively, of *D&L*: 129, 117, 123, 435, 483, and 312.

192 "Frequent borders": *D&L*, p. 346.

193 "a line of exchange": *D&L*, p. 349.

193 "Near where I live": *D&L*, p. 350.

193 "The floor of the building": *D&L*, p. 252.

194 "They are extremely touchy": JJ to Albert L. Ely III, March 29, 1962, Burns.

194 "There is something more": JJ to Ellen Perry, October 11, 1959; this account is based on phone interview and correspondence with Ellen Perry Berkeley and correspondence between her and JJ that she made available. Berkeley went on to become a senior editor at *Architectural Forum* after Jane left. She wrote to Jane in 1996, "I feel as far from those days in NYC as you probably do. But I'll never be so far from those days to [forget] how very nice you were to me."

194 "The subjects she asked me to follow": Ellen Perry Berkeley to author, June 11, 2012.

194 "People who are interested": *D&L*, p. 20.

195 "There is a quality even meaner": *D&L*, p. 21.

195 "This is the fourth draft": JJ to Jason Epstein, December 15 (1960), Random House Papers, ColumbiaRare.

196 "in an oblique way": *D&L*, p. 559.

196 "What makes an evening primrose": *D&L*, p. 563.

197 "nothing accidental or irrational": *D&L*, p. 566.

197 "the triumph of the mathematical average": *D&L*, p. 569.

197 "I am somewhat allergic": Nathan Glazer to JJ, January 30, 1961, Random House Papers, ColumbiaRare.

197 "The task of science": From a scrap headed "The New Sociology," in Burns, 19:12.

197 "the freshness and immutability": Laurence, "The Death and Life of Urban Design," p. 165.

198 "I very strongly disagree": JJ to Nat [Glazer], February 2, 1961, Random House Papers, ColumbiaRare.

198 "the most exciting book on city planning": Epstein to JJ, November 22, 1960, Random House Papers, ColumbiaRare.

198 "Here is chapter 22": JJ to Glazer, January 24 [1961], Random House Papers, ColumbiaRare.

CHAPTER 13: MOTHER JACOBS OF HUDSON STREET

199 blistering review: Lewis Mumford, "Home Remedies for Urban Cancer," in Mumford, *The Urban Prospect*. Original title: "Mother Jacobs' Home Remedies."

199 "a bunch of mothers": Kunstler, II, p. 24.

199 "a room to work in": JJ to Chadbourne Gilpatric, July 17, 1959, Rockefeller.

199 Bethune Street: Knox Burger to JJ, November 19, year uncertain, possibly 1998, Burns, 7:6; interview, Jim Jacobs.

201 Macy's: Jane to a Mr. O'Connell, January 25, 1997, Burns, 2:11.

201 "an outdoor home base": *D&L*, p. 106.

202 "Little tots are decorative": *D&L*, p. 104.

202 "Adolescents are always being criticized": *D&L*, p. 113.

202 A photograph of Jimmy and Ned: *Matter*, p. 132.

203 block printing mixed with cursive: Mary Jacobs to her grandmother, Mrs. Butzner, April 10, 1967, Burns, 23:6; see also Mary (by now Burgin) and her husband, Mel, to JJ, August 12, 2000, Burns, 7:7.

CHAPTER 14: THE PHYSICAL FALLACY

208 "How funny you are": Frank O'Hara, "Steps," in Stephen Wolf, ed., *I Speak of the City: Poems of New York* (New York: Columbia University Press, 2007).

209 "I want to get": JJ to Nathan Glazer, January 24 [1961], Random House Papers, ColumbiaRare.

209 "truly a great, important": Elias Wilentz to Jason Epstein, March 27, 1961, Random House Papers, Box 535, ColumbiaRare.

209 "thoughtful and thought-provoking": Chadbourne Gilpatric to JJ, March 27, 1961, RG 12, Series 200R, Box 390, Folder 338, Rockefeller.

209 magazines were lining up: Chadbourne Gilpatric memo, June 7, 1961, of conversation with Jason Epstein, RG12, Box 170, Rockefeller.

209 prepublication copies: September 18, 1961, memo, Random House Papers, Box 535, ColumbiaRare.

209 "Jane—TERRIFIC!": William H. Whyte to JJ, October 3, 1961, Random House Papers, Box 535, ColumbiaRare.

210 "Hers is a huge, a fascinating": Orville Prescott, *New York Times*, November 3, 1961.

210 "It is a considerable achievement": John Kouwenhoven, *New York Herald Tribune*, November 5, 1961.

210 "A new, passionately argued": "Deplanning the Planners," *Time*, November 10, 1961, p. 57.

210 "unmistakably seminal": Edward T. Chase, "Cities Should be for People," *Commonweal*, December 22, 1961.

210 "enormous intellectual temerity": John Chamberlain, *Wall Street Journal*, November 3, 1961.

211 "a window of January air": Edwin Weeks to JJ, January 29, 1962, Burns, 2:3.

211 a hot ticket: This correspondence is drawn from Burns, 2:3.

211 "Laws of the Asphalt Jungle": Account drawn from Walter McQuade, *The Nation*, March 17, 1962, pp. 241–42; press release, Museum of Modern Art, February 2, 1962; untitled summary by Sidney Frigand and Peter Lapham of MOMA panel discussion, February 14, 1962, Commissioner Goldstone Papers, New York Municipal Archives.

212 "the enchanted ballerina": Morton Hoppenfeld, *Journal of the American Institute of Planners*, 28, no. 2 (1962).

212 visiting Pittsburgh: Account drawn from James V. Cunningham, "Jane Jacobs Visits Pittsburgh," *New City*, September 15, 1962; press release, "Jane Jacobs, Anti-City Planner, Will Spend Week Here Lecturing," University of Pittsburgh, January 25, 1962; William Allan, "City Planning Critic Gets Roasting Reply," *Pittsburgh Press*, February 22, 1962.

214 "I am filled with delighted admiration": Eugene Raskin, in "Abattoir for Sacred Cows."

214 "Khrushchev see the North End": *Matter*, p. 51.

214 "What a dear, sweet character": *Matter*, p. 15.

214 Mooritania: *Matter*, pp. 53–54.

215 "like two Japanese wrestlers": Jason Epstein to JJ, December 1, 1960, Random House Papers, ColumbiaRare.

215 "a morbid and biased catalog": *D&L*, p. 28.

215 "I held my fire": Miller, p. 474.

215 "Mother Jacobs' Home Remedies": Quotations that follow drawn from reprint of article in Lewis Mumford, *The Urban Prospect*, pp. 182–207.

216 "like a chestful of combat ribbons": Miller, p. 475.

216 "born and bred New Yorker": Mumford, "Mother Jacobs' Home Remedies," p. 193.

217 Sunnyside Gardens: The community still exists.

217 in the spirit of Ebenezer Howard: In a review of a new edition of Howard's *Garden Cities of To-morrow,* Mumford calls *Death and Life* a "preposterous mass of historic misinformation and contemporary misinterpretation . . . [in which] she exposed her ignorance of the whole planning movement by seeking to make Howard responsible for all the mistakes made in modern planning." Lewis Mumford, "Revaluations I: Howard's Garden City," *New York Review of Books,* April 8, 1965.

217 "not utopia": Mumford, "Mother Jacobs' Home Remedies," p. 194.

217 "Her simple formula": Mumford, "Mother Jacobs' Home Remedies," p. 197.

217 "driven Mumford into schizophrenia": Dwight, unknown last name, on *New Yorker* letterhead, to JJ, December 6, [1961], Burns, 2:3.

217 "I laughed": Rochon, "Jane Jacobs at 81."

218 "quite a sexist": Dillon, p. 42.

218 "When two people": Miller, p. 474.

218 "I'm not sure whether": Herbert Gans to JJ, January 19, 1962, Herbert Gans Papers, ColumbiaRare.

218 "What is lively": In Gans's typed notes about *Death and Life*, Herbert Gans Papers, ColumbiaRare.

219 "No child of enterprise": *D&L*, p. 105.

219 "She doesn't accept the existence": Morton Hoppenfeld, *Journal of the American Institute of Planners* 28, no. 2 (1962).

219 "She imposes her tastes": A. Melamed, *Journal of the American Institute of Planners* 28, no. 2 (1962).

219 "a brilliant personal diatribe": Catherine Bauer Wurster, in "Abattoir for Sacred Cows."

219 "a brilliant and distorted book": Kevin Lynch, in "Abattoir for Sacred Cows."

219 "mixing apples with battleships": "North End Here to Stay, Boston Planners Declare," *Boston Sunday Globe*, October 15, 1961. The planner quoted is Donald M. Graham.

219 "no direct, simple relationship": *D&L*, p. 147.

220 "the physical fallacy": Herbert Gans, "City Planning and Urban Realities," *Commentary*; reference to the physical fallacy appears on p. 172; see also typed notes about *D&L* in Herbert Gans Papers, ColumbiaRare; Herbert Gans, "Jane Jacobs: Toward an Understanding," pp. 213–15.

220 "old-hat stereotypes": JJ to Herbert Gans, January 19, 1962, Herbert Gans Papers, ColumbiaRare.

220 "she broke off relations": Herbert J. Gans, "Jane Jacobs: Toward an Understanding," p. 213.

221 Mr. and Mrs. McLean: See Ellen Lurie, "A Study of George Washington Houses: The Effect of the Project on Its Tenants and the Surrounding Community," 1955–1956, Union Settlement Papers, Box 11, Folder 13, ColumbiaRare. For an imaginative reconstruction of Lurie see Zipp, "Superblock Stories." Lurie died, at age forty-seven, in 1978.

221 "a question to put": Jason Epstein to JJ, December 22, 1960, Random House Papers, ColumbiaRare.

222 "a poor idea": JJ to Jason Epstein, December 27, 1960, Random House Papers, ColumbiaRare.

222 "was more firmly convinced": Jason Epstein to JJ, December 28, 1960, Random House Papers, ColumbiaRare.

222 "Jason is very worried": Nathan Glazer to JJ, January 30, 1961, Random House Papers, ColumbiaRare.

222 "the discrimination which operates": *D&L*, p. 371.

223 "touched some sensitive chords": Arthur T. Row, *Yale Law Journal* 71 (1962): 1597–1602.

223 "inept introspective scholarship": Paul A. Pfretzschner, "Panning the Planners," *Antioch Review* 22, no. 1 (spring 1962): 130–36.

223 "conveniently overlooks": A. Melamed, *Journal of the American Institute of Planners* 28, no. 2 (1962).

223 "remarkable appraisal": Jerome Zukosky, letter to the editor, *Commentary*, July 1, 1962.

CHAPTER 15: WEST VILLAGE WARRIOR

224 "People who have seen her": Kramer.

226 "If you write a press release": Laura Hansen, "Claire Tankel," oral history interview, Greenwich Village Society for Historic Preservation, March 1, 1997, and February 20, 1998.

226 urban oasis was threatened: This account is built up in part from Fishman, "Revolt of the Urbs"; oral histories in the Greenwich Village Society for Historic Preservation archives; Flint, chapter 3.

226 "a cumbersome kind of name": KentVillage, p. 3.

227 the winning strategy: KentVillage, p. 5.

227 "the backroom boss": Susan DeVries, "Norman Redlich," oral history interview, Greenwich Village Society for Historical Preservation, March 6, 1997.

227 "had every reason to expect": KentVillage, p. 5.

227 "We expect you do it": KentVillage, p. 6.

227 "all these little elves": KentVillage, p. 8. When, years later, she sent her son Ned a transcript of Kent's oral history of her, Jane suggested he might want to simply "enjoy it yourself as a piece of life, in which you shared importantly in so many ways, young as you were," JJ to Ned Jacobs, January 28, 2001, Burns.

227 "passed the word": Susan DeVries, "Norman Redlich," oral history interview, Greenwich Village Society for Historical Preservation, March 6, 1997.

228 ribbon-*tying*: When *The New York Times* reported on the closure, it referred to Jane as "Mrs. Jane Jacobs, the author." This was almost three years before the publication of *D&L*, and even before she went under contract for the book with Random House.

228 "tough political pressure": *D&L*, p. 472.

228 "issue-oriented politics": KentVillage, p. 9.

228 Robert Moses: See Caro; Ballon and Jackson; Mennel, "A Fight to Forget," in which he quotes a 1962 Moses letter to an acquaintance: "Jane Jacobs isn't really worth refuting. She has the Architectural Forum following and the professional critics with her, but nobody with any experience or responsibility is impressed by such captious owl dropping . . . La Jacobs doesn't know this metropolis or any other. In an examination on facts she would not get 40%. After all, you must start with knowledge, not cyanide."

229 "All new work": Robert Moses, "What Happened to Haussmann," *Architectural Forum* (July 1942): 57–66.

229 "partisans, enthusiasts": Cited in Robert Fishman, "Revolt of the Urbs," p. 122.

229 "did more harm to New York": *Ethics*, p. 187. See also Amateau, "Jane Jacobs, Urban Legend": "It makes me sick when I hear, 'People are too timid and you need someone with the boldness of Robert Moses,' Jacobs said. 'Well, if you like a big dictatorship and life under a dictator you had the closest thing to it under Robert Moses.'"

229 "NOBODY, NOBODY, NOBODY": Kunstler, II, p. 24. Jane says here that she saw Moses only once. However, in an article in *Building Design*, May 5, 2006, p. 9, Richard Sennett recalls Jane taking on Moses at a public meeting:

In her public encounters with him, she was anything but politically naïve. Other people would scream at Moses but she just politely asked him questions like: "How do you know this is what people want?" "Do you know any of the people in this room?" "Who do you know?" It drove him crazy. Rather than telling him the community was against him, she focused on his position. I was at one meeting where she asked him "What is beautiful for you?" She put him on the defensive.

230 "cut off our sidewalks": *Matter*, pp. 67, 71. KentVillage, pp. 16–18, 23–24; see also Vicki Weiner, "Anthony Dapolito," oral history interview, New York Preservation Archive Project, October 5, 1997.

230 "this brave, inquiring little boy": KentVillage, p. 23.

230 the plan: *Matter*, p. 67.

230 "any demand of incidental play": *D&L*, p. 114.

231 "a mindless, routinized": *D&L*, p. 162.

231 "That'll be too late": *Matter*, pp. 67, 71.

231 before they went in to see him: Vicki Weiner, "Anthony Dapolito," oral history interview, New York Preservation Archive Project, October 5, 1997.

231 "I knew at once": KentVillage, p. 18.

232 fourteen-block stretch: John Sibley, "Two Blighted Downtown Areas Are Chosen for Urban Renewal," *New York Times*, February 21, 1961.

232 $300,000: Interview, Pierre Tonachel, who furnished me with "The City's Request for a Survey: What It Means to All of Us," by the Committee to Save the West Village, no date, as well as many other documents bearing on the West Village urban renewal struggle, including official documents, legal correspondence, clippings, neighborhood newsletters, and other materials related to the West Village and dating to 1961—hereafter "Tonachel papers."

232 Elizabeth Squire: Robert de Vaughan to John & Elizabeth Squire, February 15 and 26, 1961; deposition by Elizabeth Squire, April 26, 1961; Tonachel papers.

232 "disconnected the doorbell": *Dallas Morning News*, May 9, 1962.

232 The battle for the West Village: Account built up from Tonachel papers; Flint, chapter 4; *Projects*, pp. 366–68; *Transatlantic*, pp. 146–60; Stern, Mellins, and Fishman, *New York 1960*, pp. 247–49; Frigand; Moser; Hock; KentVillage, pp. 18–21, 25–31; interviews, Ned and Jim Jacobs; see also Ned Jacobs, "Changing the World by Saving Place," *Alternatives Journal* (summer 2002).

233 "kill this project entirely": Sam Pope Brewer, "Angry 'Villagers' to Fight Project," *New York Times*, February 27, 1961.

235 "We are 100% for improvement": *West Village Newsletter*, no date, but before March 23, 1961, Tonachel papers.

235 "blighting influence": *Newsletter*, Department of City Planning, May 1961.

235 "less-than-desirable area": Patricia Fieldsteel, "Remembering a Time When the Village Was Affordable," *Villager*, October 19–22, 2005.

236 "Who Says What Is a Slum?": John Crosby, *New York Herald Tribune*, March 13, 1961.

237 "generally high standards": Sam Pope Brewer, "Dudley Inspects Area in 'Village,'" *New York Times*, March 21, 1961.

237 surveyed all fourteen blocks: "Residential and Business Survey of the West Village," March 1961, and "Housing Characteristics and Business Survey of the West Greenwich Village Area," March 1961, Committee to Save the West Village, Tonachel papers.

238 "fundamentally as attractive": Daniel M. C. Hopping and Henry Hope Reed Jr. to James Felt, April 18, 1961, Tonachel papers.

238 "no romantic attitude": Bruno Zevi to Committee to Save the West Village, May 3, 1961, Tonachel papers.

239 This tack: Amateau, "Jane Jacobs Comes Back"; Gratz, *The Battle for Gotham*, p. 87; KentVillage, pp. 26–27.

239 record sound levels: KentVillage, pp. 10, 14. See also undated internal memo, *Architectural Forum*, noting that Jane "went so far as to produce an acoustical engineer who proved the West Village was quieter than Sutton Place," Haskell-Pap, 80:5.

239 "nibbled to death by ducks": Interview, Pierre Tonachel.

240 "an action-packed montage": Nathan Silver, "Jane Jacobs for Example," *Columbia Forum* (summer 1972): 47–49.

241 "unreal and almost dreamlike": "Report of the City Planning Commission on the Designation of the West Village Area," October 18, 1961, p. 7.

241 "leaped from their seats": Edith Evans Asbury, "Plan Board Votes 'Village' Project; Crowd in Uproar," *New York Times*, October 19, 1961.

241 "We were not violent": Edith Evans Asbury, "Deceit Charged in 'Village' Plan," *New York Times*, October 20, 1961.

241 "a weary father": *Housing and Planning News*, February 1962, p. 1; see also Edith Evans Asbury, "Board Ends Plan for West Village," *New York Times*, October 25, 1961; Martin Arnold, "Felt Set to Yield in 'Village' Fight," *New York Times*, January 17, 1962.

241 "eleven months and ten days": Jane Jacobs, "The Citizen in Urban Renewal: Participation or Manipulation," February 21, 1962, typescript, Burns.

241 "highly sophisticated and articulate": "Report of the City Planning Commission on the Designation of the West Village Area," October 18, 1961, p. 8.

242 "discovered beauty": Abe [Abraham E. Kazan], of United Housing Foundation, to James Felt, December 18, 1961, Goldstone Papers, New York Municipal Archives.

242 "whipped up this book": Books and Authors Luncheon.

242 "As long as it couldn't be avoided": Wachtel, p. 53. See also *Matter*, p. 82: "Fights like these are an outrageous imposition on the time and resources of citizens," eased only by having "a bang-up good time in the process, and a satisfying vengeance against the rascals at the end."

243 West Village Houses: The brochure was titled "The West Village Plan for Housing"; see also *Transatlantic*, pp. 187–91, 208–12; Stern, pp. 249–51; interviews, Pearl Broder, Katy Bordonaro.

243 "This will show": Jerome Zakowsky, "Villagers Want 5-Tier Walkups to 'Save' Area," *New York Herald Tribune*, May 6, 1963.

244 "Revolutionary in its modesty": Nichols.

244 Jane and Betty had inhabited: But in a letter to Myrna Katz Frommer and Harvey Frommer, July 12, 2000, Burns, 1, Jane writes, "There was nothing wrong with the building on Orange St. that couldn't have been fixed with installation of a small elevator," as her next apartment, on Morton Street, had been.

245 "well-publicized 'victory'": "Analysis and Comments on the West Village Plan for Housing," anonymous report, n.d., City Planning Commission Papers, New York City Municipal Archives.

245 Jane's "in fill": JJ to Ned [Jacobs], February 11, 2002, Burns: "An unwritten basic point . . . was that we hoped this infill method would teach the city a new and better way to build housing—but its Dreadful Big Thinkers were too dumb or bloody-minded or both to learn."

245 were a going industry: Intradepartmental memorandum from Theodore Berlin to Samuel Joroff, "Survey of West Village Housing Proposal Area," November 18, 1964, Ballard Papers, City Planning Commission, New York City Municipal Archives.

245 "conceived in utmost secrecy": "Analysis and Comments on the West Village Plan for Housing," anonymous report, n.d., City Planning Commission Papers, New York City Municipal Archives.

245 "startling and frightening": Jeanne Godwin, "Tenement House Revival," *Co-op Contact*, newsletter, ca. 1963, Commissioner Goldstone Papers, New York Municipal Archives.

246 "the most incredible proposal": Frank S. Kristof, Intradepartmental Memorandum, "The West Village Plan for Housing—Some Questions," June 25, 1963, Housing and Redevelopment Board, New York City Municipal Archives.

246 "classic example of conflict": Philip Will Jr. to William Ballard, November 9, 1964, Commissioner Goldstone Papers, New York Municipal Archives.

246 "a determined lot": William F. R. Ballard to Philip Will, November 16, 1964, Commissioner Goldstone Papers, New York Municipal Archives.

247 "plain brick buildings": West Village Houses, writes Michael Sorkin in "Two Critics," "fits unobtrusively within the intimate weave of its surroundings. It's a model piece of urbanism because of this careful integration."

CHAPTER 16: LUNCHEON AT THE WHITE HOUSE

248 "their patience": JJ to Jason Epstein, January 9, 1961, Random House Papers, ColumbiaRare.

249 "so clear even for us": Noriaki Kurokawa to JJ, July 10, 1963, and JJ reply, July 30, 1963, Burns, 1:14.

249 The street crime Americans: Interview, Toshiko Adilman.

249 " 'Plans Agley' ": JJ to Tom Maschler, March 29, 1962, Burns, 1:14.

249 Harvard Graduate School of Design: Laurence, "Contradictions and Complexities," p. 59.

250 "some real news for you": JJ to Mrs. Butzner, postmarked June 7, 1964, Burns, 23:6. Jane also wrote brother John with the news of what she called her "mysterious errand—the first meeting of President Johnson's task force on the Preservation of Beauty! I do not like to take the time, but I am curious about it [and] it is hard to refuse without being churlish," JJ to John and Pete, July 28, 1964, Decker Butzner papers.

250 "really appreciate, honey": *Matter*, p. 22.

250 "amenity": *Matter*, p. 59.

250 "I wanted to talk sense": *Matter*, p. 22.

250 forty-one-year-old Diane Arbus: Richard Soren, "Jane Jacobs on Diane Arbus," Q&A interview edited for unknown publication, Burns, 43:6. The photo appeared in the July 1965 *Esquire*.

251 "As you know": JJ to Peter Blake memo, March 29, 1962, HaskellPap.

251 "all of her best energies": Chadbourne Gilpatric memo, February 8, 1962, Rockefeller.

251 "It became evident to me": "Jacobs Tape," Burns, 22:5.

252 "The question of, you might say": *Matter*, p.12.

252 "Life is an end in itself": *D&L*, p. 3.

252 "cheerful and respectful curiosity": November 1963 draft of book at the time titled "Cities and Work: The Economic Principles of City Growth," Burns, 8:2.

252 "The most elementary point": December 1964 draft, Burns, 8:2

253 "I have to stop talking": JJ to John Elmendorf, August 24, 1962, Rockefeller. A copy went to Chadbourne Gilpatric.

253 "I am already so badly delayed": JJ to Noriaki Kurokawa, September 3, 1963, Burns.

253 "I'm still plugging away": JJ to Mrs. Butzner, postmarked June 7, 1964, Burns, 23:6.

254 "I'll never forget it": JJ to Chadbourne Gilpatric, October 13, 1961, Rockefeller. Two weeks later, she wrote to Gilpatric again: "Yesterday, I ran into my first published review, quite a feeling. It was in the November *Atlantic*, and was a nice one."

254 " a total knit-together book": JJ to David Gurin, September 4, 1963, David Gurin papers.

254 "distressingly and maddeningly slow": JJ to Jason Epstein, March 3, 1966, Random House Papers, ColumbiaRare.

255 "marvelous": Barbara Epstein to JJ, September 9, 1966, Burns, 2:8.

255 "Cities First": See *EofC*, chapter 1. Her new project, "which I have been heartily enjoying, is an imaginary history of the first city in the world," JJ to John and Pete, July 28, 1964, Decker Butzner papers.

256 small gems of reportage and memoir: Jane's letters home to her family from Europe are at Burns, 4:7. Some appear in *Matter*, pp. 87–96. For those that do, I supply the page number. For those that do not, I give the date of the letter and from where it was written.

256 "living room is all cleaned up": Copenhagen, January 21, 1967.

257 "I hope you get my letters": Amsterdam, January 30, 1967.

257 "dirty, garish, ugly": *Matter*, p. 87.

257 "You could play chess": *Matter*, p. 88.

257 "Snow covered, wild": *Matter*, p. 88.

257 "just enough to enhance": *Matter*, p. 89.

257 "dear, lovely letter": *Matter*, p. 90.

258 "one of those great and famous": London, February 7, 1967.

258 a foretaste: *Matter*, p. 90.

258 "in full technicolor": London, February 7, 1967.

258 "tiresome beyond belief": Chester, February 8, 1967. Fashion note, by Jane Jacobs, from Chester, England: "Many girls in London had mini-skirts that came just about to here"; here she drew a primitive stick figure of a tall, skinny girl, her skirt miles above her knees, the little bumps on her stick legs obligingly identified as "knees."

258 "took charge of the conversation": *Matter*, p. 93.

259 "complicated and wonderful": *Matter*, p. 93.

CHAPTER 17: GAS MASKS AT THE PENTAGON

260 "the building I live in": *Matter*, p. 200.

261 "Erosion of Cities": *D&L*, chapter 18.

261 garage on Greenwich Street: Interview, Jim Jacobs.

261 "we went awry": *D&L*, p. 447.

262 Lower Manhattan Expressway: See Flint, chapter 5; Anthony M. Tedeschi, "Father LaMountain: After Nine Years, It's Still War on the LME," *Villager*, April 3, 1969; Stern, pp. 259–61; Stephanie Gervis, "Artists, Politicians, People

Join Fight for Little Italy," *Village Voice*, August 30, 1962; Ballon and Jackson, pp. 213–15.

263 "consider [their] present space requirements": Stephen Freidus, "Dear Sir" form letter, October 12, 1961, Commissioner Goldstone Papers, New York City Municipal Archives.

263 "The methods that you have used": James Felt to Stephen Freidus, November 3, 1961, Commissioner Goldstone Papers, New York City Municipal Archives.

263 "I could get along": KentVillage, p. 48.

264 "I felt very resistant": KentVillage, p. 49.

264 vital middle period: KentVillage, p. 47.

265 "making us sound": KentVillage, p. 50.

265 "Los Angelize New York": Stephanie Gervis, "Artists, Politicians, People Join Fight for Little Italy," *Village Voice*, August 30, 1962.

265 "This isn't about *The New Yorker*": Rochon, "Jane Jacobs at 81."

265 "the idea dismays me": Burns, 2:1.

266 panel devoted to "the city and the freeway": Transcript, "Our Nation's Capital—The City and the Freeway," May 23, 1965, Burns.

267 sewing machines, printing presses: Or tanks of chemical solutions: My father ran a small manufacturing company, Egyptian Polishing and Plating Works, that occupied the second floor of a decaying 1890s-vintage brick loft building, on the other side of the Williamburg Bridge, adjacent to the Brooklyn Navy Yard. You'd go up a dark wooden staircase, at the landing unlock a heavy door, and enter a spacious bay whose worn, wood-planked floor glinted with tiny flecks of brass, nickel, and zinc, the scene showered by light pouring in through banks of high windows. The building no longer exists.

267 "Lofts": See Stern, pp. 263–77.

267 Margot Gayle: Carol Gayle and John G. Waite, "Margot Gayle: Passionate Crusader for Cast-Iron Architecture," *APT* [Association for Preservation Technology International] *Bulletin* (2013) 44, no. 4, pp. 5–6.

268 April 10, 1968: Account drawn from *Matter*, pp. 15, 20, 72–78; Epstein, "Introduction," in *D&L*, p. xvii; Wachtel, pp. 53–54; KentVillage, pp. 55–59; Leticia Kent, "Persecution of the City Performed by its Inmates," *Village Voice*, April 18, 1968; Flint, pp. 172–75; Alexiou, pp. 129–34; "Jane Jacobs and Margot Gayle on Phone to Her Home in Toronto, 6/4/88," typescript of notes, Burns, 5:3.

269 Susan Sontag: *Matter*, p. 168.

269 "Flanking her": Bole, p. 20.

269 "arrested again": JJ to her mother, *Matter*, p. 72.

270 "the prosecutor made such a case": Wachtel, p. 54.

270 several months later: See, for example, JJ to Richard B. Barnett, November 1, 1968, Burns, 5:3, in which she thanks Barnett for his help with a fund used to pay her legal fees: "It certainly feels awfully good to be out from under that jail shadow!" For more details on the Jane Jacobs Legal Defense Fund, see Richard B. Barnett to Jason Epstein, November 21, 1968, Random House Papers, Folder 1365, ColumbiaRare. Jane had to pay about $70 for the damage to the stenotype machine.

270 "The Social Uses of Power": Panel transcripts appear in Janeway, ed., pp. 297–316.

271 "Is it for hunting": *Esquire* (July 1965), caption accompanying Diane Arbus photo of Jane and Ned Jacobs.

271 "some horrible insect": *Matter*, p. 11.

272 "CAN YOU CONTRIBUTE": The telegram, dated November 1, 1967, and Jane's response, Burns.

272 Eight months later: Interview, Jane Henderson.

CHAPTER 18: A CIRCLE OF THEIR OWN

277 They told no one: The story of the Jacobses' move to Canada is largely drawn from interviews with Jim, Ned, and Burgin Jacobs.

278 "think kindly of Toronto": Fulford, *Accidental City*, p. 20.

278 "he phoned me up": JJ in interview with Peter Gzowski, May 18, 1993, for program *Morningside*, Burns, MS1995_029_CS08_REF.

280 "A year from now": Robert Fulford, "Lives Lived: Robert Hyde Jacobs," *Globe and Mail*, September 24, 1996. See also TV coverage on TV-UN, aired June 28, 2006, covering Jane Jacobs Day in New York City. Ned Jacobs, on hand for the event, quotes his father: " 'There's a fine country up there. I think we should go.' It was a decision none of us regretted."

280 through a darker lens: Dillon, p. 42: "Between her second and third books Jacobs 'fell out of love with America.' "

280 maybe all of them: For an example of this thinking, consider Alexander Ross, "Could Jane Jacobs Save Us Millions in Taxes?," unknown publication, ca. 1969, Burns, 31:2. For him, the Jacobses moved to Toronto "for a variety of reasons," chief among them being Bob's professional opportunities in Toronto.

280 What do you do: This and other tales of their earliest days in Toronto drawn from interview, Jim Jacobs.

281 cries of children playing: Alexander Ross, "Could Jane Jacobs Save Us Millions in Taxes," unknown publication, ca. 1969, Burns, 31:2; see also *Ethics*, p. 26.

281 a wobbly start: Paul Wilson, "Urban Legend," *Saturday Night* (March 2000); "Conversation," among JJ and friends, *Ideas That Matter Quarterly* 1, no. 1, n.d.

281 architect Eberhard Zeidler: Interviews, Jim Jacobs and Eb Zeidler.

281 "The Future of the American Hospital": *Architectural and Engineering News* (November 1965).

282 "encyclopedic brain": Interview, Alan Littlewood.

282 Mary Malfara: Jane acknowledged Malfara's help in her books.

282 "Bob is working": JJ to Doug Haskell, January 15, 1969, HaskellPap, 32:9.

283 One was Cliff Esler: Account of his relationship with the Jacobses built up from interview, email correspondence, unpublished memoir, and "Notes for Robert Kanigel, December 7, 2012," courtesy of Mr. Esler.

284 "peace, order and good government": Jane specifically referred to this Canadian-U.S. difference in an interview with Michael Valpy, Ideas That Matter conference, 1997, videotape, Toronto Reference Library, no. 2345212.

284 "is a holiday here": JJ to her mother, August 7, 1972, Burns, 4:9.

285 Spadina fight: Account drawn from extensive materials at the Burns, 48, including Margaret Daly, "People Power: Our Unhappy Citizens Are Fighting Back," *Toronto Daily Star*, March 21, 1970; Ned Jacobs, "Brief Regarding the William R. Allen Expressway," with lyrics to four songs, including "The Bad Trip" and

JJ's prepared remarks for April 7, 1970, hearing; James MacKenzie, "Committee Turning Spadina Hearing into Charade, Urbanologist Charges," *Globe and Mail*, April 7, 1970; Sewell, *The Shape of the City*, pp. 177–82; *Matter*, pp. 114–20; interviews with Ned Jacobs, Jim Jacobs, Bobbi Speck.

286   "Toronto's a very refreshing city": On CBC-TV, "The Way It Is," March 2, 1969.

286   "A City Getting Hooked": *Matter*, pp. 115–16.

286   *"Oh, we can do it here"*: JJ interview with Ann Medina, Ideas That Matter conference, 1997, videotape, Toronto Reference Library, no. 2345212.

287   New Year's Day "levee": See David Lewis Stein, "The Lady Sings the Spadina Blues," *Toronto Star*, ca. 1970, Ontario Municipal Board testimony. (The year given in *Matter*, p. 115, for the first article, "Spadina Protest at the Mayor's Levee," should be 1970, not 1969.) See also TV coverage on TV-UN, aired June 28, 2006, covering Jane Jacobs Day in New York City. "I became the group minstrel, writing and performing protest songs," said Ned Jacobs at the event, held at New York's Washington Square, "inspired by those I had learned as a child, right there"—he rises up and points—"right over there at the fountain, in 1961, when they tried to kick the singers out and failed."

287   *The Burning Would*: *Matter*, pp. 118–19.

288   "coming to a head": JJ to Jason Epstein, March 29, 1969, Random House Papers, Folder 1365, ColumbiaRare.

289   "If we are building": Bruce Fisher.

289   two or three daily newspapers: *Matter*, pp. 129–30.

289   *Are there igloos in the street?*: Interview, Jim Jacobs.

290   an extra February: Interview, Jim Jacobs.

CHAPTER 19: SETTLING IN

291   extracted from the freezer chest: According to Decker Butzner, based on his conversation with Burgin Jacobs.

291   "I will [tell] the story": *EofC*, epigraph.

292   "The new enterprises": *EofC*, p. 152. Jane was later bothered by her account of Los Angeles after the war, reports Jim Jacobs: Why, more precisely, did it not decline? "There was a big hole there." For another peek at postwar Los Angeles, see Paul Goldberger, *Building Art: The Life and Work of Frank Gehry* (New York: Knopf, 2015), pp. 43–47.

292   Manchester and Birmingham: *EofC*, pp. 86–96.

293   Ida Rosenthal: *EofC*, pp. 51, 56.

293   *"Division of labor"*: *EofC*, p. 82.

293   "where men and women": *EofC*, p. 83.

294   "New goods and services": *EofC*, p. 55.

294   "a pleasure to read": Robert Lekachman to Jason Epstein, July 15 [1968], Random House Papers, Folder 1365, ColumbiaRare.

294   "she both oversytematizes and overgeneralizes": Robert McCormick Adams to Jason Epstein, September 11, 1968, Random House Papers, Folder 1365, ColumbiaRare.

295   "permanently nuance": Carroll Keeley, "The Vision of Jane Jacobs: An Overview

and an Interpretation," in *Ethics*, p. 65. In a footnote, p. 64, Keeley suggests that Rousseau, in *Discourse on the Origins of Inequality*, comes near to supporting Jacobs's cities-before-agriculture argument: the technological arts of the city, Rousseau wrote, were "necessary to force the human race to apply itself to that of agriculture. Once men were needed in order to smelt and forge the iron, other men were needed in order to feed them."

295 "We cannot . . . envision": See Smith, Ur, and Feinman.

295 "Bless Jane Jacobs": *Matter*, p. 104.

295 "It blows cobwebs": *Matter*, pp. 101–02.

296 "provoked, stimulated": *Matter*, pp. 102–04.

296 "whole new world to think about": Roger Sale, *Hudson Review* (spring 1970).

296 "continues the search for vitality": Gans, "Dream of Human Cities," p. 28.

297 Patricia Daly: This correspondence, in Burns, begins May 20, 1969; Jane's reply is July 2, Daly's response September 5.

297 "not a single outdoor café": JJ interview with Peter Gzowski, Ideas That Matter conference, 1997, videotape, Toronto Reference Library, no. 2345212.

298 "it transformed Toronto": Fulford, *Accidental City*, p. 7.

299 "We had one or two": In "Jane Jacobs' Annex: A Guided Audio Walking Tour," produced by Sarah Elton, City of Toronto—Office of the Public Realm, CBC/Radio Canada, and Jane's Walk.

299 "We think we have bought": JJ to Jason Epstein, July 20, 1970, Random House Papers, Folder 1365, ColumbiaRare.

299 dinosaur expert: JJ to Barbara Chisholm, May 6, 1997, Burns, 5.

299 "We are going to have more room": JJ to David Gurin, no date, but listing her new address, David Gurin papers.

300 "The carpenter yesterday finished": JJ to her mother, July 16, 1971, Burns, 4:9.

300 Bloor Street's array of shops: Interview, Jim Jacobs.

300 wire scarecrow: This and some other house details drawn from Associated Press article by Hillel Italie, November 23, 2000, Burns, 44:3.

301 "You can't say no to Jane Jacobs": Interview, Robert Brown, former neighbor of Jane's at 39 Albany Avenue.

301 "white painter": Interview, Robert Brown.

301 Jane rescued her: "Jane Jacobs' Annex: A Guided Audio Walking Tour," produced by Sarah Elton, City of Toronto—Office of the Public Realm, CBC/Radio Canada, and Jane's Walk.

302 "all the threshing around": McCall.

302 Jane became a citizen: JJ to her mother, *Matter*, p. 143. See also *Ethics*, pp. 26–27.

303 Canary Islands: JJ to her mother, April 2, 1971, *Matter*, pp. 133–34.

303 bike project: JJ to her mother, *Matter*, p. 139; interview, Jim Jacobs.

304 "The inn in Kyoto": JJ to her mother, Burns, 4:9.

305 "three black squirrels": *Matter*, p. 134.

305 adventures of young life and spirit: Interview, Burgin Jacobs.

305 "went to a country fair": JJ to her mother, *Matter*, p. 135.

306 "in a little log cabin": JJ to her mother, *Matter*, p. 137.

306 "Day before yesterday": JJ to her mother, December 3, 1972, Burns, 4:9.

307 misspelling it: As, for example, in several of Jane's entries in her 1977 and 1978 date books, Burns, 37. Or in JJ to Decker Butzner, December 13, 1978, and April 22, 1979, Decker Butzner papers.

307 "Day after tomorrow": JJ to Jason Epstein, June 23, 1975, Random House Papers, Box 1365, ColumbiaRare.

CHAPTER 20: OUR JANE

308 "We made a lot of new cutters": JJ to David Gurin, December 12, 1971, David Gurin papers.

308 "down to serious work": JJ to Jason Epstein, June 10, 1970, Random House Papers, Box 1365, ColumbiaRare.

309 "work well enough": Jason Epstein to JJ, October 8, 1971. Random House Papers, Box 1365, ColumbiaRare.

309 "You are absolutely right": JJ to Jason Epstein, October 19, 1971, Random House Papers, Box 1365, ColumbiaRare.

309 signed a contract: Contract is dated November 1, 1971, and can be found in Random House Papers, Box 1365, ColumbiaRare.

309 "I'm working hard": JJ to her mother, July 16, 1971, Burns, 4:9.

309 "when was the last time": A favorite story among the family.

310 "the density turn": See Nikolai Roskamm, "Taking Sides with a Man-eating Shark: Jane Jacobs and the 1960s 'Density Turn' in Urban Planning," in Schubert, pp. 83–92.

310 "standard urban theory": Paul Goldberger, review of *Urban Utopias in the Twentieth Century* by Robert Fishman, *New York Times*, January 21, 1978.

311 "Modern architecture died": Charles Jencks, *The Language of Post-Modern Architecture* (New York: Rizzoli, 1984) p. 9. "The era of American faith in big plans came to an end, symbolically," Jane said at a panel discussion in 1980 at Faneuil Hall in Boston, "when that building in the huge Pruitt-Igoe public housing project in St. Louis was dramatically dynamited by the authorities."

311 "A poor man's penthouse": *The Pruitt-Igoe Myth*.

311 "I don't think things should be blown up": JJ, "Futility vs. Taking Chances," manuscript, no date, no place, Burns, 13.

311 "I have to hop to it": JJ to her mother, June 12, 1974, *Matter*, p. 98.

312 "Our Jane": For example, Wellman.

312 consulted with Jane: Interviews, Eb Zeidler, Max Allen, Jim Jacobs.

312 "the most important advance": "Randall Unveils Plan for $500 Million City in Toronto Harbor," *Toronto Star*, May 20, 1970.

312 "nasty, tacky collections": Memo, JJ to Eberhard Zeidler, July 14, 1970, Burns, 13.

313 "fantastic election": JJ to Jason Epstein, December 29, 1972, Random House Papers, Box 1365, ColumbiaRare.

313 "the constantly reminding background": Interview, David Crombie. Sketch of this era drawn from interviews with John Sewell, Jim Jacobs, Alan Broadbent, Max Allen, Alan Littlewood, and Crombie.

313 Jane's personal influence: See Richard White. A more typical assessment comes from Ken Greenberg, in *Walking Home*, p. 67: "Jane Jacobs' observations almost immediately resonated in Toronto . . . Her ideas quickly came close to being conventional wisdom."

313 "This morning at 6:30 am": JJ to Jason Epstein, April 5, 1973, Random House

Papers, Box 1365, ColumbiaRare. See also excerpt from apparently unpublished JJ article: "One cold early spring morning before dawn in 1973 . . ." Burns, box 13.

314 "The remark was repeated": Jane Jacobs, "Can Big Plans Solve the Problem of Renewal?"

314 Regent Park: See, for example, Mary W. Rowe; Laurie Greene; *Farewell Oak Street.*

315 live a decent life: Ryan James made this point at a conference of the Society for American City and Regional Planning History in Toronto in October 2013. See also Ryan James, "From 'Slum Clearance' to 'Revitalisation.'"

315 St. Lawrence: Account drawn from site visit; Sewell, *The Shape of the City*; Hume; David L. A. Gordon, "Directions for New Urban Neighbourhoods: Learning from St. Lawrence," CIP/ACUPP Case Study Series, ca. 1993; Jane Jacobs, "Can Big Plans Solve the Problem of Renewal?"; interview, Alan Littlewood.

315 "the best example": Leblanc.

315 "a district-scale experiment": Klemek, p. 222, caption, figure 12.2.

317 "enjoyed the activist part": Gerard.

318 "I realize I have been inflicting": JJ to Jason Epstein, December 15, 1974, Random House Papers, Box 1365, ColumbiaRare.

318 "I write a little way": Jane to John and Pete Butzner, April 2, 1976, Burns, 41:1.

CHAPTER 21: FLUMMOXED

319 "When you ask": JJ to Jason Epstein, August 12, 1976, Random House Papers, RH 1365, ColumbiaRare.

319 "I always hit some point": Alexander and Weadick, p. 30.

320 "I feel strongly": Jason Epstein to JJ, February 2, 1977, Random House Papers, Box 1365, ColumbiaRare.

321 "There is a fight to be had": "Mary Rowe on Cities, Nature, and Chaotic Systems," http://www.citybuilderbookclub.org, April 19, 2012.

322 "Islands seem to be wonderful": Sandra Martin, "An Urban Legend," p. 85. See also Alexander and Weadick, p. 29.

322 "I'm very slow": Warren, p. 16.

322 "stand the boredom": Alexander and Weadick, p. 30.

322 "tightly imprisoned": For JJ to Ned O'Gorman, December 20, 1965, and February 20, 1966 [but probably 1967], Burns, 5:3.

323 "all around 200 words or more": William Talada, "Obfuscation Overload," Amazon review, July 16, 2014.

323 "Oh, I'm so chaotic": *Matter*, p. 26.

325 "a caterpillar munching": Harvey, p. 42.

325 *The Muqaddimah*: *CityWealth*, p. 237.

325 recollections of Higgins: *CityWealth*, p. 240.

325 "in the form of a funeral description": JJ to John Butzner, April 5, 1974, Burns, 4:8.

325 extracting from the clergyman: *SofS*, pp. 86–87, 224.

325 "'such wonderful examples'": *Matter*, p. 26; see also Alexander and Weadick, p. 30.

326 " 'unaverage' clues": *D&L*, p. 574.

326 "solid statistical evidence": JJ to Stewart Brand, January 17, 1994, Burns, 6:5.

326 "an admiring puzzlement": *Ethics*, p. 34.

326 "When I start exploring": *Ethics*, p. 34.

327 favored small entities: "Perhaps the stagnation of the United States is irreversible unless and until, no doubt after great turmoil, what is now the United States has divided into a dozen or so separate countries," Jane Jacobs, "The Responsibilities of Cities," Queen's Lecture, Amsterdam, September 1984, Burns, 13:1.

328 Norway's from Sweden: *QofS*, chapter 3.

328 "Here in Toronto": *QofS*, p. 51.

328 *"a tour de force"*: Edgar Z. Friedenberg, "Splitting Up," review of *The Question of Separatism*, *New York Review of Books*, November 20, 1980.

328 "practically no reaction": *QofS*, p. 137.

328 refuted "some of the weaker arguments": Mazer.

328 "dreams in very good prose": *Matter*, p. 154.

CHAPTER 22: ADAM, KARL, AND JANE

329 "a kind of overhaul": JJ to M. Marcel Côté, June 30, 1982, Burns, 5:10.

329 "For a little while": *CityWealth*, p. 3; ensuing pages follow chapter 1.

331 Bardou: *CityWealth*, chapter 2.

332 We could beat our brains out: *CityWealth*, p. 34.

333 "was not a demonstration": *CityWealth*, p. 128.

333 "The difference between a rich backward economy": *CityWealth*, p. 63.

333 "Faulty feedback to cities": *CityWealth*, p. 158.

334 "done a great service": *Matter*, p. 106.

334 "learned, iconoclastic": *Matter*, p. 106.

334 wasn't high prices: *Matter*, p. 108.

334 "hated" by economists: JJ to Robert Brandes Gratz, June 10, 1988, Gratz papers.

335 "the mysteries of the trade": Warsh, p. 80. See Warsh's book and his "The Road Since 'The Mechanics of Economic Development,' " Economic Principals online, September 23, 2007.

335 "didn't inquire too deeply": Warsh, p. 81.

336 His subject was economic growth: Robert Lucas, "On the Mechanics of Economic Development," *Journal of Monetary Economics* 22 (1988): 3–42.

336 "The consequences for human welfare": Cited in Warsh, "The Road Since 'The Mechanics of Economic Development,' " Economic Principles online, September 23, 2007.

337 as he'd later tell the story: Martin Wolf and Robert Lucas, "Economies and Growth," *Ideas That Matter*, 3, no. 3 (undated): 11–14.

337 "Is it because innovations are so unpredictable?": JJ to Graciela Chichilnisky, June 9, 1993, Burns.

338 "I will be following very closely": Robert Lucas, "On the Mechanics of Economic Development," *Journal of Monetary Economics* 22 (1988): 37.

338 compared Jane's predictions: Edward L. Glaeser et al., "Growth in Cities, " *Journal of Political Economy* 100, no. 6 (December 1992): 1126–1152.

38 Canadian inventors: Pierre Desrochers and Samuli Leppälä, "Opening Up the

'Jacobs Spillovers' Black Box: Local Diversity, Creativity and the Processes Underlying New Combination," *Journal of Economic Geography* 11, no. 5 (2011): 843–63.

338 "an economics guru": John Barber, "Jacobs Embraced as Economic Guru," *Globe and Mail*, October 15, 1997. Examples of the literature on Jane Jacobs and economics include: Pierre Desrochers and Gert-Jan Hospers, "Cities and the Economic Development of Nations: An Essay on Jane Jacobs' Contribution to Economic Theory," *Canadian Journal of Regional Science* (spring 2007): 115–30; Clint Ballinger, "More on Jane Jacobs & Economics," http://www.open .salon.com/blog/clintballinger, accessed October 10, 2012; Sam Staley, "Disequilibrium and Time in the Urban Economy: Reassessing the Contributions of Jane Jacobs to Development Theory," *Market Process* 7, no. 1 (spring 1989): 16–21. See also Brian Tochterman, "Theorizing Neoliberal Urban Development: A Genealogy from Richard Florida to Jane Jacobs," *Radical History Review* (winter 2012): 65–87.

339 "Jane Jacobs Among the Economists": *Matter*, pp. 111–13.

339 "great novel of economic development": Robert E. Lucas Jr., "A Million Mutinies: The Key to Economic Development," excerpt from his book, *Lectures on Economic Growth* (Cambridge, MA: Harvard University Press, 2002).

340 "We have determined at last": Robert Kanigel, *On an Irish Island* (New York: Knopf, 2012), p. 223.

CHAPTER 23: WEBS OF TRUST

346 At one session: Taped, courtesy Roberta Gratz.

348 a cozy summertime community: Interviews, Toshiko Adilman, Jim Jacobs, Caitlin Broms-Jacobs, Alan Littlewood; photos and map provided by Ms. Adilman.

349 One summer day: Teleky; interview, Karen Reczuch.

349 "Thinking about a useful life": *Girl*, p. 33.

350 "enchanting": Erik Wensberg to JJ, May 4, 1989, Burns, 6:4.

350 was scarcely reviewed: "Not a first choice," wrote Maryleah Otto in *CM Archive* 17, no. 4 (July 1989).

350 "But the Sasquatch is imaginary": *Girl*, p. 48.

350 Hannover, West Germany: See *Matter*, p. 87.

350 "like an international merchant": *Matter*, p. 87. See also *Ethics*, pp. 6, 222; Jane Jacobs, "The Responsibilities of Cities," Queen's Lecture, Amsterdam, September 1984, Burns, 13:1.

351 "times of terrible piracy": *Matter*, p. 163. See also Warren, p. 6.

352 in very great time: *Systems*, p. 218, note for chapter 2. See also Alexander and Weadick; Warren, p. 7.

352 That's the guardian at work: "Eisenhower said, no, no, we never sent any spy planes over Russia," Jane told Claire Parin in a May 1999 interview [Burns 22:32], yet there it was, the wreckage of a U2 spy plane the Soviets had shot down, for all the world to see. "And nobody minded because after all that for National Security . . . A totally different point of view about the value honesty in these situations."

352 "not one over-riding system": *Ethics*, p. 211.

353 "As Machiavelli understood": *Systems*, p. 72.

353 "My characters": *Systems*, p. 13.

353 "I've become disturbed": *Systems*, p. 4.

354 "questions, answers, second thoughts": *Matter*, p. 161.

354 "It went over my head": JJ interview with Peter Gzowski, May 18, 1993, Burns, MS1995_029_CS08_REF.

354 "saved myself a lot of work": Warren, p. 9.

354 imagined as a blend: JJ to a reader, July 6, 1998, Burns, 1:6.

354 "like talking to a pillow": Interview, Margie Zeidler.

354 "were happy to seize the argumentative bit": *Matter*, p. 161,

354 "Where the Mafia most resembles": *Systems*, p. 94.

355 Mafia conclave: Account drawn from *Systems*, pp. 94, 175; JJ interview with Peter Gzowski, May 18, 1993, Burns, MS1995_029_CS08_REF.

355 "Well, it is all true": JJ to mother, February 11, 1970, Burns, 4:9.

355 "A brilliant exploration": *Matter*, p. 162.

356 "a very cold look": Alan Ryan, "Cautionary Tales," review of *Systems of Survival*, New York Review of Books, June 24, 1993.

356 "I don't think I was successful": Warren, p. 17.

356 her aunt Hannah's: Account drawn from *Alaska*, foreword.

357 "a great heroine": Radio interview with Desmond Glynn, January 10, 1996, Burns, MS1995_029_CS09.

357 birch-bark basket: JJ to John Branson, August 18, 1994, Burns, 1:7.

357 "had hooked me": *Alaska*, p. xv.

357 "got such a bang out of it": Robin Roger, p. 6.

358 "overcome ignorance": *Alaska*, p. 5.

358 "improved organization": *Alaska*, p. xviii.

358 They'd gathered brochures: Details of the family's trip to Alaska, maps, brochures, plans, and the like, can be found at Burns, mostly Boxes 1, 14–18.

359 "along a crooked airpath": *Alaska*, p. 260.

359 "I had lived in the Rocky Mountains": *Alaska*, p. 63.

359 "treasure trove": JJ to John and Pete Butzner, July 26, 1994, Burns, 1:7.

359 "demolished by the tidal wave": "Epilogue," early manuscript draft, Burns, 16:7. Compare with *Alaska*, p. 262.

359 "the three happiest months": Robin Roger, p. 6. Jane "ignored the aborted draft" she had worked on half a century before, she wrote Jason Epstein on July 25, 1996, choosing to start anew from Hannah's original manuscript instead.

360 "Every generation": Robin Roger, p. 5.

360 "tended to fall prey": Paul Goldberger, "Jane Jacobs: Still a Pioneer," *New York Times Book Review*, April 28, 1996.

361 "I have my doubts": Branson letter at Burns, 1:7.

361 "the infirmities of age": JJ to Simon Doyon, August 3, 1999, Burns, 3:4.

361 "one hell of an operation": JJ to Jason Epstein, November 21 [1973], Random House Papers, Box 1365, ColumbiaRare.

361 "stupid, stupid lady": JJ to Roberta Brandes Gratz, January 15, 1982, Gratz papers.

"such a stupid careless thing": JJ to Roberta Brandes Gratz, November 18, 1985, Gratz papers.

"white hair and a marked stoop": *Matter*, p. 13.

362 "aware we're aging": JJ to Lukas van Spengler, January 20, 1994, Burns, 3:6.

363 "lost the sight": JJ to Ellen Perry, January 31, 1996, Burns, 1.

363 Someone snapped a picture: *Matter*, p. 153.

363 "Our news is not so great": JJ to John Branson, July 26, 1996, Burns, 1:9.

363 "liked going for the treatments": Robert Fulford, "Lives Lived: Robert Hyde Jacobs," *Globe and Mail*, September 24, 1996.

363 "a happy month": JJ to John Branson, October 11, 1996, Burns, 1:15.

363 "An interesting, loveable": Obituary notice, *Globe and Mail*, September 18, 1996. Jane gave $3,000 to Princess Margaret Hospital for its radiation treatment program. "We all remember . . . the kindness and sensitivity" with which Bob was treated there; JJ to David G. Payne, November 12, 1996, Burns, 7:5.

363 "am kind of useless": JJ to Ellen Perry Berkeley, October 9, 1996, Burns, 1.

CHAPTER 24: IDEAS THAT MATTER

364 "firmly ensconced": Jefferson Medal details, Burns, 21:5.

365 "I still cannot walk down": Simon Jenkins, on five best books about cities, *Wall Street Journal*, December 24, 2011. Jenkins apparently draws from Immanuel Kant: "From the crooked timber of mankind nothing entirely straight can be built."

365 "vernacular utopia": Montgomery.

366 "connected with a generation": Sandra Martin, "Jane Jacobs, Writer, Urban Planner, Activist."

366 "car people" and "foot people": *D&L*, p. xxii.

366 "a nauseating name for an old ideal": *D&L*, p. 81.

366 "*interconnected, not interrelated*": Jamin Creed Rowan, "The New York School," p. 591.

366 sides of city life unrelated to physical form: Bramwell, in 2011, writes, "The Bedford-Stuyvesant district in Brooklyn, with its rows of pre-war brownstones, front stoops, and mixed uses, adheres almost perfectly to Jacobite principles. In movies such as 'Do the Right Thing,' Bed-Stuy native Spike Lee recreates its street life, replete with old men lounging on curbsides, children playing in the streets, mothers watching from windows, and local characters exchanging gossip. Nevertheless, for decades, strangers have not felt safe within it . . . Human capital overwhelms the influence of neighborhood design every time. On the other hand, Bed-Stuy is physically so attractive that it is now rapidly un-slumming, thus proving Jacobs's points all over again."

367 "So thoroughly internalized": Campanella, p. 144.

367 "compared to developers": Zukin, "Jane Jacobs," *Architectural Review*.

368 "we stopped building places worth gentrifying": Stephen Wickens, "Jane Jacobs Honoured in the Breach," *Globe and Mail*, May 6, 2011. See also interview Jane by Claire Perrin, May 1999, Burns, 22:32.

368 "I hope any reader": *D&L*, p. 22.

368 older, smaller buildings: "Older, Smaller, Better: Measuring How the Ch[...] of Buildings and Blocks Influences Urban Vitality," National Trust for [...] Preservation report, May 2014.

368 Did "eyes on the street" reduce crime?: Matt Bevilacqua, "Researchers Challenge Jane Jacobsian Notion That 'Eyes on the Street' Reduce Crime," *NextCity*, February 22, 2013.

368 Was gradual and piecemeal development: Eric Jaffe, "Jane Jacobs Was Right: Gradual Redevelopment Does Promote Community," *Atlantic Cities*, March 8, 2013.

369 It became the measure: For numerous examples of the influences of *Death and Life* internationally, see edited works by Hirt; Schubert; Page and Mennel.

369 correct in all she saw?: After living in the Annex, Jane herself, according to son Ned, "modified" her insistence on the central importance of very high-density neighborhoods. "I think she realized that maybe she had highballed it a bit," in response to the prevailing low-density faith of the 1950s.

370 "peak sprawl": Emily Badger, "Have We Reached Peak Sprawl?" *Atlantic Cities*, October 2, 2013.

370 "Who could have envisioned": Goldberger, "Tribute to Jane Jacobs."

371 "the influence of Jane Jacobs": Montgomery, p. 273.

371 James Marston Fitch once observed: Excerpt from *The Architecture of the American People* in Burns, 2:20.

372 "We'd strap her on the front": "An Urban Visionary," *Vancouver Sun*, April 26, 2006. See also *Matter*, pp. 187, 210–11.

372 she worried she'd hurt herself: Interview, Jim Jacobs.

373 "While I can always use more money": JJ to William K. Reilly, January 29, 1986, Burns, 6:3.

374 "Much as I feel fondly attached": JJ to George Rupp, December 4, 2000, Burns, 4:2.

374 "About a year and a half ago": Peter Laurence to JJ, February 28, 1999, Burns, 39:11.

374 "a comprehensive intellectual biography": Christopher Klemek to JJ, March 4, 2002, Burns, 43:10.

375 "Anyone with this amount of sway": Vanda Sendzimir to JJ, October 16, 1995; JJ to Sendzimir, October 20, 1995; at Burns, 6:5.

375 "Cityscapes, Sidewalks and Scranton": Michael Illuzzi to JJ, June 26, 2001; JJ to Illuzzi on June 26, his reply on July 18, her response on July 24; at Burns, 4:5.

375 "These past six months": Timothy Patitsas to JJ, January 26, 2000; JJ to Patitsas, February 12, 2000; Patitsas to JJ, March 13, 2000; at Burns, 7:1. See also "The City as Liturgy: An Orthodox Theologian Corresponds with Jane Jacobs About a Gentle Reconciliation of Science and Religion," in George D. Dragas, ed., *Legacy of Achievement* (Boston: Newrome Press, 2007), pp. 799–819.

376 "the Kings": See, for example, Eli Yarhi, "Tale of Two Kings: The Story of Toronto's Real Estate Transformation," http://www.psrbrokerage.com; "Regeneration in the Kings: Directions and Emerging Trends," Toronto Urban Development Services, City Planning Division, November 2002; interview, Ken Greenberg.

377 "It's magical": Steigerwald, p. 8.

377 "saved one neighbourhood": Wellman.

"so many parking lots": "Random Comments," *Boston College Environmental Affairs Law Review* 28, no. 4 (2001): 540.

"The first hit our city took": Geeman's Blog, October 17, 2014, http://www.geeman655.wordpress.com.

378 "shit disturber": Interview, John Downing; Downing's article, "Jane Jacobs: She Listened to No One."

378 "smiled benignly": Fulford, *Accidental City*, p. 83.

378 the Order of Canada: Burns, 21:7.

379 "Ideas That Matter": Account drawn from Cayo; interviews, Alan Broadbent, Jim Jacobs; event materials, programs, brochures, and planning documents, including John Sewell, typescript, "Rethinking Cities, Economies, Countries: A Symposium with Jane Jacobs as Mentor," April 29, 1996, Burns, 20:6–7.

379 "I agreed they could do this": JJ to John Butzner, n.d., but annotated as 1997, Burns.

379 "So bedazzling": Cayo.

379 "Have you ever been?": JJ to Ellen Perry, August 14, 1999, Burns, 1. The balloon ride was a gift from Alan Broadbent, a philanthropist and friend.

380 "At some point along the trail": *D&L*, p. xxvi.

CHAPTER 25: CIVILIZATION'S CHILD

382 "is to learn economics from nature": *Nature*, p. 8.

382 "I'm convinced": *Nature*, p. 11.

383 "a blob of multiplied generality": *Nature*, p. 17.

383 "Our remote ancestors": *Nature*, p. 23.

383 "human beings exist": *Nature*, p. ix.

383 "Those insufferable yuppies": Mike Davis, "Green Streets," review of *The Nature of Economies*, *Village Voice*, April 11, 2000.

384 "fresh and provocative": Steven Shaviro, review of *The Nature of Economies*, blog, http://www.shaviro.com, January 16, 2003.

384 "come to be seen": Taylor, "Jane Jacobs (1916–2006): An Appreciation."

384 *listened* to one another: Patrick [last name unknown] to JJ, April 4, 2000, Burns, 1:11: "Your characters are basically kind to each other and take each other's ideas seriously . . . They listen to each other, another thing I see too little of among intellectuals."

384 "learning to walk again": JJ to Myron Magnet, February 13, 2000, Burns, 1:11.

384 "I'm taking the glucosamine": JJ to Sally [?], June 19, 2000, Burns, 3:6.

384 "You were poised as a queen": Margot Gayle to JJ, April 2, 2000, Burns, 7:1.

384 "nice wheeled walker": JJ to Anneke, April 23, 2001, Burns, 7:2. The previous year, Jane had written a local medical supply company that she wished now to buy the walker she had been renting: "It now seems that I am going to need this walker indefinitely, rather than temporarily as I first supposed," JJ to Therapy Supplies and Rental, July 10, 2000, Burns, 7:7.

384 "merry leading-edge explorers": *Dark*, dedication.

385 "worked day and night": JJ to David Ebershoff, November 26, 2003, David Ebershoff papers.

385 "Crisp, entertaining": Kirkus review attached to David Ebershoff to JJ, February 24, 2004, Burns, 43:2.

385 promotional tour: 2004 tour chronology supplied by Anne Collins, Random House Canada.

386 "serfs, feudal tenants": Jane Jacobs, draft of Mumford lecture, David Ebershoff papers. The several versions of the lecture show Jane really working it over. It ends: "Thank you for your patience as I struggle, like all of us, to find sane footing in the pervading insanity and insecurity of the shaky present tense."

386 "grotesque parodies": Essay based on Mumford lecture, JJ, "The Greening of the City," *New York Times*, May 16, 2004.

386 "because people make it new": Gopnik.

386 "the first theoretical explanation": JJ, draft table of contents for unfinished book, then titled *Uncovering the Economy: A New Hypothesis,* Ebershoff papers.

387 formal contracts: Anne Collins to Aaron Milrad and Jane Jacobs, April 19, 2004, Anne Collins papers.

387 "I thought she would be with us forever": See also Sandra Martin, "Jane Jacobs, Writer, Urban Planner, Activist."

387 "first terrific pages": David Ebershoff to JJ, December 10, 2004, Ebershoff papers.

387 "You must think": JJ to David Ellerman, March 18, 2005, Burns. See also JJ to Tom G. Palmer, June 10, 2003, Burns, 43:6, where Jane takes umbrage at the few dollars an editor proposes to pay her for an article: "It is not only 'nominal,' as you characterize it, but insulting. You might do better to explain to your prospective victims or martyrs" why they offered so paltry a sum—whereupon she makes her way through a bleak litany of possible reasons.

388 "Unwinding Vicious Spirals": *Dark,* p. 215.

390 supposed to have joked: Martin, "Jane Jacobs, Writer, Urban Planner, Activist."

390 applying the word "theorist": Robert Lucas, in "Economies and Growth," *Ideas That Matter* 3, no. 3 n.d., p. 12.

391 retreat to the abstract: Several of Jane's friends observed this change in her.

391 three women: See, for example, Rebecca Solnit, "Three Who Made a Revolution," *Nation*, March 16, 2006; Urbashi Vaid, blog, "Women as Public Intellectuals: The Legacies of Jane Jacobs, Rachel Carson and Betty Friedan," November 15, 2011; "Jane Jacobs, Rachel Carson, Betty Friedan: One Provocative Evening," http://www.womenvoicesforchange.org, November 15, 2011; Josh Stephens, "50 Years Later, Jacobs Still Leads a Sorority of Dissent," *California Planning & Development Report*, December 28, 2011. The three women, Stephens writes, spoke for many "who had grown weary of the false promises of the 1950s."

392 "ladies' auxiliary": JJ, typed draft of her Mumford lecture, Ebershoff papers.

392 pushing a baby carriage: Veronica Horwell, "Jane Jacobs," *Guardian,* April 27, 2006; Sir Peter Hall, "In Context—Social Ideal Ends in Yuppy Ghettos," *Planning Resource,* June 3, 2011.

393 "the first book on the subject": JJ to Jason Epstein, January 26, 1971, Random House Papers, RH 1365, ColumbiaRare.

393 "man's fundamental propensity": Warren, p. 8.

393 "market mamas": JJ to Benjamin H. Hardy, February 2, 1985, Burns, 6:3.

394 "Like other women": JJ to Frank Mannheim, May 9, 2005, Burns, 43:8.

395 "an amateur in the professional's den": Taylor, "Jane Jacobs (1916–2006): An Appreciation," p. 1983.

"a revolutionary writer": Taylor, "Jane Jacobs (1916–2006): An Appreciation," p. 1986.

"more about restoration": Mazer.

"planning is good": "Quotation of the Day," *New York Times*, May 12, 1962.

In another version: "I'm pretty sick of people being hurt in the concrete and benefited in the abstract, and this is what is always happening in planning." *Matter*, p. 60. Or again: "There is nothing more frustrating than to be continually hurt in the concrete while you are continually assured, by persons out of touch with the realities, that you are being helped in the abstract." JJ, Alan B. Plaunt Memorial Lecture, "The Changing Economy of Canada," March 19, 1970, Burns, 42:1.

396 "Any child is more important": "Efficiency and the Commons," conversation between JJ and Janice Gross Stein, November 15, 2001, in *Ideas That Matter 2*, no. 2 (n.d).

396 "I've had a very easy life": *Matter*, p. 13.

397 Sabilla Bodine: See Jacobs/Butzner genealogical chart, Burns, 4:7. The original Sabilla Bodine died April 4, 1825.

397 "dynamics of civilization": *D&L*, p. xii.

397 "we live in a graveyard": *Dark*, p. 3.

398 "not the book": Bruce Fisher. Other harsh reviews included those of Michiko Kakutani in *The New York Times*, who called it an "extremely sloppy book"; and Peter Laurence, writing in the *Journal of the Society of Architectural Historians*, who termed her last book perhaps "her least original and least persuasive." Jane, says her son Jim, was aware it was not as strong as her other books; she did it too quickly.

398 "Even if we go into darkness": Gopnik.

398 "began by writing about sidewalks": Mazer.

399 "To civilization!": *Systems*, p. 214.

BIBLIOGRAPHY

The bibliography excludes Wikipedia and similar such online entries; routine newspaper articles, obituaries, brochures, and newsletter entries; ordinary genealogical information about the Butzners, Robisons, and Jacobses; and newspaper clippings and the like bearing on local history. When relevant, these are mostly consigned to the Notes.

The 1997 book *Ideas That Matter*, edited by Max Allen, and abbreviated in the Notes as *Matter*, is a particularly rich sampling of information about Jane Jacobs, containing hundreds of articles, letters, and excerpts culled from the Jane Jacobs Papers held at the Burns Library in Boston, as well as some original contributions. The numerous citations in the Notes to this essential book simply cite the page number; for further bibliographical reference consult the book itself. The book *Ideas That Matter* was inspired by a conference of the same name held in Toronto in 1997. The same name was used for a short-lived journal, which is referred to in the Notes by its full name.

As for Jane Jacobs's own work, writings published under her maiden name, Jane Butzner, appear under that name. Articles written for *Amerika* in Russian translation do not appear here but are referred to in the text and the Notes.

WORKS BY JANE JACOBS

BOOKS

The Death and Life of Great American Cities. 50th anniversary edition. New Modern Library. Originally published by Random House, 1961.

The Economy of Cities. New York: Vintage Books, 1970.

The Question of Separatism: Quebec and the Struggle over Sovereignty. Montreal: Baraka Books, 1980.

Cities and the Wealth of Nations: Principles of Economic Life. New York: Vintage Books, 1985.

The Girl on the Hat. Illustrated by Karen Reczuch. Toronto: Oxford University Press, 1989.

Systems of Survival: A Dialogue on the Moral Foundations of Commerce and Politics. New York: Vintage Books, 1994.

The Nature of Economies. New York: Vintage Books, 2001.

Dark Age Ahead. New York: Vintage Books, 2005.

Jacobs, Jane, ed., with introduction and commentary. *A Schoolteacher in Old Alaska: The Story of Hannah Breece.* New York: Vintage Books, 1997.

SELECTED ARTICLES *(including uncredited ones where JJ is known to be the author),* TALKS, PANEL PRESENTATIONS

"Islands the Boats Pass By." *Harper's Bazaar* (July 1947).

"Big Double Hospital." *Architectural Forum* (June 1952), unbylined.

"Self-Selection." *Architectural Forum* (November 1953), unbylined.

"Hitch-hiking with the Fish." Unpublished article, ca. 1954. Burns 22:8.

"Philadelphia's Redevelopment." *Architectural Forum* (July 1955), unbylined.

"The Missing Link in City Redevelopment." *Architectural Forum* (June 1956).

"By 1976 What City Pattern?" *Architectural Forum* (September 1956), unbylined.

"Our 'Surplus' Land." *Architectural Forum* (March 1957), unbylined editorial.

"New York's Office Boom." *Architectural Forum* (March 1957).

"Row Houses for Cities." *Architectural Forum* (May 1957).

"Metropolitan Government." *Architectural Forum* (August 1957).

"Washington." *Architectural Forum* (January 1958).

"The City's Threat to Open Land." *Architectural Forum* (January 1958), unbylined.

"Redevelopment Today." *Architectural Forum* (April 1958), unbylined.

"Downtown Is for People." In Whyte, *The Exploding Metropolis,* 157–84.

"Talk Given April 20, 1958, at a dinner panel of the New School Associates." Typescript. Burns.

"New Heart for Baltimore." *Architectural Forum* (June 1958).

"What Is a City?" *Architectural Forum* (July 1958), unbylined editorial.

"Housing for the Independent Age." *Architectural Forum* (August 1958).

"Modern City Planning: The Victory over Vitality." *Columbia University Forum* (fall 1961).

"Remarks at Ceremony at Westbeth, Late 1960s." Annotated typescript. Burns 42:1.

"The Citizen in Urban Renewal: Participation or Manipulation?" Typescript. February 21, 1962. Burns.

Unpublished, untitled two-page essay on civil disobedience, ca. November 1967. Burns.

"Strategies for Helping Cities." *American Economic Review* (September 1969).

"Response to Remarks by Mr. Rouse and Mr. Safdie." Typescript. Boston, 1980. Burns.

"Big Plans Solve the Problem of Renewal?" Typescript of lecture, for international congress, "Considerations in Urban Redevelopment," Hamburg, West Germany, 1981. Burns 13:1.

"VA Failed." *New York Review of Books,* May 10, 1984.

"The Responsibilities of Cities." Typescript. Queen's Lecture, Royal Palace, Amsterdam, September 1984. Burns.

Speech on women as business creators, November 1992. Typescript. Burns 13:1.

"Reading, Writing, and Love-Apples." In Ellen Perry Berkeley, *At Grandmother's Table*. Minneapolis: Fairview Press, 2000.

"Time and Change as Neighbourhood Allies." *Ideas That Matter* 3, no. 2 (n.d.): 4–7. Excerpted from address given on receiving 2001 Vincent Scully Prize. Burns 22:33.

Introduction to Mark Twain's *The Innocents Abroad*. New York: Modern Library, 2003.

"The Past, Present and Future of the Office Skyscraper." Lewis Mumford lecture, May 6, 2004. Typescript, in several edited versions, courtesy Anne Collins and David Ebershoff.

"The Greening of the City." *New York Times*, May 16, 2004.

SECONDARY SOURCES

"Abattoir for Sacred Cows." Brief reviews of *The Death and Life of Great American Cities*, by Charles Abrams, Henry S. Churchill, Leonard K. Eaton, Robert L. Geddes, Percival Goodman, Kevin Lynch, Eugene Raskin, and Catherine Bauer Wurster. *Progressive Architecture* (April 1962).

Alexander, Don. *Jane Jacobs: Urban Wisdom, Princeton, N.J.* Films for the Humanities and Sciences, 2006.

Alexander, Don, and Joe Weadick. Interview with Jane Jacobs. October 2000. Transcript. Burns 38:1.

Alexiou, Alice Sparberg. *Jane Jacobs: Urban Visionary*. New Brunswick: Rutgers University Press, 2006.

Allen, Max, ed. *Ideas That Matter: The Worlds of Jane Jacobs*. Owen Sound, Ont.: Ginger Press, 1997.

Amateau, Albert. "Jane Jacobs, Urban Legend, Returns Downtown." *Villager* (New York), May 14–20, 2004.

———. "Jane Jacobs, Activist Who Saved Village, Is Dead at 89." *Villager* (New York), April 26–May 2, 2006.

"Analysis and Comments on the West Village Plan for Housing." Chairman Ballard Papers, New York City Municipal Archives. (Christopher Klemek, in *The Transatlantic*, p. 291, n. 40, suggests that this was "prepared inside the City Planning Commission sometime after June 1963" and before July 1964.)

Atkinson, Brooks. "Jane Jacobs, Author of Book on Cities, Makes the Most of Living in One." *New York Times*, November 10, 1961.

Auchincloss, Eve, and Nancy Lynch. "Disturber of the Peace: Jane Jacobs." *Mademoiselle* (October 1962).

Ballon, Hillary, and Kenneth T. Jackson. *Robert Moses and the Modern City Transformation of New York*. New York: W. W. Norton, 2007.

Barber, John. "Jacobs Embraced as Economic Guru." *Globe and Mail*, October -

Beauman, Ned. "Rereading: *The Death and Life of Great American Citie* Jacobs." *Guardian*, www.guardian.co.uk., October 14, 2011.

Bébout, Rick. "Master Builders Meet Citizen Activists." http://www.r^ queen/mtc/2ptref.htm, 2002.

Berman, Marshall. *All That Is Solid Melts Into Air: The Experience of Modernity.* New York: Simon and Schuster, 1982.

Blake, Peter. *Form Follows Fiasco: Why Modern Architecture Hasn't Worked.* Boston: Little, Brown, 1976.

———. *No Place Like Utopia: Modern Architecture and the Company We Kept.* New York: Alfred A. Knopf, 1993.

Bole, William. "Urban Legend." *Boston College Magazine* (fall 2010): 14–22.

Books and Authors Luncheon, March 19, 1962. Audio. New York City Municipal Archives, wnyc_LT9522.

Bramwell, Austin. "Cobblestone Conservative." *American Conservative*, October 5, 2011.

Brand, Stewart. "Vital Cities: An Interview with Jane Jacobs." *Whole Earth* (winter 1998).

Bromley, Hank. "The Convention Follies, Part 5: A Conversation with Jane Jacobs." *Artvoice* 11, no. 30 (July 27, 2000).

The Burning World. Film. McLuhan Associates, 1970.

Butzner, Jane. "Where the Fur Flies." *Vogue*, November 15, 1935.

———. "Diamonds in the Tough." Typescript manuscript. Burns 13:1. (Article appeared in *Vogue*.)

———. "Leather Shocking Tales." *Vogue*, March 1, 1936.

———. "WANTED: Women to Fill 2,795 Kinds of Jobs." *Washington Post*, October 26, 1942.

———. "Trylon's Steel Helps to Build Big New Nickel Plant in Cuba." *New York Herald Tribune*, December 27, 1942.

———. "Daily's Effort Saves City from 'Ghost Town' Fate." *Editor & Publisher* (1943).

———. "30,000 Unemployed and 7000 Empty Houses in Scranton, Neglected City." *Iron Age*, March 25, 1943.

Butzner, Jane, ed. *Constitutional Chaff—Rejected Suggestions of the Constitutional Convention of 1787 with Explanatory Argument.* New York: Columbia University Press, 1941.

Butzner, J. I. "Non-Ferrous Metals." *Iron Age,* January 7, 1943.

———. "Silver Alloy Brazing," *Iron Age,* September 23, 1943.

Campanella, Thomas J. "Jane Jacobs and the Death and Life of American Planning." In Page and Mennel, pp. 141–60.

Caro, Robert. *The Power Broker: Robert Moses and the Fall of New York.* New York: Knopf, 1974.

Cassegard, Carl. "Jane Jacobs—Some Critical Remarks." The World (and Books) blog, http://www.carlcassegard.blogspot, January 31, 2011.

Cayo, Don. "Some Thoughts on the Matter of Ideas." *Globe and Mail*, October 25, 1997.

Charley in New Town. Animated film. Halas & Batchelor Cartoon Film Production. Central Office of Information (U.K.), 1948.

———, Edward T. Review of *The Death and Life of Great American Cities. Commonweal*, December 22, 1961.

———, Roberto, Tia Duer, and Ke Fang. "Urban Economy and Development: Interview of Jane Jacobs." Transcript. World Bank, February 4, 2002.

———, Pierre, and Olivier Balez. *Robert Moses: Master Builder of New York City.* Nobrow, 2014.

Cohen, Lizabeth. "Ed Logue and the Struggle to Save America's Cities." *Research Briefs*. Real Estate Academic Initiative at Harvard University, March 2010.

Crane, Elise. "The Full-Format American Dream: *Amerika* as a Key Tool of Cold War Public Diplomacy." *American Diplomacy* (January 2010).

Cullum, Lee. "Where Trade Began: Jane Jacobs." *Parabola* (winter 1993).

Cunningham, James V. "Jane Jacobs Visits Pittsburgh." *New City* (Catholic Council on Working Life), September 15, 1962.

Crombie, David. "Jane Jacobs: The Toronto Experience." In Goldsmith and Elizabeth, pp. 125–34.

Daniere, Amrita. "Canadian Urbanism and Jane Jacobs." *Journal of Urban Affairs* 22, no. 4 (2000).

Darley, Gillian. "Ian Nairn and Jane Jacobs, the Lessons from Britain and America." *Journal of Architecture* 17, no. 2 (2012): 733–46.

Davis, Mike. Review of *The Nature of Economies*. *Village Voice*, April 11, 2000.

De Backer, Mattias. "In Search of a Present-day Utopia: The Heritage of the Modernists." Polis, polismaster.edu European Urban Cultures Studies portal, May 30, 2012.

DeLeo, Joseph, and David L. A. Gordon. "Directions for New Urban Neighbourhoods: Learning from St. Lawrence." Case study. Canadian Institute of Planners/Association of Canadian University Planning Programs, n.d.

Dennis, Nigel. "Under the City Wall." *Sunday Telegraph* (London), May 3, 1970.

DePalma, Anthony. "At Home with Jane Jacobs, Urban Hero." *New York Times*, November 6, 1997.

"Deplanning the Planners." *Time*, November 10, 1961.

Desrochers, Pierre. Review of *The Nature of Economies*. *Le Québécois Libre*, April 29, 2000.

———. "The Death and Life of a Reluctant Urban Icon." *Journal of Libertarian Studies* (fall 2007): 115–36.

Desrochers, Pierre, and Gert-Jan Hospers. "Cities and Economic Development of Nations: An Essay on Jane Jacobs' Contribution to Economic Theory." *Canadian Journal of Regional Science* (spring 2007): 115–30.

Desrochers, Pierre, and Samuli Leppälä. "Opening Up the 'Jacobs Spillovers' Black Box: Local Diversity, Creativity and the Processes Underlying New Combinations." *Journal of Economic Geography* 11, no. 5 (2011): 843–63.

Diehl, Lorraine B. *Over Here! New York City During World War II*. New York: Harper Collins, 2010.

Dillon, David. "Jane Jacobs: Eyes on the Street." *Preservation* (January/February 1998): 39–43.

Dorfman, Nancy. Review of *The Economy of Cities*. *Journal of Economic Literature* (June 1970): 492–93.

Downing, John. "Jane Jacobs: She Listened to No One." *Toronto Sun*, April 27 2006.

Dreir, Peter. "Jane Jacobs's Legacy." *City & Community* (September 2006): 227–3

Ehrenfelt, Alan. *The Great Inversion and the Future of the American City*. New Y Alfred A. Knopf, 2012.

Epstein, Jason. "New York: The Prophet." *New York Review of Books*, Aug 2009, pp. 133–35.

———. Introduction. 50th anniversary edition of Jacobs, *The Death and Lif American Cities*, 2011.

———. "Jane Jacobs and the Republican Radicals." *New York Review of Books* blog, March 30, 2012.

Esler, Cliff. Unpublished memoir.

Farewell Oak Street. Film. Grant McLean, director. National Film Board of Canada, 1953.

Fisher, Bruce. "The War for Jane Jacobs." *Artvoice,* June 23, 2010.

Fisher, Sean M., and Carolyn Hughes. *The Last Tenement: Confronting Community and Urban Renewal in Boston's West End.* Boston: Bostonian Society, 1992.

Fishman, Robert. *Urban Utopias in the Twentieth Century: Ebenezer Howard, Frank Lloyd Wright, and Le Corbusier.* New York: Basic Books, 1977.

———. "Howard and the Garden." *APA Journal* (spring 1998): 127–28.

———. "Rethinking Public Housing." *Places* 16, no. 2 (2004): 26–33.

———. "Revolt of the Urbs." In Ballon and Jackson, pp. 122–29.

Fitch, James Marston. Review of *The Economy of Cities. Forum* (July-August 1969): 98–99.

Flint, Anthony. *Wrestling with Moses: How Jane Jacobs Took on New York's Master Builder and Transformed the American City.* New York: Random House, 2009.

Friedenberg, Edgar Z. "Splitting Up." *New York Review of Books,* November 20, 1980.

Frigand, Sidney J. "West Village—Lessons in Urban Renewal." *Pratt Planning Papers* (February 1962): 3–5.

Frigand, Sidney, and Peter Lapham. "The Laws of the Asphalt Jungle." Summary memo. Panel discussion. Museum of Modern Art, February 8, 1962. Commissioner Goldstone Papers, New York Municipal Archives.

Fulford, Robert. "When Jane Jacobs Took On the World." *New York Times Book Review,* February 16, 1992.

———. *Accidental City: The Transformation of Toronto.* Boston: Houghton Mifflin, 1996.

———. "Radical Dreamer: Jane Jacobs on the Streets of Toronto." *Azure* (October-November 1997).

———. Review of *The Nature of Economies. National Post,* March 28, 2000.

Gans, Herbert J. *The Urban Villagers: Group and Class in the Life of Italian-Americans.* New York: Free Press, 1962.

———. "City Planning and Urban Realities." Review of *Death and Life. Commentary,* February 1, 1962.

———. "The Dream of Human Cities." Review of *The Economy of Cities. New Republic,* June 7, 1969.

———. "Jane Jacobs: Toward an Understanding of 'Death and Life of Great American Cities.' " *City & Community* (September 2006): 213–15.

Gerard, Warren. "Jane Jacobs Dies at 89." *Toronto Star,* April 25, 2006.

Gladwell, Malcolm. "Designs for Working." *New Yorker,* December 11, 2000.

Glaeser, Edward. "What a City Needs." *New Republic,* September 4, 2009.

Glazer, Nathan. "Why City Planning Is Obsolete." *Architectural Forum* (July 1958).

———. "Letter from East Harlem." *City Journal* (autumn 1991).

———. *From a Cause to a Style: Modernist Architecture's Encounter with the American City.* Princeton: Princeton University Press, 2007.

———. "What Happened to the Social Agenda?" *American Scholar* (spring 2007).

———, John M., and Peter Meiser. "Housing and Urban Redevelopment: Two Case [Studi]es of Community Involvement." *Housing and Society* 5, no. 3 (1978): 2–13.

Goist, Park Dixon. "Lewis Mumford and 'Anti-Urbanism.'" *Journal of the American Institute of Planners* (September 1969): 340–47.

Goldberger, Paul. "Jane Jacobs: Still a Pioneer." *New York Times Book Review,* April 28, 1996.

———. "For William H. Whyte." Unpublished lecture, January 19, 1999.

———. "Tribute to Jane Jacobs." Lecture. Greenwich Village Historic Preservation Society, October 3, 2006.

———. "Uncommon Sense." *American Scholar* (autumn 2006).

———. *Why Architecture Matters.* New Haven: Yale University Press, 2009.

Goldsmith, Stephen A., and Lynne Elizabeth, eds. *What We See: Advancing the Observations of Jane Jacobs.* Oakland, Calif.: New Village Press, 2010.

Gopnik, Adam. "Cities and Songs." *New Yorker,* May 17, 2004.

Gordon, David L. A. "Directions for New Urban Neighbourhoods: Learning from St. Lawrence." Case study. Canadian Institute of Planners/Association of Canadian University Planning Programs, n.d.

Gratz, Roberta Brandes. *The Living City.* New York: Simon and Schuster, 1989.

———. *The Battle for Gotham: New York in the Shadow of Robert Moses and Jane Jacobs.* New York: Nation Books, 2010.

———. "Enough with 'Enough with Jane Jacobs' Already!" *Planetizen,* January 24, 2011.

Greenberg, Ken. "The Avenger of Cities." *Literary Review of Canada* (May 2004).

———. "Jane, We Miss You Terribly." *Ecoweek* (June 2006).

———. *Walking Home: The Life and Lessons of a City Builder.* Toronto: Vintage Canada, 2011.

Greene, Betsy Butzner, and Jim Greene. Butzner Family History, unpublished genealogy, January 2012.

Greene, Laurie. "Regent Park: A Brief History." *Ideas That Matter* 3, no. 1 (n.d.): 30–33.

Hacker, Andrew. "Back to Nature." Review of *The Nature of Economies. New York Review of Books,* June 15, 2000.

Hampson, Sarah. "Grand Old Jane." *Toronto Life,* November 1, 1997.

Harris, Blake. "Cities and Web Economies: Interview with Jane Jacobs." Http://www.digitalcommunities.com, 2002.

Harvey, Charlotte Bruce. "A Ruthless Mind." *Boston College Magazine* (summer 1998): 35–42.

Hill, David R. "Jane Jacobs' Ideas on Big, Diverse Cities: A Review and Commentary." *Journal of the American Planning Association* (summer 1988): 302–14.

Hirt, Sonia, ed., with Diane Zahm. *The Urban Wisdom of Jane Jacobs.* New York: Routledge, 2012.

Hock, Jennifer. "Jane Jacobs and the West Village: The Neighborhood Against Urban Renewal." *Journal of the Society of Architectural Historians* 66, no. 1 (March 2007): 16–19.

Hodge, Gerald. Review of *The Economy of Cities. Journal of the American Institute of Planners* 36, no. 2 (1970): 133–34.

Holden, Alfred. "Pillar of Community." *Taddle Creek* (May 2004).

———. "The Timely Arrival of Citizen Jane." *Toronto Star,* April 30, 2006.

———. "Jane Jacobs, 1916–2006." *Taddle Creek* (summer 2006).

Hoppenfeld, Morton, and A. Melamed. Reviews of *The Death and Life of Great ican Cities. Journal of the American Institute of Planners* 28, no. 2 (1962):

Hume, Christopher. "Big Ideas: Learning the Lessons of St. Lawrence Neighbourhood." *Toronto Star*, May 3, 2014.

Husock, Howard. "Urban Iconoclast: Jane Jacobs Revisited." *City Journal* (winter 1994).

"Industry Builds Kitimat—First Complete New Town in North America." *Architectural Forum* (July 1954): 128–47.

Isserman, Andrew M. Review of *Cities and the Wealth of Nations*. *Journal of the American Planning Association* 51, no. 2 (1985): 230–31.

Jackson, Kenneth T. *Crabgrass Frontier: The Suburbanization of the United States.* New York: Oxford University Press, 1985.

———. *WWII & NYC*. New York: New-York Historical Society, 2012.

Jacobs, John Kedzie. *The Stranger in the Attic: Finding a Lost Brother in His Letters Home*. Self-published, 2013.

Jacobs, Lucia. Video interview of Jane Jacobs, 1992. Courtesy of Lucia Jacobs.

Jacobs, Ned. "Changing the World by Saving Place." *Alternatives Journal* (summer 2002): 33–36.

Jacobs, Robert Hyde Jr. "A Structural Approach to Art Appreciation." *College Art Journal* (winter 1947–1948): 107–15.

James, Ryan K. "From 'Slum Clearance' to 'Revitalisation': Planning, Expertise and Moral Regulation in Toronto's Regent Park." *Planning Perspectives* (January 2010): 69–86.

"Jane Jacobs—The Nature of Economies." The Pinocchio Theory, blog, http://www.shaviro.com.

"Jane Jacobs Audio Tour of Toronto's Annex Neighborhood." Sarah Elton, producer. City of Toronto Office of the Public Realm, CBC/Radio Canada, and Jane's Walk, 2013.

"Jane Jacobs Speaks Out." *City* (Toronto) 1, no. 1 (summer 1969).

Janeway, Elizabeth, ed. *The Writer's World*. New York: McGraw-Hill, 1969.

Kakutani, Michiko. "A Lover of Urban Life Fears Decline and Fall." *New York Times*, June 15, 2004.

Kaunitz, Rita D. Review of Whyte, *The Exploding Metropolis*. *Journal of the American Institute of Planners* 25, no. 3 (1958): 159–61.

Kellerman, Regina M., ed. *The Architecture of the Greenwich Village Waterfront*. New York: New York University Press, 1989.

Kent, Leticia. "Jane Jacobs: Against Urban Renewal, for Urban Life." *New York Times*, May 25, 1969.

———. "Jane Jacobs." Oral history interview. Greenwich Village Society for Historic Preservation, October 1997.

Kidder, Paul. "The Urbanist Ethics of Jane Jacobs." *Ethics, Place and Environment* 11, no. 3 (October 2008): 253–66.

Kimmelman, Michael. "An Expert on Cities, at Home in the World." *New York Times*, May 31, 1993.

inkeloa, David. "Cities, Nature and Health: The Ecological Landscapes of Jane Jacobs and Rachel Carson." Paper delivered at 5th Round Table on Urban Environmental History, Berlin, July 6, 2008.

ek, Christopher. "Placing Jane Jacobs Within the Transatlantic Urban Conversa-
a." *Journal of the American Planning Association* (winter 2007): 49–67.

"Bacon's Rebellion." *Context* (spring 2007).

————. "From Political Outsider to Power Broker in Two 'Great American Cities.'" *Journal of Urban History* (January 2008): 309–32.

————. *The Transatlantic Collapse of Urban Renewal: Postwar Urbanism from New York to Berlin.* Chicago: University of Chicago Press, 2011.

Kramer, Jane. "The Ranks and Rungs of Mrs. Jacobs' Ladder." In Kramer, *Off Washington Square.* New York: Dell, Sloan & Pearce, 1963.

Krauss, Clifford. "Public Lives: War? Terrorists? No, Here's What's Really Scary." *New York Times,* June 29, 2004.

Krieger, Alex, and William S. Saunders. *Urban Design.* Minneapolis: University of Minnesota Press, 2009.

Kunstler, Jim. Interview, Jane Jacobs, September 6, 2000. *Metropolis* (March 2001). (On the Kunstler.com website, the interview transcript appears in two parts, which are preserved in the Notes as I and II, with separate page numbering.)

Kuttner, Robert. "Green Ideas." Review of *The Nature of Economies. New York Times,* March 12, 2000.

Lang, Glenna, and Marjory Wunsch. *Genius of Common Sense: Jane Jacobs and the Story of "The Death and Life of Great American Cities."* Boston: Godine, 2009.

Laurence, Peter. "Recontextualizing Jane Jacobs: Jane Jacobs and American Architecture, 1948–1968." Unpublished research thesis document. Harvard Graduate School of Design, 1999. Burns 39:10.

————. Review of *Dark Age Ahead. Journal of the Society of Architectural Historians* (March 2005): 126–28.

————. "The Death and Life of Urban Design: Jacobs, the Rockefeller Foundation, and the New Research in Urbanism, 1955–1965." *Journal of Urban Design* (June 2006): 145–72.

————. "Contradictions and Complexities: Jane Jacobs's and Robert Venturi's Complexity Theories." *Journal of Architectural Education* (2006): 49–60.

————. Review of *Jane Jacobs: Urban Visionary. Journal of Architectural Education* (2007): 52–54.

————. "Jane Jacobs Before *Death and Life.*" *Journal of the Society of Architectural Historians* (March 2007): 5–15.

————. "Jane Jacobs, American Architectural Criticism and Urban Design Theory, 1935–1965." Unpublished doctoral dissertation. University of Pennsylvania, 2009.

————. "The Unknown Jane Jacobs: Geographer, Propagandist, City Planning Idealist." In Page and Mennel, pp. 15–36.

Lawrence, Fred, ed. *Ethics in Making a Living: The Jane Jacobs Conference.* Atlanta: Scholars Press, 1989.

Leblanc, Dave. "35 Years On, St. Lawrence Template for Urban Housing." *Globe and Mail,* Feburary 8, 2013.

Lehmann-Haupt, Christopher. "Seeing Humans as Cogs in the Wheel of Nature." *New York Times,* March 2, 2000.

Littlewood, Alan. Reminiscence in *Matter,* pp. 202–04.

————. "Jane Jacobs: Memories." Unpublished typescript, October 2013. Written for the author.

Logue, Edward J. "The View from the 'Village' Is Not Enough." Typescript *Architectural Forum* (March 1962). Burns.

————. "Attack from Hudson Street." *American Scholar* (spring 1962): 343–4

Lovewell, Mark. "Micro-Enterprise Rules the Day." *Literary Review of Canada* (May 2004): 6–8.

Lurie, Ellen. "The Dreary Deadlock of Public Housing—How to Break it." *Architectural Forum* (June 1957).

———. "Community Action in East Harlem." In Leonard J. Duhl, *The Urban Condition; People and Policy in the Metropolis.* New York: Simon and Schuster, 1963.

Mannes, Marya. *The New York I Know.* Philadelphia: J. B. Lippincott, 1961.

Manshel, Andrew. "Enough with Jane Jacobs Already." Http://www.WSJ.com, June 29, 2010.

Martin, Douglas. "Jane Jacobs, Social Critic Who Redefined and Championed Cities, Is Dead at 89." *New York Times*, April 26, 2006.

Martin, Sandra. "An Urban Legend." *Maclean's*, October 20, 1997.

———. "Jane Jacobs, Writer, Urban Planner, Activist": 1916–2006." *Globe and Mail*, April 26, 2006.

———. "Jane Jacobs." In Sandra Martin, *Working the Dead Beat: 50 Lives That Changed Canada.* Toronto: Anansi, 2012.

Mazer, Alex. "City Limits." *Walrus* (May 2007).

McCall, Christina. "Let's Cherish Our Cities." *Chatelaine* (November 1970).

McCrary, Lewis. "*The Death and Life of Great American Cities* at 50." *American Conservative*, October 5, 2011.

McQuade, Walter. "Architecture." *Nation*, March 17, 1962.

Mehaffy, Michael. "The Power of Jane Jacobs' 'Web Way of Thinking.'" *Planetizen*, December 15, 2011.

Mellon, James G. "Visions of the Livable City: Reflections on the Jacobs-Mumford Debate." *Ethics, Place and Environment* (March 2009): 35–48.

Mendleson, Rachel. "How to Get Big Ideas Off the Ground: Toronto Mayors Edition." *Toronto Star*, October 10, 2014.

Mennel, Timothy. "Jane Jacobs, Andy Warhol, and the Kind of Problem a Community Is." In Page and Mennel, pp. 119–28.

———. "A Fight to Forget: Renewal, Robert Moses, Jane Jacobs, and the Stories of Our Cities." *Journal of Urban History* (2011): 1–8.

Mennel, Timothy, Jo Steffens, and Christopher Klemek, eds. *Block by Block: Jane Jacobs and the Future of New York.* New York: Princeton Architectural Press, 2007.

Miller, Donald L. *Lewis Mumford: A Life.* New York: Grove Press, 1989.

Mitchell, Joseph. *Up in the Old Hotel.* New York: Vintage, 1993.

Montgomery, Roger. "Is There Still Life in *The Death and Life?*" *Journal of the American Planning Association* (summer 1998): 269–74.

Moore, Denny. "Sunshine Spread Between States." *Presbyterian Advance*, September 15, 1932.

Morris, Jan. *Manhattan '45.* New York: Oxford University Press, 1987.

Moser, Sarah. "Jane Jacobs' West Village: Then and Now." Unpublished master's thesis. Tufts University, 2011.

Moses, Robert. "What Happened to Haussmann." *Architectural Forum* (July 1942): 57–66.

Mumford, Lewis. "Revaluations I: Howard's Garden City." *New York Review of Books*, April 8, 1965.

———. *The Urban Prospect.* New York: Harcourt, Brace & World, 1968.

Nichols, Mary Perot. "Village Housing Plan: Unslumming Without Tears." *Village Voice,* January 30, 1969.

Nowlan, David M. "Jane Jacobs Among the Economists." In *Matter,* pp. 111–13.

Osman, Suleiman. *The Invention of Brownstone Brooklyn: Gentrification and the Search for Authenticity in Postwar New York.* New York: Oxford University Press, 2011.

"Our Nation's Capital—The City and the Freeway." Transcript. May 23, 1965. Burns.

Our Presbyterian Heritage, 1706–1993. Council of the Mayland Presbyterian Fellowship (churches in Mitchell, Avery, and Yancey counties, N.C.), 1995.

Ouroussoff, Nicolai. "Outgrowing Jane Jacobs." *New York Times,* April 30, 2006.

Page, Max, and Timothy Mennel, eds. *Reconsidering Jane Jacobs.* Chicago: American Planning Association, 2011.

Pfretzschner, Paul A. "Panning the Planners." *Antioch Review* (spring 1962): 130–36.

Philpot, Robin. "An Interview with Jane Jacobs," May 2, 2005. In Jacobs, *The Question of Separatism,* 2011 edition.

Pirenne, Henri. *Medieval Cities: Their Origins and the Revival of Trade.* Princeton, N.J.: Princeton University Press, 1969. (Originally published 1925.)

Platt, Rutherford H. "Holly Whyte: Visionary for a Humane Metropolis." *Land Lines* (Lincoln Institute of Land Policy) (January 2003).

Plummer, Kevin. "Historicist: Marshall McLuhan, Urban Activist." Torontoist, blog, June 4, 2011. torontoist.com.

Pommer, Alfred, and Eleanor Winters. *Exploring the Original West Village.* Charleston, S.C.: History Press, 2011.

Powell, Michael. "An Urban Theorist Questions the Gospel of St. Jane." *New York Times* blog, February 19, 2010. cityroom.blogs.nytimes.com.

Prescott, Orville. Review of *The Death and Life of Great American Cities. New York Times,* November 3, 1961.

The Pruitt-Igoe Myth: An Urban History. Documentary. Chad Freidrichs, director. 2011.

"Regeneration in the Kings: Directions and Emerging Trends." Urban Development Services, [Toronto] City Planning Division, November 2002.

"Report of the [New York] City Planning Commission on the Designation of the West Village Area as Appropriate for Urban Renewal and as Master Plan." October 18, 1961, pp. 1–14. New York City Municipal Archives.

Richert, Evan D., and Mark B. Lapping. "Ebenezer Howard and the Garden City." *APA Journal* (spring 1998): 125–27.

Riggenbach, Jeff. "Jane Jacobs: Libertarian Outsider." Ludwig von Mises Institute of Canada, http://www.mises.ca/posts/articles/jane-jacobs-libertarian-outsider, December 13, 2012.

Rochon, Lisa. "Jane Jacobs at 81. *Metropolis* (April 1998).

———. "Time to Think Big About Jane." *Globe and Mail,* October 17, 2006.

Roger, Robin. "The Jane Jacobs of the Arctic." *Books in Canada* (November 1995): 4–6.

Rogers, Elizabeth Barlow. "Robert Moses and the Modern City." Review of thr museum exhibits devoted to Moses. *Journal of the Society of Architectural Historians* (March 2008): 130–33.

Rosenfelder, Mark. "It's the Cities, Stupid: Jane Jacobs on Cities." Http:// .zompist.com, ca. 2000.

Rothstein, Edward. "Jane Jacobs, Foe of Plans and Friend of City Life." *New York Times*, September 25, 2007.

Row, Arthur T. Review of *The Death and Life of Great American Cities*. *Yale Law Journal* (July 1962): 1597–1602.

Rowan, Jamin Creed. "The Redevelopment of 'Human and Social Values in Modern City Life': Jane Jacobs and the Rockefeller Foundation." Rockefeller Archive Center Research Reports Online, 2009.

———. "The New York School of Urban Ecology: The New Yorker, Rachel Carson, and Jane Jacobs." *American Literature* (September 2010): 583–610.

———. "The Literary Craft of Jane Jacobs." In Page and Mennel, pp. 43–56.

———. "Sidewalk Narratives, Tenement Narratives: Seeing Urban Renewal Through the Settlement Movement." *Journal of Urban History* no. 10 (2012): 1–19.

Rowe, Mary W. "Background on the Neighbourhood of Regent Park, Toronto." *Ideas That Matter* 3, no. 2 (n.d.): 20–22.

Russell, Paul. "Guest Column—Jane Jacobs: 'Toronto's Greatest Single Menace is the Spadina Expressway.'" *Toronto Life* (June 1969): 9–10.

Ryan, Alan. "Cautionary Tales." *New York Review of Books*, June 24, 1993.

Rybczynski, Witold. *Makeshift Metropolis: Ideas About Cities*. New York: Scribner, 2010.

Salisbury, Harrison. "Cities in the Grip of Revolution." Review of Whyte, *The Exploding Metropolis*. *New York Times Book Review*, October 5, 1958.

Saunders, Doug. "Citizen Jane." *Globe and Mail*, October 11, 1997.

Schwarz, Benjamin. "Gentrification and Its Discontents." *Atlantic* (June 2010).

Schubert, Dirk, ed. *Contemporary Perspectives on Jane Jacobs: Reassessing the Impacts of an Urban Visionary*. Burlington, Vt.: Ashgate, 2014.

Sennett, Richard. "An Urban Anarchist." *New York Review of Books*, January 1, 1970.

Sewell, John. *Up Against City Hall*. Toronto: James Lewis & Samuel, 1972.

———. *The Shape of the City: Toronto Struggles with Modern Planning*. Toronto: University of Toronto Press, 1993.

———. "Jane Jacobs in Conversation." *Ideas That Matter* 3, no. 3, (n.d): 31–33.

Silver, Nathan. "Jane Jacobs for Example." *Columbia Forum* (summer 1972): 47–49.

Smith, Michael E., Jason Ur, and Gary M. Feinman. "Jane Jacobs' 'Cities First' Model and Archeological Reality." *International Journal of Urban and Regional Research* 38 (2014): 1525–1535.

Soja, Edward W. "Putting Cities First: Remapping the Origins of Urbanism." In Gary Bridge and Sophie Watson, eds., *Companion to the City*. New York: Blackwell, 2002.

Solnit, Rebecca. "Three Who Made a Revolution." *Nation*, April 3, 2006.

Solow, Robert. "Economies of Truth." *New Republic,* May 15, 2000.

Soren, Richard. "Jane Jacobs on Diane Arbus." Unpublished interview, March 1, 2004. Burns 43:6.

Sorkin, Michael. *Twenty Minutes in Manhattan*. New York: North Point Press, 2013.

Sorkin, Michael, and Robert Campbell. "Two Critics Assess Jane Jacobs and Her Legacy." *Architectural Record* (June 2006).

Staley, Sam. "Disequilibrium and Time in the Urban Economy: Reassessing the Contributions of Jane Jacobs to Development Theory." *Market Process* 7, no. 1 (spring 1989): 16–21.

Starr, Roger. *Urban Choices: The City and Its Critics*. Baltimore: Penguin, 1967.

Steigerwald, Bill. "City Views." Interview with Jane Jacobs. *Reason* (June 2001).

Stephens, Josh. "50 Years Later, Jacobs Still Leads a Sorority of Dissent." *California Planning & Development Report* 26, no. 23 (December 1, 2011).

Stern, Robert A. M., Thomas Mellins, and David Fishman. *New York 1960: Architecture and Urbanism Between the Second World War and the Bicentennial.* 2nd edition. New York: Monacelli Press, 1997.

Taylor, Peter J. "Jane Jacobs (1916–2006): An Appreciation." *Environment and Planning A* 38 (2006): 1981–1992.

———. "Extraordinary Cities: Early City-ness and the Origins of Agriculture and States." *International Journal of Urban and Regional Research* online, January 19, 2012.

———. "Post-Childe, Post-Wirth: Respond to Smith, Ur and Feinman." *International Journal of Urban and Regional Research* online, December 12, 2014.

Teaford, Jon C. "Urban Renewal and Its Aftermath." *Housing Policy Debate* 11, no. 2 (2000): 443–65.

Teleky, Richard. "Editing 'Old Ladies'." *Canadian Literature* (spring 2014).

Tobin, Anne-Marie. "Urban Planning Guru Jane Jacobs on the Traps We Set for Ourselves." *All About Canoes,* March 27, 2000.

Tochterman, Brian. "Theorizing Neoliberal Urban Development: A Genealogy from Richard Florida to Jane Jacobs." *Radical History Review* (winter 2014): 65–87.

Turner, Chrisopher. "Mother Courage." *Guardian,* September 11, 2009.

"Urban Design: Condensed Report of an Invitation Conference Sponsored by Faculty and Alumni Association of Graduate School of Design, Harvard University, April 9–10, 1956." *Progressive Architecture* (August 1956): 97–112.

Vaca, Diane. "Jane Jacobs, Rachel Carson, Betty Friedan: One Provocative Evening." http://www.womenforchange.org, November 15, 2011.

Vafidis, Jen. "Jane Jacobs Looks into the Gloom." *Guernica,* December 18, 2012.

Valpy, Michael. "A Prophet for a Toxic Age." *Literary Review of Canada* (spring 2004): 9–11.

———. "Afraid of the Dark?" Review of *Dark Age Ahead.* Blog, http://www.forum.dallasmetropolis.com, May 8, 2004.

Vitullo-Martin, Julia. "West Village Houses a Monument to a 1960s Development Battle." *New York Sun,* August 30, 2007.

Von Hoffman, Alexander. "High Ambitions: The Past and Future of American Low-Income Housing Policy." *Housing Policy Debate* 7, no. 3 (1996): 423–46.

———. "A Study in Contradictions: The Origins and Legacy of the Housing Act of 1949. *Housing Policy Debate* 11, no. 2 (2000): 299–326.

Wachtel, Eleanor. "A Conversation with Jane Jacobs." *Brick* 70 (winter 2002).

Ware, Caroline F. *Greenwich Village, 1920–1930.* Berkeley: University of California Press, 1963. (Originally published 1935.)

Warren, David. "Two Ways to Live." Interview with Jane Jacobs. *Idler* (summer 1993): 6–17.

Warsh, David. *Knowledge and the Wealth of Nations: A Story of Economic Discovery.* New York: W. W. Norton, 2006.

Weiner, Vicki. "Edith Lyons." Oral history interview. Greenwich Village Society for Historic Preservation, February 19, 1997, and July 3, 1998.

Weiner, Vicki, and Anthony Wood. "Leticia Kent." Oral history interview. Greenwich Village Society for Historic Preservation, October 8, 1997.

Wellman, Barry. "Jane Jacobs, the Torontonian." Research Bulletin #30. Centre for Urban and Community Studies, University of Toronto, July 2006.

"West Village Plan for Housing." Brochure. West Village Committee, 1963. Burns.

White, E. B. *Here Is New York*. New York: Little Bookroom, 1999. (Originally published 1949.)

White, Richard. "Jane Jacobs and Toronto, 1968–1978." *Journal of Planning History* 2, no. 10 (2011): 114–38.

Whyte, William H. Jr. New introduction to *The WPA Guide to New York City*. New York: Pantheon, 1982. (Originally published 1939.)

Whyte, William H. Jr., ed. *The Exploding Metropolis*. Berkeley: University of California Press, 1993. (Originally published 1958.)

Wickens, Stephen. "*The Death and Life* at 50." *Globe and Mail*, May 7, 2011.

Wiles, Will. "Saint Jane." Urbanophile, http://www.urbanophile.com/2011/03/01/saint-jane-by-will-wiles.

Winkler, Allan M. *The Politics of Propaganda: The Office of War Information, 1942–1945*. New Haven, CT.: Yale University Press, 1978.

Wolfe, Alan. "How We Live Now." Review of *Systems of Survival*. *New York Times*, July 25, 1993.

Wurster, Catherine Bauer. "The Social Front of Modern Architecture in the 1930s." *Journal of the Society of Architectural Historians* (March 1965): 48–52.

Zeidler, Eberhard. *Buildings Cities Life: An Autobiography in Architecture*. Toronto: Dundurn, 2013.

Zipp, Samuel. *Manhattan Projects: The Rise and Fall of Urban Renewal in Cold War New York*. New York: Oxford University Press, 2010.

———. "Living for the City": On Jane Jacobs." *Nation*, April 5, 2010.

———. "Superblock Stories, or Ten Episodes in the History of Public Housing." *Rethinking History: The Journal of Theory and Practice* (2013): 38–73.

Zukin, Sharon. "Jane Jacobs: The Struggle Continues." *City & Community* (September 2006): 223–26.

———. "Reading *The Urban Villagers* as a Cultural Document: Ethnicity, Modernity, and Capital." *City and Community* (March 2007): 39–48.

———. *Naked City: The Death and Life of Authentic Urban Places*. New York: Oxford University Press, 2010.

———. "Jane Jacobs." *Architectural Review* (November 2011).

INDEX

Page numbers in *italics* refer to illustrations.

ILLUSTRATION CREDITS

Grateful acknowledgment is made to the following for the use of their photographs:

22 Courtesy of Maryann Thomas at The Ginger Press

24 Courtesy of Maryann Thomas at The Ginger Press

27 Courtesy of Maryann Thomas at The Ginger Press

45 Collage of family photographs, undated Map-case 1 Case-Drawer 17, Jane Jacobs Papers, MS.1995.029, John J. Burns Library, Boston College.

96 Courtesy of Maryann Thomas at The Ginger Press

100 Collage of family photographs, undated Map-case 1 Case-Drawer 17, Jane Jacobs Papers, MS.1995.029, John J. Burns Library, Boston College.

114 Collage of family photographs, undated Map-case 1 Case-Drawer 17, Jane Jacobs Papers, MS.1995.029, John J. Burns Library, Boston College.

116 FBI report provided by the Freedom of Information Act, Request No. 12167–000.

124 Jane Jacobs at Diner, 1950s, Box 36, Folder 6, Jane Jacobs Papers, MS.1995.029, John J. Burns Library, Boston College." Photo by Kenneth C. Welch.

133 Courtesy of the Avery Architectural and Fine Arts Library

138 Courtesy of Judy Kirk Fitzsimmons

147 Courtesy of Maryann Thomas at The Ginger Press

150 Library of Congress, Prints & Photographs Division, Gottscho-Schleisner Collection |LC-G612–60152|

150 The La Guardia and Wagner Archives, La Guardia Community College/The City University of New York and the New York City Housing Authority

168 Rockefeller Foundation records, photographs, series 100–1000: Series 100: International; Portraits; provided by the Rockefeller Archive Center

174 Courtesy of Peter Peter

200 Courtesy of Maryann Thomas at The Ginger Press

202 Courtesy of Maryann Thomas at The Ginger Press

216 Lewis Mumford Collection, Monmouth University, used with permission

228 Portrait of American public official and city planner Robert Moses (1888—1981) during the CBS Reports news program, October 1962. The segment, entitled 'The Man Who Built New York,' originally aired on April 17, 1963. (Photo by CBS Photo Archive/Getty Images)

233 Collage of family photographs, undated Map-case 1 Case-Drawer 17, Jane Jacobs Papers, MS.1995.029, John J. Burns Library, Boston College.

237 Jane Jacobs at penny sale, 1968 Box 36 Folder 10, Jane Jacobs Papers, MS.1995.029, John J. Burns Library, Boston College.

240 Library of Congress, Prints & Photographs Division, New York World-Telegram and the Sun Newspaper Photograph Collection |LC-USZ-62–137838|

Printed in the United States
by Baker & Taylor Publisher Services